A SACRED
KINGDOM

Studies in Medieval and Early Modern Canon Law

Kenneth Pennington, General Editor

Studies in Medieval and Early Modern Canon Law

VOLUME 8

A SACRED KINGDOM

Bishops and the Rise of Frankish Kingship, 300–850

MICHAEL EDWARD MOORE

THE CATHOLIC UNIVERSITY OF AMERICA PRESS
Washington, D.C.

100 009072c

Library of Congress Cataloging-in-Publication Data
Moore, Michael Edward.
A sacred kingdom : bishops and the rise of Frankish kingship, 300–850 /
Michael Edward Moore.
p. cm. — (Studies in medieval and early modern canon law)
Includes bibliographical references (p.   ) and index.
ISBN 978-0-8132-1877-9 (cloth : alk. paper)
1. France—Church history—To 987.   2. Franks—Kings and rulers.
3. Bishops—France—History—To 1500.   4. Councils and synods—
France—History—To 1500.   I. Title.   II. Series.
BR844.M63 2011
274.4'03—dc22
2011014400

In gratitude for his scholarship in
ancient philosophy, and his friendship,
this book is dedicated to Pierre Hadot:
Changer la vie!

La chair est triste, hélas! Et j'ai lu tous les livres.

Fuir! Là-bas fuir! Je sens que des oiseaux sont ivres

D'être parmi l'écume inconnue et les cieux!

—*Stéphane Mallarmé, "Brise Marine"*

CONTENTS

PREFACE

For sustaining and faithful friendship, I am ever grateful to David Nierenberg, Rob Zaretsky, and Eileen Joy. Many friends and former friends read and commented on this work as it progressed, including David, Sally Vaughn, Brigitte Bedos-Rezak, Paolo Squatriti, Nancy Aykanian, Justine Firnhaber-Baker, and Osvaldo Pardo. Intellectual and spiritual support came from Stephen Tonsor, Alain Boureau, Amos Funkenstein, Pierre Hadot, the monks of Maria Laach, and Wolfram Brandes. I was further assisted by magnificent libraries, angelic librarians, and generous research support: an Andrew J. Mellon Fellowship at the Library of Congress in Washington, D.C.; stipends at the Max-Planck-Institut für europäische Rechtsgeschichte, Frankfurt am Main; a stipend at the Herzog-August Bibliothek, Wolfenbüttel, and a fellowship from the Deutscher Akademischer Austauschdienst (D.A.A.D.).

It would be hard to have courage without love: I thank my mother, Marilyn Barclay, the excellent sir, Jerome Drummond, and my sweetie, Michaela Hoenicke Moore. With love and scholarship we can find a world to inhabit. There is an ancient saying: "To the courageous man, the whole earth is his homeland."

DUBLIN
June 30, 2010

ix

ABBREVIATIONS

AASS	Acta Sanctorum [Bollandi]
AHC	*Annuarium Historiae Conciliorum*
CCCM	Corpus Christianorum Continuatio Mediaevalis
CCSL	Corpus Christianorum Series Latina
CSEL	Corpus Scriptorum Ecclesiasticorum Latinorum
DA	*Deutsches Archiv für Erforschung des Mittelalters*
DACL	*Dictionnaire d'archéologie chrétienne et de liturgie.* Edited by Fernand Cabrol. 15 vols. Paris: 1903–1953.
De ecc.	Isidore of Seville. *De officiis ecclesiasticis*
Drobner	Drobner, Hubertus R. *The Fathers of the Church: A Comprehensive Introduction.* Translated by Siegfried S. Schatzmann. Peabody. Mass.: 2007.
DSA	Dictionnaire de spiritualité ascetique et mystique, doctrine et histoire. 19 vols.-in-23. Paris: 1932–1995.
EHR	*English Historical Review*
EME	*Early Medieval Europe*
GGB	*Geschichtliche Grundbegriffe: Historisches Lexikon zur politisch-sozialen Sprache in Deutschland.* Edited by Otto Brunner, Werner Conze, and Reinhart Koselleck. 8 vols.-in-9. Stuttgart: 1972–1997. Revised edition: 2004.
Hefele-Leclercq	Charles Joseph Hefele. *Histoire des conciles d'apres les documents originaux.* Translated and augmented by Henri Leclercq. 11 vols. Paris: 1907–1952.
HJ	*Historische Jahrbuch*
HZ	*Historische Zeitschrift*
JECS	*Journal of Early Christian Studies*

JEH	*Journal of Ecclesiastical History*
JTS	*Journal of Theological Studies*
MA	*Le Moyen Âge: Revue d'histoire et de philologie*
Mansi	J. D. Mansi. *Sacrorum conciliorum nova et amplissima collectio.* Florence/Venice: 1759–.
MGH	*Monumenta Germaniae historica*
"	Capit. *Capitularia Regum Francorum*
"	Conc. *Concilia*
"	Dipl. *Diplomatum Imperii*
"	Epp. *Epistolae*
"	Leg. *Leges nationum Germanicarum*
"	SS. *Scriptores* (= *Scriptorum*)
"	SRM *Scriptores Rerum Merovingicarum*
"	SRG in us. schol. *Scriptores Rerum Germanicarum in usum scholarum*
MScR	*Mélanges de science religieuse*
PL	Migne, Jacques-Paul. *Patrologiae cursus completus, Series Latina.* Paris: 1878–1890. Works are cited by volume no.: column no.
RB	*Revue bénédictine*
RBPH	*Revue belge de philologie et d'histoire*
RHEF	*Revue d'histoire de l'Église de France*
RHDr	*Revue historique de droit français et étranger*
SC	*Sources chretiennes*
SM	*Studi medievali*
Settimane	*Settimane di Studio del Centro Italiano di Studi sull' alto Medioevo,* Spoleto.
TCCG	*Topographie chrétienne de cités de la Gaule. des origines au milieu du VIIIe siècle.* Edited by N. Gauthier and J.-Ch. Picard. Paris: 1986 –.
TU	*Texte und Untersuchungen zur Geschichte der altchristlichen Literatur*
VC	*Vigiliae Christianae*
ZKG	*Zeitschrift für Kirchengeschichte*
ZSRG.K	*Zeitschrift der Savigny-Stiftung für Rechtsgeschichte: Kanonistische Abteilung*
ZSRG.R	*Zeitschrift der Savigny-Stiftung für Rechtsgeschichte: Romanistische Abteilung*

A SACRED
KINGDOM

INTRODUCTION

*T*HIS BOOK is an examination of the interaction between bishops and kings from the Gallic period of the fourth century to the breakup of the Carolingian Empire in about 850. We will see that kings and bishops powerfully influenced one another, and that the character of kingship was transformed in the course of the creation of the Carolingian Empire by the ideas, law, and ritual activities of bishops. Indeed, the building of the Empire and the sense of religious mission that inspired it can, to a significant extent, be attributed to the royal adoption of an episcopal platform. Royal power became ritualized and Christianized. Episcopal power was transformed at the same time, because by virtue of living in the Empire they had helped create, bishops could act on a cross-cultural, even Church-wide level. The language with which Carolingian bishops explained their role continued to draw upon the conciliar tradition of Gallic and Merovingian bishops. Ancient legal principles were used to regulate and explain the cultural role of bishops in a world that was seemingly new. To some extent this reflected the persistence of ancient social patterns, which extended from antiquity into the Carolingian era, like veins in marble.

Royal power and ideas about kingship did not result directly from the rise of royal clans or ethnic federations. Christian kingship, which became dominant in Western Europe by the end of the sixth century, must also be understood in the context of clerical and aristocratic culture and the traditions of Roman culture and ecclesiastical law that bishops possessed. Pierre Clastres has shown that power, especially in small-scale societies, may be located in social registers quite unlike the categories conceived of by Max Weber that have dominated scholarly understanding for so long: according to Weber, power is only in the hands of those who have a monopoly over the use of force.[1] A related view is that power "in its pure state" has only to do with command and obedience.[2] This type of power (pure force) certainly existed in the Frankish world, but was not the basis of its political systems, which were consensual and communal. In the subtle view of Søren Kierkegaard:

Only a wretched and mundane conception of the dialectic of power holds that it increases in proportion to the ability to compel and to make dependent. No, Socrates knew better, that the art of power lies precisely in making free. But in the relation between one human being and another this can never be done.[3]

For Kierkegaard, only Christ offered such freedom. The type of power that will most concern us here instead is the ability to govern—that is, the power to shape and guide a society rather than coerce it *(Regierung* rather than *Herrschaft).*[4] Cultural, political, and social power were shared by kings and bishops.

In reflecting on the development of kingship among the Franks, it is not my aim to trace the "rise of the secular sovereign state" in Europe, a theme that lies outside the period and scope of the present book. The role of bishops and their relation to kings and kingship—the ambitious "thin state" created by kings and bishops at the head of Frankish society, the powerful and elaborate political myths that supported this structure (aggressive political doctrines phrased as religious law, innovations in royal and episcopal symbology)—all represent the full flowering of what, at the outset of this book, we see only as a gathering of resources—something commencing—*ab illo aevo.*[5]

Sometime between 496 and 508, the Frankish king Clovis, after years of disinclination, at long last agreed to be baptized by Remigius, the founder of the

1. Pierre Clastres, *Society Against the State,* trans. Robert Hurley (New York: 1989), 7–13. Also essential to this question is J.-W. Lapierre, *Essai sur le fondement du pouvoir politique* (Aix-en-Provence: 1968).

2. Bertrand de Jouvenel, *On Power: The Natural History of Its Growth,* trans. J. F. Huntington (1948; repr., Indianapolis: 1993), 108.

3. Søren Kierkegaard, *Papers and Journals: A Selection,* trans. Alastair Hannay (London: 1996), 235.

4. The distinction was common in political discussions after World War II: "Regierung ist nicht Herrschaft," Dolf Sternberger, "Der alte Streit um den Ursprung der Herrschaft," in his *Schriften,* vol. 3, *Herrschaft und Vereinbarung* (Frankfurt am Main: 1980), 11–27, esp. this quote, 20; see also Sternberger, "Regierung, Regime, Obrigkeit," in GGB 5:361–421; and "Herrschaft," in GGB 3:1–102.

5. "Ab illo aevo, quo pereunte Romano imperio novae gentes terras, quas Urbs dominio suo subegerat, occupant novaque regna instaurant (saec. V–VIII)"; Carlos da Silva-Tarouca, *Fontes historiae ecclesiasticae medii aevi in usum scholarum selegit* (Rome: 1930), vii.

bishopric of Rheims.[6] Gregory of Tours tells that the public squares were hung with colored cloth and the churches with white cloth:

The baptistery was put in order, suffused with balm of Gilead; flaming candles gleamed, and the entire temple of the baptistery was filled with scent. God granted his grace to those present to such an extent that they believed themselves swept up into Paradise by the fragrance.[7]

As a gateway to heaven, the sacred precincts of a church were capable of transporting those who entered them away from the ordinary world.

The threshold of a church was the boundary between two levels of being, the terrestrial and the celestial, the one level subject to the power of kings, and the other to the power of bishops. To stand on the threshold of a church was, thus, to stand at the border of two worlds and of two ways of understanding power. Those excommunicated by their bishop were said to be "kept back from the threshold."[8] Royal law stopped at this threshold, so the first thought of anyone threatened by the king was to seek asylum by clinging to the altar of a church, something that was respected by the Frankish kings surprisingly often.[9] From the day Clovis crossed the doorstep of the church in Rheims, his relationship to the bishops of his kingdom was also transported to a new level. He had tacitly acknowledged the centrality of the church in the spiritual landscape of his

6. On the long controversy about this date, see Mark Spencer, "Dating the Baptism of Clovis, 1886–1993," EME 3 (1994): 97–116. Spencer settled on a date between 496 and 499. Ian Wood argued for a date of 508 in "Gregory of Tours and Clovis," RBPH 63 (1985): 249–72; and again in Wood, *The Merovingian Kingdoms, 450–751* (London: 1994), 48; Rolf Weiss earlier proposed this date in reconstructing Clovis' reign and itinerary: *Chlodwigs Taufe: Reims 508. Versuch einer neuen Chronologie für die Regierungszeit des ersten christlichen Frankenkönigs unter Berücksichtigung der politischen und kirchlich-dogmatischen Probleme seiner Zeit,* Geist und Werk der Zeiten 29 (Bern: 1971). For commemoration of the traditional date in 1996, there was an outpouring of literature on the baptism of Clovis: Elisabeth Magnou-Nortier, "La christianisation de la Gaule (VIe–VIIe siècles): Esquisse d'un bilan et orientation bibliographique," MScR 53 (1996): 5–12 [*Christianisation en Gaule de Clovis à Charlemagne*]. In this event can be found, we are still told, the origins of French catholicity, French royalty, and even the French nation: Michel Sot, "Le baptême de Clovis et l'entrée des Francs en romanité," *Bulletin de l'Association Guillaume Budé* (1996: fasc. 1): 64–75. For the ensuing study, the problematic that frames this event is instead the transformation of Frankish kingship and the eventual rise of a Carolingian state.

7. "Baptistirium conponitur, balsama difunduntur, micant flagrantes odorem cerei, totumque templum baptistirii divino respergetur ab odore, talemque ibi gratiam adstantibus Deus tribuit, ut aestimarent se paradisi odoribus collocari" (2.31); Gregory of Tours, *Gregorii episcopi Turonensis: Libri historiarum X,* ed. Bruno Krusch and Wilhelm Levison, MGH: SRM 1.1:77.

8. "A communionis consortio uel ab ecclesiae liminibus arceatur," Council of Paris (573), CCSL 148A: 213. Full citations of councils and royal law are provided in the bibliography.

9. The episcopal power to grant asylum was developed in late antiquity: Claudia Rapp, *Holy Bishops in Late Antiquity: The Nature of Christian Leadership in an Age of Transition* (Berkeley: 2005), 253–60.

kingdom. Indeed, the bishop was aware of the event's significance, for as Clovis walked toward the baptismal pool, Remigius addressed the king with a reference to the ancient origins of the Franks, saying "Meekly bow down your head, Sigamber."[10] Remigius (d. 532) believed he was quelling the destructive and primitive nature of a royal clan by drawing it across the threshold of his world.

Any reader of Gregory's *Histories* will know, however, that the early Merovingians were not so easily quelled. His pages are lurid with tales of royal violence, which he found difficult to assign a Christian meaning. The role of the early Merovingian kings was centered in their ability to rally a warband. The spear thus remained the central instrument and symbol *(indicium)* of royal power. King Gunthram resorted to this symbol in handing his kingdom over to Childebert. The spear, and other war-gear, long remained the chief ensigns of kingship.[11] The history of the Frankish kingdoms, as told by Gregory, was nevertheless dominated by king and bishop as if by two main characters. In the period dating from the baptism of Clovis to 850, there was a broad transformation of the Frankish kingdoms, from a small, warlike Roman ally to the larger-scale, "complex" society of the Carolingian Empire.[12] These changes were not merely the expansion of the political and military sphere of a few powerful families, but involved, at a deeper level, the development of a highly political state making grandiose claims.[13] Along the way, kingship was considerably changed. Royal power was Christianized as it gained new dimensions of meaning and undertook new tasks.[14] At the heart of this transformation, it will be argued, stood the figure of the bishop.

10. "Mitis depone colla, Sigamber" (2.31), Gregory of Tours, *Libri historiarum,* 77; this traditional interpretation of the phrase was confirmed by Pascale: Bourgain and Martin Heinzelmann, "Courbe-toi, fier Sicambre, adore ce que tu a brûlé: Á propos de Grégoire de Tours, Hist. II: 31," *Bibliothèque de l'École de Chartes* 154 (1996): 591–606.

11. "Post haec rex Gunthchramnus, data in manu regis Childeberthi hasta, ait: 'Hoc est indicium, quod tibi omne regnum meum tradedi'" (7.33); Gregory of Tours, *Libri historiarum,* 353. On the spear and helmet, see Margarete Weidemann, *Kulturgeschichte der Merowingerzeit nach den Werken Gregors von Tours,* Römisch-germanisches Zentralmuseum, Monographien 3; 2 vols. (Bonn: 1982), 1:20–23.

12. This is a different issue than assessing the "barbaric" vs. Roman character of the early Franks: Stéphane Lebecq, "Variations sur l'image du Barbare vu par ses contemporains et par les historiens: le cas Childeric," in *Le Barbare, le primitif, le sauvage: neuf études,* edited by Jacques Boulogne and Jacques Six, Études Inter-ethniques New Series 10 (Villetaneuse: 1995), 89–108.

13. Karl Ferdinand Werner has pointed to the revolutionary changes in Frankish society as it sought to absorb and adapt to Gallo-roman culture: "Die 'Franken': Staat oder Volk?" in *Die Franken und die Alemannen bis zur "Schlacht bei Zülpich" (496/97),* edited by Dieter Geuenich, 95–101, Ergänzungsbände zum Reallexikon der Germanischen Altertumskunde 19 (Berlin: 1998).

14. Mary Garrison, "The Franks as the New Israel? Education for an Identity from Pippin to Charlemagne," in *The Uses of the Past in the Early Middle Ages,* edited by Yitzhak Hen and Matthew Innes, 114–61 (Cambridge: 2000); see 135.

The bishops described by Gregory were evidently conscious of their solidarity as actors in the arena of history. They wrote letters to one another, met in council together, faced problems together, and prayed for one another. But their most important actions were always carried out in relation to the king, a dynamic filled with tension and often with violence. For the succeeding four centuries, the character and meaning of royal power was one of the most pressing and troubling problems faced by bishops. As they came to play a role at the highest levels of power, bishops sought to articulate the norms of political life and to announce changes in the political order.

Bishops inherited an enduring aristocratic role going back to late antiquity, often governing cities and controlling extensive properties and the people who lived on them. The premier exercise of their authority was in legislation enacted at councils. This law was wide in scope and expressive not only of moral ideals, but also of a fully elaborated social thought. I have therefore reached back into late antiquity to underscore the development of the episcopate as an elite, possessing collegiality and a legal tradition radically unlike that native to Frankish society.

While the bishop emerged as the key figure in the cult, other men and women competed with or complemented his role. Recent research on late antique Christianity often reveals how bishops formed one node within extensive religious networks linking late Roman aristocrats with one another and with their local communities: ascetical holy men and women, as well as pious aristocrats. Complex relations existed between aristocratic families and the Christian public, with many opportunities for "both tension and overlap."[15] Well into the fourth century, wealthy secular landowners provided for their own religious needs by building chapels and mausolea on their estates, establishing religious connections that included the nearby bishop, but enveloping him in a larger religious world.[16] But the urban resources of episcopal authority allowed bishops to predominate on many levels. Bishops exercised important functions of mediation and judgement, rulership and leadership, for the largest Christian communities, and were strengthened in these activities by the relative stability and safety offered by city walls.

Late antique bishops adopted the transcendent values of asceticism as their own and bound these ideals to their evolving religious and governmental poten-

15. Kim Bowes, *Private Worship, Public Values, and Religious Change in Late Antiquity* (Cambridge: 2008), 4.
16. Bowes, *Private Worship,* 50.

cy at the head of the church. They produced a body of legislation that bolstered every bishop's authority by giving him a connection to a legal tradition spanning centuries. This legislation had a very different tone than royal legislation: bishops believed that they were guided to the truth of law by the Holy Spirit. Bishops gained a mastery of all law, both secular and religious. We can even point to an early learned common law, Roman and ecclesiastical.

Alongside the legal resources wielded by bishops went a host of unique qualities. As ritual experts, bishops occupied the center of their society, in part by absorbing and dominating pre-Christian cultic practices and ancient holy places.[17] By means of their liturgical expertise, bishops had a hand in all major aspects of life: agricultural and human fertility, the birth, maturity, marriage, and death of individuals. Through the liturgy, bishops established the periodization and the very meaning of time. As the preeminent religious authorities, bishops were able to discern God's judgment in battles or judicial ordeals. Through the ritual of baptism, bishops believed they were engaged in the establishment of Christian society, a society it was their role to govern. They therefore talked about their own power in terms full of royal imagery. Many of the hieratic images so famously used to describe the Carolingian kings ("David," "Melchizidek," "Priest and King") bishops also applied to themselves, even before they applied them to kings. This was because episcopal power was held to derive from the apostles and thence from Christ, the Priest and King.

I have emphasized the social thought of these bishops and its impact upon Frankish kingship, believing that to understand the meaning of social forms is a central task of the historian. Bishops claimed that there were two governing "persons" in their society: king and bishop. As a result of this perception, they gradually elaborated their notion of kingship, until at a certain point (751), they deployed their intellectual resources on behalf of a new royal family that offered to advance their social ideals. With the Carolingians came a far-reaching combination of royal and episcopal interests. This combination, I believe, helps explain the pious, violent ideology of the Carolingian Empire, its ability to mobilize the most powerful men in Frankish society, and its rapid expansion.

The renaissance of intellectual culture in the Carolingian period has often attracted the attention of intellectual historians. I have focused on one aspect of this change, as a triumphant episcopate forged consensus in its own ranks and across society, in a reform of church and kingdom. At the same time, Frank-

---

17. Alain Dierkens, "The Evidence of Archaeology," in *The Pagan Middle Ages*, edited by Ludo J. R. Milis, translated by Tanis Guest, 39–64 (Woodbridge: 1998).

ish kings increasingly turned to episcopal ideals, redirecting and newly understanding their own social and historical role. The view has become traditional that Charlemagne dominated and directed Frankish culture, himself eager for knowledge and wishing to promote learning in his kingdom. However, the programs that Charlemagne undertook may also be seen as a royal adoption of episcopal ideals, supported by an alliance of the king with his powerful bishops. This is a story of mutuality rather than of royal domination. I have sought to illustrate this by examining Frankish royal law and its transformation in the Carolingian period, when so much royal fabric seemed to absorb an episcopal dye. The rapid expansion of the Empire by means of what I call "missionary warfare" is only a more striking example of this same logic.

Memory, Law, and Power

The episcopal council was a forum in which bishops made law. It was a unique institution in early Frankish society. Law, in all the Germanic societies that inherited the lands of the Roman Empire, was not something made, but remembered and collected. The historical memory of bishops had a very different shape from that of kings and their nobles. Bishops maintained copies of lawbooks in which secular, Roman, and conciliar law from centuries past was recorded, and they were aware that bishops of the past had exercised a legislative power that they themselves possessed in the present.

Social changes in the period 450–850 were accompanied by a continuous reinterpretation of the past. Concepts of royal and episcopal power were situated in the collective memory of a restricted group. Episcopal social thought was framed by the historical memory of bishops, with its horizon extending beyond the early church, and before Rome, to long-ago Hebrew institutions, where ancient concepts of sacred rulership could be confirmed from sacred Scripture.[18] The contrast between episcopal memory and royal memory was not merely that between literacy and orality, but also reflected their relative status. The collective memory of religious groups, as Halbwachs maintained, "either obliges others to adapt themselves to its dominant representations, or it systematically ignores them."[19] This commanding position emerged, however, from the consistent, col-

18. On the concept and symbology of sacral kingship in ancient Israel, see Geo Widengren, *Sakrales Königtum im Alten Testament und im Judentum,* Franz Delitzsch-Vorlesungen 1952 (Stuttgart: 1955), 44–58; a deeper time horizon is suggested by Jan Assmann, *Herrschaft und Heil: Politische Theologie in Altägypten, Israel und Europa* (Munich: 2000), 250–64; see also Roland de Vaux, *Ancient Israel: Its Life and Institutions,* trans. John McHugh (Grand Rapids: 1997), 91–114.

19. Maurice Halbwachs, *On Collective Memory,* trans. Lewis A. Coser (Chicago: 1992), 92.

legial operation of an elite making a claim to govern society and capable of acting with power. In conciliar legislation, bishops laid down their vision of society and their own role in it, amassing an institutional memory of legal and literary form spanning centuries.

Assemblies of bishops met frequently in the fourth and fifth centuries throughout the Christian Mediterranean. Often convoked by the Roman emperors to combat heresy, bishops could make use of the imperial post, usually restricted to the highest imperial functionaries, to travel to a council, as when more than 300 bishops traveled to the Council of Nicaea in 325.[20] By the fourth century, these assemblies had an official character because they frequently gathered in response to an imperial summons, and because the emperor or other lay officials might attend to intervene in those councils considered important for imperial policy. Imperial policy had meanwhile become implicated in the governance of the church.[21]

With Constantine's conversion in 312, bishops quickly found themselves serving as officials of the Roman Empire, in part because of the many public duties thrust into their hands, but also because their religious duties had come to impinge on the interests of the state. It has often been said that bishops were drawn almost exclusively from senatorial families, although in the fourth century this was still extremely rare. In the fifth century the rank of bishop became an alternative culmination of the ancient senatorial *cursus honorum*—the church offered very attractive paths to honor and achievement.[22] At the same time, the structure of ecclesiastical offices and the pathway of preferment were standardized in the course of the fourth century: "Ritualized" is the term used by Alexandre Faivre.[23] In imperial law, bishops were now reckoned near the top of the social pyramid, ranking as "illustrious" *(inlustri)*. Bishops thus represented the conti-

---

20. Werner Eck, "Der Einfluss der konstantinischen Wende auf die Auswahl der Bischöfe im 4. u. 5. Jahrhundert," *Chiron* 8 (1978): 561–85; see 561; Jean Gaudemet, *Les sources du droit de l'Église du IIe au VIIe siècle* (Paris: 1985), 51–56; Rapp, *Holy Bishops,* 237.

21. As, for example, the Council of Arles, which gathered "piissimi Imperatoris voluntate adducti," Council of Arles (314), CCSL 148:4. Still central to this question is Norman H. Baynes, *Constantine the Great and the Christian Church,* 2nd ed., The Raleigh Lecture on History, 1929 (London: 1972), 12–14, and the notes at 74–79.

22. On the senatorial background of bishops, see Eck, "Der Einfluss der konstantinischen," 562–63. This assumption has been refuted for the fourth century: Frank D. Gilliard, "Senatorial Bishops in the Fourth Century," *Harvard Theological Review* 77 (1984): 153–75. See Martin Heinzelmann, *Bischofsherrschaft in Gallien: Zur Kontinuität römischer Führungsschichten vom 4. bis zum 7. Jahrhundert. Soziale, prosopographische und bildungsgeschichtliche Aspekte,* Beihefte der Francia 5 (Munich: 1976), 101–11.

23. Alexandre Faivre, *Ordonner la fraternité: Pouvoir d'innover et retour à l'ordre dans l'Église ancienne* (Paris: 1992), 128–30.

nuity of an "aristocratic ethos" and a "traditional form of late Roman political behavior."[24] Their insignia and garments were accordingly drawn from the official symbology of the Roman Empire.[25] Even the social and legal terminology bishops used in their councils bore the mark of their high standing. Bishops incorporated the sonorous diction of emperors in their law, thereby expressing the high importance they attached to their governing role in society.[26] Bishops always viewed imperial and royal power from across the hedgerow of their own highly defined power and functionality.

The Figure of the Bishop

In the late nineteenth and early twentieth centuries, ecclesiastical historians examined the history of church structures to show the extent to which the preservation of orthodoxy in the Latin church had been grounded in institutional continuity.[27] Louis Duchesne was a unique case, given that he was also willing to apply critical methods to the documents of ecclesiastical history. In line with a tradition reaching back to Jean Mabillon, Duchesne brought to bear on church history all the acumen of modern historiography. For this he was attacked as a liberal, "modernist" priest.[28] Despite Duchesne's awareness of the political and social situations in which bishops found themselves, they remained for him essentially religious figures.[29]

Following the Second World War, the study of aristocratic families in the late antique and medieval world, combined with an interest in social history, led scholars away from the history of institutions and ideas toward the meticulous description of localized and personalized social pressures. German scholarship, in

24. Arnaldo Marcone, "Late Roman Social Relations," in *Cambridge Ancient History,* vol. 13, *The Late Empire, A.D. 337–425,* edited by Averil Cameron and Peter Garnsey (Cambridge: 1998), 338–70; see 349.

25. Theodor Klauser, *Der Ursprung der bischöflichen Insignien und Ehrenrechte* (Krefeld: 1949); Repr. in *Gesammelte Arbeiten zur Liturgiegeschichte, Kirchengeschichte und christlichen Archäologie,* edited by Ernst Dassmann, *Jahrbuch für Antike und Christentum,* Ergänzungsband 3 (Münster: 1974), 195–211; esp. 198–99 and 203; see also Karl Ferdinand Werner, *Naissance de la noblesse: L'essor des élites politiques en Europe* (Paris: 1998), 349–54.

26. Michael H. Hoeflich, "The Concept of Utilitas Populi in Early Ecclesiastical Law and Government," ZSRG.K 67 (1981): 36–74.

27. See for example, Germain de Montauzan, "Saint-Eucher, évêque de Lyon et l'école de Lérins," *Bulletin historique du diocèse de Lyon* 2 (1923): 81–96; "A Rome, tour à tour prise et reprise, amoindrie, annihilée presque, le pape demeure inamovible, ne perdant rien de son autorité. Dans les diverses circonscriptions ecclésiastiques, le clergé reste obéissant à ses évêques," 81–82.

28. Especially in regard to his work on the *Liber Pontificalis;* Brigitte Waché, *Monseigneur Louis Duchesne (1843–1922): Historien de l'Église, directeur de l'École française de Rome* (Rome: 1992), 230–40.

29. See Louis Duchesne's last book: *L'Église au VIème siècle* (Paris: 1925), 486–550.

particular, came to rely on historical prosopography.[30] In recent decades, scholars have taken the high social standing of bishops to mean that the episcopate was gradually absorbed by the upper levels of society: according to this view, bishops in the Gallic church were essentially senators, while later on, bishops in the Merovingian church were merely Frankish or Burgundian nobles dressed in clerical garb. The importance of the episcopal office made it an object of social competition, and hence the preserve of the most important families of Gaul. Bishops could be seen as nobles who had taken a slightly different path to power, whose activities were directed primarily by reference to family politics or faction.[31]

This trend has led some scholars to reinterpret the role of Gallo-Roman and Frankish bishops almost exclusively in terms of such pressures.[32] The more detailed such descriptions become, the more convincingly can social action be portrayed in terms of self-interest and familial loyalty. Many interpretations of elite groups in the period 450–850 assume that self-interest governs the actions of individuals—that private interest is the secret truth of institutions. In such a perspective, bishops such as Audoin of Rouen (641–684) can be stripped of nearly all other significance, given the perception that "Audoin was not important because he was a bishop, he was bishop because he was important."[33] But this opposition is a false one. Self-interest is only one facet of any complex system of social exchange, as anthropologists have long understood.[34]

30. Most notably, Karl Friederich Stroheker, *Der senatorische Adel im spätantiken Gallien* (Tübingen: 1948); and Heinzelmann, *Bischofsherrschaft.* For a discussion of this debate, and a suggestion of a new direction, which I favor, see Jean Heuclin, "Le clergé mérovingien et carolingien: Instrument de christianisation?" MScR 53 (1996): 27–42; see 31–34.

31. An overview of the literature may be found in Arnold Angenendt, *Das Frühmittelalter: Die abenländische Christenheit von 400 bis 900* (Stuttgart: 1990), 23–52.

32. Friedrich Prinz often argued that Gallo-Roman bishops were essentially equivalent to the senatorial class, and that this aristocratic episcopacy was gradually taken over by the Frankish nobility in the Merovingian era; see Prinz, "Aristocracy and Christianity in Merovingian Gaul: An Essay," in *Gesellschaft—Kultur—Literatur: Rezeption und Originalität im wachsen einer europäischen Literatur und Geistigkeit. Beiträge Luitpold Wallach gewidmet,* edited by Karl Bosl, 153–65, Monographien zur Geschichte des Mittelalters 11 (Stuttgart: 1975); also Prinz, "Die bischöfliche Stadtherrschaft im Frankenreich vom 5. bis zum 7. Jahrhundert," HZ 217 (1973): 1–35. For Jean Durliat, these powers were instead delegated by kings to bishops: Durliat, "Les attributions civiles des évêques mérovingiens: l'exemple de Didier, évêque de Cahors (630–655)," *Annales du Midi* 91 (1979): 237–54, esp. 239–40. See an assessment of this debate in Bernhard Jussen, "Über 'Bischofsherrschaften' und die Prozeduren politisch-sozialer Umordnung in Gallien zwischen 'Antike' und 'Mittelalter,'" HZ 260 (1995): 673–718.

33. Paul Fouracre and Richard A. Gerberding, *Late Merovingian France: History and Hagiography, 640–720* (Manchester: 1996), 148.

34. Claude Lévi-Strauss, *Tristes Tropiques,* trans. John Weightman and Doreen Weightman (New York: 1975), 244–46. Compare the reductionism of Pierre Bourdieu, *Homo Academicus,* trans. Peter Collier (Stanford: 1984), 78–79. Historians tend to assume a simple link between

Hilary of Arles, for example, was born to an aristocratic family, yet believed that such a "dignity of earthly origin" was something to be despised. The path of Christian wisdom led away from one's family—only in Christ could one come to the "height of nobility."[35] Such traditional statements (*topoi*) were frequently repeated because they had become central to a new language of power and the development of a stridently Christian elite.

Sidonius Apollinaris, a fifth-century aristocrat whose family connections, education, and abilities allowed him to attain the highest civil offices, nevertheless became bishop of Clermont in the end.[36] In doing so, he by no means retreated from civic duties. Bishops in southern Gaul were representatives of their cities, both before the emperor and before the kings of barbarian tribes.[37] They were mediators for and judges of their cities. The scope of episcopal authority was such that it was a natural outlet for the skills of organization and leadership fostered in aristocratic families.[38] Sidonius claimed that he was deeply unworthy of the office: although other souls were put in his care, his own sins needed the purification of tears.[39] In becoming the bishop of Clermont, this Gallic noble made a choice that took him from his beloved estates, forcing him to undertake the close life of the city, to care for the poor, and to lead the cultic observances of his community.[40] Marcone emphasizes the perceived starkness of this choice: "the freedom of the desert is for the monk, the hell of the city for the bishop."[41] The choice oriented him in the complex task of understanding the region's new Gothic kingdom.[42] In the case of Bishop Sidonius, self-interest falls short of providing a satisfactory explanation of a life.

Much recent scholarly work has highlighted the role of bishops and their po-

---

blood and interest (thinking of this as a value-neutral approach). Lineages, however, can bear all sorts of meaning: E. E. Evans-Pritchard, *The Divine Kingship of the Shilluk of the Nilotic Sudan,* the Frazer Lecture 1948 (Cambridge: 1948), 17.

35. "Nec addere nobis quicquam ad dignitatem terrenae originis decus nisi contemptu suo potest" (4.1), Hilary of Arles, *Hilaire d'Arles: Vie de Saint Honorat,* ed. Marie-Denise Valentin, SC 235 (Paris: 1977), 76.

36. Still vital is C. E. Stevens, *Sidonius Apollinaris and His Age* (Oxford: 1933) and, more recently, Jill Harries, *Sidonius Apollinaris and the Fall of Rome, AD 407–485* (Oxford: 1994).

37. André Loyen, "Le rôle de saint Aignan dans la défense d'Orléans," *Comptes rendus de l'Académie des Inscriptions et Belles-Lettres* (1969): 64–74.

38. Stevens, *Sidonius,* 130.

39. "Quem longis adhuc abluenda fletibus conscientia premat" (Epistolae 7:6.3), Sidonius Apollinaris, *Sidoine Apollinaire: Poèmes, Lettres,* ed. André Loyen, 3 vols. (Paris: 1960–1970), 3:44.

40. Philip Rousseau, "In Search of Sidonius the Bishop," *Historia* 25 (1976): 356–77; Françoise Prévot, "Sidoine Apollinaire et l'Auvergne," RHEF 79, no. 203 (1993): 243–59.

41. Marcone, "Late Roman Social Relations," 349.

42. Suzanne Teillet, *Des Goths à la nation gothique: Les origines de l'idée de nation en Occident du Ve au VIIe siècle* (Paris: 1984), 185–206.

sition in late antiquity and afterward. The brilliant work of Peter Brown set in motion a body of research addressing the "economy of the sacred" in late antiquity that has provided the framework for studies of bishops. As Conrad Leyser, Philip Rousseau, and others have shown in many parallel studies, bishops like Sidonius developed a new model of power that gave bishops a central position of moral and political authority. Brown, in *Power and Persuasion in Late Antiquity* and other works, placed the bishops in the context of the transformation of urban society and urban elites, revealing the dynamic interplay of "the Christian sacred" in this complex set of phenomena: extending from aristocratic patronage of building projects to protection of the poor and dealings with the centers of power and municipal authority.[43] The magisterial work of Alexandre Faivre, already mentioned, offers guidance to ecclesiastical self-perceptions and institutional self-crafting.[44] More recently, in a valuable treatise on the episcopate of late antiquity, Claudia Rapp highlights the figure of the bishop as it evolved in late Roman society, tracing developments that placed bishops beside other holy men and the emperor himself as figures of power and authority. Rapp's goal is to present the late antique episcopate, not as the outcome of a straightforward institutional development, but as the emergence of the bishop as a "leadership figure."[45] She illustrates the development of episcopal ascetic authority and the accumulation of social and religious prestige in a sweeping view of the late Roman scene. The ascetic distance of the bishop from ordinary life was part of a claim to control property and to govern the church.[46] Ultimately, as I will demonstrate, this new language of power served in the effort to Christianize power and to transform the nature of kingship.

These approaches are now complemented by studies reaching into the early medieval world. In a major reinterpretation of the early medieval episcopate, Steffen Patzold shows that the potent role of bishops in the Carolingian period was an episode in the long-enduring prominence of the episcopacy in the social order of Europe, from the fifth through the tenth century and beyond.[47] Like Claudia Rapp,

43. Peter Brown, *Power and Persuasion in Late Antiquity: Towards a Christian Empire* (Madison: 1992).

44. Faivre, *Ordonner la fraternité.*

45. Rapp, *Holy Bishops,* 3, 22; Rapp provides a useful survey of recent literature: 6–22.

46. See, for example, Peter Brown, *Poverty and Leadership in the Later Roman Empire,* Menahem Stern Jerusalem Lectures (Hannover: 2002); Conrad Leyser, *Authority and Asceticism from Augustine to Gregory the Great* (Oxford: 2000); and Philip Rousseau, *Ascetics, Authority, and the Church in the Age of Jerome and Cassian* (Oxford: 1978).

47. Steffen Patzold, *Episcopus: Wissen über Bischöfe im Frankenreich des späten 8. bis frühen 10. Jahrhunderts,* Mittelalter-Forschungen 25 (Ostfildern: 2008), 17–18.

Patzold highlights the bishop as a "figure" within the context of his contemporary social imagination. In Patzold's view, episcopal power should be understood as resting upon social agreements, expressed in rituals, signs, and symbols, in the framework of social knowledge (*Wissen*). Social power is ever intimately tied to the social imagination. In order to understand the construction of social power, therefore, historians should reexamine and deepen the "history of images" and the "history of perceptions."[48] Social power, according to Patzold, cannot be studied only in terms of a simple history of events, as an appendage of prosopography, or as part of the traditional narrative thematics of the rise of the later Ottonian *Reichskirche*. Rather, in an approach ranging over historiography, theology, and legal and ritual texts, Patzold examines the social power of bishops as arising from social agreement and shared perceptions. Patterns of interpretation and imagination of social reality interpose between economic, social, and political relations, and thus affect our understanding of the sources. Awareness and perceptions about society have an effect on social reality, and are thus part of historical actuality.[49] A similar approach is followed here, with the goal of describing the origins and character of episcopal social power and its effect on the imagination and institutions of Merovingian and Carolingian political and ecclesiastical culture.

To portray the role of bishops in the formation of societies they helped to govern, it is necessary to temper recent research by a certain "return to Duchesne," that is, by a renewed appreciation of the religious function of the bishop. Claudia Rapp's insistence that the bishop should be seen as a holy man offers a valuable approach that puts the historian in tune with the sources.[50] The aristocratic origin of most bishops was not seen by contemporaries as an impediment to episcopal office, but rather as an appropriate background for someone who would rule a community, in addition to governing its religious cult. The bishop had become the *homme clé* of the late Roman Empire, and retained this position in the rise of Visigothic, Burgundian, and Frankish societies.[51]

48. Cf. Patzold's discussion of *Vorstellungsgeschichte* and *Wahrnehmungsgeschichte,* which imply the study of rituals and other symbolic expressions: Patzold, *Episcopus,* 45.

49. Patzold, *Episcopus,* 37–38; Patzold follows the social analysis of Barry Barnes, *The Nature of Power* (Cambridge: 1988), for whom power is essentially an aspect of the distribution of social knowledge; Patzold, 43.

50. Compare her discussion of the bishop as combining the impress of the Holy Spirit with the accumulated prestige of ascetic diligence, and the ideal of the desert: Rapp, *Holy Bishops,* 56 and 105–06.

51. *Homme clé:* Alain Dierkens, "Christianisme et 'paganisme' dans la Gaule septentrionale aux Ve et VIe siècles," in *Franken und Alemannen,* 457. Frequently cited essay collections are cited by short title. Full information is provided in the bibliography.

Bishops, moreover, did not act as functional equivalents of senators or no-bles, but as a distinctive, cohesive group, possessing a self-conscious and unifying identity. Unlike senators, bishops ordained clerics, gave sermons, and baptized people. They made blessings of salt and water. They adopted a special hairstyle symbolically connecting them to the asceticism of the desert and a moral code that brought them into contact with the poor and that gave them a unique po-sition from which to make demands on their kings (and on the poor). The reli-gious side of episcopal activity will also occupy us.

The episcopal council was crucial to the development and durability of this identity. Although the men who attended the councils of Gaul possessed im-portant duties and powers that could be paired with those of lay officials, bish-ops argued that a unique status bound them together and created a rift between themselves and the rest of society. They claimed to be members of an "order" and called one another brothers.[52] The Council of Arles in 314, for instance, made elevated claims about the ultimate source of its spiritual authority. Despite the importance of the imperial summons that caused bishops to set sail across the Mediterranean or cross the Pyrenees, the emperor had no influence over the un-shakable certainty that ultimately arose from every council. That sense of verity came instead from the belief that whenever bishops were gathered in council, the Holy Spirit was present among them, accompanied by angels.[53]

Political Augustinianism

The records of Gallic and Merovingian councils preserve the activities of an articulate group that struggled to maintain its character and continuity, despite social and political change in the societies in which it functioned. The laws ad-vanced in episcopal councils reveal how bishops viewed themselves as a group whose duty was to govern the church, and how they squared this duty with the unavoidable and often unpredictable pressure of royal power. The perception bishops had of their role in society hinged in large measure on how they viewed the past, going back to the Apostolic Church, and the manner in which their own authority flowed out of this past. Bishops therefore thought of their power

52. The clergy as a whole formed an "ecclesiastical order" *(ordo ecclesiasticus)* distinct from the "people" *(plebs)*. For example: "Ex eo quod contra ecclesiasticum ordinem baptizare uiden-tur" *Canones suppositii ad finem canonum concilii arelatensis* CCSL 148:25; "ordinem clericatus" Council of Orange (441), CCSL 148:82. The rise of this distinction is described by Faivre, *Or-donner la fraternité,* 192–93. But bishops were a separate order of men: *(noster ordo):* "Etiam in nostri ordinis" Council of Vaison-la-Romaine (442), CCSL 148:99.

53. "Praesente Spiritu sancto et angelis eiusdem," Council of Arles (314), CCSL 148:4–5.

as having a nontemporal, structural basis (they were an *ordo*), as well as a historical basis (as the heirs and guardians of "apostolic doctrine)."[54]

The unfolding of this dual perspective will occupy us in what follows. The Roman Empire disappeared and was replaced by the (traditionally so-called) barbarian kingdoms, vying for dominance. Bishops laid out new tasks for men of power. Thus the problem of kingship became one of the most persistent concerns of bishops, because the "kings" of the peoples who swept over their ancient domains could hardly be ignored, yet were violent, often heretical, and generally difficult to deal with. All the time, however, bishops continued to insist upon their own unique role in society: "the episcopal order, both first and perfect in all things," according to a late-sixth-/early-seventh-century treatise on church offices, "is provided by the omnipotence of the Lord and Christ."[55]

Episcopal law is sometimes thought of as nothing more than a "normative source," with only a tenuous relation to social reality. It is avoided by some scholars who are in search of an "objective representation" of what actually happened in the past.[56] Indeed, episcopal and royal law should be used with caution. The legal historian Alan Watson reminds us that law should not be used uncritically as a description of society. One obvious reason is the fact that law is often borrowed, as we find so often in this period.[57] Law was accepted from other cultures, and was also "borrowed," so to speak, from the past. This book seeks to highlight instead other aspects of law: its function as holy writ, and especially its reflection of ideals and cultural aspirations. The study of law has a place in a history of early medieval concepts. In the setting of epicopal councils, bishops were able to address the powerful in society, drawing on centuries of legal tradition and the social doctrines contained therein.

In studying the law and other writings of bishops, one should maintain a certain mental reserve. For example, the bishops often talked about their concern for the poor, going so far as to rest one corner of their governmental claims, and

---

54. "Euangelica praecepta et apostolicam doctrinam," Council of Tours (461), CCSL 148:143.

55. "Septimus autem in his despositionibus episcopalis ordo est, qui et primus et perfectus in cunctis est, qui omnipotentia Domini et Christi donatur," pseudo-Jerome, *Ps.-Hieronymi De septem ordinibus ecclesiae,* ed. P. Athanasius Walter Kalff, Inaugural-Dissertation . . . Bayerischen Julius-Maximilians-Universität Würzburg (1935), 57. The question of dating was reexamined in Roger E. Reynolds, "The Pseudo-Hieronymian 'De septem ordinibus ecclesiae': Notes on its Origins, Abridgments, and Use in Early Medieval Canonical Collections." RB 80 (1970): 238–52.

56. Matthew Innes, *State and Society in the Early Middle Ages: The Middle Rhine Valley, 400–1000* (Cambridge: 2000), 47–48.

57. Alan Watson, "Uses and Abuses of Law in History," in his *Ancient Law and Modern Understanding: At the Edges,* 1–19 (Athens, Ga.: 1998).

their control of ecclesiastical property, on their care for the weak and displaced. Yet the poor were kept at the very margins of biological existence by bishops as much as by other lords.[58] From our perspective bishops did not sustain the destitute, and were part of a power structure that oppressed them.[59] No doubt it has always been true that "no one helps the poor like the poor themselves."[60]

Episcopal social ideals had a profound impact on Frankish society, especially at its uppermost reaches, toward which these ideals were primarily directed. Most historians now agree that the old assumption of sacral kingship among the Germanic peoples, rooted in a distant pre-invasion antiquity, must finally be abandoned.[61] Nevertheless, I have reexamined the notion of sacral kingship, given that, under the impact of episcopal social thought, kings and the Frankish kingdom itself were thought of in religious terms. However, I argue that special qualities associated with the Carolingian Empire, especially its sacropolitical concepts, did not derive from an ancient pagan past, but were profoundly Christian, and specifically episcopal from the beginning. An important source of this new social ideal was the model of the Visigothic kingdom and the effort of bishops there to sacralize royal power.[62]

Along the way I have reexamined the notion, arising from a misreading of the bishop of Hippo, that Carolingian politics should be thought of as "political Augustinianism."[63] Augustine offered little support for the notion that the Carolingian political order was divinely ordained, believing as he did that political states arose, not as part of a special divine plan, but from a *libido dominandi* or lust for domination.[64] In contrast, Carolingian bishops were hopeful, at times even ecstatic, about the political order they helped to create. They were prepared to find the immanence of God in a rightly ordered political structure. Major discussions of social reality did not hinge on Augustine, but rather on Isidore of Seville, pseudo-Cyprian, liturgical texts, and other sources. "Mis-

58. As forcefully stated by Paul Fouracre, "Merovingian History and Hagiography," *Past and Present* 127 (1990): 3–38.

59. Such a revision has been offered by Marie-Luise Windemuth, *Das Hospital als Träger der Armenfürsorge im Mittelalter,* Sudhoffs Archiv 36 (Stuttgart: 1995).

60. In the words of the novelist José Saramago; Saramago, *The History of the Siege of Lisbon,* trans. Giovanni Pontiero (New York: 1989), 122–23.

61. A summary of recent work is Walter Goffart, "Two Notes on Germanic Antiquity Today," *Traditio* 50 (1995): 9–30.

62. Michael Zimmermann, "Les sacres des rois wisigoths," in *Clovis* 2:9–28.

63. The phrase is from the classic statement of this theme: H.-X. Arquillière, *L'Augustinisme politique: Essai sur la formation des théories politiques du moyen-âge,* L'Église et l'etat au moyen âge 2 (Paris: 1934).

64. Amos Funkenstein, *Heilsplan und natürliche Entwicklung: Formen der Gegenwartsbestimmung im Geschichtsdenken des hohen Mittelalters* (Munich: 1965), 47.

reading Augustine" was a secondary movement of men who raised a new sacro-political ideal, yet were thoroughly committed to Augustine's saintly stature and theology. The religious purpose of the Carolingian Empire was assumed to be compatible with Augustine. Anything else would have been awful!

Culture and Political Concepts

Bishops incorporated both new and old texts in a tradition they thought of as ancient and authoritative. These texts were freely adopted from Spain, Ireland, and England, and from within Gallic traditions. The history of ideas has long centered on *catenae* of thinkers whose importance extended from their own time into some future time, in a branching, organic model of influences, organized by genre (philosophy, theology, historiography, or political thought). With its focus on reception, the history of ideas has been progressive and has tended to conceptualize influence as a type of causality. It overlooks the importance of thinkers whose influence was limited in time, but who were crucial to the development of characteristic social structures. For example, the poets who wrote the early Frankish liturgies may be ranked alongside more celebrated thinkers, although their works were abandoned and lacked influence later in the Middle Ages. I have sought to describe the intellectual resources of the period without reference to their later resonance, and thereby to address tradition-building as a creative and conscious act, in which ideals about the past were generated with one eye on the present. I believe that this approach allows a reexamination of the relation of ideology to social forms.[65] I have therefore sought to extend the traditional range of intellectual history to examine clothing, hairstyles, and landscapes, as well as law and liturgy.

I attempt to trace the role of bishops in the rise of the Carolingian Empire: an entity that can be described as a newly ambitious, piously minded, yet aggressive state (a "thin state") at the upper reaches of Frankish society. The *state* is an unfortunately ambiguous term. If by the term "state" we mean a self-perpetuating structure of coercive and administrative power, distributing its effects downward, then the term is inappropriate for the entire period of Western European history between the fall of Rome and the rise of powerful kingdoms and city-states of the fourteenth century. Such a concept would certainly not be applicable to the Carolingian Empire. Nevertheless, many historians now argue for the persistence of a Roman-style state into the Merovingian period.[66] Oth-

---

65. See the resumé of recent debate on history and ideology in Marc Zvi Brettler, *The Creation of History in Ancient Israel* (London: 1995), 1–19.

66. Innes, *State and Society,* 141. Ian Wood argues that the Merovingian kingdom was a "late Roman state"; Wood, *Merovingian Kingdoms,* 60–63; Paul Fouracre puts the "state" in inverted

ers, like Barbara Rosenwein, wish to retain the term, but reinterpret it in light of early medieval conditions. She argues for the existence of a state in this period, but one that does not fulfill the traditional assumptions about statehood: "that it is based on bureaucracy; that it thrives on centralization; and that it attempts to amass and conserve its material resources."[67] Instead, Merovingian power was massively decentralized, and Carolingian power only somewhat less so. Over this period, kings gave away huge quantities of land and wealth, even removing important lands from their own jurisdiction by grants of immunity. The purposes of such states were radically different than the purposes of modern states and modern notions of power as an end in itself. Rosenwein's view on this point is similar to my own.

What I have endeavored to describe is the creation of a piously motivated political culture in the Carolingian era that was thought of as a "sacred kingdom." The totality of the social order was conceptualized as the church: contemporaries did not identify their social and political order as a state. The old doctrine that "two persons" governed society was the basis for a thorough reinterpretation and redirection of the social order. By the time of Louis the Pious it was accepted that both *personae* were responsible for the well-being and salvation of mankind.[68] This symbolic structure had legal and institutional dimensions, and was able to mobilize and join together the most powerful men in Frankish society. Functioning only sporadically as a directive coercive force, the kingdom—in this conceptualization—was motivated by doctrines about righteous power, many of which can be traced to episcopal social thought. It is a mistake to explain away the sources by interpreting them only in light of secular power. The records of councils are a significant source for understanding changes in the nature and meaning of Merovingian and Carolingian power. As Janet Nelson has pointed out, episcopal law reflects the viewpoint of highly placed men, often involved at the highest levels of politics. The councils reflect the pressures of their historical moment and respond to social change.[69]

---

commas; Fouracre, *Late Merovingian France,* 56; see also Innes, *State and Society,* 3–7. Alan Harding reviews a spectrum of meanings for state, and the medieval *status regni,* cautioning against a teleological search for the 'origins of the modern state' in medieval sources: Alan Harding, *Medieval Law and the Foundations of the State* (Oxford: 2002), 1–9.

67. Barbara Rosenwein, *Negotiating Space: Power, Restraint, and Privileges of Immunity in Early Medieval Europe* (Ithaca: 1999), 14.

68. Patzold, *Episcopus,* 543, 521.

69. Janet L. Nelson, "The Intellectual in Politics: Context, Content and Authorship in the Capitulary of Coulaines, November 843," in *Intellectual Life in the Middle Ages: Essays Presented to Margaret Gibson,* edited by Lesley Smith and Benedicta Ward, 1–14; see 2–5 (London: 1992).

These social doctrines and concepts were persuasive, and can be shown to have affected Frankish institutions and the actions of powerful men. The ideal of a sacred kingdom involved kings, bishops, and nobles in a conversation about the nature and proper uses of power. Cultural existence is also a basic reality of the historical world. People do not merely act and behave, but also think and believe, reflecting on what they do and what is done to them. Marc Bloch rightly said that "human actions are essentially very delicate phenomena . . . which elude mathematical measurement."

Throughout this book, I have given special prominence to a major body of evidence—episcopal law, which has been used only in a limited way by historians. Records of councils are one of the most continuous source-types for the period, reflecting the social ideals, patterns of governance, and political myths of an important group of men. Nevertheless, church councils are sometimes not even mentioned in résumés of historical sources for the period.[70] Others have looked to episcopal councils to illuminate historical problems of narrative and chronology, but especially the history of religious doctrine. I have studied this body of legislation with the goal of explaining the rise of a social and intellectual elite whose influence in political and social affairs was pervasive. Political culture was shaped by political myths, and special attention is given to the formulation, tenor, and content of political myth.[71] In doing so, I have taken seriously the bishops' vision of the past—an *effective past* that formed the backdrop against which they formed their concepts and undertook action, and that is very different to our own vision of the past.

This book seeks to add another level of analysis to the important work that has been done in recent decades on the rise of the Carolingian Empire, by considering again the interrelation of political concepts and the course of history. Rather than attempt a renewal of traditional history of political thought, I have focused instead on the conceptualization of social forms: concepts of kingship, power, priesthood, and kingdom, and how these concepts were thought to be distilled in symbols and institutions. The history of these concepts is pursued in the context of cultural and social history.[72] It is a mistake to believe that a

---

70. See for example, Roger Collins, *Charlemagne* (Toronto: 1998), 1–15, although he does in fact discuss councils elsewhere in the text; see also Kathy Lynne Roper Pearson, *Conflicting Loyalties in Early Medieval Bavaria: A View of Socio-Political Interaction, 680–900* (Aldershot: 1999).

71. Maria Pétychaki-Henze, "Les fonctions sociales des mythes politiques," in *Mythe et politique: Actes du Colloque de Liège 14–16 septembre 1989,* edited by François Jouan and André Motte, 249–59 (Liège: 1990).

72. The history of concepts *(Begriffsgeschichte)* is usually aligned with social history: Reinhart

society is understood when its mechanisms have been described. In his ethnography of the village of Ballymenone, "a small place of green hills, white homes, and brown bog," Henry Glassie aptly remarked that "Culture is not a problem with a solution. There are no conclusions. Studying people involves refining understanding, not achieving final proof."[73]

The sweep of time addressed here, from the conversion of Constantine to the coronation of Charles the Bald, encompasses the epochal rise of Christian kingship in Europe and the role that bishops played in this development. The topic evokes tremendous depths of time. The story told here commends the perception of Fustel de Coulanges about the pace and nature of political and social change:

> Political institutions are never established by the will of one man; even the will of an entire people does not suffice to create them. The human facts which engender them are not such that the caprice of one generation can change them. . . . It takes many generations to found a political regime, and many more generations to build one. From this arises also the necessity for the historian to extend his research over a vast space of time.[74]

Koselleck, "Social History and *Begriffsgeschichte*," in *History of Concepts: Comparative Perspectives,* edited by Iain Hampsher-Monk, Karin Tilmans, and Frank Van Vree, 23–35 (Amsterdam: 1998).

73. Henry Glassie, *Passing the Time in Ballymenone* (Bloomington: 1982), 13.

74. Fustel de Coulanges, *La Gaule Romaine,* completed from the author's manuscript by Camille Jullian (Paris: 1994), 42.

[1]

GOVERNING THE PEOPLE
OF GOD

*T*HE ENSUING CHAPTER comprises an overview of key aspects of episcopal public life, legal activity, and governance. The social stature of bishops and the social doctrine of episcopal councils in Gaul were crafted during
the fourth century, a period corresponding to what is customarily termed the
Gallican period of episcopal law (314–506 AD). During this period, the political world of Gaul was transformed as the late imperial world of Rome gave way
to newly dominant tribal kingdoms, most notably the Visigoths, Ostrogoths,
Franks, and Burgundians. In the late Roman world, bishops served in the important role of mediating between imperial centers of power and regional communities. The level of education and aristocratic background of most bishops
gained for them the cachet of being part of the urban elite.[1]

Later on, bishops would represent their cities vis-à-vis the kings of emerging
barbarian principalities, despite the traditional Roman perception, inherited
and shared by bishops, that those kings were the leaders of pagan, heretical, and
uncouth nations (*nationes*) or tribes (*ethnici*). In the rapidly changing political
world of Gaul, bishops expressed their understanding of the church as a social
and political entity and as having an exclusive right to protected holy spaces.

In the late Roman world the texture of aristocratic life was rapidly chang-

1. Rapp, *Holy Bishops,* 208.

ing. Serving as bishops, aristocrats adopted a Christian manner and appearance and established emotional and legal ties to urban Christian communities. The social importance of bishops grew ever more significant in the late Empire and was deliberately and conspicuously advanced by bishops themselves through prominent activities such as magnificent building programs, leadership over cult and community, and unwelcome but vital service as judges in the episcopal court system. Alongside these bishops were many other types of clerics, such as deacons and priests or presbyters, although the episcopate began to distinguish itself more and more.[2]

In their councils, meanwhile, bishops developed a specialized body of law expounding their stature in an official way. In conciliar law we observe the regional actions of this cultural aristocracy partaking in ritualized gatherings in which bishops mutually heightened their stature and laid down legal procedures from which they mutually benefited. The resulting body of law expressed universalized social doctrines and developed a mode of authority looking back to the ancient Christian past.

Aristocratic Temples

Bishops of the late Roman Empire crafted a powerful public image of themselves as pious men leading lives of monastic rigor and personal discipline, and at the same time as men of aristocratic mold who could be relied upon to wield power skillfully on behalf of Christian communities. The image of the bishop was developed as a combination of holy man and governor, a figure whose authority was charismatic but also grounded in law and ecclesiastical history. Although their role as governors of church and society expanded substantially in the course of the fourth century, the bishops often claimed in their councils that their religious stature and governance were ancient prerogatives, based on the decrees of the saintly men of Christian antiquity. Connections to this ancient past were maintained especially in the medium of law.

According to Jean Gaudemet, bishops must have been involved in legal activity from an early period of the church's history. While the earliest phases of episcopal lawmaking and adjudication are not documented, this activity comes into clear view in the early fourth century in the records of councils.[3] Gathering periodically in regional bodies, the bishops discussed and debated problems

---

2. Robert Godding, *Prêtres en Gaule mérovingienne,* Subsidia Hagiographica 82 (Brussels: 2001), 5–6.

3. Jean Gaudemet, *L'Église dans l'empire romain (Ive–Ve siècles)* (Paris: 1958), 214.

relevant to their governance of Christian communities, issuing canons to address them.[4] Episcopal law conveyed a complete social vision in its lofty, moral-
istic language. The legislation of councils offers insight into the mentality of this
ecclesiastical and social elite. Episcopal claims to religious authority, an emerging governmental style, and a specialized language may all be found in the conciliar records. By the fourth century, moreover, bishops expected their voices
to be heard. They preserved a familiar type of aristocratic leadership, but transposed into a new Christian key, with a new ethical tone. By serving as bishops,
the well-educated and wealthy elites of the Empire could shape "alternative notions about leadership and authority in communities."[5] Local elites of the late
Empire were adept at mediating between the distant scene of imperial power
and the local world of their constituencies. Bishops proved to be well-prepared
to take over that mediating role as the arrival of barbarian tribes began to transform the Roman world. The lifestyles and activities of aristocratic Romans had
to change, especially inside barbarian settlements.[6]

Thus the imagination and hopes of the Roman aristocracy were turned toward the cool stone interiors of the church, where new opportunities for local
leadership and mediation could be mapped out. Ambrose of Milan remained
aware that the life of a bishop was distinct from a secular career, although it still
involved the exercise of power.[7] An ecclesiastical orientation helped to orient
and stabilize an elite whose rise to prominence was in many instances recent.
High clerical orders were absorbed into the aristocracy, which accordingly was
"cloaked in . . . sacred and secular prestige."[8] Social power acquired a new guise

---

4. A brilliant, concise introduction: Gaudemet, *Les sources du droit*. For sources and transmission: Friedrich Maassen, *Geschichte der Quellen und der Literatur des canonischen Rechts im
Abendlande bis zum Ausgang der Mittelalters*, 1 (1870; repr. Graz: 1956)—only vol. 1 appeared;
Maassen is now supplemented by Lotte Kéry, *Canonical Collections of the Early Middle Ages
(ca. 400–1140): A Bibliographical Guide to the Manuscripts and Literature* (Washington, D.C.:
1999); see also the following detailed histories: Charles Joseph Hefele, *Histoire des conciles d'apres
les documents originaux,* trans. and augmented by Henri Leclercq, 11 vols. (Paris: 1907–1952)
[Hefele-Leclercq]; Hans Barion, *Das fränkisch-deutsche Synodalrecht des Frühmittelalters* (1931:
repr. *Kanonistische Studien und Texte* 5.6 [Amsterdam: 1963]); Odette Pontal, *Histoire des conciles
mérovingiens* (Paris: 1989); Wilfried Hartmann, *Die Synoden der Karolingerzeit im Frankenreich
und in Italien,* Konziliengeschichte, Reihe A: Darstellung (Paderborn: 1989).

5. Raymond Van Dam, *Leadership and Community in Late Antique Gaul* (Berkeley: 1985), 21.

6. Ralph W. Mathisen, *Roman Aristocrats in Barbarian Gaul: Strategies for Survival in an Age
of Transition* (Austin: 1993), 35.

7. Roger Gryson, *Le prêtre selon Saint Ambroise,* Universitas Catholica Lovaniensis—Dissertationes: Series tertia 11 (Louvain: 1968), 120.

8. Giovanni Tabacco, *The Struggle for Power in Medieval Italy: Structures of Political Rule,*
trans. Rosalind Brown Jensen (Cambridge: 1989), 55.

with the dominance of these educated, elegant, and withdrawn gentlemen: the bishops maintained a style and appearance quite similar to the stoical ethos of earlier imperial elites, but they now engaged with their clientele in the intense, close-knit communal setting of Christian festivals and religious services.[9]

The governors of the church were held to a seemingly contradictory set of standards. Theological discussions of political power in this period often reflected the ambition of Christian thinkers to serve as the privileged source of doctrine for the imperial state.[10] According to Gregory the Great, the bishop should also live an ascetical life devoted to spirituality so that he could "glimpse the invisible world in contemplation," even while exercising a practical, effective, but nevertheless merciful style of government.[11]

The coherence of episcopal power with earlier elites of the late Roman Empire may also be seen in the energetic building programs of bishops, above all of episcopal churches. Church construction went on at a steady clip during the final crises of the Roman Empire. The fifth century witnessed an episcopal building boom that transformed the topography of Gallic cities.[12] In the apt phrase of Peter Brown, such foundations were "arguments in stone," meant to advertise the security of episcopal government during a period of troubling social and political change.[13] Bishops built other civic structures, notably the bishop's residence, which combined the character of an aristocratic urban household with public spaces for meetings and the reception of visitors: "building patronage was . . . a visible assertion of status within the city."[14]

Most bishops had an aristocratic background and were accepted as highly qualified, therefore, to offer leadership for their communities. Most bishops came from curial and senatorial families.[15] The church and its higher offices were an attractive alternative source of prestige and social position for the local

9. Rita Lizzi, "I vescovi e i *potentes* della terra: definizione e limite del ruolo episcopale nelle due *partes imperii* fra IV e V secolo d.c.," in *L'Évêque dans la cité du IVe au Ve siècle: Image et autorité,* edited by E. Robillard and C. Sotinel, 81–104; 83 (Rome: 1987); see also Van Dam, *Leadership and Community,* 64.

10. Alexander Demandt, *Geschichte der Spätantike: Das Römsiche Reich von Diocletian bis Justinian* (Munich: 1998), 411–12.

11. Carole Straw, *Gregory the Great: Perfection in Imperfection* (Berkeley: 1988), 91.

12. S. T. Loseby, "Bishops and Cathedrals: Order and Diversity in the Fifth-Century Urban Landscape of Southern Gaul," in *Fifth-Century Gaul: A Crisis of Identity?* edited by John Drinkwater and Hugh Elton (Cambridge: 1992).

13. Peter Brown, *The Rise of Western Christendom: Triumph and Diversity, A.D. 200–1000,* 2nd ed. (Oxford: 2003), 108.

14. Rapp, *Holy Bishops,* 221; 209–10.

15. Gilliard, "Senatorial Bishops," 153–75; Rapp, *Holy Bishops,* 183–95.

aristocracy in Gaul and elsewhere in the Empire.[16] These men were well-known to one another as the bluebloods of society, the "best men" (*optimates viri*), or even, in the phrase of Symmachus, "the better part of humankind" (*pars melior humani generis*), possessing a sensitive awareness of rank and hierarchy and always on the lookout for any slighting of their carefully nurtured prestige.[17]

Mamertus, Bishop of Vienne (ca. 461–477) was one such, who relied on the weight of his personal background and his office when he established Rogations processions during a period of crisis in his city.[18] When he built the Basilica of the Holy Apostles in Vienne in about 475, the church took its place in a cityscape already dense with Christian chapels, monasteries, and baptisteries.[19] Bishops such as Mamertus were frequently involved in the basic planning of such building programs, right down to organizing the work of craftsmen and builders.[20] His new basilica was intended to serve as the chief episcopal church of the city, a monument to Vienne's grand tradition of bishops going back to the time of the apostles. He also wished it to serve as a resting place for the bishops of Vienne, whose worthy bodies could be archived there as a tangible record of religious accomplishment and continuity. Indeed, as time went on, the church was overcrowded with the close-set ranks of stone tombs and graves of many bishops.[21] The edifice conveyed a wonderful sense of confidence as Mamertus led his city in dealing with the Burgundians and their kings, who had occupied the city from the middle of the fifth century. The basilica announced that episcopal continuity would be maintained even under the dominance of the heretical Burgundians.

A bishop's cathedral was the centerpiece of his ritual stature in social affairs and his role as judge and governor. The cathedral, baptistery, and bishop's palace, arranged around the edges of the main square or forum in the heart of a city, gave the bishop a central stage of power befitting his governing role.[22] Seated on

---

16. Ralph W. Mathisen, *Ecclesiastical Factionalism and Religious Controversy in Fifth-Century Gaul* (Washington, D.C.: 1989), 7.

17. Demandt, *Geschichte der Spätantike*, 245.

18. Mamertus may have revived older Roman ceremonies of placation: Geoffrey Nathan, "The Rogation Ceremonies of Late Antique Gaul: Creation, Transmission and the Role of the Bishop," *Classica et Mediaevalia* 49 (1998): 275–303.

19. Jacques Biarne, et al., eds., TCCG, vol. 3, *Provinces ecclésiastiques de Vienne et d'Arles (Viennensis et Alpes graiae et poeninae)* (Paris: 1986), 17–35.

20. Claire Sotinel, "Le personnel épiscopal: Enquête sur la puissance d l'évêque dans la cité," in *L'Évêque dans la cité du IVe au Ve siècle: Image et autorité,* edited by E. Robillard and C. Sotinel, 105–26; see 115–16 (Rome: 1987).

21. Jeremy K. Knight, *The End of Antiquity: Archaeology, Society and Religion A.D. 235–700* (Stroud: 1999), 76.

22. Loseby, "Bishops and Cathedrals," 152; see also Marc Heijmans, *Arles durant l'antiquité tardive: De la Duplex Arelas à l'Urbs Genesii* (Rome: 2004), 262; Rapp, *Holy Bishops,* 209–10.

his episcopal throne (*cathedra*), with his clergy gathered around him, the bishop faced his congregation much like a civil magistrate seated in one of the former city basilicas.[23] This was a position both lofty and protective. For the bishops of Vienne, rivals of the bishops of Arles for religious prominence in Gaul, the basilica was a great jewel flashing the depth and extent of their significance. From such a center, the bishop's influence could be seen to extend over all Vienne's ecclesiastical institutions and the Christian people whose salvation he safeguarded.

A bishop's preeminence took visible shape in such buildings. The central basilica represented the government of the bishop over his community. Le Goff calls this the "remodeling of space."[24] Episcopal prestige was also demonstrated in legal activities and ecclesiastical struggles. The bishops of Vienne had played a role in episcopal legislation and politics as early as 314, when Bishop Verus, accompanied by his exorcist, Beflas, attended the Council of Arles.[25] In 398 Bishop Simplicius of Vienne sought to challenge the presumptive dominance of Arles before a council in Turin. A generation later Bishop Claudius, his deacons, and his suffragans were at the Council of Orange in 441. This was a time of disruption as the invading Alans settled in the region.[26] We know that Bishop Mamertus, in his turn, attended a council held in Arles in 470 to settle a dispute over the theology of predestination between Faustus of Riez and Lucidus.[27] The participation of bishops in these councils gave them a voice in the operation of regional networks of aristocratic government.

The Ancient Canons

Ever since the days of St. Paul, Christian leaders had claimed a unique prerogative and responsibility to assemble and judge and make rules for the Christian community. In the late Empire, there were two types of councils, the big ecumenical or church-wide councils, meeting with the direct patronage and explicit interference of the emperor, and smaller regional councils. The latter were by far the most numerous. The records of such regional councils display many differences of style, relevant problems, and organization. African councils tended to be highly centralized, well-organized events. Councils held in Carthage pos-

23. Knight, *End of Antiquity*, 68.

24. Jacques Le Goff, *The Birth of Europe*, trans. Janet Lloyd (Malden, Mass.: 2005), 25.

25. Council of Arles (314), CCSL 148:14–15.

26. Council of Turin (398), CCSL 148:52–60; Council of Orange (441), CCSL 148:76–93; Mathisen, *Ecclesiastical Factionalism*, 108–9.

27. Council of Arles (c. 470), CCSL 148:159–60; see also Mathisen, *Ecclesiastical Factionalism*, 244–50.

sessed a special prestige and formed an unbroken order of authority throughout the fifth century. These were grand affairs: Carthage (398) was attended by 240 bishops.[28] Gallic councils, in contrast, were more localized and dispersed, meeting in various cities. As a consequence they were often rather small. The Council of Riez (439) gathered eleven bishops to discuss an austere set of seven canons in this metropole of the old Roman province of the Maritime Alps.[29] Two years later, the Council of Orange brought together seventeen bishops.[30] Despite such small numbers of attendees, Gallic councils gave bishops an opportunity to assemble as a privileged group and to forge personal ties with other bishops, sometimes across considerable distances.

As modest as these occasions may seem, given the numbers involved, the bishops presented their activities in tones of high seriousness. As legislators and governors, bishops claimed that it was their role to uphold "authority and tradition"— if need be, even in opposition to the power of emperors and kings. "Let us risk our souls for the flock," Hilary of Poitiers exclaimed, "because thieves came in, and a raging lion walks about." The raging lion in this case was Constantius II, a precursor of the Antichrist, Hilary declared, because of his interference in episcopal action and his promotion of the Arian heresy.[31] The aristocratic groups of southern Gaul attempted to moderate the impact of imperial power and its intervention in the affairs of the church. The participation of bishops in regional governance, as religious figures protected by the sanction of holiness, added the subtle complicating element of religion. In the setting of the episcopal council the bishops of Gaul created and elaborated a legal and moral tradition to which they soon looked back as if it were something ancient and authoritative. By no means was this tradition simply inherited, but it was actively assembled, transposed into a Christian frame of meaning, and expanded.

The ideal of conciliar freedom and the mutuality of bishops were sometimes declared to be fundamental values, for in theory the will of God appeared to a council through the miraculous agreement of the attending bishops. Mutual recognition of episcopal power took the form of acquiescence in the exclusivity

---

28. Hefele-Leclercq, *Histoire des conciles* 2:102.

29. Council of Riez (439) CCSL 148:61–75; Hefele-Leclercq, *Histoire des conciles* 2:423.

30. There are several versions of the subscription list: Council of Orange (441), CCSL 148:87–90.

31. "Ponamus animus pro ouibus, quia fures introierunt, et leo saeuiens circuit," Hilary of Poitiers, *Contre Constance,* ed. André Rocher, SC 334 (Paris: 1987), 166; "Antichristum praeuenis," Hilary of Poitiers, *Contre Constance,* 180; see also Bertrand Fauvarque, "Eschatologie: Conversion et mission à la fin de l'Empire romain," MScR 53 (1996): 13–26, esp. 18–19; see also Berthold Altaner, *Patrologie: Leben, Schriften und Lehre der Kirchenväter,* 3rd ed. (Freiburg: 1951), 315–19.

of each bishop's territory.[32] It was believed that the Holy Spirit and attending angels were present at such assemblies. The brevity and reticence of council records do not enable us to peer into the actual give and take of debates within the council meetings, but conciliar decisions were always presented as certain and unanimous. While they continued the functionality of regional aristocratic assemblies, the councils possessed a new, distinctive religious dimension, as well.

Despite the claim of unanimity, the canons of many councils appear to record the successful arguments made by one victorious side in a dispute. In a study of the use of the Bible in later Merovingian councils, for example, Brigitte Basdevant-Gaudemet argued that bishops looked for a confirmation of their ideas and arguments from biblical passages, and did not find in them "an imperative juridical norm." Her findings seem applicable to the Gallic period, as well. In preparing to attend an important and possibly contentious council, it seems that leading bishops would prepare dossiers of legal and sacred texts for presentation. Strategies, debates, and arguments have left for us only subtle traces in the quotation of Biblical texts, as we see in the councils of Macon (581–583) and Lyon (583).[33] The same can be said about the earlier Gallic councils: we know that debates were part of the basic functioning of the councils, but little trace of those debates remain. The presentation of dossiers of texts at Gallic councils is amply testified, and these were seemingly supported by Biblical passages or by collections of canon law. The values of collegiality and unity seem to have dampened the open expression of hostility.[34]

The increasing depth and luster of the conciliar tradition provided bishops with a platform from which to view and attempt to shape the world around them. The legal tradition was crafted so as to offer stability to every bishop, filled as it was with directives and justifications for episcopal government.[35] For that very reason, it can be difficult to distinguish the idealism of episcopal law from the actual activities of bishops.[36] Often the councils were concerned with current problems arising from their governance over clerics, chapels, and monasteries and their control of land and buildings. Beyond this, moreover, episcopal

32. Jean Gaudemet, "La législation des conciles gaulois du IVe siècle," in *Proceedings of the Third International Congress of Medieval Canon Law*, Strasbourg, Sept. 3–6,1968, edited by Stephen Kuttner, 1–13; see 7, *Monumenta Iuris Canonici* ser. C, Subsidia, vol. 4 (Vatican City: 1971).

33. Brigitte Basdevant-Gaudemet, "La Bible dans les canons des conciles mérovingiens," in *Église et Autorités: Études d'histoire du droit canonique médiéval;* Cahiers d l'Institut d'Anthropologie Juridique 14 (Limoges: 2006), 201–12; quoting 206.

34. Gaudemet, "La législation des conciles gaulois," 6.

35. Alexandre Faivre, *Naissance d'une hiérarchie: Les premières étapes du cursus clérical,* Théologie historique, 40 (Paris: 1977), 259–68.

36. See the entirely relevant remarks of Heuclin, "Le clergé mérovingien et carolingien," 28.

law had a spacious horizon. The law of episcopal councils included wide-ranging social doctrines regarding the nature of Christian society, which were expressed as the authoritative, communal decisions of episcopal authority. Good power was legal power. The concept of *legality* was an ancient Roman principle that shaped episcopal understanding of their role as regional judges and governors.

The bishops legislated as governors of the People of God, the Christian society that bishops themselves brought into existence through baptism. As will be seen, this society, the "people of God" (*populus Dei*), "Christian people" (*plebs christiana*), or "holy people" (*plebs sancta*) was intended as a contrasting category to the many clans or tribes (*gentes*) out of which it was created.[37] In the developing Christian and episcopal social model it was the task of bishops to bring the *gentes* into the sheep-fold of the Christian people, and subsequently to govern them. New political federations of the Goths, Burgundians, and others were incorporated within the frame of ancient patterns of organized space, which continued to provide, in Christian guise, the unity and interconnectedness of the old Roman regions.[38] Christian space largely adhered to this pattern.

From the fourth to fifth century, one can observe a flexible Christian historical vision: under the still-flourishing Roman Empire many Christians had come to believe that Divine Providence allowed the Roman Empire to arise in order to secure and pave the way for the Christianization of the world, the familiar concept of *praeparatio evangelii*.[39] With the gradual collapse of Rome and the establishment of new barbarian kingdoms in its place, the historical perspective of Christians was transmogrified into a program of missionary expansion with a more central and independent role for bishops in bringing about the conversion of these barbarian peoples before the approaching end of time.[40] Eschatological energy was added to the magnificence of episcopal government.

---

37. Cf. Tertullian's expression of the wide diffusion of Christianity even among "abditarum multarum gentium"; cited in Ilaria Ramelli, "Alcune osservazioni sulle origini del cristianesimo in Spagna: la tradizione patristica," *Vetera Christianorum* 35 (1998): 245–56. On the ambiguity of *gens* and other ethnic designations, see Susan Reynolds, "Our Forefathers? Tribes, Peoples and Nations in the Historiography of the Age of Migrations," in *After Rome's Fall: Narrators and Sources of Early Medieval History—Essays Presented to Walter Goffart,* edited by Alexander Callander Murray, 17–36 (Toronto: 1998).

38. Camille Jullian, *Gallia: Tableau sommaire de la Gaule sous la domination romaine* (Paris: 1892), 304.

39. See the classic discussion of Theodor E. Mommsen, "St. Augustine and the Christian Idea of Progress: The Background of the City of God," in his *Medieval and Renaissance Studies,* edited by Eugene F. Rice, Jr. (Ithaca: 1959), 265–98; Jean Daniélou, *Message évangélique et culture hellénistique aux IIe et IIIe siècles,* Bibliothèque de théologie 2 (Paris: 1961), 41–72.

40. Edward O. James, *Europe's Barbarians A.D. 200–600* (Harlow: 2009), 219. On Jerome's despair over barbarian incursions see J. N. D. Kelly, *Jerome: His Life, Writings and Controversies*

The great ecumenical councils of Christian antiquity cast a significant shadow over bishops who held councils later on, especially in Europe.[41] The dramatic role those ancient bishops had played in laying down the foundations of Christian doctrine left later bishops in awe of them.[42] Canons of the great "ecumenical" councils were customarily read aloud at the outset of later councils of bishops. The meticulous record of debates and conflicts of the old councils were now transformed into short, authoritative precepts. Old canon law was something to be adored and adhered to, rather than questioned or reexamined, except in unusual cases. By adopting this pious view of the great early councils, bishops developed a mode of authority and an understanding of history that sustained their actions over centuries and enhanced the authority of their own legislation by association with an illustrious past.

Collections of canon law were a further form of the admiration of old conciliar authority and the development of Christian legal scholarship. The chief legal accomplishments of fourth- and fifth-century bishops were summarized sometime around the year 500. Dionysius Exiguus gathered the canons of the ecumenical councils in a collection known as the *Dionysiana,* a widely used source of knowledge about the early councils that espoused their *magna auctoritas.*[43] This collection of texts was worked out in two recensions. The first contained the Canons of the Apostles and the canons of Nicaea, Ancyra, Neocaesarea, Gangra, Antioch, Laodicea, Constantinople, Sardica, the first session of Carthage (419), and Chalcedon. The second recension added the rest of Carthage (419) and incorporated an earlier collection of African councils, especially those taking place in Carthage, the *Codex Canonum Ecclesiae Africanae.*[44]

(London: 1998), 296–97; see also G. J. M. Bartelink, *De Geboorte van Europa: Van laat-romeins imperium naar vroege middeleeuwen* (Muiderberg: 1989), 51–65; Fauvarque, "Eschatologie," 21–22.

41. This meant the "four holy councils": Nicaea I (325), Constantinople I (381), Ephesus (431), and Chalcedon (451). In the Merovingian period were added the Council of Constantinople II (553) and Constantinople III (680–681); in the Carolingian period, Nicaea II (787) was added, although the Franks contested this council. The decrees of these councils are conveniently found in *Conciliorum oecumenicorum decreta,* ed. Joseph Alberigo, et al., 3rd ed. (Bologna: 1973); English trans. *Decrees of the Ecumenical Councils,* ed. Norman P. Tanner, 2 vols. (Washington, D.C.: 1990).

42. Paul Mikat, "Zu Bedingungen des frühchristlichen Kirechenrechts," ZSRG.K 64 (1978): 309–20.

43. *Die Canonessammlung des Dionysius Exiguus in der ersten Redaktion,* ed. Adolf Strewe, Arbeiten zur Kirchengeschichte 16 (Berlin: 1931), Prologue: "magna est siquidem auctoritas," 1; Proem of the Council of Chalcedon: "Regulas sanctorum partum," 98. See further on this collection, known as the *Dionysiana:* Jean Gaudemet, *Sources du droit,* 134–37; Maassen, *Geschichte der Quellen,* 103–7. On Dionysius Exiguus: Gustave Bardy, *Littérature latine chrétienne* (Paris: 1929), 194–95.

44. Hamilton Hess, *The Canons of the Council of Sardica A.D. 343: A Landmark in the*

The collections attributed to Dionysius became a basic resource of canonical authority in Rome and Gaul. Later on, records of the ecumenical councils served as the basis for ever larger collections, which gradually added the canons of successive Gallic councils, set out in chronological order.[45] Thus the Gallic tradition could always be linked to the prestigious past of the early church. As will be explained in more detail in the following chapter, this took the form of a scholarly and aristocratic legal culture.

The most typical conciliar activity in the fourth and fifth centuries gathered the bishops of a province or region under the authority of the most important bishop of the region, the "metropolitan" bishop, usually in his city, thus giving shape to independent regional churches.[46] As we have seen, the African Church met regularly under the bishops of Carthage and developed a conciliar tradition that was widely admired and circulated in several early collections, which were accepted as a valuable source of law by the Church of Rome and incorporated in the *Dionysiana*.[47] In the same way, the bishops of Gaul created a distinctive legal tradition tailored to regional Gallic concerns and conditions, often shaped by bitter local disputes, but that could also be seen as having general application and authority.[48]

The aristocratic bishops who assembled in these councils adopted the parliamentary procedures of the Roman Senate as their own. According to Hess, at first the early conciliar manuscripts consisted of complete stenographic records of council debates and the protocol to which they adhered: the short address opening a discussion (*relatio*), followed by lengthy debates, or interrogations, often emotional in the case of struggles to claim and define orthodoxy. At this point the members, in order of precedence, expressed their opinions (*sententiae*), followed by a majority vote for one of these resolutions. This parliamentary procedure was followed at Carthage (256), Ephesus (431), and Chalcedon (451). A conclusion was announced with the proclamation *omnes episcopi dixerunt,*

Early Development of Canon Law (Oxford: 1958), 153. For other African collections, see Gaudemet, *Sources du droit,* 79–82. According to Doujat, Dionysius completed the first redaction in about 496, relying upon an earlier Latin collection; J. Doujat, *Histoire du droit canonique* (Paris: 1685), 54–55.

45. Ralph Mathisen, "The 'Second Council of Arles' and the Spirit of Compilation and Codification in Late Roman Gaul," JECS 5 (1997): 511–54; see 528; and Maassen, *Geschichte der Quellen,* 640–42.

46. F. Kempf, "Primatiale und episkopal-synodale Struktur der Kirche vor dem gregorianischen Reform," *AHC* 16 (1978): 27–66; see esp. 27–29.

47. Kéry, *Canonical Collections,* 1–2 and 9–13; Gaudemet, *L'Église dans l'empire,* 39.

48. Faivre, *Naissance d'une hiérarchie,* 262–63; and a brilliant article by C. H. Turner, "Arles and Rome: The First Developments of Canon Law in Gaul," JTS 17 (1916): 236–47.

recording a vote by acclamation.[49] Other early councils, such as Arles (314), are not preserved in complete stenographic reports, but in a much shorter form of publication, ending with the identity of the place of assembly and a subscription list of those who attended. Parallels between senatorial procedure and that of councils of bishops have often been noted, although somewhat different modes of procedure were used from one council to another. Stenographers recorded the conciliar proceedings and decisions following an austere, laconic pattern.[50] In some cases we can point to an imitation of senatorial form, while in others we can only speculate that other forms of procedure might have been used.[51]

Philippe Buc has insisted that rituals such as those recorded in conciliar records should not be viewed in line with the "functionalist baggage" of anthropology. The written documents that record ritual may be carefully, even deceptively, crafted to create a textualized ritual that masks the original event. Even if we do not follow Buc in his thoroughgoing skepticism, we must approach conciliar records with caution. Bishops' rituals of discussion and decision-making were recycled and transposed in their new setting.[52] Nevertheless, the conciliar records reveal certain rites of mutual recognition, the fraternal character of powerful men gathering as an exclusive club. As Patzold suggests, ritual (such as episcopal ordinations) served to crystallize and disseminate doctrines regarding the *ministerium* and religious centrality of the bishops.[53] In the councils, age-old parliamentary formulae and rituals were given new Christian purposes. Ancient senatorial rituals were adopted because they were eminently suited to the class and character of the bishops and to the task in which these men were engaged. Parliamentary ritual served to regulate the public interactions of this elite group and to highlight its claim to exercise a prerogative of religious direction for a community. As each bishop entered his name in the subscription list at the end of the canons of a council, he thus agreed not to disturb the placid surface of the canons, and at the same moment asserted his rightful place in an exclusive aristocratic group. Theological, ecclesiastical, and social order was projected by the canons and assumed episcopal control over ritual order.

49. Hess, *Canons of Sardica*, 29–31.
50. Sotinel, "Le personnel épiscopal," 108.
51. Gaudemet, *L'Église dans l'empire*, 451–52.
52. Philippe Buc, "Political Rituals and Political Imagination in the Medieval West from the Fourth Century to the Eleventh," in *The Medieval World*, edited by Peter Linehan and Janet L. Nelson (London: 2001), 189–213; see esp. 190. On the crafting of textualized rituals, see also Buc, *The Dangers of Ritual: Between Early Medieval Texts and Social Scientific Theory* (Princeton: 2001), 9.
53. See Patzold's critical discussion of Buc: *Episcopus*, 527–30.

In their councils bishops often asserted that their authority and social function had come to them out of the sacred past. They had evidence of an ancient backdrop in the records of old councils and in the apparent fact that they still engaged in the same religious and social activities as their predecessors.[54] The legislation of Gallic bishops was therefore conceived to be entirely coherent with older law, which had been "established by our fathers as an expression of authority."[55] The bishops were the direct heirs and continuators of the work of the "elders," and their own law constantly referred to "what our holy fathers established" and the "ancient authority of the canons."[56] Such expressions gave an ancient patina even to the recent activities of bishops.

The Rule of Truth

Gallic bishops of the fourth and early fifth centuries looked to the Mediterranean and Rome as their intellectual and cultural homeland. Their councils served as a vehicle for maintaining official contact with this broader Mediterranean world by addressing theological struggles that preoccupied the Roman Church. The first Gallic council whose records we possess took place in 314 in Arles, a city that played a central role in imperial politics and later in the post-imperial world of the barbarian kingdoms. The council announced a new era for a church that was coming under the power of the Roman state and would remain so for nearly a century.[57] The law that the bishops defended, however— "our law" (*lex nostra*)—was episcopal law derived from the "rule of truth" that lay in the bishop's hand.[58]

In the fourth century the Christian emperors thought of bishops as imperial

54. Michael Durst, "Nizäa als 'autoritative Tradition' bei Hilarius von Poitiers," in *Stimuli: Exegese und ihre Hermeneutik in Antike und Christentum, Festschrift für Ernst Dassmann*, edited by Georg Schöllgen and Clemens Scholten, 406–22, Jahrbuch für Antike und Christentum, Erganzungsband 23 (Munster: 1996).

55. "Et licet a patribus nostris emissa auctoritate id fuerit constitutum," Council of Tours (461), CCSL 148:144.

56. "Secundum instituta seniorum," Council of Arles (ca. 442–506), CCSL 148:123; "Quod sancti patres nostri synodali sententia statuerunt," Council of Agde (506), CCSL 148:211; "Prisca canonum praecepit auctoritas," Council of Agde (506), CCSL:208.

57. Sebastian Scholz, "Die Rolle der Bischöfe auf den Synoden von Rome (313) und Arles (314)," in *Köln: Stadt und Bistum in Kirche und Reich des Mittelalters, Festschrift für Odilo Engels zum 65. Geburtstag*, 1–21, Kölner historische Abhandlungen 39 (Cologne: 1993).

58. "Ubi grauem ac pernitiosam legis nostrae atque traditionis [. . .] effrenatae mentis homines pertulimus; quos et Dei nostri praesens et auctoritas et traditio ac regula ueritatis, *Epistula ad Siluestrum*, Council of Arles (314), CCSL 148:4. The authenticity of the letter has been challenged, among other reasons, for an anachronistic use of *papa* to mean "pope": I. M. Mazzini, "Lettura del concilio di Arles," VC 27 (1973): 282–300. On the rule of truth, see Damien Van den Eynde, *Les normes de l'enseignement chrétien dans la littérature patristique des trois premiers*

agents and dignitaries and were intent on creating consensus among them, putting considerable pressure on one group or another to accomplish this.[59] From Constantine onward, direct control over the church became central to concepts of imperial government, a culmination of the developing association of monotheism and imperial autarchy.[60] Eusebius portrayed Constantine as a new imperial model, making Christian legislation, convoking and attending synods: a unifying "episcopal" figure, a *koinos episkopos*.[61] In the West, bishops such as Athanasius and Hilary of Poitiers rankled at imperial activism. Nevertheless, imperial laws on religious matters, developed with the aid of episcopal advisors, were widely accepted as authoritative. Evidence of this is provided by compilations of Roman law, relevant to church affairs, such as the *Constitutiones Sirmondianae,* a collection made sometime between 425 and 438.[62] Just as the regional elites of the Roman Empire had served as mediators between the imperial center and local communities, bishops now performed a similar service in a Christian context.

Long afterward the struggle between competing orthodoxies, such as Nicene doctrine *versus* Arianism, shaped relations between orthodox bishops and the Arian-faithed Germanic peoples and colored the interaction of bishops with imperial or royal power. In 385, Ambrose of Milan (374–397), with the enthusiastic support of his parishioners, was able to resist attempts by the emperor Valentinian II to put some of his churches in the hands of the Arians.[63] Ambrose was an unusually sophisticated and well-entrenched bishop, well able to "pull the Nicene rabbit out of the hat in the West," but his reaction reveals the social and political tensions many bishops experienced, tensions intertwined with fundamental questions of theology.[64]

siècles, Universitas catholica Lovaniensis, Dissertationes Ser. 2.25 (Paris: 1933), 281–313; Faivre, *Ordonner la fraternité,* 276–80.

59. Timothy D. Barnes, *Constantine and Eusebius* (Cambridge, Mass.: 1981), 224–44.

60. On the centrality of the church to Constantine's conception of "Weltherrschaft": Eduard Schwartz, *Kaiser Constantin und die Christliche Kirche: Fünf Vorträge* (Leipzig: 1913), 69–71; on the relation between monotheism and imperial ideals: Pierre Hadot, "La fin du paganisme," in *Histoire des religions,* edited by Henri-Charles Puech, 2:81–113, see 84 (Paris: 1970–1976) and Barnes, *Constantine and Eusebius,* 245–60.

61. Charles Pietri, "La politique de Constance II: Un premier 'césaropapisme' ou l'*Imitatio Constantini*," in his *Christiana Respublica: Éléments d'une enquête sur le christianisme antique,* Collection de l'École française de Rome 234 (Rome: 1997), 1:281–346.

62. Kéry, *Canonical Collections,* 5–6.

63. Boniface Ramsey, *Ambrose* (London: 1997), 26; more generally on Ambrose and his struggle with Arianism, F. Homes Dudden, *The Life and Times of St. Ambrose* (Oxford: 1935), 1:185–206; and Daniel H. Williams, *Ambrose of Milan and the End of the Nicene-Arian Conflicts* (Oxford: 1995).

64. G. R. Evans, "Eutyches, Nestorius and Chalcedon," in *The First Christian Theologians:*

Gentes—Gentiles—Populus

Imperial politics provided the unavoidable backdrop of episcopal activity for the second half the fourth century and into the fifth century. Yet the "Roman Empire" was not a constant, unchanging value. The Empire had been undergoing rapid change before the fifth century, and the meaning of imperial politics was also changing.[65] The settlement of peoples from outside the empire was ever faster and less susceptible to control, becoming the most difficult social problem faced by late Roman society.[66] The Danube frontier was absorbed by a proto-kingdom of the Goths. As the pace of change accelerated, the attention of bishops was more and more directed toward the tribes entering Western Europe from beyond the borders of a fading Roman hegemony. The bishops thought about these peoples in a complex manner, combining traditional Roman cultural perspectives with concepts drawn from the Bible.

In accord with an old traditional Roman perspective, people from the Rhine-Danube frontier were barbarians, occupying a secondary, inferior cultural rank.[67] The Romans often raided, burned houses, and destroyed crops on the barbarian side of the line, and in this sense, Roman ethnography and border policy worked together.[68] In the eyes of the Gallic bishops, these were the "the peoples" (*gentes*) nations or ethnic groups from outside the Roman world.[69] Their distance from Roman culture could be measured by their *gentilitas*—the extent to which they clung to their own legal customs and culture rather than adopting Roman ways. In the social imagination of the late empire, *gentiles* were permanent outsiders, despised even when their help was needed.

As the Goths and other *gentes* entered the territories of the old Roman cities, the bishops thought about them in a complex, ambiguous way. This was reflected in the terminology used to describe these peoples. In translating the Hebrew *goyim* by the Latin *gentes* (or *gentiles*), Jerome and other translators of the Bible

---

An Introduction to Theology in the Early Church, edited by G. R. Evans, 243–47; quoting 243 (Oxford: 2004).

65. John Moorhead, *The Roman Empire Divided* (Harlow: 2001), 24.

66. Demandt, *Geschichte der Spätantike,* 285.

67. Such was Emperor Julian's perception of European peoples outside the limits of the Empire: Jean Bouffartigue, "L'Empereur Julien et les barbares: Réalisme et illusion," in *Haut moyen-âge: Culture, éducation et société—Études offertes à Pierre Riché,* edited by Michel Sot, 49–58 (La Garenne–Colombes: 1990); see also Bartelink, *Geboorte van Europa,* 24–28.

68. James, *Europe's Barbarians,* 40.

69. Yves Albert Dauge, *Le Barbare: Recherches sur la conception romaine de la barbarie et de la civilisation,* Collection Latomus 176 (Brussels: 1981), 424–31; Teillet, *Des Goths à la nation gothique,* 24–31.

produced a complex new word, which absorbed at the same time the Roman concept of non-Roman barbarian peoples (*barbari*), and the Hebrew notion of non-Jews: unbelievers or pagans.[70] For the Spanish priest Eutropius, writing at the end of the fourth century, that the Suevi were a barbaric tribe (*ethnici barbari*) was shown equally by their language and their idolatrous mentality.[71] Like many another bishop, Ambrose of Milan drew a connection between barbarism and the Arian heresy.[72] However, in the context of the successor kingdoms of the post-Roman world, from Britain to Spain, even the Romans could appear as just another *gens,* the *Romani.*[73]

Christ had told the disciples that his message should be proclaimed to all the nations (*testimonium omnibus gentibus*).[74] The bishops of Gaul, as heirs of the apostles, believed that they inherited this special duty, conceiving of the task as the creation of a new people: the People of God (*populus Dei*). Their missionary concepts were tinged with expectations that completion of this task would usher in the Second Coming.[75] The contrast between the *gentes* and the people of God were highlighted in the conflict between the social demands of Christian legislation and the sexual and social customs of the peoples toward whom it was directed.[76] Viewed broadly, Christianity was a possession of the "people of the faithful" (*fidelium populus*), but as an empirical society it took shape in

70. H. Lesètre, "Gentils," in *Dictionnaire de la Bible,* by F. Vigouroux (Paris: 1907–1912), 3:189–92; see also Charles du Fresne du Cange, "Gentiles," *Glossarium mediae et infimae latinitatis,* edited and supplemented by D. P. Carpenter and G. A. L. Henschel (Graz: 1954), 4:57: "Ces cinq éléments permettent une multiplicité de combinaisons, et donc de slogans," François Paschoud, "Le mythe de Rome à la fin de l'empire et dans les royaumes romano-barbares," in *Passaggio dal mondo antico al medio evo da Teodosio a san Gregorio Magno (Rome: April 25–28, 1977),* atti dei convegni Lincei 45 (Rome: 1980), 123–38; see 134.

71. Eutropius, "Sur quelques textes littéraires relatifs aux grandes invasions," *De similitudine carnis peccati,* edited by Pierre Courcelle, RBPH 31 (1953): 23–37; see 29–31.

72. Catherine Lheureux-Godbille, "Barbarie et hérésie dans l'oeuvre de saint Ambroise de Milan (374–397)," MA 109 (2003): 473–92.

73. Like other peoples, the *Romani* had their own customary law; Luisa Pelliciari, *Sulla natura giuridica dei rapporti tra Visigoti e impero romano al tempo delle invasioni del Vo secolo;* Publicazioni della facoltà di giurisprudenza della università di Modena 3 (Milan: 1982), 47.

74. Mt 24:14. The Bible contains a host of passages in which the concept was elaborated; see "Gens, gentes," in François Pascal Dutripon, *Bibliorum sacrorum concordantiae* (1880; repr. Hildesheim: 1976), 561–65. The contrast between the People and the nations—peoples—gentiles is a major theme in the Book of Acts, cf. "Lumen annuntiaturus es populo et gentibus" (Acts 26:23).

75. Fauvarque, "Eschatologie," 21–26; see also Lucien Cerfaux, "Le peuple de Dieu," in *Populus Dei: Studi in onore del Card, Alfredo Ottaviani per il cinquantesimo di sacerdozio: 18 marzo 1966,* edited by H. Cazelles and R. de Vaux, Communio 10 and 11 (Rome: 1969): 2:803–926.

76. The conflict especially centered on marriage-customs, concubinage and feuding. In regard to Merovingian conciliar legislation, see J. M. Wallace-Hadrill, *The Frankish Church* (Oxford: 1983), 108.

local communities, gathered under its bishops, the people of a church (*plebi ec-clesiae*).[77] Outside the church were those unbelievers who still clung to their *gen-tilitas*, a word which for churchmen now combined the concepts of paganism and cultural backwardness.[78] Barbaric stupidity (*gentilis stultitia*) therefore dis-gusted the learned Maximus of Turin (†408/423).[79] Imperial law was brought to bear against the public existence of paganism in the harsh and combative legisla-tion of the late fourth century.[80] A new social order was imagined based on the norms of Christian communities and their guidance by a Christian aristocracy.

Ius—Potestas—Gubernatio

The Gallic councils were ordinarily preoccupied with a limited number of themes, such as strictures regulating the penance of murderers and other crimi-nals, the establishment of standards of discipline for clerics, and, to a lesser ex-tent, the Christianization of pagan populations. Ecclesiastical law was directed toward civil and political life. The bishops tended to restrict their legislation to matters of discipline and jurisdiction, producing a lean, practical set of laws.[81] At the heart of Gallic episcopal legislation was the working out of institutional norms for bishops themselves, how they should govern and be governed, and how to treat one another. The boundaries of each bishop's power and control of sacred space were considered to be sacrosanct, and were said to have an ancient and religious origin. This was governed by right (*ius*):

Regarding the presumptuous, it was fittingly observed that if some bishop makes an attempt to assert his power (*potestas*) over his brother's jurisdiction (*ius*), so that he

77. "Fidelium populus," Council of Vaison-la-Romaine (442), CCSL 148:99; on the "people of a church," see the address to the church of Fréjus: "Dilectissimus fratribus clero et plebi eccle-siae Foroiuliensium," *Epistula Foroiulienses,* in Council of Valence (374), CCSL 148:44; also "Huic autem etiam in ecclesiarum plebibus per loca tamen magis quam per urbes," Council of Riez (439), CCSL 148:68.

78. "De puellis fidelibus quae gentilibus iunguntur," Council of Arles (314), CCL 148:11; the sense of otherness extended to Germanic institutions: Arnold Angenendt, "Princeps impe-rii—Princeps apostolorum: Rom zwischen Universalismus und Gentilismus," in *Roma—Caput et fons: Zwei Vorträge über das päpstliche Rom zwischen Altertum und Mittelalter,* edited by Ar-nold Angenendt and Rudolf Schieffer, 7–44, see 8, Gerda Henkel Vorlesung (Opladen: 1989).

79. Maximus of Turin, *Contra paganos,* L.56, ed. A. Spagnolo and C. H. Turner, in "Maximus of Turin Against the Pagans: Contra paganos," JTS 17 (1916): 321–37; see 322.

80. With laws against the continuation of sacrifice, for example: Theodosian Code XVI.10.7; see Périclès-Pierre Joannou, *La legislation imperiale et la christianisation de l'empire romain (311–476),* Orientalia christiana analecta 192 (Rome: 1972), 81.

81. Gaudemet, "La législation des conciles gaulois," 11–12; Gunther Gottlieb, "Die formalen Bestandteile in der Überlieferung der gallischen Konzilien des 4. und 5. Jahrhunderts," AHC 16 (1984): 254–63.

either invades another's diocese, by transgressing the borders established by the Fathers, or presumes to remove clerics ordained others, let him not doubt that he alienates himself from the communion of all brothers and his fellow priests. We know from the Apostle's words that one may have no contact with unordained, wandering brothers, not established "according to tradition" by the Fathers.[82]

The antiquity and religious sanction of these arrangements were insisted on, although the boundaries of dioceses were in a state of almost constant change.[83] The "borders" (*termini*) should, in any case, not be thought of as lines on a map. Instead, the terminology makes it clear that the borders in question were the borders of a bishop's *ius*—his sphere of influence and the buildings, land, and people under his authority.[84] As the Council of Agde declared in 506:

As the ancient authority of the canons ordains, little houses, slaves, and church plate should remain under the legal authority (*ius*) of the church, preserving the intention of donations made in faith.[85]

The Council of Orange in 441, led by Hilary of Arles, declared that while it would be sinful to prevent a bishop from building a church in the *territorium* of another bishop, the bishop who governed that territory would also govern the new church, with sole authority to ordain and govern its clerics. Only the bishop of a territory had the capacity of governance (*gubernatio*) within its bounds. A bishop's territory coincided with the region around the city (*territorium civitatis*) of which he was bishop—the region dominated by and officially attached to a city.[86] The bishop inherited this aspect of late Roman municipal structure and the dominance of *civitas* over *territorium*.[87] Despite their religious purposes, the councils were also working out institutional and governmental norms and vo-

82. "De praesumptoribus etiam placuit obseruari ut si quis episcopus in ius fratris sui suam conatus fuerit inserere potestatem, ut aut dioceses alienas, transgrediendo terminos a patribus constitutos, peruadat, aut clericos ab aliis ordinatos promouere praesumat, ab uniuersorum fratrum et consacerdotum suorum communione se alienum efficiendum non dubitet, quia Apostolo dicente cognoscimus nullam nos cum fratribus inordinate ambulantibus et 'non secundum traditionem' (II Pet. 2:22) a patribus contitutam, posse habere participationem," Council of Tours (461) CCSL 148:146.

83. Maurice Chaume, "Le mode de constitution et de délimitation des paroisses rurales aux temps mérovingiens et carolingiens," *Revue Mabillon* 27 (1937): 61–73, esp. 64–66; Godding, *Prêtres en Gaule,* 104–6.

84. Chaume, "Le mode de constitution," 61.

85. "Casellas uero uel mancipiola ecclesiae episcopi, sicut prisca canonum praecepit auctoritas, uel uasa ministerii, quasi commendata fideli proposito integro ecclesiae iure possideant," Council of Agde (506) CCSL 148:195.

86. Council of Orange (441), CCSL 148:80–81.

87. Michael Kulikowski, *Late Roman Spain and Its Cities* (Baltimore: 2004), 242–43.

cabulary, drawing on existing situations, assimilating the new to the old, sometimes listening to papal advice.[88]

The sphere of a bishop's power was centered in a city. Ambrose of Milan was perhaps the sterling example of a bishop who firmly established his episcopal authority on the old stone foundations of aristocratic privilege and urban communal power. Rural churches began to appear in the late fourth century, but these were always subject to the bishop of a city.[89] The bishop's *territorium,* or sphere of influence, included the rural areas surrounding the city, where it was his duty to extirpate paganism.[90] The *territorium* was long established in the municipal structure of the late Empire, whereby a territory was attached to a city for purposes of administration and taxation and marked by such signs as "territorial markers, the path of the *limites,* and inscriptions, that is, [marked by] inscribed stones, and often by rivers and stone altars."[91] Episcopal government enacted the Christianization of such well-recognized late imperial spaces. Bishops were able to extend their influence by serving as the representatives of their cities in the imperial scene. As episcopal churches grew in number and became central to city life, traditional themes of power were newly mobilized in Christian form. The charity of wealthy citizens now coursed through the coffers of these churches as care for the poor became a feature of Christian social privilege.[92]

Claiming to undertake the traditional duty to protect and care for the poor, bishops could often emerge as the "city defender" (*defensor civitatis*). The late Roman *defensor civitatis* had been a judge devoted to defend the causes of the poor.[93] In the setting of episcopal judgment and arbitration, this role was taken over by the *defensor ecclesiae,* a legal agent associated with the activity of episcopal courts.[94] The change of terminology, from "city defender" to "church defend-

---

88. Jean Gaudemet, "Charisme et droit: Le domaine de l'évêque," ZSRG.K 74 (1988): 44–70, esp. 52.

89. Pierre Imbart de la Tour, *Les paroisses rurales dans l'ancienne France du IVe au XIe siècle* (Paris: 1898), 6–17.

90. "Si in alicuius episcopi territorio infideles aut faculas accedunt aut arbores, fontes uel saxa uenerantur," Council of Arles (ca. 442–506) CCSL 148:119. Such combinations were proverbial: "Colunt adhuc pagani et montes et arbores et fontes," Maximus of Turin, *Contra paganos,* L.143:325.

91. According to the surveying manual *Commentarium de agrorum qualitate,* a *territorium;* text in Brian Campbell, *The Writings of the Roman Land Surveyors,* Journal of Roman Studies Monograph No. 9 (London: 2000), 53; see also Kulikowski, *Late Roman Spain,* 14.

92. Peter Brown, *Poverty and Leadership in the Later Roman Empire,* Menahem Stern Jerusalem Lectures (Hannover: 2002), 28–30.

93. Robert M. Frakes, *Contra Potentium Iniurias: The Defensor Civitatis and Late Roman Justice,* Münchner Beiträge zur Papyrusforschung und antiken Rechtsgeschichte 90 (Munich: 2001).

94. Henry Chadwick, "Bishops as Monks," *Studia Patristica* 24 (Louvain: 1993): 45–61, see 52.

er," may reflect a shift in social terminology as much as a shift in competence. In moments of crisis, the bishop's role as patron of the poor and defenseless also took the form of negotiating with or repulsing an external enemy. The term *defensor civitatis* also referred to such acts of defense: thus the term was applied to St. Aignan when he confronted Attila the Hun, and to Germanus of Auxerre when he faced pillaging Alans.[95] Indeed, many bishops were said to have "confronted Attila": the list also includes Albinus of Châlons and Memorius of Troyes.[96] Such events provided uncanny and dramatic evidence of the bishop's benevolent religious power. When Pope Leo successfully negotiated with Attila to avoid hostilities, the news was received in Rome as a religious miracle.[97]

Episcopal Courts

Ecclesiastical and wealthy, religiously ascetic and socially potent: as the Roman aristocracy applied its energies to governing the Christian communities in Gaul, Italy, and elsewhere, episcopal courts grew in splendor.[98] Ambrose might counsel that a bishop should avoid secular entanglements, yet he was adept at combining ecclesiastical and secular politics.[99] The development of the institutions of the episcopal court went hand in hand with the ever growing range of power and responsibility accepted by bishops. Imperial law reveals the gradual expansion of episcopal authority as local justice and leadership were placed in the hands of the bishops.[100]

Beginning in 318, Constantine established episcopal courts by edict.[101] According to this law, Christians could choose to have their cases heard by an episcopal court (*episcopale iudicium*) and a judgment rendered according to Christian law (*lex christiana*).[102] Such cases were at the same time removed from the

95. Herwig Wolfram, *The Roman Empire and its Germanic Peoples,* trans. Thomas Dunlap (Berkeley: 1997), 137; André Loyen, "Le rôle de saint Aignan dans la défense d'Orléans," *Comptes rendus de l'Académie des Inscriptions et Belles-Lettres* (1969): 71–72.

96. "Confronting Attila" as a *topos*: Albinus, bishop of Châlons, described in *Vita Alpini,* AASS, September 3:85–89; and Memorius, bishop of Troyes, described in *De S. Memorio et sociis MM.,* AASS, September 3:70–72; see also Constantius of Lyon, *Vie de Saint Germain d'Auxerre,* SC 112:39.

97. Paschoud, "Mythe de Rome," 130.

98. Sotinel, "Le personnel épiscopal," 110–11.

99. Gryson, *Le prêtre selon Saint Ambroise,* 252–53.

100. Maurizio Lupoi, *The Origins of the European Legal Order,* trans. Adrian Belton (Cambridge: 2000), 26–27.

101. According to Barnes, the existence of this law must be deduced: Barnes, *Constantine and Eusebius,* 51.

102. Giulio Vismara, *La Giurisdizione civile dei vescovi (secoli I–IX),* Pubblicazionei dell'Istituto di Storia del Diritto Italiano 18 (Milan: 1995); see also Jill Harries, *Law and Empire in Late Antiquity* (Cambridge: 1999), 191–96.

praetorial court system. Even more dramatically, the decisions of an episcopal court, or episcopal audience (*episcopalis audientia*), were not subject to review, but were held to have the same stature as imperial decisions. The ability and authority to judge arose out of the historical development of the bishop and the role of the bishop in judging his Christian community.[103] By transforming this into an imperial function, Constantine thereby opened an enormous chasm in the Roman legal system and allowed episcopal power to pour into it. The law placed an onerous and unwelcome burden on bishops who might have preferred to spend their time hunting and fishing, or reading their Bibles, rather than listening to the quarrels of their neighbors.[104] It was fully expected that the trials conducted by bishops would result in *arbitrium* and *iudicium*.[105] When Synesius of Ptolemais judged the crimes of an adulterer of wine in 412, he had no qualms about consigning the man to prison.[106] Despite episcopal complaints, the duty of judging can be defined as a status obligation: a duty that is also a prerogative, marking the stature of a social elite.

In time, bishops were left as the only effective judicial tribunal in their cities, and by combining pastoral care with municipal leadership, were a source of social cohesion in an era of upheaval.[107] The relegation of a case to the episcopal audience was "to transfer to Christian law" (*Ad legem Christianam transferre*).[108] Episcopal courts were surely one of the last roses to bloom in the autumn of the late Western empire.

Bishops accepted the tasks of governing and judging with a lofty sense of purpose, ready to play the role of civic patrons. Ambrose declared that the Apostle Paul and the emperor together had placed the power of judgment in his hands: religious and secular business alike flowed toward the episcopal residence.[109]

The style of this ecclesiastical aristocracy was first worked out in Italy. It often took the form of an austere life. Petronius, bishop of Bologna from 432 until his

---

103. Harries, *Law and Empire,* 210.

104. John C. Lamoreaux, "Episcopal Courts in Late Antiquity," JECS 3 (1995): 143–67; see 143.

105. Walter Selb, "Episcopalis audientia von der Zeit Konstantins bis zur Nov. XXXV Valentiniens II," ZSRG.R 84 (1967): 162–217; see 180–81.

106. Lellia Cracco Ruggini, "Prêtre et fonctionnaire: L'essor d'un modèle épiscopal aux IVe–Ve siècles," in *Antiquité tardive—Antigüedad Tardía—Late Antiquity—Spätantike—Tarda Antichità,* 7 (1999)], 175–86; see 175.

107. William Klingshirn, "Charity and Power: Caesarius of Arles and the Ransoming of Captives in Sub-Roman Gaul," *Journal of Roman Studies* 75 (1985): 183–203; see 199; see also Mathisen, *Roman Aristocrats,* 97–104. On episcopal leadership and the bishop's tribunal, see especially Henry G. Beck, *The Pastoral Care of Souls in South-East France during the Sixth Century,* Analecta Gregoriana 51 (Rome: 1950), 317–44.

108. Selb, "Episcopalis audientia," 184.

109. Lamoreaux, "Episcopal Courts," 154–57.

death in 450, came from a pious, wealthy family. Petronius ended by devoting himself to the church. Adopting the sober life of a monk, he went on to become a bishop, and was believed, probably wrongly, by the historian Gennadius of Marseille (d. 492–505) to have written about the lives of Egyptian monks.[110] The ascetic life became a familiar dimension of a new ideology and style of power.

Paulinus, bishop of Nola (353–431), also came from a wealthy family of Bordeaux, and was destined for an elegant life, receiving an education from Ausonius and going on to become senator and later consul. After his baptism as a Christian, however, Paulinus moved to Nola, where he became devoted to Felix, a saint associated with the city. Then, as his admirer Augustine of Hippo tells us, Paulinus "willingly abandoned immense wealth and became exceedingly poor, yet abundantly holy."[111] Paulinus' dramatic change of direction allowed his biography to serve as an exemplary life, frequently referred to by Christian authors such as Jerome, Eutropius, and Eucherius of Lyon.[112] He succeeded Paulinus as bishop of the city in 409, and soon began to express his devotion to St. Felix, and his position at the head of his city, by means of a great building program. Paulinus called on Felix to protect Nola from the Goths. He crafted his own literary persona by means of this affiliation with Felix, writing a *Vita Felicis* and fashioning Felix as his *comes*.[113] His membership in a Christian elite was further demonstrated by the letters he exchanged with Augustine of Hippo and Ambrose of Milan. Like Ambrose, Paulinus built many new churches, and refurbished and decorated old ones, with an eye toward the conversion and religious education of the lower classes.[114] Paulinus exulted, in his *Carmen* 27, about the crowds who were drawn to his churches. The majority of these visitors were illiterate peasants, only recently won over from pagan cults. Paulinus felt it was important to dominate their rustic souls with the grandeur of his churches, and to educate them by means of the pictures adorning the walls:

Therefore it seemed to us useful to work gaily to embellish Felix' houses all over with sacred paintings in order to see whether the spirit of the peasants would not be surprised by this spectacle and undergo the influence of the colored sketches which are explained by inscriptions over them.[115]

---

110. Ruggini, "Prêtre et fonctionnaire," 185; Gennadius, *De viris inlustribus,* ed. E. C. Richardson, TU 14.1 (Leipzig: 1896), 41.
111. Augustine of Hippo, *The City of God against the Pagans,* trans. R. W. Dyson (Cambridge: 1998), I.10, 17–18.
112. Dennis E. Trout, *Paulinus of Nola: Life, Letters, and Poems* (Berkeley: 1999), 5–7.
113. Trout, *Paulinus,* 165–67.
114. Rudolf Carel Goldschmidt, *Paulinus' Churches at Nola* (Amsterdam: 1940), 1–5.
115. Goldschmidt, *Paulinus,* 65.

The passage is interesting for its anticipation of Gregory the Great's argument, in his famous letter to Serenus, that pictures can serve as books for the illiterate.[116] The whole point of Paulinus' poem, and of the churches it described, was to demonstrate the benevolent dominance of a highly literate, aristocratic bishop over his humble patrons. In his writings and his building programs "Paulinus set about orchestrating the cult of Felix at Nola by recalibrating sacral space and time."[117] The benevolence of Paulinus toward the poor could wear thin, however.

Paulinus was greatly annoyed by the proximity of two peasant hovels that spoiled the view of his newly refurbished religious compound. Paulinus had built a courtyard with a fountain, enclosed by a cloister and flanked by a pair of little churches—but right in front stood two ugly huts. He tried to reason with their owner, but the man refused to leave. Then came a miracle, which clearly approximated Paulinus' own wishes: a fire burned one of the huts to the ground, without harming the churches, while the owner, strangely enough, tore down the second hut himself, apparently in a fit of self-destructive anger. Paulinus was pleased. He clearly believed that the peasantry should make way for episcopal improvements and the glory of St. Felix.[118] By transferring his interests and ambitions to the church, Paulinus reflected a new, successful strategy for the Roman aristocracy.[119]

Farther north, the Mediterranean tradition of the ascetic bishop was combined with a heroic missionary ideal. The asceticism of Martin of Tours (371/372–397) was idealized after his death as an exceedingly harsh personal regimen. Martin was remembered as a charismatic holy man and a countercultural figure.[120] While his direct influence as a founder or promoter of monasticism was negligible, largely restricted to individual hermitages, nevertheless his aggressive image appealed very much to later bishops of Frankish Gaul as a symbolic figure more than a practical model, especially as the wonder-working opponent of paganism. Martin's direct influence was limited: the monastery of Lérins would instead become the predominant model for monasticism in Gaul.[121]

116. Robert A. Markus, *Gregory the Great and His World* (Cambridge: 1997), 175.
117. Trout, *Paulinus*, 173.
118. Goldschmidt, *Paulinus*, 71–79.
119. Van Dam, *Leadership and Community*, 308.
120. José María Blázquez, "El monacato de los siglos IV, V y VI como contracultura civil y religiosa," in *Intelectuales, ascetas y demonios al final de la Antigüedad*, 221–55 (Madrid: 1998); Sulpicius was himself an "homme d'opposition"; E.-Ch. Babut, "Saint Martin de Tours," *Revue d'histoire et de littérature religieuses*, New Series 1 (1910): 466–87, see 532.
121. On Martin's influence on eremeticism: Jean Heuclin, *Aux origines monastiques de la Gaule*

The figure of Martin really came into prominence as a mental image, or literary ideal, through the writings of his hagiographer, Sulpicius Severus. When Bishop Perpetuus held a council in Tours in 461, he drew on the authority of Martin's saintly image as the council opened on Martin's feast-day.[122] Sulpicius' *Life of Martin* was a major hagiographical model, gaining an unparalleled popularity in Gaul and elsewhere.[123] As a literary figure Martin combined the monastic ideal to the office of bishop; and yet Sulpicius boasted of his hero that he hardly ever sat in his bishop's *cathedra*—indeed scarcely set foot in his church. He was much more likely to be found in his rustic woodland cell.[124] The concept was persuasive and appealing. According to Sulpicius' account, Martin heroically confronted paganism and stood as an angry prophet against his episcopal enemies and the Emperor Maximus himself.[125] Martin had moved outside the familiar ambit of the Roman Mediterranean and its ancient traditions of aristocratic prestige, and Martin himself adopted a new ethos, ascetic but distinctly nonaristocratic. In the view of Arnaldo Marcone, "it is easy to see in the difficulties encountered by Martin a manifestation of the attachment of the rural population to their own pagan traditions and their opposition to Roman civilization."[126] Here was a different style than the cultured episcopal heirs of Rome. The emphasis for Martin and his followers was upon a prophetic distance from political power, a "distant saint" standing out as a reproach to ordinary ways of living.

Law and Sanctity

The Gallo-Roman city of Arles had been home to a Christian community since the mid-third century. By the first half of the fifth century, when Honoratus and then Hilary of Arles (†449) occupied the episcopal throne, the city possessed only a modest set of Christian spaces: a basilica called the *ecclesia publi-*

---

du nord: Ermites et reclus du Ve au XIe siècle (Lille: 1998), 28; see also Ivan Gobry, *Les moines en occident* (Paris: 1985–1987), 2:81–124; Dieter Von der Nahmer, "Martin von Tours: Sein Mönchtum—seine Wirkung," *Francia* 15 (1987): 1–41.

122. "Cum ad sacratissimam festiuitatem qua domni nostri Martini receptio celebratur," Council of Tours (461) CCSL 148:143. Hefele-Leclercq, *Histoire des conciles* 2.2:898.

123. René Aigran, *L'Hagiographie: Ses sources, ses méthodes, son histoire* (Paris: 1953), 298–99; Adalbert de Vogüé, *Histoire littéraire du mouvement monastique dans l'antiquité* (Paris: 1991–), 4:19–91; Sulpicius Severus, *Vie de Saint Martin*, ed. Jacques Fontaine, SC 133–35, 3 vols. (Paris: 1967–1969).

124. "Illud non praeteribo, quod in secretario sedens numquam cathedra usus est: nam in ecclesia nemo umquam illum sedere conspexit" (*Dialogues,* 2:1), in Augello, *Sulpici Severi Dialogi,* 68.

125. De Vogüé, *Histoire littéraire,* 4:56.

126. Marcone, "Late Roman Social Relations," 387.

ca, a second basilica dedicated to St. Genesius (*Basilica beati Genesii*), a further sanctuary preserving the column of St. Genesius, and two Christian cemeteries.[127] For the bishops of Arles, however, these modest edifices and sacred spaces were only the hub of a more wide-ranging power. Hilary, bishop from about 429 until his death in 449, was intent, as had been his predecessors, on having the church of Arles recognized as the most important see of southern Gaul.[128]

Behind Arles and its powerful bishops lay the prestige of Lérins, an island monastery just off the Mediterranean coast. It has been argued that Hilary, along with others trained in Lérins, formed a cohort of disaffected nobles who turned toward the church in a competitive search for social position because the imperial government could no longer provide secure positions for the Gallic aristocracy.[129] The island became a training ground for bishops, where men were schooled in a genteel culture of asceticism and learned silence and imbibed an elegant form of Christianity marked by a deep attachment to tradition.[130] Hilary of Arles was one of the most formidable of these Lérinian bishops.[131] With his aristocratic background and connections to the most powerful men of Gaul, he was in a position to play a leading role in shaping the Gallic Church of the invasion period. His immediate predecessor, Honoratus (d. 429/430), founded Lérins in 410, and Hilary was trained in the desert ethos of this island monastery.[132]

In the cultured, literate atmosphere of Lérins aristocrats could develop a new sensibility suited to the changing political world of Gaul.[133] At Lérins, turmoil

127. Biarne, *Provinces ecclésiastiques de Vienne,* 73–84; see also Jean Hubert, "La topographie religieuse d'Arles au VIe siècle," *Cahiers archéologiques* 2 (1947): 17–27.

128. This was a long-term project of the bishops of Arles: William E. Klingshirn, *Caesarius of Arles: The Making of a Christian Community in Late Antique Gaul,* Cambridge Studies in Medieval Life and Thought 22 (Cambridge: 1994), 66–67; Louis Duchesne, *Fastes épiscopaux de l'ancienne Gaule,* 2nd ed. (Paris: 1907–1915), 1:86–119; Eric Vanneufville, "L'Église en Provence du Ve au VIIIe siècles," MScR 53 (1996): 61–81; see 62–63.

129. Martin Heinzelmann, "The 'Affair' of Hilary of Arles (445) and Gallo-Roman Identity in the Fifth Century," in *Fifth-century Gaul,* 239–51; Friedrich Prinz, "Il monachesimo occidentale," in *Passaggio dal mondo antico,* 415–34. R. W. Mathisen has stressed that Hilary's rise and fall was characterized by aristocratic infighting; Mathisen, "Hilarius, Germanus and Lupus: The Aristocratic Background of the Chelidonius Affair," *Phoenix* 33 (Toronto: 1979): 160–69.

130. Columba Stewart, *Cassian the Monk* (New York: 1998), 16–19; on Lérins as a "pépinière d'évêques,"see Vanneufville, "L'Église en Provence," 62; see also Prinz, "Il monachesimo occidentale," 422.

131. Léon Cristiani, *Lérins et ses fondateurs* (Paris: 1946), 127–40.

132. Gobry, *Les moines en occident,* 2:235–70; Cristiani, *Lérins,* 113–26.

133. Pierre Courcelle, "Nouveaux aspects de la culture lérinienne," *Revue des études latines* 46 (1968): 379–409; and Michel Carrias, "Vie monastique et règle à Lérins au temps d'Honorat," RHEF 74 (1988): 195–211.

in the church and the collapse of Rome served as the backdrop of a greater literary and spiritual theme—the ingrained, sorrowful decline of the world.[134] In response to this perception, Lérinian scholars sought to gather documents of the Christian past in *compendia* and to base their intellectual life on the Bible and the most highly regarded authors of the early church in an effort to provide themselves with sure pathways of authority.[135] Vincent of Lérins (d. 450), evoking the "shipwreck of this present life," was at the forefront of those engaged in a project of preserving and distributing such sources of authority.[136] With Hilary of Arles, too, one recognizes a combination of harsh asceticism, learned conservatism, and aristocratic calm characteristic of those trained in Lérins.[137] The ascetic traditions of the monastery were avidly promoted as a salvific model for a corrupt world: the aura and reputation of Lérins were highlighted in a rhetorical project of many hands. The alumni of Lérins never tired of praising their fellow members, who together with them formed "a group of men whose fierce ambition was matched only by their exquisite self-consciousness."[138]

Gallic law compilations also included important materials from Rome—lists of the popes, papal rescripts, and collections of Roman synodal decisions.[139] This was especially true in Arles. The expansionism of the bishops of Arles had been sustained for generations, resulting in a burgeoning archive of old law, papal letters, and other legal documents. Until the mid-sixth century Arles was the most important center of canonical scholarship and compilation.[140] The councils held under Hilary: Riez (439), Orange (441), and Vaison (442), were characterized by

---

134. Salvatore Pricoco, *L'isola dei santi: Il cenobio di Lerino e le origini del monachesimo gallico,* Filologia e critica 23 (Rome: 1978), 192–204; Bartelink, *Geboorte van Europa,* 68–70.

135. Clemens M. Kasper, *Theologie und Askese: Die Spiritualität des Inselmönchtums von Lérins im 5. Jahrhundert,* Beiträge zur Geschichte des alten Mönchtums und des Benediktinertums 40 (Munster: 1990), 1–20.

136. "Praesentis uitae naufragia," Vincent of Lérins, *The Commonitorium of Vincentius of Lérins,* ed. Reginald Stewart Moxon (Cambridge: 1915), 5. This mood was at the heart of the *Traditionskonzept* of Lérins: Kasper, *Theologie und Askese,* 262–66.

137. On the 'ideology' of Lérins, see Pricoco, *Isola dei santi,* 189–92; these qualities were all emphasized in the Life of Hilary, by Honoratus of Marseilles: P. Benedikt Kolon, *Die Vita S. Hilarii Arelatensis: Eine eidographische Studie,* Rhetorische Studien 12 (Paderborn: 1925), 35–39.

138. Conrad Leyser, "'This Sainted Isle': Panegyric, Nostalgia, and the Invention of Lerinian Monasticism," in *The Limits of Ancient Christianity: Essays on Late Antique Thought and Culture in Honor of R. A. Markus,* edited by William E. Klingshirn and Mark Vessey (Ann Arbor: 1999), 188–206.

139. Charles Pietri, *Roma Christiana: Recherches sur l'Église de Rome, son organisation, sa politique, son idéologie de Miltiade à Sixte III (311–440),* Bibliothèque des Écoles françaises d'Athènes et de Rome 224 (Rome: 1976), 1:765.

140. Detlev Jasper and Horst Fuhrmann, *Papal Letters in the Early Middle Ages* (Washington, D.C.: 2001), 32–33.

a legal sophistication not shared by Vienne.[141] Increasingly these bishops could call upon legal resources from within the Gallic Church's own past—and older traditions assembled and tailored toward Gallic purposes.

In this way Arles (with Lérins) was at the center of a twofold movement, creating a legal tradition so attractive and authoritative that it formed the basis for Gallic law as a whole while promoting a learned asceticism. With the backing of the papacy, the bishops of Arles managed to extend their theoretical jurisdiction over most of southern Gaul and to act as papal vicars for the whole of Gaul. The bishops of Arles were proud of their special privileges and traditions. Pope Celestine complained that in their pride, the bishops of Arles had begun to dress in a manner that seemed grandiose and foreign.[142]

Hilary of Arles wrote about the life of Honoratus, his predecessor as bishop and founder of Lérins. This life (*Sermo de uita Honorati*) was probably written on the first anniversary of Honoratus' death to console those who still remembered the great monk-bishop and to reinforce the Lerinian ideal.[143] We are told that when Honoratus was first attracted to the religious life, he found many in his neighborhood engaged in a friendly competition, working out different ways of leading a true Christian life—some reading a great deal, others less so, some fasting constantly, others only moderately.[144] According to Hilary, these men were bishops in all but name.[145] After a religious *Wanderjahre* that took him to Greece and back by way of Italy, Honoratus was given the island of Lérins by Leontius, the bishop of Fréjus. Eventually he became a priest to meet the needs of the little community; as Hilary pointed out, none of the bishops of the region dared think of themselves as the equal of this simple priest (*presbyter*). The life of ascetic discipline and serenity that he led on Lérins was the "angelic life," which remained at the center of Honoratus' later role as bishop. This was why, according to Hilary, Honoratus could offer a special form of government unlike that of kings or emperors, "to rule with love rather than to dominate by terror."[146] Behind the grandeur and legal mastery of the bishops of Arles lay the

---

141. Hefele-Leclercq *Histoire des conciles* 2.1:423–60.

142. On the adoption at Arles of a "tentative de costume ecclésiastique," see Léon Cristiani, "Essai sur les origines du costume ecclésiastique," *Orientalia christiana periodica* 13 (1947): 69–80; on the privileges of Arles, see Vanneufville, "L'Église en Provence," 62.

143. Hilary of Arles, *Hilaire d'Arles: Vie de Saint Honorat*, ed. Marie-Denise Valentin, SC 235 (Paris: 1977); C. Kaspar, "Hilarius von Arles," *Lexikon der antiken christlichen Literatur*, 291.

144. Perhaps this is an accurate description of the earliest, "anarchic" phase of Gallic monasticism; Prinz, "Monachesimo occidentale," 419.

145. "Privatus quidam iam tunc in conuersatione eorum episcopatus gerebatur" (9.4), Hilary of Arles, *Vie de Saint Honorat*, 92.

146. "Studebat praeterea amore potius regere quam terrore dominari, ut uoluntaria magis

"most splendid temple" of Lérins, with its ideals of wisdom, virtue, justice, and truth nourished in the "squalor of the desert."[147]

The Mediterranean world in which the popes had long operated was reduced to an axis between Ravenna and Byzantium, a case of diminished expectations as Roman hegemony in the West gave way to the Visigothic kingdom of Toulouse, the Ostrogothic kingdom in Italy, and the Burgundian kingdom.[148] From the letters of Sidonius Apollinaris one can gain a vivid picture of what these new kingdoms and their masters looked like—at once off-putting and impressive— to their Roman contemporaries.[149] The cultural identity of bishops was crafted especially in southern Gaul, where Christianization had reached furthest, and where cities and their institutions were the least disturbed. Basilicas of the fourth and fifth centuries, with the exceptions of Trier, Metz, Reims, and Cologne, were almost exclusively to be found in southern Gaul.[150]

Meanwhile, the history of the bishops of Gaul became all but disjoined from the history of the papacy. From the turn of the fifth century, the bishops of Britain, Gaul, and Iberia developed institutions and customs with little steady contact with Rome. Papal letters and decrees were deemed a major source of authority, however, ranking beside conciliar canons in this respect.[151] But communication and travel between Gaul and Rome became more arduous and increasingly rare.[152]

As mentioned earlier, bishops thought of themselves as a distinct group in the church and in society—they sometimes spoke of themselves as forming an "order" (*ordo*).[153] As such, by means of conciliar law, bishops sought to bolster their personal prestige, as a cultural aristocracy and as the leading figures of the cult, by declaring a monopoly over the government of the church. The stature of a governor could take the form of ruling individual churches and the clerics who

---

quam coacta correctio" (28.2), Hilary of Arles, *Vie de Saint Honorat,* 148. On the angelic life, see also Mireille Labrousse, *Saint Honorat: Fondateur de Lérins et évêque d'Arles* (Bégrolles-en-Mauges: 1995), 53–56.

147. "In squalore heremi" (20.3), Hilary of Arles, *Vie de Saint Honorat,* 126. On the virtues espoused on Lérins, see (17.3), 114.

148. Wolfram, *Roman Empire,* 183–203.

149. James, *Europe's Barbarians,* 199; see also Teillet, *Goths,* 185–206; Alain Chauvot, "Images positives, images négatives des Barbares dans les sources latines à la fin du Ve siècle et au début du VIe siècle après J.-C.," in *Clovis,* 1:3–14.

150. Émile Mâle, *La fin du paganisme en Gaule et les plus anciennes basiliques chrétiennes* (Paris: 1950), 123–61.

151. Jasper and Fuhrmann, *Papal Letters,* 17.

152. Mathisen, *Roman Aristocrats,* 29–30.

153. Held under Hilary of Arles, "Placuit praeterea accusandi licentiam etiam in nostri ordinis," Council of Vaison-la-Romaine (442), CCSL 148:99.

pertained to them, of overseeing the initiation of new Christians, and judging their disputes and determining penances for their sins. Over their local churches bishops declared that they exercised "power and judgment."[154] In turn they agreed to adhere to their own mutual decisions, the canon law of metropolitan councils.[155] Gallic councils declared that the bishops themselves were responsible for reconciling any disagreements in their ranks: they were a self-governing body.[156] By meeting in council, they could present themselves as a distinctive cultural force, united around the act of legislation. This collegiality must often have seemed forced and artificial, for we know of many factional disputes dividing the bishops and lurking beneath the smooth surface of the canons.

Pater—Rector—Sacerdos

A bishop sought to represent the catholic, universal church in his city. But how exactly was this to be done?[157] According to the Council of Turin, the good bishop was a *pius pater*, a pious father.[158] Some idea of what was wanted in a bishop can be found in the instructions for the ordination of a bishop, compiled in a collection of canons made in southern Gaul in the late fifth century, called the *Ancient Statutes of the Church*. The work is thought by some to have been compiled by Gennadius of Marseille, and is discussed further in chapter 2. Here our interest is in the legal construction of the bishop.[159]

According to the *Ancient Statutes*, every bishop should undergo an examination in which right belief and ordination were carefully intertwined. The directions include a brief *symbol*, which the candidate was expected to know and be able to "declare in simple terms." The future bishop was expected to be prudent,

154. "In potestate tamen uel arbitrio sit episcopi, ut si eos ex animo errorem deflere et agere paenitentiam uiderit, ad communionem pro ecclesiastica humanitate suscipiat," Council of Arles (ca. 442–506), CCSL 148:116. On the bishop's power within the diocese, see Gaudemet, "Charisme et droit," 48.

155. "Hoc etiam placuit custodiri ut nihil contra magnam synodum metropolitani sibi aestiment uindicandum," Second Council of Arles (ca. 442–506), CCSL 148:125.

156. "Dissidentes episcopos, si non timor Dei, synodus reconciliet," *Statuta ecclesiae antiqua* (c. 475), CCSL 148:162–88; see 174.

157. See, for example, the incipit of the Council of Vaison-la-Romaine (442): "CONSTITVTIONES SANCTAE SYNODI HABITAE IN CIVITATE VASENSI APVD AVSPICIVM EPISCOPVM ECCLESIAE CATHOLICAE"; CCSL 148:96.

158. Council of Turin (398), CCSL 148:55.

159. *Statuta ecclesiae antiqua* (c. 475), CCSL 148:161–88; See the remarks of Ralph W. Mathisen, "The 'Second Council of Arles' and the Spirit of Compilation and Codification in Late Roman Gaul," JECS 5 (1997): 511–54, see 548; see also Charles Munier, *Les Statuta ecclesiae antiqua* (Paris: 1960); Alban Dold, "Alte, teilweise unbekannte Väterfragmente auf dem Doppelblatt N I 6 Nr. 9 der Universitätsbibliothek Basel," RB 63 (1953): 239–45; Turner, "Arles and Rome," 240–45.

docile, temperate, chaste, sober, "affable to the humble," merciful, literate, "instructed in the Law of God," and "trained in ecclesiastical dogma." Having met all these conditions, he could be accepted as a bishop by the common consent of the assembled laymen and clerics and by a "convention of the bishops of the whole province."[160] In the idealized portrait provided by this collection of canon law, the bishops are portrayed as a literate and specialized group that prized orthodoxy as a kind of learned lore.

The bishop was still imagined in this collection as a figure elected by the entire community, just as described much earlier in the *Apostolic Tradition* of Hippolytus.[161] In early Roman liturgies for the consecration of a bishop, after a series of solemn prayers the assembled clerics imposed their hands on the new bishop as he received a blessing and ultimately was installed on his episcopal throne (*cathedra*).[162] Similarly, according to the *Ancient Statutes,* a bishop was "taken up into the episcopate in the name of Christ, not by his own wish or thoughts, but because he acquiesced in these definitions of the Fathers."[163] In the Gallic Church, imbued with the historical vision of Lérins, adherence to antiquity took pride of place. The saintly but departed Fathers could surely guide the course of their institution. The bishop was imagined as an august figure whose governing capacity was symbolized in his throne and in the solemnity of his consecration.

Bishops hoped that by refurbishing "rules of discipline concerning ecclesiastical matters," as at the Council of Tours (461), they could keep the church permanently pure and immaculate. In this way they could preserve the "evangelical precepts," "apostolic doctrine," and the "statutes of the Fathers."[164] This basic motivation of the Gallic councils is illuminated by an exceedingly rare glimpse, in the records of the Council of Agde in 506, of how an episcopal council began its proceedings. Having met in the city of Agde with the permission of the Visigothic king, everyone in the "holy synod" bent their knees to the ground and prayed to the Lord for the kingdom, the health of the king, and the people.[165]

160. *Statuta ecclesiae antiqua* (c. 475), CCSL 148:164. Like the *Statuta,* the Council of Orléans (533) insisted on literacy for priests, and added a knowledge of liturgy: Godding, *Prêtres en Gaule,* 51.

161. Hippolytus of Rome, *La Tradition apostolique d'apres les anciennes versions,* ed. B. Botte, SC 11 (Paris: 1984); see also Pierre Batiffol, "La liturgie du sacre des évêques dans son évolution historique," *Revue d'histoire ecclésiastique* 23 (1927): 733–63; see 734–35.

162. Batiffol, "La liturgie du sacre," 737.

163. "Suscepto in nomine Christi episcopatu, non suae delectationi nec suis motibus, sed his patrum definitionibus adquiescat," *Statuta ecclesiae antiqua* (c. 475), CCSL 148:165–66.

164. "Ut secundum euangelica praecepta et apostolicam doctrinam patrum statuta seruantes, ecclesia Domini pura et immaculata permaneat," Council of Tours (461) CCSL 148:143.

165. "Ibique flexis in terram genibus, pro regno eius, pro longaeuitate, pro populo Dominum

The first order of business was to read aloud "the canons and statutes of the fathers," thereby linking the council's present business to the venerable past.[166] The bishops then, as so often, turned their attention to questions of "discipline and the ordination of clerics and bishops."[167] The councils provided the bishops a privileged circle of conversation. At the same time the cultural stature, way of life, and religious meaning of this Christian aristocracy were further shaped by monastic ideals cultivated along the Mediterranean shore.

---

deprecaremur," Council of Agde (506), CCSL 148:192; J. Champagne and R. Szramkiewicz, "Recherches sur les conciles des temps mérovingiens," RHDr 49 (1971): 7–49; see 8–10; Hefele-Leclercq, *Histoire des conciles* 2.2:973–1002.

166. "In primo id placuit, ut canones et statuta patrum per ordinem legerentur," Council of Agde (506), CCSL 148:193.

167. "De disciplina et ordinationibus clericorum atque pontificum . . . tractaturi," Council of Agde (506), CCSL 148:192.

[2]

THE SPIRIT OF THE
GALLICAN COUNCILS

D ELICATE, ANCIENT PATTERNS OF LIFE, thought, and public activity took enduring form in the opalescent, hard shell of law. The meaning and function of ecclesiastical law and the legal authority of bishops were developed in councils of the fourth century and afterward. This chapter offers an approach to the Gallic councils, with their ancient legacy of law and aristocratic activity. The legal activity of bishops of the late Roman Empire contained new elements, but in other regards connected the bishops to ancient structures of law and aristocratic cultural values. The lives of these bishops in the cities of southern imperial Gaul, living as they did in the ancient landscapes of the Mediterranean littoral and Maritime Alps, seem to confirm the historical vision of Fernand Braudel, revealing the patterns of a history "slowly rhythmical: one would willingly say, if the expression had not been detoured from its plain sense, a *social* history, of groups and of groupings."[1] The old wine of aristocratic life, poured out into the new bottles of the church, involved bishops in immemorial patterns of regional and community leadership and mediation. "A privileged

---

This chapter is based on an earlier article: Michael Edward Moore, "The Spirit of the Gallican Councils," AHC 39 (2007): 1–52. I gratefully acknowledge permission granted by the editors of *Annuarium Historiae Conciliorum* to use material from that article here.

1. Fernand Braudel, *La méditerranée et le monde méditerranéen a l'époque de Philippe II,* 2nd ed. (Paris: 1966), 1:13.

social background thus often translated into privileged access to the episcopal office," in the phrase of Claudia Rapp.[2]

Bishops, Law, and the Rise of the Councils

After Constantine's conversion, bishops were engaged in all the legal questions affecting their communities, and were forced into the role of mediators between their churches and imperial centers.[3] Bishops were also compelled to serve as judges in courts intended for Christian communities (*episcopalis audientia*). As Gaudemet explains, "The justice of the church was recognized as the equal of secular justice," and while the exact procedures are unknown, it seems that legal methods of inquest and evidence-gathering were simply adopted from secular courts.[4] Episcopal courts gradually absorbed the function of imperial courts—and transferred to episcopal hands a familiar aristocratic sense of legal privilege and elite dominance over the legal system. Bishops naturally turned to Roman law as a basis for judging the many complex property and family disputes that came their way. Christian principles were translated into legal norms.[5] Augustine of Hippo, for one, possessed a general familiarity of Roman law, but little scientific legal knowledge, and so episcopal *audientiae* gave life to a flexible, mixed style of law comprising Roman and Christian elements in a distinctive, new *lex christiana*.[6] The transfer to Christian law (*ad legem Christianam transferre*) implied new developments and accommodations. The bishops were expected to issue their judgments "according to the precepts of law and equity," or "according to the laws of truth and equity," thereby gaining a different moral tone and conceptual location than the decisions of imperial courts.[7]

Serving as a judiciary required a constant engagement of bishops with Roman law, which characterized the legal decisions of bishops as they began to assemble for purposes of judgment and decision-making.[8] There was a close con-

2. Rapp, *Holy Bishops,* 202.

3. Rapp, *Holy Bishops,* 243.

4. Jean Gaudemet, *Église et Cité: Histoire du droit canonique* (Paris: 1994), 112. Both civil and criminal cases were heard: Bertrandus Kurtscheid and Felix Antonius Wilches, *Historia iuris canonici* (Rome: 1943–1951), 2:207–16.

5. Anton Stiegler, *Der kirchliche Rechtsbegriff: Elemente und Phasen seiner Erkenntnisgeschichte* (Munich: 1958), 75–79.

6. Daniel Edward Doyle, *The Bishop as Disciplinarian in the Letters of St. Augustine,* Patristic Studies 4 (New York: 2002), 75, 107; see also Vismara, *Giurisdizione,* 86; Chadwick, "Bishops as Monks," 56, with references; and Rapp, *Holy Bishops,* 244–45.

7. "Praecepta legis et aequitatis" or "Secundum leges veritatis et aequitatis": Walter Selb, "Episcopalis audientia," 184.

8. Vismara, *Giurisdizione,* 112.

nection between the rise of episcopal councils and the overall involvement of bishops in the legal world of the late empire. As the "illusion" of imperial unity, maintained through the potency of ritual and panegyric, fell apart in regional divisions and civil wars, bishops were well positioned to pick up the legal pieces.[9]

In the fourth century, episcopal councils gained prestige and authority primarily by participating in imperial religious politics. As the world of late Rome was rapidly transformed in cultural and political terms, bishops were careful to preserve their own aristocratic and legal functions. In the course of the fifth century what emerged in southern Gaul was an insistence that bishops should form a Christian cultural and religious elite, steeped in a monastic philosophy of the desert, directed by particular centers of authority and by men with a certain monastic training and personal style.[10] These values were inscribed in episcopal law. The island monastery of Lérins trained a cohort of men who pursued the way of life practiced at the monastery, which the monks called "the discipline" (disciplina).[11] The theme of ascetic power was combined with the distinctiveness of bishops as rulers of the church. Monastic in lifestyle and rhetorical stance, the bishops presented themselves as humble, austere men acting in the service of Holy Law, while weaving a very complex legal world incorporating Roman elements, in the context of governing their Christian communities and forming regional associations of bishops.

The legacy of Rome implied that good forms of power should possess legality, and that law was concomitant to the exercise of power. Roman law had served to formalize privilege and power and to regulate forms of dominance.[12] Increasingly, episcopal law and judgment provided the shifting gears needed to mediate between centers of power, regional elites, and local communities. Thus the Roman legal patrimony nurtured the scholarly and aristocratic connotations of Christian law.

Perhaps twenty-three councils were held during the Gallic period, traditionally extending from A.D. 314 to 506.[13] Most of these councils met in southeastern Gaul or in nearby Turin, and while we often have little specific information about the reason for the meeting or the substance of their doctrinal debates, it is

---

9. Van Dam, *Leadership and Community,* 11.

10. Rapp, *Holy Bishops,* 105–6.

11. Carrias, "Vie monastique et règle à Lérins," 196.

12. Peter Garnsey, *Social Status and Legal Privilege in the Roman Empire* (Oxford: 1970), 243–35.

13. Gottlieb, "Formalen Bestandteile," 254. On the place of these councils in the overall conciliar documentation: Gaudemet, *Sources du droit,* 49–56.

clear that dogmatic and disciplinary questions often dominated conciliar business. The councils were at first shaped by the context of the late Empire and the intervention of emperors in the disputes over dogma that dominated the life of the church in this period. Later, during the military crises of the late fourth century, the rise of independent barbarian regimes put new pressures on bishops, culminating in the presence of the Gothic king Alaric II at the Council of Agde in 506, which Wolfram rightly describes as a "Gothic-Gallic territorial council."[14]

In the course of the Gallic period, a characteristic conciliar format was developed, spare and almost reticent.[15] The councils deployed a special terminology and expressed typical aristocratic concerns of consensus-building, mutuality, and arbitration. A constant preoccupation with law provided a cultural space for the resolution of conflicts, for mediating between imperial or royal centers and among the churches of southern Gaul. We can view the councils as mirrors partially clouded by time, but reflecting the steady development of the episcopate as an aristocratic body engaged in the wholesale transfer of Roman aristocratic cultural ideals to the church and the emerging governance by bishops over their regional Christian communities. Upper-class values were an important dimension of episcopal character and activities.[16]

It is often assumed that small regional councils had only a limited territorial competence, their law binding only the bishops who attended, in contrast to the great ecumenical councils, which were "universal." This is emphasized in the modern scholar's distinction, based on Gratian, between a "council" and a mere "synod." However, these terms were synonyms in the Gallic period, alongside *coetus,* or "assembly." The Gallic councils frequently made reference to African and Spanish regional councils and accepted them as good law. As we shall see in the course of this discussion, authentic law was widely collected and accepted as sound episcopal law if it came from a known region with famous, admirable traditions, or if it appeared to be authentic and valuable. Although no official diplomatic format existed for councils, certain types of documentation were accepted as a sign of authority. Then conciliar law could function as a body of authoritative texts in a commonly recognized legal universe.

The first council held in Gaul, in the future conciliar center of Arles (314), was also the first body of bishops to assemble under imperial orders.[17] In the

---

14. Wolfram, *Roman Empire,* 155.
15. Gaudemet, "Législation des conciles gaulois," 4–5.
16. Rapp, *Holy Bishops,* 188–95.
17. Council of Arles (314), CCSL 148:3–25; and Jean Gaudemet, *Conciles Gaulois du IVe siècle,* SC 241 (Paris: 1977), 35–67.

years preceding this council, Constantine had involved himself more and more in ecclesiastical affairs, apparently out of a fear that the truth of religion and of Catholic law (*leges catholicae*) might be confused by disputes over doctrine and church order. At Arles the ordination of Caecilian of Carthage was reconfirmed, despite a challenge from the Donatists. Constantine claimed that only bishops could resolve such ecclesiastical matters: "the judgement of bishops ought to be looked upon as if the Lord Himself were sitting judgement."[18]

Whether or not this was mere verbiage, Arles (314) was intended to be a grand affair. Bishops were allowed to travel by the imperial post, indicating that attendance at the council was imperial business of the highest order. In the period leading up to the council, the look and feel of the imperial court had been transformed by Christian politics and symbols. The battle standard of Constantine, the labarum, a spearhead forming a cross, with the Chi Rho enclosed in a circle (memorializing the well-known vision of Constantine) was established in the palace and attended by an honor guard of fifty men.[19] The regular engagement of the emperor in ecclesiastical matters was a victory for the theologico-political ideals of Eusebius.[20]

Arles, "the Rome of the Gauls," was chosen as the location for the assembly in recognition of Arles' traditional commercial and administrative importance.[21] The council was only the first step in a long-maintained dominance of Arles over the Gallic Church and the early character of ecclesiastical law.[22]

The council reveals the extent to which the cities of Gaul could already be represented by a bishop, among them Marseilles, Arles, Vienne, Vaison-la-Romaine, Orange, Nice, Apt, Rheims, Rouen, Autun, Lyon, Cologne, Javols, Bordeaux, Trier, and Eauze, all of which gradually accepted the dominance of Arles.[23] Many churches were represented by presbyters or deacons rather than bishops. Lectors and exorcists were also present, seemingly forming the entourage of certain bishops or presbyters.[24] The dominant figure of the bishop, coming into view at Arles, reflects the wish to draw a dark line between bishops

18. Cited in Baynes, *Constantine the Great,* 14.

19. Demandt, *Geschichte der Spätantike,* 48–51; Barnes, *Constantine and Eusebius,* 43.

20. Barnes, *Constantine and Eusebius,* 254.

21. Camille Jullian, *Gallia: Tableau sommaire de la Gaule sous la domination romaine* (Paris: 1892), 258–62.

22. Turner, "Arles and Rome," 236–47.

23. Mathisen, *Ecclesiastical Factionalism,* 5. The early rise of Arles is sketched in Klingshirn, *Caesarius of Arles.*

24. Godding, *Prêtres en Gaule,* 459, provides charts detailing the attendance of priests (i.e., presbyters) at councils.

and other clerics. Bishops, presbyters, and deacons might share the prestige of asceticism, but bishops controlled sacred places and offices. At Arles (314) bishops were emerging as masters of ascetic power, masters of law and dispute-resolutions, and as the wielders of sacred things.[25]

The council was attended by *missi* of Pope Silvester and was later accepted in Rome as an authoritative source of doctrine.[26] The participation of clerics from across the Latin-speaking church is significant. Attending were bishops and deacons of other Italian cities: Syracuse in Sicily, Campania, Apulia, Aquileia in Dalmatia, Milan, and Rome itself. From Britain, bishops of York, London, and Lincoln; from Spain came bishops, presbyters, or deacons from Merida, Betica, Ossuna, Tarragona, and Saragossa; and of course, a small band of sympathetic clerics arrived from the African Church to support Caecilian of Carthage, who also attended.

Stunningly, for a church so recently persecuted by the state authorities, local church battles, high ecclesiastical politics, and questions of sacramental theology could now be resolved in the context of a convening authority dominated by bishops: they made decrees "by common counsel" (*quid decreuerimus communi consilio*), thus using a prestigious, communal setting to lay claim to law and authority.[27] *Auctoritas,* the grave dignity of influence and power associated with the Roman Senate, was seemingly adopted by this council. As a quality pertaining to the Christian bishop, *authority* had already been highlighted in apologetic and theological writings, but here the term retained its luster as part of the Roman vocabulary of privilege.[28] Special terminology reveals a mature set of concepts about the importance of ecclesiastical law and its ability to stabilize the community. Theological ructions in the church were dismissed as a disruption of social order by mere "agitators." Bishops agreed to respect one another's decisions. The legal authority of the meeting was highlighted as a defense of "our law and tradition," as a statement of "authority and tradition and the rule of truth."[29] The establishment of these rules was announced by the ancient senatorial *placuit:* that a motion "pleased" the council was recorded in a stenographic, ritual formula.

25. Faivre, *Naissance d'une hiérarchie,* 129.

26. Silvester sent the deacons Eugenius and Quiriacus as *missi:* Council of Arles (314) CCSL 148:14; see also Robert Somerville and Bruce C. Brasington, *Prefaces to Canon Law Books in Latin Christianity* (New Haven: 1998), 37.

27. *Canones ad Silvestrum,* Council of Arles (314), CCSL 148:9.

28. Garnsey, *Social Status,* 225; see also the doctrinal treatment of Hans Urs Von Campenhausen, *Ecclesiastical Authority and Spiritual Power in the Church of the First Three Centuries,* trans. J. A. Baker (Stanford: 1981), 280–81.

29. *Epistula ad Siluestrum,* Council of Arles (314), CCSL 148, Proem, 4.

Despite the participation of other clerics (presbyters, deacons, exorcists, and lectors) at the council, in its published proceedings, the bishops assembled at Arles in 314 ignored the presence of lesser clerics and described themselves as forming an exalted and independent group. The scale of Arles (314) was possible only because of direct imperial promotion and a stable political situation. All later Gallic councils were to some degree local and regional, based in one or another important city and church, as an institution of the "localized hierarchical networks" now reorganizing social order in Gaul.[30]

Constantius II (337–361) interfered with conciliar activity in a direct, crude manner once he governed alone.[31] He allied himself with the Arian party and set out to impose those religious views on bishops across the Empire, to insist upon religious unity as an adjunct of imperial unity.[32] While staying in Arles in 353, he assembled a council at which the bishops were forced to denounce Athanasius and trinitarian theology and to accept Arianism.[33] A council in Milan (355) likewise condemned Athanasius.

Such methods and the sudden prominence of Arianism caused Bishop Hilary of Poitiers (ca. 315–367) to react vehemently: "You imprisoned bishops, setting your army to terrorize the church; you assembled synods and pushed the faith of the westerners to impiety."[34] In his *Liber contra Constantium,* a fierce little work published only after the death of Constantius II, Hilary denounced the emperor as an oppressive tyrant.[35] To the bishops who folded under imperial pressure, Hilary contrasted the good bishops, "apostolic men" who remained faithful to the truth.[36] Martin of Tours and Ambrose also reacted strongly against the interference.[37] Hilary of Poitiers and his fellow bishops were meanwhile crafting an ideal of episcopal activity as the achievement of a social elite animated by

30. Van Dam, *Leadership and Community,* 11.

31. R. P. C. Hanson, *The Search for the Christian Doctrine of God: The Arian Controversy, 318–381* (Edinburgh: 1993), 329–86.

32. Joannou, *La legislation imperiale,* 31–43 and 72–75.

33. Council of Arles (353), CCSL 148:30; see also Timothy D. Barnes, *Athanasius and Constantius: Theology and Politics in the Constantinian Empire* (Cambridge, Mass.: 1993), 115–16; Hefele-Leclercq, *Histoire des conciles,* 1.2:869–75.

34. "Sacerdotes custodiae mandas, exercitus tuos ad terrorem Ecclesiae disponis; synodos contrahis et Occidentalium fidem ad inpietatem conpellis," Hilary of Poitiers, *Contre Constance,* 180. It is possible that this work was not published until after the death of Constantius: Hanns Christof Brennecke, "Hilarius von Poitiers," *Theologische Realenzyklopädie* (Berlin: 1977–2004), 15:315–22.

35. Demandt, *Geschichte der Spätantike,* 66.

36. See the discussion in Hilary of Poitiers, *Hilary of Poitiers' Preface to his Opus historicum: Translation and Commentary,* ed. and trans. P. Smulders (Leiden: 1995), 65–71.

37. Mathisen, *Ecclesiastical Factionalism,* 14.

strictly religious ideals and a concept of conciliar authority associated with the Council of Nicaea (325). This was the Nicene faith (*fides Nicaena*).[38]

Constantius II used this strategy again in 359, in councils summoned to Rimini and Seleucia, where bishops were again forced to sign pro-Arian statements.[39] The emperor meanwhile adopted Eusebian political theology for himself, using "Emperor Constantine" as a historical and political symbol. The legend of Constantine's conversion, centering on the story of the Battle of the Milvian Bridge, the emperor's vision of the Chi Rho symbol in the heavens, and the phrase *In hoc signo vincis*—all served as a political myth.[40] Such symbols seemed to give the emperor an ecclesiastical aura. But Gallic episcopal identity was sharpened by reaction against this potent political mythos.

In 360 or 361 a council of bishops gathered in Paris to reverse the extortive councils of Rimini and Seleuca. This was a regional Gallic assembly, assembling under the newly crowned co-emperor Julian, at a point in his career when Julian found it expedient to maintain a façade of Christianity.[41] Julian allowed Hilary of Poitiers to return to Gaul in time to participate in the council to be held in Paris.[42]

The "Gallican bishops" (*Gallicani episcopi*), for so they identified themselves, now directed a synodal letter to the eastern bishops, declaring their opposition to the proceedings at Rimini and trumpeting their return to what were held up as the universal beliefs of the church. Directing bitter remarks against Constantius II, the bishops complained that they had been constrained by "worldly judgment" and were now freed from the "error of the world."[43] Eastern bishops were roundly blamed for their complicity: "many . . . were compelled to silence by the authority of your name."[44] Those who clung to such doctrines, the bishops declared, should be deposed from their sees as blasphemers and "apostate bishops."[45] Imperial struggles made it possible for Gallic bishops, following the lead of Hilary of Poitiers, to oppose the bishops of the East, and to exercise con-

38. Durst, "Nizäa als 'autoritative Tradition,'" 407.
39. Hanson, *Search for the Christian Doctrine,* 329–34; 362–80; Hefele-Leclercq, *Histoire des conciles,* 1:947; Durst, "Nizäa," 418.
40. Pietri, "La politique de Constance II," 1:337–46.
41. Analysis in Barnes, *Athanasius and Constantius,* 152–55; Demandt, *Geschichte der Spätantike,* 74. For a crisp review of the evidence: Glen W. Bowersock, *Julian the Apostate* (Cambridge, Mass.: 1978), 46–51.
42. Drobner, 254–56.
43. "Iudicio saeculi teneremur"; "liberans nos ab errore mundi": Council of Paris (360/361) CCSL 148: 32–33; Hefele-Leclercq, *Histoire des conciles,* 1.2:960.
44. Council of Paris (360/361), CCSL 148:33.
45. Council of Paris (360/361), CCSL 148:34.

ciliar authority with little imperial interference. In this respect, the Council of Paris was something of a watershed.

The statement of faith propounded at Paris (360) and preserved in the *Collectanea antiariana parisina* of Hilary of Poitiers expressed the Nicene doctrine of a triune God (*fides Nicaena*) in simple Latin terminology.[46] The dignity of a regional aristocratic assembly in this case was closely connected to imperial struggles and aligned against Constantius II's religious policies, which the Gallican bishops considered to be abusive. Ironically, it was the ambition and religious skepticism of Julian that made possible the holding of such a council and provided the setting for the bishops to adopt an openly combative tone and to act as an independent institution.

Angels and "the Discipline"

Divisions over questions of doctrine could sometimes be transposed into the terms of clerical procedure. This seems to have been the tack taken at the Council of Valence in 374, where disputes over Priscillianism were deliberately muted during an unfolding military crisis faced by the Empire.[47] Emperor Valentinian had recently launched attacks against the Alamanni. The subscription list from Valence (374) records the participation of a large number of clerics from Gaul and the western Mediterranean.

Florentius of Vienne must have led the proceedings, as the senior cleric and bishop of a very powerful see, and therefore his name was entered first in the subscription list. Bishop Amilianus of Valence did not claim precedence, although the council assembled in his city. Others who can be identified and definitely connected to a city are Chrestus of Syracuse, Simplicius of Autun, and Britto of Trier. Most of the bishops said to have been present are otherwise little-known. Paulus may have been bishop of Paris, Justus may have been bishop of Lyon, Concordius perhaps of Arles. This leaves many opaque figures, such as Eumerius, Artemius, Evodius—twelve unknown men in all, assumed by the editor Munier to be bishops.[48]

The Council of Valence was concerned primarily with the religious discipline

---

46. Hilary of Poitiers, *Collectanea antiariana parisina*, in *S. Hilarii episcopi Pictaviensis Opera*, edited by Alfredus Feder (Vienna: 1916), CSEL 65: 43–46; see also Hefele-Leclercq, *Histoire des conciles*, 1:903–62.

47. Council of Valence (374), CCSL 148:35–42; Maassen, *Geschichte der Quellen*, 100–11.

48. For discussion of the subscription list, see Maassen, *Geschichte der Quellen*, 574–85; see also Kéry, *Canonical Collections*, 44–45; Gaudemet, *Sources du droit*, 144; Kurtscheid and Wilches, *Historia iuris canonici*, 1:98.

of Christian communities. There were strictures against the return of "persons" to pagan practices after Christian baptism (a significant use of the legal term *persona* to designate a legally recognized member of the Christian community). Thus the bishops hoped to distinguish their communities from the surrounding cultural world and draw it more closely to episcopal guidance.[49]

The Pricillianist controversy created conflict over what should be considered the highest form of Christian life. Although Valence was an early expression of episcopal authority, it took note of the fact that some clerics viewed ascetical retreat to be preferable to engagement with the world as a bishop, a dissonance that was not resolved until the rise of Lérins after 410, when episcopal power and asceticism were combined in a convincing, permanent manner.[50]

The same issues recurred at a council held in Nîmes either in 394 or 396.[51] Twenty-one bishops were said to be present.[52] The subscription list does not record the cities of the bishops present, and little can be said about them as individuals. Geniales was bishop of Cavaillon, Eusebius of Rouen, Remigius of Dax (Aquae Civitas), and Ingenuus of Arles. The city connections of the remaining bishops are unknown. Nevertheless, we can assert that the council was a primarily southern Gallic assembly connected to the larger scene of imperial-ecclesiastical politics. The transactions of the council are so brief in content that they seem not to warrant the presence of the long list of bishops who attended the assembly. Why had so many bishops travelled to Nîmes?

In addition to the twenty-one bishops, at least one angel was present, according to a charming tale in the *Dialogues* of Sulpicius Severus. Martin of Tours was eager to learn about the decisions of this council, because he believed they would touch upon the persecution of Priscillian of Avila. The angel arrived to provide Martin with news of the council proceedings. Chadwick notes that this story is the only reason to associate the council with the Pricillianist controversy, because the affair was not treated directly in any of the canons.[53] The

---

49. "Circa eorum uero personas, qui se post unum et sanctum lauacrum, uel profanis sacrificiis daemonum uel incesta lauatione polluerint," Council of Valence (374), CCSL 148:39.

50. Henry Chadwick, *Priscillian of Avila: The Occult and the Charismatic in the Early Church* (Oxford: 1976), 13–14.

51. Council of Nîmes (394/396), CCSL 148:49–51; see also Hefele-Leclercq, *Histoire des conciles*, 2:94–97; Maassen, *Geschichte der Quellen*, 191; and Gaudemet, *Conciles Gaulois*, 124–31.

52. The records are preserved in the late-sixth or early-seventh-century manuscript mentioned earlier, the *Collectio Coloniensis* (Cologne: Dombibliothek 212); Maassen, *Geschichte der Quellen*, 577.

53. Sulpicius Severus, *Dialogues*, II.13.8, cited in Hefele-Leclercq, *Histoire des conciles*, 2:91, n. 2, and Chadwick, *Priscillian of Avila*, 158.

brief set of canons is instead quite similar to the proceedings at Valence (374), and reveals no obvious engagement with theological controversies. The council prohibited the ordination of women, thus promoting the trend toward making the clergy an entirely male preserve.[54] However, the brevity of the canons does not exclude a preoccupation with other matters and discussions that could not be safely recorded. The angel was probably right to say that Priscillianism was discussed at Nîmes.

Thus at Nîmes, too, we see a council serving as a regional aristocratic assembly, providing an occasion for rites of mutual recognition, consultation, and discussion. The principle of mutuality had been expressed at Arles (314) in the collegial recognition of every bishop's disciplinary decisions. At Nîmes (394/396) the bishops went on to establish the corollary that no deposed cleric should be received from another bishop's territory.[55] The coolness in regard to theological conflict reflects an emphasis on conciliation and mediation rather than assertion and decision-making. And theological reticence was a counsel of wisdom in periods of political and religious antagonism.

In 398, Stilicho moved the capital of the prefecture of Gaul to Arles, making a dramatic new arrangement for the Rhine border regions involving new treaties with the Franks and Alamanni.[56] A brief, welcome period of calm ensued, which encouraged the bishops of Gaul to focus on their own formal organization as a regional elite. At a council held in Turin in this same year, Gallic bishops set out to organize themselves around the primacy of metropolitan bishops (i.e., bishops of provincial capitals).[57]

Turin (*Augusta Taurinorum*), lying on the upper Po River in the Piedmont, was associated with the southern Gallic Church. If it ever existed, the subscription list of the Council of Turin (398) was not preserved, although episcopal authority was the only concern at this evidently mean-spirited gathering.[58] Nevertheless, the records of this council allow us to see an ecclesiastical and aristocratic elite attempting to regulate and routinize its interactions—in other words, to clarify or establish the dominance of certain bishops and certain cit-

54. Council of Nîmes (394/396), CCSL 148:50.

55. "Neque sibi alter episcopus de clerico alterius, inconsulto episcopo cuius minister est, iudicium uindecit," Council of Nîmes (394/396), CCSL 148:50; see also Gaudemet, "Législation des conciles gaulois," 7.

56. J.-R. Palanque, "La date du transfert de la préfecture des Gaules de Trèves à Arles," *Revue des études anciennes* 36 (1934): 359–65; also by Palanque, "Du nouveau sur la date du transfert de la préfecture des Gaules de Trèves à Arles?" *Provence historique* 23 (1973): 29–38.

57. Élie Griffe, *La Gaule chrétienne à l'époque romaine,* 2nd ed. (Paris: 1964–1966), 1:336–40.

58. Council of Turin (398), CCSL 148:52–60; Maassen, *Geschichte der Quellen,* 191–92.

ies. The council also attempted to adjudicate battles shaped by the presentation of competing legal dossiers (*allegationes*), in response to which judgment (*iudicium*) was expected from the assembled bishops.[59] Proculus of Marseilles sought acceptance of his authority to ordain clergy in the province Narbonensis II. In this dispute, the authority of metropolitan bishops was being asserted (or created), on the model of the eastern Pentarchy. The second canon records the council's cautious effort to employ the metropolitan principle to resolve the struggle (sometimes exaggerated in modern scholarship) between Vienne and Arles.[60]

Questions of orthodoxy were thereby transformed into legal questions of ordination and precedence, mutual recognition and acts of governance. The bishops implied that a satisfactory theological outcome was expected not from soul-searching or gazing into heaven, but from the smooth functioning of principles of order, seniority, and rules of etiquette. The assembly further served as a tribunal for disputes involving bishops, such as the aggrieved Bishop Triferius. At Turin the council of bishops appears as a source of law, possessing judicial competence, which could serve as an organ of self-government.

To pass decrees by the "authority of the council" (*synodi decreuit auctoritas*), or to issue an official verdict (*sententia definitum est*) in a dispute, appears as the consuming preoccupations of the Gallic bishops. Meanwhile the political and social setting of imperial politics was almost wholly replaced by new regional political confederations. Bishops no longer waited for imperial initiatives, but focused their activity on coordinating their governmental and legal activities and integrating them with newly emerging regimes.

Ascetic Masters of Law

The Council of Riez held in 439 illustrates a cultural transformation within the episcopate of southern Gaul. Confronted by political upheavals, the bishops devised new forms of organization and adopted a new cultural and scholarly style, drawing upon the monastic traditions of the Mediterranean coast. By the early fifth century, the imperial and Roman context of Gallic councils was changing rapidly with the rising prominence of new tribal federations. The relevance of the emperors was waning, as the most important arrangements were now made in the intimacy of local networks and negotiation with newly arriv-

---

59. "Auditis allegationibus episcoporum, eorum uidelicet qui ad iudicium nostrum fuerant congregati," Council of Turin (398), CCSL 148:54.

60. Chadwick, *Priscillian of Avila*, 160–61; see also Hefele-Leclercq, *Histoire des conciles*, 2:133–34.

ing peoples. The western Empire experienced devastating events, such as the migration of the Vandals after 406, the sack of Rome by the Goths in 410, and the sudden rise of Attila's Hunnic Empire. The unified context of the Roman state dissolved in the divisions between Germanic and Roman elements in the army and aristocracies of western regions.[61]

Such events presented challenges for local sources of authority. This was a maximal period of responsibility for Gallic bishops, who served as key figures representing cultural, historical, and political continuity in their cities and communities.[62] In many regions the kings of barbarian federations were able to force recognition of their successful seizures of power. In 439 the capital of the Burgundian kingdom was established in Lyon, where one of the oldest western Christian communities was led by a cultured ecclesiastical echelon with ties to Lérins.[63] The bishop of Lyon lived in a well-appointed episcopal residence and governed several churches and monasteries, such as the nearby *Monasterium Insulae Barbarae.*[64] The bishops of southern Gaul were forced to adapt themselves to a world in which new zones of power arose, and as suddenly melted away, according to shifting fortunes in the "game of the powerful."[65]

The bishops of Arles cultivated their affiliation with the monastery of Lérins, founded on an island off the Mediterranean coast in 410. Arlesian clerical culture gained luster by its connection to this monastery, which served as a center of book-learning and authority, a school of ascetic discipline, and a refuge of religious significance. The carefully nurtured and widely advertised "desert ethos" associated with the monastery formed the basis for a close-knit aristocratic cultural circle. The contrast between the role of monk and bishop, painfully examined in the Priscillian affair, was reconciled in this cultural circle.[66] Lérins and Arles were sources of cultural persistence in terms of aristocratic leadership, a meaningful form of life, and the bright thread of learning.

The circle of Lérins was masterful in its accumulation of sanctity and in shaping a network of closely cooperating urban and monastic centers of regional authority, bound by men sharing a personal sense of solidarity.[67] In 439, Hilary of

61. Tabacco, *Struggle for Power in Medieval Italy,* 50.

62. Brown, *Power and Persuasion,* 103, 134.

63. Wolfram, *Roman Empire,* 252.

64. *Province ecclésiastique de Lyon (Lugdunensis prima),* ed. Brigitte Beaujard, et al., TCCG 4 (Paris: 1986), 28; on the episcopal residence, see 26.

65. Phrase of Wolfram, *Roman Empire,* 103.

66. Chadwick, "Bishops as Monks," 47.

67. Mathisen, *Ecclesiastical Factionalism,* 83. In the case of Eucherius of Lyon, Prinz suggests

Arles called a council in Riez, in the Maritime Alps of Provence, to address the improper ordination of a bishop in Embrun.[68] Although the subscription lists do not identify the attending bishops by city, we know that the council included the ecclesiastical *beau monde* of the southern Rhone valley, the Mediterranean coast, and the Milanese Church. Thirteen bishops recorded their attendance and acceptance of the proceedings: Severianus of Thorame, Adentius of Die, Iulius of Apt, Arcadius (bishopric unknown), Auspicius of Vaison-la-Romaine, Severus of Milan, Claudius of Castellane, Valerianus of Cimiez, Nectarius of Avignon, Asclepius of Cavaillon, Theodorus of Fréjus, and Maximus of Riez.

This was a group guided not only by the concept of episcopal power, but by the added project of a monastic ideal, severe in its stated character but at the same time cultivated, practical, and easily combined with positions of authority. We know the commitments of some of these men: Maximus of Riez wrote an encomium for Honoratus, the founder of Lérins. It is possible that Valerianus of Cimiez can be identified as the author of an *Epistle to Monks,* which emphasized a Pauline spirituality in which the idea of manual labor was subtly translated into a broader commitment to "do the work of God."[69] With such subtleties the road was open to provide aristocratic activities with the cachet of asceticism.

Episcopal law was gaining a sense of depth and perceived antiquity: the council declared that it followed the statutes of the Fathers (*statuta Patrum secutus*), thereby connecting the council to the setting of fourth-century Christianity and the bishops of old.[70] In scolding tones the council-record frequently reminds the reader of the absolute and holy nature of synodal law, which embodies the historical weight of earlier assemblies of bishops. The council-record was crafted so as to function as an *authority-bearing* written document, a record of judgment, to be associated with the bishops who subscribed to the verdicts (*definitiones*) of the council. The tone, vocabulary, and style of the document reflect an awareness of "a council" as a developing legal genre. There are signs that the bishops of Arles had begun to build up a library of canon law to serve them in their assertions of privilege. The Council of Riez (439) was therefore able to draw

---

a connection between the bishop and the Jura monasteries: Friedrich Prinz, *Frühes Mönchtum im Frankenreich: Kultur und Gesellschaft in Gallien, den Rheinlanden und Bayern am Beispiel der monastischen Entwicklung (4. bis 8. Jahrhundert)* (Munich: 1965), 66–67.

68. Council of Riez (439), CCSL 148:61–75; Hefele-Leclercq, *Histoire des conciles,* 2.1:423–30; see also Maassen, *Geschichte der Quellen,* 192–93.

69. Valerianus, *Epistola ad monachos,* PL 52:755–58; discussion in Vogüé, *Histoire littéraire du mouvement monastique,* 7:129–31.

70. Council of Riez (439), 71 and (subscriptions contained in the *Collectio Coloniensis*), 72.

upon canons from the councils of Nicaea (325), Toulon (398), and Elvira (306).

By thus exercising control over Embrun, Hilary was making clear that the power of Arles extended that far; that he exercised power only in accordance with the statutes of the fathers, in accordance with legal authority, and supported by evidence known in Arles and brought to bear on the case through legal scholarship.[71] The organized regional power of bishops and their government over Christian communities were seen to take shape through law. Thus we can observe the communal activities of the bishops and a characteristic legal procedure and mentality. The jurisdiction (*ius*) of a bishop, even a metropolitan bishop, was only as large and as real as he could make it by engaging in authoritative acts, forcing men to recognize him over a certain area. Arles made such claims throughout the fifth century, asserting its metropolitan status against Vienne's reluctance to cede any of its own authority.[72] Any supposed imperial setting had faded completely from view, while episcopal governance was highlighted.

At the Council of Riez, Hilary and his fellow bishops were engaged in "making real" the diocese of Arles and "making legal" the shape of aristocratic prestige. In this case the procedure required the exclusion or punishment of opposing groups. Yet the mutuality of episcopal power had to be recognized. By no means could Hilary act by fiat in matters that touched on the sources of episcopal authority. Old law, scholarly and spiritual resources, and ascetic power formed a potent combination that placed the bishop of Arles at a pinnacle of authority. The ideal of collegial mutuality was stressed in spite of the effective seizure of power by Hilary of Arles:

Whatever is established by the common will, in the will of God, must be preserved by common consent: otherwise, God forbid, someone might prescribe something that goes beyond it, and yet not face the opprobrium of everyone as well as of God.[73]

The bishops claimed to make their decisions "in common" (*in commune*). Beneath the quiet surface, we can see the fierce struggle of Hilary of Arles and his circle against the bishop of Vienne unfolding as law.[74] Thus bishops reacted to the hypertrophy of Roman order and the ubiquity of military force by pulling

---

71. See for example Hilary's subscription to the council: "Ego Helarius iuxta id quod uniuersis sanctis episcopis meis qui mecum subscripserunt placuit, statua patrum secutus," Council of Riez (439), CCSL 148:72.

72. On this claim of Arles, see Hefele-Leclercq, *Histoire des conciles*, 2.1:424–28 (no. 1).

73. "Quae uoluntate communi in uoluntate Domini constitua, omnes communi consensu conseruanda neque, quod absit, sine offensa omnium ac Dei a quoquam transgredienda definiunt," Council of Riez (439), CCSL 148:70.

74. Hefele-Leclercq, *Histoire des conciles*, 2:423–30.

together as a tight-knit regional organization through formal, mutually accepted ritual and legal procedures.

Orange, an old Roman center of the Vaucluse, with its baths, triumphal arch, and splendid theatre, was the setting for a further Arlesian council in 441.[75] The ascetic master Hilary of Arles again presided over an assembly of bishops from across southern Gaul to inscribe the dominance of Arles in legal terms.[76] Legal knowledge, or what might be called the very concept of legality, was a principal feature of this council, as select canons were presented to the council and incorporated in its own records: from the councils of Arles (314), Nicaea (325), Turin (398), Elvira (306), and Riez (439). The bishops displayed a knowledge of Roman law. Significantly, we also see the incorporation of older Gallic canon law as a valued legal tradition.

The use of canons from councils held in Carthage (397 and 399) probably reflects the possession at Arles of an African canon collection.[77] These impressive African councils circulated in several early collections, such as the *Codex canonum ecclesiae africanae,* also called the *Registri ecclesiae Carthaginensis excerpta.* This collection was known at Rome as well as Arles and later incorporated in larger collections such as the *Dionysiana*. It appears that Hilary used the Council of Orange (441) as an opportunity to publish and declare valid for the Gallic Church the bodies of law that were known in Arles. Mastery of sacred law, Hilary had discovered, allowed a mastery of situations.

In this way a mixed law was coming into existence that involved the highly significant transfer of law from one regional church to another (in this case from Africa to Gaul). This meant that the scholarly *collection* and widespread *acceptance* of law through the medium of collections were coming to rival the importance of "new legislation" as the means of creation and dissemination of legal doctrines, legality, and corresponding terminology. The acceptance of such "regional" councils by the Gallic churches shows that canon law was not conceived of as territorial in its purview. Instead, the councils were informed by legal scholarship that focused on the compilation of law.[78] The mastery of this learned law accords well with the ascetic and scholarly connotations of the monk-

75. *Provinces ecclésiastiques de Vienne et d'Arles,* ed. Biarne, TCCG 3: 95–99.

76. Council of Orange (441), CCSL 148:76–93; see also Maassen, *Geschichte der Quellen,* 193.

77. African councils: Gaudemet, *Sources du droit,* 50–51; Maassen, *Geschichte der Quellen,* 149–86; Roland Minnerath, *Histoire des conciles* (Paris: 1996), 24–25; Kurtscheid and Wilches, *Historia iuris canonici,* 1:92–93; Hefele-Leclercq, *Histoire des conciles,* with analysis of contents, 2:201–9.

78. In contrast to the view of Gaudemet, who suggests a limited regional competence for such councils: "Législation des conciles gaulois," 1.

bishop of Arles and the backdrop of Lérins as a scholarly center of authority.

Concluding the records of the Council of Orange (441) are the subscriptions of seventeen bishops in attendance, recording their assent and participation by entering not only their names, but also the city and province of which they were bishop. Hilary of Arles led the assembly, accompanied by the presbyter Ravennius and Petronius, a deacon. About one-half of the attending bishops, such as Claudius of Vienne, Eucherius of Lyon, Salonius of Geneva, Constantianus of Carpentras, and others, noted that they were similarly accompanied by presbyters or deacons. Having an entourage must have contributed to the prestige of each bishop, and may also reflect the intellectual efforts of episcopal ateliers engaged in compiling and manipulating the legal dossiers so evident in the conciliar record.

The council reflects the dominance among these bishops of the desert ethos of Lérins and of men associated with the monastery. Eucherius of Lyon expressed the ideal that equated the "love of the desert" with the "love of God" in his *De laude eremi*.[79] According to Eucherius, the ascetic tradition established in Biblical times with Moses and David culminated in the monastery of Lérins, and thus was inherited by the echelon of bishops connected to the monastery. Those affiliated with Lérins described it as a place of austerity and monastic training, but it clearly also served as a regional retreat and center of learning, where men such as Eucherius could explore dialectic, grammar, and the study of Scripture.[80]

The Lérins cohort included many highly literate and prolific authors, who were often connected by the friendly connection of student and pupil: one of the bishops named above, Salonius of Cologne, was a pupil of Salvian of Marseilles, who had introduced him to the "discipline of spiritual things."[81] His teacher Salvian may have been a native of Cologne, entering Lérins in about 426.[82] For his part, Salonius authored the exegetical treatise *Expositiones mysticae*. The Lérinians were connected by family ties as well: Salonius was the son of another learned bishop attending the council, Eucherius of Lyon.[83] Salonius was later present at the Council of Vaison-la-Romaine (442), and signed the synodal letter of the Council of Arles sometime between 449 and 461. Salonius of

79. Eucherius of Lyon, *De laude eremi*, PL 50:701–12; see Altaner, *Patrologie*, 404–5, and the sketch in de Montauzan, "Saint-Eucher," 81–96.

80. Pierre Riché, *Éducation et culture dans l'Occident barbare, VIe–VIIIe siècle* (Paris: 1995), 89.

81. "Spiritualium rerum disciplinae," in the testimony of Eucherius of Lyon, *Instructiones ad Salonium,* edited by C. Wotke, CSEL 31:1 (Vienna: 1894), 65.

82. Drobner, 490.

83. Salonius of Cologne, *Expositiones mysticae in parabolas Salomonis et in Ecclesiasten*, PL 53:967–1012.

Cologne, although stationed farther north, was able to maintain a close cooperation with other men of learning and thus share in the ascetical reputation of
this emerging elite.[84] Such bonds encouraged the concept that the episcopate
and clergy should become a strictly male association, united only by scholarly,
ecclesiastical, or regional ties.

The Council of Vaison-la-Romaine in 442 was a further council under the
leadership of Hilary of Arles.[85] His organization of so many apparently effective assemblies demonstrates Hilary's central position in this regional network
of like-minded clerics and their communities. A presiding bishop could exert
pressure to sway the results and decisions of the council.[86] But this often had to
take the form of conciliation and recognition of others: while we imagine Hilary as the bishop providing the energy and impetus of this council, Auspicius,
the bishop of Vaison, was allowed to inscribe his name first in the subscription
list and, nominally, at least, must have presided. Auspicius was one of the Lérins
circle and had been ordained in Arles. In Mathisen's view this arrangement may
have been an attempt to lighten the oppressive sense of Hilary's dominance over
the southern Gallic church. It is even possible that the bishops who were disci-
plined at Riez (439) were brought back into the fold.[87] In so small a world, the
tense presence of unreconciled men was difficult to bear.

The subscription list contained in the *Collectio Coloniensis* reveals again the
attendance of bishops accompanied by other clerics, in this case from no fewer
than twenty-three cities.[88] Subscriptions provided a record of who had agreed
to potentially divisive canons. The name of Claudius of Vienne was entered immediately after Hilary's, suggesting that their stature was comparable, despite
the underlying tension of competition for regional prominence. Salonius of Geneva was present, but not his father.

On the nature of episcopal prestige and mutuality, Vaison-la-Romaine (442)
accepted as canonical the First Epistle of pseudo-Clement, thus revealing that
they were in tune with Pope Leo's interest in this document, which Leo was using, in combination with principles from Roman law, to limn the legal nature

84. Van Dam, *Leadership and Community*, 73.
85. The council-record: Council of Vaison-la-Romaine (442), CCSL 148:94–104; see also
Maassen, *Geschichte der Quellen*, 193–94; see also Hefele-Leclercq, *Histoire des conciles*, 2:454–
60. On the ecclesiastical landscape of Vaison-la-Romaine: Biarne, ed., *Provinces ecclésiastiques de
Vienne et d'Arles*, 89–93.
86. Prinz, *Frühes Mönchtum im Frankenreich*, 51; Gaudemet, *Sources du droit*, 53.
87. Mathisen, *Ecclesiastical Factionalism*, 97, 112.
88. Vaison-la-Romaine (442), CCSL 148:102; Maassen, *Geschichte der Quellen*, 577.

of Roman authority.[89] The bishops attempted to make regional councils such as Vaison the ordinary court for all appeals in ecclesiastical disputes.[90] It was declared that bishops formed an order: "our order" (*noster ordo*), which should not readily listen to accusations injurious to collegial activity and cooperation.[91] The bishops were shaping this ideal order as an affiliated group with special training and monastic connections. As portrayed in the council-record, this *ordo* possessed a special sacred aura combined with an equally supported aura of legality.

In summarizing Hilary's career Peter Brown aptly suggests, "as befitted an aristocrat, backed by aristocrats, Hilary was an empire-builder."[92] This is certainly justified by Hilary's dominant role in the Gallic councils of his day. Hilary could marshal the resources of Arles and the Lérins circle and, with their assistance, successfully maintain his ecclesiastical decisions even over the opposition of Pope Leo I. Hilary's deposition of Chelidonius of Besançon also created friction with the monastic communities of the Jura.[93] The image of Hilary as an ecclesiastical campaigner should be complemented by an appreciation of his role in shaping and strengthening the very meaning of the episcopate in the context of his councils as a brotherly *ordo*.

As a result of invasions and civil wars of the early fifth century, Gallic bishops became isolated from the eastern Mediterranean world that had harbored the late antique church, and regular contact among themselves became the decisive factor in preserving their ability to act as an institution.

Ancient Networks, New Worlds

One such council (location unknown) sent a synodal letter to Pope Leo I in 451. The pope had conveyed to these bishops a document that he had "sent to the east for the assertion of the Catholic faith."[94] Pope Leo's letter to Flavian of Con-

89. Council of Vaison-la-Romaine (442), CCSL 148:98; text of First Clement: M. J. Rouët de Journel, *Enchiridion patristicum*, 2nd ed. (Freiburg: 1962), 5–11; see also Walter Ullmann, *A Short History of the Papacy in the Middle Ages* (New York: 1982), 20; see further on First Clement: Drobner, 47–49.

90. "Si quis episcopi sui sententiae non adquiescit, recurrat ad synodum," Council of Vaison-la-Romaine (442), CCSL 148:98.

91. "Placuit praeterea accusandi licentiam etiam in nostri ordinis si qua existit leuitate comprimere," Council of Vaison-la-Romaine (442), CCSL 148:99.

92. Brown, *Rise of Western Christendom*, 113.

93. See the account in Élie Griffe, *La Gaule chrétienne*, 2:160–70; and Maurice Jourjon, "À propos du conflit entre le Pape Léon et Hilaire, évêque d'Arles," in *La Patrie gauloise d'Agrippa au VIème siècle: Actes du Colloque (Lyon: 1981);* Centre d'Études Romaines et gallo-romaines 3 (Lyon: 1983), 267–71. On the reaction in the Jura communities: Vogüé, *Histoire littéraire du mouvement monastique*, 7:330–31.

94. "Perlata ad nos epistola beatitudinis uestrae, quam ad Orientem pro catholicae fidei

stantinople on the two natures of Christ, known as the *Tome of Leo*,[95] had been rejected at the Council of Ephesus in 449, so Leo recruited the support of the Gallic bishops for his effort to overturn that council, which he succeeded in doing at the Council of Chalcedon in 451.[96] Gallic bishops were thus drafted for the church-wide struggles of the time, yet there were signs, in their letter of reply to the pope, of how difficult their participation was: "it was difficult for us, because we could not quickly come together, either because of the long distances which separate us, or because of the weather, which, as is customary in our regions, was intemperate."[97] This was an oddly diffident statement, given that many bishops were then enduring invasion by the Huns, who were defeated in a horrible battle on the Catalaunian Plains that same year.[98] The contrast with the eastern Church was great, where councils gathering many hundreds of bishops met repeatedly throughout the fifth century and continued to rely on the emperor's protection.

Leo must have been gratified by this support. The bishops made an extended declaration of faith in the Apostolic See, and of their joy at having heard Leo's authoritative voice, which the bishops accepted as a "symbol of the faith."[99] The Apostolic See was described as the "font and origin of our religion."[100] Far from being intimately involved in this debate, the bishops felt that the pope had taken up arms against "a heresy developing in secret for a long time."[101] In the very act of declaring their reverence toward Rome the bishops of Gaul betrayed the extent to which they were absorbed by their own profound troubles and their

---

assertione misistis," *Epistola synodica episcoporum Galliae ad Leonem Papam post concilium incerto in loco adunatum* (451), CCSL 148:107.

95. *Tomus Leonis,* in Alberigo, ed., *Conciliorum oecumenicorum,* 77–82.

96. On Chalcedon, see Eduard Schwartz, *Aus den Akten des Concils von Chalkedon:* Abhandlungen der Bayerischen Akademie der Wissenschaften, Philosophisch-philologische und historische Klasse, 32/2 (Munich: 1925); Aloys Grillmeier, *Le Christ dans la tradition chrétienne,* trans. Sister Pascale-Dominique, vol. 2.1, *Le Concile de Chalcédoine (451): réception et opposition (451–513)* (Paris: 1990).

97. "Nisi nobis difficultatem, qua in unum celeriter non potuimus conuenire, uel spatia, quibus a nobis dispalati sumus, longa terrarum uel aurarum, quae in regionibus nostris praeter consuetudinem fuit, intemperies attulisset," *Epistola synodica episcoporum Galliae,* CCSL 148:107.

98. Wolfram, *Roman Empire,* 136–39.

99. "Quae Apostolatus uestri scripta, ita ut symbolum fidei, quisquis redemptionis sacramenta non negligit, tabulis cordis adscribit, et tenaci . . . memoriae commendauit," *Epistola synodica episcoporum Galliae,* CCSL 148:107.

100. "Tantaeque doctrinae Apostolicae Sedi, unde religionis nostrae, propitio Christo, fons et origo manauit, Antistitem dederit," *Epistola synodica episcoporum Galliae,* 108. The bishops thereby applied to the pope the same epithet which they applied to themselves; see, for example, "Presbytero uel diacono sine antistitis sui epistolis ambulanti cummunionem nullus inpendat," Council of Épaone (517) CCSL 148A:25.

101. "Meritis autem Apostolatus uestri pius Dominus praestitit, ut haeresim iamdiu occulte nutritam uestris temporibus proderet," *Epistola synodica episcoporum Galliae,* 108.

efforts to find local solutions. An attitude of worshipful obedience to Rome was combined with a degree of disconnection from the debates in which the popes were engaged.

The continuity of aristocratic networks was nourished, and at times enforced, by the continuity of councils during times of profound change. A further council was held in Arles during the episcopate of Bishop Ravennius (449–461), but the date cannot be further specified.[102] It was the first council held there following the death of Hilary of Arles (†449). The council-record takes the form of a synodal letter recording the decision of the bishops in the affair of Faustus, Abbot of Lérins.[103] This involved a dispute between the abbot and Theodorus, bishop of Fréjus, over the liturgical precedence of the bishop whose territory included the island monastery.

The synodal letter confirmed the principle of mutuality, restating that clergy must not seek the chrism from bishops other than their own, and that "peregrine clerics" should not be given a position when they have fled the territory of another bishop.[104] Most of the bishops who signed this synodal letter were also signatories of the letter to Pope Leo, discussed above: Ravennius of Arles, Rusticus of Narbonne, Nectarius of Avignon, Florus (of Lodève?), Constantius of Carpentras, Asclepius of Cavaillon, Maximus (not the same bishop of Riez mentioned earlier), Iustus of Orange, the learned Salonius of Geneva, and Ingenuus, the new bishop of Embrun. This group of bishops continued to be a well-connected and learned group. Rusticus had corresponded with Jerome, who replied with detailed instruction in the monastic life.[105] Within the circle of this aristocratic community, drawn from several southern metropolitan provinces, it appears that all matters touching Lérins still formed a point of concern for most of the southern Gallic bishops.[106] The large number of bishops involved in the dispute settlement highlights the importance, for southern Gallic bishops, for matters affecting the collegial and legal construction of their aristocratic echelon. The agony of discord was expressed in the following terms: "Each time that a member suffers some kind of infirmity, it cannot be that the other members of the

---

102. Hefele-Leclercq, *Histoire des conciles*, 2:881.

103. Jacques Sirmond, *Conciliorum antiquorum Galliae a Iac: Sirmondo S.I. editorum Supplementa* (Paris: 1666), 27–32; Charles Munier, ed., *Concilia Galliae A. 314–A. 506,* Council of Arles (449–461), CCSL 148:131–34.

104. "Peregrini clerici absque ipsius praecepto in communionem uel ad ministerium non admittantur," Council of Arles (449–461), CCSL 148:133.

105. Jerome, Letter 125; see Kelly, *Jerome,* 297.

106. See the analysis of Vogüé, *Histoire littéraire du mouvement monastique,* 7:319.

body do not suffer."[107] An affair that touched on the proper distribution of the monastic prestige associated with Lérins was something that harmed the college of bishops, who were said to form a single, vividly imagined social and religious body (*corpus*), a term that appears to acquire a social or political sense referring to the clergy alone, rather than to Christian community, as in Tertullian.[108]

The norms and patterns of these councils continued to function even when new political conditions caused the centers of royal power to move beyond the familiar Mediterranean regions. With the council of Tours (461) we leave the close-knit world of southern Gaul and its Lérinian connections and observe a new generation of bishops grappling with new conditions.[109] The Gothic kingdom now reached out into Spain, where in 455 the Suebi and their Roman allies were defeated and absorbed by the Gothic kingdom of Toulouse. The bishoprics of Clermont-Ferrand and Tours were a kind of refuge, protected by the miraculous power of St. Martin and by the Frankish general Childeric. Alliances frequently cut across the traditional opposition of *Romani* and *barbari* in these conditions.[110] The Roman aristocracy increasingly turned to the church: Avitus himself was (forcibly) made bishop of Piacenza.[111]

The church of St. Martin was the setting of this assembly of bishops, who declared that they were "preserving the statutes of the fathers according to evangelical precepts and apostolic doctrine."[112] Led by Perpetuus of Tours, the council assembled nine bishops from the surrounding region on the feast day of St. Martin. The unusual reliance of this council on citations from Scripture fits into the total picture presented by this council: that it focused on recounting old law in a quest for the most widely known and ancient sources of authority. Out of the total of thirty-six scriptural citations contained in all the councils of the Gallic period, about one-half were presented at Tours (461).

Perpetuus corresponded with the elegant occupant of the see of Clermont-Ferrand, Sidonius Apollinaris, and may have overseen an early episcopal school in

107. "Quotiens membrum aliquod quolibet infirmitatis genere laborat, fieri non potest quin etiam cetera membra corporis doleant," *Exemplar Epistulae generalis quae ad episcopos invitandos in causa insulae Lerinensis missa est,* Council of Arles (449–461), CCSL 148:132.

108. It is highly significant that *corpus* here does not refer to the church but to the bishops of southern Gaul; compare citations in GGB 4:538–541; see also Henri de Lubac, *Corpus mysticum: L'Eucharistie et l'église au moyen âge, Étude historique,* 2nd rev. ed. (Paris, 1949), 94.

109. Council of Tours (461), CCSL 148:142–49.

110. Wolfram, *Roman Empire,* 152.

111. Mathisen, *Ecclesiastical Factionalism,* 199.

112. "Ut secundum euangelica praecepta et apostolicam doctrinam patrum statuta seruantes," Council of Tours (461), CCSL 148:143.

Tours.[113] Such schools existed in a number of Gallic cities, operated by bishops and providing for the training of the priesthood.[114] We should probably imagine a kind of education directed toward practicalities basic to the priestly life: chant, liturgy, and administration. Such presbyters/priests might be found residing in the *domus ecclesiae*. In Gap in the sixth century the bishop's residence contained a dormitory for clerics.[115] Thus new resources for clerical culture were gradually developed.

Tours had its own ascetic tradition, initiated by Martin of Tours, who made a point of conducting his episcopal business while seated on a homely tripod. The bishops of Tours could draw upon the resonance of those associations and the continued presence of Martin's monastic community in neighboring Marmoutier.[116] Also present at the Council of Tours (461) were Victorius of Le Mans, Leo of Bigorre (Tarbes), Eusebius of Nantes, Amandinus of Chalons-sur-Marnes, Germanus of Rouen, and Athenius of Rennes. A British bishop, Mansuetus, might have represented a British refugee community in the Loire.

Like the councils of Hilary, this council likewise drew upon ancient conciliar tradition, including decrees of Ancyra (314), Nicaea (325), Turin (398), and Angers (453). The effect was to publish the ancient canons and support them with Scripture, as in the council's stricture against usury: "We believe thereto exactly according to the authority of Scripture and the additional constitution of the fathers."[117] Generally the content of these canons regarded the discipline of Christian communities and of bishops themselves. Fundamental, traditional dictates were prominent. It was forbidden to violate the norms of collegiality by accepting foreign clerics or to attempt to exercise power in another's territory: a violation of another bishop's rights (*ius*). Thus in conditions of tremendous pressure, in a key city in the power struggle underway between the emerging Franks and the Gothic kingdom of Toulouse, the bishops made the recovery and promotion of ancient law the centerpiece of their own regional cooperation. The ascetic aura of this meeting was guaranteed by the saintly presence of Martin, for whose intercession the bishops prayed in closing the council.[118]

Perpetuus presided, possibly only at a distance, at a council held in Vannes (461–491). The council appears to have been a continuation, or follow-up, on

---

113. Riché, *Éducation et culture,* 74. On the possible existence of a school in Tours, 106.

114. Godding, *Prêtres en Gaule,* 53–59; Rapp, *Holy Bishops,* 178–83.

115. Godding, *Prêtres en Gaule,* 63–64, 223–24.

116. Vogüé, *Histoire littéraire du mouvement monastique,* 7:340.

117. "Illud etiam secundum scripturarum auctoritatem uel patrum constitutionem addendum credidimus," Council of Tours (461), CCSL 148:147.

118. Council of Tours (461), CCSL 148: 146–47.

some intitiative coming out of Tours (461). The first canon repeated the rejection of murderers from communion as propounded at Tours, also drawing on a canon of the Council of Elvira (306), which had concerned women who had beaten their servants to death.[119] In the early Gallic *Collection of Rheims (Collectio Remensis)* (Berlin: Phillipps 1743), compiled in the second half of the sixth century, the council is connected to six attending bishops, although Perpetuus might not have been physically present.[120] Paternus of Vannes was not permitted to preside, although the council met in his church. Nonechius of Nantes was present, with Albinus and Liberalis, obscure bishops. The presence of Athenius of Rennes was another point of continuity with Tours (461).

Conflict with the new, unstable, and competitive kingdoms was evident. The council adopted a lofty tone in its express return of the region to ecclesiastical law and order (*regula ecclesiastica*). The bishops sought to prevent clerics from being dragged before secular courts and maintained the special dignity and competence of the episcopal *audientia* as a court that should not be interfered with by "secular power."[121] The council forbade clerics from indulging in auguries "under the banner of a made-up religion" that was known as consulting the oracles of the saints (*sanctorum sortes*).[122]

The council was primarily concerned with marshalling and ordering the monastic life, allowing for the growing numbers of monks who wished to retreat into the life of a hermit. Vogüé considers the Council of Vannes (461–491) as evidence for an eremitical tone in the monastic life of the region.[123] By organizing and ruling over monasteries and hermitages, bishops such as Perpetuus could ensure their own contact with the ascetic sources of religious authenticity.

The Council of Agde (506)

A new political and religious figure loomed over the council that met in the Gothic city of Agde in 506: the council noted the permission granted to their meeting by a "most-glorious, most-magnificent, most-pious king." The triple soubriquet of King Alaric outshined the recognition of Constantine long ago at

---

119. Council of Vannes (461–491), CCSL 148:151; see also Brown, *Rise of Western Christendom,* 64 with refs.

120. Kéry, *Canonical Collections,* 50–53; Maassen, *Geschichte der Quellen,* 638–40.

121. "De proprietate aliqua aduersus ipsum episcopum fuerit nata contentio, aliorum episcoporum audientaim no saecularium potestatem debebit ambire," Council of Vannes (461–491), 153.

122. It is certainly possible that such references indicate a written oracle-text: William E. Klingshirn, "Defining the *Sortes Sanctorum*: Gibbon, Du Cange, and Early Christian Lot Divination," JECS, 10 (2002): 77–130; see also Council of Vannes (461–491), 156.

123. Vogüé, *Histoire littéraire du mouvement monastique,* 7:386.

Arles (314), who had only been termed "most-pious." The proem of the council-record is worth quoting at greater length:

When in the name of the Lord, the holy synod gathered in the city of Agde, with the permission of our most-glorious, most-magnificent, most-pious king, and there bent our knees to the earth, praying for his reign, for his longevity, for the people of God.[124]

Alaric II succeeded his father in ruling the Kingdom of Toulouse in 484. Throughout his reign, conflict with the Franks was becoming ever more inevitable as the Franks expanded across northern Gaul toward the Visigothic frontier. At the same time the Visigoths began to conquer Spain from the Suebi and their Roman allies. Beginning in about 500, the Frankish and Visigothic kingdoms began to skirmish. Throughout the two decades of Alaric's reign these two confederacies confronted each other as rivals, each kingdom endeavoring to consolidate its new possessions effectively. In both the Frankish kingdom and the Kingdom of Toulouse, this required reaching an accommodation with the valuable aristocratic networks of bishops and their well-entrenched government over cities, monastic communities, and Christian churches.[125] In Wolfram's view, "Alaric II's great achievement was his legal and ecclesiastical policy."[126] This achievement soon came to an end. In the year following the council of Agde, Alaric was spectacularly defeated and killed at the Battle of Vouillé. From that point onward the Visigothic kingdom was restricted to Spain, while the Franks under King Clovis now extended their rule across Gaul.[127]

Alaric was a king who recognized the value of law as a point of contact with his Roman subjects and bishops, who also believed that social and religious order could be shaped by law. The explanation for Alaric's extensive legal activities probably lies with aristocratic, and possibly episcopal, advisors. The result was a coordination of "royal" law with canon law.[128] *Collection* rather than legislation was the form taken by Alaric's legal program. The Council of Agde (506) was an assembly of bishops as well as of other leading men of the Kingdom of Toulouse. The ecclesiastical portion of the council was a fitting summary and coda for

124. "Cum in nomine Domine ex permissu domni nostri gloriosissimi magnificentissimi piissimique regis in Agatensi ciuitate sancta synodus conuenisset, ibique flexis in terram genibus, pro regno eius, pro longaeuitate, pro populo Dominum deprecaremur," Council of Agde (506), CCSL 148:192.

125. Mathisen, "'Second Council of Arles,'" 533.

126. Wolfram, *Roman Empire*, 155.

127. Demandt, *Geschichte der Spätantike*, 160.

128. Ralph W. Mathisen, "D'Aire-sur l'Adour à Agde: Les relations entre la lois séculière et la loi canonique à la fin du royaume de Toulouse," in *Le Bréviaire d'Alaric: Aux origines du Code civil,* edited by Michel Rouche and Bruno Dumézil (Paris: 2008), 41–52.

the Gallic legal tradition. The large body of canon law that issued from the council was widely collected in early Gallic collections of canons.[129] Despite the new political context of the Gothic kingdom, Agde (506) was considered to belong to Gallic conciliar tradition, given its inclusion in chronologically ordered collections of Gallic canon law. One example is the sixth- to seventh-century *Collection of Corbie,* originally compiled in Vienne.[130] The late-sixth-century *Collection of Rheims* (Berlin: Phillipps 1743) also records the council of Agde among its chronological series of councils.[131] Because of the sudden political changes following the death of Alaric, some recorded versions of Agde (506) expunged the name of King Alaric from the council-record, seemingly to make the text "more acceptable in a Frankish context."[132]

Scholars agree that Agde (506) was the occasion for the issuance of the *Lex Romana Visigothorum,* an anthology of Roman law designed for the Roman inhabitants of the Kingdom of Toulouse. The *Lex Romana Visigothorum* contained an abridgment of the *Institutes* of Gaius.[133] Also known as the *Breviary of Alaric,* this simplification of the Theodosian Code was tailored to the conditions in Gaul and built upon an earlier initiative of King Euric, the *Codex Euricinianus.*[134] We will return to these Visigothic collections of Roman law in chapter 4. One clear signal of this event was a declaration of peace and cooperation between the Arian Gothic nobility and the Catholic Roman subjects of the Kingdom of Toulouse. The religious division separating ruler and ruled would not preclude the continuation of Gallic Christianity and the dominance of bishops within that system.

The Council of Agde (506) gathered perhaps twenty-four bishops from across the region dominated by the Goths. This was the first council held in Agde, reflecting the importance of Languedoc in the new configuration of Visigothic power in southern Gaul. The changed shape of power did not prevent the see of Arles from maintaining its leadership role, now in the person of Caesarius of Arles. For this council Caesarius was able to rely on the traditional conciliar cities of southern Gaul, represented by Cyprian of Bordeaux, Clarus of Eauze, Tetradi-

129. See the discussion by Munier: Council of Agde (506), CCSL 148:189–91; also Hefele-Leclercq, *Histoire des conciles,* 2:973–1004.

130. This work, the *Collectio Corbeiensis,* is contained in Paris, B.N. Lat. 12097 (St. Gall, Cod. Sangerm. 936): Maassen, *Geschichte der Quellen,* 556–74.

131. Munier's text A is the version of the council-record preserved in the ninth-century Carolingian manuscript, Paris, Bibliothèque Nationale, lat. 3846: Kéry, *Canonical Collections,* 10 and 16.

132. Mathisen, "Second Council of Arles," 552–54.

133. Herbert Felix Jolowicz, *Historical Introduction to the Study of Roman Law* (Cambridge: 1932), 394; Kurtscheid and Wilches, *Historia iuris canonici,* 1:118.

134. Lupoi, *Origins of the European Legal Order,* 76–78.

us of Bourges, and Heraclianus of Toulouse. But this southern grouping of cities was joined to a newly emergent and wider network of bishoprics. Only after the Arlesian worthies did Sofronius of Agde enter his name in the subscription list, followed by many other bishoprics stretching across southwest Gaul: Boethius of Cahors, Gratianus of Dax, Galactarius (var. Galectorum) of Lescar, Gratus of Oloron, and other cities within the province of Éauze.[135] Verus of Tours, who surely found it difficult to attend a council in Visigothic territory when his city was under Frankish protection, was represented by his deacon Leo.[136]

The integration and consolidation of royal power and the southern and southwestern Gallic episcopal aristocracy were thereby demonstrated in communal acts of law-giving. The "royal" side of law was represented by the promulgation of a simplified code of Roman law. The "episcopal" side of law was reflected in the canons of Agde (506), a compendium of important earlier conciliar law, similar to the learned procedure of Orange (441), described earlier.

"In the first place it pleased the council the canons and statutes of the fathers be read concerning order *(ordo),*" by which was meant old canon law regarding the character of clergy.[137] The ensuing text of the first canon of the council seemingly relied on the first canon of Valence (374) and the twenty-fourth canon of Orange (441), denying ordination to those who had been married more than once. Such men could retain their positions, but were forbidden to conduct the rites.[138] Similarly the council made reference to canons of the following councils, many of which have been discussed here: among them Neocaesaria (314), Nîmes (394 or 396), Vaison-la-Romaine (442), and Vannes (461–491). The Council of Agde thus gives the feeling of a summary and promotion of important old law, considered vital for the organization of episcopal regional networks of prestige, aristocratic mutuality, and ecclesiastical culture. Among the topics developed in this way: the problem of an unjust punishment by a bishop, who must allow the appeal of such cases to the judgment of a synod (following a canon from Vaison-la-Romaine, 442).[139]

135. *Province ecclésiastique d'Éauze (Novempopulana),* ed. Louis Maurin, et al. TCCG 13 (Paris: 2004), 13.

136. The subscription list survives in a number of different versions: the list contained in Paris, B.N. Lat. 1564, allows us to identify the cities of attending bishops, including those indicated here: Council of Agde (506), 213–19.

137. "In primo id placuit, ut canones et statuta patrum per ordinem legerentur," Council of Agde (506), CCSL 148:193.

138. "Quibus lectis placuit de bigamis aut internuptarum mariti," Council of Agde (506), 193; similar to canon one on *digami,* Council of Valence (374), CCSL 148:38; see also "duplicata matrimonia," canon 24 of Council of Orange (441), CCSL 148:84.

139. Council of Agde (506), CCSL 148:193–94; see also Council of Vaison-la-Romaine (442),

The solution to contemporary problems was sought in the books of canon law, which by this time had assuredly taken the form of canon law collections. Two such sources, relied upon by Caesarius and the bishops assembled in Agde, are of particular interest to this discussion, reflecting the earliest stage of canon collection and the development of learned Christian law: these were the so-called "Second Council of Arles" and the *Statuta ecclesia antiqua,* collections of canons made by anonymous scholars or bishops and presented as actual councils.[140] Agde (506) sought to highlight the special dignity of vestments and distinctive appearance of clerics, who should not grow their hair long or wear the vestments or slippers appropriate only to a clerical order higher than their own.[141] This canon of Agde combined two canons of the *Statuta ecclesia antiqua.*[142] The latter work was seemingly compiled in order to synthesize laws concerning clerical discipline, church order, and the appropriate cultural attributes of clerics.

At Agde (506) and at later, similar councils in the Frankish and Burgundian kingdoms, important collections of Roman and barbarian law were published in the context of councils, which served as major expressions of law and legality, grand ritual events evoking the religious and cultural basis of law. Like the other councils examined here, Agde (506) was an aristocratic assembly dedicated to the notion of legality, possessing the competence of an ecclesiastical court and including members who had abundant legal resources at their fingertips. The episcopal assembly at Agde was concerned with presenting a compendium of old law, with the goal of making it relevant for a new aristocratic network, assembling in new conditions. Caesarius of Arles was a master at maintaining clerical orientation and discovering new resources for episcopal power in the post-Roman world. He managed to work closely with King Alaric II, who may have agreed to the nomination of Caesarius as bishop.[143]

Like Roman law, conciliar law itself was increasingly preserved in canon collections. An early version of that scholarly activity took the form of pseudo-councils, which attempted to provide a canon collection with the dignity and

---

CCSL 148:98. Hefele-Leclercq considers such reproductions in light of their later incorporation in the Corpus Iuris Canonici, although the contemporary context is more important: Hefele-Leclercq, *Histoire des conciles,* 981–83.

140. Mathisen, "Second Council of Arles," 538–39.

141. "Clerici qui comam nutriunt, ab archidiacono, etiam si noluerint, inuiti detundantur; uestimenta uel claceamenta etiam eis nisi quae religionem deceant," Council of Agde (506), CCSL 148:202.

142. "Clericus nec comam nutriat" and "Clericus professionem suam," *Statuta ecclesia antiqua,* CCSL 148:171.

143. Mathisen, "Second Council of Arles," 536.

weight of an actual council. All this legal material, much of it old, some of it new, was intended to bear the weight of what the "ancient authority of the canons prescribes" (*prisca canonum praecepit auctoritas*).[144]

Factitious Councils (Canon Collections)

Following is a discussion of two important cases of the forgery or composition of a pseudo-council. In each case, these conciliar records prove to be canon-collections, compiled in an episcopal or monastic atélier, rather than a record of the actual legislation of a meeting of bishops: these include the so-called "Second Council of Arles (442–506)" and the *Statuta ecclesiae antiqua* from about 475. We have already noted the development of legal knowledge and the focus on old law, possibly with the assistance of canon collections or legal libraries, in several of the Gallic councils. One can speak of an ideological preference for repetition, not merely as an awareness of "legal precedent" but as a sign of connectedness to the holy past and to the religious power embedded in the law.

These pseudo-councils were in fact a type of canon collection. On the one hand, their existence demonstrates the prestige accorded to real council-records as authority-bearing documents, and on the other hand, they illustrate an intimate connection between conciliar activity and the emergence of a *learned law*. They are an important phase in the overall history of canon law collections.

It was mentioned in connection with Orange (441), above, that episcopal councils sought to bind together and reconcile the frequently divided regional networks of governance that replaced the wider, unified associations of the Empire. Legal collections developed as a concomitant to the overall life of episcopal law as one of the principal means of disseminating law, and especially as a way to heighten the authority of old law. By means of such legal work a scholar or the workshop of a bishop, monastery, or school could prepare a legal counterbalance to phenomena of theological discord and social fission. A close parallel can be observed in the development of *codices* of Roman law. Varied types of Roman law collections were compiled in this period, in addition to the grand imperial collections such as the *Theodosian Code* (discussed in chapter 4).

In the case of canon law, imperial initiatives gave way to regional associations of bishops, often under the leadership of prominent figures such as Hilary of Arles. Ecclesiastical politics came to the fore, involving negotiations and consensus-building among the representatives of aristocratic regional power.

---

144. Council of Agde (506), CCSL 148:195.

These trends were reflected in the development of archives and codices containing law. The judgment of Bellomo, that the fifth century was an "age without jurists," is technically correct, but by no means was the period devoid of legal activity and scholarly interest in law, especially on the part of bishops.[145] As Mathisen has demonstrated, legal scholarship took the characteristic form of compilation and codification and was part of a trend in which the primary concern was the preservation and gathering of sources of authority. The factitious council known as the "Second Council of Arles" was in actuality a collection of earlier conciliar law, although it is certainly possible that the work was promulgated at a gathering of bishops.[146] The presentation of this material as a pseudo-council deliberately blurred the line between conciliar legislation and the literary authority possessed by conciliar law when collected and disseminated in an authoritative, learned compilation.[147] This was one of the first such deliberate collections of Gallic canon law, compiled sometime after 442.[148] Collections of this kind became one of the most important dimensions of canon law. In other words, the collection of law was a type of legal activity that could take the place of legislation and have the same impact as a council. In order to achieve such a result, the collection known as the "Second Council of Arles" had to accord with traditions of canon law and correspond to known canons of earlier councils.[149] The earliest manuscript containing this set of canons is the *Collectio Coloniensis,* mentioned earlier. This *codex* is an important testimony of the history of canon law compilation and scholarship, containing the canons of many councils as well as papal decretals.[150] Later compilations always relied heavily upon earlier collections. The *Statuta ecclesiae antiqua,* a compilation presented as a council-record, was possibly made by Gennadius of Marseilles, working in southern Gaul, perhaps in Arles itself.[151] For many centuries the work was accepted as the "Fourth

145. Manlio Bellomo, *The Common Legal Past of Europe, 1000–1800,* trans. Lydia G. Cochrane (Washington, D.C.: 1995), 34–36.

146. Mathisen, "Second Council of Arles," 551.

147. The so-called "Second Council of Arles" (c. 442–506), CCSL 148:111–30; see also Maassen, *Geschichte der Quellen,* 194–200.

148. Mathisen, *Ecclesiastical Factionalism,* 114.

149. Knut Schäferdiek argued that the Second Council of Arles was a forgery intended to bolster the metropolitan claims of Arles: "Das sogenannte zweite Konzil von Arles und die älteste Kanonessammlung der arelatenser Kirche," ZSRG.K 71 (1985): 1–19; Turner, "Arles and Rome," 240; see also Hefele-Leclercq, *Histoire des conciles,* 2.1:460–76; and Kéry, *Canonical Collections,* 6–7.

150. Gaudemet, *Sources du droit,* 88–89.

151. *Statuta ecclesiae antiqua,* CCSL 148:162–88. Munier also edited and studied the work separately: Charles Munier, *Les Statuta ecclesiae antiqua,* Bibliothèque de l'Institut de droit canonique 5 (Paris: 1960); see also Kéry, *Canonical Collections,* 7; Maassen, *Geschichte der Quellen,* 202–4.

Council of Carthage" (398), no doubt because of the predominance of African councils in the collection.[152] In fact it is a collection of eastern and Gallic councils, with decretals.[153] The legal concerns behind this collection are specific to questions of church order, the selection and ordination of various grades of clerics, and the qualities that should distinguish them from each other and from the surrounding world. In the first place, the collection offered a statement of faith in Nicene Catholicism, "confirming that Father and Son and Holy Spirit are one God, and the coessential and total deity of the Trinity, coeternal and consubstantial and coeternal."[154] Such an understanding and statement of faith should be required of a man to be ordained bishop.

The overall portrait of an ideal bishop included here is highly instructive. Among other fine qualities, bishops should be knowledgeable in the "Law of the Lord," which probably means the very kinds of law and doctrine contained in the *Statuta ecclesiae antiqua*.[155] The ability of the bishop to govern in the best style of conciliation and moderation between communities was to be safeguarded by consultation. The bishop should govern in harmony with his clerics and the local community of his church.[156] Clerical culture should be distinguished from that of the surrounding nobility, not only in the matter of not wearing long hair, marking clerical status by means of specialized clothing, but also in abstention from women (*extraneae mulieres*), and preserving the property of his church from the creeping effects of sale and involvement in local arrangements. A significant portion of the *Statuta ecclesiae antiqua* regards liturgical order and oversight of the cult. The bishop as a ritual expert and master of ascetic discipline is presented side by side with the bishop as a master of law and government.

The *Quesnelliana,* possibly made in Gaul at the end of the fifth or early sixth century, was a canon collection that brought together the oldest threads of conciliar tradition, Nicaea (325) and other eastern councils such as Ancyra, Neocaesarea, and Gangra, conciliar documents from Africa, and papal decretals through Pope Gelasius.[157] The work takes its name from the first editor of the

---

152. The contents are analyzed by Hefele-Leclercq, *Histoire des conciles,* 108–21.

153. Kurtscheid and Wilches, *Historia iuris canonici,* 1:96–97.

154. "Patrem et Filium et spiritum sanctum unum Deum esse confirmans, totamque in Trinitate deitatem coessentialem et consubstantialem et coaeternalem," *Statuta ecclesiae antiqua* (c. 475), CCSL 148:164.

155. "In lege Domini," *Statuta ecclesiae antiqua* (c. 475), CCSL 148:164; see also "legis et prophetarum," 165; Kéry, *Canonical Collections,* 7.

156. "Ut episcopus absque consilio compresbyterorum suorum clericos non ordinet, ita ut civium conniuentiam et testimoniusm quaerat," *Statuta ecclesiae antiqua* (c. 475), CCSL 148:168.

157. Maassen, *Geschichte der Quellen,* 486–500.

collection, the Jansenist theologian and orator Pasquier Quesnel (1634–1719), who believed it to have been a Roman collection (*Codex ecclesiae Romanae*).[158] According to Maassen and others, it was probably made in southern Gaul. Because of its wide-ranging contents and its possible reflection of the ecclesiastical and scholarly resources of Arles, some have assigned the *Quesnelliana* to the legal *atélier* of Caesarius of Arles (†542) himself.[159] The collection was foundational in the sense that it later served Dionysius Exiguus (†537–555) in crafting his own collection, known as the *Dionysiana*. The collection is an early example of the development of ecclesiastical *learned law* and the historical ambitions of such collections. In this sense, it should be viewed in the context of the early pseudo-conciliar collections. Council records were ordinarily assembled in chronological sequence, thereby emphasizing the historical character of the unfolding authority of episcopal law.

Beginning in the sixth century there was a kind of awakening of religious legal scholarship taking the form of many local collections of canons.[160] Despite their inclusion of the most highly regarded sources of conciliar authority, these collections were tailored to local needs, "local perceptions of priorities and local understandings of the history of the church," which in the theory of R. McKitterick would explain why many canon collections only exist in unique copies.[161]

As a religious phenomenon, the "unrolled carpet" of canon law seems generally devoid of emotional flights or inscribed beauty. The barren language of the law conveys little more than the practical framing of institutions and regulations. This *askesis* of law, the reduction of complex matters to prudential conclusions, was part of the legacy of Roman law. Conciliar law focused on governmental concepts and the arrangement of aristocratic status and privilege. Interactions within the aristocratic coterie of southern Gaul were regulated and mediated. Episcopal government over regional Christian communities was often fortified in the context of these regional aristocratic assemblies. The councils were more than that: they served also as tribunals for dispute resolution and provided theological and ritual leadership to Christian communities.

What has been shown in this examination of the Gallic councils is the development of a legal tradition that suited the needs and aims of aristocratic groups

---

158. Pasquier Quesnel, *Ad S. Leonis Magni Opera Appendix 2* (Paris: 1675), 13–242.

159. Kurtscheid and Wilches, *Historia iuris canonici*, 1:96.

160. A brief conspectus of sixth-century canon collections: Kurtscheid and Wilches, *Historia iuris canonici*, 1:97–98.

161. Rosamond McKitterick, *History and Memory in the Carolingian World* (Cambridge: 2004), 254.

and the communities they governed in littoral and southwestern Gaul during the collapse of the Roman Empire and the rise of new barbarian political confederations. The breakdown of imperial unity allowed the bishops of Gaul to center their activities in the needs of a southern Gallic aristocratic elite and its efforts to provide guidance and orientation to Christian communities.

Roman law affected the life of the councils by providing legal concepts and terminology, the parameters of the institutional possibility and episcopal cooperation, conciliation, and mutual recognition. The most powerful forum in which this transfer of Roman aristocratic values was made, for the purposes of Christian community, was among Gallic bishops trained and inspired by the ascetic masters of Lérins and the collegial cohort of like-minded men who dominated the church after 410. As powerful new barbarian regional dominions transformed the social landscape of Gaul, the bishops continued to rely on their mastery of law as a basic medium for negotiating between Roman and barbarian, royal, or military centers of power, aristocratic networks, and regional Christian communities. In these activities of the Gallic aristocracy we confront the slow movement of institutional and political change and the "necessity for the historian to extend his research over a vast space of time," in the phrase of Fustel de Coulanges.[162]

Ultimately such activities gave rise to a learned law as the activity of the councils was supported by legal collections and scholarly mastery over canon law. Seemingly on this basis, the episcopal councils became the appropriate setting for kings such as Alaric, who wished to play a role in the legal universe. In turn, the council was briefly transformed into a territorial meeting bringing the Gothic nobility and Roman bishops together to promulgate collections of the two bodies of old law relevant to the church and its episcopal governors: Roman law and canon law. Both of these laws were in the special domain of bishops. In the famous phrase of the *Lex Ribuaria,* "the Church lives according to Roman law."[163]

---

162. "La nécessité pour l'historien d'étendre ses recherches sur un vaste espace de temps," Fustel de Coulanges, *La Gaule Romaine*, 42.

163. "Secundum legem Romanam, quam ecclesia vivit," (61.1) *Lex Ribuaria,* ed. F. Beyerle and R. Büchner, MGH Leges 3.2 (Hannover: 1954), 109. The famous expression is often wrongly quoted as "Ecclesia vivit lege Romana"; see for instance: Henry Osborn Taylor, *The Mediaeval Mind: A History of the Development of Thought and Emotion in the Middle Ages*, 3rd ed. (New York: 1919), 2:294. I myself repeated Taylor's fruitful error in Moore, "The Spirit of the Gallican Councils," 52; see also Gaudemet, *Sources du droit*, 67–68.

[3]

BISHOPS AND THE
"NATIONS"

*T*HE PREVIOUS CHAPTER examined the ways in which aristocratic bishops attempted to raise their social prestige and religious profile in the last
decades of the Roman Empire, and the role of conciliar law as an authoritative
expression of episcopal social doctrine. Here the story is carried forward into
the sixth century and the creation of what are ordinarily termed the "barbarian kingdoms." Bishops in Gaul sought to craft a Christian ideology relevant to
the post-Roman world and to gather religious and ritual resources to confront
the disquieting religious diversity (Arianism, paganisms) of the barbarian kingdoms. The figure of the bishop was developed mythically in the miracles of saintly bishops, which were fervently recounted and avidly read. Meanwhile several
key thinkers—Ambrose of Milan, Julian Pomerius, and Gregory the Great—
developed a practical, severe model of ascetic power and an ethos of saintly stoicism.

Two major figures of this period provide a focus and eloquent examples of an
emerging episcopal ideology. Caesarius of Arles in southern Gaul reflected the
active, sophisticated approach of a cultivated and self-assured aristocrat as he led
the Christian community of Arles under Burgundian overlordship. In northern
Gaul, Gregory of Tours wrote a history of the Frankish Church. In this history,
an aristocratic episcopal view of history was expressed as a struggle between the
violence of kings and the religiosity of bishops and holy hermits who sought to

educate, defy, and control those kings. The barbarian kingdoms brought stability to post-Roman Europe, but also new sources of conflict. Both Caesarius and Gregory believed that the transformed political world of Gaul called for new politico-historical concepts and for a new social vocabulary, especially in regard to the problem of kingship. These were expressed as religious, episcopal ideals.

Mirrors of Bishops

Guides for the proper conduct of clerical life focused on the role of the bishop, whose burdens were greater than those of other clerics. These ideals were frequently presented in sermons and treatises.[1] Ambrose of Milan, Julian Pomerius, and Gregory the Great added to the developing model of the bishop. According to these men, at the heart of episcopal power was a monastic style of life, an attitude of personal retreat, and religious seriousness, which then "returned to the world" in acts of governance and social authority. Often the protection of the poor was offered as the signature of a new style of Christian power. This was a theme of privilege and dominance for the centers of Christian charity. Episcopal government and charity reflected the government of God and the "dependence of all creatures on the generosity of an all-powerful giver."[2]

Ambrose of Milan, writing in the late 380s, took Cicero's *De officiis* ("On Obligations") as a model for his work of the same title on the responsibilities of important clerics.[3] As a metropolitan bishop, Ambrose (ca. 339–397) was very active in the area of ecclesiastical law and the life of the councils in the region around Milan.[4] Descended from an aristocratic family with Gallic ties, Ambrose trained as an advocate and later rose to become a consular governor for Aemilia-Liguria before becoming the bishop of Milan.[5] Cracco Ruggini distinguishes the three elements of an "Ambrosian model" of the bishop: a severely ascetic form of life, combined with a charismatic style of power; tireless activity as a pastor and evangelist, and thus an ability to mobilize his people around a civic and religious patriotism; and loyalty to the faith of Nicaea and to Ambrose himself.[6] In Milan, Ambrose gradually built a cultural setting in which loyal, orthodox, and well-educated clerics could be produced. He dominated the Aquilean Church by overseeing the ordination of bishops and by intervening in clerical affairs

---

1. Rapp, *Holy Bishops*, 41.
2. Brown, *Poverty and Leadership*, 87.
3. Ambrose of Milan, *De officiis*, ed. and trans. Ivor J. Davidson, 2 vols. (Oxford: 2001).
4. Gryson, *Le prêtre selon Saint Ambroise*, 155–61.
5. Drobner, 307–18.
6. Ruggini, "Prêtre et fonctionnaire," 183.

across the region.[7] His career exemplifies the transfer of aristocratic values and governmental ideals from the empire to the church.[8]

Ambrose sought to prepare clerics for the equally public and engaged life of a Christian priest or bishop. Even more important was his focus on the bishop. While he had words of advice for the humble exorcist or doorkeeper, most of his remarks were intended for the *sacerdos,* by which he sometimes meant "priest," but usually "bishop." The same usage of the term was retained in Gallic and Merovingian councils.[9] The Christian stoicism of the book, in which asceticism was projected as a public ethos, was intended to instruct clerical men of power.[10] The bishop must possess sufficient *gravitas* of character to distinguish himself from the crowds of the city.[11] He ought to be "sober, chaste, distinguished, hospitable, a good teacher, not greedy, not quarrelsome, and in proper control of his own household."[12]

The bishop assured his readers that the duties (*officia*) he had in mind were truly Christian.[13] Under the influence of Cicero, traditional episcopal duties, such as ransoming prisoners and giving aid to the poor, were reinterpreted by Ambrose as requiring balance. To hit the right mark was to achieve a "beautiful generosity" (*pulchra liberalitas*). One traditional act of pious generosity was the ransom of hostages held by barbarian armies.[14] The bishop must be a source of calm, sound judgement, since so many rely on him. Nor should he be deficient in faith.[15] Ambrose's ideal bishop had the quiet, steadfast demeanor of a Hellenistic sage.

Ambrose argued that only clerical obedience could bind the church together, but the relation between bishop and clergy should be mild and familial.[16] Indeed, he ensured that his clergy would form a loyal and effective cadre of followers, trained under his aegis and fiercely devoted to himself and to the Nicene faith.[17] Not surprisingly, then, *De Officiis* addresses the possibility of struggles

7. Gryson, *Le prêtre selon Saint Ambroise,* 149–64.

8. Judith Herrin, *The Formation of Christendom* (Princeton: 1987), 64.

9. Godding, *Prêtres en Gaule,* 173–77.

10. Ambrose, *De officiis* (I.183), 1:224–25.

11. Vincenzo Monachino, *S. Ambrogio e la cura pastorale a Milano nel secolo IV* (Milan: 1973), 41.

12. Ambrose, *De officiis,* trans. Davidson (I.246), 1:258–59.

13. Ambrose, *De officiis* (I.24), 1:130–31.

14. "Praecipua est igitur liberalitas redimere captivos et maxime ab hoste barbaro," Ambrose, *De officiis* (II.71), 1: 306–7.

15. Ambrose, *De officiis* (I.256), 1:266–67.

16. Ambrose, *De officiis* (II.134), 1:343–44 and (II.121), 1:334–35.

17. N. B. McLynn, *Ambrose of Milan: Church and Court in a Christian Capital,* Transformations of the Classical Heritage 22 (Berkeley: 1994), 253.

between the bishop and his clergy.[18] There are clear signs that Ambrose faced resistance among his own clergy and undertook such battles with energy.[19] According to Ambrose, the bishop should see his clergy as members of his body. If any need healing, he should try to heal them, but he must also be prepared to amputate.

Ambrose held that to build and adorn churches was an admirable occupation for the *sacerdos*.[20] He expected every bishop to be a builder and overseer of churches and institutions: thus everyone could see at a glance that the bishop dominated his city. Surely Ambrose dominated Milan with his building program and his grand new basilica, completed in 386.[21]

Philip Rousseau argues that Ambrose, by pursuing an ascetic form of life, thereby strengthened his claim to an independent style of power. It allowed him to carve out his own sphere of influence in the shadow of imperial authority.[22] This may be seen especially in Ambrose's ability to combine the role of priest with that of a high imperial official in dispensing justice within Milan.[23] He established a splendid and influential Christian court in Milan: he has even been called an "urban demagogue."[24] It was possible for Ambrose, with his aristocratic background and religious prominence, to deal directly with Emperor Theodosius (347–395) and to effectively represent the interests of his church at the imperial level.[25] In doing so, he developed a new model of episcopal power that would resonate powerfully in northern Italy and Gaul.

The relations of Ambrose to Theodosius were sometimes antagonistic, despite the fact that Theodosius was also devoted to the Nicene faith and had fostered the church by forbidding pagan worship and closing the temples.[26] In 390, Theodosius ordered a massacre of the citizens of Thessalonica as a collective punishment for a riot in which imperial troops had been killed. Ambrose and his fellow bishops were shocked, and the bishop of Milan denied communion to Theodosius unless he would do penance for the massacre. In a stunning "ritual proof-text" of the relation between emperor and bishop, Theodosius under-

---

18. Ambrose, *De officiis* (II.135), 1:342–43.

19. Williams, *Ambrose,* 121–22.

20. Ambrose, *De officiis* (II.111), 1:329–31.

21. McLynn, *Ambrose,* 158–219; for a survey of the Milanese churches in the time of Ambrose, see Monachino, *S. Ambrogio,* 1–19.

22. Rousseau, *Ascetics, Authority,* 89.

23. Ruggini, "Prêtre et fonctionnaire," 178.

24. John F. Matthews, *Western Aristocracies and Imperial Court, A.D. 364–425* (Oxford: 1975), 191.

25. Matthews, *Western Aristocracies,* 202.

26. Demandt, *Geschichte der Spätantike,* 106–7.

went the penance, appearing publicly in church without his imperial robes. In his own, unreliable record of these events, Ambrose had no qualms about presenting himself in the guise of the prophet Nathan confronting King David.[27]

It must be admitted that the episode was dramatic. Episcopal power was revealed as a potent nucleus of religious authority, in regard to which the emperor must position himself. Ambrose readmitted the emperor to communion on the following Christmas.[28] In Gaul, even as political horizons were narrowed, the model of the powerful, wise, religiously strict, ascetic "Ambrosian bishop" was very influential.[29] Ambrose himself was the model: a highly cultured figure, learned in Scripture and philosophy. Such bishops fulfilled the old Christian dream of providing a new intellectual basis for the political world.

Later outlines of clerical duties developed the Ambrosian model. Julian Pomerius, in his work *On the Contemplative Life,* was close to Ambrose in proposing a model of ascetic authority, presenting himself as an "ascetic expert in power."[30] Like Ambrose, Julian also directed his work toward the bishops, applying to them the terms *sacerdos, pontifex* or even *dominus.*[31] Despite Pomerius' sense that the bishop was a lord (*dominus*), his power and command over the properties of the church should be directed above all toward helping the poor. In the admirable translation of Joseph Plumpe:

This is why it is expedient to hold the goods of the church, not to satisfy and foster pleasure, but to provide for the community life (*congregandis*) of the brethren (*fratribus*) and their support (*aut alendis*) so that, while one person shoulders the care of all living in his company (*uno sollicitudines omnium in sua societate viventium sustinente*), all those under him may enjoy spiritually a fruitful leisure and quiet.[32]

Thus the bishop must labor and be active in the world so that the church as a whole can flourish under his government in the peaceful leisure necessary to the spiritual life. This is what the goods of the church are for. The bishop oversees this wealth in order to nurture the religious life of his congregation, never acting as if the property of the church were his own.

As will be seen, although Pomerius' treatise was not widely known in his own

27. John Moorhead, *Ambrose: Church and Society in the Late Roman World* (London: 1999), 121–22.

28. Matthews, *Western Aristocracies,* 234–36.

29. Ruggini, "Prêtre et fonctionnaire," 184.

30. Leyser, *Authority and Asceticism,* 80; see also Rapp, *Holy Bishops,* 50–53.

31. Joseph C. Plumpe, "Pomeriana," VC 1 (1947): 227–39; see 227–28.

32. For the text of Julian's treatise: Julian Pomerius, *De vita contemplativa,* PL 59:415–520; Plumpe, "Pomeriana," 236.

day, it became exceptionally prominent in Frankish libraries in later centuries. Fascinating evidence for the early knowledge and use of Pomerius in Gaul can be seen in the *Vetus Gallicanum*, a sixth-century lectionary containing long passages from Pomerius' *On the Contemplative Life*, especially the sections relevant to the duties of bishops.[33]

Julian was from Africa, but made his home in Gaul, where he became a priest, and died probably in the first years of the sixth century.[34] His little treatise was intended to resolve the question of where the bishop should stand in the traditional distinction between the active and the contemplative life. According to Julian, the bishop is a holy man, but he also has to work in the world and take part in the business and law of the city. Those who seek spiritual perfection, according to Julian, must lay down all worldly business, but the bishop must also practice justice, which is a social virtue. Thus the bishop, as the model of a good shepherd, is a figure halfway between the active and contemplative forms of life. Despite his many duties, he must still find time for the study of divine literature.[35] He should live in voluntary poverty and practice asceticism in imitation of Christ.[36]

For Julian had no doubt that the contemplative life was the highest form of life, and the active life received short shrift. Nevertheless, activity is a crucial aspect of the bishop's function: he must defend the oppressed and take responsibility for his flock.[37] In a striking and beautiful phrase, Julian insists that the the bishop must see to it that we are liberated from tyrannical domination (*tyrannicam vindicemus*).[38] Thus the bishop's duties are so grave and important that he must allow them to impinge on his own desire for spiritual gains and his preference for quiet religious reading.

Pope Gregory the Great (590–604), in his treatise *On Pastoral Care*, likewise placed the religious function of the bishop uppermost, viewing the government of souls as the *ars artium*.[39] The bishop undertook an unpleasant task, "for the benefit of his neighbors," that took him away from his own desire for a life of contemplation and study.[40] The true bishop, in Gregory's view, was utterly

33. Wolfenbüttel: Herzog-August Bibliothek; Cod. Guelf. Weissenb. 76.
34. The scant details that are known of Julian's life were assembled by F. Degenhart, *Studien zu Julianus Pomerius* (Eichstätt: 1905); see also "Julien Pomère," in DSA 3: 1594–1600.
35. Julian Pomerius, *De vita contemplativa*, PL 59:429.
36. Julian Pomerius, *De vita contemplativa*, PL 59:455 and 466.
37. "Pastori pastorum omnium reddat," Julian Pomerius, *De vita contemplativa*, PL 59:431.
38. Julian Pomerius, *De vita contemplativa*, PL 59:437.
39. Rapp, *Holy Bishops*, 43–44.
40. "Dum solius contemplationis studiis inardescunt, parere utitlitati proximorum in praedi

without worldly ambition, and indeed would try to avoid becoming a bishop in the first place. Thus the figure of the bishop, as illuminated by Gregory, was informed by Mediterranean ideals of aristocracy, combining skill in rhetoric with stoic-Platonic traditions.[41] The bishop "does not delight in ruling over men, but in serving them" (*Nec praesse se hominibus gaudent sed prodesse*).[42] The bishop must maintain his sense of distance from a world populated by wicked men, as Carole Straw phrases it: "though mingling with the unclean, the righteous must retain a sense of separateness."[43] According to Gregory, St. Peter should serve as the model for episcopal government: Peter had preeminence over the whole church, and yet refused to accept any sign of obeisance, even from the lowly centurion Cornelius. Thus the desire for a life of ascetic retreat and study became the *sine qua non* of a Gregorian ideal of episcopal power.

Moreover, Gregory often expressed his own sense of vulnerability and suffering during his tenure as pope. Such statements should be seen as a feature of Gregory's claim to rule as an ascetic figure: liberated from the the realm of power, and not desiring to participate in it, the bishop was therefore more capable of exercising power in an authentic way. Thus according to Conrad Leyser, his expressions of pain and doubt are a "necessary component of his authority."[44]

Such views did not prevent Gregory from becoming a pope of unprecedented activism and effectiveness, especially in his dealings with the barbarian kings to the north. From another perspective, Gregory insisted on the correct use of power by bishops and by other Christian governors (*rectores*). Gregory's concept of the *rector* has sometimes been interpreted as an image of Christian kingship or a generalized form of Christian power. Gregory, as argued by R. A. Markus, helped to create a political tradition in which "secular space" all but disappeared.[45] In contrast to this view, it can be suggested that Gregory (like Augustine) was skeptical about the prospects for Christian kingship. His primary concern was for the leadership of the church and its bishops as the best

catione refugiunt," Gregory the Great, *Régle pastorale,* ed. Bruno Judic and Floribert Rommel, SC 381, 382, 2 vols. (Paris: 1992); this quote: I.5, 1:148.

41. Rita Lizzi, "I vescovi, e i *potentes* della terra: definizione e limite del ruolo episcopale nelle due *partes imperii* fra IV e V secolo d.c.," in *L'Évêque dans la cité du IVe au Ve siècle: Image et autorité,* edited by E. Robillard and C. Sotinell, 83 (Rome: 1987).

42. Pierre Batiffol, *Saint Grégoire le Grand,* 3rd ed. (Paris: 1928), 85–94.

43. Carole Straw, *Gregory the Great: Perfection in Imperfection* (Berkeley: 1988), 4.

44. Conrad Leyser, "'Let Me Speak, Let me Speak': Vulnerability and Authority in Gregory's Homilies on Ezekiel," in *Gregorio magno e il suo tempo XIX incontro di studiosi dell'antichità cristiana. . . . Roma 9–12 maggio 1990,* Studia Ephemeridis "Augustinianum" (Rome: 1991), 2:169–82.

45. Robert A. Markus, "The Sacred and the Secular: From Augustine to Gregory the Great," JTS 36 (1985): 84–96.

form of power.[46] Yet Gregory tried to instruct kings that they should bend their efforts to the same spiritual ends as the church.[47] The bishop is not at home in this world, and thus his rulership here is awkward and ambiguous. Kings are too much at home in the world, and thus they are often subject to the temptations of pride and anger.

Episcopal government was a form of good power, refreshed by the spiritual life of the bishop: "the *rector* should be a neighbor in compassion to each person, and be raised up above everyone in contemplation."[48] The bishop must undertake public tasks, even though his own heart is longing for a life of contemplation. In his own role as bishop of Rome, Gregory certainly exploited both the religious prerogatives of his position and the political dimension of his power. *On Pastoral Care* was a basic statement of Gregory's beliefs, and the doctrine it propounds is similar to the ascetic doctrine of power developed by Ambrose and Julian Pomerius. As G. R. Evans has argued, the bishop and his duties, as imagined by Gregory, were far from the otherworldly church of St. Augustine. The Ambrosian bishop, as developed further by Pomerius and Gregory, presented to later bishops of Gaul a legacy of power combining the moral claims of the contemplative life with the activity of beneficial Christian power. The bishop, as a Christian governor (*rector*), must focus on the world around him, the world of city market stands, the villas of the rich, and the squalor of the poor, although his concerns were religious.[49]

The bishop was a dual figure who combined in himself the religious potency of a holy man with the responsibility, seductive power, and cares of political and legal governance over his city. The radical duality of power perceived by St. Augustine was left behind. His own expertise as a pastor of his flock was offered as "a case for his own ability to command" and to assert his own brand of power.[50] As the barbarian kingdoms came to replace the structures of imperial Rome, this dual role of the bishop would prove to be a flexible and successful model of power in Europe, capable of shaping the churches and kingdoms of Western Europe.

46. Christian Brouwer, "Egalité et pouvoir dans les 'Morales' de Grégoire le Grand," *Recherches augustiniennes* 27 (1994): 97–129. Gregory's *Regula pastoralis* is often viewed as the principal source for the early medieval image of the bishop, but Gregory's homilies were also influential: Steffen Patzold, *Episcopus: Wissen über Bischöfe im Frankenreich des späten 8. bis frühen 10. Jahrhunderts,* Mittelalter-Forschungen 25 (Ostfildern: 2008), 519.

47. Carole Straw, "Gregory's Politics: Theory and Practice," in *Gregorio magno,* 1:47–63; see esp. 57–58.

48. "Sit rector singulis compassione proximus, prae cunctis contemplatione suspensus," Gregory the Great, *Règle* (II.5), 1:196.

49. G. R. Evans, *The Thought of Gregory the Great* (Cambridge: 1986), 119, 121.

50. Conrad Leyser, "Expertise and Authority in Gregory the Great: The Social Function

Caesarius of Arles

The end of the Roman Empire in Gaul and the establishment of a number of smaller successor kingdoms in Europe by the Goths, Burgundians, and Franks placed bishops in a new and often uncomfortable position. It was a world in which direct, personal contact with royal power was frequent, especially for important bishops.[51] Bishops such as Sidonius Apollinaris, Caesarius of Arles, and Mamertus of Vienne had to establish relationships with the Goths, Franks, and Burgundians, even as those peoples were crafting a distinctive political mentality relevant to their changed situation.[52] The prevalence of Arianism was a troubling feature of the identity taking shape among Germanic peoples.[53] Catholic bishops nevertheless struggled to preserve their public and official character in the new circumstances. Caesarius of Arles (ca. 470–542) expounded the concept of the people of God (*populus Dei*) in exegetical sermons that portrayed the Christian people as having a coherent and stable identity and a historical mission undisturbed by the disappearance of the Roman Empire.[54] In fifth-century Provence, unlike Spain and northern Gaul, bishoprics and monasteries were all intact, while the preeminence of Arles was strengthened.[55] As we have seen, Arles and its bishops provided a model of the post-Roman Christian community and its shaping under aristocratic rule. All of these factors were evident at the Council of Agde, which found Caesarius of Arles cooperating with the Visigothic king Alaric, an Arian.[56]

Caesarius of Arles was a crucial figure in maintaining the centrality and presence of the church of Arles in these new circumstances. He helped to craft the basic ideals of Gallic bishops and aggressively fought for a new vision of orthodoxy. A cultured man with far-reaching connections, especially those he made while in the monastery of Lérins, Caesarius became bishop of Arles only with the help

---

of *Peritia*," in *Gregory the Great: A Symposium,* edited by John Cavadini, 38–61 (Notre Dame: 1995); see esp. 45, 49.

51. Élie Griffe, *Gaule chrétienne à l'époque romaine,* 2nd ed. (Paris: 1964–1966), 3:94–107.

52. Lotte Hedeager, "Migration Period Europe: The Formation of a Political Mentality," in *Rituals of Power from Late Antiquity to the Early Middle Ages,* edited by Frans Theuws and Janet L. Nelson, 15–57 (Leiden: 2000).

53. José Orlandis, *La conversión de Europa al Cristianismo* (Madrid: 1988). 55–67.

54. William M. Daly, "Caesarius of Arles: A Precursor of Medieval Christendom," *Traditio* 26 (1970): 1–28; see also Karl Ferdinand Werner, "La place du VIIe siècle dans l'évolution politique et institutionnelle de la Gaule franque," in *Le Septième siècle,* 173–211; see 182–83.

55. Eric Vanneufville, "L'Église en Provence du Ve au VIIIe siècles," MScR 53 (1996): 68–73.

56. Hefele-Leclercq, *Histoire des conciles,* 2.2:980.

of the Visigothic king.[57] As a leader of the southern Gallic echelon of bishops, he was forced to participate in the dangerous politics of the Visigothic kingdom of Alaric II, even suffering arrest and exile.[58] Caesarius had strong ties to the papacy, whose interests he sometimes represented in the councils under his direction.[59]

At a time when Arles was under siege by the Franks and Burgundians, probably after 508, Caesarius delivered a sermon exploiting Augustinian themes as a means of understanding the war as a "just judgment of God."[60] The turmoil of his age was often reflected in his sermons. Caesarius himself faced danger. His own background lay in Burgundy, and he was accused of wanting to hand Arles over to the Burgunds.[61] "The world is agitated by the clamors and evil customs of many," he said, in order to reveal the qualities of men: "just as filth and perfume are agitated with the same movement, the former gives off fumes, while the latter is sweetly redolent."[62] This is why good and evil people must equally endure the same tribulations. The suffering of this life, as Caesarius described it, is an annex to the Judgment, when good and evil will at last be separated.[63] Because God's judgment is hidden, and we cannot understand the ultimate meaning or purpose of historical events, "the hope of the good is not placed in this world."[64] The Franks eventually captured the city of Arles, as well as most of the old province of Gaul. Their kings, the Merovingians, had begun to intervene in episcopal elections farther north, much to the dismay of bishops there.[65] In Arles, however, bishops continued to be elected by the Christian community in the traditional manner until the late sixth century.[66]

Caesarius was well supplied with copies of Augustine's writings, above all the

57. Mathisen, *Ecclesiastical Factionalism,* 275.

58. Caesarius was accused of aiding the Burgundians against the Visigoths; see William E. Klingshirn, *Caesarius of Arles,* 93–97; and Carl Franklin Arnold, *Caesarius von Arelate und die gallische Kirche seiner Zeit* (Leipzig: 1972), 215–23.

59. Arnold, *Caesarius von Arelate,* 285–304.

60. Sermon 70, in Caesarius of Arles, *Sancti Caesarii Arelatiensis Sermones,* edited by D. Morin, 2nd ed., 2 vols., CCSL 103/104 (Turnhout: 1953), vol. I, CCSL 103:295–99; the siege is described in Klingshirn, *Caesarius of Arles,* 107–10.

61. Heijmans, *Arles,* 254–56.

62. "Multorum enim malis moribus atque clamoribus exagitatus est mundus; et ista exagitatio malorum atque bonorum, sicut caenum atque unguentum pari quidem motu exagitatum, illud exhalat, hoc suaviter fraglat," Caesarius of Arles, Sermon 70, CCSL 103:295.

63. "Ita simul boni atque mali indiscrete quidem turbati, sed alto dei iudicio separati," Caesarius of Arles, Sermon 70, CCSL 103:295.

64. "Non enim spes bonorum in isto est mundo posita," Caesarius of Arles, Sermon 70, CCSL 103:296.

65. Ian Wood, "The Ecclesiastical Politics of Merovingian Clermont," in *Ideal and Reality in Frankish and Anglo-Saxon Society: Studies Presented to J. M. Wallace-Hadrill,* edited by Patrick Wormald, Donald Bullough, and Roger Collins, 34–57; see 42–43 (Oxford: 1983).

66. Vanneufville, "L'Église en Provence," 68.

homilies, which he mined for his own sermon writing, along with the works of other authors such as Quodvultdeus.[67] In more than a hundred sermons, Caesarius offered a practical Augustinianism to an audience facing continual warfare in which, as he lamented, whole provinces were led into captivity, mothers abducted, the dead left unburied.[68] In several of the sermons, Caesarius reflected on the connection between right belief and the textual sources of Christian faith: reading, understanding, and believing. The promise of salvation contained in the Scriptures was a communication from an invisible society parallel to the city of Arles and its Visigothic king:

The Divine Scriptures are like letters sent to us from our homeland. In fact our homeland is paradise: our parents are the patriarchs, prophets, Apostles, and martyrs: our citizens are indeed angels, our king is Christ.[69]

Despite its appealing imagery of integration, the passage also announced a sense of exile and a longing for a safer, transcendent, alternative community.

Caesarius' perspective was that those who had received the Scriptures had a duty to read and understand them, if possible.[70] Those who could not read were bound to receive their understanding of the faith from those who could read.[71] Most of his sermons, indeed, conveyed to the illiterate what he himself had read in the Scriptures.[72] The literate and illiterate would then have in common a *symbol* of the faith in brief, authoritative statements that all should believe and memorize.[73]

In the same spirit, the works of late antique Christian authors, particularly the writings of St. Augustine, were encapsulated in anthologies of sentences

67. Raymond Étaix, "Le texte complété du sermon 178 de saint Césaire d'Arles," *Sacris Erudiri* 34 (1994): 59–66.

68. "Quando totae provinciae in captivitatem ductae sunt, sustinuimus matres familias abductas . . . nec mortuos permissae sunt sepelire," Caesarius of Arles, Sermon 70, CCSL 103:297.

69. "Quia scripturae divinae quasi litterae sunt de patria nostra nobis transmissae. Patria enim nostra paradisus est: parentes nostri sunt patriarchae et prophetae et apostoli et martyres: cives enim angeli, rex noster Christus est," Caesarius of Arles, Sermon 7, CCSL 103:38.

70. "Qui divinas scripturas de patria aeterna transmissas dissimulat legere, timere debet, ne forte praemia aeterna non accipiat," Caesarius of Arles, Sermon 7, CCSL 148:39.

71. "Primum est, quod lectionem divinam etiamsi aliquis nesciens litteras non potest legere, potest tamen legentem libeneter audire," Caesarius of Arles, Sermon 6, CCSL 148:31; see also Alberto Ferreiro, "'Frequenter Legere': The Propagation of Literacy, Education, and Divine Wisdom in Caesarius of Arles," JEH 43 (1992): 5–15.

72. These sermons were explanations of the lessons (Bible readings) during the Mass. As for example: "DE EO QUOD SCRIPTUM EST IN EVANGELIO," Caesarius, Sermon 152, CCSL 104:622; and "DE EO QUOD SCRIPTUM EST," Caesarius, Sermon 159, CCSL 104:650.

73. "Qui symbolum et orationem domincam memoriter tenet, et filios vel filias suas ut et ipsi teneant fideliter docet," Caesarius, Sermon 16, CCSL 103:78.

and paragraphs, which extracted an authoritative kernel of statements on topics that had come to define orthodoxy, such as the problem of predestination.[74] Caesarius himself made an epitome of Augustine so that he could have on hand the opinions of his mentor in the councils over which he presided, seemingly attempting (like his contemporary Eugippius) to avoid conflict over the thorny question of predestination.[75] His collection, *De gratia,* was complemented by a larger collection of Augustine's phrases and opinions compiled by Prosper of Aquitaine, and both were used at the Council of Orange of 529, which Caesarius directed.[76] At the council he continued the tradition of Arlesian leadership and mastery of law.[77] Here Caesarius attempted the delicate task, requiring both theology and diplomacy, of bringing the bishops of his church, among whom were many adherents of Pelagianism, into line with other western churches.[78] The southern Gallic network was represented by bishops primarily from within the regions dominated by Arles: Julan of Carpentras, Constantius of Gap, Cyprian of Toulon, Eucherius of Avignon, Heraclius of St.-Paul-Trois-Chateaux, and Alicius of Vaison. Also present were Fylagrius of Cavaillon, Maximus of Aix, Praetextatus of Apt, Lupercianus of Fréjus, and Vindimialis of Orange, who humbly entered his name last in the presence of Caesarius. Non-clerical nobility were also present, including Liberius, a praetorian prefect who had recently built a church in Orange, newly dedicated in 529. Thus the council and its theological impetus proved to be an important occasion for regional cooperation.[79]

It was natural enough that Caesarius and the bishops at Orange might turn to Augustine as they endeavored to define the nature of grace and the status of our "efforts, labors, prayers, vigils."[80] The bishops nevertheless adopted a version

74. Conrad Leyser, "Shoring Fragments against Ruin? Eugippius and the Sixth-Century Culture of the Florilegium," in *Eugippius und Severin: Der Autor, Der Text und der Heilige,* edited by Walter Pohl and Maximilian Diesenberger, Forschungen zur Geschichte des Mittelalters 2, 65–75 (Vienna: 2001).

75. Leyser, "Shoring Fragments," 74.

76. Prosper of Aquitaine, *Sententiae* PL 51:427–96; see Arnold, *Caesarius von Arelate,* 536–41; D. M. Cappuyns, "L'origine des 'Capitula' d'Orange 529," *Recherches de théologie ancienne et médiévale* 6 (1934): 121–42.

77. The Council of Orange (529): CCSL 148A:53–76; see also Hefele-Leclercq, *Histoire des conciles,* 2:1085–1108; Odette Pontal, *Histoire des conciles mérovingiens* (Paris: 1989), 94–99.

78. Robert A. Markus, "From Caesarius to Boniface: Christianity and Paganism in Gaul," in *Le Septième siècle: Changements et continuités/The Seventh Century: Change and Continuity,* edited by Jacques Fontaine and J. N. Hillgarth, 154–72; see 156, proceedings of a joint French and British Colloquium at the Warburg Institute, July 8–9, 1988, Studies of the Warburg Institute 42 (London: 1992).

79. Subscriptions: Council of Orange (529), CCSL 148A:64–65.

80. "Conantibus, laborantibus, orantibus, uigilantibus," Council of Orange (529), CCSL 148A:57. On this council see Arnold, *Caesarius von Arelate,* 533–67.

of Augustine's skeptical assessment of Rome, saying that "worldly desire is the gentile's strength, whereas God's love generates the fortitude of Christians."[81] The Council of Orange is significant because it turned the Gallic church toward an Augustinian theology that would remain the bedrock of belief for councils in succeeding centuries. In the "Definition of the Faith" with which the council ended, the bishops encapsulated their "essential Augustinianism": stressing the priority of grace and denying predestination to damnation.[82] The intention of the bishops at Orange was to produce a clipped, utilitarian handbook on grace and free will, "gathered from the ancient fathers."[83] This Augustinian theology, which went against the traditions of monasteries in southern Gaul, may have helped pave the way for worldly engagement by the bishops.

In many ways, the bishops assembled at Orange faced a world quite similar to that which Augustine had known. Like Augustine, they were confronted by a well-established paganism, still supported by the impressive edifice of Hellenistic and Roman philosophy.[84] Late Roman worship extended far beyond the borders of officially sanctioned cults to an array of privately cultivated deities and rituals. The patrons of altars and shrines, both pagan and Christian, were typically aristocratic and prominent. The members of the aristocracy who continued to maintain private worship on their estates have been misunderstood as nonconformist and pagan, but were in fact participants in a more amorphous and eclectic religious world. When these same aristocrats adopted Christianity, they continued to provide the space and furnishings for religious life.[85] Caesarius was a close observer of the religious practices of his people and a knowledgeable, even sympathetic opponent of pagan philosophy and literature. He believed that his

81. "Furtitudinem gentilium mundana cupiditas, furtitudinem autem Christianorum Dei caritas facit," Council of Orange (529) CCSL 148A:60.

82. The phrase "essential Augustinianism" is Jaroslav Pelikan's; see Pelikan, *The Christian Tradition: A History of the Development of Doctrine*, vol. 1, *The Emergence of the Catholic Tradition (100–600)* (Chicago: 1971), 327–29; Council of Orange (529) CCSL 148A:62–64.

83. "Ab antiquis patribus de sanctarum scripturam voluminibus in hac precipue causa collecta sunt," cited in Pontal, *Histoire des conciles mérovingiens*, 96.

84. R. Thouvenot, "Saint Augustin et les Païens (d'après *Epist.*, XLVI et XLVII)," in *Hommages à Jean Bayet,* edited by Marcel Renard and Robert Schilling, Collection Latomus 70 (Bruxelles-Berchem: 1964), 682–90. For the traditional view of an "exhausted" paganism, and the "insuffisance de la philosophie," see Gustave Bardy, *La conversion au christianisme durant les premiers siècles,* Théologie 15 (Paris: 1947), 84–89. On the struggle of paganism with Christianity, and their intertwining, see Hadot, "Fin du paganisme,"2:101–7; the connections between Christian and pagan were social, intellectual and familial: Maurice Testard, "Observations sur le passage du paganisme au christianisme dans la monde antique," *Bulletin de l'Association Guillaume Budé* (1988; fasc. 2): 140–61. The survival and influence of paganism is also addressed in Ramsay MacMullen, *Christianity and Paganism in the Fourth to Eighth Centuries* (New Haven: 1997).

85. Bowes, *Private Worship*, 11, 38–49.

task was to bring the power of Christian culture and reading (*lectio*) against the pagans.[86] He nevertheless spoke of this paganism in quite traditional terms—denouncing the worship of stones, fountains, and groves.[87] The achievement of Caesarius is notable—he did not struggle with the complex factors that have been mentioned as if against a seven-headed hydra. Facing the mutation of the sixth century—a transformed ethnic and political world, a new intellectual and religious context—Caesarius moved with great facility and tact in a setting that he understood perfectly and to which he already belonged.[88]

The tradition of Arlesian leadership reached a high point with Caesarius and the series of councils he directed. The city had been an important center long before the time of Caesarius, the site of an imperial residence from the time of Constantine, and the ideal location for the transfer of the Gallic prefecture as a "last bastion of *romanitas*."[89] The original religious topography of the city was modest, consisting of an ancient baptistery and the fourth-century church. Caesarius demonstrated his committment to asceticism by building a monastery for women (dedicated to Mary), and another for men (*in suburbans insula*), thus extending Christian space into the region outside the city walls. Caesarius and his successors continued to expand the Christian landscape of the city, adding baptisteries and an episcopal residence for the bishop and cathedral clergy.[90] It is possible that an expanded cathedral was later built over the site of a former temple of Diana.[91]

Tyrants and Fanatics

Farther north, in Frankish realms, Gregory of Tours would also learn to despise the gullibility of countryfolk and their veneration of a statue of Diana "as if it were a god."[92] "Diana" was the Roman interpretation of a Celtic goddess who

86. Ferreiro, "Frequenter Legere," 10; Vanneufville, "L'Église en Provence," 63–65.

87. Christian understanding of Gallo-Roman and Germanic paganism seems close to the norms of Roman ethnography: compare Jane Webster, "Sanctuaries and Sacred Places," in *The Celtic World,* edited by Miranda J. Green, 445–64 (London: 1995).

88. On the facility Caesarius showed in dealing with the many kingdoms of his day, see Wallace-Hadrill, *Frankish Church,* 98.

89. Heijmans, *Arles,* 43.

90. Heijmans, *Arles,* 257–92.

91. Heijmans, *Arles,* 292. On the expansion of the Christian built landscape in Arles: Hubert, "Topographie religieuse," 19–27. On the absorption of pagan temples by Christian churches: Jacques Moreau, "La lutte entre le christianisme et le paganisme gréco-romain dans la Guale du nord-est," in *Rome et le christianisme dans la région rhenane: Colloque du Centre de recherches d'histoire des religions de l'Université de Strasbourg, 19–21 mai, 1960* (Paris: 1963), 109–26; see 123–26.

92. "Repperi tamen hic Dianae simulacrum, quod populus hic incredulus quasi deum adorabat" (8.15), Gregory of Tours, *Libri historiarum,* 381. On the figure of Diana, see Moreau, "Lutte

held a prominent place in the paganisms confronting the Gallic Church of the sixth century.[93] "Numerous types of paganism" existed, although the possible connections between them are hard to determine or verify.[94] Changing perceptions of paganism revolved around the interpretation of old gods and goddesses. For the Romans, the gods of non-Romans were recognizable as Roman gods in foreign dress. For Christians, such gods were nothing more than demons. A council held in Orléans (541) held that sacrifices made in the name of the old gods were actually offered to demons (*immolata daemonum*).[95] The syncretic paganisms of the recently arrived Germans, as well as their troubling Arian version of Christianity, were added to the familiar paganism of the Gallo-Romans to produce a more complex religious framework.[96]

In the course of the late fifth and early sixth centuries, cultural identity took on a distinctive religious dimension as peoples arranged their sense of belonging and identity around three basic poles of belief: Catholicism, Arianism, and paganism. Such claims of identity were complicated. In literature of the period, the contrast between Roman and barbarian was mingled in every possible combination with the possible religious polarities: pagan-Arian-Catholic. Arianism, once embraced by the emperors, had invoked the opposition of Gallic bishops. This was now the religion of most of the barbarians. When the emperors dropped their support of Arianism, it became a marginal form of religiosity, thereby adding to the oppositional identity of the barbarians *versus* the Romans they conquered.[97] The self-consciousness of Gallic bishops, formed in a struggle against

entre le christianisme et le paganisme," 119–20. On shifting understandings of Germanic and Gallic paganism, see Jan De Vries, *Altgermanische Religionsgeschichte,* Grundriss der germanischen Philologie 12.1, 3rd ed. (Berlin: 1970), 1:163–66; see also Dieter Timpe, "Tacitus' Germania als religionsgeschichtliche Quelle," in *Germanische Religionsgeschichte: Quellen und Quellenprobleme,* edited by Heinrich Beck, Detlev Ellmers, and Kurt Schier, 434–85, esp. 458–62, Ergänzungsbände zum Reallexikon der germanischen Altertumskunde 5 (Berlin: 1992).

93. MacMullen, *Christianity and Paganism,* 74–76.

94. James, *Europe's Barbarians,* 215.

95. Council of Orléans (541), CCSL 148A:136.

96. Reinhard Wenskus, "Religion abâtardie: Materialien zum Synkretismus in der vorchristlichen politischen Theologie der Franken," in *Iconologia Sacra: Mythos, Bildkunst und Dichtung in der Religions- und Sozialgeschichte Alteuropas. Festschrift für Karl Hauck,* edited by Hagan Keller and Nikolaus Staubach, 179–248, Arbeiten zur Frühmittelalterforschung 23 (Berlin: 1994). The overlapping of Mediterranean paganism with that of peoples outside the Greco-Roman world was explored long ago by Franz Rolf Schröder, *Germanentum und Hellenismus: Untersuchungen zur germanischen Religionsgeschichte* (Heidelberg: 1924). On the conversion of the Goths to Arianism, see Wolfram, *Roman Empire,* 75–79 and 204–13; Manlio Simonetti, "L'incidenza dell'Arianesimo nel rapporto fra Romani e barbari," in *Passaggio dal mondo antico,* 367–79; see also J. M. Wallace-Hadrill, "Gothia and Romania," *Bulletin of the John Rylands Library, Manchester* 44 (1961): 213–37, 235.

97. On Arianism as an oppositional stance: James, *Europe's Barbarians,* 222–24; Simonetti,

the Arianism of the Roman emperors, now continued to labor, in a different key, against the Arianism of the Burgundians, the Visigoths, and the Ostrogoths in Italy. For their part, Arian churches frequently were not led by bishops.[98]

For centuries Christianity had appeared to be only one convincing path among many as a number of religious philosophies competed for attention in late antique Europe.[99] For fifth-century bishops, however, the contrast was one of stark opposition: culture and salvation confronted violent ignorance. Episcopal self-assurance—a sure sense of governmental authority, backed up by a potent story of the origins of episcopal power, rooted in the rich soil of a privileged legal and historical inheritance—seemed to thrive in these new circumstances. Opposition to paganism was a powerful argument in favor of episcopal power.

Recent scholarship has focused on the continuities to be observed from the Roman to the post-Roman period, an approach that harmonizes, it must be said, with the propaganda of the Ostrogothic kingdom. With the help of thinkers like Cassiodorus, the Goths sought to formulate a new "Roman" identity.[100] Indeed, Theodoric's kingdom gained the recognition of Byzantium and began to serve as a kind of intermediary between the empire and the new kingdoms arising in western Europe.[101] Nevertheless the changes were dramatic enough that contemporaries struggled to describe them. It was difficult to fit the barbarian kings into an older social vocabulary inherited from the Roman Empire: the task of assimilation required a reorientation of regional aristocracies.[102]

In Gothic Italy, the reign of Theodoric was the subject of a brief chronicle, the *Theodoriciana*.[103] Writing in the mid-sixth century, the author of the *Theodoriciana* recorded the early years of Theodoric's reign as a relatively peaceful time,

---

"Incidenza dell'Arianesimo," 374; Wallace-Hadrill, "Gothia and Romania," 233; see also Ralph W. Mathisen, "Barbarian Bishops and the Churches 'in barbaricis gentibus' during Late Antiquity," *Speculum* 72 (1997): 664–95.

98. Mathisen, "Barbarian Bishops," 673.

99. John F. Matthews, *The Roman Empire of Ammianus* (Baltimore: 1989), 425.

100. James, *Europe's Barbarians*, 108–10; see also Teillet, *Des Goths à la nation*, 281–303; and Andrew Gillett, "The Purposes of Cassiodorus' *Variae*," in *After Rome's Fall: Narrators and Sources of Early Medieval History—Essays Presented to Walter Goffart*, edited by Alexander Callander Murray (Toronto: 1998), 37–50; and W. Wattenbach, E. Dümmler, and Franz Huf, *Deutschlands Geschichtsquellen im Mittelalter* (Kettwig: 1991), 1:65–72.

101. Werner, *Naissance de la noblesse*, 229.

102. Wolfram, *Roman Empire*, 117.

103. This is the second part of the *Excerpta Valesiana*, so called after its first editor, the seventeenth-century humanist Henri de Valois: *Excerpta Valesiana*, ed. Jacques Moreau (Leipzig: 1968). The work has two distinct (unrelated) sections: the "Pars prior," or *Origio Constantini imperatoris* (1–10), and the "Pars posterior," or *Theodoriciana* (10–27). See also J. N. Adams, *The Text and Language of a Vulgar Latin Chronicle (Anonymus Valesianus II)*, University of London, Institute of Classical Studies Bulletin Supplement 36 (London: 1976), 3–6.

when he "governed two peoples as one, Romans and Goths," and although an Arian himself, took no actions against the Catholic religion.[104] This happy situation did not last long, however, as the king was soon revealed as an oppressive tyrant. The author did not fail to mention that Theodoric was illiterate, something that starkly distinguished him from the Roman world and foreshadowed his developing brutality.[105]

Theodoric was a great builder who sought to restore the cities of Italy, and in this way to promote the idea of continuity with Rome.[106] He even adopted the imperial role of enforcing unity in the church—resolving a disputed papal election, for example, despite his Arianism, and afterward walking to the relics of Peter in Rome "most devoutly and as if he were Catholic."[107] However, the strident show of continuity seemed false to the chronicler, meant to mask profound changes. One of the more significant of these changes was the total sway now exerted by kings. Kingship had long been understood by Romans to be a type of tyranny.[108]

Therefore the devil soon found a place in Theodoric's kingdom.[109] A poor Gothic woman lay down beneath a portico near the king's palace in Ravenna and gave birth to four dragons, two of which flew from west to east and plunged into the sea as the people watched. The other two dragons shared one head.[110] The sudden change of tone suggests that the author of the *Theodoriciana* was struggling to find words for painful changes, the monstrous union that Theodoric's kingdom represented. Moreover, this was the prelude of a tragedy that seemed to concentrate all the sorrows of the age in a single event. Soon there-

104. "Nihil etiam perperam gessit, sic gubernavit duas gentes in uno, Romanorum et Gothorum, dum ipse quidem Arrianae sectae esset, tamen nihil contra religionem catholicam temptans" (60), *Excerpta Valesiana,* ed. Moreau, 17.

105. *L'Anonymus valesianus II, ch. 79–96: texte et commentaire,* ed. Wouter Bracke (Bologna: 1992), 30. On the crises faced by Theodoric, see Gregorio Caravita, *Teoderico: I Goti a Ravenna V–VI secolo* (Rimini: 1993), 81–86 and 148–51.

106. "Erat enim amator fabricarum et restaurator civitatum" (70), *Excerpta Valesiana,* ed. Moreau, 20.

107. "Post factam pacem in urbis ecclesia ambulavit rex Theodoricus Romam et occurrit beato Petro devotissimus ac si catholicus" (65), *Excerpta Valesiana,* ed. Moreau, 19.

108. Cf. the republican tradition, as in Cicero, which saw Tarquin the Proud as the archetypal figure of a king-tyrant: "Monarchie," GGB, 4:133–214, esp. 138; see also Marc Reydellet, *La Royauté dans la littérature latine de Sidoine Apollinaire à Isidore de Séville,* Bibliothèque des Écoles Françaises d'Athènes et de Rome 243 (Rome: 1981), 22–46.

109. "Ex eo enim [tempore] invenit diabolus locum" (83), *Excerpta Valesiana,* ed. Moreau, 24.

110. "Item mulier pauper de gente Gothica, iacens sub porticu non longe a palatio Ravennati, quattuor generavit dracones: duo de occidente in orientem ferri in nubibus a populo visi sunt et in mare praecipitati sunt, duo protati sunt unum caput habentes" (84), *Excerpta Valesiana,* ed. Moreau, 24.

after, the philosopher Boethius was imprisoned by Theodoric on suspicion of conspiring with Byzantium and, without a hearing, was put to death.[111] Announced by the birth of dragons, the death of Boethius was the loss of a better and much-regretted world.[112] Theodoric's treatment of the philosopher was the ultimate expression of tyranny, or so it seemed to the anonymous chronicler. This had certainly been the position of poor Boethius.[113] We have to do with intellectual responses to a world permeated by change, but already an unavoidable new reality.

In northern Gaul, a very different setting unfolded as the Franks carved out a stable, strong kingdom under the leadership of their pagan kings. Gregory, bishop of Tours (c. 539–594) recorded the history of the Franks in his *Ten Books of Histories,* a work that allows us to observe the relations between kings and bishops in the most powerful and successful of the barbarian kingdoms, and above all to examine how one influential bishop, quite learned in canon law, developed concepts of royal power early in the history of the Frankish kingdoms. At the outset of the *Histories,* Gregory attempted to discover the origins of the royal clan, the Merovingians, whom he knew in his own day as the central figures of Frankish social identity.[114] Their origins were obscure, and although Gregory researched the rise of the Merovingians in a number of history books, he could learn little about the inauguration of the dynasty.[115] The earliest rulers were war leaders (*dux, duces*) rather than kings. Later, after a period of wandering, the Franks came to recognize the preeminence of a single royal family—the long-haired Merovingian

---

111. Catherine Morton, "Marius of Avenches, the 'Excerpta Valesiana,' and the Death of Boethius," *Traditio* 38 (1982): 107–36; on the death of Boethius see 124–26.

112. "Tunc Albinus et Boethius ducti in custodiam ad baptisterium ecclesiae. rex vero vocavit Eusebium, praefectum urbis, Ticinum et inaudito Boethio protulit in eum sententiam. quem mox in agro Calventiano, ubi in custodia habebatur, misere fecit occidi. Qui accepta chorda in fronte diutissime tortus, ita ut oculi eius creparent, sic sub tormenta ad ultimum cum fuste occiditur" (83), *Excerpta Valesiana,* ed. Moreau, 24.

113. As "Philosophia" explained: "Indignissima tibi videbatur malorum potestas" (4.4); Boethius, *Philosophiae consolationis libri quinque,* ed. Karl Büchner, Editiones Heidelbergensis 11 (Heidelberg: 1977), 82; see also Pierre Courcelle, "Le tyran et le philosophe d'après la 'Consolation' de Boèce," in *Passaggio dal mondo antico,* 195–224.

114. On Gregory, see Martin Heinzelmann, *Gregor von Tours (538–594), "Zehn Bücher Geschichte": Historiographie und Gesellschaftskonzept im 6. Jahrhundert* (Darmstadt: 1994); Walter Goffart, *The Narrators of Barbarian History (A.D. 550–800): Jordanes, Gregory of Tours, Bede, and Paul the Deacon* (Princeton: 1988), 112–234; Reydellet, *Royauté dans la littérature latine,* 345–437; Wattenbach, et al., *Deutschlands Geschichtsquellen,* 1:101–11.

115. "De Francorum vero regibus, quis fuerit primus, a multis ignoratur" (2.9), Gregory, *Libri historiarum,* 52; see also F. L. Ganshof, *Een Historicus uit de VIe Eeuw: Gregorius van Tours; Mededelingen van de Koninklijke vlaamse Academie voor Wetenschappen, Letteren en schone Kunsten van België, Klasse der Letteren—Jaarg. 28, no. 5 (Brussels: 1966), 9–13.*

kings. Gregory vaguely concluded that the Franks "produced" or "established" kings over themselves (*super se creare*).[116] There was something arbitrary about the origins of Frankish kingship. Gregory was either reticent about or lacked knowledge of a Frankish royal origin-myth: it is likely that the Franks, like other Germanic peoples, would have imagined a mythic origin for their war leaders.[117] The lack of clear royal origins may also point to the historical disruption of Frankish society and their self-creation within the late Roman world.[118]

The grave of one of these pagan Frankish kings, Childeric, was unearthed in the seventeenth century, its contents revealing how kingship was displayed and performed among the Franks.[119] Surrounded by ritual horse-burials, the grave contained a warrior's finery, including a sword in a garnet-inlayed sheath, a purse full of coins, a jewelled purple cloak, a battle-axe, and a spear.[120] Childeric's famous seal-ring was also discovered, with its striking visual testimony of Frankish kingship at the time of Clovis, still bound up with the status of a war captain in the service of the Roman Empire.[121] On the ring, an engraved portrait of Childeric reveals a long-haired warrior, wearing a breastplate and holding a spear in his right hand, expressing his ability to compel. The legend surrounding the figure declares him to be a king (CHILDERICI REGIS).[122] The ambiguous impression given by Childeric of a royal war chief is recognizable in many of the kings described by Gregory, even after their conversion to Christianity.[123] Was Childeric a Roman official? The royal elements of his grave-ensemble do not

116. "Iuxta pagus vel civitates regis crinitos super se creavisse de prima" (2.9), Gregory, *Libri historiarum,* 57.

117. J. M. Wallace-Hadrill, *Early Germanic Kingship in England and on the Continent,* The Ford Lectures 1970 (Oxford: 1971).

118. Gabriele Zanella, "La legittimazione del potere regale nelle 'Storie' di Gregorio di Tours e Paolo Diacono," SM ser. 3, vol. 31 (1990): 55–84; see 64; Hedeager, "Migration Period," 29–30.

119. Wallace-Hadrill, *Early Germanic Kingship,* 18.

120. Joachim Werner, "Childerics Pferde," in *Germanische Religionsgeschichte: Quellen und Quellenprobleme,* edited by Heinrich Beck, Detlev Ellmers, and Kurt Schier, 145–61, Ergänzungsbände zum Reallexikon der germanischen Altertumskunde 5 (Berlin: 1992): see also R. C. Van Caenegem, *De Instellingen van de Middeleeuwen: Geschiedenis van de westerse Staatsinstellingen van de Ve tot de XVe Eeuw* (Ghent: 1967), 1:29–31; Wallace-Hadrill, *Frankish Church,* 23.

121. Werner, *Naissance de la noblesse,* 197–204; Ian Wood, The *Merovingian Kingdoms, 450–751* (London: 1994), 38–41.

122. Weidemann, *Kulturgeschichte der Merowingerzeit,* 1:20–23; see also Wattenbach, et al., *Deutschlands Geschichtsquellen,* 1:95–96; see further Averil Cameron, "How Did the Merovingian Kings Wear Their Hair?" RBPH 43 (1965): 1203–16. On the iconography of long hair in royal portraits: Percy Ernst Schramm, *Herrschaftszeichen und Staatssymbolik: Beiträge zu ihrer Geschichte vom dritten bis zum sechzehnten Jahrhundert,* Schriften der Monumenta Germaniae historica 13 (Stuttgart: 1954–1956), 1:228–233.

123. Lebecq, "Variations sur l'image du Barbare, 89–108.

preclude such an assertion, but they certainly demonstrate that a *royal* theme was foremost in the design of the burial.[124]

Moreover, the earliest Frankish kings were pagan, "obedient to fanatic cults."[125] To Gregory's mind, the paganism of the early Franks was similar to that of the Romans whom they conquered, who were also bound to fanatic cults (*fanatici cultus*).[126] Being quite familiar with the history of the Goths, who dominated Italy, southern Gaul, and Spain, Gregory wished to present a contrasting history of the Franks in light of the three poles of religious identity: Paganism—Catholicism—Arianism.[127] The first pages of his book, therefore, announced the theme of orthodoxy in a credo that focuses on the trinity and thus seems directed especially against Arianism.[128] Gregory's account of the conversion of the Franks to Catholicism was framed by this religious dialectic and the issue of social identity. At first Clovis and his army had gone on rampages in which they destroyed many churches because of their adherence to "fanatical errors."[129] In the view of Le Jan, such activities can be understood as the barely contained mythic-sacral expression of royal power in a violent circuit of the kingdom.[130]

With the baptism of King Clovis, perhaps in 508, Frankish identity was reshaped and distinguished from its neighbors by the adoption of Catholic Christianity.[131] The action seems to reflect a new accommodation of the king to his Gallo-Roman subjects and the regional networks of its aristocratic leadership. This is confirmed by Gregory of Tours' religious interpretation of the confrontation of the Visigothic and Frankish kingdoms. Shortly after his conversion,

124. James, *Europe's Barbarians*, 80.

125. "Sed haec generatio fanaticis semper cultibus visa est obsequium praebuisse" (2.10), Gregory, *Libri historiarum*, 58.

126. "Senatores vero vel reliqui meliores loci fanaticis erant tunc cultibus obligati" (1.31), Gregory, *Libri historiarum*, 24; see also Wallace-Hadrill, *Frankish Church*, 18–19.

127. Johann Weissensteiner, "Cassiodors Gotengeschichte bei Gregor von Tours und Paulus Diaconus? Eine Spurensuche," in *Ethnogenese und Überlieferung: Angewandte Methoden der Frühmittelalterforschung*, edited by Karl Brunner and Brigitte Merta, 123–28, Veröffentlichungen des Instituts für Österreichische Geschichtsforschung 31 (Vienna: 1994).

128. "Credo ergo in Deum patrem omnipotentem. Credo in Iesum Christum, filium eius unicum, dominum nostrum, natum a patre, non factum" (1.1), Gregory, *Libri historiarum*, 3; on this credo, see also Wallace-Hadrill, *Frankish Church*, 51.

129. "Eo tempore multae aecclesiae a Chlodovecho exercitu depraedatae sunt, quia erat ille adhuc fanaticis erroribus involutus" (2.27), Gregory, *Libri historiarum*, 72.

130. Régine Le Jan, "La sacralité de la royauté mérovingienne," *Annales: Histoire, Science Sociales* 58 (2003): 1217–41.

131. Ian Wood dated the baptism of Clovis to 508 in "Gregory of Tours and Clovis," 249–72; and again in *Merovingian Kingdoms*, 48; perhaps following Rolf Weiss, who proposed this date in reconstructing Clovis' reign and itinerary in *Chlodwigs Taufe: Reims 508— Versuch einer neuen Chronologie*.

Clovis wished to drive the Visigoths out of Gaul, according to Gregory, because of their adherence to Arianism.[132]

In the tableau of Frankish society as painted by Gregory, king and bishop stand out as the two primary figures dominating the social landscape.[133] Moving back and forth between portrayals of saintly bishops or monks and unflattering pictures of violent kings, Gregory nevertheless drew a number of parallels between bishops and kings—for example, in his many references to their parallel seats of power: the *cathedra episcopalis* and the *cathedra regis*.[134] Bishoprics were the building blocks of Merovingian kingdoms, and thus the parallel was not merely literary and symbolic. Bishoprics served to organize the space of the kingdoms and to stabilize the integration of Gallo-Roman bishops with the Frankish nobility. As kings sought to bring these networks under their control, laymen were sometimes imposed as bishops.[135] Bishoprics were lucrative prizes in the game of power. The wealth and noble background of the bishops and the continuous collection of pious donations by their churches meant that the wealth and power of bishops could rival that of kings.[136]

Councils played a role in the movement of integration, and Gregory himself was at times involved in efforts to preserve the independence of the church and to maintain the quality of bishops and other clerics, as at the Council of Lyon (567–570), held under Nicetius of Lyon. King Guntram had accused Salonius of Embrun and Sagittarius of Gap of certain crimes.[137] In Gregory's account of the history of the Franks, the church is depicted not as a group of institutions gradually melding with Frankish society, but as an entity sharply marked off by its severe religious goals and the ascetic sanctity of individuals.[138]

---

132. Gregory of Tours, *Libri historiarum* (2.37), 87–88; discussion in Reydellet, *Royauté dans la littérature latine*, 430.

133. Adriaan H. B. Breukelaar, *Historiography and Episcopal Authority in Sixth-Century Gaul: The Histories of Gregory of Tours Interpreted in their Historical Context*, Forschungen zur Kirchen- und Dogmengeschichte 57 (Göttingen: 1994), 227–30.

134. For episcopal *cathedrae*, see Gregory of Tours, *Libri historiarum* (2.1), 38; (2.13), 63; (3.2), 98; (4.5), 138; (9.18), 432, and elsewhere. For royal *cathedrae*, see *Libri historiarum* (2.7), 50; (2.38), 89; (4.22), 155; (5.17), 216; (10.28), 521. Similarly, Gregory sometimes described kings as having a *sedes*—a "seat," or "see," again using a term often used of bishop's seat of power. For royal *sedes*, see *Libri historiarum* (4.22), 154; (4.22), 155; (7.27), 346. For episcopal *sedes*, see *Libri historiarum* (2.1), 38; (4.26), 158.

135. Pontal, *Histoire des conciles mérovingiens*, 146.

136. Martin Heinzelmann, "L'aristocratie et les évêchés entre Loire et Rhin jusqu'a la fin du VIIe siècle," RHEF 62 (1976): 74–90.

137. The Council of Lyon (567–570), CCSL 148A:200–3; see also Pontal, *Histoire des conciles mérovingiens*, 166–67.

138. Heinzelmann, *Gregor von Tours*, 145–50.

Peregrination and Kingship

Gregory spoke as one who had labored to Christianize the landscape of Tours and promote the cult of St. Martin.[139] Thus Gregory wished to highlight the existence he perceived, of a considerable gulf between kingship and saintliness: he represented monasteries and monks (and saintly bishops) as points of interruption in historical time, tears in the fabric, as peepholes offering a view of ultimate reality. Their disruption of history is usually dramatic, as told by Gregory, but small in apparent impact—they were at once subversive and marginal.

Although Gregory insisted on the fact that his history was based on older models, this is hard to verify.[140] At any rate these models were subordinated to his own complicated agenda, contributing to what has been called the "subterannean structure" of the work.[141] For one thing, Gregory had contemporary problems constantly on his mind as he composed. By means of self-censorship he hoped to avoid offending powerful men who were still on the scene.[142]

Gregory was destined for his position as bishop of Tours, coming as he did from a solid old senatorial family of Gallic nobles. On his mother's side the family included Bishop Sacerdos of Lyon (†552). All told the family could boast six bishops before Gregory took the see of St. Martin.[143] It has been argued suggestively that the *Histories* are essentially an ideology presented in literary form that sought to maintain the prerogatives of this old Gallic aristocracy in a Christian guise, but still consistent with late-Roman senatorial concepts.[144] It seems further that there is an intimate connection between Gregory's opinions about royal power and his intellectual and *theological* response to the Merovingian world. He was not very concerned to portray the ordinary functioning of Merovingian secular society with its communitarian organization of nobles from across the Frankish world. Other features of Frankish society were downplayed, as well.

139. Ian Wood, "Topographies of Holy Power in Sixth-Century Gaul," in *Topographies of Power in the Early Middle Ages,* edited by Mayke de Jong, Frans Theuws, and Carine van Rhijn, 137–54, The Transformation of the Roman World 6 (Leiden: 2001).

140. Massimo Oldoni, "Gregorio di Tours e i 'Libri Historiarum': Le fonti scritte" in *Gregorio di Tours,* Convegni del centro di studi sulla spiritualità medievale 12 (Spoleto: 1977), 282–90.

141. Oldoni, "Gregorio di Tours," 318.

142. Ian Wood, "The Secret Histories of Gregory of Tours," RBPH 71 (1993): 253–70.

143. See the prosopographical study of Heinzelmann, *Gregor von Tours,* 10–21; and Luce Pietri, *La ville de Tours du IVe au VIe siècle: Naissance d'une cité chrétienne,* Collection de l'École française de Rome 69 (Rome: 1983), 247–57.

144. Following Heinzelmann, Breukelaar argues that the *Histories* purvey an aristocratic ideology: Breukelaar, *Historiography and Episcopal Authority,* 13. Gregory was proud of his senatorial family background: Ganshof, *Een Historicus uit de VIe Eeuw,* 4.

As Ian Wood has remarked, "the romanizing aspect of Merovingian ideology seems not to have impressed Gregory," and he is right to say that Gregory was more concerned with ecclesiastical ideals.[145] For all his fascination with kings, Gregory did not believe that royal power could set the moral tone in a kingdom.

The assassinations and acts of brute force that Gregory catalogued give every appearance of exaggeration and special pleading. No doubt genuine acts of violence were deliberately selected in order to provide a background of blood and flames against which the purity of the religious episcopal order could be revealed. Frankish history revealed to Gregory that the spiritual life could only be perfected in a retreat from the world, radically separating and protecting the ascetic from the world of royal power. Thus Gregory's own stature, as illustrated in his account, was elevated by his promotion and appreciation of asceticism. Gregory may have been born in Auvergne, and was especially interested in promoting the saints of that region. Thus part of Gregory's projection of episcopal power consisted of the deepening of a sacred landscape of chapels and monasteries dedicated to the saints.[146] This is the real landscape of the *Histories*.

In the terms of Gregory's account, bishops and saints offered Archimedean points from which truth and justice could radiate and offer hope to the world. This is the gist of Gregory's portrayal, even though Merovingian cloisters must have been closely connected to the world around them.[147] The contrast between kingship and the religious life was not the opposition of two powerful and alternative institutions, but the radical disjuncture between two forms of life, portrayed, nevertheless, as having an intimate setting that brought them together. This is to argue that Gregory's *Histories* are descriptive, if one-sided; they are based on observation, although selective; they are inflected by theological concerns. Gregory sought to lay out the boundaries and norms of Christian power, and to present saintly monks and bishops as possessing the most righteous types of power and law.

It has long been known that a number of stories about saintly personages were inserted into the *Histories* in the course of a second, or final, redaction late in Gregory's life.[148] What intrigued Gregory was how a holy life provided

145. Wood, *Merovingian Kingdoms*, 68.

146. Ian Wood, "Constructing Cults in Early Medieval France: Local Saints and Churches in Burgundy and the Auvergne, 400–1000," in *Local Saints and Local Churches in the Early Medieval West*, edited by Alan Thacker and Richard Sharpe, 155–87 (Oxford: 2002).

147. Wallace-Hadrill, *Frankish Church*, 58–59.

148. M. Gabriel Monod, *Études critiques sur les sources de l'histoire mérovingienne: Première partie—Introduction—Grégoire de Tours—Marius d'Avenches* (Paris: 1872), 46–48; see discussion in Heinzelmann, *Gregor von Tours*, 171–72.

access to the invisible reality behind the world of spearings, assassinations, and poisonings that were so pervasive in the historical world. This is why, in recording the deeds of holy monks, he sometimes made no reference to place, person, or time. There are many examples of such historically stripped accounts, even where Gregory apparently knew a lot about the person he was describing.[149]

These stories were stitched into the text to highlight and deepen an important aim of the *Histories,* for while Gregory contrasted a historical world of violence and power with a nonhistorical world of monastic retreat, his addition of exemplary lives was intended to make this contrast more severe and unmistakable.[150] The preambles of these stories made clear that the narrative flow was being deliberately interrupted for the sake of adding an interlude, but also argued that the flow of history had been interrupted by the presence of these saints in the world of the Franks. Gregory put it this way at the beginning of Book 2, in which he stated his policy: "As we follow the order of the ages, mixed and confused, we relate the virtues of the saints as much as the slaughter of peoples."[151] History, here characterized as a violent, meaningless flux, was to be contrasted with the lives of saints, in whom meaning could be located. History itself was political and religious.

Gregory introduced the story of St. Salvius, in the preamble to Book 7, in the same way: "Although it might be proper to continue the history, which the order of the preceeding books has abandoned, nevertheless first something must be said about the death of St. Salvius."[152] He would sometimes close such an account by saying, "let us return to our story."[153] The deeds of the saints provided Gregory with an extrahistorical standpoint from which to view the flow of time.

The recitations of violence that fill the pages of the *Histories* imply that the historical world was separated by a gulf from the divine, in a manner perhaps comparable to the thought of St. Augustine.[154] Unlike Augustine, however, for whom things created by purely human endeavor were internally coherent, Gregory thought that the world he surveyed was not self-explanatory. It seems unlikely

149. For example, Gregory describes an apparently vague personage in this manner: "De horum vero discipulis quidam Bituricas civitatem adgressus, salutare omnium, Christum dominum populis nuntiavit" (1.31); Gregory, *Libri historiarum,* 24. The name is left out, although Gregory had written about this person, St. Ursinus, in his own *Glory of the Martyrs.*

150. Wood, *Merovingian Kingdoms,* 31; on the "lurid" tone of Gregory's history see Wallace-Hadrill, *Frankish Church,* 37.

151. "Prosequentes ordinem temporum, mixte confusequae tam virtutes sanctorum quam strages gentium memoramus" (2.1), Gregory, *Libri historiarum,* 36.

152. "Licet sit studium historiam prosequi, quam priorum librorum ordo reliquid, tamen prius aliqua de beati Salvii obitu exposcit loqui" (7.1), Gregory, *Libri historiarum,* 323.

153. "Ergo, ut ad historiam recurramus" (4.38), Gregory, *Libri historiarum,* 169.

154. The comparison is made by Goffart, *Narrators of Barbarian History,* 181.

that Gregory had read Augustine, although he would have been introduced to an abbreviated Augustinian theology by the Gallic councils to which he so often turned. In Orosius he would also have found an Augustinian perspective, but this did not strongly influence him.[155] Further, while Gregory may have adopted from Orosius the structure of a "universal history," this framework was in considerable conflict with Gregory's own perception of the Frankish kingdoms, in which power was isolated in individuals, whose actions could be redeemed only by the intervention of divine justice. In other words, the sphere of historical action was punctuated by the divine, rather than constantly guided by it.[156] Like a late antique school, this was a world guided by slaps and blows of the cane.

The idea that monasteries and their occupants stood outside of the historical realm in which power and kingship were exercised was something that occurred to early medieval monks themselves. They expressed this by describing the monastery as a prison.[157] Their lives behind walls perhaps naturally led to such a comparison, but what is most remarkable about the image is that monasteries were in fact used as prisons by Frankish kings and bishops alike. Gregory imprisoned the rebellious Riculf in a monastery after his attempt to usurp the see of Tours.[158] King Guntram dealt similarly with the unruly bishops Salonius and Sagittarius.[159] As a sacred precinct marked off from the world, the monastery served as a place in which people could be forcibly removed from the world. It was also a relatively secure place of retreat from political violence, for honorable and temporary withdrawal from conflict.[160]

The church was a sacred precinct outside the historical world. Within its confines, those pursued by royal anger or law could seek asylum by clinging to the altar. Gregory was clearly eager to defend this important privilege of his churches, and to portray it as a clear and powerful right. The right was asserted at many Gallic councils.[161] One group of men, being sent into exile by their king,

155. Oldoni, "Gregorio di Tours," 258–61, 322.

156. Benedetto Vetere, *Strutture e modelli culturali nella società merovingia: Gregorio di Tours—una testimonianza,* Università degli studi di Lecce, Saggi e Ricerche 3 (Lecce: 1979), 49–50 and 92–93; see also Oldoni, "Gregorio di Tours," 295.

157. Gregorio Penco, "Monasterium—Carcer," *Studia Monastica* 8 (1966): 133–43.

158. "Cum consilio provincialium eum in monasterio removeri praecipio" (5.49), Gregory, *Libri historiarum,* 262.

159. "His auditis, rex commotus valde, tam equos quam pueros vel quaecumque habere poterant abstulit; ipsosque in monasteriis a se longiori accensu dimotis, in quibus penitentiam agerent" (5.20), Gregory, *Libri historiarum,* 228.

160. Mayke de Jong, "Monastic Prisoners or Opting Out? Political Coercion and Honour in the Frankish Kingdoms," in *Topographies of Power,* 291–328.

161. Pontal, *Histoire des conciles mérovingiens,* 285–87.

escaped when their guards fell asleep. It was enough for them to reach a basilica to be liberated from their punishment.[162] Through the concept of asylum, the world was marked off into two distinct spheres, one of which was governed by the bishop, and the other by the king. Each sphere had its own law. Not surprisingly, fugitives fleeing to his church often put Gregory at uncomfortable loggerheads with the king. To surrender a fugitive in response to royal pressure would be, Gregory thought, to violate the holy basilica.[163] The monasteries and saints Gregory admired were at a far remove from the world of royal power. That they played so large a role in Gregory's history tells us a lot about his perspective on the history of the Merovingian kings.

Let us return to Gregory's friend, St. Salvius. When the abbot of his monastery died, Salvius was forced to become abbot of the Holy Cross. Instead of fulfilling his duties, however, the saint fled to a more remote chamber of the establishment. The whole course of Salvius' spiritual pilgrimage was the result, in Gregory's view, of the entry of the Holy Spirit into the very fiber of his being.[164] For Salvius, inner pilgrimage and solitude were combined with ascetic extremism, including a regimen of fasting that seems to have ruined his health, and that was certainly one aspect of his eventual flight from the world. As he lay suffering, "He stretched forth his hands to heaven, and as he gave thanks he breathed forth his spirit." Next morning, as his fellow monks began to wash the body and prepare it for burial, Salvius began to stir, and awakened. After three days of abstinence, he called in his fellows to tell them about his adventure.

First of all, Salvius declared, "understand that what you see in this world is nothing."[165] He then went on to tell about his visionary journey.[166] The solitude

---

162. "Quos statim in exilio direxerunt. Sed die altera depraessis somno custodibus, ipsi se liberos sentientes, ad beati Iuliani basilicam confugiunt, et sic ab exilio liberantur" (4.13), Gregory, *Libri historiarum,* 145.

163. "Nuntios ad nos dirixit, ut scilicet Gunthchramnum, qui tunc de morte Thudoberthi inpetebatur, a basilica sancta deberemus extrahere. . . . Quo audito, mittimus ad eum legationem, dicentes, haic ab antiquo facta non fuisse, quae hic fieri deposcebat, sed nec modo permitti posse, ut basilica sancta violaretur" (5.4), Gregory, *Libri historiarum,* 199; see also Marc Reydellet, "Pensée et pratique politiques chez Grégoire de Tours," in *Gregorio di Tours,* Convegni del centro di studi sulla spiritualità medievale 12 (Spoleto: 1977), 173–205; see 182.

164. "Iam cum divini spiramenti odor interna viscerum attigisset, relicta saeculari militia, monasterium expetivit" (7.1), Gregory, *Libri historiarum,* 323.

165. "Audite, o delectissimi, et intellegite, quia nihil est, quod cernitis in hoc mundo; sed sunt iuxta id quod Solomon propheta cecinit: 'Omnia vanitas'" (7.1), Gregory, *Libri historiarum,* 324.

166. For a unique discussion of these visions as "near-death experiences," see M. Van Uytfanghe, "Les *Visiones* du très haut Moyen Age et les récentes 'expériences de mort temporaire': Sens ou non-sens d'une comparison, Première partie," in *Aevvm inter vtrvmqve: Mélanges offerts à Gabriel Sanders,* Instrumenta Patristica 23 (The Hague: 1991), 447–81.

and asceticism of the abbot reached the extreme point of a journey into "death." Moreira has argued that the dramatic visionary journey of Salvius was directed toward establishing his earthly authority.[167] Gregory hoped to confirm his own episcopal authority with the assistance of these noteworthy examples of ascetic distance and power and to demonstrate that he stood in the tradition of St. Martin. The experience was grounded in his attempt to seek radical purity of body and spirit, something only possible in complete isolation from other people, and therefore far from the scene of royal power.[168] Lifted up by angels into the heavens, he was able to see the saints and martyrs. He was then addressed by a voice from a glimmering cloud, which ordered him to return to the world "since our churches need this."[169] His vision was consistent with liturgical imagery of the afterlife as a "place of light," populated by the saints.[170]

Gregory's sympathy for ascetics and hermits resulted in a tension that ran throughout the *Histories*. The noble origins of bishops contrasted with the humbler origins of the hermits: it is significant that the elegant Gregory wished to associate himself with these sometimes wild visionary figures.[171] This is the key to Salvius' story, because he was not allowed to remain in the otherworld. The voice in the glimmering cloud told him to return to earth and resume his duties, "for the churches have need of him." Salvius protested in vain: "and I turned back through the gate by which I had entered, weeping as I went." Upon his return to the world, he was forced to become the bishop of Albi.[172] In this story, Gregory painted a vivid picture of tension between kings and bishops. The family background of many Merovingian bishops connected them directly to the late Roman episcopate, and their understanding of episcopal power was consistent, as well. Episcopal power was a righteous form of rulership, vindicated, as in the old Ambrosian or Gregorian model, by contemplative flight and stoic acceptance of unwanted power and responsibility.

Recent scholarship has emphasized the extent to which Roman cultural and

167. Isabel Moreira, *Dreams, Visions, and Spiritual Authority in Merovingian Gaul* (Ithaca: 2000), 152–55.

168. Giselle de Nie, "Le Corps, la fluidité et l'identité personnelle dans la vision du monde de Grégoire de Tours," in *Aevvm inter vtrvmqve*, 75–87.

169. "Revertatur hic in saeculo, quoniam necessarius est aeclesiis nostris" (7.1), Gregory, *Libri historiarum*, 325.

170. J. Ntedika, *L'Évocation de l'au-delà dans la prière pour les morts: Étude de patristique et de liturgie latines (IVe–VIIIe s.)*, Recherches africaines de théologie 2 (Louvain: 1971), 185–93.

171. Heuclin, *Aux origines monastiques*, 98–99.

172. Gregory, *Libri historiarum* (7.1), 326; Jean Dufour, *Les Évêques d'Albi, de Cahors, et de Rodez, des origines à la fin du XIIe siècle*, Mémoires et documents d'histoire médiévale et de philologie 3 (Paris: 1989), 22–23.

political models persisted among Frankish bishops and their kings.[173] This im-
plies that bishops and kings moved within the same living world inherited from
Rome. Frankish kings hearkened back to a Roman past in their attempts to
purvey a royal ideology.[174] Like the fading colors of an aquatint, however, Roman and Frankish features were bleeding across their original borders. Roman
themes were selected and interpreted with considerable freedom in a developing
Franco-Roman order. In the view of Le Jan, this assertion of Roman symbols
was an effort to adopt Roman signs of legitimacy so as to unify many peoples
under the sovereign.[175]

A poignant instance of Roman survivals, often discussed, is when the Emper-
or Anastasius conferred the title of "consul" upon Clovis.[176] The Franks had just
driven the Visigoths out of Gaul in a major battle, and Byzantine envoys were
immediately on the scene, perhaps waiting to reward the winners.[177] It is clear
that the Byzantine mission was understood to be a "promotion" of the king, intended to make an impression, and thereby to recruit the king and his men. Clovis, clad in purple, stood in St. Martin's Church and crowned himself. Mounting his horse, he rode out throwing gold and silver coins into the crowd.[178] Here
was a ceremony seemingly created on the spot, with Roman themes providing a
certain tone, but this is not the same as a real survival of Roman state forms.[179]

173. "Das antike Lebensgefühl spielte eine dominierende Rolle": Georg Scheibelreiter, *Der
Bischof in merowingischer Zeit*, Veröffentlichungen des Instituts für österreichische Geschichts-
forschung 27 (Vienna: 1983), 56; Michael McCormick, *Eternal Victory: Triumphal Rulership in
Late Antiquity, Byzantium and the Early Medieval West* (Cambridge: 1986); Werner, *Naissance
de la noblesse*, 188–96; and McCormick, "The Liturgy of War in the Early Middle Ages: Crisis,
Litanies, and the Carolingian Monarchy," *Viator* 15 (1984): 1–23. On the rusticity of Gregory, see
Oldoni, "Gregorio di Tours," 263–64; Vetere, *Strutture e modelli culturali*, 10; Heinzelmann,
Bischofsherrschaft, 118–22.

174. Wood, *Merovingian Kingdoms*, 66–70.

175. Le Jan, "La sacralité de la royauté mérovingienne," 1226.

176. Jean Gaudemet, "Survivances romaines dans le droit de la monarchie franque du Vème
au Xème siècle," *Tijdschrift voor Rechtsgeschiedenis/Revue d'histoire du droit* 23 (1955): 157; Gabriele Zanella, "La legittimazione del potere regale nelle 'Storie' di Gregorio di Tours e Paolo Diacono," SM ser. 3, vol. 31 (1990): 66.

177. Louis Levillain, "La crise des années 507–508 et les rivalités d'influence en Gaule de 508
à 514," in *Mélanges offerts à M. Nicolas Iorga par ses amis de France et des pays de langue française*
(Paris: 1933), 537–67.

178. "Igitur ab Anastasio imperatore codecillos de consolato accepit, et in basilica beati Martini tunica blattea indutus et clamide, inponens vertice diadema. Tunc ascenso equite, aurum
argentumque in itinere illo, quod inter portam atrii et eclesiam civitatis est, praesentibus populis
manu propria spargens, voluntate benignissima erogavit, et ab ea die tamquam consul aut augustus est vocitatus" (2.8), Gregory, *Libri historiarum*, 88–89.

179. Michael McCormick, "Clovis at Tours, Byzantine Public Ritual and the Origins of Medieval Ruler Symbolism," in *Das Reich und die Barbaren*, edited by Evangelos K. Chrysos and
Adreas Schwarcz (Vienna: 1989), 155–80.

The trappings of Rome had been redirected toward the prestige of a war-leader "in the lap of his own people."[180] The adoption of the title "augustus" by Clovis reflects a Frankish culture set free from Roman models and in the process of creating itself. Everything about this ceremony was upside-down, viewed from a Roman perspective.[181] Put simply, here was a royal "exit" rather than an advent![182] What did the title "consul" meant to Clovis? One Roman consul with whom Clovis came in contact was the learned philosopher Boethius, and this is an awkward comparison. The ceremony has more to do with Clovis' claim to kingship over his newly aquired territory.[183] He appears in the familiar guise of an old-fashioned federate king.[184]

The Sword of God's Wrath

The Franks associated some archaic features of sacrality with their kings. Much of the tension, ambiguity, and incomprehensibility of Gregory's account arise from the shifting notions of a society undergoing change.[185] Gregory of Tours described Frankish kingship without reference to its sacrality, and other evidence for it is scanty.[186]

Gregory's account avoids the "bad sacrality" of the old Frankish kings, which the bishop of Tours felt to be in violent contrast to the holy men and women he praised. In this he is close to Pope Gregory the Great, who tartly informed Childebert II that Christian orthodoxy was more important than earthly kingship.[187] Gregory did not discover (or failed to record) a divine ancestor of the

180. The phrase is Pierre Clastres, "La question du pouvoir dans les sociétés primitives," in his *Recherches d'anthropologie politique* (Paris: 1980), 103–9; see 106. On the details of this ritual, see Ralph W. Mathisen, "Clovis, Anastase et Grégoire de Tours: consul, patrice et roi," in *Clovis: Histoire et mémoire,* edited by Michel Rouche (Paris: 1997), 1:395–407.

181. Sabine G. MacCormack, *Art and Ceremony* (Berkeley: 1981), 194–95; see also Michael E. Moore, "The King's New Clothes: Royal and Episcopal Regalia in the Frankish Empire," in *Robes and Honor: The Medieval World of Investiture,* edited by Stewart Gordon, 5–135 (New York: 2000).

182. On the tradition of *adventus:* Ernst Kantorowicz, "The 'King's Advent' and the Enigmatic Panels in the Doors of Santa Sabina," in his *Selected Studies,* 37–75, esp. 42–51 (Locust Valley, N.Y.: 1965).

183. Mathison, "Clovis, Anastase," 404.

184. Wallace-Hadrill, *Early Germanic Kingship,* 19.

185. Alexander Callander Murray, "Post vocantur Merohingii: Fredegar, Merovech, and 'Sacral Kingship,'" in *After Rome's Fall,* 121–52; see 121; Angenendt, "Princeps imperii," 8–9.

186. Murray argues that the concept of Germanic sacral kingship is not well supported in Merovingian sources: Murray, "Post vocantur Merohingii: Fredegar, Merovech, and 'Sacral Kingship,'" 121–52; but now see Le Jan, "La sacralité de la royauté mérovingienne," 1229–34.

187. Brouwer, "Egalité et pouvoir," 129.

Merovingians, as would later emerge in the writings of Fredegar.[188] From the perspective of Gregory there was no cosmic-political myth associated with Frankish kingship that could serve to guarantee the social order.[189] Quite to the contrary, their activities inspired Gregory with sadness and evident disdain.

Gregory's views on kingship were intimately linked to his perception of the role of bishops, men who could combine their religious role with an earthy practicality. Thus Leo of Tours was "an active man and also handy at carpentry."[190] Gregory also offered himself as a good model of a bishop. There is evident continuity between the late antique model of episcopal power and the bishops whom Gregory advanced as ideals. Nicetius, bishop of Lyon, he described as a saintly and chaste figure who offered his love to all. He was slow to anger and quick to forgive those who undertook penance.[191] He gave alms and was "strenuous in his labor, taking very diligent care in erecting churches, building houses, sowing fields and cultivating vineyards. But none of these things disturbed his prayers."[192] Nicetius was also at the Council of Lyon (567–570), and may have had a hand in the council's insistence on the quality of bishops.[193] The qualities of a good bishop were thus a combination of practical management, a good temper, and religious fervor. Building churches and concern for the poor were two sides of a single project, centered in the bishop's government of his city.[194] At the heart of the bishop's sphere of action were the buildings and vineyards attached to the *domus ecclesiae,* but his cares extended as well to the refurbishment and protection of his city.[195]

Care for the poor went beyond alms-giving to providing protection against the powerful. The funeral procession of the recluse Eparchius was accompa-

188. On the mythological genealogy of the Merovingians in Fredegar, see J. M. Wallace-Hadrill, "Fredegar and the History of France," *Bulletin of the John Rylands Library, Manchester* 40 (1958): 527–50; 540.

189. On the support that divine kingship can offer to the social order, see Evans-Pritchard, *Divine Kingship,* 9.

190. "Hic fuit vir strenuus atque utilis in fabrica operis lignarii" (3.17), Gregory, *Libri historiarum,* 117.

191. "Nam si et commotus contra aliquem pro neglegentia fuit, ita protinus emendatum recepit, tanquam si non fuisset offensus" (4.36), Gregory, *Libri historiarum,* 168; on Gregory's view of the ideal bishop, see Wallace-Hadrill, *Frankish Church,* 80.

192. "Elemosinarius atque strenuus in labore; ecclesias erigere, domos componere, serere agros, vineas pastinare diligentissime studebat. Sed non eum hae res ab oratione turbabant" (4.36), Gregory, *Libri historiarum,* 168.

193. Council of Lyon (567–570), CCSL 148A:202.

194. On Gregory's portrayal of bishops and their functions, see Reydellet, "Pensée et pratique politiques," 174–81.

195. Fabienne Cardot, *L'Espace et le pouvoir: Étude sur l'Austrasie mérovingienne,* Histoire ancienne et médiévale 17 (Paris: 1987), 155–63; see further Godding, *Prêtres en Gaule,* 223.

nied by a crowd of people whom he had defended.[196] Maurilio, Bishop of Cahors, "was just in his judgements and in defending the poor of his church from
the hand of evil judges."[197] Such protection could not always be provided: both
Gregory and Bishop Eunius faced the ire of King Chilperic when they attempted to prevent him from pressing the poor into military service contrary to custom.[198] Antagonism between bishops and kings frequently centered on issues
of law. Bishops assembled either on their own initiative or at the request of the
king, to serve as an impromptu court in important cases, although the results
were usually unsatisfactory. Such a court failed to resolve a dispute between
Guntram and Sigibert, because the men refused to listen to the bishops.[199] In
judging a dispute between Count Nantinus and Bishop Heraclius, the bishops
were unable to control the Count after deciding against him at a council held
in Auvergne (of uncertain date).[200]

Gregory portrayed a stark contrast between kings and bishops. Unlike a good
bishop, Frankish kings often acted without reference to law. Instead, many of the
royal actions Gregory relates were undertaken out of anger.[201] Royal and noble
anger accounted for the extremes of violence characterizing the upper levels of
society.[202] Guntram was "deranged by anger" at Dynamius, the Bishop of Marseilles, and sent men to beat and arrest him.[203] Guntram was also angered at Ber-
tram and Palladius.[204] Chilperic's anger led him to launch a war from which the
church suffered more than during the Diocletian persecution.[205] On learning
that Merovech had married the widow of his rival Sigibert, Chilperic was "huge-

---

196. "Magnus autem conventus, ut diximus, de redemptis in eius processit exsequiis" (6.8),
Gregory, *Libri historiarum*, 278.

197. "Fuit etiam et in iudiciis iustus ac defendens pauperes ecclesiae suae de manu malorum
iudicum" (5.42), Gregory, *Libri historiarum*, 249.

198. "Post haec Chilpericus rex de pauperibus et iunioribus eclesiae vel basilicae bannos iussit
exigi, pro eo quod in exercitu non ambulassent. Non enim erat consuetudo, ut hi ulolam exsolv-
erent publicam functionem" (5.26), Gregory, *Libri historiarum*, 232–33.

199. "Gunthchramnus rex apud Parisius omnes episcopus regni sui congregat, ut inter utrusque
quid veritas haberit edicerent. Sed ut bellum civili in maiore pernicitate cresceret, eos audire, peccatis facientibus, distulerunt" (4.47), Gregory, *Libri historiarum*, 183–84.

200. Gregory, *Libri historiarum* (5.36), 242–43; and Pontal, *Histoire des conciles mérovingiens*, 178.

201. As was noted by Reydellet, *Royauté dans la littérature latine*, 386–89.

202. Barbara Rosenwein, "Worrying about Emotions in History," *American Historical Review* 107 (2002): 821–45, esp. 843–44.

203. "At ille ira commotus, iubet contra fas religionis, ut pontifex summi Dei artatus vinculis
sibi exhiberetur" (6.11), Gregory, *Libri historiarum*, 281.

204. "Cum haec rege nuntiata fuissent, valde commotus est" (8.2), Gregory, *Libri historiarum*,
372.

205. "Chilpericus autem in ira commotus" (4.47), Gregory, *Libri historiarum*, 184.

ly embittered."[206] Bitterness also overwhelmed Guntram when he learned King Childebert had received Bishop Egidius.[207] Such examples could easily be multiplied.[208] These powerful emotions were, according to Gregory, what drove kings toward violent expressions of power. Anger was something shared by the kings of whom Gregory approved and those whom he disliked. Power inhered in the person of the king, and every important person had to deal with him.[209] The *Histories* make a plea for a greater Christianization of power. According to Gregory, the realm should be seen as a Christian space, anchored in churches and monasteries, organized by committed religious men and obedient Christian kings.

Discussions of Gregory's views on kingship have tended to focus, with reason, on two important kings described by Gregory, Chilperic, and Guntram.[210] While Chilperic has been taken as the typically bad king, Guntram has often been advanced as the king in whom Gregory placed his hopes, and whose portrait was intended as one of ideal kingship. Yet neither king was drawn in broad strokes. While Chilperic and Guntram each represented a different aspect of kingship, Gregory did not attempt to reduce them to symbols. For this reason, the two portraits share a certain number of features, such as indulgence in anger or polygamy. Both kings engaged in harsh exercises of power to eliminate rivals and seize their treasure, then to expand their kingdoms.

According to Gregory, Chilperic composed hymns and even Masses, but the clerics did not want to perform them because of his heretical leanings.[211] Chilperic's Arianism presented Gregory with a further problem. Despite his antagonism toward Chilperic, Gregory could scarcely avoid the king and was forced to rely on him. The king could provide the setting for grand occasions, such as the public disputation between Gregory and the Jew Priscus, and could call episcopal councils. The portrait of Chilperic is necessarily an ambiguous one. While the King was clearly interested in maintaining a certain continuity with Roman government, and was learned enough to write Latin poetry in the style of Sedu-

206. "Valde amarus" (5.2), Gregory, *Libri historiarum*, 195.

207. "Unde rex Guntchramnus valde in amaritudine excitatus est" (9.14), Gregory, *Libri historiarum*, 428.

208. Of Guntram: "Addita est etiam huic causae aliud amaretudinis incendium" (9.32), Gregory, *Libri historiarum*, 451. Of Chramn: "Semper adversus Cautinum episcopum invidiam tenens" (4.16), Gregory, *Libri historiarum*, 147.

209. Reydellet, "Pensée et pratique politiques," 195–96; idem, *Royauté dans la littérature latine*, 389–90; Zanella, "La legittimazione," 59.

210. Breukelaar, *Historiography and Episcopal Authority*, 230–40; Reydellet, *Royauté dans la littérature latine*, 416–29.

211. Ulysse Chevalier, *Poésie liturgique du moyen âge: Rythme et histoire* (Paris: 1893), 83.

lius, Gregory felt oppressed by him because of the king's Arianism.[212] Nevertheless, when the King asked Gregory for his blessing, the bishop could hardly refuse.[213] In telling of a council that gathered in Paris for the trial of Praetextus of Rouen, Gregory painted a vivid picture of his fellow bishops, totally cowed in a conflict with royal power.[214] The bishops felt the trial was a travesty, yet "they feared the King and his raging, on whose impulse these things were being done. Constrained, pressing their fingers to their lips."[215]

Gregory condemned Chilperic for the devastation caused by his wartime brutality, comparing him to Nero.[216] Not only did he fail to defend the poor, but actively hated them, just as he hated the bishops and their churches.[217] After Chilperic was assassinated, King Guntram was inclined to blame the bishops for his brother's death, because they had been opposed to him. At a terrifying dinner, a group of bishops gathered at the king's table had to listen to an exchange between Gregory and Guntram, in which it emerged that both men had been warned of Chilperic's death in their dreams. Gregory declared that Chilperic was responsible for his own death because of his wickedness, and that even King Guntram had prayed for Chilperic's downfall.[218] The contrast between royal and episcopal power had appeared to Gregory in an eerie dream:

I saw this in a dream-vision, when first I saw him [Chilperic] with his head tonsured, as if he were ordained a bishop; then placed on an iron throne, and plain, merely covered in black, with lighted candles and torches before him.[219]

Guntram responded that he too had foreseen Chilperic's death in a dream. In this vision, Chilperic was brought into his presence, bound in chains, by three bishops. The bishops judged Chilperic, and breaking his bones, threw him into

---

212. Wood, *Merovingian Kingdoms*, 68.

213. "Ait enim: 'Dicam,' inquid, 'tibi, o sacerdos, quod Iacob dixit ad angelum, qui ei loquebatur: Non demittam te, nisi benedixeris mihi' (Gen. 32:26)" (6.5), Gregory, *Libri historiarum*, 271.

214. Pontal, *Histoire des conciles mérovingiens*, 148–49.

215. "Timebant enim regine et fururem, cuius instinctu haec agebantur. Quibus intentis et ora digitis conpraementibus" (5.18), Gregory, *Libri historiarum*, 217–18.

216. "Nam regiones plurimas sepius devastavit atque succendit; de quibus nihil doloris, sed laetitiam magis habebat, sicut quondam Nero" (5.46), Gregory, *Libri historiarum*, 319.

217. "Causas pauperum exosas habebat. Sacerdotes Domini assiduae blasphemabat" (5.46), Gregory, *Libri historiarum*, 320.

218. "Et quis Chilpericum interemit, nisi malitia sua tuaque oratio?" (8.5), Gregory, *Libri historiarum*, 374.

219. "Quod ut dicam, valde hoc per visionem somnii inspexi, cum viderem eum, ante tonsorato capite, quasi episcopum ordinari; deinde super cathedram puram, sola fuligine tectam, inpositum ferri, praelucentibus coram eo lyghnis ac cereis" (8.5), Gregory, *Libri historiarum*, 374.

a cauldron.[220] The contrast between bishops and kings was a stark and haunting one, and was felt on both sides.

For Guntram, who did have Gregory's approval, the story is no less equivocal. Despite this, Guntram has often been referred to as an important example of the existence of sacral kingship among the Merovingian Franks. For Gregory remarked that Guntram, when he commanded his kingdom to engage in fasts and processions, had acted like a priest and a king.[221] It is remarkable how much weight this passage has been made to bear. For Anton, this was Gregory's ideal of Merovingian kingship and proof of the antiquity of the "priest-king" among the Germanic peoples.[222] Indeed, Gregory's description of Guntram has been called "hagiographical."[223]

Do we have here a type of kingship that might "better be described as sacerdotal than as governmental"?[224] In Gregory's account there is substantial continuity between Chilperic's rule and that of Guntram. Guntram was also capable of devastating the countryside in wartime, and did not shy away from killing his rivals or from attacking bishops. As had Chilperic, Guntram tried to force the people of Gregory's church to take part in his military campaigns, fining them when they refused.[225] On the other hand, he did attempt to undo some of the harm Chilperic had caused. King Guntram restored lands that had been expropriated,[226] and allowed Praetextus to return to his bishopric at Rouens.[227] Yet Gregory gives little indication that Guntram was an ideal king. In 585, when the city of Poitiers refused to give its allegiance to him, Guntram marched against it, and when his envoys were rebuffed by the bishop, the lands of Poitiers were burned and looted and the inhabitants massacred. As the army returned, Tours was subjected to the same treatment; Guntram burned churches there as well.[228]

220. Gregory, *Libri historiarum* (8.5), 374.
221. "Ipse autem rex, ut saepe diximus, elymosinis magnus, in vigiliis atque ieiuniis promptus erat. Nam tunc ferebatur, Masiliam a luae inguinaria valde vastare et hunc morbum usque ad Ludgunensim vicum Octavum nomine fuisse caeleriter propalatum. Sed rex acsi bonus sacerdos providens remedia, qua cicatrices peccatoris vulgi mederentur, iussit omnem populum ad eclesiam convenire et rogationes summa cum devotione celebrare" (9.21), Gregory, *Libri historiarum,* 441.
222. Hans Hubert Anton, *Fürstenspiegel und Herrscherethos in der Karolingerzeit,* Bonner Historische Forschungen 32 (Bonn: 1968), 53 and n. 38.
223. Vetere, *Strutture e modelli culturali,* 111.
224. Evans-Pritchard, *Divine Kingship,* 16.
225. "Post haec edictum a iudicibus datum est, ut qui in hac expeditione tardi fuerant damnarentur" (7.42), Gregory, *Libri historiarum,* 364.
226. Gregory, *Libri historiarum* (7.19), 338–39.
227. Gregory, *Libri historiarum* (7.16), 337–38.
228. "At illi infra terminum ingressi, praedas, incendia adque homicidia faciebant. Hii vero qui cum praeda revertebantur, per Toronicum transeuntes, similiter illis qui iam sacramenta dederant faciebant, ita ut ipsae quoque aeclesiae incenderentur" (7.24), Gregory, *Libri historiarum,* 344.

On another occasion, Guntram sent men to arrest Eberulf, whom he suspected in Chilperic's death. Eberulf took refuge in "the church of St. Martin," that is, Gregory's own cathedral in Tours. The men seized Eberulf within the church and killed him.[229] Although Gregory considered Guntram to be preferable to his brother, he did not portray him as a paragon. The right of asylum was something that Gregory defended with great passion, and Guntram violated it in the worst possible way.

Let us return to the well-known phrase in which Gregory compared Guntram to a priest and a king. With evident pleasure, Gregory told of a gathering of bishops, whom Guntram encouraged to hold more frequent councils. At a subsequent feast, he promised to build churches and to help the poor. Gregory was quite cheered by the food and conversation on this occasion. Guntram's good actions were at this point minimal, to say the least. Nevertheless, the king's piety impressed Gregory—for example, when he ordered the people of Marseilles to undertake Rogations processions in response to a plague.[230] In doing so, Gregory said, Guntram acted "like a bishop providing a remedy."[231] The key to this remarkable passage lies in what follows: "For three days he indeed gave more alms than usual, having so much fear for all the people that he seemed to be, not so much a king, but a bishop of the Lord."[232] Gregory wished to highlight the possibility of conversion, in line with Biblical histories. Gregory goes on to say that threads from Guntram's cloak could cure a fever, and that by calling on his name, people were freed from demonic possession. This sounds suspiciously similar to the funeral of the Ostrogothic king Theodoric. Despite his heretical views and tyrannical rule, Theodoric's body was able to cure a demoniac, and the assembled people began to tear bits of clothing from the corpse as it lay in state.[233]

The portrait of Guntram was thus composed of glaring contradictions, but taken as a whole, left the impression that this king, by taking seriously the episcopal model of government, was capable of approaching the powers of those saints whom Gregory ordinarily contrasted with kingship. The qualities that

---

229. Gregory, *Libri historiarum* (7.29), 346–49.

230. On Rogations: T. Bailey, *The Processions of Sarum and the Western Church,* Pontifical Institute for Medieval Studies, Studies and Texts 21 (Toronto: 1971), 95–97; and for the ancient context of the ritual: Nathan, "Rogation Ceremonies," 275–303.

231. "Sed rex acsi sacerdus providens remedia" (9.21), Gregory, *Libri historiarum,* 441.

232. "Per triduum enim ipsius elimosinis largius solito praecurrentibus, ita de cuncto populo formidabat, ut iam tunc non rex tantum, sed etiam sacerdus Domini putaretur" (9.21), Gregory, *Libri historiarum,* 441.

233. "Quod videntes populi et senatores coeperunt reliquias de veste eius tollere" (93), *Excerpta Valesiana,* ed. Moreau, 27.

gave Guntram an episcopal air were the very qualities Gregory praised in saintly bishops. Gregory is deliberately vague about Guntram's pious activities. In order to understand the portrait of Guntram, it is not necessary to postulate a sacral kingship that Gregory was only recognizing. Guntram could be compared to a bishop because he emulated episcopal government and had gone at least some distance toward cooperating with the bishops of his kingdom. He was saintly to the extent that he ceased to act like a traditional king, but according to episcopal norms of behavior.

For the bishop of Tours, kingship was not inherently good, with its angry impulses, blood feuds, fratricide, and brute violence against the innocent. A good king was one who emulated and supported the bishops and other saints. History, the deeds of people, had no internal coherence on which an order of government might be erected. A saintly person, capable of having visions, could at times step outside the historical realm dominated by kings and their minions, and meaning was located in that mysterious "outside."

One evening Gregory of Tours strolled and talked with his visionary friend Salvius, now bishop of Albi. Salvius (ca. 571–584), like Gregory, worked for reform of the church and to preserve Christian space in the kingdom. Salvius had joined Gregory at the Council of Berny in 580, and helped defend him from the accusations of Leudast when Chilperic gained control of Tours.[234] The two comrades were saying good-bye after a very trying meeting with King Chilperic, at which the king had declared that there was no distinction in the Trinity. Walking before the king's house, Salvius suddenly stopped.

"Do you see what I am looking up at, over that roof?" I said to him: "I see the new tiles which the king recently ordered." And he said: "Don't you see anything else?" I replied: "I see nothing else." Indeed, I suspected he was jesting. And I added: "If you discern something else, tell me what it is." That man, drawing a deep breath, said: "I see the sword of God's wrath, drawn from its sheath, hanging over this house."[235]

While Gregory, through his familiarity with Gothic history, could conceive of a higher possibility for kingship, this was not the theme of his portrayal of Frankish kingship and society. Gregory observed and described a harsh contrast

234. The Council of Berny (580), CCSL 148A:220; see also Pontal, *Histoire des conciles mérovingiens*, 147.
235. "'Videsne super hoc tectum quae ego suspicio?' Cui ego: 'Video enim supertegulum, quod nuper rex poni praecepit.' Et illi: 'Aliud,' inquid, 'non aspicis?' Cui ego: 'Nihil aliud video.' Suspicabar enim, quod aliquid ioculariter loquaretur. Et adiaci: 'Si tu aliquid magis cernis, enarra.' At ille, alta trahens suspiria, ait: 'Video ego evaginatum irae divinae gladio super domum hanc dependentem'" (5.50), Gregory, *Libri historiarum*, 263.

between sanctity and royalty that amounts to a bipolar structure, a division of society into two moieties, in which one person was aligned with kings and another with the saints.[236]

Bishops sought to maintain their identity as religious leaders and governors of cities, especially through membership in a select group. This group consisted of all bishops going back to the time of the apostles, a sacred fraternity whose contemporary members, meeting in council, sought to preserve and renew the legislation of their predecessors, the "ancient statutes." Every bishop could thus draw upon the past, even the recent past, as a venerable antiquity vindicating his own authority. As the Roman Empire faded and bishops confronted a changed political landscape in successor kingdoms, the council became an increasingly important forum for the preservation of the episcopal institution. In the Frankish context, bishops looked to one another, not to the papacy, to support their institutional claims. They did this on the basis of what might be called a "vest pocket" Augustinianism, reduced to a set of theological *dicta* to be memorized. Gregory of Tours, perceiving the Merovingian world as brutally violent, promoted an ethic of withdrawal and retreat. Gregory did not conceive of kingship as a Christian institution, but as a restraining force in a wicked world. Frankish life did not revolve around the king or within a framework imposed by royal power: social power was diffused among men—dukes, counts, and bishops—whose local prestige was integrated into the kingdom by their participation in communal decision-making, all of which make it a typical "late-Roman state."[237] With his fascination for kings and the overriding importance he saw for saintly monks and bishops, Gregory scarcely lets us see the role of the nobility in the Frankish system. His great themes were the conversion and gradual discipline of the barbarous and sinful Frankish kings. According to Gregory, bishops, not nobles, were the leading figures in Frankish society beside the king. Gregory hoped that Christian discipline, haltingly and painfully accepted by kings, might be diffused among the Frankish nobility and people.

236. This terminology is taken from Evans-Pritchard, *Divine Kingship,* 27.

237. Wood, *Merovingian Kingdoms,* 60–63. On the Merovingian nobility in a later period, see Paul Fouracre and Richard A. Gerberding, *Late Merovingian France: History and Hagiography, 640–720* (Manchester: 1996), 56–57.

[4]

THE DIGNITY OF POWER

*I*N THE COURSE of the late sixth and seventh centuries, bishops became functionally and structurally central to the Frankish system. Frankish kingdoms were organized around cities and dioceses governed by bishops, and kings recognized their importance by attempting to control the selection of bishops to important sees. This system served to stabilize an enormous region extending from the foothills of the Pyrenees to the forests along the Rhine. Acting on their position as a cultural aristocracy and serving as ritual leaders of the cult, bishops were increasingly drawn from the Frankish aristocracy and cooperated extensively with the Frankish kings. The effort to conceptualize kingship on the part of bishops went hand in hand with efforts to Christianize kingship and to participate in royal governance. A major dimension of these changes was in the realm of law. Bishops aquired learned and religious claims over law, developing their own special law and maintaining books of canon law, so that even traditional tribal law codes and royal edicts were issued ordinarily at episcopal councils. Episcopal Christianity constituted a cultural overlay, papering over tribal institutions as the episcopal council became the ultimate locus of law.

The problem of kingship was understood from within the bishops' own substantial tradition and an ideology that now recognized the social power, wealth, and grandeur of Frankish bishops. The conceptualization of kingship in the barbarian kingdoms was complicated by these cross-currents. In Visigothic Spain,

the bishop-scholar Isidore of Seville helped resolve this problem of categoriza-
tion and understanding. Isidore turned to liturgy and patristic vocabulary for
an understanding of kingship in the successor kingdoms. His liturgical concept
of kingship was extremely influential in Gaul, and merits the close reading with
which this chapter ends.

The Problem of Kingship

As bishops looked to the new kingdoms of Europe, they were confronted by
the problem of kingship: what was the proper relation of bishops and the church
to these kings? At the end of the Roman era many of these kings were either
non-Christian or Arian heretics. As the kings were gradually converted to Catholicism, the relation between episcopal and royal power was worked out as the
terms of an alliance and partnership between bishops and kings in the creation
of a Christian society ruled by law. Along the way, bishops developed a unique
level of expertise and knowledge about law. Their function and duties were laid
down most authoritatively in law and ecclesiastical tradition, although these
principles were often defeated by royal interference and the tantalizing prospect
of cooperation, as we have seen in the case of the Council of Agde (506) and its
recognition of King Alaric.

Bishops frequently claimed that they were the heirs and representatives of
an unchanging tradition connecting them to the times of Christ and earlier to
the kings and priests of ancient Israel. Bishops formulated a social theology anchored in this understanding of the past, insisting on their unique status, their
governmental role, and their "dignity of power" (*dignitas potestatis*).[1] In doing
so, they drew on a late antique inheritance embedded in law and liturgy. Conciliar law was central to this vision of the past and, as a result, the manuscripts
in which it was preserved often juxtaposed historical texts with the legislation
of councils arranged in chronological order.[2]

Collections of canon law, such as the *Concordia canonum* of Cresconius (compiled in Italy in the mid-sixth century), the *Quesnelliana,* and other fifth-century
compilations, were guided by this historical awareness, incorporating "all the
canonical enactments which both the holy apostles and apostolic men promul-

---

1. In the words of Isidore of Seville: Letter 8, Isidore to Bishop Eugenius, *The Letters of St.
Isidore of Seville,* ed. and trans. G. B. Ford, 2nd ed. (Amsterdam: 1970), 46.

2. Bernard Guenée, *Histoire et culture historique dans l'Occident médiéval* (Paris: 1980), 33;
Maassen, *Geschichte der Quellen,* 640–42; see also Gérard Fransen, *Les collections canoniques,*
Typologie des sources du moyen âge occidental 10 (Turnhout: 1973), 17–19.

gated from the very beginning of the Christian struggle through the course of time."[3] Thus law books could be seen as sacred history.

Frankish bishops were very open to the law and writings of bishops in other successor kingdoms—Ireland, Spain, and England. Thinkers in those kingdoms were often ahead of Frankish bishops in adapting episcopal ideology to the relatively new scene of small kingdoms and their warrior kings. It is often stressed that the bishops of Gaul and Spain represented the continuity of Roman culture in the new kingdoms. However, the Roman identity of these bishops was remade as a Catholic and Christian idea in a new, barbarian context.[4] From the *Histories* of Gregory of Tours, we gain a clear picture of one prominent scion of an old Roman family—Gregory himself.[5] Here was a man totally engaged in a Frankish world, whose concepts were formed by an episcopal training and his love of monastic Christianity. The distinction between Frank and Roman was increasingly unclear and difficult to determine from the sources. Ethnicity was certainly less important than historians have assumed, as Romans adopted Frankish names and adopted barbarian culture as their own.[6] Intense royal interest in the crucial border city of Tours seems to have prevented Gregory from full engagement in the conciliar life of his day.

Gregory's ideas of kingship were based on his observation of Frankish kings, rather than Roman models. Taxation was prominent in his view of royal power.[7] The late Roman historians interested him only because of the sparse information they contained about Frankish history. Gregory wished to understand Frankish kingship on its own terms, and this is why he was so intent on discovering the earliest phase of the Frankish kings. Nevertheless, historians such as Sulpicius Alexander and Orosius frustrated his effort to discover the names of the earliest Frankish kings and how they came to have their dominance over the Franks. Sulpicius Alexander spoke only of unnamed "princes" (*regales*).[8] Did the rise of the Frankish kings represent anything more than lionlike force, signaled by the brandished spear?[9] Episcopal social thought focused on the understanding that good power should possess legality.

3. Cresconius, *Die Concordia canonum des Cresconius, Studien und Edition* 1–2, ed. Klaus Zechiel-Eckes, Freiburger Beiträge zur mittelalterlichen Geschichte 5 (Frankfurt: 1992), 419–22; translation in Somerville, *Prefaces to Canon Law,* 51; see also Kéry, *Canonical Collections,* 33–37.

4. Edward O. James, "Gregory of Tours and the Franks," in *After Rome's Fall,* 51–66.

5. On Gregory's family connections: Heinzelmann, *Gregor von Tours,* 7–21.

6. Godding, *Prêtres en Gaule,* 5–6; James, *Europe's Barbarians,* 121–26.

7. James, *Europe's Barbarians,* 248; see also James, "Gregory of Tours," 65.

8. Wood, *Merovingian Kingdoms,* 36–38; J. M. Wallace-Hadrill, *The Long-Haired Kings* (Toronto: 1982), 153–58.

9. Royal power as pure strength was symbolized by the lion. On the ancient and medieval

When it came to kingship, the centerpiece of social identity in the new king-doms, the Romans had left behind an ambivalent legacy. The Romans proudly thought of themselves as a people liberated from kings early in their history.[10] The emperors were considered to be a different and higher social phenomenon, to be contrasted with the rulership to be found in the smaller and inferior so-cieties that they conquered or negotiated with, the *principes* (chief men), *duces* (war leaders) and *reges* (kings) that were customary figures in Roman ethnog-raphy, deemed suitable for describing the simple structure of barbarian societ-ies.[11] The Romans also helped to develop a limited type of kingship in Germanic societies to organize them as armies in border alliances.[12] The figure of an "em-peror" and the entire structure of imperial power could still be observed in the Byzantine east. Imperial government was a higher type of royalty, arising out of republican institutions, defined by law, and unfolding in law.[13] On the other hand, as the center of an imperial cult retaining many pagan elements, even the Christian emperors were still addressed as the "deified one" (*divus*).[14] The prob-lems raised by kingship could not be resolved simply by applying such imperial terms to a warlord.

Nor were the popes ready to provide a new concept of kingship, since their own political doctrine was shaped by Roman imperial ideals. It was possible for Pope Gregory the Great (590–604) to apply the terminology of empire to cajole the barbarian kings, but these kings did not seem fully valid and independent: Gregory still hoped that, with the help of divine grace, the emperor would "bend

association of kings and lions: Werner, *Naissance de la noblesse*, 113; Jacques Le Goff, "Le roi dans l'occident médiéval: caracteres originaux," in *Kings and Kingship in Medieval Europe*, edited by Anne J. Duggan, King's College London Medieval Studies 10 (London: 1993), 1–39; esp. 31; see also Cicero's famous analogy of the "fox and the lion," in which the lion represents pure force: *De officiis*, 1.41; he contrasts the spear to fellowship, 2.29. Compare Hilary's description, mentioned earlier, of Constantius II as a raging lion"leo saeuiens": Hilary of Poitiers. *Contre Constance*, 166. The spear symbol was also used by the Roman emperors: Andreas Alföldi, "Zum Speersym-bol der Souveränität im Altertum," in *Festschrift Percy Ernst Schramm*, edited by Peter Classen and Peter Scheibert (Wiesbaden: 1964), 1:3–6; Wallace-Hadrill suggests that among the Franks, the spear retained its pagan association with Woden: Wallace-Hadrill, *Long-Haired Kings*, 201.

10. See discussion in "Monarchie," GGB, 4:133–214, esp. 138. For Cicero, kings represented a failure of fellowship, the highest political ideal: *De officiis*, 1.26; see also Tacitus: "Vrbem Roman a principio reges habuere; libertatem et consulatum L. Brutus instituit," *Annals* (1.1), The Annals of Tacitus, edited by Henry Furneaux, 2d ed. (Oxford: 1896), 1:179.

11. Brenda M. Bell, "The Contribution of Julius Caesar to the Vocabulary of Ethnography," *Latomus* 54 (1995): 753–67; Reydellet, *La royauté dans la littérature*, 7–21.

12. Wolfram, *Roman Empire*, 14–20; Werner, *Naissance de la noblesse*, 197–210.

13. Harries, *Law and Empire*, 19–21. On the *lex regia* as the basic legal formula of the Princi-pate: Fustel de Coulanges, *La Gaule romaine*, 122–31.

14. Ramsay MacMullen, *Christianity and Paganism in the Fourth to Eighth Centuries* (New Haven: 1997), 34–36.

the necks of the nations into subjection to the Christian Empire."[15] In his book *On Pastoral Care,* Gregory instead developed the significant concept of the *rector,* the Christian governor, to describe the governmental role of bishops.[16] This ascetic model of power was not easily fitted to the wilder nature of early Frankish kingship. Kingship, as a new social form, remained a problem of conceptualization facing the bishops of Gaul and the other successor kingdoms. This was reflected in the absence of royal inauguration rituals for the rulers of the new kingdoms.[17] Among the Franks, royal power remained the personal accomplishment of members of the Merovingian family, based on a king's ability to rally a band of supporters. In the civil wars of the sixth century described so luridly by Gregory, the fortunes of kings rose or fell as the nobles shifted allegiances.

The creation of a royal doctrine was welcomed by the leaders of barbarian societies as an additional layer of prominence and association with law: a "juridico-religious authority," as Le Jan has suggested.[18] The dominance of the barbarian kings was often based on little more than military success and the ability to remain at the center of a social identity through sheer physical vigor and good luck.[19] Royal power existed at the level of incarnation.[20] Clovis' interest in the "consulship" reflects a kind of indecision. The older model of a Roman general and war chieftan was still in the air. The power of a king like Clovis was personal, serving as a temporary center of social gravitation. The rise of many contemporary royal dynasties, such as the Gothic Amals, was accompanied by mythic genealogies, drawing on cycles of traditional tales vaunting the heroic power and authenticity of the family.[21]

Among all the Germanic peoples who built up successor kingdoms after the fall of Rome, cultural identity was formed around a story of origins (*origo gentis*)[22] and the construction of such genealogies for their royal families (*stirps regia*).[23] These themes of cultural identity reached toward a distant past imbued

15. Markus, *Gregory the Great,* 84–85.

16. Bruno Judic, "Grégoire le Grand et le pouvoir royal," *Studia Patristica* 33 (Louvain: 1997): 434–40.

17. Janet L. Nelson, "Symbols in Context: Rulers' Inauguration Rituals in Byzantium and the West in the Early Middle Ages," in her *Politics and Ritual in Early Medieval Europe* (London: 1986), 259–307; esp. 260–65.

18. Le Jan, "La sacralité de la royauté mérovingienne," 1227.

19. Wolfram, *The Roman Empire,* 16.

20. Zanella, "Legittimazione," 59.

21. Peter Heather, *Goths and Romans, 332–489* (Oxford: 1991), 19–21.

22. Wolfram, *Roman Empire,* 22–34.

23. Jörg Jarnut, "Genealogie und politische Bedeutung der agilolfingischen Herzöge," in *Mitteilungen des Instituts für Österreichische Geschichtsforschung* 99 (1991): 1–22.

with mythic qualities, despite the fact that the Franks, Burgundians, and others were constructing new identities in Gaul.[24] A warlike identity centered on the person of the king was thus equipped with archaic prestige in a narrative expressing something distinctive about the society and its ways.[25] Such collective beliefs could become the nucleus for a tribe or group of tribes.[26] Early Gothic kingship had been, as among the Franks, primarily a war leadership developed in partnership with Rome.[27] Nevertheless, the Franks saw their royal line, the Merovingians, as having an origin in the coupling of a noble woman with a *Quinotaur,* a fantastic sea creature.[28] Such a tale was dramatic and interesting, but something of an embarassment in a Christian context, especially following the baptism of Clovis in about 508. Gregory of Tours suppressed the story, if he knew it. Perhaps the tale was not widely believed.[29] In any case, the content and explanatory power of such mythic tales was limited.

Bishops developed a political theology from their own traditions, perceiving a dualism in the field of power.[30] Relying on the Bible and liturgical imagery, they were able to draw on ancient Near Eastern traditions of rulership to help them understand the present world of power. These same ancient traditions and their symbology (throne, sceptre, diadem, the purple *chlamys*) had been absorbed by Rome as it adopted Hellenistic forms of monarchy and the cult of rulership.[31] For this reason, early medieval concepts of power can be viewed against an ex-

24. Karl Hauck, "Lebensformen und Kultmythen in germanischen Stammes- und Herrschergenealogien," *Saeculum* 6 (1955). Genealogy had also served as a mythic formula for the ancient Greeks: Paula Philippson, "Genealogie als mythische Form (Studien zur Theogonie des Hesiod)," in her *Untersuchungen über die Griechischen Mythos* (Zurich: 1944), 7–42. For a discussion of recent scholarship: Patrick Amory, "The Meaning and Purpose of Ethnic Terminology in the Burgundian Laws," EME 2 (1993): 1–28; see 3. On ethnogenesis, see Walter Pohl, "Tradition, Ethnogenese und literarische Gestaltung: Eine Zwischenbilanz," in *Ethnogenese und Überlieferung,* 9–26.

25. On myths as "social representations" and the obscure border between myth and history, see Georges Dumézil, *Mitra–Varuna: An Essay on Two Indo-European Representations of Sovereignty,* trans. Derek Coltman (New York: 1988), 110.

26. Pétychaki-Henze, "Mythes politiques," 257.

27. Herwig Wolfram, *History of the Goths,* trans. T. J. Dunlap, 2nd ed. (Berkeley: 1988), 211–17; Werner, *Naissance de la noblesse,* 204–6.

28. Wallace-Hadrill, *Long-Haired Kings,* 84; Reinhard Wenskus, "Religion abâtardie," 181–88.

29. Alexander Callander Murray, "Post vocantur Merohingii: Fredegar, Merovech, and 'Sacral Kingship,'" in *After Rome's Fall,* 124–27; see also Wood, *Merovingian Kingdoms,* 37.

30. On dualism in political theologies (and on the concept of a political theology), see Assmann, *Herrschaft und Heil,* 15–28.

31. On the sceptre, see Ferdinand Joseph M. de Waele, *The Magic Staff or Rod in Graeco-Italian Antiquity* (Ghent: 1927); on the throne, H. U. Instinsky, *Bischofsstuhl und Kaiserthron* (Munich: 1955), 11–25; on the "purple": Heinke Stulz, *Die Farbe purpur im frühen Griechentum: Beobachtet in der Literatur und in der bildenden Kunst,* Beiträge zur Altertumskunde 6 (Stuttgart: 1990).

tremely long horizon of time.[32] Bishops insisted on their own unique and austere sources of authority and frequently called for the redirection and Christianisation of power.

The authority and explanatory power of this historical-theological myth were
not shared by Germanic kingship. Within their encompassing memory, bishops could frame well-developed ideas about the proper shape of society, which
included kings and gave them an important and stable role to play. It was a role
kings could play only in tandem with the "dignity of power" that bishops possessed and the law they wielded. Cooperation opened the prospect of integrating important aristocratic networks of sacred space and centers of social and
economic power under royal power. By the seventh century, success in warfare
remained a basic requirement, but increasingly the Merovingian kings could rely
on their ritual stature, at the center of exchanges of gifts, as a means of organizing space and rallying powerful men. The tendency of kings to make donations
to churches and to promote churchmen was another aspect of this polycentric
organization.[33]

Royal Law and Bishops' Law

In the late Empire, a theoretical gulf had opened between the competency
of the Christian emperors and their bishops. Only bishops could expound doctrine, and even emperors were thought to be subject to clerical discipline. The
local power of bishops came to rival that of imperial administrators, while the
church formed a cultural overlay with its own law.[34] Christian city dwellers
could choose to have their cases heard before an episcopal rather than imperial
court, and this became an increasingly common choice in the fifth century. In
essence, Christians could move between jurisdictions by laying claim to one or
another side of their identity. Bishops moved with ease between the official role
of judge and the informal role of mediator, based on the relationship between
the bishop and his church, but operating within a space opened by imperial law.[35]

The cultural stature of bishops was retained and expanded in the new king-

---

32. Werner suggests a vast comparative context: "L'histoire de nos institutions, malgré toute
la richesse de leurs diversités régionales, est donc européene, voire eurasienne"; Werner, *Naissance de la noblesse,* 113. A horizon of extreme antiquity is suggested by Assmann, *Herrschaft und
Heil,* 250–64.

33. Rosenwein, *Negotiating Space,* 23.

34. Tony Honoré, *Law in the Crisis of Empire, 379–455 A.D.: The Theodosian Dynasty and Its
Quaestors* (Oxford: 1998), 3–6.

35. Harries, *Law and Empire,* 191–211.

doms of Western Europe. With the further Christianization of Gaul, more bishoprics were created. There were more bishops, now drawn increasingly from the
ranks of the Frankish nobility.[36] Despite the shift in social background and cultural possibilities of its bishops, the Merovingian Church continued to maintain
traditions inherited from the Gallo-Roman Church, a continuity especially to
be seen in the preservation and recapitulation of old conciliar law, "renewing
the ancient canons." Bishops had a special mastery of law and were able to wield
imperial edicts, papal letters, and councils from across the Christian world, as
well as their own Gallic conciliar law.[37] The prestige of episcopal law and the
stature of bishops as the masters of law were to have a transformative impact on
the customary law of the Franks.

Clovis' baptism was soon followed by a publication of traditional Frankish
law, translated into Latin in the form of numbered *capitula* marked off with rubrics.[38] The *Pactus legis salicae* was in origin a body of custom, now presented
as a prestigious code of law, but still retaining pre-Christian elements. The first
part of the *Pactus* appears to document the regulation of the Franks by their
war chiefs during their existence as Roman military allies.[39] As Clovis' kingdom
expanded across Gaul, his power also unfolded in Latin documents, despite the
fact that this language did not have words for the many technical terms of Salic
law, such as the *Racemburgii,* judges whose function it was to "tell" the law.[40]

Yet another body of law must be taken into account: the Roman law that
still regulated those thought of as Roman, both in the Frankish and Visigothic

36. Heinzelmann, "L'aristocratie et les évêchés," 75–90; Wood, *Merovingian Kingdoms,* 102–19.
37. Stefan Esders, *Römische Rechtstradition und merowingische Königtum: Zum Rechtscharakter politischer Herrschaft in Burgund im 6. und 7. Jahrhundert,* Veröffentlichungen de Max-Planck-
Instituts für Geschichte 134 (Göttingen: 1997), 43.
38. *Lex Salica: 100 Titel Text,* ed. Karl August Eckhardt, *MGH Leg.* 4.2; see also Jean Marie Pardessus, *Loi salique ou recueil contenant les anciennes rédactions de cette loi et le texte connu
sous le nom de Lex emendata* (Paris: 1843), 67. Unlike Eckhardt, Pardessus published entire texts
with great care, rather than attempting to reconstruct an "original" that may never have existed.
On the contrast between the work of Pardessus and Eckhardt, see Ernst Andersen, *The Renaissance of Legal Science after the Middle Ages: The German Historical School no Bird Phoenix* (Copenhagen: 1974), 46–47.
39. Élisabeth Magnou-Nortier, "Remarques sur la genèse du *Pactus Legis Salicae* et sur le privilège d'immunité (IVe–VII siècles)," in *Clovis: Histoire et mémoire,* edited by Michel Rouche
(Paris: 1997), 1:495–538; in this sense, such law codes should not be viewed as "primitive": James,
Europe's Barbarians, 248.
40. "Si Racimburgi lege noluerint dicere in mallo residentes," Pardessus' "Fourth Text,"
Pardessus, *Loi salique,* 113–56; see 153; see also Ruth Schmidt-Wiegand, *Fränkische und franko-
lateinische Bezeichnungen für soziale Schichten und Gruppen in der Lex Salica,* Nachrichten der
Akademie der wissenschaften in Göttingen, philologisch-historische Klasse, Jahrg. 1972, no. 4
(Göttingen: 1972), 8.

kingdoms.[41] As was noted earlier, it was held that the church "lived by Roman law." The *Theodosian Code,* an imperial compilation developed by a scholarly collective working between 424 and 438, was widely circulated and its texts redeployed in many later legal texts. Based upon earlier private collections (the *Codex Gregorianus* and the *Codex Hermogenianus*), the *Theodosian Code* gathered laws of general, rather than regional, significance, in an effort to produce a unified law for the eastern and western Empires.[42] After the fall of the western Empire, this law continued to circulate, no longer backed up by imperial power, but possessing its own textual and methodical power, reflecting its continuing relevance to social organization. The study of law was maintained in Italy and Gaul throughout the fourth and fifth centuries, although increasingly only in the limited activity of individual scholars, as evidenced by the reception of the *Theodosian Code* compiled in 438 and commentaries made on it (*interpretationes*).[43] An example of legal scholarship in the late Empire is the *Summaria antiqua Codicis Theodosiani,* which Sirks dates between 465/467 and 474. This private collection was produced in Italy. The *Summaria* provided abbreviated versions of the laws contained in the *Theodosian Code,* with brief commentaries, while deliberately excluding other laws. One sign of the times is the interest of the author in distinctions between *Romani* and *barbari.*[44] The work is one example of a fifth-century Western trend in aquiring law and achieving intellectual mastery over it.

At the Council of Agde (506), the Visigoths created a code of Roman law adapted to life in their kingdom, which was later widely used in Gaul: the *Lex romana Visigothorum,* or *Breviary of Alaric,* compiled in about 506, with the assistance of aristocratic clerics of Roman culture.[45] The Burgundians likewise soon produced their *Lex romana Burgundionum,* which also cited the *Theodosian Code* at length, confirming the adage that codes travel easily.[46] Such com-

41. Ian Wood, "The Code in Merovingian Gaul," in *The Theodosian Code: Studies in the Imperial Law of Late Antiquity,* edited by Jill Harries and Ian Wood (London: 1993), 161–77; see 161.

42. Honoré, *Law in the Crisis,* 127–29; and Lupoi, *Origins of the European Legal Order,* 33.

43. From the late fifth century, there is also the *Veteris cuiusdam iurisconsulti consultatio:* Jolowicz, *Historical Introduction,* 472. Later the *Papianus* was created in Burgundy in about 502: Taylor, *Mediaeval Mind,* 2:271.

44. A. J. Boudewijn Sirks, "The Summaria Antiqua Codicis Theodosiani in the ms. Vat. Reg. Lat. 886," ZSRG.R 113 (1996): 243–67.

45. *Legis romanae Wisigothorum fragmenta ex codice palimpsesto sanctae legionenensis ecclesiae,* ed. Francisco de Cardeñas y Espejo (Madrid: 1896); Jean Heuclin, "Identité et rôle du clergé à l'époque du Bréviaire d'Alaric," in *Le Bréviaire d'Alaric: Aux origines du Code civil,* edited by Michel Rouche and Bruno Dumézil, 57–71 (Paris: 2008).

46. Wood, "The Code," 162–63. As Nicholas points out, codes travel easily: Barry Nicholas, *An Introduction to Roman Law* (Oxford: 1962), 52.

pendia of Roman law in turn influenced the Germanic customary law codes.[47] Gone were the traditions of legal reasoning and interpretation embedded in this law, and gone, too, was the dialectic between precedent and reform that had produced this law.[48] The *Lex romana Visigothorum* drew upon the Theodosian Code and post-Theodosian *novellae,* but excluded substantial sections of the Code relating to imperial officials, senatorial regulations, and other administrative matters of little relevance to the Visigothic kingdom.[49] Roman law had come to life in trial and dispute settlement, a complex and flexible interplay between legal norms, specific evidence, and pleading.[50] The laws were summarized and explained in simpler *Interpretationes,* drawing on the work of Gallic commentators of the late fifth century.[51]

The political and institutional context of Roman law had changed, but its continued textual power meant that it could still "come to life" in the barbarian kingdoms. The publication of Visigothic and Burgundian codes of Roman law may well reflect the effort of kings to accomodate their Gallo-Roman subjects, especially the bishops, who believed that their own law was Roman.[52] The *Breviary of Alaric* proclaims the authority of the king at the outset (*auctoritas Alarici regis*), but these were not his laws, as was clear from the carefully retained attribution of each title and *novella.* Nevertheless, according to the *Interpretationes* in the Visigothic code, the laws themselves command and instruct: "this

47. The Visigoths long continued to incorporate this law in later codes, such as that of Recceswinth in 654: Luis A. García Moreno, *Historia de España visigoda* (Madrid: 1989), 168–69. The *Lex romana Visigothorum* is also known as the "Breviary of Alaric." On the use of this code in Gaul, see Michael McCormick, "An Unknown Seventh-Century Manuscript of the Lex romana Visigothorum," *Bulletin of Medieval Canon Law,* New Series 6 (1976): 1–13; Katherine Fischer Drew, *The Laws of the Salian Franks* (Philadelphia: 1991), 22–23; an early version of the Breviary of Alaric was published under the care of the Cathedral of León, *Codigo de Alarico II: Fragmentos de la "Ley Romana" de los Visigodos conservados en un codice palimpsesto de la Catedral de Leon* (1896; repr. León: 1991); see also the useful survey in Hans Julius Wolff, *Roman Law: An Historical Introduction* (Norman: 1978), 174–76; and Mathisen, "D'Aire-sur l'Adour à Agde."

48. On the disappearance of jurists: Bellomo, *Common Legal Past,* 44–46; see also Lupoi, *Origins of the European Legal Order,* 37; Honoré, *Law in the Crisis,* 133; and Nicholas, *Introduction to Roman Law,* 28–31.

49. John F. Matthews, *Laying Down the Law: A Study of the Theodosian Code* (New Haven: 2000), 87–89.

50. Harries, *Law and Empire,* 96–98.

51. Lupoi, *Origins of the European Legal Order,* 76; Peter Stein, *Roman Law in European History* (Cambridge: 1999), 31–32.

52. See this volume, chapter 2, n. 173; "Legem Romanam, quam ecclesia vivit" (61.1), *Lex Ribuaria,* ed. F. Beyerle and R. Büchner, MGH Leges 3.2:109. The expression is often wrongly cited, perhaps following Taylor: "The Church lives according to Roman law" ("Ecclesia vivit lege Romana"): see, for example, Dafydd Walters, "From Benedict to Gratian: The Code in Medieval Ecclesiastical Authors," in *The Theodosian Code: Studies,* 200–16; see 200; on this theme see also Wallace-Hadrill, *Long-Haired Kings,* 37–41.

law especially commands."[53] Roman law, with its impressive language ringing with command and authority, was accepted as a valuable legal inheritance: it was accepted as good law, without any reference to an enforcing power or to zones of competence or "jurisdiction."

In the Frankish kingdom, as in the Visigothic kingdom, each "people" possessed its own law. When a Roman faced a Frank in a legal dispute, each could insist on being judged by his law, a principle that was restricted only in the early seventh century.[54] In a major reassessment of this familiar concept, Maurizio Lupoi has recently emphasized the manifold versions of this rule in early medieval kingdoms: "personality of law" was no primeval archetype, but rather a mere tendency, subject to wide regional variation.[55] Despite the diversity that Lupoi has uncovered, it remains true that among the Franks and Visigoths, law was an important marker of cultural identity as a body of custom that tied a people to its ancient and mythic origins and that distinguished them from other peoples, in particular from the Romans. Thus customary law, as part of a people's story of origins (*origo gentis*), was sacralized, intimately tied to a mythic story of origins.[56] The telling or remembering of the law, usually at an annual assembly, was thought to be in the hands of old wise men, guardians of a traditional lore, conceived of, in Fritz Kern's famous phrase, as "good old law."[57] As Janet L. Nelson has observed, in view of the actual flexibility of this law in practice, we should recognize that "Kern's ritualistic and unchanging medieval law . . . is a myth."[58] It remains true, however, that ceremonies of legal memory always harkened back to the period of ethnogenesis, to the original creation of a social identity, and such law therefore always adopted the patina of great antiquity.[59]

53. "Haec lex specialiter jubet" 1.3, Interp.: Cardeñas y Espejo, *Legis romanae Wisigothorum*, 249; "Haec lex hoc praecipit" 12.6, Interp., 215.

54. The classic statement of legal "personality": Paul Vinogradoff, *Roman Law in Mediaeval Europe* (London: 1909), 15–18; now see Luisa Pelliciari, *Sulla natura giuridica*, 46–47. Recourse of the *Romani* to Roman law was curtailed in a law of Clothar II: "Inter Romanus negutia causarum romanis legebus praecepemus terminari" (4), *Praeceptio Chlotharii*, edition in Esders, *Römische Rechtstradition*, 82; see also Wood, *Merovingian Kingdoms*, 114.

55. Lupoi, *Origins of the European Legal Order*, 388–405.

56. Karol Modzelewski, "*Legem ipsam vetare non possumus*: Il re codificatore dinanzi alla forza della consuetudine," *Bulletino dell'Istituto storico italiano per il Medio Evo* 101 (1997–1998): 1–12; on sacralized custom, see esp. 3.

57. "Gutes altes Recht": Fritz Kern, "Recht und Verfassung im Mittelalter," HZ 120 (1919): 1–79.

58. Janet L. Nelson, "On the Limits of the Carolingian Renaissance," in *Politics and Ritual*, 49–67; this quote, 62, in reference to a once-influential work: Fritz Kern, *Kingship and Law in the Middle Ages*, trans. S. Chrimes (Oxford: 1939).

59. Rothar's Edict, a promulgation of Lombard law made in about 643, associated the law with

The publication of Frankish and Burgundian customary law in Latin reflects their entry into a legal universe that included many other bodies of law—all having a claim to antiquity, and all offering a means of giving legal expression to one side or another of a person's social identity: Roman law, barbarian Roman law codes, barbarian customary codes, and episcopal law. The way in which these many laws circulated shows a certain longing for law and for gathering up legal documents in a locale. Certain places, most notably Lyon, became centers of legal study and compilation.[60]

Kings tried to associate themselves with law. Its publication in Latin represented a royal seizure of the law, with the aid of episcopal advisors and its presentation as a royal accoutrement, with symbolic or ritual significance.[61] Like the publication of codes of Roman law, such promulgations under royal authority can be viewed as emblems of the king's prestige, like his long hair, seal-ring, and spear.[62] It is possible to view a law code as a royal gift, but a dubious one. The king presented law but did not legislate. Unlike its original issuance, it did not descend from royal power, and the king had an anomalous role in all of this. There was an important distinction to be drawn between all these law codes, on the one hand, and episcopal law, on the other. Conciliar law was the result of legislation by men with a special prerogative to make law, drawing on all its ancient connotations of deep regionalism and elite collegiality.

Four points can be made about this complex legal universe:

First: law codes like the *Lex salica* or the *Lex ribuaria* were not *official*. This is reflected in the fact that the *Lex Salica* was not carefully preserved in the Merovingian period. Likewise, the vulgar Roman law codes and the *Theodosian Code* no longer radiated the legal omnipresence of imperial authority. They no longer had sharp teeth—but by means of these codes, Frankish, Burgundian, and Visigothic kings could be seen as gatherers and providers of law.

Second: the codes were maintained by *erudition*. By and large, it was bishops

---

a story of Lombard origins, a list of kings, and the lineage of Rothar himself; *Le leggi dei Longobardi: Storia, memoria e diritto di un popolo germanico,* ed. Claudio Azzara and Stefano Gasparri, Le Fonti 1 (Milan: 1992), 2–9; see also Modzelewski, *"Legem ipsam vetare,"* 7.

60. Wood, "The Code," 163–65.

61. Hubert Mordek, "Kapitularien und Schriftlichkeit," in *Schriftkultur und Reichsverwaltung unter den Karolingern: Referate des Kolloquium der Nordrhein-Westfälischen Akademie der Wissenschaften am 17./18. Februar 1994 in Bonn,* edited by Rudolf Schieffer, Abhandlungen der Nordrhein-Westfälischen Akademie der Wissenschaften 97 (Opladen: 1995), 34–66; see 36.

62. Wolfgang Sellert, "Aufzeichnung des Rechts und Gesetz," in *Das Gesetz in Spätantike und Frühen Mittelalter,* 67–102; see 75–76.

who collected and preserved law of every kind through a "tradition savante."[63]
The law codes thus functioned with textual power as genuine sources of law,
cheek by jowl with other bodies of law, including custom and oral law. They
were in the hands of the learned, but came to life in the resolution of conflicts.

Third: these bodies of law were not *directive*. The various bodies of written
law functioned together and in a complex and layered arena of dispute resolution. The laws functioned as rules, but not as commands. Overhead was a constellation of many stars that might shine on the actions of a single problem:
memory, custom, informal claims, and traditional procedures, as well as several written codes of law that might prove relevant to the particular case.[64] The
normativity of the law was muted in this sense, yet it had the cachet of ancient
holy writ.

Fourth: the collection and maintainance of all these written codes reflect an
episcopal preoccupation with law, reflecting the belief of bishops that they had
a special mandate to bring old law to bear on modern griefs. Codes of royal law,
like collections of canon law, conveyed the idea that social order could be shaped
and preserved by established legal order.

The *Lex salica,* perhaps issued by Clovis and often reissued thereafter, was
thought of as the law of the Salian Franks (i.e., not of all the Franks). The law
was thought of as a "pact" defining and binding a particular people.[65] The Ribuarian Franks had their own code, as did the Burgundians and other peoples
within the kingdom.[66] Bishops, on the other hand, believed their law extended
to the "people," the "Catholic people," or the "Christian people."[67] Bishops were
delighted to have the aid of Catholic kings in governing, but their stature as governors over that vast society did not derive from those kings. When bishops pro-

---

63. Jean Gaudemet, "Survivances romaines," 149–206: see 158–59.

64. The point is made succinctly by Paul Fouracre, *The Age of Charles Martel* (Harlow: 2000),
23–24: see also his "'Placita' and the Settlement of Disputes in Later Merovingian Francia," in
The Settlement of Disputes in Early Medieval Europe, edited by W. Davies and Paul Fouracre
(Cambridge: 1986), 23–43.

65. This code was variously called the "Capitula in pacto salicae," Pardessus, *Loi salique,* 195;
"Lex Zalica," Pardessus, *Loi salique,* 195; "Pactus legis salicae," Pardessus, *Loi salique, 226;* see
also Jean Pétrau-Gay, *La notion de "lex" dans la coutume salienne et ses transformations dans les
capitulaires* (Grenoble: 1920), 108–11; see also Magnou-Nortier, "Remarques sur la genèse," 504–6.

66. *Lex Ribuaria,* ed. F. Beyerle and R. Büchner, *MGH Leges,* 3.2; see also *Lex Ribuaria,* in
Die Gesetze des Karolingerreiches, 714–911, edited by Karl August Eckhardt, Schriften der Akademie für Deutsches Recht, Gruppe V: Rechtsgeschichte; Germanenrechte, Texte und Ubersetzungen (Weimar: 1934), 1:137–207.

67. "Ne Iudaei Christianis populis iudices deputentur," Council of Mâcon (581–583), CCSL
148A:226.

claimed: "With God's help we take our place under the dominion of Catholic kings," their grammatical *we* did not include those kings.[68]

The legal activity of Frankish kings began to dovetail with the interests of their bishops and to adopt forms and vocabulary of the law-codes that bishops preserved and mastered. Indeed, the first legislative act that can be associated with a Frankish king is an act of Clovis, associated with the Council of Orléans in 511.[69] The occasion was similar to Adge (506) in providing new sources of legitimacy to kingship. This was the first Frankish synod, called by King Clovis to deal with ecclesiastical matters in the wake of his conquest of Visigothic Gaul. The power of legislation was a major addition to the concept of kingship, drawing upon conciliar and Roman models.[70] The bishops, many of them from sees in Aquitaine, were especially concerned to protect the property of their churches in the new regime.[71] Beginning with Clovis, the Merovingians legislated under their own authority, at times in concert with bishops' councils that gathered under their protection. The concerns of early Merovingian legislation were dominated by old episcopal preoccupations and their language. Childebert I (511–558), for example, published a circular throughout his realm condemning the persistence of pagan practices such as the making of "likenesses" or "images" (*simulacra*) and idols "dedicated to a demon." The vocabulary of this law was similar to biblical texts deployed in the *Histories* of Childebert's contemporary, Gregory of Tours, which suggests an episcopal atmosphere.[72]

The Council of Macon, held sometime between 581 and 583 under the direction of Bishop Priscus of Lyon, stressed discipline and decorum. The council

68. "Quia Deo propitio sub catholicorum regum dominatione consistimus," Council of Orléans (538), CCSL 148A:126.

69. Esders, *Römische Rechtstradition*, 46. Dierkens believes that Clovis here tried to play the part of a Roman emperor: Alain Dierkens, "Christianisme et 'paganisme' dans la Gaule septentrionale aux Ve et VIe siècles," in *Die Franken und die Alemannen bis zur "Schlacht bei Zülpich" (496/97)*, edited by Dieter Geuenich, 457, Ergänzungsbände zum Reallexikon der germanischen Altertumskunde 19 (Berlin: 1998).

70. Wood, *Merovingian Kingdoms*, 107–8.

71. Council of Orléans (511) CCL 148A:3–19; on the property concerns of the Aquitainian bishops, see Wallace-Hadrill, *Frankish Church*, 95; Wood, *Merovingian Kingdoms*, 48; and Maassen, *Geschichte der Quellen*, 204.

72. "Ubicumque fuerint simulacra constructa vel idola daemoni dedicata," *Childeberti I regis praeceptum* (511–558), MGH Cap I.1, 2–3. There is a parallel with two Psalm verses assembled by Gregory on this theme: "Quia omnes dii gentium daemonia, Dominus autem caelos fecit?" (Ps 96 [Vulg. 95]:5); and "Simulacra gentium argentum et aurum, opera manuum hominum" (Ps. 135 [Vulg. 134]:15): (2.10); Gregory, *Libri historiarum*, 59. On the tradition-context of this law in the *Codex Corbeiensis*, see Esders, *Römische Rechtstradition*, 46; see also Wallace-Hadrill, *Frankish Church*, 96.

highlighted the distinction of clerics from laymen in their manner of dress and denounced any attempt to bring a cleric before a secular law court.[73] The council drew on the *Theodosian Code* as well as the edict of Childebert I, and may have had a hand in preserving the *Collectio Sirmondiana,* an ancient little compendium of law used by the compilers of the *Theodosian Code.*[74] Lyon was a city with a strong legal tradition. The cooperation of King Childebert with Priscus and other bishops of his kingdom was expressed in legal activity.

King Guntram (561–592)[75] also urged the bishops of his kingdom to destroy pagan shrines in an edict of 585. What is so striking about the *Edict of King Guntram* is not merely the preoccupation of royal legislation with episcopal concerns, but the mutual expression of episcopal and royal power.[76] The "sacrosanct bishops, to whom divine clemency gave over the office of paternal power," were paired with the king, to whom "the authority of the celestial King had committed the capacity of ruling."[77] This is an important early statement of *utraque lex.*[78]

The royal doctrine of the Merovingian councils introduced themes similar to the political ideas of Pope Gelasius (492–496).[79] Gelasius, in an influential phrase, contrasted royal and priestly spheres of activity: "There are two powers by which this world is principally ruled," said Gelasius, "the sacred authority of bishops and royal power, of which the authority of bishops is so much weightier because they will have to answer even for kings themselves to the Heavenly Lord."[80] Gelasius thus contrasted not only kings and bishops, but also authority and power.

73. Council of Mâcon (581–583), CCSL 148A:222–30.

74. Translation in *The Theodosian Code and Novels and the Sirmondian Constitutions,* trans. Clyde Pharr, The Corpus of Roman Law (Corpus Juris Romani), vol. 1 (Princeton: 1952), 477–87. See discussion in Mark Vessey, "The Origins of the *Collectio Sirmondiana:* A New Look at the Evidence," in *Theodosian Code: Studies,* 178–99. See further on the *Collectio Sirmondiana* (also known as the *Constitutiones Sirmondianae*): Kéry, *Canonical Collections,* 5–6.

75. J. R. Martindale, *The Prosopography of the Later Roman Empire,* vol. 3a (Cambridge: 1992), 568–71.

76. "If we find it hard to square this sense of divine mission with a good Merovingian career in the field of vendetta, the fault may be ours, not his"; Wallace-Hadrill, *Long-Haired Kings,* 201.

77. "Sacrosancti pontifices, quibus divina clementia potestatis paternae concessit officium," and later, "nos, quibus facultatem regnandi superni regis commisit auctoritas," *Guntchramni regis edictum* (585), MGH Cap 1.1:10–12; see 11.

78. Lupoi, *Origins of the European Legal Order,* 249.

79. Jean Heuclin, "Le concile d'Orléans de 511, un premier concordat?" in *Clovis,* 1:435–50; esp. 434–36.

80. "Duo quippe sunt . . . quibus principaliter mundus hic regitur: auctoritas sacra pontificum et regalis potestas, in quibus tanto gravius est pondus sacerdotum quanto etiam pro ipsis regibus Domino in divino reddituri sunt examine rationem," PL 59:42, as cited in Arquillière,

In the *Edict of Guntram,* however, the terms of this relation were reversed: it was bishops to whom power was conceded, and the king who claimed authority. This "confusion" was possible because bishops and kings in the Frankish realms thought about royal and episcopal power in terms of mutuality and parallelism, a conceptual "cross-entry."[81] In the terms of the *Edict,* the king undertook to help his sacrosanct and apostolic bishops (*sacrosancti/apostolici pontifices*) to exercise their power of governing and correcting (*corrigere*) Frankish society.[82] The need for royal and episcopal cooperation was shown by many signs of divine anger: storms and the death of men and cattle due to illness or the violence of war.[83] Who had noticed and pointed out this divine anger? The *Edict* reveals that kings were listening to highly placed clerical advisers. Upon his death, Guntram was buried in the Church of St. Marcellinus, which he had built in Chalon-sur-Saône.[84]

Kings offered their own legislative efforts within this complex constellation of laws without any nativist sensibility. Toward the end of his life, Childebert II (575–596) issued a law at an assembly of his kingdom's great men (*optimates*), the annual Marchfeld. Childibert's *Decretum* is revealing because of the flexibility with which it drew upon Burgundian law and its Roman antecedents.[85] Like his bishops, this king was open to the gathering, acceptance, and redeployment of old law.

In 614, Chlothar II (584–629) reissued many of the canons of the Council of Paris, held a week earlier, as royal law. Only the wording was slightly different.[86] The setting was a major council of bishops, followed by a grand assembly of the nobility. Among other strictures, the council endeavored to shelter clerics from secular justice. The precept, requiring permission of the bishop before a cleric could be judged outside of the church, was confirmed by the assembly

L'Augustinisme politique, 71, n. 3; see also Walter Ullmann, *Gelasius I (492–496): Das Papsttum an der Wende der Spätantike zum Mittelalter,* Päpste und Papsttum 18 (Stuttgart: 1981), 199–206; A. K. Ziegler, "Pope Gelasius I and His Teaching on the Relation of Church and State," *Catholic Historical Review* 27 (1942): 412–37; see also Georges Duby, *The Three Orders: Feudal Society Imagined,* trans. Arthur Goldhammer (Chicago: 1980), 77–78.

81. "*Umbuchung*" is Jan Assmann's phrase, in his discussion of the creation of a sacralized royal doctrine in ancient Israel: *Herrschaft und Heil,* 50.

82. "Frequenti praedicatione studeatis corrigere et pastorali studio gubernare," *Guntchramni regis edictum,* 11.

83. "Et ex hoc procul dubio indignatione coelesti per diversas seculi tempestates homines ac pecora aut morbo consumi cenentur aut gladio," *Guntchramni regis edictum,* 11.

84. Martindale, *Prosopography,* 571.

85. *Childeberti secundi Decretio* (594–596), MGH Cap 1.1:15–17; discussion in Wood, "The Code," 173–74.

86. *Chlotharii II edictum* (614), MGH Cap 1.1:20–23.

of nobles and issued in an edict of the king.[87] This was an exceptional council, perhaps the greatest of the Merovingian period, gathering seventy-nine bishops (including twelve metropolitans) from across Gaul, including Aridius of Lyon and Florianus of Arles, whose old conciliar cities were now eclipsed by the prestige of Paris as a royal center.[88] The council coordinated the ancient networks and sacred landscapes of Provence with emerging northern centers and Frankish strongholds. The council announced the significance of ancient law in the self-authenticating mode of recapitulation. Chlothar also believed that divine favor would flow from his support for the bishops and bring about the happiness of the kingdom.[89] The council marked his unification of the Frankish kingdoms, which he ruled until his death in 629.[90] The coordination of royal and episcopal law was momentous: royal law gained prestige from the setting of a council, while conciliar law gained stature and force from royal promulgation. Royal and episcopal power took the ideal form of a diarchy.

Merovingian bishops, heirs of Gallo-Roman aristocratic sensibility and administrative ability, built up centers of power that competed effectively with royal centers. A patrimony (*patriarcha*) was attached to the bishop's office to support the bishop and his clergy and to provide for the continuance of cultic observance. This *patriarcha* was under his direct control.[91] Some bishops carved out extensive and independent domains.[92] But these privileges and estates were a strong reason for cooperation with royal power.[93] Friedrich Prinz argued that Gallo-Roman bishops were essentially equivalent to the senatorial class, and that this aristocratic episcopacy was gradually taken over by the Frankish nobility in the Merovingian era.[94]

A more nuanced and complete perspective on this debate is offered by Bernhard Jussen, who argues that episcopal power after 400 reflected a new situation and a broader cultural transformation as the Gallic aristocracy searched for new forms of legitimation. In order to understand this transformation, one

---

87. Godding, *Prêtres en Gaule*, 322–23.

88. The Council of Paris (614), CCSL 148A:274–85; Pontal, *Histoire des conciles mérovingiens*, 205–11.

89. "Felicitatem regni nostri," *Chlotharii II edictum*, 20.

90. Wallace-Hadrill, *Frankish Church*, 104; Martindale, *Prosopography*, 300–1.

91. F. Cardot, *L'Espace et le pouvoir*, 151–52.

92. Werner, "La place du VIIe siècle dans l'évolution politique," 186–87.

93. Reinhold Kaiser, "Bistumsgründungen im Merowingerreich im 6. Jahrhundert," in *Beiträge zur Geschichte des Regnum Francorum: Proceedings of a Colloquium for the 75th Birthday of Eugen Ewig 28 May 1988,* edited by R. Schieffer, 9–35 (Sigmaringen: 1990).

94. This is argued by Friedrich Prinz in his "Aristocracy and Christianity," 153–65; and in his "Die bischöfliche Stadtherrschaft," 1–35. In contrast, Durliat, "Les attributions civiles," 237–54.

must examine the new symbolic modes of action and new form of thought that emerged in the relations among bishops, nobility, and kings.[95]

Bishops were endowed with a prestige that derived, in part, from the beneficial effect they could offer their society, combining governmental authority with religious potency.[96] Bishops built up estates that kings could only envy, giving rise to the well-known complaint of King Chilperic: that ecclesiastical estates were so large that "only bishops rule nowadays."[97] This peculiar saying reveals a new pattern of cultural meaning in which bishops were prominent.

Merovingian Councils and Kingship

During the course of the seventh century, despite the fact that episcopal and royal power often clashed, especially over these very estates, bishops had begun to think about royal power in a different way. Kings relied on bishops to give institutional and structural shape to their kingdoms.[98] Bishops, for their part, relied on royal support to hold their councils.[99] Kings selected men with legal expertise, such as Priscus of Lyon, as bishops and councillors. Childeric II was aided in his legal reforms by Leodgar, and it was Leodgar's legal training, in turn, that suited him to become bishop of Autun.[100] Councils became the setting for compilations of Roman and customary Germanic law. In the meantime, royal legislation was subtly transformed in line with conciliar law. Bishops saw their legislation as the religiously sanctioned activity of a holy order of men, to be fostered and protected by good kings. Conciliar legislation was potent, and kings sought an association with it—here we can see a desire on the part of kings to gain a protective and benevolent role.

This was portrayed in the liturgical arrangement and etiquette of a council. The most influential liturgical order for the celebration of councils was that of Isidore, known and adopted by Frankish bishops from the canon law collection known as the *Hispana Gallicana*.[101] The bishops entered the church in order of

95. Jussen, "Über 'Bischofsherrschaften,'" 673–718; see summary discussion in Patzold, *Episcopus*, 26.

96. Friedrich Prinz, "Der fränkische Episkopat zwischen Merowinger- und Karolingerzeit," *Settimane* 27 (1981): 1:102–33; 110–11.

97. Prinz, "Der fränkische Episkopat," 110; "only kings rule": Wallace-Hadrill, *Frankish Church*, 124.

98. Pontal, *Histoire des conciles mérovingiens*, 251–52.

99. Wood, *Merovingian Kingdoms*, 105.

100. Wood, "The Code," 167–69.

101. Charles Munier, "L'Ordo *De celebrando concilio* wisigothique," *Revue des sciences religieuses* 37 (1963): 250–71, which is cited here. Munier's text of the *Ordo* was reprinted in PL *Supplementum*, vol. 4 (Paris: 1969), col. 1865–1876. On the *Hispana Gallicana:* Hans Barion, *Das*

their date of ordination, elders first, reflecting a principle of rank and precedence similar to that of Pachomian and Benedictine monasticism.[102] Then came the presbyters and deacons. The bishops took their seats in a circle (*corona facta*), their clerics ranged behind them. The archdeacon of the church called the clerics to pray, at first silently, "with weeping and groans." The bishops then rose to pray aloud, after which all the clerics threw themselves to the earth at the moment their prayers were answered by the awesome influx of the Holy Spirit, who is always present "where two or three are gathered in my name."[103] After praying for help, a series of the church's most ancient canons were read aloud, establishing the norms of all conciliar action by invoking the six ecumenical councils. The ritual of the council was a *tableau vivant* depicting a social order that also expressed firm adherence to a sacred past.

Only then did the king enter with his nobles, as the clerics began another series of prayers for the aid of their king. At this point everyone who had come to attend the council entered to hear the business proceed. The legislation of a council was arrived at by unanimous vote, a unanimity that itself was a sign of divine inspiration.[104] At the conclusion, the council's decisions were read publicly, and the council ended with further prayers for the bishops.[105] Episcopal councils were the most interesting, potentially successful, and liturgically grand events in which kings could participate. Kings were offered a lofty role they could play only in concert with bishops. The legislation of such councils records the social doctrine of an active, cohesive elite, eager to shape society.[106]

Merovingian kings took on the responsibility for convoking councils, and this was one aspect of a growing partnership between royal and episcopal power.[107] Bishops believed in their capacity to govern, despite the fact that Merovingian kings began to intervene in episcopal elections.[108] Like their kings, bishops

---

fränkisch-deutsche Synodalrecht, 55–110; Jacques Merlin, *Conciliorum quatuor generalium Niceni, Constantinopolitani, Ephesini, et Calcedonensis* (Cologne: 1530), 1:fol. 1a–1b.

102. Terrence G. Kardong, "Benedict's Insistence on Rank in the Monastic Community: RB 63:1–9 in Context," *Cistercian Studies Quarterly* 42 (2007): 243–65.

103. Munier, "L'Ordo *De celebrando concilio,*" 265–66.

104. Barion, *Fränkisch-deutsche Synodalrecht,* 99.

105. Munier, "L'Ordo *De celebrando concilio,*" 268–71.

106. Gabriel Le Bras, *Introduction à l'histoire de la pratique religieuse en France* (Paris: 1942–1945) 1:32–33; Wallace-Hadrill, *Frankish Church,* 108–9.

107. Reinhold Kaiser, "Royauté et pouvoir épiscopal au nord de la Gaule (VIIe–IXe siècles)," in *La Neustrie: Les pays au nord de la Loire de 650 à 850,* edited by Hartmut Atsma, 1:143–60, Beihefte der Francia 16 (Sigmaringen: 1989); see 145–50.

108. On disputed elections in Clermont, and royal pressure: Wood, "Ecclesiastical Politics of Merovingian Clermont," in *Ideal and Reality,* 34–57.

"ruled."[109] The relation between the king and his bishops was not that of a master and his followers. Although bishops had to take note of the king's will (*voluntas regis*), conflicts between kings and bishops were typically complex, involving negotiation and posturing.[110] One example is the important council held in Orléans in 511, in the last year of Clovis' life and only a few years after his conversion to Christianity and Catholicism.[111] The council was clearly a long-delayed reply to the initiative of King Theodoric at Agde (506). The council record begins with a letter to the king, whose conversion seemed to offer an important new vista to the bishops of his kingdom:

To their lord Clovis, son of the Catholic church, the most glorious king; from all the bishops whom you bid come to the council. You, who with so much concern for the cultivation of the glorious faith of the Catholic religion will have bid the bishops gather, as one assembly instilled with a priestly mind, to treat of needful matters; we respond by pronouncement what seemed best to us, according to your will, consultation, and the titles you gave us.[112]

The bishops went on to legislate about homicide, kidnap, criminal clerics, and the conversion of heretics, as usual by "renewing the ancient canons."[113] Seated among his bishops, the warrior Clovis could play the role of adviser to a council, which replied to the king's requests with its canons.[114] Such statements reveal the conceptualization of a relation between king and council. It is unlikely that Clovis drew up this list of "titles." Rather, the letter reveals the coopera-

109. Albert Hauck, *Die Bischofswahlen unter den Merovingern* (Erlangen: 1883), 1–19. The length of a bishop's term was called the time when he ruled (*rexit*): Louis Duchesne, *Fastes épiscopaux,* 1:189; see also "[Agilmarius] qui rexit ecclesiam suam," Duchesne, *Fastes épiscopaux,* 1:201. In the case of a "joint appointment," "rexeruntque ecclesiam Turonicam simul annis duobus et sepulti sunt in basilica sancti Martini" (10.31), Gregory of Tours, *Libri historiarum,* 532.

110. *Voluntas regis:* Wood, "Ecclesiastical Politics," 42. Royal initiative was fundamental to conciliar activity: Wood, *Merovingian Kingdoms,* 105.

111. Heuclin, "Concile d'Orléans," 435–38.

112. "Domno suo catholicae ecclesiae filio Chlothouecho gloriosissimo regi omnes sacerdotes, quos ad concilium uenire iussistis. Qui tanta ad religionis catholicae cultum gloriosae fidei cura uos excitat, ut sacerdotalis mentis affectum sacerdotes de rebus necessariis tractaturos in unum collegi iusseritis, secundum uoluntates uestrae consultationem et titulos, quos dedistis, ea quae nobis uisum est definitione respondimus," Council of Orléans (511), CCSL 148A:4.

113. "Antiquos canones religentes priora statua crededimus renouanda," Council of Orléans (511), CCSL 148A:9.

114. Hubert Mordek, "Karolingische Kapitularien," in *Überlieferung und Geltung normativer Texte des frühen und hohen Mittelalters: Vier Vorträge, gehalten auf dem 35. Deutschen Historikertag 1984 in Berlin,* edited by Hubert Mordek, Quellen und Forschungen zum Recht im Mittelalter 4 (Sigmaringen: 1986), 25–50; see 28.

tion of the king and his episcopal advisors.[115] The councils gave kings a religious role to play.[116]

Sigismund, the Burgundian king, came to the throne in 516 soon after his conversion to Catholicism.[117] Seeking recognition from Byzantium, he seemed to think of his kingdom as "an old-style federated regnum," and he wrote letters to the emperor proclaiming the obedience of himself and his people to the Empire.[118] The bishops saw his conversion as the inauguration of a new Catholic kingdom. As in the case of Clovis, the bishops again reacted to these events by staging a major council. Led by Avitus, bishop of Vienne, twenty-four bishops gathered at Epaon in 517.[119] Avitus (†518), ascetic master and poet, was a man who specialized in royal conversions and had seen the baptism of the Frankish king Clovis as the opening of a new, victorious period for Catholicism.[120] Sigismund's Catholicism allowed the Burgundian bishops to contemplate a complete integration of the kingdom in accordance with their ideals: they dreamed of uprooting the Arian Church once and for all.[121] The bishops were again ready to pounce on the opportunity offered by a strong and Catholic king. Thus three councils, Agde (506), Orléans (511), and Epaon (517), sealed the alliance of the episcopal echelons of Gaul with their new barbarian rulers, Visigothic, Frankish, and Burgundian. When Sigismund fell into the hands of his enemy, the Frankish King Chlodomer, Bishop Avitus negotiated to save the king's life, but to no avail. Sigismund and his family were thrown into a well.[122]

A more exceptional case is that of the Frankish King Theodebert I, who cooperated with the bishops of his realm in an unprecedented way, allowing them to dominate the tenor of his court and to direct his policies concerning ecclesiastical affairs.[123] At a council held in Clermont in 535, this happy turn of events led the bishops to offer a lesson on the nature of power and the social order:

---

115. Heuclin, "Concile d'Orléans," 438.

116. For Angenendt, this amounted to sacralized kingship: argued extensively in Arnold Angenendt, "Princeps imperii." On Clovis' conversion: Orlandis, *Conversión de Europa,* 67–73.

117. Ian Wood, "Kings, Kingdoms and Consent," in *Early Medieval Kingship,* edited by P. H. Sawyer and I. N. Wood, 6–29; see 22 (Leeds: 1979); and Wood, *Merovingian Kingdoms,* 51–52.

118. Wolfram, *The Roman Empire,* 256.

119. On Avitus' life and writings, see Altaner, *Patrologie,* 426–29.

120. Wood, *Merovingian Kingdoms,* 43–44; Wallace-Hadrill, *Long-Haired Kings,* 171; Franz Brunhölzl, *Histoire de la littérature latine du moyen âge;* trans. Henri Rochais (Turnhout: 1990–1996), 1:116 and 145.

121. Council of Epaon (517), CCSL 148A:33.

122. "Statimque interfecto Sigimundo cum uxore et filiis, apud Colomnam Aurilianinsim urbis vicum in puteum iactare praecipiens" (3.6), Gregory, *Libri historiarum,* 102.

123. Roger Collins, "Theodebert I, 'Rex Magnus Francorum,'" in *Ideal and Reality,* 7–33; Breukelaar, *Historiography and Episcopal Authority,* 231–33.

When the holy synod had convened in the city of Clermont, in the name of the Lord, gathering in the Holy Spirit, with the accord of our most glorious and pious King Theodobert, we there bent our knees to the earth and prayed to the Lord for his reign, longevity, and for the people; so that our Lord might bring felicity to the kingdom; that he might grant us, assembled, power that may rule the *imperium,* and direct justice, sitting with us in the church, as is customary.[124]

Royal power protected the bishops and allowed them to gather: the bishops' power, inspired by the Holy Spirit, could call down the blessing of the Lord to protect the kingdom and the king himself. Their prayers could, moreover, suggest how a king should govern. At Clermont, king and bishop sat together in harmony and, more importantly, were seen to govern together. One distinction remained firm: the Holy Spirit descended on bishops alone. The Christianization of royal power arose from this otherworldly source.

Similarly, when bishops assembled in Arles in 549 to "revive the ancient canons" and establish the "norm of living," King Childebert I was cloyingly termed "the most clement prince, unconquered lord, endowed with triumphs."[125] At Paris in 552, he was simply "most glorious" as he took his seat among the bishops.[126] Indeed, Childebert was that *rara avis,* a Frankish king who died in bed. Nevertheless, in every case the bishops made clear, as they did in Tours in 567, that it was they who assembled to govern the church, though with the protection and encouragement of the king sitting with them, in this case Charibert I, the adulterous king of Paris.[127]

By the seventh century, as Wallace-Hadrill noted, a new phase had opened in the history of Germanic kingship as royal power came to be viewed as a good part of the Christian order of society.[128] The promotion of justice and the protection of councils and cooperation with episcopal advisors had already begun to connect these kings to their bishops. Civilized power was reclaimed by the assertion of legality.

124. "Cum in nomine Domini congregante sancto Spiritu, consentiente domno nostro gloriosissimo piissimoue regi Theudebertho in Aruerna urbe sancta synodus conuenisset, ibique flexis in terram genibus pro regno eius, pro longeuitate, pro populo Dominum depraecaremur, ut, qui nobis congragationis tribuerat potestatem, regnum eius Dominus noster felicitatem attolleret, imperio regeret, iustitiam gubernaret, in ecclesiam cumsedentes ex more," Council of Clermont (535), CCSL 148A:105.

125. "Clementissimus princeps domnus triumphorum titulis inuictissimus Childeberthus rex," Council of Orléans (549), CCSL 148A:148.

126. "Domini regis gloriosissimi Childiberthi," Council of Paris (552), CCSL 148A:167.

127. "In Toronica ciuitate consilio concordante iuxta coniuentiam gloriosissimi domni Chariberthi regis adnuentis coadunati," Council of Tours (567), CCSL 148A:176. On Charibert's adultery and excommunication, see Wood, *Merovingian Kingdoms,* 73.

128. Wallace-Hadrill, *Early Germanic Kingship,* 47–48.

The Council of Clichy, in about 626, poured out their praises on King Clothar, who had called his bishops to this suburb of Paris.[129] Clothar was called a "glorious" and "pious" king, who had commanded the bishops gather "to treat of the rules of canons." He commanded this to "arrange whatever was necessary for the status of the Church" and for the "peace of the Church."[130] In so doing, the bishops declared, Clothar was "governing, just like David, the empire of the kingdom," and fulfilling a "prophetic ministry."[131] Clothar was like David because he had gathered a great synod to preserve the ancient canons.[132] Historians have been fascinated by the application of biblical titles to the Frankish kings. David, the anointed king and poet of the Psalms, possessed the powers of priest and king. Less well-known is that bishops had long believed that they were also like David.[133] In applying this title to a Frankish king, the bishops were draping his figure with their own special terminology of power, developing this possibility from a historical reflection.

Bishops believed they could embrace kingship in the Frankish kingdoms if only these kings would foster the work of episcopal councils. They were prepared to redirect their vocabulary of power, and their own titles, to accommodate such kings. Such kings were rare, however, and they were not always very significant. In contrast to this leitmotif of royal-episcopal accommodation was probably the reign of Dagobert I (623–639), who unified and ultimately ruled the Frankish kingdom alone. His tours of the Frankish world demonstrated his acceptance by the regional nobility almost everywhere, and he was able to dominate and defend the border regions. He may have been present for the Council of Clichy (636), but in general he did not promote the activities of bishops, being more enthusiastic about the expansion of Irish monasticism.[134] Legal and

129. Council of Clichy (626–627), CCSL 148A:290–98.

130. "Venissemus ibique clementia uestra canonum regulas tractare iussisset hac pro statu ecclesiae, quaeque sunt necessaria disponere precepisset . . . ut non minus pro pacem ecclesiae," Council of Clichy (626–627), CCSL 148A:291.

131. "Preuenitis hac uelut illi Dauid et regni imperium gratia prouide gubernantes et ministrationem propheticam adimpletis," Council of Clichy (626–627), CCSL 148A:291.

132. "Vobis presentibus in uniuersali Gallearum et magna synodum iuxta prisca canonum institutionem constitui precepistis," Council of Clichy (626–627), CCSL 148A:291; Wallace-Hadrill, *Frankish Church,* 105–6.

133. "Videte, fratres, unde in libro Regum legimus de duobus regibus Saul et Dauid; sed si de eorum uitam pensamus, possumus aliquid ad nostram imitationem collegi. Iste prior et presens regnum perdedit et caelestem amisit, ille sequens et presentem habuit et caelestem adeptus est," Marseilles (533), CCSL 148A:84–97; see 96. This document, appended to the records of the council, was called an "Epistle of John III." There was a John II (533–535) who ascended the papal throne three months earlier than the council, but the origins of this item are not known. The bishops may have produced this text themselves.

134. Council of Clichy (636), CCSL 148A:300. Evidence for Dagobert's monastic policy:

conciliar silence echoes through the long years of his reign; nevertheless, his name was later deemed suitable for numerous forged charters. Authentic charters show that he granted the village of Ursines to the Abbey of St. Denis to help the poor and clerics "for the stability of the realm and the salvation of our soul."[135] He could intervene in the church in a major way, as when he appointed his treasurer Desiderius as bishop of Cahors.[136] Old grievances and criticism are preserved in the *Chronicle of Fredegar,* which says that eventually Dagobert "forgot the justice he once loved" and "longed for ecclesiastical property."[137] He was able to bind together traditionally hostile and separate regions—the Mediterranean world and the Frankish heartland of Austrasia—and managed to conciliate the nobility and bishops of Neustria.[138] This was an early strengthening of the notion of Frankish identity, or a trauma, depending on your side.[139] Given that the Frankish kingdom was unified and so extensive under Dagobert, his reign has often been seen either as a harbinger of Carolingian times or as the reign of the last good Merovingian king. But Dagobert's accomplishment was fragile and unique, and was followed by a period of further division and royal weakness, although Yitzhak Hen points to a culture enlivened by a "vibrant aristocracy" in the setting of itinerant royal courts.[140] Dagobert was buried in the Abbey of St.-Denis, a monastery that was long nourished by the Merovingian kings and that responded by offering a sacred setting for the cult and remembrance of royalty.[141]

Sometime after 673 bishops assembled at Jean-de-Losne praised King Childeric II (662–675) as the "most glorious prince," who could listen to the council meetings, even though the proceedings were (it was apologetically noted) in Lat-

Dagobertus I. rex monasterio Resbacensi, a Dadone referendario et fratribus eius Adone et Radone in fisco Meldensi constructo privilegium liberatis atque immunitatis concedit (635), MGH Dip. 1:16–18.

135. "Pro regni stabiletate vel remedium animae nostrae"; text in "Dagobert Ier," DACL 4.1:9.

136. *Dagobertus I. rex Desiderium, thesaurarium suum. . . . Cadurcensis episcopum consituit* (629) MGH Dip. 1:15.

137. *The Fourth Book of the Chronicle of Fredegar with its Continuations,* ed. J. M. Wallace-Hadrill (London: 1960), 50.

138. Yitzhak Hen, *Roman Barbarians: The Royal Court and Culture in the Early Medieval West* (Houndmills/Basingstoke: 2009), 95–96; see also Louis Dupraz, *Contribution à l'histoire du Regnum Francorum pendant la troisième quart du VIIe siècle (656–680)* (Fribourg: 1948), 204–19.

139. In the context of Merovingian developments, the concept "Frank" meant "a sense of political integration"; see Helmut Reimitz, "Omnes Franci: Identifications and Identities of the Early Medieval Franks," in *Franks, Northmen, and Slavs: Identities and State Formation in Early Medieval Europe,* edited by Ildar H. Garipzanov, Patrick J. Geary, and Przemslaw Urbanczyk, 51–68 (Turnhout: 2008); quoting 57.

140. Hen, *Roman Barbarians,* 99–100.

141. Harding, *Medieval Law,* 19.

in.[142] Again, so the bishops declared, it was Childeric himself who commanded the bishops to renew what the "most holy fathers" had established at the six ecumenical councils.[143] The bishops declared that their councils would allow the inheritence of those holy fathers to be "established and preserved for all with a firm stability through declining ages."[144] Participants in episcopal councils believed that their inspired law could overcome the deterioration and mutability of temporal existence. Kingship, however, remained mired in time. King Childeric was assassinated shortly after the Council of Jean-de-Losne.

The ability to rule in Frankish Gaul was something given more than taken. Power was recognized in symbolic actions and granted by the society rather than siezed by the powerful.[145] Recent studies of Frankish political life emphasize that it emerged out of the organization of powerful men and their estates around communal activities, such as annual gatherings, gift exchanges, and consensual decision-making. A royal ideology emerged that drew on the theme of Roman origins and Roman survivals.[146] But for activities of a political power to be recognized and accepted, there must exist a general agreement over the leader's position. This is the process that placed bishops alongside kings. There was a developing consensus about the role of kings, which remained intact until late in the seventh century. Thus royal power, with its traditional origins in the history of a royal clan, was actualized from below, rather than asserted from above. No barrier was put in the way of "royal blood"—in fact this claim was strengthened.[147] Bishops were incorporated in the communal system of Frankish governance, but meanwhile they insisted on their meaningful distinction from the rest of society and on their own ancient, independent origins. Justifications of episcopal power were expounded as doctrine and developed as part of the legacy of Gallic and Merovingian councils. These justifications were also embedded in images and signs that operated on their own. Images and symbols of religious function and social power provided a shortcut, drawing a direct line from function to sign and from sign to function.

---

142. "Nos Latina in praesentia gloriosisimi principis nostri domni Childerici regis congregati eramus," Council of Jean-de-Losne (673–675), CCSL 148A:315. Since all councils were in Latin, mention of this fact must refer to the presence of the king and nobles.

143. "Quod sanctisimi patres quinque principalibus synodis congregati pro statui sancae aecclesie," Council of Jean-de-Losne (673–675), CCSL 148A:315.

144. "Nobis quoque stabilire atque conseruare in omnibus firma stabilitate per succidua tempora conueniat," Council of Jean-de-Losne (673–675), CCSL 148A:315.

145. Patzold, *Episcopus,* 509.

146. Wood, *Merovingian Kingdoms,* 66–70.

147. Le Jan, "La sacralité de la royauté mérovingienne," 1229–31.

A Social Model and a Hairstyle

In Visigothic Spain, meanwhile, the model of episcopal-royal cooperation was deepened following its ceremonial debut at the Council of Agde (506). Isidore of Seville (c. 560–636), in the course of preserving the learning and lore of the Christian and classical past, recast some of the major categories of late antique thought in the process. He did this in an effort to apply those categories to his own society, governed as it was by kings who could only draw vicariously on the intellectual resources and imagery that had validated the Roman Empire. The persuasive and encyclopedic way he did this made his works highly relevant to other bishops in the barbarian kingdoms of Europe, to such an extent that he became extremely influential in succeeding centuries. For Frankish bishops of the eighth century, therefore, the most authoritative book on the nature of their office was Isidore's *On Ecclesiastical Offices,* written *circa* 598–615.[148] The work stands in the lineage of the old Mirrors of Bishops of Caesarius, Pomerius, and Gregory the Great, but everything is changed in the direction of formality, liturgical stiffness, and extremism. Copies of this book were in the hands of Frankish clerics from as early as 700, and the work was early taken to Ireland, where it was used by the compilers of the *Collectio canonum Hibernensis* between 690 and 725.[149] It was at hand in Lindisfarne when the *Life of Cuthbert* was written, in about 700.[150] Similarly, it arrived in Northern Italy just before 700.[151] What follows is a description of how Isidore, in explaining the nature of episcopal authority, developed a social theology widely accepted by bishops across Europe.

148. Isidore of Seville, *Sancti Isidori episcopi Hispalensis: De ecclesiasticis officiis,* ed. Christopher M. Lawson, CCSL, 108 (Turnhout: 1989), 14. On Isidore generally, see Jacques Fontaine, *Isidore de Séville et la culture classique dans l'Espagne wisigothique,* 2 vols. (Paris: 1959); H. J. Diesner, *Isidor von Sevilla und seine Zeit* (Berlin: 1973); P. D. King, *Law and Society in the Visigothic Kingdom,* Cambridge Studies in Medieval Life and Thought, 3rd ser., vol. 5 (Cambridge: 1972); J. N. Hillgarth, "The Position of Isidorian Studies: A Critical Review of the Literature 1936–1975," SM 3d ser., vol. 24 (1983), 817–905.

149. See Isidore, De ecc., 127. On the diffusion of Isidore's writings in Ireland and elsewhere, see J. N. Hillgarth, "Ireland and Spain in the Seventh Century," *Peritia* 3 (1984): 1–16.

150. Wilhelm Levison, *England and the Continent in the Eighth Century* (Oxford: 1946), 282; see also editorial comment of Lawson in Isidore, *De ecc.,* 127.

151. Lawson, "X. History of the Text," in Isidore, *De ecc.,* 122–34; see also Appendix B, "The Indirect Tradition," 146–59, where a list of authors and groups using *De ecc.* is given, from which I extract the following: Benedict of Aniana (*Concordia regularum*); the *Institutio Canonicorum* (Aachen 816); Amalarius of Metz (*Liber officialis*); the Pseudo-Isidorean Decretals; Pirmin (*Scarapsus*); the Council of Mainz (813); the *Collectio Hibernensis;* the *Via sancti Cuthberti;* Pseudo-Bede (*De officiis libellus*); Pseudo-Alcuin (*De diuinis officiis liber*); Paul the Deacon; Jonas of Orléans (*De institutione laicali*); Hraban Maur (*De institutione clericorum*); and Beatus of Liebana (*Aduersus Elipandum*).

The first book of *On Ecclesiastical Offices* contained a discussion of the origins of Christian churches. This reflects Isidore's historical vision and his personal situation in a Visigothic kingdom so recently turned to Catholicism.[152] He attempts to explain the origins of the hymns, psalms, and other liturgical observances governing the church's activities. For every Christian observance, ritual, and office, an antecedent was found in the Judaic past, reflecting the post-Augustinian tendency of Christians to read the Old Testament as prefiguring the New, and hence as prefiguring contemporary institutions.[153] Like Eusebius and Augustine before him, Isidore believed that he lived in the sixth and last age of the world. This was basic to his exegetical and political vision. He turned to the Old Testament as a mysterious, encoded prophecy of every feature of Christian history. Christian priesthood was a continuation of Jewish priesthood. The Christian Church replaced the Jewish Temple, continuing the worship and divine origins of Jewish institutions. A similar "broken continuum" can be seen in a work attributed to Isidore, *On the Rise and Death of the Fathers,* in which the Jewish and apostolic fathers fell under a single terminological and historiographical category.[154] Analogy was used to depict Judaism as a symbolic predecessor of Christianity.

The guiding impulse of *On Ecclesiastical Offices* was to explain the establishment of the episcopate as an order and to lay down the principles of its governing and teaching authority.[155] Isidore had little use for bishops detached from the structures of the church (the "headless" ones), or for clerics subject only to their own will.[156] These "have the sign of religion but not the office of religion." Obedience within a structure was thus asserted as a defining feature of ecclesiastical office.[157] Also basic was the seclusion of clerics from ordinary ways of

---

152. An old handbook, outdated in part, is Carlos Cañal, *San Isidoro: Exposición de sus obras é indicaciones acerca de la influencia que han ejercido en la civilización española* (Seville: 1897), 21–24; on Isidore's histories of the Goths see 55–61.

153. J. Coppens, *Le sacerdoce chrétien: Ses origines et son développement,* Analecta lovaniensia biblica et orientalia Ser. 5, Fasc. 4–5 (Leiden: 1970), 38.

154. Isidore of Seville [Isidoro de Sevilla], *De ortu et obitu patrum: Vida y muerte de los santos,* ed. and trans. C. Chaparro Gómez, (Paris: 1985). Its authenticity was challenged by R. McNally, "Christus in the pseudo-Isidorian Liber de ortu et obitu patriarchum," *Traditio* 21 (1965): 167–83.

155. *A History of Christian Spirituality,* vol. 2, *The Spirituality of the Middle Ages,* ed. Jean Leclercq, F. Vandenbroucke, and L. Bouyer. Trans. the Benedictines of Holme Eden Abbey (London: 1968), 52.

156. Isidore struggled against the *Akephaloi:* Herrin, *Formation of Christendom,* 241; Cañal, *San Isidoro,* 34 and 100.

157. "Quique dum nullum metuentes explendae uoluptatis suae licentiam consectantur, quasi animalia bruta libertate ac desiderio suo feruntur. Habentes signum religionis non religionis officium," Isidore, *Sancti Isidori,* 2.3:54.

living. They were to avoid delightful spectacles and pleasurable occupations, giving their whole attention to the duties of office. This required mental obedience. Simplicity and chastity were crucial methods of self-discipline, allowing the cleric to pursue the study of doctrine, reading, psalmody, hymnody, and chanting.[158]

An accurate symbol had for Isidore a reality greater than other objects in the world. Such a symbol revealed a transcendent phase and the participation of worldly things in a higher reality. This use of symbols can be seen in his interpretation of many features of nature in the *De natura rerum*. Clouds, for example, signified preachers bringing the rain of the divine word.[159] The cleric could only become a cleric by this double effort of internalization by self-discipline and externalization by symbol. Thus, in the discussion of the tonsure Isidore reached the heart of his theme, because this way of cutting the hair linked the moral and physical worlds. In adopting the tonsure, the cleric himself became a symbol.

"Sign" and "office" could become interchangeable through obedience, Isidore argued. Tonsure was the outward mark of an internal transformation; it was something "figured on the body but done in the soul," and marked on the head because the mind was thought to dwell there.[160] The tonsure was above all a royal sign, a crown meant to indicate the government of the church by the priesthood:

The head being shaved on top, a lower circular crown is left, and I judge their priesthood and government of the church to be figured in them. Indeed, among the ancients, a tiara was placed on the head of priests (this was made of cotton, and circular as if it were a half-sphere), and this is symbolized in the shaved part of the head. A crown, moreover, is the golden circular band which adorns the heads of kings. Consider therefore whether the same sign is not expressed on the head of clerics so that it can accomplish by a certain similitude of the body what was written by Peter the Apostle, who taught "You are the royal, elect race of priests."[161]

158. "Postremo in doctrina, in lectionibus, psalmis, hymnis, canticis exercitio iugi incumbant," Isidore, *De ecc.,* 2.2:54.

159. "Nubes autem sancti praedicatores intelliguntur, qui verbi diuini pluuiam credentibus," Isidore of Seville, *De natura rerum,* 32; Isidore de Séville, *Traité de la nature,* ed. Jacques Fontaine (Paris: 2002), 287; Cañal, *San Isidoro,* 63–64.

160. "Est autem in clericis tonsura signum quoddam quod in corpore figuratur sed in animo agitur . . . quam renouationem in mente oportet fieri, sed in capite demonstrari ubi ipsa mens noscitur habitare," Isidore, *De ecc.,* 2.4:55.

161. "Quod uero, detonso superius capite, inferius circuli corona relinquitur, sacerdotium regnumque ecclesiae in eis existimo figurari. Thiara enim apud ueteres constituebatur in capite sacerdotum (haec ex bysso confecta rotunda erat quasi sfera media), et hoc significatur in parte capitis tonsa; corona autem latitudo aurea est circuli quae regum capita cingit. Utrumque itaque signum exprimitur in capite clericorum ut impleatur etiam corporali quadam similtudine quod scriptum est Petro apostolo perdocente: *Vos estis genus electum regale sacerdotium* (I Pet. 2:9)," Isidore, *De ecc.,* 2.4:55f.

Priests bore a double symbol, marked on their bodies, connecting Christian priesthood to its ancient Jewish counterpart, and indicating government of the church at the same time.

The concept of the "priest as king" appeared at roughly the same time as the concept of the "king as priest."[162] For Isidore the concept of priesthood, no less than kingship, revolved around the fascinating image of the crown: among ointments, diadems, bracelets, and robes, the crown was a superior ornament, representing superiority. The crown had an ancient resonance that, as a symbol of triumphant religious qualities, had fascinated Christian thinkers as early as Origen and Tertullian, and had been adopted by the Roman emperors, as well.[163] Insignia and garments flourished with the development of a Christian imperial ideal.[164]

At the heart of Isidore's theory of the priesthood lay the notion that it was a legal office, established by authority. It was only the attachment to a traditional order that gave the priesthood its meaning and authenticity.[165] Aaron was the first man who "caused the order of bishops to flourish in the world." The earlier priests had carried out sacrifices "by their own will, not by priestly authority." But "Aaron first took the priestly name in law, and first, wearing the woolen fillet and episcopal stola, offered sacrifices at the Lord's command."[166] Thus Isidore rejected any charismatic basis for the priesthood in favor of legal ordination. Aaron's offer of sacrifice *prefigured* Christ's death—an inversion of the *commemoration* of that death in the Christian Mass.[167]

God established and announced the lines of priestly authority. Moses, in

---

162. Reydellet, *Royauté,* 539; see also Lucien Cerfaux, "Regale sacerdotium," repr. in *Recueil Lucien Cerfaux,* 2:283–315 (Gembloux: 1954).

163. Tertullian, *Q. Septimi Florentis Tertulliani De corona/Tertullien: Sur la couronne,* ed. Jacques Fontaine, Érasme 18 (Paris: 1966). On the Persian backdrop of the diadem, see Hans Werner Ritter, *Diadem und Königsherrschaft: Untersuchungen zu Zeremonien und Rechtsgrundlagen des Herrschaftsantritts bei den Persern, bei Alexander dem Grossen und im Hellenismus,* Vestigia 7 (Munich: 1965); for its adoption in Rome: Nikolaus Gussone and Heiko Steuer, "Diadem," in *Reallexikon der germanischen Altertumskunde* (Berlin: 1973–), 5:351–75. On the crown in Isidore, see Cañal, *San Isidoro,* 89–90. Origen on crowns: Carla Noche, *Vestis Varia: L'immagine della veste nell'opera di Origene,* Studia Ephemeridis Augustinianum 79 (Rome: 2002), 30.

164. Moore, "King's New Clothes," 86–114.

165. "Quasi animalia bruta libertate ac desderio suo feruntur," Isidore, *De ecc.,* 2.4:54.

166. "Initium quidem sacerdotii Aaron fuit; quamquam et Melchisedech prior obtulerit sacrificium et post hunc Abraham, Isaac et Iacob; sed isti spontanea uoluntate, non sacerdotali auctoritate, ista fecerunt. Ceterum Aaron primus in lege sacerdotale nomen accepit, primusque pontificali stola infulatus uictimas obtulit iubente domino," Isidore, *De ecc.,* 2.5:56.

167. "Hic per hostiam uictimarum et sacrificium sanguinis futuram Christi passionem expressit; his ius et principatum sacerdoti per ordinem generis et successionis suae transmisit," Isidore, *De ortu et obitu patrum,* 26.1:143–44.

the First Order of Priesthood, functioned as mediator between God and man, and established the priesthood, although he was not a priest. Just as Aaron was the image (*figura*) of the high priest (*id est episcopum*), so Moses was the *figura* of Christ, who established the Second Order of Priests. Christ however, unlike Moses, "is the true leader of peoples, the true prince of priests, and lord of bishops, to whom there is honor and glory in *saecula saeculorum,* amen."[168] *Dux, princeps, dominus*—this regal aspect of Christ was embodied in the priesthood and marked by the tonsure.

By insisting on ordination as the origin of priesthood, Isidore described Moses and Christ as parallel founders of two priesthoods. There were biblical passages that suggested that Christ was a priest.[169] In the writings of Paul, Christ was portrayed as a minister to the people, establishing the cult and liturgy of the Christian priesthood and offering the first Eucharist.[170] In the Apocalypse, the Son of Man appeared clothed in a robe that can be said to represent a priestly vestment.[171] A crucial difference between the Jewish and Christian priesthood was that Moses, the founder of the first order of priests, was a man and was not a priest. Christ, the founder of the second order of priests, was God and was also a priest.

Isidore immediately turned from his discussion of Peter to explain that, although Peter was the first to receive the power of binding and loosing, power and honor were shared by the other apostles in the evangelical calling. This meant that, like Cyprian, Isidore believed that the priority of Rome was not exclusionary or of a different kind. The honor and power of other apostolic sees were equal to Rome.[172] This Cyprianic doctrine led Isidore's contemporaries to wonder if he really meant to say that, and his reply to a question from Bishop Eugenius attempted to place the priority of Rome and the equality of all bishops within a single framework.[173]

168. "Si enim filii Aaron presbiterorum figuram faciebant et Aaron summi sacerdotis, id est episcopi, Moyses cuius/ Indubitanter Christi, et uere per omnia Christi, quoniam fuit similitudo mediatoris dei qui est inter dium et hominem Iesus Christus, qui est uerus dux populorum, uerus princeps sacerdotum et dominus pontificum, cui est honor et gloria in saecula saeculorum, amen," Isidore, *De ecc.,* 2.5:57.

169. "Tu es sacerdos in aeternum secundum ordinem Melchisedech," Heb. 5:6; Similarly in 7:15, 17, 21.

170. Coppens, *Sacerdoce chrétien,* 12–13.

171. "Et in medio septem candelabrorum similem Filio hominis vestitum podere et praecinctum ad mamillas zonam auream," Apoc. 1:13; see Coppens, 13.

172. Isidore, *De ecc.,* 2.5:57.

173. Duchesne misconstrued this incident; Duchesne, *L'Église au VIème siècle,* 586.

But concerning the question of the equality of the apostles, Peter takes precedence over the others because he deserved to hear from the Lord: "You will be called Cephas; you are Peter" (John 1:42) and other things; and he first received in the Church of Christ the honor of the priesthood not from any other but from the Son of God himself, and the Virgin. . . . Although his dignity of power is transferred to all bishops of the Catholics, yet in a special way and with a singular privilege it remains forever higher to the bishop of Rome as the head than to all the other members.[174]

Every apostolic see had an independent claim to this fundamental power and could transmit that authority from successor to successor without dilution. Only a bishop could ordain a priest or another bishop. This was accomplished by the imposition of hands and a blessing, so that this *traditio* literally involved the "handing over" of authority.[175] *Honor, dignitas, potestas.* Again the discussion hinged on questions of government and power.

According to Isidore, unlike the Jewish priesthood, whose members were chosen by blood filiation, the selection of a Christian bishop was based on merit. Judaism "prefigured" Christianity, but without understanding. The contrast between the Jewish and Christian priest was a contrast between ignorance and knowledge. Isidore aggrandized the Jewish past by taking it as a symbol imprinted in history.

Tonsure was a sign of the priest as governor, and so were the other symbols of the bishop's office, the ring and the staff. Notice in this passage the combination of medical and royal images:

When he is consecrated, he is given the staff, so that by its sign he may rule or correct the people put under him, or so that he may stave off the illnesses of the sick. And the ring is given as a sign of pontifical honor or as a little sign of the mysteries: for there are many things which conceal carnal and (less often) spiritual things—priests as if under that little sign establish that the sacraments are not displayed by anyone unworthy of them.[176]

174. "Quod vero de parilitate agitur apostolorum, Petrus praeeminet caeteris, quia a Domino audire meruit: Tu vocaberis Cephas, tu es Petrus (Joan. I:42) et caetera, et non ab alio aliquo, sed ab ipso Dei et virginis filio honorem pontificatus in Christi Ecclesia primus suscepit. . . . Cujus dignitas potestatis etsi ad omnes catholicarum episcopos est transfusa, specialius tamen Romano antistiti singulari quodam privilegio, velut capiti, caeteris membris celsior permanet in aeternum," Isidore, Letter 8, Isidore to Bishop Eugenius, *Letters of St. Isidore,* 46.

175. Godding, *Prêtres en Gaule,* 160–62; "Quod vero per manus inpositionem a praecessoribus dei sacerdotibus episcopi ordinantur, antiqua est institutio," Isidore, *De ecc.,* 2.5:59.

176. "Huic autem, dum consecratur, datur baculus ut eius indicio subditam plebem uel regat uel corrigat uel infirmitates infirmorum sustineat. Datur et anulus propter signum pontificalis honoris uel signaculum secretorum; nam multa sunt quae, carnalium minusque intellegentium

This was the less severe side of episcopal authority. Bishops were provided to the world to offer a beneficial and healing power, the "medicine of God."[177] Crozier and ring were signs of episcopal office only in Spain and Gaul, and were unknown in Rome. Isidore's mention of the staff, alongside that of the Fourth Council of Toledo, is the earliest evidence for its use as an episcopal sign. The ring, on the other hand, was another adoption of a royal symbol by the bishops.[178] Taken together, these principles represent a projection of the ancient gestures and signs of the liturgy onto the screen of social life.

Unction and the Two Orders of Society

Toward the end of the work, Isidore moved on to a discussion of "unction," or the anointing with oil that accompanied baptism, drawing on ancient traditions about the church as a "mystical body." Patristic thinkers had believed that, because the body of Christ entered all Christians by means of the Eucharist, they were thereby incorporated into one body, the body of Christ.[179] Isidore transposed these categories in a significant way, first by thinking of baptism as the means whereby Christians became "one body," and, secondly, by equating the church and Visigothic society, thereby taking an old tradition far outside its original boundaries. This doctrine offered the possibility of rethinking Visigothic social identity by looking to the origins of the *Populus Christi* rather than a Gothic *origo gentis*.

Isidore explained that Christ received his title (*Christus*) from the fact that Moses established the use of chrism for the anointing of priests, using it first in Aaron's ordination:

Then kings were also anointed with the same chrism, whence they were called *christi*, as is written, "Do not touch my anointed." At that time there was a mystical unction both for kings and priests by which Christ was prefigured (whence his name itself

---

occultantes, sacerdotes quasi sub signaculo condunt ne indignis quibusque dei sacramenta aperiantur," Isidore, *De ecc.,* 2.5:60.

177. Isidore, *De ecc.,* 2.2:53, where it is forbidden to receive payment for this power: "pro beneficiis medicinae dei munera non accipiant."

178. "Recipiat coram altario de manu episcoporum orarium, annulum et baculum," Fourth Council of Toledo (633), in José Vives, *Concilios visigóticos e hispano-romanos*, España Cristiana, Textos 1 (Madrid: 1963), 203; On these symbols, see further: Louis Duchesne, *Christian Worship, Its Origin and Evolution: A Study of the Latin Liturgy up to the Time of Charlemagne*, trans. M. L. McClure, 5th ed. (London: 1931), 397; and Klauser, *Ursprung der bischöflichen Insignien*, 201. On the episcopal ring, see Verena Labhart, *Zur Rechtssymbolik des Bischofsrings*, Rechtshistorische Arbeiten 2 (Cologne: 1963), 10–14.

179. De Lubac, *Corpus mysticum*, 89–135.

comes from the chrism) (2). But after our Lord, the true king and eternal priest, the celestial and mystic ointment was spread out by God the Father, and now not only bishops and kings but the whole church is consecrated with the unction of chrism because it [the church] is a part of the eternal king and priest. Therefore because "we are a priestly and royal people," we are anointed after baptism so that we can be wreathed in the name of Christ.[180]

I mentioned earlier Isidore's practice of examining reality by analyzing symbols. Symbols were also capable of shaping reality. Anointing was a powerful symbol, able to govern and control reality: every Christian was anointed in order to establish the church as the body of Christ. As the Body of Christ, moreover, the church combined the royal and priestly offices of Christ.[181] Isidore saw the church as having these two natures, embodied in the offices of priest and king, developing this idea from the ancient liturgical blessing of the chrism. Society itself was mapped out by this simple conjuncture of two forms of government. Unlike the earlier Mirrors of Bishops, Isidore's treatise was resolutely political and social.

Isidore presented society, as had Pope Gelasius, as a twofold structure, each "order" of which was embodied by its governing person. For Gelasius, this placed power in the hands of the emperor and authority in the hands of the pope. With Isidore, a major transposition of categories had taken place, for now it was the *church,* not the world, that was expressed in the double image of priest and king. Royal power no longer represented, as it did for Gelasius, a secular realm distinct from the church, but had been absorbed by the church. Priest and king were united as aspects of Christ, and as aspects of the body of Christ—the church—now identified with society. This was a departure from patristic social thought, and was far from Augustine's social thought, with which Isidore was so familiar. Isidore's *On Ecclesiastical Offices* drew on a Christological tradition of Christ's kingship and priesthood, which became a way of seeing Christian society.[182] Reydellet found this concept elsewhere in Isidore, but did not think

---

180. "Deinde quoque et reges eodem crismate sacrabantur; unde et christi nuncupabantur, sicut scriptum est: *Nolite tangere christos meos.* Eratque eo tempore tantum in regibus et sacerdotibus mystica unctio qua Christus figurabatur. Vnde et ipsud nomen a crismate ducitur. (2) Sed postquam dominus noster, uerus rex et sacerdos aeternus, a deo patre caelesti ac mystico unguento est dilibutus, iam non soli pontifices et reges sed omnis ecclesia unctione crismatis consecratur, pro eo quod membrum est aeterni regis et sacerdotis. Ergo quia genus sacerdotale et regale sumus, ideo post lauacrum unguimur ut Christi nomine censeamur," Isidore, *De ecc.,* 2.26:106.

181. On the royalty of Christ, see Lucien Cerfaux, "Le titre *Kyrios* et la dignité royale de Jésus," in *Recueil Lucien Cerfaux,* 1:1–63.

182. J. G. Sagüés, "La doctrina del Cuerpo místico en San Isidoro," *Estudios eclesiásticos* 17 (1943): 227–57, 329–60, 517–46; see esp. 354–60.

it supported the power and domination of the priesthood.[183] What should be added to Reydellet's picture is the pairing of Christological elements in human kings and priests, both of whom partake of Christ's royalty and priesthood.

This image of the kingdom as the Body of Christ underpinned Isidore's attempt to promote Christian kingship in Spain. His political thought, therefore, was grounded in exegesis, liturgy, and the patristic concept of Christ's kingship and priesthood. It should be emphasized, at the same time, that Isidore developed his sociology neither from Roman political thought, nor from a source like Pope Gelasius, but from the liturgy.

In the mid-fourth century, the first representations of Christ as king of the world, or cosmocrator, appeared.[184] In patristic literature Christ was often portrayed as king, but more importantly as king and priest, what Beskow calls the "twofold office." Unction linked these offices in the patristic conception.[185] As early as 200, Tertullian described unction at baptism in terms recalling the anointing of Jewish kings: "from which ye are called 'christs' (*christi dicti a chrismate*) from the chrism, that is the anointing, which also lent its name to the Lord."[186] Certainly the most influential text containing these notions was the *Apostolic Tradition,* the source of so much Latin liturgical development.[187] Thus in Gelasian and Gregorian sacramentaries, chrism was described as the oil "with which you anointed kings and priests and prophets."[188] It inspired the prayer in the Gelasian rite (early sixth century): "Mix in the power of the Holy Spirit through the might of thy Christ, from whose holy name chrism received its name, with which thou didst anoint thy priests, kings, prophets and martyrs."[189]

Isidore's use of the image tied it to the concept of the church as the body of

183. Reydellet, *Royauté,* 557–62.
184. Peter Beskow, *Rex Gloriae: The Kingship of Christ in the Early Church,* trans. E. Sharpe (Uppsala: 1962), 23.
185. Beskow, *Rex Gloriae,* 111; see also 119, concerning Eusebius' interest in anointment and the threefold office.
186. Tertullian, *De baptismo* (7–8), trans. by L. L. Mitchell, in *Baptismal Anointing,* Alcuin Club Collections 48 (London: 1966), 10.
187. On Hippolytus and the Apostolic Tradition, see G. W. H. Lampe, *The Seal of the Spirit: A Study in the Doctrine of Baptism and Confirmation in the New Testament and the Fathers,* 2nd ed. (London: 1967), 128–42; see also J. A. Jungmann, *The Early Liturgy to the Time of Gregory the Great,* trans. F. A. Brunner, University of Notre Dame Liturgical Studies 6 (Notre Dame: 1980), 52–73; and Mitchell, *Baptismal Anointing,* 1–9.
188. "Ut oleum hoc sanctificans das, deus, sanitatem utentibus, et percipientibus, unde unxisti reges, sacerdotes et profetas, sic et omnibus gustantibus confortationem et sanitatem utentibus illud praebat" (5.2), *La tradition apostolique de saint Hippolyte: Essai de reconstitution,* edited by B. Botte, 18–19 (Munster: 1963); see also G. Ellard, *Ordination Anointings in the Western Church before 1000 A.D.* (Cambridge: 1933), 108.
189. Trans. in Mitchell, *Baptismal Anointing,* 107.

Christ; as such, the image of Christ's priesthood and kingship expressed the structure of a society entirely coincident with the church, in which nothing was secular. By approaching the Visigothic kingdom from this perspective, Isidore resolved in a convincing manner the relationship between bishops and kings in the successor kingdoms of Europe. He also made a convincing claim for the importance of a Spanish Christian kingdom against the (continued) competing claims of Byzantium.[190]

At the same time, Isidore refused to recognize force, or the pure function of ruling, as the conceptual origin of kingship. He addressed the issue in his *Etymologies*.[191] Isidore was dissatisfied with the traditional etymology that derived the word "king" (*rex*) from the mere activity of ruling (*rex a regendo*). He went on to derive the second term, *regendo,* from acting justly—"to act rightly" (*recte agendo*). For Isidore, "a king who fails to rule in the right way is no king but a tyrant."[192] For this reason, Isidore thought it right to instruct King Sisebut about the eternal truth of the course of the stars: for such things should be a guide for the stability and wisdom of kingship.[193] Isidore's interpretation of the liturgy was not an attempt to Christianize or legitimate an older form of government. This was the inauguration of a new and better type of kingship, which would be worthy of the name (*nomen*) of a king. For Isidore, the liturgy of anointing, which portrayed all Christians as a royal priesthood, had clear social and political ramifications.[194]

Isidore's writings cannot be proven to be the source for the anointing of kings and bishops in Visigothic Spain.[195] The first known instance of this ritual may have been thirty years after Isidore's death, when King Wamba, in 672, was anointed by Julian of Toledo in a ceremony full of priestly allusions.[196] Isidore

190. Herrin, *Formation of Christendom,* 237.
191. Isidore of Seville, *Etymologiae IX,* ed. Marc Reydellet (Paris: 1984), 121.
192. Wallace-Hadrill, *Early Germanic Kingship,* 53.
193. Isidore of Seville, *De natura rerum,* (Praef. 2), 167–68.
194. On the concept of a royal priesthood in Maximus of Turin and Isidore, see Lampe, *Seal of the Spirit,* 220.
195. E. Eichmann, "Königs- und Bischofsweihe," *Sitzungsberichte der Bayerischen Akademie der Wissenschaften: Philosophisch-philologische und historische Klasse* 6 (1928): 1–71; see 23–24; see also Reydellet, *Royauté,* 565, with bibliography at 567; and Achim Thomas Hack, "Zur Herkunft der karolingischen Königssalbung," ZKG 110 (1999): 170–90.
196. Julian of Toledo recorded this event in his *Historiae Wambae regis,* ed. W. Levison, MGH SRM 5:486–535. The "first instance" of royal anointing is a highly controversial topic. See, within a vast literature, Eichmann "Königs- und Bischofsweihe," 24; Roger Collins, "Julian of Toledo and the Royal Succession in Late Seventh-Century Spain," in *Early Medieval Kingship,* 30–49; and C. A. Bouman, *Sacring and Crowning: The Development of the Latin Ritual for the Anointing of Kings and the Coronation of an Emperor before the Eleventh Century,* Bijdragen van het Instituut

made an important claim about the olive oil, with which both king and priest were anointed, in which balsam and herbs had been steeped, and which embodied the importation of the Holy Ghost.[197] The anointing of kings derived from baptismal ritual as a recognition of their ability to represent an aspect of Christ in the church, prefigured in the anointed kings of the Old Testament. Bishops would eventually be anointed, as well.[198] This new institution drew on the ability of a historical vision to generate a political myth.

Liturgical imagery must have seemed especially appropriate in the baptismal anointing of newly converted kings, such as the baptism of Clovis described by Gregory of Tours.[199] The reception of baptized heretics was also solemnized by anointing.[200] Such an event had taken place not long before Isidore was writing, when Reccared converted to Catholicism and was crowned in 586. It is therefore unlikely that royal anointing was introduced in Visigothic Spain as an imitation of Old Testament practice.[201] Isidore relied instead on the liturgy. A doctrine of royalty drawing upon the model of the Old Testament kings would emerge perhaps fifty years after Reccared's conversion to Catholicism.[202] Eventually this ritual would provide kings with a kind of religious prestige.[203] The practice resulted from a new interpretation of baptismal liturgy.[204]

For Isidore, society could be identified with the church because of the conversion of the Visigoths and their kings from Arianism. As the Body of Christ,

---

voor Middeleeuwse geschiedenis der Rijks-Universiteit te Utrecht 30 (Groningen: 1957), esp. xi; Jean Devisse, "Le sacre et le pouvoir avant les carolingiens, l'héritage wisigotique," in *Le Sacre des rois: Actes du Colloque international d'histoire sur les sacres et couronnements royaux* (Reims and Paris, 1975), 27–38; Michael Zimmermann, "Les sacres des rois wisigoths," in *Clovis,* 2:9–28, esp. 11–13.

197. Eichmann, "Königs- und Bischofsweihe," 22.

198. Nelson, "National Synods, Kingship as Office, and Royal Anointing," in her *Politics and Ritual,* 249–50, Bouman, *Sacring and Crowning,* 112–13, noted the likelihood that the blessing of chrism was at the heart of later anointing rituals.

199. Recounted in Mitchell, *Baptismal Anointing,* 121.

200. Mitchell, *Baptismal Anointing,* 121–26.

201. The argument of P. D. King, "The Barbarian Kingdoms," in *The Cambridge History of Medieval Political Thought, c. 350–c. 1450,* edited by J. H. Burns, 123–53, see 144 (Cambridge: 1991); compare Nelson, "National Synods," 250.

202. José Orlandis, "Bible et royauté dans les conciles de l'Espagne wisigotho-catholique," AHC 18 (1986): 51–57.

203. Nelson, "Symbols in Context," 279–81. On the baptism of Clovis, see Wood, "Gregory of Tours and Clovis," 267–72. The baptism of Clovis has been seen as the first "royal anointing" since the time of Hincmar, a view still to be found in modern scholarship: Jean de Pange, "Doutes sur la certitude de cette opinion que le sacre de Pépin est la première époque du sacre des rois de France," in *Mélanges d'histoire du Moyen Âge dédiés a la mémoire de Louis Halphen,* edited by Charles-Edmond Perrin, 557–64 (Paris: 1951); similarly Mitchell, *Baptismal Anointing,* 121.

204. Zimmermann, "Sacres des rois wisigoths," 15–16.

therefore, the kingdom combined the royal and priestly functions of Christ, represented in human kings and bishops. Such a combination appeared possible after the conversion of Reccared (586–601) and the subsequent ecstatic pronouncement of Catholic union at the Third Council of Toledo in 589.[205] As among the Franks, there ensued a gradual interpenetration of royal and episcopal law.[206] Nevertheless, the statement of official consensus at Toledo screened many continuing conflicts from view.[207]

The Catholicism of King Sisebut (612–621) seemed to offer the hope that history had culminated in the *regnum Christi*.[208] Sisebut himself may have been influenced by Isidore's "Christological sociology." In a letter to Bishop Eusebius, he explained that Christ was sent to earth to lead mankind to the "aetherial thrones," and that "with Christ is the plenitude of the body of Christ, while he came to be the connection of all his members at the head."[209] The Arian heresy could be seen as an amputation from the body of Christ;[210] hence a return to Catholicism was to become a part of his body again, as Sisebut urged the Lombards.[211] The task of uniting Christ's body entailed ending heresy and bringing about cooperation among the diverse claims of society.

Priest and king could imitate Christ by their cooperation and unity, although this was often in doubt. Julian of Toledo was involved in an attempt to remove

205. "De eius conversione quam de gentis Gothorum innovatione in Domino exultarent et divinae dignationi pro tanto munere gratias agerent," Third Council of Toledo (589), in J. Vives, *Concilios visigóticos*, 107; see also J. Orlandis and D. Ramos-Lisson, *Die Synoden auf der Iberischen Halbinsel bis zum Einbruch des Islam (711),* Konziliengeschichte, Reihe A: Darstellung (Paderborn: 1981), 95–117. Zimmermann argues that this was the first instance of royal anointing: "Sacres des rois wisigoths," 25.

206. Knut Schäferdiek, *Die Kirche in den Reichen der Westgoten un Suewen bis zur Errichtung der westgotischen katholischen Staatskirche,* Arbeiten zur Kirchengeschichte 39 (Berlin: 1967), 205–33; see also Roger Collins, *Early Medieval Spain: Unity in Diversity, 400–1000* (Houndmills/Basingstoke: 1983), 116–17.

207. Rachel Stocking, *Bishops, Councils, and Consensus in the Visigothic Kingdom, 589–633* (Ann Arbor: 2000), 59–68.

208. Reydellet, *Royauté,* 556–57, and Herrin, *Formation of Christendom,* 235. Now also see the account in Hen, *Roman Barbarians,* 124–52.

209. "Nam omnium creaturum creator pia miseratione iussit ad terras descendere, ut in aethereis sedibus per opulentiam bonitatis humanum genus perduceret, quatenus credatur cum Christo Christi corporis plenitudo, dum ad caput in supernis pervenisset omnium membrorum compago," King Sisebut, Letter to Eusebius (c. 614–620), MGH Epp. 3.1:670.

210. "Quando execranda Arriana pernicies de generosa prosapie pellitur et effosa vel suffocata radicitus e Christi corpore Christi gratia amputatur," King Sisebut, Letter to Adualuald, King of the Lombards (c. 616–620), MGH Epp. 3.1:671–75; this quote, 671.

211. "Unde praecamur vestram clementiam verbis, praecamur votis, precamur et mentibus puris, tantorum praemiorum vestram fore gentem participem et adunatam in Christi corpore simul vobis esse consortem," Sisebut to Adualuald, King of the Lombards (c. 616–620) MGH Epp. 3.1:672.

Wamba, and to crown his rival, in 680. The Isidorean project involved a radical rejection of the idea of a secular, independent society and was a viewpoint that could not accommodate internal pluralism. Isidore's anti-Semitism, and that expressed by the bishops at the Fourth Council of Toledo, may have its source in this assimilation of kingdom to church.[212] In fact, from the moment Reccared converted to Catholicism, episcopal law began to have an important impact on Visigothic royal legislation regarding the Jews.[213] At the same time, Reccared was able to influence episcopal law.[214]

It appears that royal anointing began in Spain as a method of ensuring stable succession to the throne. It was an outgrowth of efforts such as that at the Fourth Council of Toledo (633), strongly influenced by Isidore, to introduce legal and regular means of selecting a king.[215] The type of Christian kingship Isidore promoted at court, and in councils over which he presided, was intimately tied to his ideas about episcopal authority and to his conception that king and priest were the two orders that together should govern the kingdom-church.[216] The unity of the Visigothic kingdom under a Catholic king, and that king's cooperation with the bishops of his realm, allowed this profound shift in social thought, amounting to a redefinition of Gothic kingship as a quasi-clerical office.[217] The Fourth Council of Toledo, in presenting its picture of how a monarch might die peacefully and be succeeded without violence, described a process like an episcopal succession: "the prince having died in peace, let the leadership of the whole people along with the priests establish the successor of the realm in common council."[218] One who would use force or fraud to acquire

212. Orlandis and Ramos-Lisson, *Synoden,* 164–66.

213. Jean Juster, "La condition légale des Juifs sous les rois Visigoths," in *Études d'histoire juridique offertes à Paul Frédéric Girard* (Paris: 1913), 2:275–335. The idea of forced baptism was known among the Franks, as well. According to Fredegar, Dagobert forced the Jews of his kingdom to become baptized: *The Fourth Book of the Chronicle of Fredegar,* 54.

214. Stocking, *Bishops, Councils,* 68–71.

215. Orlandis and Ramos-Lisson, *Synoden,* 167. Irish origins are proposed in Michael J. Enright, *Iona, Tara and Soissons: The Origin of the Royal Anointing Ritual,* Arbeiten zur Frühmittelalterforschung, Schriftenreihe des Instituts für Frühmittelalterforschung der Universität Münster 17 (Berlin: 1985). The earliest possible example of royal anointing is the supposed "ordination" of Aidán circa 574, described by Adomnán between 688 and 704. The *Collectio canonum hibernensis* (c. 690–725) connects the problem of kingship to the anointing of Saul by Samuel: *Die irische Kanonensammlung,* ed. H. Wasserschleben (1885; repr. Aalen: 1966), 76.

216. Stocking, *Bishops, Councils,* 172–73; On Isidore's political efforts, see Collins, *Early Medieval Spain,* 61–62.

217. Wallace-Hadrill, *Early Germanic Kingship,* 55.

218. "Defuncto in pace principe primatus totius gentis cum sacerdotibus successorem regni concilio conmuni constituant," Fourth Council of Toledo (633), Vives, *Concilios visigóticos,* 218; see also Orlandis and Ramos-Lisson, *Synoden,* 169–70.

the kingdom was to be bound with anathema "in the sight of Christ and of his apostles."[219] King-priest and priest-king emerged as bipolar, reflecting sides of a holy structure.[220] The accuracy of the structure allowed it to express Christ's nature and hence to claim transcendence. The rite of Christian initiation had become a way of establishing society.

The kingdom itself could become a symbol. Like the tonsure, it could be something "figured in the body but done in the soul."[221] As will be seen, the sacralized kingdom of Visigothic Spain was an influential model for bishops of the Frankish kingdom, despite the ultimate failure of the experiment and the conquest of Spain by the Moslems in 711. Frankish kingship, meanwhile, had been harnessed to a modest set of aims: preserving the kingdom and offering the locus for ritual and period meetings at which the reality of the kingdom could be made plain. Kings also offered law and coordinated the activities of the bishops.[222] The doctrine of Isidore and the model of a theocratic kingdom in Spain offered the possibility of deepening the concept of kingship and providing it with a political theology based in a persuasive vision of the past. To assimilate this vision, however, it would be necessary for all parties to accept a totally Christian vision for society and for kingship.

219. Fourth Council of Toledo (633), *Concilios visigóticos,* 219.
220. Rosine Letinier, "Le rôle politique des conciles de l'Espagne wisigothique," RHDr 75 (1997): 617–26.
221. "In corpore figuratur sed in animo agitur," Isidore, *De ecc.,* 2.4:55.
222. Zanella, "Legittimazione," 68–69.

[5]

OCCUPATION OF
THE CENTER

THIS CHAPTER offers an interpretation of Frankish liturgy in the
Merovingian and early Carolingian period as a poetical and religious
achievement coherent with the legal and political activities of bishops. The history of liturgy moves at a glacial pace, with changes of rituals or garments recorded only seldom and subtly over the centuries. Like episcopal law, liturgy
also provided a deep connection of the Frankish bishops to the ancient past of
the church. Liturgy involved bishops in a unique theatre of rituals and gestures
repeated over many centuries. As in episcopal law, emphasis was laid on the du-
plication of antiquity. As we have already seen in the case of the clerical tonsure
and the ritual of anointing, the meaning of these ancient gestures was puzzling
and inspired reflection and allegorical interpretation. The goal here is to understand the role of rites, special garments, and prayers in the development of what
is here termed the *persona* of the bishop. The composite of social doctrine, ritual
action (performative action), and special forms of dress together went into the
conceptual and social construction of the bishop. As a specialized elite drawn
from the ranks of the aristocracy, bishops occupied the center of society in ritual
terms, but also in economic and in political terms.

In the seventh century bishops profited equally from a rapid acceleration of
the Christianization of Frankish society and from the profound Christianization of kingship. The aristocratic and ascetic legacy of the episcopate took new

forms. The very meaning of royal power began to change in line with episcopal social concepts, so that bishops gained positions of closeness to the king.

The *Persona* of the Bishop

Governmental authority was asserted by bishops not only in literary expressions of authority such as legislation or in theological works like Isidore's *On Ecclesiastical Offices,* but also in symbolic ways of dressing and ritualized ways of acting. It is sometimes overlooked that episcopal government was *priestly:* a manifestation of sacred order, supported and explained by a historical mythology of origins.[1] Bishops were said to be agents (*vicarii*) of the apostles, who preserved an ancient tradition in their councils, whose government over Christian communities brought into the present all the power and functionality of the apostles. Bishops at the Council of Macon in 585 identified themselves as "holy fathers,"[2] claiming that they revived the sacred past in their legislation and in their very persons as each new bishop assumed the throne, garments, and regalia of an ancient high priest.

To be a bishop was not merely to hold an office, but to assume a *persona.*[3] Marcel Mauss once suggested that in certain social phenomena one may speak of an individual being possessed by his role.[4] This seems applicable to the bishops of Gaul, as well. The assertion of religious status by bishops operated at a deeper level than theological assertion, arguments from Scripture, or expository claims to represent an older civilization. Like other similar attempts to act out a mythic claim to social prominence studied by the anthropologist Jonathan Z. Smith, this was a wide-ranging and persistent effort, since "a total world-view [is] implied and involved in assuming these postures."[5]

Bishops sought to occupy the center stage of their society in a variety of

1. For "historical mythology": Dumézil, *Mitra–Varuna,* 163.

2. "Vniversi episcopi dixerunt: Congratulamur et nos, patres sanctissimi," Council of Mâcon (585), CCL 148A:238.

3. On the *persona* in early Christian thought see Pierre Hadot, "De Tertullien à Boèce: Le développement de la notion de personne dans les controverses théologiques," in *Problèmes de la personne: Colloque du Centre de Recherches de Psychologie comparative,* edited by Ignace Meyerson, 123–34, École Pratique des Hautes Études—Sorbonne: Congrés et colloques 13 (Paris: 1973).

4. "Cette prise de possession de l'individu par son rôle": Marcel Mauss, "Fait social et formation du caractère (1938): Notes inédites de Marcel Mauss, transcrites et présentées par Marcel Fournier," *L'ethnographie* 93 (1997): 7–14; this quote 13; see also Mauss, "Une catégorie de l'esprit humain: la notion de personne, celle du 'moi,' Un plan de travail," Huxley Memorial Lecture 1938, *Journal of the Royal Anthropological Institute* 68 (1938): 263–81.

5. Jonathan Z. Smith, "The Influence of Symbols upon Social Change: A Place on Which to Stand," in *Map Is Not Territory: Studies in the History of Religions,* Studies in Judaism in Late Antiquity 23 (Leiden: 1978), 129–46.

ways—in their liturgical and legal activities, in their building programs, in controlling large tracts of land and governing the people who lived on them. Episcopal government occupied a broad sphere of activity, spilling over from lordship into all aspects of religious life. Historians have long discussed episcopal lordship as a typical early medieval phenomenon, often implying a contradiction between the religious claims of bishops and their involvement in estate management and lordship. This was a contradiction contemporaries did not see. It was the extensive range of episcopal power that allowed bishops to participate in the Christianization and integration of the Frankish kingdom, overcoming the separatism of the Franks.[6]

Bishops claimed to govern according to ancient precepts handed down from bishop to bishop from the time of Christ. By occupying the center of religious life, bishops claimed to offer access to divine reality and the hope of salvation. They also proposed to reorient society through the institution of righteous forms of government and the reform of royal power. At the same time, bishops bolstered their position by developing a theory of property based upon protection of the poor. In what follows, episcopal power is shown to have been rooted in the fact that bishops occupied the center of cultic observance and, by extension, the center of society itself. The bishop claimed to bring the interior realm of the soul into harmony with the exterior realm of meaning: this congruence was brought about and expressed in gestures and signs.[7] A similar kind of harmony was looked for at the level of the kingdom in the Christianization and reform of society.

Liturgy and Power

As was seen in the Gallic period, bishops jealously guarded their control over sacred space and the sacred substances of the liturgy. Standing at the center of cultic observance, bishops not only exercised authority over other clerics, but also embodied, as the successors of the apostles, the point of contact between ritual and the religious realities toward which it was directed.[8] Liturgical imagery was not only directed "upward," so to speak, but also "outward," toward the portrayal of correct social structures. This was especially true in baptismal rituals, which had come to be seen as means of creating a Christian society. Isidore's

6. Werner, *Naissance de la noblesse,* 386–87, 346–52; Dierkens, "Christianisme et 'paganisme' dans la Gaule," 462.

7. Jean-Claude Schmitt, *La raison des gestes dans l'Occident médiéval* (Paris: 1990), 66.

8. Brigitte Basdevant-Gaudemet, "L'évêque, d'après la législation de quelques conciles mérovingiens," in *Clovis,* 1:471–94.

On Ecclesiastical Offices was widely accepted as an authoritative discussion both of the liturgy and of the social implications of liturgical government by bishops. As we have seen in the case of Isidore, social thought could draw upon and expand the significance of liturgical symbols.

Liturgical practice and texts traveled between Spain and Gaul, bringing about a significant degree of coherence between Visigothic liturgy and Gallic ritual. The difficulty of determining what the Gallic liturgy was like is due to the incomplete nature of the sources and to regional variation. Mabillon's belief that the *Missale Gothicum* represented a practice common to Gaul has not withstood detailed study.[9] Variation and the fragmentary nature of the sources have led to attempts to produce a synthetic, complete picture of this liturgy, especially of the Mass, where the Mozarabic liturgy supplies important clues to its nature.[10] Yitzhak Hen argues that many of the surviving liturgical texts may be associated with Frankish monastic centers in Burgundy and reflect the focus of these cultural centers on the problem of authority.[11] Kings were often linked to the liturgy, and special masses for the king were composed, as in the *Bobbio Missal,* which reflect the continuing Christianization of kingship.[12] Els Rose has suggested that liturgical texts such as the *Missale Gothicum* reveal connections of piety and alliance with distant centers, especially Rome.[13] While these texts were preserved in a monastic milieu and therefore illustrate the role of monasteries as an expression of royal aspirations, they also presuppose the central role of priests (in the Mass, for example) and the governing role of the bishop in establishing the orders of the church, in creating sacred space, in baptism, and in blessings of substances and people.

The religious centrality of the bishops seems to accord with other aspects of their activity, such as building and occupying important urban religious cen-

9. Jean Mabillon, *De liturgia gallicana libri tres* (Paris: 1685), repr. PL 72: 99–448; see Duchesne, *Christian Worship,* 151; and W. S. Porter, *The Gallican Rite* (London: 1958), 10.

10. Duchesne, *Christian Worship,* 189–227; Porter, *Gallican Rite,* 19–53; Klaus Gamber, *Die Messfeier nach altgallicanischem Ritus,* Studia patristica et litugica quae edidit Institutum Liturgicum Ratisbonense 14 (Regensburg: 1984), 30–31; and Yitzhak Hen, *Culture and Religion in Merovingian Gaul, A.D. 481–751,* Cultures, Beliefs and Traditions 1 (Leiden: 1995), 67–75.

11. Hen, *Culture and Religion,* 43–60; and Cyrille Vogel, *Medieval Liturgy: An Introduction to the Sources,* trans. William G. Storey and Niels Krogh Rasmussen (Washington, D.C.: 1986), 61–78.

12. Mary Garrison, "The *Missa pro principe* in the Bobbio Missal," in *The Bobbio Missal: Liturgy and Religious Culture in Merovingian Gaul,* edited by Yizhak Hen and Rob Meens (Cambridge: 2004), 187–203; see 189.

13. Els Rose, "Liturgical Commemoration of the Saints in the *Missale Gothicum* (Vat. Reg. Lat. 317): New Approaches to the Liturgy of Early Medieval Gaul," VC 58 (2004): 75–97.

ters and their role as patrons and civic governors. Bishop Desiderius of Cahors was seen as a "great benefactor of his city" because of his religious status.[14] The terms and scholarly methods of liturgiology focus on historical morphology rather than the meaning of the texts, since, after all, many of these meanings are recognizably ancient. The great liturgical scholar Callewaert emphasized that liturgical formulae and gestures should be studied in their liturgical context and analyzed so as to reveal their "principes fondamentaux."[15] Yet the traditional connection between the *lex orandi* (the mode and rule of prayer) and the *lex credendi* (the mode and rule of belief) means that liturgy must also be understood in the larger context of contemporary belief and theology. The liturgy was a preeminent "cultural text"; therefore, in what follows, these sources will be read *as if meant*.

An early and important example of the implications of the liturgy for the expression of social thought, and of a historical vision, may be found in the *Exposition of the Ancient Gallic Liturgy*.[16] It is a vital source of knowledge about the liturgy of Gaul around the year 700, and offers (sometimes cryptic) explanations of the importance of various rituals. The work was long considered to be relevant and valuable, and was copied well into the Carolingian period.[17] Perhaps twenty years earlier is the *Missale Gothicum,* which provides a fairly complete sacramentary for the period.[18] Also important is the *Bobbio Missal,* compiled a bit later (sometime after 700).[19] The *Bobbio Missal* may copy a sixth-century

14. On the building program and urban government of Desiderius, see Wood, *Merovingian Kingdoms,* 76, 79. In the view of Jean Durliat, as mentioned earlier, civil and military powers were delegated to bishops by kings: Durliat, "Les attributions civiles," 239–40.

15. Camillus Callewaert, "La méthode dans l'étude de la liturgie," in *Sacris Erudiri: Fragmenta liturgica collecta a monachis Sancti Petri Aldenburge in Steenbrugge ne pereant,* edited by Camillus Callewaert, 25–40 (Steenbrugge: 1940).

16. Although Duchesne and others had accepted the attribution of the work to the sixth-century Germanus of Paris (Cf. Duchesne, *Christian Worship,* 155), André Wilmart dated it to the turn of the eighth century, in Wilmart, "Germain de Paris (Lettres attribuées à saint)," DACL 6:1049; text in *Expositio antiquae liturgiae gallicanae,* edited by E. C. Ratcliff, Henry Bradshaw Society 98 (London: 1971); see also Vogel, *Medieval Liturgy,* 11, 108.

17. Yitzhak Hen, *The Royal Patronage of Liturgy in Frankish Gaul, to the Death of Charles the Bald (877),* Henry Bradshaw Society, Subsidia III (London: 2001), 5–7; see also Hen, *Roman Barbarians,* 118–23.

18. *"Missale Gothicum": A Gallican Sacramentary. MS. Vatican. Regin. Lat. 317,* ed. H. M. Bannister, Henry Bradshaw Society 52 and 54, 2 vols. (London: 1916–1917); see also Klaus Gamber, *Codices liturgici latini antiquiores,* Spicilegii Friburgensis subsidia 1 (Freiburg: 1963), 30–31; Vogel, *Medieval Liturgy,* 108.

19. *The Bobbio Missal: A Gallican Mass-book (MS. Paris. Lat. 13246) Text,* ed. E. A. Lowe, Henry Bradshaw Society 58 (London: 1920). On the influence of Milan, see Duchesne, *Christian Worship,* 158–60. This is confirmed by M. P. Vanhengel, "Le Rite et la formule de la chrismation postbaptismale en Gaule et en Haute-Italie du IVe au VIIIe siècle d'apres les sacramentaires

Gallic compilation.[20] Both the *Missale Gothicum* and the *Bobbio Missal* derive from somewhere near Luxeuil and are marked by Roman and Spanish influences.[21] The liturgy of these Gallic missals was composed without Isidore, while the *Expositio* may rely on an earlier source that Isidore also used to explain the liturgy. The caveat must be repeated that these works cannot provide evidence for the whole of Gaul. Local centers of worship developed along independent lines, partly because of poor communications, but also because of the localized authority of bishops to govern without constant contact with Rome or other outside interference.[22] Prayers and hymns were composed by locally important charismatic bishops and abbots.[23]

Perhaps the most important ritual bishops performed was baptism, one of the oldest rituals of the Christian Church.[24] In this ceremony the governing authority of bishops was most on display, for they thereby brought into existence the very society they claimed to govern. In the late antique church, baptism came after a period of instruction and reflection. Cyril of Jerusalem, writing sometime around 350, expected that those who wished to enter the Church of Jerusalem would be adult converts. They would advance their names at the beginning of Lent and come to church over these forty days to hear special sermons and explanations of the importance of baptism.[25] "Persist in the catechizings: though my discourse is long, do not weary. For you are receiving an armour against the enemy power."[26] But as early as the end of the third century, infants were being baptized alongside adults. The resulting alteration in the performance and meaning of baptism was profound. The ceremony gradually became a ritual manipulation on the part of the bishop. All aspects of the ritual were thereby transformed: the subject of the baptism, the infant, was objectified (the rite was "per-

---

gallicans: Aux origines du rituel primitif," *Sacris Erudiri* 21 (1972/73): 209–12; see further Gamber, *Codices liturgici,* 35; Vogel, *Medieval Liturgy,* 323–24. See also "Liturgical Latin in the Bobbio Missal," in *The Bobbio Missal: Liturgy and Religious Culture in Merovingian Gaul,* edited by Yizhak Hen and Rob Meens (Cambridge: 2004), 67–78.

20. For a survey of these sources: Hen, *Culture and Religion,* 43–60.

21. The dating, provenance, and relationship of these works are summarized and a stemma is proposed in Vanhengel, "Le Rite et la formule de la chrismation postbaptismale," 222.

22. Cardot, *L'Espace et le pouvoir,* 159; Hen, *Culture and Religion,* 59.

23. Hen, *Royal Patronage of Liturgy,* 28.

24. André Benoît and Charles Munier, *Die Taufe in der Alten Kirche (1.–3. Jahrhundert),* trans. Annemarie Spoerri, *Traditio christiana* 9 (Bern: 1994); Simon Légasse, *Naissance du baptême,* Lectio divina 153 (Paris: 1993).

25. Introduction, *St. Cyril of Jerusalem's Lectures on the Christian Sacraments: The Procatechesis and the Five Mystagogical Catecheses,* ed. F. L. Cross (London: 1951), xxii.

26. Cyril of Jerusalem, *Procatechesis,* 10, in *St. Cyril of Jerusalem's Lectures,* 46; I have adjusted the translation.

formed over him/her"), and the physical actions of the rite were freighted with significance. With the Christianization of Merovingian Gaul, infant baptism became the norm.[27] The transformation of the rite in favor of infant baptism, however, proved to be appropriate for the baptism of adult converts, as well—especially in a missionary setting.[28]

This shift awakened an intense interest in the question of how baptismal water could effect a transformation in the candidate, who was now viewed as a passive infant. Tertullian explained that the water used in baptism could offer an exit from the darkness into which man had fallen with Adam, because God somehow inhabited the water. As Tertullian put it, "And so, made holy by the holy, the nature of water has itself taken up the power to make holy."[29] In a work of the late fifth century, Pseudo-Jerome's *On the Seven Orders of the Church,* the water of baptism was compared to the water that poured from Christ's wounded side at the Passion. The salvific power of baptismal water was put succinctly: "the spirit of Life is in the water."[30]

The earliest Western liturgy known in detail is the *Apostolic Tradition* of Hippolytus, which still seems to picture the initiation of adults who have undergone a period of education as catechumens.[31] Hilary of Arles, describing the baptism of his predecessor Honoratus, explained that he had learned the "first rudiments of the faith" during his instruction as a catechumen.[32] In the period leading up to baptism, as in the ritual described by Cyril, candidates were exorcised daily to rid them of demonic influences lingering after their education.[33] During the

27. Hen, *Culture and Religion,* 155–57.

28. Senn, *Christian Liturgy, Catholic and Evangelical,* 192–94.

29. "Ita de sancto sanctificata natura aquarum et ipsa sanctificare concepit," Tertullian, *De baptismo* (1.4), in *Quinti Septimi Florentis Tertulliani Opera,* edited by August Reifferscheid and Georg Wissowa, 204, CSEL 20 (Vienna: 1890); Timothy D. Barnes, *Tertullian: A Historical and Literary Study,* 2nd ed. (Oxford: 1985). Discussion in Peter Cramer, *Baptism and Change in the Early Middle Ages, c. 200–c. 1150* (Cambridge: 1993), 57; see also Paul De Clerck, "Les origines de la formule baptismale," in *Rituels: Mélanges offerts à Pierre-Marie Gy, O.P.,* edited by Paul De Clerck and Éric Palazzo (Paris: 1990), 199–213.

30. "Baptismus uero aqua est, quae tempore passionis de latere Domini exiuit et nullum aliud est elementum, quod in hoc mundo purget uniuersa, quod animarum poculum sit, quod uiuificet cuncta; et ideo, quia spiritus uitae in aqua est, et congregatio aquarum mare nomen accepit," Pseudo-Jerome, *Ps.-Hieronymi De septem ordinibus ecclesiae,* ed. P. Athanasius Walter Kalff (Diss., Bayerischen Julius-Maximilians-Universität, Würzburg 1935), 76.

31. Hippolytus of Rome, *Traditio apostolica* (Diataxeis), 5.2; see also Henry Asgar Kelly, *The Devil at Baptism: Ritual, Theology, and Drama* (Ithaca: 1985), 81–82; and J. D. C. Fisher, *Christian Initiation: Baptism in the Medieval West. A Study in the Disintegration of the Primitive Rite of Initiation,* Alcuin Club Collections 47 (London: 1965), 2; Vogel, *Medieval Liturgy,* 31–32.

32. "Inter prima fidei rudimenta," Hilary of Arles, *Vie de Saint Honorat* (5.6), 82.

33. This account is from Kelly, *Devil at Baptism,* 85–86.

actual baptismal ritual, the bishop breathed into the catechumen's face, perhaps as a final exorcism, and then signed him or her on the forehead, ears, and nose with oil that itself had previously been exorcised. The initiate was then asked to renounce Satan and all his works before being immersed in the water. All these features were retained in the baptismal liturgies of Gaul. Infants were exorcised at the beginning of the ceremony and then anointed with the "oil of exorcism," which itself had been exorcised with this formula:

I exorcise you, creature of oil, by the almighty God, who made heaven and earth, the sea, and all that is in them. Every power of the adversary, every army of the devil, every attack, every phantasm of Satan, be uprooted and be put to flight from this creature of oil, so that it might become for all who are to be anointed with it [a means] for their adoption as sons, through the Holy Spirit, in the name of God the Father almighty, and in the charity of Jesus Christ our Lord, who is to come in the Holy Spirit to judge the living and the dead and the world by fire.[34]

The exorcism thus passed from Creation to Judgment, encapsulating in one sweep the beginning and end of created beings. The oil was addressed as a distinct being, as though it were a person being commanded. The bishop thereby liberated the oil from Satan's influence and incorporated it under his own government as a newly purified substance. Thus purified, the oil could be entered by the Holy Spirit, which it could impart to those whose skin absorbed it.[35] This oil was used to seal the infant on its ears, nostrils, and between the shoulder blades to drive out and exclude the demons inevitably hidden there. "Catechism" accordingly became a ritual performed over the infant:

Nor does it escape you, Satan, that punishments threaten you. . . . Therefore, damned one, give honor to the living and true God, give honor to Jesus Christ his Son, and to the Holy Spirit, in whose name and power I command you to go out and depart from this servant of God.[36]

The as yet pagan child was viewed as a mere creature, assumed to harbor demons. By means of infant baptism, the bishop lay claim to the child as a human territory. This is why bishops, like those assembled in Mâcon in 585, commanded

---

34. Gel. 617, trans. in Kelly, *Devil at Baptism,* 211; see also G. G. Willis, *A History of Early Roman Liturgy, to the Death of Pope Gregory the Great,* Henry Bradshaw Society 1 (London: 1994), 120–21.

35. "Descendat super hoc oleum potentie tue donum; descendat claritas et origo virtutum; descendat benignitas et puritas sanitatis," cited in Adolph Franz, *Die kirchlichen Benediktionen im Mittelalter* (Freiburg im Breisgau: 1909), 1:346.

36. From the Roman Ordo XI:83–83, cited in Kelly, *Devil at Baptism,* 220.

that all must appear in church with their newborn children on the first Sunday in Lent so that they might receive the imposition of hands, be anointed with the sacred tincture of oil, and be regenerated by holy baptism.[37] With a motion of his hand, the bishop made "le signe chrétien par excellence," the sign of the Passion, exerting a metaphysical power over the new Christian.[38] Unlike late antique churches, Merovingian churches were no longer believing assemblies providing themselves with bishops as their chosen leaders, but a domain of the bishops, who established and expanded the society they governed through baptism.[39] The *personage* of the child was conceived only as what Ricoeur has called the "subject of imputation."[40] Through baptism, the child was impressed with an identity—given a name and enrolled in society, in a liturgy of imputation. Therefore the history of infant baptism should not be viewed only in terms of the problem of original sin, as a phase in the history of dogma. As we shall see in the next chapter, pagan adults were also baptized in just this mood of triumph and conquest, as if they were children.

Baptism and anointing could only be performed by a bishop, who alone could create and wield the sacred substances involved. An exception was made for the deathbed reconciliation of heretics. In this case, chrism could be used by a presbyter if a bishop could not be present.[41] Water was not the only element of the ceremony of baptism. In a sense, the water purified the child, but the application of oil after baptism was the defining moment, the "sealing" and establishment of a new member of society. In thinking about the oil, bishops connected their own rulership with the ancient anointed "offices" which they inherited.

A connection between baptismal anointing and the "anointed offices" of ancient Judaism was established by John III (the Deacon), pope from 561 to 574, in a letter to Senarius (c. 500):

Having donned the white vestments, his head is anointed with the unction of sacred chrism, so the baptized might know that a kingship and priestly mystery befits him. In fact priests and princes were anointed with the oil of chrism. . . . To express more fully

37. "Reuocati omnes omnino a die quadragensimo cum infantibus suis ad ecclesiam obseruare praecipimus, ut inpositionem manus certis diebus adepti et sacri olei liquore peruncti ligitimi diei festiuitate fruantur et sacro baptismate regenerentur," Council of Mâcon (585), CCSL 148A:40.

38. Schmitt, *Raison des gestes*, 321.

39. Jungmann, *Early Liturgy*, 248–52; Dierkens, "Christianisme et 'paganisme,'" 461.

40. Paul Ricoeur, "Ipséité, altérité, socialité," *Archivio di filosofia* 54 (1986): 17–33.

41. The necessity of chrism at baptism was specified at the Council of Orange (441), canon 2. Canon 1 allowed a presbyter to do it in emergencies; CCSL 148:78; see also Willis, *History of Early Roman Liturgy*, 126.

the image of a priest, the head of the reborn person is beautifully arranged with wool. For the priests of those days always adorned their heads with a kind of mystic veil.[42]

The combination of allusions here seems to coincide neatly with Isidore's treatment of tonsure and the chrism. This letter and a related text, Pseudo-Maximian's *De Baptismo,* have been shown to have influenced the Gallic rite of unction, although not all of their allusions were retained.[43] John the Deacon's letter was still being excerpted in Frankish *florilegia* of the late eighth century.[44] According to Gy, this text still envisioned the initiation and baptism of adults.[45]

In the *Bobbio Missal* one finds the image of the "twofold office" of king and priest in the rite of extreme unction: "I anoint you with the sanctified oil just as Samuel anointed David as a king and a prophet."[46] David's significance for the rite of unction was that he combined the offices of king and priest, anticipating the union of these functions in Christ. Every Christian could therefore be compared to David. At baptism, unction was associated with being given a vestment.[47] While applying the chrism, the *Missale Gothicum* said that this vestment was first received by Christ, which therefore also seems to refer to Christ's royal and priestly status.[48] John the Deacon and Pseudo-Maximian together provided images that became attached to baptismal unction in both the *Missale Gothicum* and the *Bobbio Missal,* images joining royal and priestly characteristics— crowns, vestments, and anointing—prefigured by the ancient Jewish priests and kings.[49] The initiate was "baptized and crowned in Christ."[50]

42. "Sumptis dehinc albis vestibus, caput eius sacri chrismatis unctione perungitur, ut intellegat baptizatus regnum in se ac sacerdotale convenisse mysterium. Chrismatis enim oleo sacerdotes et principes unguebantur. . . . Ad imaginem quippe sacerdotii plenius exprimendam renascentis caput lintei decore conponitur. Nam sacerdotes illius temporis quodam mystico velamine caput semper ornabant," John the Deacon, *Epistola ad Senarium,* in André Wilmart, "Un florilège carolingien sur le symbolisme des cérémonies du baptême, avec un Appendice sur le lettre de Jean Diacre," in Wilmart, ed., *Analecta Reginensia: Extraits des manuscrits latins de la reine Christine conservés au Vatican,* 174, Studi e Testi 59 (Rome: 1933), 174.

43. Vanhengel, "Le Rite et la formule de la chrismation postbaptismale," 214.

44. P. Bouhout, "Explications du rituel baptismal à l'époque carolingienne," *Revue des études augustiniennes* 24 (1978): 278–301; see 282–83.

45. Pierre-Marie Gy, *La liturgie dans l'histoire* (Paris: 1990), 152.

46. "Ungo te oleo sanctificato sicut unxit samuhel david in rege et propheta," *Bobbio Missal,* 74; see also J. B. Bord, *L'extrême onction d'après l'épître de saint Jacques (V.14.15), examinée dans la tradition,* Museum Lessianum—Section théologique (Brussels: 1923), 86–92.

47. "Accipe vestem candidam quam inmacolatam perferas ante tribunal christi," *Bobbio Missal,* 75.

48. "Perungo te crisma santitatis Tonicam inmortalitatis qua[m] dominus noster iesus christus traditam a patre primus accepit ut eam integram et inlibatam perferas ante tribunal christi et uiuas in saecula saeculorum," *Missale Gothicum,* 1:77.

49. Vanhengel, "Le Rite et la Formule de la chrismation postbaptismale," 214–15.

50. "Baptizatis et in christo coronatis," *Missale Gothicum,* 1:78.

In a blessing of oil, the *Bobbio Missal* gestured toward this interpretation:

I adjure you, creature of oil, in the name of Jesus Christ of Nazareth, son of the living God, that you be for the sanctification and and purgation of men, because our kings and judges were anointed by you, or taken up whom God called to his grace.[51]

This can be interpreted as a social application of Christology like that of Isidore's, one that was widespread in early medieval Europe.[52] The focus of baptismal liturgy was on the governing elements of society, viewed as anointed offices.

As in the writings of Isidore, these formulae tried to give social concepts a strong connection to Scripture they did not objectively have. Having appeared in the slow accretion of liturgical tradition, they could only be rooted in the Bible by means of allusion and analogy. Preoccupation with kings and priests, their interrelation, and the source of their authority turned on Christology. Bishops sought to locate their social ideals in liturgy just as they did in their legislation. Royal images were used to elaborate the role of the bishop as governor of a church that assumed, in baptism, the royal and priestly character of Christ. The Gelasian rite was oriented toward the baptism of infants.[53] By means of baptism, bishops established a Christian's membership in society and the bishops' right to govern him.

Bishops in the Merovingian period believed that their power was grounded in an authoritative tradition of several interwoven strands. First, there was the tradition of episcopal succession, which provided contact with the establishment of the church by Christ. With apostolic authority came the power to bind and loose, and hence to govern the church. Second, there was the bishop's participation in legislative councils, which preserved and refurbished the orthodox faith of the ancient fathers. Thus, a sacred antiquity could be called upon and redeployed by the contemporary holder of an episcopal see. His social status was thought to be grounded in these same traditions. The bishop's power derived from his personal revival of apostolic prerogatives. The movement from government over the church to government over society was indicated by the complex images of the liturgy. Ritual, gesture, law, and government all came together at the point of the liturgy.

51. "Aiuro te criaturi oliae i nomene iesus christi nacariae filiae dei uiui reges et iudices nostri ut sis sanctefecacio et purgacio hominum quia ex te ongendi fuerent uel sumti quos deus ad suam graciam uocare," *Bobbio Missal*, 173.

52. See the references to Bede in Yves Congar, *L'ecclésiologie du haut moyen âge de Saint Grégoire le Grand à la désunion entre Byzance et Rome* (Paris: 1968), 85.

53. Gy, *La liturgie*, 152.

Vestments and Tonsure

Early ecclesiastical garments were similar to other official garments of the Roman Empire. Ordinary priests did not wear any distinctive garments until the fifth century, when they were criticized for wearing overly elaborate costumes.[54] A light-colored tunic was covered by a brown or violet *planeta,* or cloak.[55] In the cities of Gaul, this meant that the identification of bishops as the last representatives of the old Gallo-Roman nobility could also be seen in their dress. The exception to this was the *pallium.* Originally a garment marking consular authority, it long retained this official quality. Duchesne believed that it was granted to the pope as an imperial gift, just as is recounted in the *Donation of Constantine,* but that it came to be regarded as a relic of St. Peter's mantle.[56] Beginning in 1997, a set of garments, preserved as relics of St. Caesarius, was examined and restored by a team led by Anastasia Ozoline, allowing us to have a close look at the style of a late antique bishop's tunic and pallium (in fact, two palliums).[57] Caesarius was the first bishop aside from the bishop of Rome to be granted a pallium. This special dignity demonstrated the prominence of Arles relative to Vienne, and thus it was also politically significant. The pallium would be lowered into Peter's tomb so as to become Peter's own before being sent to the see on which it was being conferred. Under Pope Gregory the Great Arles lost its exclusive claim to wear the pallium, and its use was gradually extended to become the shared mark of metropolitan, and then all episcopal, dignity.[58] In Gaul and Spain it became a general mark of episcopal authority in the sixth century, and by the late sixth century it was felt that no bishop should presume to conduct a Mass without the pallium.[59]

Typically the pallium was a long scarf of white wool, marked with black or

54. Godding, *Prêtres en Gaule,* 28–29.

55. Duchesne, *Christian Worship,* 380; Wharton B. Marriott, *Vestiarum Christianum: The Origin and Gradual Development of the Dress of Holy Ministry in the Church* (London: 1868), xlvii–xlviii.

56. Duchesne, *Christian Worship,* 385. But the impossibility of dating such an event makes it subject to interpretation: J. Braun, *Die liturgische Gewandung im Occident und Orient: Nach Ursprung und Entwicklung, Verwendung und Symbolik* (Freiburg im Breisgau: 1907), 652–64.

57. On the preservation of these garments as relics: Anastasia Ozoline, *Trésors de la Gaule chrétienne: Histoire et restauration des reliques textiles de saint Césaire d'Arles (470–542)* (Arles: 2008), 17.

58. Ozoline, *Trésors,* 29–32; Braun, *Liturgische Gewandung,* 653.

59. Duchesne, *Christian Worship,* 384–90; Braun, *Liturgische Gewandung,* 675–76; "Vt episcopus sine palleo missas dicere non praesumat," Council of Macon (581–583), CCSL, 148A:224. Also useful is the translation in *Les canons des conciles mérovingiens (VIe–VIIe siècles),* trans. J. Gaudemet and B. Basdevant, SC 353, 354, 2 vols. (Paris: 1989).

red crosses at each end: it was looped over the right shoulder, and draped over the left shoulder so that it hung straight down in back and front.[60] The preserved palliums of Caesarius are of two types: one was a simple band of cloth marked by three red crosses (one at each end, and one in the center). A second, highly remarkable pallium was embroidered with a Chi Rho or labarum.[61] By the Carolingian period, the pallium went around the neck and was joined in front to hang straight down from the breast.

Such historical details are only a minor part of the story, however, since all such garments had long been given a symbolic and myth-historical interpretation. Origen, for example, was much given to this type of discourse, expounding on the linen tunic of Christ, the true High Priest, and of the priestly *mitra*.[62]

In this vein the *Exposition of the Ancient Gallic Liturgy* offered an explanation of the origin of the pallium radically different than that of the modern historian of costume, thus complicating our understanding of the history of episcopal garments, and especially the more important history of their meaning:

The pallium, which goes around the neck down to the breast, was called a *rationale* in the Old Testament, that is to say, a sign of sanctity over the memory of the breast, as the prophet said in the person of the Lord: "The Spirit of the Lord is upon me."

The prophet Isaiah had long ago described the vestments of a high priest in terms that showed that Christian bishops had inherited their garments from an ancient and holy tradition:

That I might give glory to the mourners of Zion, and give them a crown for ashes, the oil of joy for mourning, a garment (*pallium*) of praise for the spirit of grief (Is. 61:3).

The *Exposition* went on to explain that "Ancient custom adorns the neck because kings and priests were enveloped with a pallium over their shining vestments which was a sign of grace."[63] Far from looking to the Roman past, the author's

---

60. Duchesne, *Christian Worship*, 387.

61. There is some mystery as to why Caesarius might have had two palliums: one may have been the pallium sent by Pope Symmachus, and the other a pallium given by the bishops of Gaul: Ozoline, *Trésors*, 46.

62. Noche, *Vestis Varia*, 153.

63. "Pallium uero quod circa collum usque ad pectus uenit rationale uocabatur in ueteri {testamento} scilicet signum sanctitatis super memoriam pectoris dicente proph[a]eta ex persona domini 'Spiritus domini super me' Et post pauca 'Ut ponerem gloriam lugentibus Sion et darem eis coronam pro cinere. oleum gaudii pro luctu. Pallium laudis pro spiritu meroris' quod autem collum cingit anitquae sonsuetudinis est quia reges et sacerdotes circumdati erant pallio {super} ueste[m] fulgente{m} quod gratia{m} praesignabat," *Expositio antique liturgiae gallicanae* (2.16), 23.

instinct was to explain the bishop's pallium by a Christological reference to the Judaic offices and to anointing. Like Isidore, the author wished to anchor the episcopal office in ancient Israel.[64]

Gallic bishops tended to think about their own past along the lines laid down by Isidore, hence the tradition of their special vestments was not at all seen by them as a "Roman survival." The preservation of ecclesiastical dress was not only a sign of religious conservatism.[65] The actual origin of the vestments was not remembered, and so has little relevance to this discussion. What did the vestments mean in the sixth and seventh centuries? Though Braun argued that there are scant traces of mystical interpretation of vestments before the Carolingian period, it has already been shown that speculation on the part of Isidore and the litugical poets led toward the hermeneutic assimilation of Christian priesthood to Judaic priests and kings through their vestments, tonsure, and anointing. For clerics, these were signs of a prerogative to rule, based on their assumption of the Old Testament offices of priest and king.[66]

Distinctive dress has everywhere been used for marking social categories and stature, but it is always questionable how applicable general anthropological data can be to any specific historical case.[67] As a language, it is the specific, historically rooted meaning of clothing, rather than its place in a structure, that is its most outstanding feature. On the one hand, there was a clerical understanding of priestly clothing, a closed language of Christology and Old Testament exegesis. At the same time episcopal vestments were a dynamic language, not at all incompatible with clerical interpretations, but presenting a compact, hieratic symbology of stature and religious power. The way bishops interpreted their vestments, and the hieratic symbology they saw in them, were therefore divorced from the historian's idea of the "development of clerical vestments." By the late sixth century, the distinction between secular and clerical dress was prized and emphasized. The Council of Macon (581) said that clerics should not dress like ordinary Franks, and it seems that a special clerical garb was recognized.[68]

Among the garments of Caesarius that have been preserved, there is a tunic.

---

64. It is useful to compare Isidore's description of Aaron's vestments: tunic, crown, bracelet, and superhumeral; Isidore, *De ecc.* (2.5), 57.

65. M. E. Roach and J. B. Eicher, "The Language of Personal Adornment," in *The Fabrics of Culture: The Anthropology of Clothing and Adornment,* edited by J. M. Cordwell and R. A. Schwartz, 7–21; see 17 (The Hague: 1979).

66. Braun, *Liturgische Gewandung,* 702.

67. O. Blanc, "Historiographie du vêtement: un bilan," in *Le Vêtement: Histoire, archéologie et symbolique vestimentaires au moyen âge,* edited by M. Pastoureau, 7–33 (Paris: 1989).

68. Godding, *Prêtres en Gaule,* 29.

This tunic was a sleeved garment of plain cream-colored cloth, cut in a simple T-shape, of a type well-known as a male garment in late antiquity.[69] The dalmatic, a sleeved gown often refined and decorated, went over the tunic, which could sometimes be seen beneath it. This garment often had vertical stripes or was decorated with a key motif.[70] The chasuble (*casula*), a richer development of the *planeta,* tended to be a costly garment, which made it available to few. It came to be restricted to priests and bishops.[71] The history of clerical vestments reveals two contrasting pressures: one toward a visible expression of dignity and prestige, and the other toward a declaration of ascetic simplicity. Caesarius forbade his monks to wear anything but the plainest type of clothing, and he seems to have worn the same.[72] Later on Boniface would complain, in a letter to Cuthbehrt, that vestments in England were being decorated with a broad purple stripe and meanders.[73] In Spain and Gaul, as was mentioned earlier, the crozier and ring were added to the assemblage of episcopal signs.[74] The idea of tying these developments to the "style" of the period in which they existed seems insuperable.[75] There is no question that the garments were thought to be beautiful and impressive, shining white (*candida*) or ornamented, made from expensive imported fabrics. Springing from an extremely durable tradition, their early development is discussed by scholars in terms of centuries, encompassing large-scale disruptions and migrations. As a style they are hardly tied to social changes.

Ecclesiastical vestments were the specialized garments of a group claiming rulership. They were carefully restricted to that group, and when gathered in assembly, bishops would have recognized all the marks of their elite status. It would have been rare for more than one bishop to be seen in any one place, and on ritual occasions episcopal garb marked a unique individual standing above other clerics, and even more distinctly marked off from townsmen and farmers. Although everyone in the society would be marked by clothing appropriate to

69. Ozoline, *Trésors,* 28.

70. L. Trichet, *Le costume du clergé: Ses origines et son évolution en France d'après les règlements de l'église* (Paris: 1986), 22–23; see also C. Callewaert, "De dalmatica," in his *Sacris Erudiri,* 219–22.

71. Duchesne, *Christian Worship,* 381; Braun, *Liturgische Gewandung,* 156–57.

72. Ozoline, *Trésors,* 27.

73. "Quia illa ornamenta vestium, ut illis videtur, quod ab aliis turpitudo dicitur, latissimis clavis et vermium imaginibus clavata," Boniface to Archbishop Cuthbehrt of Canterbury (747), *Die Briefe des Heiligen Bonifatius und Lullus (S. Bonifatii et Lullii epistolae),* ed. M. Tangl, Letter 78:170, MGH Epistolae Selectae 1 (Berlin: 1916).

74. Duchesne, *Christian Worship,* 397–98.

75. See Blanc's discussion of Viollet-le-Duc's notion of style, "Historiographie du vêtement," 8–12.

his age, status, and employment, this clothing formed a "sartorial set" outside of which the bishop stood, particularly in an agricultural setting.[76] Chasuble and pallium were divorced from local customs of ornamentation and group identity.[77]

At the same time, bishops employed a liturgical language distinct from the language of daily life, structured by its own tradition.[78] In the view of Mohrmann, liturgical Latin was distinctive: "it is as though contact with the divine draws man out of his ordinary life, and this is reflected in his language"— giving rise to a special holy diction.[79] Sacral language was the special language of an inner group. This view has been energetically countered by Els Rose: in the earliest liturgies of Gaul, the language is plainly close to the language of daily life. In Rose's view, "only when the Carolingians extended their reform program to the field of liturgical Latin, did the liturgical language become incomprehensible to the masses."[80] Together, ritual and vestment were "otherworldly," and if they performed a "function within a system of functions," they were powerfully distinguished from the cohesive functional elements of the rest of society.[81] While marking bishops off from those around them, vestments also served to join bishops together as a distinct, cohesive group of ritual specialists and governors.

Tonsure was another of these potent separations. Whereas taking the tonsure removed a person from the secular world, its duties, and expectations, it was considered requisite to ask permission of the king.[82] When Austrigisilus wanted to leave the service of King Guntram to enter the priesthood, he first obtained

76. See P. Mane, "Émergence du vêtement de travail à travers l'iconographie médiévale," *Vêtement,* 93–122.

77. Such customs are described in E. M. Maurer, "Symbol and Identification in North American Indian Clothing," in *Fabrics of Culture,* 119–42; see esp. 134–35.

78. After 400, the development of specialized literary Latin: Michel Banniard, *Genese culturelle de l'Europe: Ve–VIIIe siècle* (Paris: 1989), 178–214; see also Brian Stock, *The Implications of Literacy: Written Language and Models of Interpretation in the Eleventh and Twelfth Centuries* (Princeton: 1983), 3–24. Compare Hen, *Culture and Religion,* 21–42, who argues that the barrier between literacy and orality was very permeable.

79. Christine Mohrmann, *Liturgical Latin, its Origins and Character: Three Lectures* (Washington, D.C.: 1957), 13.

80. Els Rose, "Liturgical Latin in the *Missale Gothicum* (Vat. Reg. lat. 317): A Reconsideration of Christine Mohrmann's Approach," *Sacris Erudiri* 42 (2003): 97–121; see 113.

81. A reference to the Prague School which gave rise to structural anthropology. The phrase is P. G. Bogatryev's: *The Functions of Folk Costume in Moravian Slovakia,* trans. R. G. Crum, Approaches to Semiotics 5 (Mouton–La Haye: 1971). See the discussion in Blanc, "Historiographie du vêtement," 16–25.

82. Godding, *Prêtres en Gaule,* 15–16.

permission in the form of a royal letter.[83] The aesthetic impact of the style cannot be recovered. It is possible that clerics thereby adopted the look of an older, balding man, and thereby the venerability of age. Clerics had a range of interpretations available to them that were quite distinct from the tonsure's immediate impact. It could be seen, for example, as an imitation of Christ's crown of thorns.[84] As Isidore noted, it was a symbolic transformation of the body to make it express an inner transformation, and could be seen as both a kind of crown and a kind of priestly headdress.

The tonsure came to be considered a divine institution as writers pushed the origins of the practice back to Peter. The circular hairstyle thus came to be known as the "Petrine" tonsure. In their attempts to understand the practice, writers such as Isidore looked for an explanation in the various uses of crown imagery in the Bible, where it stood as a sign of "joy, plenitude, and supreme power."[85] It was inevitable that the crown of thorns and the adoption of clerical humility were not seen as symbols of weakness, but of Christ's victory: such a sign of humility stood for a victory over death itself, and hence over the human condition. The tonsure was a symbol that could express a host of important truths, which helps to explain why the Irish tonsure provoked the bitter opposition of Bede.[86] It has been incorrectly said that the crown-shaped tonsure was first mentioned by Gregory of Tours, but it is certainly older than that.[87] It can be seen, for example, in mosaics commissioned by Justinian for churches in Ravenna. The mosaics of San Vitale, completed from 546 to 549, show Archbishop Maximian wearing a circular tonsure, while a mosaic in St. Apollinare Nuovo shows St. Martin holding a martyr's crown, whose shape is mirrored in his circular tonsure.[88]

83. *Vita Austrigisilus, episcopi Biturgi,* ed. Bruno Krusch, MGH SRM 4. 188–208; see 195.

84. St. Germanus of Constantinople, *Rerum ecclesiasticarum theoria,* cited in Marriott, *Vestiarum Christianum,* 83; see also L. Trichet, *La Tonsure: Vie et mort d'une pratique ecclésiastique* (Paris: 1990), 77.

85. Trichet, *Tonsure,* 81–82.

86. Edward James, "Bede and the Tonsure Question," *Peritia* 3 (1984): 85–98.

87. Despite Trichet, *Tonsure,* 69–75. Trichet points to Gregory as the first mention of the circular tonsure, but it is not clear that Gregory refers to it. There are two instances in Gregory where a tonsure is connected with the idea of "round" or "around," but neither has to do with the shape of the tonsure. It was the enemies of Chararic who "surrounded" him: "Quem circumventum dolis coepit cum filio vinctusque totondit" (2.41), Gregory, *Libri historiarum,* 91. It was a dove that flew "around" the head of Aredius: "Cumque in huius studii flagrantia cum antestete memorato degeret, tonsorato iam capite, quadam die, psallentibus clericis in eclesia, discendit columba e camera, quae leviter volitans circa eum, resedit super caput eius" (10.29), Gregory, *Libri historiarum,* 522.

88. On the churches at Ravenna, see Herrin, *Formation of Christendom,* 148–49.

More importantly, among the Franks, the tonsure as an episcopal sign of power came up against a royal counterpart.[89] This time the contrast was a violent one, as kings forcibly distinguished themselves and their sphere of competence from that of clerics. For Merovingian kings, long hair was associated with a capacity to rule.[90] Forced tonsure, under both the Merovingians and Carolingians, was used to humble men and to bring about their political incompetence, usually a temporary and flexible state of affairs.[91] Though scholars no longer believe that such forced tonsures amounted to scalping, it can be presumed that such occasions were not very pleasant.[92] In a Frankish milieu, tonsure was bound to carry this other meaning, of humiliation and "not-royal." King Clovis expressed his domination over Chararic by cutting off the man's hair.[93] King Childebert, enraged by jealousy of his mother's affection for his half-brothers, forced her to choose between having their hair tonsured or seeing them dead. She chose death, so powerfully did she fear such a humiliation.[94]

Gregory of Tours also tells the story of a typical family squabble in the household of the counts of Brittany. Count Chanao attempted to destroy all competing authority by killing three of his brothers, a perfectly ordinary event in the world Gregory was describing. But Chanao's fourth brother, Macliaw, managed to escape. He fled to Vannes, where he had himself tonsured and ordained bishop. When Chanao died, Macliaw renounced his clerical vows, and having grown back his hair, returned to Brittany to become count. He was excommunicated, of course, but he had already made his decision to return to the scene of royal power—a decision symbolized by the way he wore his hair.[95]

When Clovis captured Chararic and his son, he had them forcibly tonsured, the father made a priest, the son a deacon.[96] Antagonism between episcopal and royal power here took a crude form. The Frank Gundovald, returning to Gaul

---

89. More generally on the symbolic role of hair: Robert Bartlett, "Symbolic Meanings of Hair in the Middle Ages," *Transactions of the Royal Historical Society,* 6th ser., 4 (1994): 43–60.

90. Moore, "King's New Clothes," 95–135; see also Dupraz, *Contribution à l'histoire,* 326–27.

91. Mayke De Jong, "Monastic Prisoners or Opting Out? Political Coercion and Honour in the Frankish Kingdoms," in *Topographies of Power,*" 293–94; Wallace-Hadrill, *Long-Haired Kings,* 245–46.

92. The suggestion that forced tonsure was actually scalping: J. Hoyoux, "Reges criniti: Chevelures, tonsures et scalps chez les mérovingiens," RBPH 26 (1948): 479–508.

93. Gregory, *Libri historiarum* (2.40), 91.

94. Gregory, *Libri historiarum* (3.18), 118–19.

95. "Macliavus autem desub terra consurgens, Veneticam urbem expetiit ibique tonsoratus et episcopus ordinatus est" (4.4), Gregory, *Libri historiarum,* 138.

96. "Quem circumventum dolis coepit cum filio vinctusque totondit et Chararicum quidem presbiterum, filio vero eius diaconem ordinari iubet" (2.41), Gregory, *Libri historiarum,* 91.

from exile in Byzantium, reappeared with his hair "as is the custom of their kings, loose and flowing down his back."[97] His hair was seen as a challenge by the Frankish kings among whom he landed. It was shorn twice, first by his putative father, Chlothar, and then by his supposed protector, King Charibert.

Bishops were quite capable of meting out the same punishment. At the reform council of 742 held under Boniface, it was decreed that clerics or monks guilty of fornication were to be incarcerated and have all their hair cut off. The wording was meant to indicate that this punishment was distinct from the tonsure such a cleric would already wear.[98] Bishops saw in their curtailed and meaningfully shaped hairstyle an expression of their capacity for power, alternative and opposed to the violence and worldliness of royal power.

Meanwhile, the *persona* of the king was undergoing change in the course of the seventh century. The king became a more stable figure, whose role in society was associated with certain royal estates and their palaces. The king sometimes sat on a throne, wearing costly imported garments, offering law, and presiding over the kingdom as a peacetime activity, providing limited police protection and distributing judicial immunities.[99]

Both kings and priests marked their special status by means of their hair. Kings marked their stature with the magic power of long hair and its mythic and biblical resonance. Only the tonsure, in contrast to the flowing hair of royalty, signified religious potency.[100] With the collapse of the Merovingian dynasty and the forced tonsure of the last Merovingian king, Childeric, their hair became an object of Carolingian taunts. Einhard's description of the long-haired kings portrayed their flowing hair as an empty presumption.[101] As will be seen, the Carolingians continued the practice of tonsuring those whom they wished to remove from the stage of power. Yet in the end, kings could neither evade nor redefine that class of men who tonsured themselves as a sign of their royal and priestly dignity.

Conceptually, a bishop's authority was based upon his unique separation from

97. "Ut regum istorum mos est, crinium flagellis per terga dimissis" (6.24), Gregory, *Libri historiarum*, 291.

98. "Radantur omnes capilli capitis eius," Carlomann's relation of the Concilium Germanicum (after 742), *Briefe des Heiligen Bonifatius*, MGH Epistolae Selectae 1, Letter 56, 101.

99. Alexander Callander Murray, "Immunity, Nobility and the Edict of Paris," *Speculum* 69 (1994): 18–39; see 32–33.

100. Wallace-Hadrill, *Long-Haired Kings*, 156; Le Jan, "La sacralité de la royauté mérovingienne," 1231–32.

101. "Crine profuso, barba summissa," *Einhardi vita Karoli magni*, ed. O. Holder Egger, MGH SRG in us. schol., 3 (Hannover: 1911).

those around him, in spite of the reality of royal interference and integration within royal spheres of power. Since the fourth century, the bishops wanted to be seen as stoic sages, engaged in prayer and study, and turning to this world only with a sense of heavy responsibility and regret. In the Merovingian period, the bishop's *persona* was elaborated by the addition of supernatural symbols and claims. This was in harmony with the bishop's perception that his office was continuous with the governing and teaching authority of Christ. Bishops carried on the apostles' work not merely by intention, but by identification, since apostolic authority lived in them. Their clothing and hairstyle emphasized this identification and were explained as royal and priestly symbols.[102] Episcopal authority therefore operated on the level of what Lévy-Bruhl termed a "mystic participation."[103] The equivalence between the bishop and his apostolic *persona* may help to explain the remarkable signs of respect that clerics could expect from laymen. A layman on horseback was expected to descend to the ground to pay honor to a cleric.[104]

Blessings and Episcopal Government

In imagining how Christ had fulfilled the office of bishop, the *Bobbio Missal* found such power in his blessing of the disciples. Ordination was the creative and establishing act of episcopal government over the orders of the church. The act of blessing was a reenactment of Christ's establishment of the church, a reenactment of his authoritative gesture, and the continuation of Christ's royal and priestly prerogatives by his representatives. The act of blessing was expanded along many lines, but all the blessings of the Gallic and Carolingian liturgies led back to this archetype. Such blessings were a ritual repetition of primordial and divine actions.[105] The blessing was, moreover, the primary liturgical expression of the bishop's place at the center of all cultic ritual. By means of the power of blessing bishops created a sacred space that they alone governed.[106] In this and other blessings, the bishop challenged and, in the end, swept away other competing cultic observances from their society.[107]

102. Compare the vestment of Oro Efe described in H. J. Drewal, "Pageantry and Power in Yoruba Costuming," in *Fabrics of Culture,* 189–230, esp. 209–12.

103. "Ceux qui, de leur vivant, ont tenu un rang éminent, et rempli de fonctions importantes, continuent de les exercer après leur mort, quoiqu'ils aient des successeurs," Lucien Lévy-Bruhl, *La Mentalité primitive,* 2nd ed. (Paris: 1922), 72.

104. Schmitt, *Raison des gestes,* 59.

105. Mircea Eliade, *The Myth of the Eternal Return, or, Cosmos and History,* trans. Willard Trask, 2nd rev. ed., Bollingen Series 46 (Princeton: 1971), 22.

106. Franz, *Kirchlichen Benediktionen,* 2:46–47.

107. Dierkens, "The Evidence of Archaeology," 39–64; Hen, *Culture and Religion,* 155–97; Franz, *Kirchlichen Benediktionen,* 1:44–45.

Blessing was the formulaic expression, by someone with a claim to represent God, of a hope that God would bless the person or object in question. Man cannot bless; only God can. In ancient Judaism, blessing was done by a person of authority, usually accompanied by the imposition of hands, by which the power of the blessing passed.[108] The gesture was taken up by the church as well. Bishops were ordained by the "laying on of hands," by which the Holy Spirit was imparted.[109] The gesture was also made when the bishop ordained other officials of the church, such as presbyters and doorkeepers.[110] The gesture was a special sign of the hand, often depicted in iconography: the right hand is lifted, with the first two fingers raised, slightly apart and relaxed, the ring and little fingers held with the thumb against the palm. This gesture, known as the *benedictio latina,* as L'Orange has shown, descended from the "speech gesture of antiquity" that connoted truth-telling. It became part of early iconography portraying Christ as a philosopher.[111] When Christ came to be depicted as the cosmocrator, the *benedictio latina* absorbed something of the "gesture of the magic right hand" used by Hellenistic and Roman rulers to show their assimilated role as cosmocrators.[112] Early descriptions of the "blessing of the people" show that from the first this gesture was restricted to the bishop. The raised hand was thought to represent Christ's own hand, the "hand of truth."[113] The blessing therefore signaled the bishop's governing role.

The most solemn of Western liturgical blessings, the *benedictio in populo,* was usually offered by a bishop.[114] The bishop, his hand raised in an authoritative gesture, appeared at that moment to represent the governing Christ. The function of this blessing was to prepare the people to receive communion, but seems

108. J. L. McKenzie, "Bless, Blessing," in *Dictionary of the Bible,* 98–99 (New York: 1965). For the benediction in the Gallic Rite, see Duchesne, *Christian Worship,* 222–24; de Vaux, *Ancient Israel,* 457.

109. *The Study of Liturgy,* ed. Cheslyn Jones, et al. (London: 1992), 86–94.

110. "Officium, quo eos episcopus dignos esse censuerit, cum impositae manus benedictione suscipiant," Council of Orléans (511), CCSL 148A:8. A potential cleric who was not denounced during a probationary period was deemed "worthy of the blessing" *(benedictionem inspectus mereatur accipere),* Synod of Bishop Aspasius (551), CCSL 148A:164.

111. H. P. L'Orange, *Studies in the Iconography of Cosmic Kingship in the Ancient World* (Oslo: 1953), 180. This gesture clearly survives in the cub-scout "oath" gesture.

112. L'Orange, *Studies in Iconography,* 194–97. Raised right hand of emperors, see 139–70.

113. "Extendo manum super hunc populum et oro, ut extendatur manus veritatis et detur benedictio huic populo propter humanitatem tuam, Deus misericordiarum," The Euchologion of Serapion XV (III), in *Monumenta eucharistica et liturgica vetustissima: Pars 1,* ed. Johannes Quasten (Bonn: 1935), 65, cited in *Corpus benedictionum pontificalium,* ed. E. Moeller, CCCM 162, 162A, 162B, 162C (Turnhout: 1971–1979), 2:ix.

114. Hefele-Leclercq, *Histoire des conciles,* 2.1:429, n. 1.

to have done more. It could protect the people from "nocturnal terrors."[115] The radiating power of episcopal authority could bring peace (the *Pax Domini*) to those receiving the blessing.[116] The offer of grace, protection, and tranquillity at the blessing formed a circle of safety, related to the status of the basilica as a sanctuary and to the fact that, within its walls, tapestries, candles, and clouds of incense offered a means of leaving the profane world and entering a holy one.[117] The formulae of blessing were most highly developed in Mozarabic and Gallic liturgies, an Eastern and African tradition that may have passed to them from Milan. Eventually the Frankish development of the blessing overcame the contrary custom of the Roman liturgy.[118]

Many other blessings existed besides the *benedictio in populo*. The peace and safety of the church could be extended to individual houses: "Bless, O Lord God, this person, his house, and all who dwell in it."[119] Blessings of a nun, an abbess, or a widow, like those of exorcists and doorkeepers, sought God's recognition and help for the orders of the church. Other blessings, such as those given at marriages, established the church's role in major events of life.[120] In the Mozarabic liturgy, the first fruits of the fields, seeds, vine-shoots, grapes, and new bread were blessed.[121] Similarly, the *Bobbio Missal* contains a "Blessing of every creature of fruit": "Bless, Lord, these new fruits which the mildness of the weather and of rain and of times was worthy to produce in serenity and maturity."[122] The baptismal blessing of infants and prayers for the dead complete the picture. Liturgical recognition of these central events tied the church strongly to the people, despite their lack of theological understanding.[123] Participation

115. In the *Missale Gothicum,* "Et ne nocturnis terroribus fatigetur, invisibilia cum attactu sanctifica. Amen"; cited in *Corpus benedictionum pontificalium,* CCCM 162B:xxiv.

116. *Corpus benedictionum pontificalium,* CCCM 162B:xvi–xvii.

117. "In prosperitate praeparet (vel temperet), in iniquitate emendet, in tranquillitate sublimet," the Benedictional of the 8th c.; cited in *Corpus benedictionum pontificalium,* CCCM 162B:xxviii. On sanctuary in Merovingian ecclesiastical law, see Pontal, *Histoire des conciles mérovingiens,* 285–86. For a description of the church interior and its meaning, see Van Dam, *Leadership and Community,* 239–41.

118. *Corpus benedictionum pontificalium,* CCCM 162B:ix–xx; see also Hen, *Royal Patronage of Liturgy,* 60.

119. "Benedic domine deus ello et domom suum et omnes qui habitant in eom," *Bobbio Missal,* 177.

120. *Bobbio Missal,* 166–69. On the entire liturgical recognition of these events, called the "personal cycle" by liturgical scholars, see Hen, *Culture and Religion,* 121–53.

121. *Le Liber Ordinum en usage dans l'église wisigothique et mozarabe d'Espagne du cinquième au l'onzième siècle,* ed. M. Ferotin, Monumenta ecclesiae liturgica 5 (Paris: 1904), 166–74.

122. "Benedic domine et hos fructus nouos ill. quos per temperamentum aeris et pluuie et temporum serenitate ad maturitate perducere dignatus est," *Bobbio Missal,* 170.

123. Gabriel Le Bras, *Études de sociologie religieuse* (Paris: 1955–1956), 1:228–30; Hen, *Culture and Religion,* 155–57.

in this transaction was itself constitutive. Belief was measured by observance of, and participation in, a vital series of rituals.[124]

Blessings of items to be used in liturgical practice had a marked tendency to link their immediate purpose to cosmological themes. Cabrol, who felt this tendency was due to a "love of nature" on the part of liturgists, missed some of the implications of these rituals.[125] Blessings expressed an intense interest in materiality—the salt, cattle, and houses of daily life. The blessing of baptismal water considered the mystery of God's spirit moving on the waters during Creation. Holy water was exorcised so that it could have a beneficial effect commensurate to its cosmic purpose:

I exorcise you, creature of water, through the living God, through God the creator who in the eternal beginning separated you into four rivers. This was fitting because you would be drunk or aspersed everywhere. May the Enemy be fled from, and overcome all his corruption, so that you might be exclusively dedicated to God.[126]

The blessed water could provide a connection to the Lord of creation and overcome history by rehearsing the Creation through the effect of the episcopal blessing. Hence it could serve in the "new birth" of Christian initiation and purify dwellings and people. It had aquired the world-creating power needed to battle Satan.[127] Caesarius of Arles could thus use it to expel demons from a house.[128] The liturgy offered bishops the means of creating sacred space and Christianizing landscapes. Substances such as water and salt could be purified and freed from the malevolent influences of this world, and such water could be used for protection against the "raging of men and beasts."[129] By means of episcopal prayer and blessing, the very power of God could descend into the sacred oil of chrism.[130]

A similar logic underpinned the blessing of fire on Easter Eve. The lighting of a new fire struck with a flint symbolized the renewal of the world by Christ.[131]

124. Le Bras, *Introduction à l'histoire de la pratique religieuse,* 1:45–46.

125. Fernand Cabrol, *Liturgical Prayer: Its History and Spirit,* trans. a Benedictine of Stanbrook (London: 1925), 218–36.

126. "Exorcizo te creatura aquae per deum uiuum per deum creatorem qui te in principio aeterna separauit et in quattuor fluminibus diuidere dignatus est uel ubicumque potata uel asparsa fueris effugiatur et expugnetur inimicus et omnes putridines eius ut sit propria deo decata," *Bobbio Missal,* 165. The editor takes "aeterna" as "terra" (n. 5).

127. On the battle against Satan at baptism, see Duchesne, *Christian Worship,* 302. On the connection between baptism and Creation, see Eliade, *Myth of Eternal Return,* 59.

128. Franz, *Kirchlichen Benediktionen,* 1:83.

129. Franz, *Kirchlichen Benediktionen,* 1:135.

130. "Descendat super hoc oleum potentie tue donum; descendat claritas et origo virtutum; descendat benignitas et puritas sanitatis," cited in Franz, *Kirchlichen Benediktionen,* 1:346.

131. F. Cabrol, *Liturgical Prayer,* 228–30.

Such ritual re-creation was a means of abolishing the past and overcoming the darkness of chaos. The church liturgically commemorated and suffered the barren darkness of the tomb and rejoiced in triumph over it. A closely related rite was the blessing of the paschal candle and all other church lights in the church. There is a splendid poem, conserved in the *Gothic Missal* and attributed there to Saint Augustine, in honor of the candle, praising with Virgilian flourish the labor of the bees that produced it.[132] The darkness of the tomb that Christ overcame was represented in the extinguished lights and their rekindling. This ritual was present in the Mozarabic Rite, and the Gallic Rite conveyed much of the same symbolism.[133] The ritual of extinguishing the lights was connected to the hope of individual triumph over chaotic night:

Omnipotent eternal God who illuminated, defend this most sacred night throughout the world, a glorious space of lordly resurrection; preserve in the new family of your children the spirit of sanctification you granted so they might exhibit, rejuvenated in body and mind, a pure spirit and soul to you.[134]

Indeed, the darkness that fell every night recalled the battle against shadows in the mind and the darkness of death and Hell, as can be seen in Vesper prayer.[135] This mood reached a crisis in the days from Maundy Thursday to Easter. The themes of threatening darkness and death are everywhere in the liturgies for Easter Eve, countered by straining and hope for light:

Beloved brothers, let us venerate the author of light, prince of light, inspector of the heart, redeemer of believers, with all our confessions, so that at day-break He might hear our resounding voices. And let him illuminate the approaching darkness of night with the splendor of his light.[136]

132. According to Duchesne, the source of the poem is Augustine, *City of God*, 15.22; see L. Duchesne, *Christian Worship*, 251–52. See the version of Augustine's prayer in *Missale Gothicum*, 67. Rose, "Liturgical Latin in the Missale Gothicum," 116–17.

133. Duchesne, *Christian Worship*, 250–51, on the contrary, says that this was a Celtic and Anglo-Saxon custom which has left no sign "in the ancient Merovingian books."

134. "Omnipotens sempiterne deus qui hanc sacratissimam noctem per uinuersa mundi spacia gloriosa dominice resurrectionis inlustras conserua in noua familie tuae progeniae sanctificacionis spiritum quem dedisti ut corpore et mente renouati puram tibi animam et purum pectus semper exhibeant," *Bobbio Missal*, 77.

135. See the "Oracionis uespertinas," esp. "inlumina quaesumus domine tenebras nostras et tocius noctis insidiis repelle propicius per," *Bobbio Missal*, 171.

136. Fear is traced in the strange shift of person in the verbs: "Auctorem lucis principem luminis inspectorem cordis credencium redemptorem fratres dilectissimi cunctis confessionibus ueneremur ut uergente die uoces rugitus exaudiat Et superuenientem caliginem nosctis luminis sui splendore inlustret," *Missale Gothicum*, 66.

The blessings of water and of fire established a connection to cosmological events by means of the ability of bishops to reenact them and make them new. The bishop was the very heart of a ritual and periodic remaking of the world, organizing the Christianization of time itself.

Such intense involvement in material transactions raises the question of whether this type of activity amounts to a Christianized form of benevolent magic.[137] Magic and religion have been too casually distinguished, and if the distinction is to have any use as a historical category, then "magic" should perhaps be restricted to rituals that have a notional certainty of success combined with an element of manipulation.[138] The comparative irrationality of religious belief is no less difficult to define. Rudolf Otto long ago argued that irrational dread was the very essence of religious phenomena, while superstition has been condemned by religious thinkers in all times.[139] Episcopal blessings do not seem to be especially magical or irrational.

The act of blessing could radiate outward from the church to protect the *civitas* and its surrounding countryside. Episcopal protection was not restricted to the heavenly atmosphere of the basilica, but from that center extended over the vital interests of peasant life, connecting the power of the ritual center to the prosperity of the fields in a protective liturgical umbrella sheltering the whole district. This was especially emphasized in Spain and Gaul by the development of the Rogation procession, held in the three days before Ascension.[140]

During Rogations, a procession of the people left the church, followed by the cathedral clergy and ultimately the bishop himself.[141] Circumambulating the city in a procession, the participants thus instantiated the cathedral as a spiri-

---

137. Valerie Flint, *The Rise of Magic in Early Medieval Europe* (Princeton: 1991), assumes the existence of an "original Christianity" that was distorted in early medieval Europe. Likewise James C. Russell, *The Germanization of Early Medieval Christianity,* 193–94 dismisses Germanic "magicoreligious" Christianity as neither a full nor an authentic Christianity.

138. J. N. Bremmer, "The Birth of the Term 'Magic,'" *Zeitschrift für Papyrologie und Epigraphik* 126 (1999): 1–12. Still basic is the essay of Henri Hubert and Marcel Mauss, "Esquisse d'une théorie générale de la magie," *Année sociologique* 7 (1902–1903): 1–146.

139. MacMullen describes the rise of irrationalism in popular religion from 300–700 ("after the Decline") as an increasing remoteness reason and thus "from the Rome that Pliny knew": MacMullen, *Christianity and Paganism,* 97–102. For Rudolf Otto, the perception of holiness is always set apart from "the Rational": Rudolf Otto, *The Idea of the Holy: An Inquiry into the Non-Rational Factor in the Idea of the Divine and its Relation to the Rational,* trans. John W. Harvey (Oxford: 1931), 4. A similar view of priestly functions imbues Mircea Eliade, *Shamanism: Archaic Techniques of Ecstasy,* trans. Willard Trask, Bollingen Series 76 (Princeton: 1964).

140. Nathan, "Rogation Ceremonies," discusses the late-antique backdrop of these rituals. A useful treatment with much early material is T. Bailey, *The Processions of Sarum and the Western Church,* Pontifical Institute for Medieval Studies, Studies and Texts 21 (Toronto: 1971).

141. Hen, *Culture and Religion,* –64.

tual and cosmic point of gravity.[142] Walking throughout the district, providing blessings of many kinds for the health of fields and cattle, for rain in drought or fair weather in a rainy season, the bishop spread his beneficence as broadly as possible. According to Gregory of Tours, Bishop Mamertus of Vienne instituted such processions sometime around 470 after a series of disasters and portents: packs of wolves and stags invading the city, earthquakes, and the destruction of the royal palace by fire.[143] The Council of Orléans in 511 attempted to make the practice universal.[144] Exceptional processions had often been held before, but Sidonius Apollinaris seems to have thought that an annual procession was a Gallic innovation unknown in Rome. The ceremony was widely known in Gaul by about 600.[145] There were many kinds of processions in Gaul.[146]

The entire people (*plebs universa*) were expected to gather and take part in the procession, and it was provided that even slaves would be released from their work for this one day.[147] It was a period of communal fasting and propitiation, making reparation for the sins of the people, so that God would "set aside the vicissitudes of the times."[148] It was felt that the people as a whole should make amends for their sins, because it was as a people that they needed the aid of heaven.[149] Moving slowly and deliberately through the lanes, the procession disclosed a hierarchical model of society in which the liturgy served as a cohesive force, shaping the community and reinforcing local solidarity under episcopal government.[150]

The antiphons for Rogations were a highly developed literature of prayers for mercy. Troubled times evoked a fear of damnation and ruin that seems boundless. "Hear us, Lord, who heard Jonah in the belly of the whale; hear our cries

142. Nathan, "Rogation Ceremonies," 290–91.

143. "Has ipsas rogationes, quas ante ascensionis dominicae triumphum caelebramus, a Mamerto ipsius Viennensis urbis episcopo, cui et hic eo tempore praeerat, institutas fuisse" (2.34), Gregory, *Libri historiarum*, 83.

144. "Rogationes, id est laetanias, ante ascensionem Domini ab omnibus ecclesiis placuit celebrari," Council of Orléans (511), 11–12; Nathan, "Rogation Ceremonies," 285; see also Bailey, *Processions of Sarum*, 95–97. A valuable early guide to the canons of councils: R. P. Ch.-L. Richard, *Analyse des conciles généraux et particuliers, contenant leurs canons sur le dogme, la morale, et la discipline tant ancienne que moderne* (Paris: 1772) 4:688–90.

145. Nathan, "Rogation Ceremonies," 278; see also Bailey, *Processions of Sarum*, 96–97, n. 9.

146. Bailey, *Processions of Sarum*, 107–19.

147. "Rogationes, id est laetanias, ante ascensionem Domini ab omnibus ecclesiis placuit celebrari, ita ut praemissum triduanum ieiunium in Domenicae ascensionis festiuitate soluatur; per quod triduum serui et ancellae ab omni opere relaxentur, quo magis plebs uniuersa conueniat," Orléans (511), CCSL 148A:3–19, 11–12.

148. "Vicissitudines temporum desposuisti," *Missale Gothicum*, 95.

149. "Petimus omnipotens deus ut accipias cuncta plebis uota," *Missale Gothicum*, 97.

150. Le Bras, *Études de sociologie religieuse*, 1:225–26.

who heeded David prostrate and cast down in the dust."[151] Other prayers addressed an immediate problem. Prayers were said during storms: "Lord, the waters burst over our heads; we invoke your name because of these unheard-of waters; Don't turn your face from our tears."[152] Also for deliverance from war: "Deliver, Lord, from the hand of death your people; with your right hand protect that people, so that living we might bless you, the Lord our God."[153] Such prayers sought to reconcile a vulnerable people and an angry God. The bishop was at the center of such efforts. By his government he attempted to purify the people of sin, and by his prayers to intercede for them.[154] The governmental capacity of the episcopate was based in part on its strangely encoded claims to royalty and priesthood. But only in part. The exercise of the bishop's claim to represent and lead the church, and hence society, was based on what he offered that society.[155] This involved taking account of popular custom, recognizing the fears of the community, and offering an access to vitality and prosperity for a society of stuggling farmers.[156] One should view the bishops' prayers for their king as they went into battle against this same backdrop.[157] In the course of the seventh century, "chants and prayers became an instrument by which heavenly protection could be sought for the benefit of the kingdom and its ruler."[158]

A Gateway to Heaven

Bishops, it has been shown, considered themselves governors—literally "straighteners" (rectores) of the church. Ritual action extended this role by a hundred lines of connection to the central events of life—birth, death, and marriage. All these events were accompanied by episcopal blessings long before

151. "Exaudi nos, Domine, qui exaudisti Ionam de ventre ceti; exaudi nos clamantes, qui exaudisti David prostratum et iacentem in cilicio," cited and trans. in Bailey, *Processions of Sarum,* 128.

152. "Inundaverunt aque, Domine, super captia nostra; invocavimus nomen tuum de lacu novissimo ne avertas faciem tuam a singultu nostro," cited and trans. (which I revise) in Bailey, *Processions of Sarum,* 129.

153. "Libera, Domine, populum tuum de manu mortis, et plebem istam protegat dextera tua, ut viventes benedicamus te Domine Deus noster," cited and trans. (which I revise), in Bailey, *Processions of Sarum,* 129.

154. "Omnipotens sempiterne deus qui beato petro apostolo conlatis clauibus regni caelestis animas legandi atque soluendi pontificium tradedisti Exaudi propicius praeces nostras in die ieiunii huius et intercessione eius quaesomus ut a peccatorum nostrorum nexibus liberemur," *Missale Gothicum,* 98–99.

155. Le Bras, *Études de sociologie religieuse,* 2:629.

156. Georges Duby, *The Early Growth of the European Economy: Warriors and Peasants from the Seventh to the Twelfth Century,* trans. H. B. Clarke (Ithaca: 1978), 25–30 and 55–56.

157. On the iconography of prayer for victory in battle, see Schapiro, *Words and Pictures,* 17–36.

158. Hen, *Royal Patronage of Liturgy,* 34.

the church sought to "sacramentalize" them.[159] To the agricultural year with its natural rhythm was added a rich calendar upon which the liturgy was built.[160] All of these may be described as features of episcopal government, a government that laid claim to much more than lands and incomes.

The threshold of a basilica marked the point of contact between two worlds.[161] Outside was the profane world, constantly struggling to deserve blessing and fruitfulness, a world whose margins blended with a dark, chaotic wilderness.[162] A prayer from shortly after 800 sought to protect those who had to leave the protected space of the church on a dangerous journey over mountains, down valleys, over fields and rivers, and into the solitude of the forest.[163]

The basilica, and the Christian-built world of which it was the center, implied a kind of rejection, a rebuttal, of wild landscapes, where the old demonic gods lingered and still dominated their worshippers. The *Sacramentary of Gellone* contains a prayer of protection against such "ancient places."[164] Within the basilica was the land of the blessed, filled with light, sanctity, and order.[165] Religious symbolism pervaded the building in every detail of its furnishings. Cleansed and purified, its most sacred confines could only be entered by those whose very bodies had been ritually purified.[166] The gradual Christianization of the landscape of Gaul was centered in the basilica, radiating outward from old sanctuaries inside the cities. From the Christian city with its basilica, a Christian physical and spiritual topography extended Christian space toward the countryside.[167] In Tours, a series of basilicae came to connect the city to the sanctuary of St. Martin and to monasteries founded by Radegund and Monegund.[168]

159. Frederick S. Paxton, *Christianizing Death: The Creation of a Ritual Process in Early Medieval Europe* (Ithaca: 1990).

160. L. Pietri, *Ville de Tours*, 431–84. For a useful summary of the calendar: John Harper, *The Forms and Orders of Western Liturgy from the Tenth to Eighteenth Century* (Oxford: 1991), 45–57.

161. Mircea Eliade, *The Sacred and the Profane: The Nature of Religion*, trans. Willard Trask (New York: 1959), 25–26.

162. Eliade, *Sacred and Profane*, 29–32; and Eliade, *Myth of Eternal Return*, 9. Duby has described how a Mediterranean agricultural system was imported to Gaul. The forests were for hermits and hunters; Duby, *Early Growth*, 20. On the mythic associations of the forest and hunt, Dumézil, *Mitra–Varuna*, 124.

163. "Prosperum iter faciat nobis deus salutarium nostrorum pateantque in vias nostras ardua montium, convexa vallium, plana camporum, vada fluminum, secreta silvarum," from the *Libellus Coloniensis*, ca. 802–805, in André Wilmart, *Precum libelli quattuor aevi Karolini* (Rome: 1940), 52.

164. *Liber Sacramentorum Gellonensis*, ed. A. Dumas, CCSL 159 (Turnhout: 1981), 450.

165. Van Dam, *Leadership and Community*, 239.

166. De Nie, "Le Corps, la fluidité," 82–83.

167. Charles Pietri, "L'espace chrétien dans la cité: Le vicus christianorum et l'espace chrétien de la cité Averne (Clermont)," RHEF 66 (1980): 177–209.

168. L. Pietri, *Ville de Tours*, 405–20.

This may be described as a nonterritorial spatial organization, based upon nodes and nuclei rather than districts; and it was this form of organization that gave Frankish kingdoms their shape and pattern.[169]

Objective geography, whatever it may be, has little application to the intellectual world of Merovingian Gaul. The world and its shape were conceived in an essentially symbolic manner. Churches, as has been mentioned, were often located on the site of former pagan shrines, a practice encouraged since the time of Emperor Constantine.[170] For this reason, the conceptual centrality of churches and monasteries had ramifications for social organization. Local geographical knowledge was undoubtedly much richer, incorporating waterways, berry patches, crossroads, and fortifications. In an isolated community, orientation would have been based upon tracing the paths of connection between royal centers, noble estates, monasteries and churches, and home. Detailed knowledge can be compiled in this way and allow a complex view of fairly large districts.[171] One feature of episcopal activity was its reorientation and redefinition of the spiritual landscape that parallels and overlies geography.[172] The building and dedication of churches inserted new points in that landscape, with a powerful predetermination of their meaning. From pre-Christian times, the landscape of Gaul had been organized around sanctuaries and shrines and a principle of centrality. Churches built over the remains of a formerly pagan cult-site could draw upon and preserve ancient topographic structures.[173] A church was, moreover, an idealized city, erected on a different level than that of the "found" sacred place. It had an elaborate and explicable rhetoric linking it to a cosmological scheme.[174] There was a language of scale and complexity, first of all. Larger churches were built as early as the fifth century with more windows and columns. A plain ex-

169. An example of such a spatial organization is described Evans-Pritchard, *The Divine Kingship,* 7–9; see also Bonnie Effros, "Monuments and Memory: Repossessing Ancient Remains in Early Medieval Gaul," in *Topographies of Power,* 93–118.

170. MacMullen, *Christianity and Paganism,* 125.

171. See Yi-Fu Tuan, *Topophilia: A Study of Environmental Perception, Attitudes, and Values* (Englewood Cliffs, N.J.: 1974), 34–35.

172. What Evans-Pritchard refers to, in the case of the Shilluk, as the "politico-religious kingdom"; Evans-Pritchard, *Divine Kingship,* 9.

173. Gisela Cantino Wataghin, "La conversion de l'espace: quelques remarques sur l'établissement matériel chrétien aux IVe–Ve siècles, d'après l'exemple de l'Italie du Nord," in *Clovis,* 1:127–39, esp. 136. On the ancient Celtic backdrop of this religious landscape, see Webster, "Sanctuaries and Sacred Places," 445–64.

174. On cosmological cities, see Tuan, *Topophilia,* 150–68; see also Sabine G. MacCormack, "Loca Sancta: The Organization of Sacred Topography in Late Antiquity," in *The Blessings of Pilgrimage,* edited by R. Ousterhout, Illinois Byzantine Studies 1 (Urbana: 1990), 7–40; see esp. 28.

terior clothed and defended the riches within. Such churches were widespread and close to the centers of population.[175]

Episcopal occupation of the center of society involved the building of churches and the gradual expansion of the physical plant with other buildings and lands attached to the bishop's office. Great bishops were expected to be great builders.[176] Each bishop was expected to be the governor of a domain (*patriarcha*) of some significant size. An assemblage of buildings— baptisteries, oratories, funeral chapels, and monasteries—reached out from the city into the surrounding country. At the heart of this grouping was the church (*ecclesia* or *basilica*).[177] At the Council of Orléans in 511, bishops asserted their complete authority over all these buildings: "It was now resolved, according to the rule of previous canons, that all churches that were built in various places or are daily being built, lie in the power of the bishop in whose territory they are situated."[178]

Duchesne gives a detailed reconstruction of the rites used in Gaul for the consecration of a new church.[179] The bishop, after entering and praying prostrate before the altar, rose and, with his pastoral staff, traced the alphabet in two diagonals across the church floor in ashes that had been sprinkled for the purpose. It is likely that this way of marking out sacred space was an expansion of the Alpha and Omega, expressing the dominion of the Word over nature.[180] This inscription was followed by lustration of the altar and walls with a bundle of hyssop, and then their anointing. The last act was the translation of saintly relics, without which, by the sixth century, no church would be established.[181] The translation, or movement and arrival, of such relics was a major event, and deepened the religious potency of the holy place.[182] Lustration and anointing of the walls clearly marked the whole interior of the building as a sacred region, an environment exorcised of worldly and demonic influence.

The establishment of sacred space allowed a concrete point of contact with the divine, a gate to heaven (*porta caeli*).[183] Jacob's vision of the ladder was re-

---

175. Hen, *Culture and Religion,* 150–53.

176. Heinzelmann, *Bischofsherrschaft in Gallien,* 150–51.

177. Cardot, *L'Espace et le pouvoir,* 149–63.

178. "Omnis autem baselice, quae per diuversa constructae sunt uel cotidie construuntur, placuit secundum priorum chanonum regulam, ut in eius episcopi, in cuius territurio sitae sunt, potestate consistant," Council of Orléans (511), CCSL 148A:9.

179. Duchesne, *Christian Worship,* 407–18.

180. Duchesne, *Christian Worship,* 417, also derives it from Roman surveying methods.

181. Duchesne, *Christian Worship,* 410–13; Jungmann, *Early Liturgy,* 186–87.

182. L. Pietri, *Ville de Tours,* 507–20.

183. From the dedication mass of the *Bobbio Missal,* 114.

called to explain the nature of the new place, where angels were to descend.[184] Indeed, angels were believed to be present at the Eucharist.[185] The liturgy was not merely a symbolic portrayal of divine reality, as if at a distance, but a participation in that reality, by joining the perpetual liturgy of heaven, as described in the book of Revelation.[186] Because the cult to be maintained there participated in the liturgy of heaven, the church was an image of the Heavenly Jerusalem, reproducing a cosmic reality in stone:

offering you in thanks a sacrifice of praise in the temple of your glory, sacrificing with prayer in that holy Jerusalem among the Elect, which you establish as an ornament of the celestial kingdom.[187]

Part of the basilica's ability to provide access to heaven rested on its assumption of a cosmic pattern.[188] Church interiors were shaped to accommodate the liturgical uses to which they would be put, influencing the arrangement of altars and shrines for individual saints. Groups of churches provided the topography of stational devotions.[189] These arrangements, moreover, made use of number symbolism so that the the entire structure might express the nature of the Trinity or assimilate features of Christ's life to the four quarters of the globe.[190]

The basilica was a sacred space, liberated from demons, imbued with divine power, and governed directly by the bishop. It was also a space freed from royal power. Bishops could offer asylum in their churches to those who fled prosecution for a crime or endured the persecution of a king. Bishops defended this privilege with considerable vigor. Frankish councils sought to confirm the right of asylum soon after Clovis' conquest of Visigothic Gaul, beginning with the Council of Orléans in 511.[191] A later council, also gathered in Orléans, declared:

184. *Bobbio Missal,* 114; see also Eliade, *Sacred and Profane,* 37.

185. On the descent of angels as the mass, see Jean Daniélou, *The Angels and Their Mission,* trans. D. Heimann (Westminster, Md.: 1987), 62–67. The comparison of the altar to the Ark is ancient; see M. E. Isaacs, *Sacred Space: An Approach to the Theology of the Epistle to the Hebrews,* Journal for the Study of the New Testament, Supplement Series 73 (Sheffield: 1992), 209–10.

186. Pierre Prigent, *Apocalypse et liturgie,* Cahiers théologiques, 52 (Paris: 1964), 46–76; Robert Douglas Richardson, "Introduction and Supplementary Essay" for the translation: Hans Lietzmann, *Mass and Lord's Supper: A Study in the History of the Liturgy,* trans. Dorothea H. G. Reeve (Leiden: 1972), fasc. 8, 473.

187. "Que tibi in templo glorie tuae sacrificium laudis gratulantes/ immolant uotis in illa sancta hierusalem inter elicta celestis regie ornamenta constituas," *Bobbio Missal,* 116.

188. See Tuan, *Topophilia,* 153–55.

189. C. Heitz, "L'architettura dell'età carolingia in relazione alla liturgia sacra," in *Culto Cristiano: Politica imperiale carolingia* (Todi: 1979) 337–62.

190. C. Heitz, "Symbolisme et architecture: Les nombres et l'architecture religieuse du haut moyen âge," *Settimane* 23 (1976), 1:387–420; see esp. 391–96.

191. Heuclin, "Le concile d'Orléans de 511," 441–42.

If someone compelled by necessity should flee to the enclosure of a church, and the bishop or governor of that church has allowed him in, even if the man is to be despised, whoever might possibly presume to disturb or drag him away from sacred places or their precincts by force, violence or trickery, shall be hurled from its threshold as an enemy of the church.[192]

Seventy years later, a council in an unknown city expressed the same principle:

Concerning those who have sought refuge in our churches. In order that the state of the church may persist with a firm strength in all things, let no one be violently dragged from a church, especially those who have fled to the church for protection. If someone should presume to do it, let him be deprived of communion. Moreover, let those who have fled to the church not be bound with chains or iron.[193]

Gregory of Tours placed a high premium on this aspect of his power, and included in his *Histories* many tales in which an offer of sanctuary stirred up intense conflicts between bishops and kings. When Merovech sought shelter in Gregory's own Church of St. Martin, King Chilperic threatened to set the countryside of Tours on fire, yet Gregory remained firm.[194] At times, however, the sacred confines were violated. King Childebert's men were hunting down his enemy Berthefried, and learned he had taken refuge in the church of Bishop Ageric, in Verdun. The men surrounded the oratory and, climbing to the roof, tore off the tiles, raining them down on Berthefried until they killed him.[195] The concept of asylum clearly had a hold on the men's imagination, who did not simply storm the building: the rules of the game forbade this.

A revealing anecdote in the *Earlier Annals of Metz* shows how directly the concept of asylum was based on the notion of sacred space and the extent to which it was defined by its boundaries. A group of men, pursued by the followers of Charles Martel, the Mayor of the Palace, ran for shelter into a church:

192. "Si quis necissitatis inpulsu ad ecclesiae septa confugerit et sacerdote seu praeposito ecclesiae praetermisso adque contempto eum quisque de locis sacris uel atriis seu ui seu dolo abstrahere aut sollicitare fortasse praesumpserit, ut inimicus ecclesiae ab eius liminibus arceatur," Council of Orléans (541), CCSL 148A:137; see discussion by Pontal, *Histoire des conciles mérovingiens,* 285–87.

193. "De his qui ad aeclesias confugium faciunt. Vt eclesiae status in omnibus firmo robore persistat, nullus de aeclesiam uiolenter tragatur, nec confugientibus in ecclesiam subtragatur. Quod si quis hoc facere praesumpserit, communione priuetur, se nec uinculis aut ferrum, qui in ecclesia confugerit, conlegetur," Council in a Place Unknown (after 614), CCSL 148A:288.

194. "Eiecite apostatam illam de basilicam; sin autem aliud, totam regionem illam igne succendam" (5.14), Gregory, *Libri historiarum,* 208.

195. "Ascendentes supra tectum, eum ab ipsis tegulis ac materiis, quibus oraturium opertum erat, inlidentes interficerunt" (9.12), Gregory, *Libri historiarum,* 427.

And as one of them hastened to enter [the church] in flight, one of his pursuers quickly lopped off with his sword the man's hindmost foot which was outside the threshold of the church. And when his comrades, moved by piety, complained that he had violated the enclosure of the church, he is said to have replied that he had been careful to respect what the church contained: on the other hand, he declared that what in hot pursuit he found outside the enclosure, he rightly cut off.[196]

The chase, and the legal justification for violence, came to an end at the boundary of this sacred enclosure. This story, with its functional realism, seems crafted to make this point about the power and importance of asylum.

The places bishops occupied had become formidable centers of power, but had not ceased to be something more. Episcopal activities were tied to society in ways that went beyond the barrier of liturgical Latin, and there are significant signs that this was understood by the laity. Clerics assembled by the bishop of Auxerre in the late sixth century complained that choirs of "secular men or girls" were singing inappropriate songs in their churches.[197] At the Council of Chalon (647–653), the assembled bishops also addressed this evidently common problem—that during the dedication of churches or on feasts of the martyrs, the solemnities were interrupted by the chanting of "choirs of women," when people ought to be listening to the clerics chanting psalms. They were to be chased away or excommunicated if they would not stop.[198]

Incidents such as these have been viewed, as they were by the bishops themselves, as a competition between a native religious tradition and an imported Christian one. It appears, however, that the gathering of such choirs of women was a recognition of the religious tone and centrality of the church and a wish to participate. It should also be noted that the women were viewed by the

196. "Quam cum quidam in ipsius fugae alacritate ingredi properaret, unus ex persequentibus posteriorem pedem foris limen ecclesiae gladio celeriter amputavit. Quem cum socii pie mentis affectu, cur basilicae septa macularet, arguerent, respondisse fertur, id quod ecclesia contineret se observasse, not contingeret, quod autem extra claustra illius celeritate cursus invenerat, iure se amputasse firmabat" (Anno 716), *Annales Mettenses Priores,* MGH SRG in us. schol., 23. My translation: but see also Fouracre and Gerberding, *Late Merovingian France,* 367–68.

197. "Non licet in ecclesia chorus saecularium uel puellarum cantica exercere nec conuiuia in ecclesia praeparare," Diocesan Synod of Auxerre (561–605), 266.

198. "Valde omnibus nuscetur esse decretum, ne per dedicationes basilicarum aut festiuitates martyrum ad ipsa solemnia confluentes obscina et turpea cantica, dum orare debent aut clericus psallentes audire, cum choris foemineis, turpia quidem, decantare uideantur. Vnde conuenit, ut sacerdotes loci illos a septa basilicarum uel porticus ipsarum basilicarum etiam et ab ipsis atriis uetare debiant et arcere et, si uoluntarie noluerint emendare, aut excommunicare debeant aut disciplinae aculeo sustinere," Chalon-sur-Saôn (647–653), CCSL 148A:302–10, 307. On the view of the councils on paganism, see Hen, *Culture and Religion,* 176–80.

bishops as communicating members of the church. Clearly this reflects a complex religious situation in which the boundary between Christian and pagan was blurred at the level of practice.[199] The corporate and constitutive nature of baptism meant that the church was established ritually and took in the people as a whole. As Ramsay MacMullen has remarked on the consequences of this phenomenon, "the elite of the church . . . opposed no barrier to the basic religious ideas of the masses, even from the poorest corners of town or the remotest villages."[200] A mixture of struggle and accommodation was under way. Christian and pagan were not exclusive categories, since religious orientations were blended and complex. Faced by the centrality of Christianity with its buildings, personnel, and official cult, people were able to accommodate and incorporate it within their own syncretic perspectives.[201] One should not be overly skeptical of Fortunatus' paean to the impact of the churches being built in his day, when he claimed that "the people avidly gathered from everywhere to the new temples."[202]

As a gateway to heaven, through which angels could pass to stand in the corners of the basilica during the Mass, the church marked the focus of the ritual organization of society around the bishop as a living symbol. It was also the center of an accumulation of property on a grander scale than that of royal centers.[203] The impact of episcopal centers was such that they provided the frame of spatial and spiritual organization, especially as royal power was eclipsed at the end of the Merovingian period.[204] This became more true as old Gallic and Merovingian churches aquired the pathos of great age and rootedness.

The Meaning of the Poor

Helping the poor, clothing the naked, and ransoming hostages were defining activities of episcopal office, and such deeds were duly noted in episcopal epitaphs.[205] Closely connected were the records of the gratitude felt by the "citizens" toward their bishop. The bishop brought about peace by these actions, forming

---

199. Dierkens, "Christianisme et 'paganisme,'" 461.

200. MacMullen, *Christianity and Paganism*, 153.

201. Wenskus, "Religion abâtardie," 181–82.

202. "Ad nova templa avide concurrunt undique plebes," cited in Samuel Dill, *Roman Society in Gaul in the Merovingian Age* (London: 1926), 443.

203. Prinz, "Der fränkische Episkopat," 112.

204. Cardot, *L'espace et le pouvoir,* 144–45 and 155–57; Prinz, "Der fränkische Episkopat," 116.

205. See the description of St. Naamatus: "Pauper laetus abit, nudus discedit opertus, captivus plaudit liver sese esse redemptum," Duchesne, *Fastes épiscopaux,* 1:191. For St. Pantagathus, "pauperibusque dedit, caelica regna petens," 189.

a bulwark of mercy and justice against the raging outsider.[206] Protection of the poor and the preservation of peace were viewed as two aspects of a single project.

This protective, charitable government can be described as paternalistic, absorbing the ancient senatorial system of patronage and protection.[207] The bishop was a father: the *pater ecclesiae,* the *pater pauperum,* and *pater populi.*[208] What could be gained, in terms of lordship, from protecting the penniless, the poor, the helpless and wretched? The Psalms, of course, are full of exhortations to protect the poor against the powerful and wealthy, often asserting the paradox that the poor are greater than the rich because they are closer to God. "Raising up the humble from the earth, lifting the poor from the mire, so that He might place them among the princes, with the princes of his people."[209] Early Christian writings such as the Epistle of Clement took up this theme of Jewish spirituality, as did the sayings of Jesus. The Fathers elaborated on the bishop's responsibility for the poor and constrained.[210] As in so many aspects of episcopal activity, one is faced with an ancient, impermeable fabric of tradition. Yet this tradition meant something new in Frankish Gaul. Peter Brown has argued that it was not the destitute, but socially connected middling groups, who were the main recipients of Christian charity in the late antique church.[211]

Caesarius of Arles used the biblical and patristic mandate that bishops ransom hostages in a new manner. While it had long been the duty of bishops to ransom Christians from captivity under barbarians or Jews, Caesarius set about ransoming even pagan citizens, explaining that he feared they might convert to Arianism or Judaism before having the chance to receive Catholicism. Caesarius here emerged not only as a religious leader, but also as the guardian and protector of a people, positioned at the social and cultural pinnacle of his city. Bishops dreamed of social transformation. The poor, whom Christ had said would be first, and the powerful, whom he had said would be last, exchanged positions in the rhetoric of power. Powerful bishops strove to be meek and to protect and

206. For Blessed Avitus, "Cultibus Christi sapienter haerens/ fautor et pacis studuit furentes/ reddere cives speciali voto mentis amicae," Duchesne, *Fastes épiscopaux,* 1:190. For St. Naamatus, "civis agit grates tantoque antistite gaudet," 1:191.

207. Brown, *Poverty and Leadership,* 24–30.

208. Heinzelmann, *Bischofsherrschaft in Gallien,* 155.

209. "Qui suscitat de terra humilem, et de stercore exaltat pauperem, ut collocet eum cum principibus, cum principibus populi sui," Psalm 112 [113]:7–8, as cited at Orange (529), CCSL 148A:53–76, 75.

210. Klingshirn, "Charity and Power," 184–87; David Ganz, "The Ideology of Sharing," in *Property and Power in the Early Middle Ages,* edited by Wendy Davies and Paul Fouracre, 17–18 (Cambridge: 1995).

211. Brown, *Poverty and Leadership,* 49.

nurture the poor.[212] This option for the poor was supported by the ascetic Ambrosian model of episcopal power. Bishop Germanus of Auxerre, for example, was described by his biographer, Constantius of Lyon (writing sometime between 475 and 480), as a severe ascetic, whose devotion to his mission imposed on him an austere, businesslike simplicity and voluntary poverty. "His clothing in every time of year was a cloak and tunic. This was neither added to in winter, nor lightened in summer."[213] Germanus, the great opponent of demons and heretics, was constantly surrounded by admiring crowds of common people. Demonstrating the *persona* of the good bishop, he seemed to care for workmen and for the poor. Constantius carefully crafted a scene in which Germanus, upon leaving a very wealthy city, met some poor people begging along the road. He asked his deacon what money was left, and insisted that it all be given to the paupers. When the deacon asked what they themselves should live on, the saint replied, "God will feed his poor. Give what you have to these poor men." Thus the ascetic poverty of Germanus gave him a special connection to the poor and the wisdom for right action.[214] The lives of heroic figures such as Germanus instructed the comfortable bishops of wealthy cities how to act. Indeed, the *Life of Germanus* shows that the ascetic mastery and saintliness of Germanus could be shared by ordinary bishops through venerating the man. Elegant bishops assembled at a council humbly venerated him for his displays of religious power.[215]

Conciliar legislation therefore gave considerable attention to the poor, but it is difficult to learn exactly who the poor were. Analysis of terminology is the only readily available tool.[216] Walter Ullmann saw episcopal concern for the poor as an early example of social welfare. It marked the bishops' attempt to turn Christian tenets into "socially realizable measures."[217] A major dimension of protecting the poor was the connection of this to the right to accumulate and

212. Klingshirn, "Charity and Power," 190–97.

213. "Indumentum cuculla et tunica fuere temporibus. Nam neque hieme accessit adiectio, neque aestate leuamen admissum est," Constantius of Lyon, *Vie de Saint Germain d'Auxerre,* ed. René Borius, SC 112 (Paris: 1965) (1.4), 126.

214. "Respondens ait: 'Pascit Deus pauperes suos'; tu, quod habes, indigentibus praesta," Constantius of Lyon, *Vie de Saint Germain,* (6.33), 182–84.

215. "Episcopi omnes sanctum Dei digna humilitate uenerantur," Constantius of Lyon, *Vie de Saint Germain,* (6.32), 182.

216. Karl Bosl, "Potens und Pauper. Begriffsgeschichtliche Studien zur gesellschaftlichen Differenzierung im frühen Mittelalter und zum 'Pauperismus' des Hochmittelalters," in *Alteuropa und die moderne Gesellschaft,* edited by Alexander Bergengruen and Ludwig Deike, 60–87; see 62 (Göttingen: 1963).

217. Walter Ullmann, "Public Welfare and Social Legislation in the Early Medieval Councils," in *Councils and Assemblies,* 1–39, Studies in Church History 7 (Cambridge: 1971), see 1–2.

preserve church property and donations. Linking them was religious meaning conveyed by material goods and places devoted to a sacred purpose. Although the issue of illicit seizure of church property was doubtless a constant and real concern, the problem was also an occasion for expressing the principles of episcopal government. Bishops could at a single stroke reaffirm their position as guardians of the people, as guarantors of social order, and as having the capacity to govern large territories and specific categories of people.

Protection of the poor, orphans, and widows were nearly always linked. Determining who these widows were would do much to shed light on the other categories.[218] It seems clear that the frequent mention of widows in the sources is not due to a high mortality rate among husbands, but to the frequency of rape, abandonment, or repudiation of women, leaving them without protection or legal status.[219] Such women would sometimes be recruited for service on monastic estates.[220] By acting as advocate for a wealthy widow, a bishop could thereby bring her property under his government, while acting on her behalf in legal transactions in which women could not engage. He could also angle for donations from property he helped to protect.

On the other hand, there was a patristic tradition that made widows an "order" in the church, just as deacons or doorkeepers were "orders."[221] As a category of unmarried women, not engaging in sex, their chastity merited religious recognition. As Isidore of Seville put it, "the virgin is therefore happy because she is intact; the widow is stronger because she knows what it's about."[222]

Merovingian canon law attempted to establish a "peace" for the poor, orphans, and widows, and threatened the "murderers of the poor" with a curse.[223] This was the Malediction against Judas (from Psalm 108:14–17):

218. Bernhard Jussen, "On Church Organization and the Definition of an Estate: The Idea of Widowhood in Late Antique and Early Medieval Christianity," *Tel Aviver Jahrbuch für deutsche Geschichte* 22 (1993): 25–42; see also Jussen, "Der 'Name' der Witwe: Zur 'Konstruktion' eines Standes in Spätantike und Frühmittelalter," in *Veuves et Veuvage dans le haut moyen âge,* edited by M. Parisse, 137–75 (Paris: 1993).

219. Michel Mollat, *The Poor in the Middle Ages: An Essay in Social History,* trans. Arthur Goldhammer (New Haven: 1986), 28–29.

220. Daniel Herlihy, *Medieval Households* (Cambridge: Mass.: 1985), 67.

221. See the texts assembled in Josephine Mayer, *Monumenta de viduis diaconissis virginibusque tractantia,* Florilegium patristicum 42 (Bonn: 1938).

222. "Felix ergo uirgo quia intacta, fortior uidua quia expert," Isidore, *De ecc.,* 87.

223. Élisabeth Magnou-Nortier, "Les évêques et la paix dans l'espace franc (VIe–XIe siècles)," in *L'Évêque dans l'histoire de l'Église: Actes de la 7me rencontre d'histoire religieuse—Fontevrault Abbey,"* 36 (Angers: 1984).

May the iniquity of his fathers remain in the sight of God, and may the sin of his mother not be forgotten / let them be against the Lord forever, and let their memory perish from the earth, because he did not remember to practice mercy / and he persecuted the helpless man and the beggar and the broken-hearted, and put them to death.[224]

Protection of the poor became a central concern of epicopal government because it linked the moral imperative of Christian charity to the bishops' responsibility and prerogative to rule.[225] The *necatores* and *pervasores* against whom the bishops fulminated were interfering with an ideal of social order of which bishops occupied the apex. To again cite Isidore, "A layman fulfills his duty of hospitality by taking in one or two, but the bishop is inhumane unless he receive everyone."[226] The layman, in other words, had a small-scale domestic duty, while the bishop's eyes were turned toward society as a whole. His was a public social duty to protect and rule the church. Protection of the poor thus had ramifications for the concept of ecclesiastical ownership of property.

Church property had presented Roman law with a new problem: that of property owned by a juridical or fictional person. It was a kind of ownership that was especially troubling to a legal system that did not recognize the concept of agency.[227] This concept was established in Roman law and survived into the post-Roman world.[228] By the fifth century church goods were being termed the property of the poor. Julian Pomerius, a late-fifth-century priest, tutor of Caesarius of Arles and author of the *De vita contemplativa,* described ecclesiastical property in a manner that had an important influence on Frankish councils and thinkers.[229] The governors of the church, he said, hold church property not as possessors, but as "overseers":

224. "In memoriam redeat iniquitas patrum eius in conspectu Domini et peccatum matris eius non deleatur / fiant contra Dominum semper, et dispereat de terra memoria eorum / pro eo quod non est recordatus facere misericordiam / et persecutus est hominem inopem et mendicum et conpunctum corde mortificare." On the importance of this Psalm in medieval curses, see Lester K. Little, *Benedictine Maledictions: Liturgical Cursing in Romanesque France* (Ithaca: 1993), 64–65.

225. Brown, *Poverty and Leadership,* 89.

226. "Laicus enim unum aut duos suscipiens imleuit hospitalitatis officium, episcopus nisi omnes receperit inhumanus est," Isidore, *De ecc.,* 63.

227. Nicholas, *Introduction to Roman Law,* 201.

228. Émile Lesne, *Histoire de la propriété ecclésiastique en France,* vol. 1, *Époques Romaine et Merovingienne,* Mémoires et travaux des facultés Catholiques de Lille 4 (Lille: 1910), 3–4.

229. See DSA, article "Julien Pomère," 8:1594–1600. Carolingians generally believed that Pomerius' *De vita contemplativa* was written by Prosper of Aquitaine; Jean Devisse, "L'influence de Julien Pomère sur les clercs carolingiens: De la pauvreté au Ve et IXe siècles," RHEF 56 (1970): 285–95; see also Jean Leclercq, et al, eds., *Spirituality of the Middle Ages,* 73.

And this is why the goods of the church are known to be nothing other than the prayers of the faithful, the ransom of sinners, and the patrimony of the poor. They do not lay legal claim to them for their personal use, but distribute them as things entrusted to them on behalf of the poor.[230]

The poor, in other words, did not receive alms because they were the objects of pity. They were held to have a right to be sustained.[231]

Julian Pomerius was encapsulating an old principle, already addressed in early Gallic and Roman councils. As the church's wealth increased through pious donations of money, ornaments, and land, the issue of economic supervision was carefully laid out. Such donations were made to lighten the retribution for sin after death, and to secure the prayers of the church.[232] Pomerius thus called these donations the "prayers of the faithful" and the "ransom of sinners." To disturb these arrangements was therefore to disturb the provision made for the salvation of the dead, and to risk casting them into shadow. As the "patrimony of the poor," church property was held in trust by bishops for its true owner. In some Merovingian churches, the words of Pomerius were regular reading.[233]

To disturb the property of the church was thus to harm the poor and to take food from their mouths. Councils, such as Agde 506, led by Caesarius of Arles, condemned those who would unlawfully retain the "gifts of relatives or donations left in testaments," or who would dare to take back what they had given to a monastery or church. Such people were to be excluded from the church as "murderers of the poor."[234] The bishops gathered in Vaison in 442 said that those who take the oblations of the faithful dead were to be thrown from the church as unbelievers, because the dead are thus deprived of arrangements made for their salvation, and the poor are cheated of necessary sustenance. Such people were "murderers of the destitute."[235]

230. "Non ut possessores, sed ut procuratores facultates ecclesiae possidebant. Et idcirco scientes nihil aliud esse res ecclesiae, nisi vota fidelium, pretia peccatorum, et patrimonia pauperum ; no eas vindicaverunt in usus suos, ut proprias, sed ut commendatas pauperibus diviserunt," Julianus Pomerius, *De vita contemplativa* 2.9 (PL 59:454).

231. Ullmann, "Public Welfare," 6.

232. Lesne, *Histoire de la propriété,* 167–85.

233. The *Vetus gallicanum* contained long extracts from Pomerius: Wolfenbüttel: Herzog-August Bibliothek, Cod. Guelf. Weissenb., 76.

234. "Necatores pauperum," Agde (506) CCSL 148:194.

235. "Egentium necatores," Council of Vaison-la-Romaine (442), 97. See the interesting discussion in Rosenwein, *Negotiating Space,* 42; and Michael Edward Moore, "The Ancient Fathers: Christian Antiquity, Patristics and Frankish Canon Law," in *Millenium: Jahrbuch zu Kultur und Geschichte des ersten Jahrtausends n. Chr./Yearbook on the Culture and History of the First Millennium C.E.,* 7 (2010): 293–342; see esp. 321–22.

Throughout the regions dominated by the Franks, the seventh century was marked by a "massive advance" of Christian culture and the Christianization of rural areas.[236] Among the nobility, this process was accompanied by the donation of estates to churches and monasteries, often as gifts to missionaries. The effect of this on Austrasian nobles and their estates was to bring about a higher level of integration within the kingdom, serving to overcome the Frankish tendency to fission and "regulated anarchy" and establishing some degree of royal dominance. In the region around Maastricht, as Frans Theuws has shown, the royal presence was thus impressed in the landscape.[237] Those in the strongest position could find external support for their power by looking for a connection to the Frankish realm, a trend that would reach its high point under Charles Martel.[238] These local tendencies came together under the aegis of a Christian kingdom and its king, acting in cooperation with episcopal advisors.[239] Protection of the poor, taking the form of protecting church property, was the theoretical construction of a sacred space and regional order in which Frankish nobles and kings could participate.

Bishops participated in dramatic ways as the Frankish kingdoms were repeatedly unified under exceptional kings. The grand Council of Paris in 614 was held to mark the domination of the Frankish realms by Clothar II.[240] Developing a special association with the cult of St. Denis, late Merovingian kings such as Dagobert were eager to accumulate religious sources of power and an association with the sacred connotations of law.[241] The abbey church of St. Denis became a favored site for royal burials and for demonstrating the Christian dimension of kingship. Dagobert and his son, Clovis II (d. 657), wanted the monastic community of St. Denis to enact a perpetual liturgy on behalf of themselves and the royal family.[242]

Kings and bishops developed their concepts of royal and episcopal power in a

236. Fouracre and Gerberding, *Late Merovingian France,* 51; see also Hen, *Culture and Religion,* 154–206.

237. F. C. Theuws, "Maastricht as a Centre of Power in the Early Middle Ages," in *Topographies of Power,* 155–216.

238. F. C. Theuws, "Centre and Periphery in Northern Austrasia (6th–8th centuries): An Archaeological Perspective," in *Medieval Archaeology in the Netherlands: Studies Presented to H. H. von Regteren Altena,* ed. J. Besterman, J. Bos and H. Heidinga, 41–69 (Aasen: 1990).

239. Werner, *Naissance de la noblesse,* 341–59.

240. Wood, *Merovingian Kingdoms,* 154.

241. Wallace-Hadrill, *Long-Haired Kings,* 224–25; Wood, *Merovingian Kingdoms,* 155; Le Jan, "La sacralité de la royauté mérovingienne," 1227.

242. Hen, *Royal Patronage of Liturgy,* 35–36; see also Wallace-Hadrill, *Early Germanic Kingship,* 50.

dynamic conversation that stressed their mutuality. The cooperation of bishops was an important asset in such efforts of consolidation, but late in the seventh century the Frankish kings proved unable to overcome local resistance. The late Merovingian kings, whom the historian Fredegar thought of as "lesser beasts," were capable only of meager projects.[243] Royal legislation, the holding of prestigious councils, and even the role of war-leader were largely abandoned. According to Ian Wood, the evidence of charters shows a continued ability on the part of these kings to act as judges and to gather powerful men around themselves. Dupraz noted the increasingly sparse evidence of charters during this period.[244] Nevertheless, their role was increasingly overshadowed by the rise of the Pippinid (later Carolingian) Mayors of the Palace.[245]

As the episcopate was absorbed by the Frankish nobility, the bishops of this period sometimes have the appearance of territorial magnates only nominally different from lords of equivalent stature.[246] There were egregious cases of bishops who took little notice of traditional episcopal responsibilities and made the office a mere adjunct of noble prestige and a source of wealth.[247] Such a view is reinforced by the state of the Frankish Church in the late seventh and early eighth centuries. Patrick Geary has said that in the period between 700 and 730, episcopal activity was rapidly transformed into simple lordship: "the new bishops' power and prestige came exclusively from their control of the material resources of one or more dioceses."[248] Indeed, the higher clergy had been "ennobled," ranking alongside other members of the governing elite, and were caught up in secular duties under the impetus of Charles Martel's rise to power.[249] This describes the bishops at a point just prior to the reform councils held under Boniface, who complained that the Frankish bishops had not met in council for 80 years.[250] Yet the reform councils of Boniface beginning in 742 retrieved legal

243. Wallace-Hadrill, *Long-Haired Kings*, 231.

244. Dupraz, *Contribution à l'histoire*, 226–27.

245. Wood, *Merovingian Kingdoms*, 261–65.

246. Heinzelmann, *Bischofsherrschaft in Gallien;* Friedrich Prinz, *Herrschaft und Kirche: Beiträge zur Entstehung und Wirkungsweise episkopaler und monastischer Organisationsformen* (Stuttgart: 1988). The case is argued extensively in Reinhold Kaiser, *Bischofsherrschaft zwischen Königtum und Fürstenmacht: Studien zur bischöflichen Stadtherrschaft im westfränzösischen Reich im frühen und hohen Mittelalter,* Pariser historische Studien 17 (Bonn: 1981).

247. On Milo, for example, see Wood, *Merovingian Kingdoms*, 277–79.

248. Patrick Geary, *Before France and Germany: The Creation and Transformation of the Merovingian World* (Oxford: 1988), 211–12.

249. Werner, *Naissance de la noblesse*, 355–59. See the discussion in Fouracre and Gerberding, *Late Merovingian France*, 48–50.

250. Eugen Ewig, "Milo et eiusmodi similes," in *Sankt Bonifatius Gedankgabe zum zwölfhundersten Geburtstag,* 412, 2nd ed. (Fulda: 1954).

and intellectual traditions that do not appear to have suffered any interruption. Boniface, moreover, it will be argued in the following chapter, found a circle of bishops and other powerful men willing to reform kingship itself and to participate in the rise of the Carolingian dynasty. Bishops continued to occupy the center of society, and were poised to reach even loftier heights.

Scholars have long pointed to the many ways in which bishops functioned much the same as other notables, offering patronage and even building episcopal dynasties, wielding formidable resources of land and thus influence.[251] Bishops were an important, distinctive group of participants in the regional power system of the kingdom, who could also call on the entire range of spiritual claims made here. Unlike their noble counterparts, they continued to maintain a mastery of law and to legislate on that basis. Late in the Merovingian period a twofold movement can be observed as part of the increasing Christianization of the kingdom: there was a continuous redistribution of wealth and land toward monasteries and churches. Although prayer, blessings, and the sacraments lay in the bishop's governing hand, the "hand of truth," bishops nevertheless thought constantly about their kings and how to understand royal power. With the rise of the Carolingian dynasty in the early eighth century, this peculiar combination of powers was brought to bear in a reform of the Frankish Church and kingdom. These dramatic events often revolved around the *persona* of the bishop.

251. Innes, *State and Society,* 174–75.

[6]

MISSIONARY WAR AND REFORM
OF KINGSHIP

THIS CHAPTER DESCRIBES the mobilization of episcopal power and ideology in the Carolingian seizure of power. Episcopal social doctrines embedded in law and liturgy were developed in a missionary theory of power that
called for the use of force in pagan regions, especially to the east. The missionary
bishop Boniface, and bishops established and influenced by him, shaped a new
ideology of royal power based around the theme of a conflict with paganism.
Boniface's mission and the letters recording his activities served as the preamble
for ambitious programs of reform. The most highly placed bishops were seemingly aware of the vast potential of a righteous form of royal power to reshape
the political and social landscape. At the same time, Frankish kings and bishops
forged ties with the papacy in Rome. The Franks came to think of themselves
as the indispensible guardians of the church. These themes soon coalesced in
Frankish aggression in Saxony and Bavaria. The reform of church and society
provided the theoretical basis for royal activism and for the development of a
new form of kingship soaked in religious symbology.

A Vision of Order

The first half of the eighth century witnessed a reconfiguration of power and
the emergence of a new political order in the Frankish kingdom, accompanied
by altered relations between the bishops and their king. The backdrop to this

lay in the gradual and repeated unification of the late Merovingian kingdoms alongside efforts to extend Frankish control to the east and north. The office of mayor of the palace came to be dominated by a powerful Austrasian family, the Pippinids (later the Carolingians), in the 650s, just as the Frankish kingdoms were being consolidated under the domination of the kingdom of Austrasia.[1] The Carolingian mayors gradually absorbed functions associated with Frankish kingship and extended them, as an expansion of noble privilege and prestige, so successfully that the mayors came to eclipse royal power. One of these mayors, Grimoald, seized power in 656, driving the Merovingian heir into exile.[2] The experiment ended in Grimoald's death, but was a harbinger of Carolingian ambitions. By the time of Charles Martel (ca. 688–741), the preeminence of these mayors was so great that it seemed to call for new titles comparable to those of the Byzantine nobility.[3] Charles Martel's raids for plunder in Frisia, Thuringia, and Bavaria, with Martel at the head of large and successful armies, could sometimes take on a religious tone, as if their aim were only to protect and cooperate with the missionaries active in Frisia and elsewhere. The support of bishops and missionaries was a crucial part of Martel's success, as was the expropriation of ecclesiastical property.[4]

The Carolingians went on to overthrow the Merovingians and establish themselves as a new royal dynasty in 751. As will be argued below, the usurpation was conceived as a reform of kingship based on theocratic concepts of royal power that we have traced to episcopal social thought. Assertions of royal power came to be suffused with a "rhetoric of reform."[5] At the same time it was intended as a revival of the Frankish Church, especially the episcopate, which was accused of having abandoned its most important duties.[6] Boniface would complain that bishops went hunting, took part in war, or were married.[7]

Historians have revised the old idea that the Franks abandoned the ancient

---

1. Fouracre and Gerberding, *Late Merovingian France,* 18–26; Rosamond McKitterick, *The Frankish Kingdoms under the Carolingians, 751–987* (London: 1983), 23.

2. Fouracre, *The Age of Charles Martel,* 37.

3. Werner, *Naissance de la noblesse,* 301.

4. Richard A. Gerberding, "716: A Crucial Year for Charles Martel," in *Karl Martell in seiner Zeit,* edited by Jörg Jarnut, Ulrich Nonn, and Michael Richter, 205–16, Beihefte der Francia 37 (Sigmaringen: 1994). Brown describes Martel's armies as "spasmodically pious": Peter Brown, *Rise of Western Christendom,* 255.

5. Paul Fouracre, "Carolingian Justice: The Rhetoric of Improvement and Contexts of Abuse," *Settimane* 42 (1995): 2:771–803.

6. Criticisms of the Frankish Church in this period have long been taken as evidence for the collapse of the episcopate into simple lordship: Ewig, "Milo et eiusmodi similes," 412–40.

7. Pierre Riché, "Le renouveau culturel à la cour de Pepin III," *Francia* 2 (1974): 59–70.

Merovingian line of kings because it had sunk into incompetence.[8] The sources creating this impression of the late Merovingian kings are not contemporary and are colored by later propaganda, which belittled the Merovingian royal line so as to vindicate the Carolingian seizure of power. Instead, one can point to the potency of the reform ideal to generate change and to provide transitions from one historical phase to another.

In frontier regions, acceptance of Christianity was equated with political submission.[9] The political skills and military might of the Carolingian family made a profound impression on bishops. Their success in battle gained the allegiance of the powerful among the upper nobility and the bishops. Even more attractive to the bishops was the fact that this family was willing to consistently foster episcopal power on a scale unlike that of the Merovingian kings. The mayors' drive to expand Frankish dominion eastward opened the further prospect that the People of God would also be expanded, and with it the dominion of the bishops, who joined in these wars and saw the possessions of their churches devoted to fighting in them.[10] With the rise of the Carolingian family, cooperation between bishops and royal power was newly intensified, creating what has been called a Carolingian model of power.[11]

A major figure in this period of transition was the Anglo-Saxon Boniface, who traveled in 719 to Rome, where he was specially appointed as a missionary by Pope Gregory II (715–731). Working at first with his mentor Willibrord in Frisia, Boniface ultimately set off on his own to undertake the conversion of the Hessians and Thuringians on the eastern side of the Rhine, and later turned his efforts toward a reform of the Frankish Church and kingdom.[12]

Anglo-Saxon missionaries such as Willibrord had been active in these regions for more than a generation, gaining the support and cooperation of Frankish

8. Edward Peters, *The Shadow King: Rex Inutilis in Medieval Law and Literature 751–1327* (New Haven: 1970), 47–55; as earlier, R. Macaigne, *L'Église mérovingienne et l'état pontifical* (Paris: 1929), 354–537; but now, see Fouracre and Gerberding, *Late Merovingian France,* 26–58.

9. Nancy Gauthier, *L'Évangélisation des pays de la Moselle: La province romaine de Première Belgique entre antiquité et moyen âge (IIIe–VIIIe siècles)* (Paris: 1980), 269–70.

10. Friedrich Prinz, *Klerus und Krieg im früheren Mittelalter: Untersuchungen zur Rolle der Kirche beim Aufbau der Königsherrschaft,* Monographien zur Geschichte des Mittelalters 2 (Stuttgart: 1971), 61–62.

11. Werner, *Naissance de la noblesse,* 371.

12. Generally on Boniface, see Brown, *Rise of Western Christendom,* 254–75; Lutz E. von Padberg, *Mission und Christianisierung: Formen und Folgen bei Angelsachsen und Franken im 7. und 8. Jahrhundert* (Stuttgart: 1995); G. W. Greenway, *Saint Boniface* (London: 1955); Theodor Schieffer, *Winfrid-Bonifatius*; Albert Hauck, *Kirchengeschichte Deutschlands,* 5th ed. (Leipzig: 1935), 1:432–535; Levison, *England and the Continent,* 70–93; Wallace-Hadrill, *Frankish Church,* 150–61; M. Coens, "Saint Boniface et sa mission historique," *Analecta Bollandiana* 73 (1955): 462–95.

nobles there.[13] Boniface's mission marked an intervention by the papacy and the Anglo-Saxon Church in Frankish affairs at a time when the mayors of the palace intensified their efforts to expand in the very regions that Boniface sought to convert.[14] Carloman and Pippin wanted Boniface's help in "integrating politically and assimilating culturally the eastern reaches" of the Frankish realm.[15]

This intervention was even more pronounced when Boniface turned his attention to reforming the Frankish Church. The particular quality of his mission is therefore important for understanding the change in episcopal prospects that accompanied the Carolingian usurpation. At the outset, it is useful to begin with a study of religious symbolism in Boniface, especially the symbols in which the social world was conceptualized, in the correspondence recording Boniface's thirty years in Hesse and Thuringia and among the Franks.[16] This feature of Boniface's thinking is in many ways similar to that of Isidore and the traditional social thought of Merovingian bishops, expressing a political theology in the terminology of liturgy and exegesis. As Le Goff has remarked, to establish the legitimacy of a monarchy, "symbolic arguments have always been necessary alongside arguments of fact derived from force."[17] Boniface's involvement in the Carolingian usurpation gives a special interest to his symbolic arguments about the social order.

The Merovingians had long desired to expand their rule in the east, culminating in a great expedition against the Alemans, Thuringians, and Bavarians by Charles Martel in 725.[18] Frequent military activity in these regions brought together the interests of the Carolingian mayors and the Anglo-Saxon missionaries who worked in the region.[19] These campaigns also offered major opportunities for plunder and reward to Frankish warriors.[20] In observing the rise of warrior bishops and their cooperation with the earliest Carolingian conquests, we will see that, although bishops still believed that they brought salvation to mankind, this belief was linked to an aggressive expansion of the church and

13. F. C. Theuws, "The Integration of the Kempen Region into the Frankish Empire (550–750): Some Hypotheses," *Helinium* 26 (1986): 121–36; Wallace-Hadrill, *Frankish Church,* 144–47.

14. David Parsons, "Some Churches of the Anglo-Saxon Missionaries in Southern Germany: A Review of the Evidence," EME 8 (1999): 31–67.

15. Schutz, *The Carolingians in Central Europe,* 32.

16. *Die Briefe des Heiligen Bonifatius und Lullus,* ed. Michael Tangl, MGH Epistolae Selectae 1 (Berlin: 1916).

17. Le Goff, "Le roi dans l'occident médiéval," 8.

18. On specific campaigns: Walter Schlesinger, "Zur politischen Geschichte, 9–61.

19. Prinz, *Frühes Mönchtum,* 232–33.

20. Timothy Reuter, "Plunder and Tribute in the Carolingian Empire," *Transactions of the Royal Historical Society,* 5th ser. 35 (1985): 75–94; see 75.

kingdom. The warlike expansionism of the Franks, like the missionary perspective of the bishops, was guided by a topographic and religious sense that Europe was divided into two parts—a Christian world and a pagan world, set in constant tension and conflict.[21] The perceived dichotomy was effective and influential despite the close similarity of societies on either side of the line dividing "inside" from "outside."[22] Furthermore, as will be seen, the division between Christian and pagan was by no means as clear as it appeared in missionary doctrine. Reform of the Frankish Church and the rise of the Carolingian dynasty were intimately linked.

Missionaries such as Boniface were able to provide a social model and a political myth for a new redemptive model of kingship and for the eventual expansion of the Frankish kingdom into an empire. As the center of moral and political gravity of the Frankish world shifted toward the east and north, missionary bishops such as Boniface, followed by a next generation of disciples, were able to set the tone of the new Carolingian regime. Boniface is a central figure in a reconceptualization of the kingdom and the emergence of a sacralized state within Frankish society.

Boniface's efforts as a missionary and reformer were guided by his perception of the relation between divine reality and this world. Many of the texts examined in this study, particularly those of Isidore, the liturgy of Gaul, and now the writings of St. Boniface, were encoded, dense texts that served as sacramental gestures, signs of sacred things.[23] Boniface cultivated a "double vision" that could see this world and the otherworld at the same time. It was this privileged vision that gave him insight into the proper order of the social world as an "order of orders."[24]

Sign and Symbol in Boniface

Boniface thought of faith as a heightened perception of reality that could overcome the limitations of the body and its senses. The problem of faith was thus a problem of vision and hence, in turn, was connected to Boniface's perception of the body and its limitations. Faith was a type of vision that transcended bodily vision and yet maintained a connection to the body. Heightened vision moved in the same channels of perception as ordinary sense experience, even

---

21. Von Padberg, "Odin oder Christus? Loyalitäts- und orientierungskonflikte in der frühmittelalterlichen Christianisierungsepoche," *Archiv für Kulturgeschichte* 77 (1995): 149–278; see 258.

22. Reuter, "Plunder and Tribute," 91.   23. Schmitt, *La raison des gestes,* 83.

24. Duby, *Three Orders,* 74–75.

though it involved being "snatched out of the body" and seeing "in spirit."[25]

In relating a monk's vision of the afterlife, Boniface made clear that the monk saw with his own eyes, and heard with his own ears, a higher reality that is always present, but usually invisible. It was as though "the eyes of a man, when he is looking, are veiled with a very thick covering, and suddenly the veil is snatched away, and all things are clear, which before were unseen and veiled and unknown."[26] This unveiled sight was still limited by human capacity. Being suddenly able to see the angels around him, the monk could not look at them because their splendor was too great.[27] The same thing happened when "the pupils of his eyes were struck" with the sight of the Heavenly Jerusalem.[28] On returning to his body, blood trickled from the monk's eyes and he could not see in this world. His eyes had suffered the impact of an excessive vision.

In order to see the things of faith, the body and its senses had to be purified, and even exchanged for a spiritual body. Yet a connection between the noncorporal plane and the physical body was maintained. The other world was always present and at hand, but invisible. As for Gregory of Tours, so for Boniface religious knowledge was acquired by fasting and discipline. Straining to see the other side, the devoted cleric could hope one day to see ultimate reality. As Boniface wrote to his supporter, Bishop Daniel of Winchester, "You have, my father, just as Antony of Didymus was said to have, eyes with which God can be seen, and his angels, and the joyful glories of the supernal Jerusalem."[29] The effort to actually see the truths of religion derived from a perception that those truths had a very concrete, "bodily" form. Visionary perception allowed religious men to see the invisible consequences of action in this world.

25. "Locutus sum et ille mihi stupendas visiones, quas extra corpus suum raptus in spiritu vidit," Boniface to Abbess Eadburg (716), *Die Briefe des Heiligen Bonifatius,* Letter 10:8.

26. "Et simillimum esse conlatione veluti si videntis et vigilantis hominis oculi densissimo tegmine velentur; et subito auferatur velamen, et tunc perspicua sint omnia, quae antea non visa et velata et ignota fuerunt," Boniface to Abbess Eadburg (716), *Die Briefe des Heiligen Bonifatius,* Letter 10:8.

27. "Ut nullatenus pro nimio splendore in eos aspicere potuisset," Boniface to Abbess Eadburg (716), *Die Briefe des Heiligen Bonifatius,* Letter 10:8.

28. "Ut reverberatis oculorum pupillis pro nimio splendore in eos nullatenus aspicere potuisset," Boniface to Abbess Eadburg (716), *Die Briefe des Heiligen Bonifatius,* Letter 10:12; see also Marie-Thérèse Gousset, "La Représentation de la Jérusalem céleste à l'époque carolingienne," *Cahiers archéologiques* 33 (1974): 47–60.

29. "Habes, pater mi, sicut Antonius de Didimo fertur dixisse, oculos, quibus potest Deus videri et angeli eius et supernae Hierusalem gloriosa gaudia speculari," Boniface to Bishop Daniel (742–746), *Die Briefe des Heiligen Bonifatius,* Letter 63:131. Boniface is referring to the Alexandrian exegete Didymus the Blind (313–398). On Didymus, see Anne-Marie Malingrey, *La littérature greque chrétienne* (Paris: 1996), 84–85.

A king's sins could destroy the image of God in him and make him an image of the devil instead.[30] It was perhaps the troubling figure of Aethelbald of Mercia that first raised for Boniface the task of reforming kingship, which he would undertake in the Frankish kingdom. Anglo-Saxon missionaries had long focused on securing the aid and protection of kings for their efforts. They sought closeness to the king, and so were horrified by royal sin.[31] Boniface wrote to King Aethelbald to complain of his scandalous life, assuring the king that two of his predecessors had been "cast down from the royal peak of this life, and were denied, by their untimely and terrible deaths, the perpetual light." As exiles they were "submerged in the depths of hell and the abyss of Tartarus."[32] What is odd about Boniface's attitude is that Aethelbald had cooperated with his clerics, summoning the great synod of Clofeshoe in 746.[33] Boniface had asked Archbishop Cuthbert for copies of the council-record.[34] Aethelbald was murdered by his bodyguard in 757.[35] Such a capacity for "double vision" nevertheless determined the way Boniface thought about his missionary activity. In attempting to reform the kingdom and its bishops, Boniface in effect sought to reify symbolic expressions of the nature of reality, of social order and its points of contact with the otherworld.

Baptism and Conquest

Some important aspects of Boniface's worldview have a classical resonance. Leaving the rural, still heavily forested landscape of England for the fairly similar landscapes of Germany, his feelings about those lands were nevertheless almost identical to those they had inspired in the Romans.[36] Boniface and his

30. "Ut imaginem Dei, que in te creata est, per luxoriam ad imaginem et similitudinem maligni diaboli convertas," Boniface to King Aethelbald (746–747), *Die Briefe des Heiligen Bonifatius,* Letter 73:149.

31. Von Padberg, *Mission und Christianisierung,* 96.

32. "Hi duo reges . . . iusto iudicio Dei damnati de culmine regali huius vitae abiecti et inmatura et terribili morte praeventi a luce perpetua extranei in profundaum inferni et tartarum abyssi demersi sunt," Boniface to King Aethelbald (746–747), *Die Briefe des Heiligen Bonifatius,* Letter 73:146.

33. Patrick Wormald, "Bede, the *Bretwaldas* and the Origins of the *Gens Anglorum,*" in *Ideal and Reality,* 126–27; Margaret Deanesly, *The Pre-Conquest Church in England,* An Ecclesiastical History of England 1 (London: 1961), 212–15; and Catherine Cubitt, *Anglo-Saxon Church Councils c. 650–850* (London: 1995), 220–21.

34. Cubitt, *Anglo-Saxon Church Councils,* 19–20.

35. "þyilcan geare mon ofslog Æþelbald Miercna cyning on Seccan dune" (Parker ms., year 755–7), in *Two of the Saxon Chronicles Parallel,* edited by Charles Plummer, 8 (Oxford: 1892); see also Frank Stenton, *Anglo-Saxon England,* 3rd ed. (Repr. Oxford: 1989), 205.

36. Daniel Garrison, "The *Locus Inamoenus:* Another Part of the Forest," *Arion,* 3rd ser. 2.1 (Winter 1992): 98–114.

supporters described his mission east of the Rhine using the same lugubrious imagery of forests and swamps that had so appalled the Romans who attempted military conquest there.[37] *Germania,* with its darkness and mire, vast forests and strange, preternatural fires (*niedfeor*), inspired fear and dread of a place beyond the pale of culture and light.[38] This learned topographic and cultural perspective also determined how the Franks would view their eastern neighbors. Unlike the Romans, however, Christian missionaries went to this region with a sense of confidence that in the waning years of the world, the pagan hinterland would be gathered into the church: that "those outside should be inside."[39] Boniface's Anglo-Saxon patron, Bishop Daniel, told him to explain to the Germans that their pagan religion and uncultivated forests were features of a primitive and uncivilized life.[40] Daniel believed that Boniface should undermine paganism by pointing out its inconsistencies and the poverty of its conceptions.[41] Conversion should begin with subversion. Missionary work was still underway even within Francia, in areas long subject to episcopal control, and its results were incomplete. The task was less easy in Frisia and Germany.[42] In Frisia, Boniface's efforts were fruitless in a "sterile land," a plowed field from which the "dew of celestial fruitfulness" had dried, and so he returned to England.[43] Perhaps as a result of this initial failure, Boniface began to think of his project in more aggressive terms. In recounting Boniface's second mission, this time to Germany, his biographer Willibald, writing not long after Boniface's death, drew often on the connection between Christianity and cultivation, contrasting it with paganism and the forest:

he was directed by the most blessed pope to inspect the monstrous peoples of Germany: to consider whether the uncultivated fields of their hearts, turned by an evangelical ploughshare, would wish to receive the seed of preaching.[44]

37. "Silvis, paludibus," Tacitus, *Annals* (2.5), 1:296.

38. "Sive sacrilegos ignes, quos niedfeor vocant," Majordomus Carlomann, letter summoning the Council of Lestinnes (743), *Die Briefe des Heiligen Bonifatius,* Letter 56:100. The same concern appears in the *Indiculus superstitionum et paganiarum* appended to the Council of Lestinnes (743), "De igno fricato de ligno id est Nodfyr," Mansi, 12:376. These fox-fires were also part of Lucan's Germanic stage-setting: Garrison, "Locus Inamoenus," 103.

39. Wallace-Hadrill, *Frankish Church,* 143.

40. Bishop Daniel to Boniface (723–724), *Die Briefe des Heiligen Bonifatius,* Letter 23:40.

41. Richard E. Sullivan, "Carolingian Missionary Theories," *Catholic Historical Review* 62 (1956): 273–95; see 276.

42. See Boniface's condemnation of paganism in Frankish territory: Boniface to Daniel (742–746), *Die Briefe des Heiligen Bonifatius,* Letter 63:130.

43. "Iam arida caelestis rore fecunditatis relinqueret arva" (4), Willibald, *Vita sancti Bonifatii archiepiscopi Moguntini,* ed. Wilhelm Levison, 23, MGH SRG in us. schol. (Hannover: 2003).

44. "A beatissimo papa ad inspiciendos inmanissimos Germaniae populos directus est; ut, an

The process of conversion was so difficult that it was accompanied, according to Willibald, by a program of mass baptism. As in Frankish Gaul, the peoples of the mission-region of Germany were gathered into the People of God by the wholesale aggrandizement of populations, a determined and aggressive effort to reorient cultures that were viewed as unwholesome. Boniface, "having baptized many thousands of people, purged them of their age-old paganism."[45] Willibald related the most famous of Boniface's deeds, felling the ancient oak of Geismar, center of an autochthonous cult. The pagans, who stood about cursing him, were silenced and awed when the great tree fell at his touch, and "formerly devoted pagans turned to the Lord."[46] Boniface then used the wood to build an oratory dedicated to St. Peter. Relying on traditions that placed bishops at the center of society, this aggrandizement was also viewed as the incorporation of a violent, uncouth people into the cultivated and civilized world.

In the Anglo-Saxon world in which Boniface had been trained, the occupation and reorientation of pagan cult-sites was backed by an august tradition going back to Pope Gregory the Great (590–604). Gregory had explained to the missionary Mellitus that if a pagan temple were solidly made, the idols within them should be destroyed, but the temple itself preserved, blessed with water, and turned to Christian use.[47] The people should be allowed to keep their ancient customs, still directed toward the age-old cult site, now transformed into a Christian center.[48] This was a tactic of mixing and blending, rather than separation and strict division. If pagan custom dictated killing animals in sacrifice to the demons, the people should be allowed to kill animals for the sake of feasting at a Christian solemnity, such as the dedication of a church.[49] Boniface was a great fan of Bede's, and would certainly have known Gregory's letter.[50] Frankish

---

inculta cordium arva, euangelico arata vomere, praedicationis semen recipere voluissent, consideraret" (5) Willibald, *Vita Bonifatii*, 26.

45. "Multisque milibus hominum expurgata paganica vetustate baptizatis" (6), Willibald, *Vita Bonifatii*, 30.

46. "Willibald, *Vita Bonifatii*, 33.

47. Von Padberg, *Mission und Christianisierung*, 151–54.

48. The letter is preserved in Bede's *Ecclesiastical History*: "Quia, si fana eadem bene constructa sunt, necesse est, ut a cultu daemonum in obsequio ueri Dei debeant cummutari" (1.30), Bede, *Venerabilis Baedae Historiam ecclesiasticam gentis Anglorum, Historiam abbatum, Epistolam ad Ecgberctum, una cum Historia abbatum auctore anonymo*, ed. Charles Plummer (Oxford: 1896), 65.

49. "Et quia boues solent in sacrificio daemonum multos occidere, debet eis etiam hac de re aliqua sollemnitas immutari, ut die dedicationis" (1.30), Bede, *Historiam ecclesiasticam*, 65. Gregory's position represents the traditional Christian rejection of pagan gods as demons: De Vries, *Altgermanische Religionsgeschichte*, 1:163–66; see also Dieter Timpe, "Tacitus' Germania," 458–62.

50. He wrote to Ecberth asking for Bede's writings: "Ut mihi de opusculis Bedan lectoris aliquos tractatus conscribere," Boniface to Archbishop Ecberth, *Die Briefe des Heiligen Bonifatius*, Letter 75:158; see also Deanesly, *Pre-Conquest Church*, 236.

tradition was harsher. The bishops at Orange in 541 were aware that some Christians continued to "swear on the head of a cow or a wild animal." Their impulse was to eliminate pagan customs.[51] As for those who continued to adore the sacred stones, trees, or fountains of the "gentiles," they should at once be deprived of Communion.[52] Despite what the bishops said, occupying old cult-sites and attempting to redirect pagan festivals toward Christian ones had been the Gallic response since the time of Caesarius.[53] Boniface attempted to combine Gregorian mildness with Frankish harshness—although, as we have seen, there was considerable intermingling of religious concepts in Gaul, as well. Missionaries such as Boniface thought of themselves as warriors in a battle against demons.

This was especially true in the "marginal cultures" of Germany, long used to blending their polytheistic paganism with elements of Christianity.[54] Pope Gregory III (731–741), apparently in response to queries from Boniface, repeatedly reminded him not to conduct any rebaptisms in regions of clerical decline, even where the language and the "ethnic paganism" (*gentilitas*) of the ceremony seemed strange. Such initiates should only be confirmed by the laying on of hands and anointing.[55] According to Gregory, rebaptism was required only when a baptism had been conducted by a pagan! We see Boniface in the position of making calculations about the nature of such ceremonies, based on how his informant described them.[56] The borders separating Christian ceremonies from heretical or merely unusual ceremonies, or pagan ceremonies based on Christian themes, were dim. The Franks in this way learned to deploy a powerful language of centrality against their neighbors.

There were many Christian enclaves in Germany—especially the remnants of old Irish monastic foundations founded by wandering missionary-monks such as Kilian.[57] Fulda, the foundation most closely identified with Boniface's name,

---

51. "Si quis Christianus, ut est gentilium consuetudo, ad caput cuiuscumque ferae uel pecudis, inuocatus insuper nominibus paganorum, fortasse iurauerit," Council of Orange (541), CCSL 148A:136.

52. "Ad nescio quas petras aut arbores aut ad fontes, designata loca gentilium, perpetrare, quae ad ecclesiae rationem non pertinent, eos ab ecclesia sancta auctoritate reppellant," Council of Tours (567), CCSL 148A:191.

53. Pierre Audin, "Cesaire d'Arles et le maintien de pratiques paiennes dans la Provence du VIe siècle," in *La Patrie gauloise d'Agrippa au VIème siècle: Actes du Colloque, Lyon 1981* (Lyon: 1983), 327–38.

54. Von Padberg, "Odin oder Christus?" 254–57.

55. "Illi quippe, qui baptizati sunt per diversitate et declinatione linguarum gentilitatis, tamen, quod in nomine trinitatis baptizati sunt, oportet eos per manus inpositionis et sacri crismatis confirmari," Gregory III to Boniface (739), *Die Briefe des Heiligen Bonifatius,* Letter 45:73.

56. Gregory III to Boniface (732), *Die Briefe des Heiligen Bonifatius,* Letter 28:50.

57. Prinz, *Frühes Mönchtum,* 239; Wilhelm Levison, "Die Iren und die Fränkische Kirche," HZ 109 (1912): 1–22.

was itself a dilapidated Merovingian stronghold.[58] Nevertheless, the Christianity of the clerics that Boniface met seemed questionable and the border between paganism and Christianity difficult to discern. Boniface was confronting a "bastardized" or mixed religious culture.[59] In this complex setting he sought to impose his own sense of clarity, feeling that his understanding of Christianity was the correct (and therefore "Roman") one.

The picture arises of old Christian enclaves blending into their environs, where Christianity appeared as "one cult among many."[60] At just this moment, however, the mayors of the palace were hitching their wagons to the missionary impulse. In 742 Mayor Carloman put his name at the head of a document thoroughly imbued with the sentiments of his Frankish bishops, complaining of "stupid people engaging in pagan rites next to churches."[61] Here the Frankish mood of extirpation was pure, now having been linked to the potential use of military force. As the *Concilium germanicum* (742), led by Boniface, would declare, the bishop "who is the defender of the church" should make sure "the people of God not do pagan things, but that it cast out and reject every filth of paganism (*gentilitas*)."[62] The bishops also complained of pagan rituals carried out beside their churches (*iuxta aecclesias*).[63] The same complaint was made at the Council of Lestinnes in the following year. Significantly, these unpleasant rites were performed "in the name of the holy martyrs or confessors."[64] This coincides exactly with Willibald's portrait of a rapid and secure occupation of the spiritual and geographical center of a society, accompanied by impressive displays of effi-

58. Geary, *Before France and Germany,* 216; and Wallace-Hadrill, *Frankish Church,* 157. This was also the case at Willibald's establishment at Eichstätt: Parsons, "Some Churches of the Anglo-Saxon Missionaries," 37–38.

59. Von Padberg, "Odin oder Christus?" 255.

60. Brown, *Rise of Western Christendom,* 258.

61. "Quas stulti homines iuxta ecclesias ritu pagano faciunt," *Karlmanni principis capitulare* (742), MGH Capit. 1.1:24–26; see 25.

62. "Episcopus in sua parrochia sollicitudinem adhibeat, adiuvante gravione, qui defensor aecclesiae est, ut populus Dei paganias non faciat, sed ut omnes spurcitias gentilitatis abiciat et respuat," *Concilium germanicum* (742), MGH Conc. 2.1:3–4.

63. *Concilium germanicum* (742), MGH Conc. 2.1:4.

64. "Incantationes sive hostias immolaticias, quas stulti homines iuxta ecclesias ritu pagano faciunt sub nomine sanctorum martyrum vel confessorum," *Die Briefe des Heiligen Bonifatius,* Letter 56:100. The *Indiculus superstitionum et paganiarum* appended to the conciliar records lists this phenomenon among its condemned practices: "De incertis locis quae colunt pro sanctis," and "De petendo quod boni vocant sanctae Mariae," Mansi, 12:376. On the *Indiculus superstitionum,* see Heinrich Albin Saupe, *Der indiculus superstitionum et paganiarum: Ein Verzeichnis heidnischer und abergläubischer Gebräuche und Meinungen aus der Zeit Karls der Grossen, aus zumeist gleichzeitigen Schriften erläutert,* Program des städtischen Realgymnasiums 551 (Leipzig: 1891), 3–34; see also Richard, *Analyse des conciles,* 1:701–2.

cacy and power. Although there was so much continuity between Boniface's perceptions of paganism and those of the Gallic bishops whose councils he studied, Boniface engaged in a far more radical attempt to create a Christian society.[65]

Pirmin, a contemporary of Boniface and a fellow missionary bishop, also had the protection and help of the mayors of the palace.[66] Pirmin left a valuable description of such baptisms in the *Scarapsus,* a missionary pamphlet that presented the basic tenets of Christianity.[67] In it, he asked his audience to think back to their own baptisms. Note how he described the baptisms of people who did not know the meaning of the Latin words, either because they were infants, or because in a missionary setting, the catechumen did not understand what was happening:

Therefore, brothers, let us recall to your mind what pact we made with God in the baptismal font, that is, when one at a time we were asked by the bishop to tell what our names were, and either you answered, if you could, or the one who stood faith for you, who took you up from the font and said "he is called John" or some other name. And the bishop asked "John, do you renounce the devil and all his works, and all his pomps?"[68] You answered, "I renounce (*abrenuntio*)," that is, I despise and forsake all evil and diabolical works. [There was then an interrogation on the Gallic creed.] Behold how your pact and promise or confession is held by God. And believing, you were baptized in the name of the Father, and the Son, and the Holy Spirit in the remission of all sins, and you were anointed by the bishop with the chrism of salvation into eternal life, and he draped your body with a white vestment, and Christ covered your soul with celestial grace, and a holy angel was assigned to watch over you. Having taken a Christian name in the catholic church, you were counted and made a member of Christ, as the Apostle said: "You are the body of Christ, and limbs of his limb," because Christ is our head, and we are his members.[69]

65. Markus, "From Caesarius to Boniface," 167.

66. Prinz, *Frühes Mönchtum,* 210.

67. Wallace-Hadrill, *Frankish Church,* 149; Sullivan, "Carolingian Missionary Theories," 286–88.

68. On the origin and meaning of this phrase, see the classic article of J. H. Waszink, "Pompa Diaboli," in his *Opuscula selecta,* 288–316 (Leiden: 1979).

69. "Ideo, fratres, ad memoriam vestram reducimus, qualem pactum in ipso baptistirio cum deo fecimus, verbi gratia, cum interrogati singuli nomen nostrum a sacerdote fuimus, quomodo diceremus, respondisti aut tu, si iam poteras respondere, aut certe qui pro te fidem fecit, qui de fonte suscepit, et dixit: Joannis dicitur, aut aliut nomen. Et interrogavit sacerdus: Joannis, abrenuncias diabulo et omnibus operibus eius et omnibus pompis ejus? Respondisti: Abrenuntio, hoc est, dispitio et derelinquo omnia opera mala et diabolica. [credal interrogation] Ecce qualis pactio et promissio vel confessio vestra apud deum tenetur. Et credens baptizatus es in nomine patris, et filii, et spiritui sancto in remissione omnium peccatorum, et unctus es a sacerdote crisma salutis in vitam eternam, et induit corpus tuum veste candita, et Christus anima tua induit

Here the social body, viewed as the Body of Christ, comes into existence in baptism as the result of a binding "pact," described in language close to that of Isidore and the Gallic liturgy.[70] The pact was marked by naming, and thus there is an interest in names and their ability to envelop (the name of Christ)—or to transform (the name of a Christian).[71] With Pirmin we see the formula of baptism at a point when the Body of Christ was expanding beyond the traditional bounds of Frankish power.

It would be wrong to conclude that missionaries like Boniface and Pirmin were content with the inclusion of peoples in the church by baptismal fiat. As Pope Gregory II wrote to the Thuringians, baptism and teaching went hand in hand. He instructed them to obey Boniface like a father and to incline their hearts to his doctrine.[72] To this end, by the 740s, the missionaries had provided themselves with a Germanic baptismal formula of abjuration (*abrenuntio*).[73] The content is significantly simpler than Pirmin's:

Forsachistu diabolae? *Et respons.* Ec forsacho diabolae. End alium diobol gelde? *Resp.* End ei forsacho allum diobol gelde. . . . *Resp.* Ec gelobo in got almehtigan fadaer. Gelobistu in Crist godes suno? *Resp.* Ec gelobo in Crist godes suno. Gelobistu in halogan gast? *Resp.* Ec gelobo in halogan gast.

Do you forsake the devil? *And it is replied:* I forsake the devil. And all the devil's work? *It is replied:* And I forsake all the devil's works. . . . *It is replied:* I believe in God the Almighty Father. Do you believe in Christ the Son of God? *It is replied:* I believe in Christ the Son of God. Do you believe in the Holy Ghost? *It is replied:* I believe in the Holy Ghost.

---

gratiam caelestem, et adsignatus est tibi sanctus angelos ad custodiendum te, et acceptum nomen Christianum in aecclesia catholica anumeratus factus es membrum Christi, ut ait apostolus: 'Vos estis corpus Christi, et membra de membro,' quia Christus capud nostrum est, et nos membra eius," Pirmin, *Scarapsus,* 2.12, in *Die Heimat des Hl. Pirmin des Apostels der Alamannen,* edited by Gall Jecker, Beiträge zur Geschichte des alten Mönchtums und des Benediktinerordens, 13 (Münster in Westf.: 1927), 43–44.

70. The text is very close to the formula of Quodvultdeus, as transmitted in a sermon of Caesarius of Arles: "Pactum enim cum Christo fecimus quando baptismi sacramenta suscepimus," Raymond Étaix, "Le texte complété du sermon 178 de saint Césaire d'Arles," *Sacris Erudiri* 34 (1994): 66.

71. On the significance of Christian naming, see G. J. M. Bartelink, *Het vroege Christendom en de antieke Cultuur* (Muiderberg: 1986), 166–67.

72. Gregory II to the Thuringians (724), *Die Briefe des Heiligen Bonifatius,* Letter 25:43.

73. On "Theodisca," see Heinz Thomas, "Frenkisk: Zur Geschichte von *theodiscus* und *teutonicus* im Frankenreich des 9. Jahrhunderts," in *Beiträge zur Geschichte des Regnum Francorum: Proceedings of a Colloquium for the 75th Birthday of Eugen Ewig 28 May 1988,* edited by R. Schieffer, 67–95 (Sigmaringen: 1990); and Werner Betz, "Karl der Grosse und die Lingua Theodisca," In *Karl der Grosse: Lebenswerk und Nachleben,* edited by W. Braunfels, 2:300–306 (Dusseldorf: 1965).

This document was preserved among the records of the Council of Lestinnes.[74] The simplicity of the *Scarapsus* reflects the practical needs of missionaries, bringing a set of doctrines that had long been accommodated in one social milieu into contact with a very different social world. On the other hand, the *Scarapsus* reflects the Biblical fundamentalism of the missionaries.[75] Missionaries left patristic tradition to one side on behalf of social transformation in the Germanic world.

The next step in this structural expansion was the establishment of ecclesiastical centers in the newly encompassed lands. That these centers were meant to forcibly reorient the landscape and culture of the Germans is evident in Boniface's use of military and governmental language, writing in 742 to Pope Zacharias (741–752):

We must also point out, father, that having beaten down or corrected the peoples of Germany, by the grace of God, that we ordained three bishops and established a province of three parishes; and we pray that the three forts or cities in which they were constituted and ordained might be confirmed and strengthened through your written authority.[76]

Boniface believed that he had been charged with the task of battling paganism, which should be distinguished from conversion. Indeed, the archeological remains of Anglo-Saxon missionary centers, as at Echternach, can usually be associated with a nearby fortification.[77] Perhaps the main hindrance to conversion lay not in language barriers, but in the boundaries of allegiance. Acceptance of Christianity was associated with accepting Frankish dominance. As in fifth-century Gaul, social identity continued to focus on questions of religion. Boniface complained that even clerics could lapse into paganism, something that suggests the early recruitment of clerics from the local population.[78] The inclusion of whole populations by means of baptism and the erection of a governmental church over them was a method that called naturally for the aid of military force. The occupation of the center could not proceed without the protection of the center. Meanwhile, the close involvement and interest of may-

74. This abjuration was appended to the proceedings of Lestinnes (743), Mansi, 12:375.

75. Sullivan, "Carolingian Missionary Theories," 280–81.

76. "Necesse quoque habemus indicare paternitati vestrae, quia per Dei gratiam Germaniae populis aliquantulum percussis vel correctis tres ordinavimus episcopos et provinciam in tres parrochias discrevimus; et ella tria oppida sive urbes, in quibus constituti et ordinati sunt, scriptis auctoritatis vestrae confirmari et stabiliri precantes desideramus," Boniface to Zacharias (742), *Die Briefe des Heiligen Bonifatius,* Letter 50:81.

77. Parsons, "Some Churches of the Anglo-Saxon Missionaries," 40–57.

78. Boniface to Daniel (742–746), *Die Briefe des Heiligen Bonifatius,* Letter 63:130.

ors of the palace seemed to hold out the prospect of combining missionary and military activity in Germany.

But military protection was not consistently available in Germany, and this difficulty may explain why Boniface turned his attention to Francia in later years. Boniface had attempted to involve the Frankish mayors of the palace in his project of reshaping Germany, but Frankish efforts to the east were sporadic—limited to lightning raids for plunder:[79]

Without the patronage of the prince of the Franks, I am not able to rule the people of the church nor to defend presbyters, clerics, monks, or the handmaidens of God. Nor can I prohibit those rites and sacrileges of pagan idols in Germany without his mandate and the fear he inspires.[80]

The *Concilium germanicum* (742) was aware that the People of God might "do pagan things."[81] Clearly, the ancient phrases "People of God" or "Christian people" did not refer to a church of believers, but to a vast social entity united under the government of its bishops. The Council of Lestinnes also legislated to restrict paganism, while at Soissons in 744, each bishop was warned "to take care in his own parish, that the Christian people not be pagan."[82] Once again, these missionary sentiments were echoed in documents issued by the mayors of the palace.[83] The connection between paganism, culture, and language was thought to be very close.

The missionary project assumed that the social world could be reshaped in the image of divine patterns. These patterns could be clearly seen by missionary bishops, who called on Frankish leaders to help impose them. The confluence of Boniface's reform councils and the legislation of the mayors of the palace seem to show that his mission was constantly in danger of redirection and absorption by the mayors and bishops close to them. What missionaries could do, particularly when aided by soldiers, was to sweep away the public functions

79. Reuter, "Plunder and Tribute," 76.

80. "Sine patricinio principis Francorum nec populum ecclesiae regere nec presbiteros vel clericos, monachos vel ancillas Dei defendere possum nec ipsos paganorum ritus et sacrilegia idolorum in Germania sine illius mandato et timore prohibere valeo," Boniface to Daniel (742–746), *Die Briefe des Heiligen Bonifatius,* Letter 63:130.

81. "Ut populus Dei paganias non faciat," *Concilium germanicum* (742), MGH Conc. 2.1:3–4.

82. "Unusquisque episcopus in sua parrochia sollicitudinem habeat, ut populus Christianus paganus non fiant," Council of Soissons, MGH Conc. 2.1:35; see also Jorg Jarnut, "Bonifatius und die fränkischen Reformkonzilien (743–748)," ZSRG.K 66 (1979): 1–26; see 3–4.

83. "Ut populus Dei paganias non faciat," *Karlmanni principis capitulare* (742), 25; and "Ut populus christianus paganus non fiant," *Pippini principis capitulare suessionense* (744), MGH Capit. 1.1:28–30; see 30.

of other religious elites, transforming them into a marginalized and anachronistic feature of cultural identity.

Reform and Kingship

The missionary perspective of bishops in the barbarian kingdoms transformed the otherwordly piety of the Merovingian Church into a social doctrine in which bishops played a central transformative role. The symbolic incorporation of peoples into the "People of God" was carried out through baptism. The sacramental church, viewed as a clerical group organized in obedient unity, was for Boniface centered around a very different symbol, the "body of St. Peter." This was, on one level, the actual body of Peter, interred beneath the altar of the papal basilica in Rome. Oaths of obedience to the popes were taken on these relics, as when Boniface swore he would uphold "the canonical way," that is, the customs and beliefs of Rome.[84] Indeed, Rome kept itself informed about the Frankish reform councils.[85] The image of Peter's body also represented the obedience and orthodoxy of the church as a unified order of clerics. It could refer to the pontiff and Roman clergy, as when Boniface sent the confessions of obedience of the Frankish clerics to the "body of St. Peter, Prince of the Apostles."[86] Pope Zacharias actively promoted this usage, using the image of a "spiritual body" to refer to a church unified under his direction.[87] Along the way, his own personality and the personalities of obedient clerics were submerged in that of Peter, becoming "one pastor":

And now, through God's help, your sanctity is gathered together in society with us as one herd of sheep, and is one pastor with us, who was established as the Prince of Apostles and our doctor by the Pastor of Pastors, our Lord God, and by our savior Jesus Christ.[88]

84. "Nam ego de illa communione culpam timeo, quia recolo me ordinationis meae tempore iuxta preceptum Gregorii pape iurasse in corpore sancti Petri talium communionem me declinaturum, si eos ad viam canonicam convertere nequiverim," Boniface to Bishop Daniel (742–746), *Die Briefe des Heiligen Bonifatius,* Letter 63:130. The text of the oath that Boniface made is preserved in Letter 16.

85. Jarnut, "Bonifatius und die fränkischen Reformkonzilien," 11.

86. "Et isti confessioni universi consensimus et subscripsimus et ad corpus sancti Petri principis apostolorum direximus. Quod gratulando clerus Romanus et pontifex suscepit," Boniface to Archbishop Cuthberht of Canterbury (747), *Die Briefe des Heiligen Bonifatius,* Letter 78:163. See the discussion in Ingrid Heidrich, "Synode und Hoftag in Düren im August 747," DA 50 (1994): 415–40; esp. 422–23.

87. "Ut sitis unum corpus spiritalis matris vestrae sanctae catholicae et apostolicae Dei ecclesiae," Pope Zacharias to an unknown Frankish bishop (748), *Die Briefe des Heiligen Bonifatius,* Letter 82:183.

88. "Et nunc Deo cooperante est aggregata sanctitas vestra nostrae societati in uno pastorali

The strength of this association may be seen in Boniface's adoption of the papal incipit ("Boniface, servant of the servants of God").[89] As papal legate, or vicar, he spoke with the very sound of Peter's voice. In 738, he styled himself the "Germanic legate of the universal Church and servant of the apostolic see."[90] Although it has been noticed that Boniface's mission-field, stretching from Bavaria and Thuringia into the heart of the Frankish kingdom, coincided with the sphere of Frankish political interests, this was not a cultural unity.[91] Its unity was, for Boniface, founded on very different principles. This was the expanding universal church, united under the direction of its bishops (themselves united as the Body of St. Peter). Because the mayors of the palace could provide little protection beyond the Rhine, Boniface turned his efforts toward Frankish Gaul, a project Pope Zacharias eagerly supported, which took shape in a series of reform councils.[92]

Something new was underway, the springs of which are now difficult to find. It may be that the popes were already flirting with the Frankish mayors, or that the mayors of the palace (or their bishops) had become aware of the political power promised by the missionary vision of social unification and expansion. Nevertheless there were significant problems in the Frankish Church from Boniface's perspective. He was particularly angered to find ordinary nobles at the head of monasteries, redirecting the income and neglecting religious duties.[93] Church lands were granted as ordinary benefices. A layman was given the bishopric of Reims, and Charles Martel gave his nephew the churches of Paris, Bayeux, and Rouen. He distributed monasteries among his followers as rich

---

ovili et est nobis unus pastor, qui a pastore pastorum domino deo et salvatore nostro Iesu Christo princeps apostolorum et noster doctor est institutes," Pope Zacharias to an unknown Frankish bishop (748), *Die Briefe des Heiligen Bonifatius,* Letter 82:183–84.

89. "Bonifatius servus servorum Dei," Boniface to Geppan and others (738), *Die Briefe des Heiligen Bonifatius,* Letter 41:66; see also Boniface to Archbishop Ecberth (746–747), *Die Briefe des Heiligen Bonifatius,* Letter 75:156; and Boniface to Fulrad of St. Denis (752), *Die Briefe des Heiligen Bonifatius,* Letter 93:212. Compare the usage of Pope Gregory III, "Gregorius episcopus servus servorum Dei," Gregory to bishops, priests, and abbots (738), *Die Briefe des Heiligen Bonifatius,* Letter 42:67, and of Pope Zacharias, "Zacharius episcopus servus servorum Dei," Zacharias to Boniface (751), *Die Briefe des Heiligen Bonifatius,* Letter 87:194. Mabillon thought of this phrase as a uniquely papal incipit: Jean Mabillon, *De re diplomatica libri VI* (Paris: 1681), 2.2:61–62.

90. "Universalis ecclesiae legatus Germanicus et servus sedis apostolice Bonifacius," Boniface to the Anglo-Saxons (738), *Die Briefe des Heiligen Bonifatius,* Letter 46:74.

91. Levison, *England and the Continent,* 77.

92. Wallace-Hadrill, *Frankish Church,* 156.

93. Boniface to Archbishop Cuthberht (747), *Die Briefe des Heiligen Bonifatius,* Letter 78:169–70; see also K. Voigt, *Die karolingische Klosterpolitik und der Niedergang des westfränkischen Königtums: Laienäbte und Klosterinhaber,* Kirchenrechtliche Abhandlungen 90 and 91 (1917; Repr. Amsterdam: 1965), 44–50.

rewards for loyalty. Recent studies have focused on the "traditional" nature of these distributions, suggesting that the bad reputation of Charles Martel is due to the later condemnations of Boniface and his allies.[94] Indeed, our general impression of the late Merovingian Church has been affected by the grim portrait left by Boniface, who complained that administration, consecration of bishops, holding of synods, and the authority of metropolitan bishops had all collapsed in the Frankish Church.[95]

Boniface's perspective is belied by the obvious persistence of episcopal activity in the Frankish realm. It is likely that the creation of missals and liturgical treatises in the early eighth century shows that liturgy was being maintained at the local level. The peculiar Latin of the *Bobbio Missal* tells a tale of local struggles to maintain a tradition without many books and with painful learning.[96] It was in the early eighth century, too, that penitential literature from Ireland, such as the *Poenitentiale* of pseudo-Theodore of Canterbury and the *Excarpsus* of Cummeanus, began to circulate in Francia.[97] It is often said that the Frankish liturgy was in decline in this period, and that new sources were imported from Rome to help revive the cult, although the renewal and copying of local liturgical sources was much more basic to this effort.[98]

Boniface found a congenial circle of bishops ready to participate in his reform councils. Internal reform and a reintegration of the episcopate into royal politics had begun even before his arrival in Francia.[99] Eugen Ewig has identified a number of these reform-minded men who cooperated with Boniface: the bishops of Lyon and Vienne; Baldobert, bishop of Basel; Dubanus, bishop-abbot of Honau; Hiddo of Autun, and Lull of Mainz.[100]

There were also independent reformers and missionaries at work in the same period. Chrodegang, according to Paul the Deacon, came from a family of the

94. Alain Dierkens, "Carolus monasteriorum multorum eversor et ecclesiarum pecuniarum in usus proprios commutator? Notes sur la politique monastique du maire du palais Charles Martel," in *Karl Martell*, 277–94.

95. Gauthier, *L'Évangélisation*, 269.

96. See E. A. Lowe's note on the *Bobbio Missal*, 1, n. 2; see also Michel Banniard, "Seuils et frontières langagières dans la Francia romane du VIIIe siècle," in *Karl Martell*, 171–91; and Els Rose, "Liturgical Latin in the Bobbio Missal," in *The Bobbio Missal: Liturgy and Religious Culture in Merovingian Gaul*, edited by Yizhak Hen and Rob Meens, 67–78 (Cambridge: 2004).

97. Hubert Mordek, "Kanonistische Aktivität in Gallien in der ersten Hälfte des 8. Jahrhunderts: Eine Skizze," *Francia* 2 (1974): 19–25; see 19–21.

98. Hen, *Royal Patronage*, 47–52.

99. Prinz, "Fränkische Episkopat," 118.

100. Eugen Ewig, "Saint Chrodegang et la reforme de l'église franque," in his *Spätantikes und Fränkische Gallien: Gesammelte Schriften (1952–1973)*, edited by Hartmut Atsma, *Beihefte der Francia* 3 (Munich: 1976–1979), 2:232–59.

highest nobility, and was sent to the palace of Charles Martel for his early education.[101] Best known for his reform of the cathedral clergy, Chrodegang also
founded the monastery of Gorze in 748, with the assistance of Pippin, and
worked to replace the Gallic chant with Roman-style chant and liturgy.[102] As
we have noted, the Roman ideal was valued, but resulted in liturgies and efforts
that were not "Roman" so much as something new and distinctively Frankish.[103]
A similar phenomenon can be seen in the Anglo-Saxon world and in the expectations and hopes attached to Rome by the monks at Wearmouth-Jarrow.[104] Pirmin should also be included in the list of reformers and missionaries active at
this time.[105] These were bishops with far-reaching temporal power, which was
shortly to be harnessed not only to missionary expansion, but also to the reform
of the church and kingship itself.

The period also saw the creation and circulation of several important canon
law collections, incorporating materials from Africa, Spain, and Ireland, forming the basis of early Carolingian conciliar activity. Boniface's reform councils
drew upon a firm knowledge of Gallic and Merovingian conciliar law.[106] At the
Council of Lestinnes (743), for example, the bishops expressed their intention
"to take up the ancient canons."[107] At Soissons (744), this law's authority was
expressed more piously as "the canonical judgments of the other saints which
they established in their synods."[108] This precious inheritance was, like liturgical knowledge, maintained by local efforts, often of particular bishops.[109] Boniface became familiar with the ancient traditions of councils held in Gaul. Condemning someone who might seize church property in a letter of 747, Boniface
drew on the vocabulary of the "ancient fathers" to describe such a man a "rap-
tor" and a "murderer of the poor."[110] At a synod held in Düren in 747, the bish-

101. On Chrodegang's background, see Ewig, "Saint Chrodegang," 232.
102. Hen, *Royal Patronage,* 47–48.
103. M. A. Claussen, *The Reform of the Frankish Church: Chrodegang of Metz and the Regula
Canonicorum in the Eighth Century* (Cambridge: 2004), 2–3.
104. Michael E. Moore, "Bede's Devotion to Rome: The Periphery Defining the Center," in
Bède le Vénérable entre tradition et postérité, edited by Stéphane Lebecq, Michel Perrin, and Olivier Szerwiniack (Lille: 2005), 199–208.
105. Ewig, "Saint Chrodegang," 245–46.
106. Mordek, "Kanonistische Aktivität," 19–25; see also Mordek, *Kirchenrecht und Reform im
Frankenreich: Die collectio vetus Gallica: die älteste systematische Kanonensammlung des fränkisch-
en Gallien: Studien und Edition* (Berlin: 1975), 102; and Maassen, *Geschichte der Quellen,* 638–40.
107. Council of Lestinnes (743) MGH Conc. 2.1:7.
108. "Iudicias canonicas aliorum sanctorum, que constituerunt in synodis suis," Council of
Soissons (744) MGH Conc. 2.1:34.
109. Rosamond McKitterick, "Knowledge of Canon Law in the Frankish Kingdoms before
789: The Manuscript Evidence," JTS 36 (1985): 97–117; see 101–3.
110. "Talem hominem antiqui patres nominabant raptorem et sacrilegum et homicidam

ops described themselves as "apostolic fathers," despite the recent founding of many of their sees.[111]

Although Charles Martel gave Boniface his special protection (*mundeburdium*) and offered to hold a council of the Frankish Church, this did not come to fruition in Charles' lifetime.[112] Both Boniface and Pirmin were well aware of the importance of military power to the project of creating clerical centers.[113] Upon Charles' death, the realm and the office of mayor of the palace were shared between his two sons, Carloman and Pippin III. Carloman had closely allied himself with Boniface's mission, but he soon left the kingdom to end his days in the monastery of Montecassino. Quite probably he thereby removed himself from a dangerous struggle for power, a frequent solution to power struggles in Anglo-Saxon royal families. As in the case of Chlodovald (as told by Gregory of Tours), by having his hair cut in a tonsure Carloman sought to disengage from a power struggle.[114]

Before abandoning political power, however, Carloman fostered Boniface's reform project and presided over a series of councils, of which the first, the "German Council" (742), aimed to coordinate new German sees with those in the Austrasian region of the Frankish realm.[115] Its canons were issued independently, in the traditional way. But they were also issued as capitularies under the authority of the mayors of the palace, as were the acts of the Council of Lestinnes the following year.[116] During the decade leading to the Carolingian usurpation, the legislation of the mayors was dominated by such episcopal concerns, enacted at great gatherings at which assemblies of the lay nobility met in tandem with an important episcopal council.[117] This had long been the pattern in England, where councils of bishops usually met at the same time and place as a royal assembly.[118] These occasions were potent displays of organized mutuality.

---

pauperum," Boniface to Archbishop Cuthberht (747), *Die Briefe des Heiligen Bonifatius,* Letter 78:169.

111. "Apostolici patres": Heidrich, "Synode und Hoftag," 439; see also Hefele-Leclercq, *Histoire des conciles,* 3.2:911–16.

112. Levison, *England and the Continent,* 83.

113. Arnold Angenendt, "Pirmin und Bonifatius: Ihr Verhältnis zu Mönchtum, Bischofsamt und Adel," in *Mönchtum: Episkopat und Adel zur Gründungszeit des Klosters Reichenau,* edited by Arno Borst, Vorträge und Forschungen 20 (Sigmaringen: 1974), 251–304, esp. 270–75.

114. Clare Stancliffe, "Kings Who Opted Out," in *Ideal and Reality,* 158.

115. On this council, see Wilfried Hartmann, *Synoden der Karolingerzeit,* 47–63.

116. *Karlmanni principis capitulare liptinense* (743), MGH Capit. 1.1:26–28.

117. Heidrich, "Synode und Hoftag," 416.

118. Hannah Vollrath, *Die Synoden Englands bis 1066,* Konziliengeschichte, Reihe A: Darstellungen (Paderborn: 1985), 122; see also Deanesly, *The Pre-Conquest Church,* 24.

As mentioned earlier, a synthesis of royal and episcopal law had been underway for some time in the Frankish and Visigothic kingdoms. Boniface would have been familiar with such a procedure, given that English episcopal legislation sometimes affected royal law.[119] Sometime between 690 and 693, King Ine of Wessex addressed a number of clerical concerns in a series of laws, confirming church sanctuary and punishing failure to baptize infants.[120]

By adopting this method of promulgating episcopal legislation, the Carolingians succeeded in bringing the bishops within their government.[121] At the same time, bishops had gained the cooperation of a newly effective instrument of central control, one capable of staging more ambitious projects. Once incorporated into royal law, canonical legislation had greater force and compass, and could now be enforced in ways inconceivable two generations before. A means had been found to reduce (though certainly not to end)[122] the power of lay bishops and abbots in the church, enabling intensive cooperation between royal and religious authorities.

Pippin was equally interested in the reform effort. In 746 he sent a commission to Rome to seek guidance on topics ranging from clerical discipline to the ecclesiastical hierarchy. His court administration came to be dominated by clerics, a development that seems related to a general revival of culture under Pippin.[123] Episcopal cooperation was a genuine asset for the assertion of royal power. Bishops served as guarantors of a religious and legal order. The reform therefore centered on a retrieval of episcopal law, the *antiquorum patrum canones*.[124]

On the eve of their destruction, the Merovingian kings were blamed for the decline of the Frankish Church, which the *Concilium Germanicum* tried to repair. The council seems to represent a missionary perspective. Carloman, in his preface to this council, laid out the aims of this reform effort in an aggressive way, essentially mounting an attack on the previous dynasty, and coming close to claiming kingship. The council documents were phrased as if Carloman were instructing his bishops:

119. Levison, *England and the Continent,* 84–85.

120. Laws of Ine: *Councils and Ecclesiastical Documents relating to Great Britain and Ireland,* ed. A. W. Haddan and W. Stubbs (Oxford: 1871), 2:214–19.

121. Geary, *Before France and Germany,* 217.

122. Friedrich Prinz, "Monastische Zentren im Frankenreich," SM Ser. 3.19 (1978): 571–90.

123. Riché, "Renouveau culturel," 63.

124. Hubert Mordek, "Kirchenrechtliche Autoritäten im Frühmittelalter," in *Recht und Schrift im Mittelalter,* Vorträge und Forschungen 23 (Sigmaringen: 1977), 237–55; esp. 240, 243.

that they counsel me on how the law of God and ecclesiastical religion might be recovered, which fell into ruins in the days of former princes; and just how the Christian people might come to the salvation of their souls and not perish, by being deceived by false priests.[125]

The Carolingians had decided to remove the Merovingian dynasty. The "German Council" was a crucial moment when the interference and irrelevance of the long-haired kings were publicized in a major document issued by a mayor of the palace. Dissatisfaction with the Merovingians coalesced around Boniface's reform movement. Carloman made as direct a claim to kingship as he could, styling himself the "war-leader and chief of the Franks" (*dux et princeps Francorum*), and referring to "my kingdom," presenting himself as defender of the "law of God" (*lex Dei*) against the Merovingian kings. The intimate connection between church reform and usurpation could not have been more clearly stated.

Aligning himself with Boniface, a group of German bishops, and his nobility (*optimates*), Carloman was bent on overturning the power of both the "false priests" and the Merovingian dynasty.[126] The false priests against whom the council fulminated were represented, in Boniface's mind, by the powerful magnate Milo, member of a family that had specialized in ecclesiastical power. Milo's father Liutwin had been bishop of Trier *and* of Rheims, and Milo, while remaining a simple cleric, inherited his father's control of these churches, gaining a reputation for tyranny.[127] Yet the bishops who played the most prominent role at the council were from the German mission-fields—Würzburg, Cologne, Buraburg, Erfurt, and Eichstätt. This was a revolutionary moment, linking the disruptive, radical impact of missionary bishops and the military might of the mayors of the palace. Eastward expansion, the missionary project of uniting and saving the *populus christianus,* and episcopal reform all provided the basis for a new style of kingship. Reform efforts were phrased in missionary terminology and driven by the momentum of missionary ideals.[128] Under the Merovingians,

125. "Ut mihi consilium dedissent quomodo lex Dei et ecclesiastica religio recuperetur, quae in diebus preteritorum principum dissipata corruit, et qualiter populus christianus ad salutem anime pervenire possit et per falsos sacerdotes deceptus non pereat," Carlomann's proem to the Concilium Germanicum (after 742), *Die Briefe des Heiligen Bonifatius,* Letter 56:99; see also Jean Heuclin, *Hommes de Dieu et fonctionnaires du roi en Gaule du Nord du Ve au IXe siècle (348–817)* (Villeneuve-d'Ascq [Nord]: 1998), 246.

126. "Ego Karlmannus dux et princeps Francorum . . . cum consilio servorum Dei et optimatum meorum episcopos, qui in regno meo sunt," Carloman's proem to the Concilium Germanicum (after 742), *Die Briefe des Heiligen Bonifatius,* Letter 56:98–99.

127. Ewig, "Milo et eiusmodi similes," 421; Prinz, *Klerus und Krieg,* 67.

128. These missionary themes are summarized in von Padberg, *Mission und Christianisierung,* 350–57.

We decreed that it is appropriate for a metropolitan, according to the canonical statutes, to investigate the mores of bishops and their care for the people . . . and that bishops, returning from a synod to their own parishes, hold a meeting (*conventus*) with their abbots and presbyters, gently admonishing them to obey the precepts of the synod.[143]

The council went on to declare that the relationship of bishops to the metropolitan should be like the relationship of bishop and pope. This was an attempt to reify the symbolic assertion, mentioned above, that the higher clergy constituted the "Body of St. Peter." Boniface also insisted that bishops should take care to deploy conciliar legislation when they returned to their home city. By no means did Boniface attempt to remake the Frankish Church from whole cloth. Internal Frankish problems and concerns largely governed the timing of councils and the bishops who would be present. One effect of the reforms was to further integrate episcopal power with royal power, and bishops were chosen who were close to the mayors.[144]

The bishops involved in these councils were therefore more than purely religious leaders. In calling the Council of Soissons, Pippin, like Carloman, called himself the *dux et princeps Francorum*. Many of the bishops assembled at the council would have been bound to follow Pippin in his very capacity as war-leader (*dux*). Among its canons was a significant new recognition of this duty of the bishops. For the first time, the council legally freed the higher clergy from old strictures against the bearing of arms by clerics, whether in hunting or war. It is not clear that the restriction against violence had ever been applied to bishops. Bishops were full participants in Pippin's military operations.[145]

At the same time, bishops had long been involved in litanies and processions for success in warfare and for protection against invasion. Liturgical participation in warfare was an important aspect of the cooperation of the mayors of the palace and their bishops. These warlike activities were especially promoted by Pippin after he became king.[146] Liturgical and armed participation in war were

143. "Statuimus, quod proprium sit metropolitani iuxta canonum statuta subiectorum sibi episcoporum investigare mores et sollicitudinem circa populos, qualis sit, et moneat, ut episcopi a sinodo venientes in propria parrochia cum presbiteris et abbatibus conventum habentes precepta sinodi servare insinuando precipiant," Boniface to Cuthbert (747), *Die Briefe des Heiligen Bonifatius,* Letter 78:164.

144. Prinz, *Klerus und Krieg,* 70.

145. "Et abbati legitimi ostem non faciant, nisi tantum hominis eorum transmittant," Concilium of Soissons (744) MGH Conc., 2.1:34: see also Heidrich, "Synode und Hoftag," 418–19; Prinz, "King, Clergy and War," 315–16; Jarnut, "Bonifatius und die fränkischen Reformkonzilien," 15.

146. McCormick, "Liturgy of War," 15–20.

a unique combination offered by bishops. Their importance was also due to their control of large estates, many of which had been appropriated by Charles Martel and by Pippin. As the Council of Lestinnes (743) noted (in Pippin's voice):

> We declare, with the counsel of the servants of God and of the Christian people, that because of threatening wars and the persecutions of the other peoples that surround us, we retain, for a certain time, in the form of estates with official military obligations, a certain portion of the church's wealth to help our army, with the indulgence of the Lord.[147]

Boniface considered the Christianization of kingship to be an urgent, holy mandate, and believed that failure would result in the destruction of the people. Writing to King Aethelbald of Mercia, he warned that the peoples of Spain had been punished for their sins by the Muslim invasion of 711.[148] Nor was this only a distant danger. Bishoprics in southern Gaul were subject to Muslim pressure over the ensuing decades, until Charles Martel defeated them at the battle of Poitiers in 733.[149] A year earlier, Pope Zacharias had written to Boniface to recommend the organization of fasts and litanies to prevent the danger of Muslim conquest.[150] Such was Boniface's grim perspective on the importance of reform!

With Pippin, who governed the entire kingdom, and seized the throne, as well, the reform of church and kingdom came to be seen as a single project. Pippin also sought to bring the old Salic law under his banner of reform, issuing among others the revised, more systematic version of the *Pactus Legis Salica,* now known as the *Recensio Pippina.*[151] He also oversaw the creation of a shorter version, Eckhardt's *65-Title Text.*[152] It is not always clear how closely Pippin should be associated with these texts, but it does seem that he recognized in this body of law, if not an instrument of control, then a means of promoting a unified Frankish identity under his own leadership. Some versions of the code contain a

147. "Statuimus quoque cum consilio servorum Dei et populi Christiani propter inminentia bella et persecutiones ceterarum gentium, que in circuitu nostro sunt, ut sub precario et censu aliquam partem aecclesialis pecuniae in adiutorium exercitus nostri cum indulgentia Dei aliquanto tempore retineamus," Council of Lestinnes (743), MGH Conc. 2.1:7.

148. "Sicut aliis gentibus Hispaniae et Prouinciae et Burgundionum populis contigit," Boniface to King Aethelbald (746–747), *Die Briefe des Heiligen Bonifatius,* Letter 73:151; see Claude Dietrich, "Untersuchungen zum Untergang des Westgotenreiches (711–725)," HJ 108 (1988): 329–58; esp. 347.

149. Josef Semmler, "Die Aufrichtung der karolingischen Herrschaft," 19–41.

150. McCormick, "The Liturgy of War," 17.

151. *Pactus Legis Salicae,* ed. Karl August Eckhardt, I.2: *Systematischer Text;* Germanenrechte Neue Folge (Göttingen: 1957).

152. *Pactus Legis Salicae,* ed. Karl August Eckhardt, II.1, *65 Titel-Text,* Germanenrechte neue Folge (Göttingen: 1955).

fascinating preface, known as the *Shorter Prologue,* to distinguish it from a longer version produced under Charlemagne.[153] The *Shorter Prologue* recalled, in the tones of a national epic, how the ancient Franks "shook the oppressive yoke of the Romans from their necks." Their conversion to Catholicism was portrayed as a direct outcome of this "rebellion" and a turning point leading to their later triumph. The hinge of Frankish history was the baptism of their king, the "impetuous and beautiful Clovis."[154]

The prologue reminds us that one significant function of such law codes was the assertion of cultural identity. The rejection of any Roman inheritance is striking. The Roman Empire was remembered as a pagan state that had burned the holy martyrs, in contrast to the Franks, who still preserved the relics of those martyrs, "ornamenting them with gold and precious stones."[155] Patrick Wormald reflects that in this prologue, we may hear "the first chords of the anthemic arrogance that would one day give western Europeans mastery of the world."[156] Arrogance there certainly was, which found in Frankish history the equal and heir to Roman greatness—but this arrogance would only tower when it adopted Rome as its own.

At the Council of Soissons in 744, Pippin repeated nearly verbatim the charge Carloman had made against the Merovingian dynasty. Pippin and his bishops had gathered, it was said, to see how "the law of God (*lex Dei*) and ecclesiastical rule might be recuperated, after dissipating and collapsing under former princes."[157]

In the blunt phrase of Friedrich Prinz, "the Frankish clergy was nothing other than the imperial aristocracy in ecclesiastical vestments and part of the Carolingian ruling structure both by birth and by function."[158] The Council of Soissons marked an important stage in this process. The council's final canon presented a radical new procedure, by which decisions of episcopal councils would be enforced by the prince, bishops, or counts of the realm. Obedience to conciliar legislation was now equated with obedience to royal power.[159]

153. Eckhardt, *Systematischer Text,* 12–14.

154. "Rex Francorum Chlodevius torrens et pulcher," Eckhardt, *Systematischer Text,* 12.

155. "Romanorum iugum durissimum de suis cervicibus excusserunt pugnando, atque post agnicionem baptismi sanctorum martyrum corpora quem Romani igne cremaverant vel ferro truncaverant, vel besteis lacerando proiecerunt, Franci [reperta] super eos aurum et lapides preciosos ornaverunt," Eckhardt, *Systematischer Text,* 14. The *Prologue* may be compared to certain sentiments in Fredegar: Wallace-Hadrill, "Fredegar and the History of France," 537.

156. Wormald, *The Making of English Law: King Alfred to the Twelfth Century,* vol. 1, *Legislation and its Limits* (Oxford: 1999), 41.

157. "Lex Dei et ecclesiastica regula recuperetur, que in diebus priorum principum dissipata corruit," Council of Soissons (744), MGH Conc. 2.1:34.

158. Prinz, "King, Clergy and War," 315.

159. "Si quis contra hanc decretum, quam XXIII episcopi cum aliis sacerdotibus vel servis Dei

Pippin carried out the usurpation that Carloman had only warned of. According to later Carolingian sources, in 750 a combined lay and ecclesiastical mission went to Rome, led by Burchard of Würzburg and Fulrad, future abbot of St. Denis, to ask the pope whether or not the mayors of the palace should have the royal title, since they in fact exercised royal power. Scholars have focused on this dramatic event, with the pope presiding over a change of regime and helping to install the Carolingian dynasty. Rosamond McKitterick has cast doubt on this version of events, so persuasive and intriguing to contemporaries and modern historians alike. The earliest evidence is in the *Royal Frankish Annals* (compiled in the late 780s or 790s), the continuations of the Chronicle of Fredegar (perhaps after 768), and the *Clausula de unctione Pippini* (a ninth-century forgery). According to these documents, the pope was presented with a deeply cowled vocabulary of Carolingian self-vindication and impending destruction for the Merovingians.[160] A further, very influential version of this event is a record in the *Annals of Lorsch*:

In the year 750 of the Incarnation of our Lord, Pippin sent legates to the Roman Pope Zacharias, to ask about the Frankish kings, who were of royal lineage and called kings, and who had no power in the realm, except for the charters and privileges that were written in their names, and who in fact have no royal power at all, save what the Frankish Mayor of the Palace wants them to have—that they did have. . . . Pope Zacharias therefore answered their question according to apostolic authority, that it would seem to be better and more useful, that he should be called king and be king, who had the power in the kingdom, rather than he who was falsely called king.[161]

Pippin formed an alliance with the papacy, but only in the time of Pope Stephen, the successor of Zacharius. The political myth of the judgment of Pope Zacharius was to serve as the prolegomena of a regime that would wear a religious

---

una cum consenso principem Pippino vel obtimatibus Francorum consilio constituerunt, transgredire vel legem inrumpere voluerint vel dispexerint, iudicatus sit ab ipso principe vel episcopis seu comitibus, conponat secundum quod in lege scriptum est unusquisque iuxta ordine suo," Council of Soissons (744), MGH Conc. 2.1:36.

160. Rosamond McKitterick, "The Illusion of Royal Power in the Carolingian Annals," EHR 115 (2000): 1–20, esp. 4–8.

161. "Anno 750. incarnationis domincae mittit Pippinus legatos Romam ad Zachariam papam, ut interrogarent de regibus Francorum, qui ex stirpe regia erant et reges appellabantur, nullamque potestatem in regno habebant, nisi tantum quod cartae et privilegia in nomine eorum conscribebantur, potestatem vero regiam penitus nullam habebant, sed quod maior domus Francorum volebat, hoc faciebant. . . . Zacharias igitur papa secundum auctoritatem apostolicam ad interrogationem eorum respondit, melius atque utilius sibi videri, ut ille rex nominaretur et esset, qui potestatem in regno habebat, quam ille, qui falso rex appellabatur" (Anno 750), *Annales Laurissenses minores*, ed. G. H. Pertz, MGH SS. 1:112–23; see 116.

mantle and pursue an unprecedented missionary agenda. Although the papal-Frankish alliance has attracted most scholarly attention, the most significant factor in the historiography of these events is the crucial role played by bishops and other clerics at a key moment of transition.[162]

It is possible that Pope Zacharias tried to ally himself with the most powerful family in a kingdom in which he had an interest, and whose help he needed.[163] Therefore, little light can be shed on this event by wondering how a "useless" king, bearing the title (*nomen*) but not the power (*potestas*) of a king, might have caused distress.[164] The Carolingians seized power in acts that had ritual potency and provided religious authorization at the highest level.

The compiler of the *Royal Frankish Annals* imagined that Boniface must have had a hand in the subsequent anointing of Pippin as king, an unprecedented event in Frankish politics, and an act that sealed the Carolingian seizure of power. Instead, by 751, long after the departure of Carloman from the scene, Boniface's influence was on the wane.[165] The origins of the ritual of anointing are obscure, but the theocratic model of Visigothic Spain and the royal doctrine of Isidore seem to be the most important antecedents for Frankish royal anointing.[166] The doctrine relied on the cooperation of king and priest, especially as expressed in a council.[167] Reinhard Elze has also pointed to the powerful image of I Peter, "You are the royal, elect race of priests." (I Pet. 2:9).[168] Isidore cited this passage in his discussion of baptismal anointing in *On Ecclesiastical Offices*.[169] Early Carolingian liturgies therefore soon assimilated the king to the figures of Samuel and David.[170] In this context, the ceremony also has the quality of an inaugural political myth, cloaking the emergence of a new royal line in a sacred history.

162. For a discussion of the historiography: Patzold, *Episcopus,* 51–52.

163. McKitterick, *Frankish Kingdoms,* 47.

164. Carolingian perceptions of the Merovingians are discussed in Peters, *Shadow King,* 48–52; see Le Goff, "Le roi dans l'occident," 24.

165. Wallace-Hadrill, *Frankish Church,* 167; McKitterick, *Frankish Kingdoms,* 35. For a revision of these events: McKitterick, "The Illusion," 15–16.

166. Bouman, *Sacring and Crowning,* xi; Devisse, "Le sacre et le pouvoir," 27–38.

167. Hans Hubert Anton, "Der König und die Reichskonzilien im westgotischen Spanien," HJ 92 (1972): 257–81.

168. "Vos estis genus electum regale sacerdotium"; see Reinhard Elze, "Le consacrazione regie," *Settimane* 33 (1987): 1:43–55; see 49–51.

169. Isidore, *De ecc.,* 2.4:55–56.

170. See, for example, the blessings in the Sacramentary of Gellone (c. 790–800): *Ordines Coronationis Franciae: Texts and Ordines for the Coronation of Frankish and French Kings and Queens in the Middle Ages,* ed. Richard A. Jackson, 1:51–54 (Philadelphia: 1995–2000); Bouman, *Sacring and Crowning,* 92–93.

Having so carefully elaborated the meaning of kingship, it no longer made sense to the bishops of Gaul to see at the pinnacle of their society a mere "war-leader" (*dux*) or "chief man" (*princeps*), as Carloman styled himself in 742.[171] Significantly, the new ritual was said to have been done as "ancient usage demanded" and "according to the custom of the Franks."[172]

The fall of the Merovingian dynasty was thus imagined, in later Carolingian perceptions of these events, as taking place in a ritualized meeting of Frankish emissaries with Pope Zacharias in Rome. The premise of this mythic event was that there should be an absolute connection between "names" and "reality": the Frankish emissaries lamented that the words and reality of power had fallen apart in Francia. The power of names had been recognized in theologies (*théologie du Nom*) that equated the "name" with the reality, as in references to the "name of Christ."[173] In the Roman Empire, the *Romanum nomen* had referred to the power and essential character of the empire.[174] Likewise we have noted the significance attached, in the *Scarapsus,* to taking on (or imposing) the "name of a Christian" during baptism, a phrase that had taken on a social dimension as early as the sixth century.[175] In this range of ideas, words were recognized as having potency and gravity. As Georges Dumézil reminds us, the border between historical myth and history can be difficult to locate, and mythical events can have a major impact on real events.[176] An imagined, agreed-upon vision of the past formed the backdrop for political action, and acts of royal and episcopal power were deliberately rooted in the soil of mythic and ritual truth.

The overthrow of the Merovingians was justified by the dream of instituting a religious kingdom wholly transparent to Roman Christianity.[177] We have seen that Isidore had sought to create a kingship in Spain that would be worthy of its *nomen,* a Catholic king capable of "acting rightly" (*rex a recte agendo*). By allying himself with his bishops, Pippin's political desires found a home in

171. Peters, *Shadow King,* 52–53.

172. The continuation of Fredegar described the ritual as being "ut antiquitus ordo deposcit." The Royal Frankish Annals declared that it had been done: "secundum morem Francorum," Hack, "Zur Herkunft der karolingischen Königssalbung," 177.

173. Cf. Hilary of Poitier's phrase "instilled with devout love for His name" (*nomini eius caritate pietatis infusa*): *Hilary of Poitiers' Preface,* ed. Smulders, 32; see also Jean Daniélou, *Théologie du Judéo-Christianisme* (Tournay: 1958), 199–216.

174. Gerd Tellenbach, *Römischer und christlicher Reichsgedanke in der Liturgie des frühen Mittelalters,* Sitzungsberichte der Heidelberger Akademie der Wissenschaften, Philosophisch-historische Klasse 1 (Heidelberg: 1934), 12.

175. Daly, "Caesarius of Arles," 10–11.

176. Dumézil, *Mitra–Varuna,* 163.

177. Schutz, *Carolingians in Central Europe,* 17–18.

a world of power that had a depth in time and a geographical reach unlike the relations between strongmen in the Frankish kingdom. Language and reconceptualization of the past were used as an instrument of power in overthrowing the Merovingians. "Pippin was called king, and Childeric, who was falsely called king, was tonsured and placed in a monastery."[178]

The revolution took a legal form, enacted first in conciliar law as a reform to restore the law of God (*lex Dei*) and surrounded with symbolic expressions of religious order and divine sanction.[179] Here was a new type of kingship, conceived and instituted from the beginning as the expression of a social doctrine, a sacralized kingship projected against the backdrop of a war against paganism.

The Missionary Bishops

A circle of bishops with close connections to the king took up the reform movement, which revolved around the royal abbey of St. Denis and its powerful abbot, Fulrad. As Fulrad's testament shows, the clerics who assumed control of eastward missionary activity came from families establishing far-flung estates in those areas as part of Frankish expansion in southern Germany.[180] Boniface had long been isolated, and was losing influence at court. With Carloman's departure for Montecassino his sphere of influence gradually diminished.[181] Despite the fact that when he built Fulda he had expressed a desire to spend the last days of his life there, he returned instead to Frisia, where he would soon meet his death, also in 754.[182] The construction of a strict hierarchy in Francia was only partially achieved, so the Council of Ver (755), under Pippin's protection, had to assert that "we establish bishops in a metropolitan city so that other bishops might obey them in all things."[183] The religious precedence of metropolitan cities still faced resistance.

Meanwhile, Chrodegang of Metz, connected by birth to the Carolingians, was given the pallium by Pope Stephen as a successor to Boniface.[184] Chrode-

---

178. "Appellatur Pippinus rex, et Hildricus qui falso rex appellabatur, tonsoratus in monasterium mittitur," *Annales Laurissenses minores,* MGH SS 1:116.

179. Le Goff, "Le roi dans l'occident," 15–16.

180. Josef Fleckenstein, "Fulrad von Saint-Denis und der fränkische Ausgriff in den süddeutschen Raum," in *Zur Geschichte der Alemannen,* edited by W. Müller, Wege der Forschung Bd. C (Darmstadt: 1987), 354–400; see 368–67.

181. Schüssler, "Die fränkische Reichsteiling," 103–6.

182. Boniface to Zacharias, *Die Briefe des Heiligen Bonifatius,* Letter 86:193.

183. "Episcopos qos in vicem metropolitanorum constituimus ut ceteri episcopi ipsis in omnibus oboediant," cited in Lesne, *Hiérarchie épiscopale,* 53, n. 3.

184. Prinz, *Frühes Mönchtum,* 218–20.

gang proved to be a tireless reformer and builder, refurbishing the episcopal complex in Metz. He rose to prominence in Frankish affairs, and was even more influential as a reformer than had been Boniface. As a liturgical reformer, Chrodegang laid the groundwork of later Carolingian reform efforts, with their Roman tone.[185]

Metz was a center of missionary activity and closely linked to royal aspirations. The Frankish mission to the east was now an aggressive encompassing of souls, and tended to become a precursor of and even a preparation for royal expansionism.[186] Boniface had designated Würzburg, Büraburg, and Erfurt as new bishoprics, centers of a missionary church.[187] These new episcopal "cities," alongside other, older cities in the east, such as Eichstätt, Bremen, Bamberg, and Mainz, would soon be developed as centers of Frankish ecclesiastical culture and royal power.

A later example of this movement can be seen in the stern figure of Lebuin, who confronted the Saxons at their annual assembly at Marklo sometime in the late eighth century.[188] He acted like a holy fool, holding up his cross and preaching to the Saxons, protected only by his clerical garments, although Lebuin might have known that he could count on the protection granted to emissaries. After failing to gain a mass conversion at the Saxon assembly, Lebuin denounced them and uttered a dire prophecy: that because they had no king, and refused to accept the King of Heaven, their land would be laid waste by a king "who was ready in a neighboring land."[189] The *Life of Lebuin* was written between 840 and 864, so the prophecy of Lebuin was clearly retrospective. The significance of missionary confrontations like the one staged by Lebuin's were clear. They were so many thunderclaps warning of the impending expansion of the Frankish world.

The implications and power of this missionary political theology are illustrated in the history of conciliar and royal activity in Bavaria, a church that had been given its basic shape by Boniface. A recent book has suggested that "in a very real sense, it can be said that Bavaria and the Bavarians have no history before

185. Claussen, *Reform of the Frankish Church,* 27–28, 271–72.

186. Tellenbach, *Römischer und christlicher,* 36–38.

187. Helmut Flachenecker, "Der Bischof und sein Bischofssitz: Würzburg—Eichstätt—Bamberg im Früh- und Hochmittelalter," *Römische Quartalschrift* 91 (1996): 148–81; esp. 148–58; Prinz, *Frühes Mönchtum,* 244–45.

188. *Vita Lebuini antiqua,* ed. A. Hofmeister, MGH SS, 30.2 (Leipzig: 1934), 789–95.

189. "Praeparatus est in vicina terra rex quidam, qui vestram terram ingredietur, praedabit vastabitque, variis vos bellis fatigabit, in exilium adducet, exhereditabit vel occident," *Vita Lebuini antiqua,* 794.

the late seventh century."[190] Jarnut, for his part, believes that upon reaching the mid-sixth century, the historian is able to leave behind the scene of "half-dark, hypothesis-rich historical reconstructions." There are only faint traces of Bavaria or Bavarians in the historical record of the sixth century. In the seventh century come signs of Frankish interest and involvement in this region as Bavarian lords formed connections with the Merovingian royal house and made ties with the Avars and Lombards.[191] The *Notitia Arnonis*[192] shows that the Agilolfing clan established itself as a ducal family in the course of the seventh century, a status that was written into the Bavarian Laws (*Lex Baiwariorum*) in the early eighth century.[193] As Frankish clients, a sense of tact or trepidation kept this family from claiming anything loftier than the title of duke.[194] The Franks continually strove to dominate the region, culminating in a great invasion by Charles Martel in 725. The ambitions of the Carolingians in Bavaria were aided by rulers who wished to enhance their position by association with the Franks, while maintaining an independent realm with its own church.[195]

Nevertheless, the sense of a Bavarian identity seems to have come about in the course of these events and is closely related to the Christianization of the region. This is certainly the perspective of a major ninth-century source, *The Conversion of the Bavarians and Carinthians,* which describes the history of the region in just those terms.[196] Frankish missionaries, most notably St. Rupert, arrived

190. Pearson, *Conflicting Loyalties,* 1.

191. Herwig Wolfram, "Baiern und das Frankenreich," in *Die Bajuwaren von Severin bis Tassilo, 488–788: Gemeinsame Landaustellung des Freistaates Bayern und des Landes Salzburg, Rosenheim/Bayern/Mattsee/Salzburg 19. Mai bis 6. November 1988,* edited by Hermann Dannheimer and Heinz Dopsch, 130–35 (Munich: 1988).

192. *Notitia Arnonis,* ed. W. Hauthaler, Salzburger Urkundenbuch 1 (Vienna: 1910). See now the more recent edition: *Notitia Arnonis und Breves notitiae: Die Salzburger Güterverzeichnisse aus der zeit 800, Sprachlich-historische Einleitung,* ed. Fritz Losek (Salzburg: 1990); see also Jörg Jarnut, *Agilolfingerstudien: Untersuchungen zur Geschichte einer adligen Familie im 6. und 7. Jahrhundert,* Monographien zur Geschichte des Mittelalters 32 (Stuttgart: 1986).

193. *Lex Baiuvariorum,* in *Die Gesetze des Karolingerreiches, 714–911,* edited by Karl August Eckhardt, Schriften der Akademie für Deutsches Recht, Gruppe V: Rechtgeschichte; Germanenrechte, Texte und Übersetzungen Bd.2 (Weimar: 1934), 2:78–187. One may also consult *Leges Baiwariorum/Lex Baiwariorum,* ed. E. Freiherr von Schwind, MGH Leges 1, *Legum nationum Germanicarum* 5.2.

194. Stuart Airlie, "Narratives of Triumph and Rituals of Submission: Charlemagne's Mastering of Bavaria," *Transactions of the Royal Historical Society,* 6th ser. 9 (1999): 93–119. On the ducal status of the Agilolfings, see 97–98.

195. Joachim Jahn, *Ducatus Baiuvariorum: Das Bairische Herzogtum der Agilolfinger,* Monographien zur Geschichte des Mittelalters 35 (Stuttgart: 1991), 178–87, and 192–202.

196. *Conversio Bagoariorum et Carantanorum,* ed. Milko Kos, Razprve Znanstvenega Drustva Ljubljani 11, Historicni Odsek 3 (Ljubljana: 1936); a more recent edition: *Die* Conversio Bagoariorum et Carantanorum *und die Brief des Erzbischofs Theotmar von Salzburg,* ed. Fritz Losek, MGH Studien und Texte 15 (Hannover: 1997).

in Bavaria from about 700 onward.[197] In the 740s, as was mentioned, missionary activity was given greater scope and impetus with the activities of Boniface. The integration of the Bavarian Church into the Frankish Church, with the help of Boniface and others, went hand in hand with the domination of Bavaria by Frankish royal power.[198] Almost immediately the Bavarian Church was itself sending missionaries farther afield, especially into Carinthia, which came to be dominated by Bavaria in the same period.[199]

An important Bavarian council was held at Ascheim around 756, under the aegis of Duke Tassilo III.[200] Pippin had imposed Tassilo on the Bavarians after they vainly attempted to reassert their independence after Duke Odilo's death.[201] The bishops reflected on the unique situation of the missionary church, but did so with remarkable self-confidence, perhaps due in part to the successful exercise of power that had placed Tassilo over the Bavarians. Tassilo and the Bavarian Church were soon engaged in an aggressive mission to the Slavs of Carinthia, acting very much in imitation of the Frankish kingdom.[202]

The Council of Ascheim opened with an explanation of the historical meaning of the occasion. A canon was cited from a council held in Ver the previous year, indicating that Christians should lead a life guided by "the norm of the early Fathers," while adding a significant caveat: "nevertheless it is compelled to change according to the diversity of times and the diverse necessity of constructing it." The bishops sought not only to address Tassilo, but to understand him as a sign or articulation in history:

The One who taught the pastors and fathers who came before us, will also teach us, as the Truth said "Just as the Father sent me, so I send you" (Jn 20:21). . . . So we offer unending thanks to God, who established you as prince in our times, because although you are of very tender years, nevertheless you appear more mature than your predecessors in your sense of sacred scripture.[203]

197. Lothar Waldmüller, "Salzburg als Zentrum der bairischen Slawenmission des achten Jahrhunderts," in *Bavaria Christiana: Zur Frühgeschichte des Christentums in Bayern. Festschrift Adolf Wilhelm Ziegler,* 111–27, Beiträge zur altbayerischen Kirchengeschichte 27 (Munich: 1973).

198. Airlie, "Narratives of Triumph," 96. Airlie argues that this triumphal Frankish narrative was one-sided and imperialistic.

199. Charles R. Bowlus, "Die militärische Organisation des karolingischen Südostens (791–907)," *Frühmittelalterliche Studien* 31 (1997): 46–69. Missionary activity followed the same pattern: Herbert Klein, "Salzburg an der Slawengrenze," *Südostdeutsches Archiv* 11 (1968): 1–14.

200. Hartmann, *Synoden der Karolingerzeit,* 90–92; McKitterick, *Frankish Kingdoms,* 67–68.

201. Airlie, "Narratives of Triumph," 98–99.

202. Prinz, *Frühes Mönchtum,* 341.

203. "Nam qui hos precessores pastores et patres nostros docuit, ipse et nos docebit, sicut veritas ait: *Sicut misit me pater, et ego mitto vos.* Misit nos qui missus erat. Ideo indesinentes Deo

The bishops engaged in reorganizing the Bavarian Church spoke of protecting the poor from oppression and injustice: "And in these days the priest ought always to be at hand, lest the judges of the world be corrupted by bribes, the innocent be oppressed or the criminal be justified."[204] More strikingly, the council presented the Bavarians with a difficult message:

It is right to admonish you about the oppression of the poor, as you ought to direct your governors, judges, centurions and vicars, that even without injustice, false accusations might remain. Concerning which the Evangelist testified: "He hurled the powerful from their seat and exalted the humble" (Lk 1:52).

Luke's powerful words must have had a particular ring, coming so soon after the Frankish intervention in Bavarian politics. The tone of the council is one of dominion, and referred, in these pious words, to the bishops' right to gather and preserve its property.

Protection of the poor was a constant concern of this priesthood, which believed that it had an apostolic mandate to shape and direct society. It was a mandate so radical it could only be carried out, in the end, through an alliance with royal power. Because of their power to bind and loose, and their protection of the poor, bishops could assert a right to control ecclesiastical property.[205] The duke, meanwhile, was bound to respect the church, which, although rooted in his kingdom, represented a much greater world: *diffusus orbs oriens occidensque*.[206] As in the Frankish kingdom, the combination of royal and episcopal power offered tangible benefits for both sides. At Dingolfing in 770, a council of bishops and abbots trumpeted the universal application of conciliar law, episcopal oversight of monasteries, and the irrevocable nature of donations to the church.[207] At the same time, Bavarian law was confirmed on questions such as inheritance and *wergelds*. The Dingolfing assembly was an official group, with an exclusive ability to legislate, by referring to an ancient, written body of law.

In this sense, the intervention of a new and foreign tradition at the top of

---

deferimus grates, qui te nostris temporibus constituit principem, quia si in aetate tenerulus, in sensu sanctae scripturae precessoribus tuis maturior appareris," Council of Ascheim (754–763), MGH Conc. 2.1: 56–58; see 56.

204. "Et in his diebus semper sacerdus adesse debeat . . . ut ne iudices terreni propter praemias causas torquantur et innocentes obprimantur aut nocentes iustificentur," Council of Ascheim, MGH Conc. 2.1:58.

205. "De potestate episcoporum, qui claves polique ligandi atque solvendi deveuntur et curam pastoralem exerceunt in pleve, unde et sine dubio rationem reddituri sunt, ut ecclesiasticis rebus dominentur," Council of Ascheim, MGH Conc. 2.1:57.

206. Council of Ascheim, MGH Conc. 2.1:57.

207. Council of Dingolfing (c. 770), MGH Conc. 2.1:93–97.

Bavarian society, whose reach had extended as well to native Bavarian law, now required an authority only bishops could provide. Nor was this simply the imposition of a foreign elite. Appended to the records of the Council of Neuching was a note explaining the role clerics had played at this assembly, giving some clues about the extent of native recruitment. The abbots at the council promised "that the people committed to them might be dissuaded from assuming popular titles, and remain under the power of bishops."[208] It was further decreed that, once having taken the tonsure, these new clerics should not presume to grow their hair back "like everyone else" (in usu populari).[209]

Tassilo wanted to establish the independent prestige of the Bavarians, and signaled this with an impressive new church in Salzburg, with Virgil of Salzburg as bishop.[210] The independence and power of Tassilo's court at Regensburg were partly due to the establishment of a Bavarian church on the Carolingian model, which recruited native elites and which was in close contact and cooperation with Tassilo and his nobles.[211] These nobles sought burial within sight of their local churches, adorned with their fine jewelry, buckles, and swords.[212] The Bavarians found that the reforming bishops in their midst could occupy the center of their society and transform it with great rapidity.

At Neuching in 772, it became clear that episcopal councils could trump native law.[213] Again, in numbered capitula on the model of episcopal law, Tassilo issued Bavarian law, but in Latin, strewn, however, with many Bavarian words for crimes or duels.[214] Although entitled "Concerning the Laws of the People," this law had undergone several important shifts—the nature of the issuing body was a clerical assembly, and the law was now in Latin, composed in conciliar form. Seeing the Bavarian words afloat like irreducible but isolated elements in a Latin fabric, it does not seem right to call the bishops' activity an "intervention." The effect was identical to the transformation of Salian Law 265 years earlier.[215]

208. "Unde ab universis abbatibus facta professio, ut minime titulis popularibus se ingerere depellerentur et haec cui commissae sunt plebes sub potestate episcoporum permanerent," Council of Neuching (772), MGH Conc. 2.1:105.

209. Council of Neuching (772), MGH Conc. 2.1:103.

210. Schutz, The Carolingians in Central Europe, 44–45.

211. Prinz, "Fränkische Episkopat," 123.

212. Hermann Dannheimer, Lauterhofen im frühen Mittelalter: Reihengräberfeld—Martinskirche—Königshof, Materialhefte sur Bayerischen Vorgeschichte 22 (Oberpfalz: 1968).

213. Council of Neuching (772), MGH Conc. 2.1:98–105.

214. "Qui furtivam rem, quod zögenzuht dicunt," Council of Neuching (772), MGH Conc. 2.1:102.

215. The status of Bavarian words such as zögenzuht is identical to that of the "Malburgic" words that float in the latinized Lex Salica: "Si quis caballum carrucaricium involaverit, cui

Bishops had occupied the public center and had remade it in accordance with their own principles, based on decrees "plowed through by holy synods and the earliest Fathers."[216]

Although the earliest manuscript of the great code of Bavarian law—*Lex Baiuvariorum*—dates from about 800, its promulgation might be associated with the Council of Dingolfing or Neuching.[217] The Carolingians later claimed that they had endowed the Bavarians with this law, a perspective made clear in the learned prologue of the code. Almost entirely drawn from Isidore's *Etymologies,* the prologue places Bavarian law in the perspective of deep antiquity.[218] The text gives a resume of the great legislators: Moses, who gave law to the Hebrews, Solon for the Athenians, Mercurius Trismegistus for the Egyptians, and Numa Pompilius for the Romans. Just so, it was implied, the Frankish kings gave law to the Bavarians.

The Prologue goes on to explain how Theodoric collected Bavarian law with the help of wise men: "and those [laws] that were according to pagan custom he changed in accord with the law of Christians."[219] It is remarkable that Isidore's learned disquisition was found to fit the Bavarian code so exactly. It was used to show that Frankish domination, and Frankish gifts of law, lifted Bavarian society from the rule of ancient custom to the higher rule of law, for, according to the prologue (Isidore), long custom is taken as law, but "law is so-called from writing" (lex a legendo vocata).[220] The prologue thus clearly reflects a Carolingian perspective.[221]

When Charlemagne (768–814) and his brother Carloman came to the throne in 768, their father had already extended Frankish dominion into Alemannia and other regions east of the Rhine Valley. With Carloman's death in 772, Charlemagne began a series of campaigns, waged without stint for the next thirty years. Bishops were intimately involved in these campaigns, accompanying the army and holding councils, even in the field.

---

fuerit adprobatum, excepto capitale et dilatura, MALB. *anzacho*" (Pardessus' second text, 38.1), Pardessus, *Lois salique,* 20.

216. "Sicut in sanctis sinodicis vel decretis priscorum patrum perarata." Council of Neuching (772), MGH Conc. 2.1:105.

217. *Lex Baiuvariorum: Lichtdruckwiedergabe der Ingolstädter Handschrift des Bayerischen Volksrechts,* ed. Konrad Byerle (Munich: 1926), xxi, lxxxviii–lxxix.

218. Isidore, *Etymologiae* (V.1): *Lex Baiuvariorum,* ed. K. A. Eckhardt, 74–76.

219. "Et quae erant secundum consuetudinem paganorum, mutavit secundum legem Christianorum," *Lex Baiuvariorum,* ed. K. A. Eckhardt, 76.

220. *Lex Baiuvariorum,* ed. K. A. Eckhardt, 76.

221. Bruno Krusch, *Die Lex Bajuvariorum: Textgeschichte, Handschriftenkritik und Enstehung* (Berlin: 1924), 259.

At one such council, held in an unknown location in 779 or 780, the bishops decreed that "each bishop should say three masses and three psalters, one for the king, one for the Frankish army, and the third for the present tribulation." Each presbyter was to say three masses, while monks and canons were enjoined to say three psalters.[222] The prayers of these clerics were considered vital to the success of Charlemagne's wars.[223] One of the first regions to attract Charlemagne's attention was Bavaria. According to the *Royal Frankish Annals,* Duke Tassilo violated the pledges of fidelity and vassalage he had made to Pippin. After a confrontation at Lechfeld in 787, Tassilo submitted, but was soon negotiating with the Avars farther east, attempting to create an alliance against the Franks.[224] His strategy came to nothing.

In the 790s, Charles invaded Avar territory repeatedly, finally sacking the Avar stronghold in 795.[225] Bishops took part, alongside other Carolingian nobles, in a defeat of the Avar kingdom north of the Danube, destroying its ancient royal seat, the "ring" (*hrinch, hringe*)[226] and laying hold of the great treasure accumulated there.[227] In 796, missionary bishops who accompanied the army on this dramatic campaign paused on the banks of the Danube to hold a council about the Christianization of the new conquest.[228] Led by Arno of Salzburg, the bishops contended that the Avar's destruction was a "just judgment of God," a historical revelation of God's presence, causing them to ponder the nature of history itself. The war showed that "all the things that are to come were predestined before all ages, and are distributed through particular moments."[229] Arno, like other Bavarian churchmen, found that his interest in the Frankish Church,

222. "Ut unusquisque episcopus tres missas et psalteria tria cantet, unam pro domno rege, alteram pro exercitu Francorum, tertiam pro praesenti tribulation," Frankish Council (c. 779–780), MGH Conc. 2.1:108–9.

223. McCormick, "The Liturgy of War," 8–9.

224. *Annales regni Francorum,* (Anno 787), ed. G. H. Pertz and Friedrich Kurze, MGH SRG in us. schol. (Hannover: 1895), 72–78; Airlie, "Narratives of Triumph," 106–8.

225. Collins, *Charlemagne,* 88.

226. "Domnus Pippinus rex ad locum celebre Hunorum qui hrinc vocatur pervenit," (anno 796) *Annals of Maximinianus:* see *Chronicon universale—741, cum continuatione (annalibus Maximinianus),* ed. G. Waitz, MGH SS 13 (Hannover: 1881), 1–25; "Pervenit ad locum, ubi reges Avarorum cum principibus suis sedere consueti erant, quem in nostra lingua Hringe nominant" (Anno 796), Annals of Lorsch: see *Annales Lauresbamenses,* ed. G. H. Pertz, MGH SS 1 (Hannover: 1826), 22–39.

227. "Perveniens usque ad celebrem eorum locum qui dicitur rinch," Kos, *Conversio Bagoariorum,* 132; see the account in Riché, *The Carolingians: A Family who Forged Europe,* trans. Michael Idomir Allen (Philadelphia: 1993), 108–9; Collins, *Charlemagne,* 95.

228. Council on the Banks of the Danube (796), MGH Conc. 2.1:172–76; see also the discussion in Sullivan, "Carolingian Missionary Theories," 277.

229. Banks of the Danube (796), MGH Conc. 2.1:172.

ops the prospect of engaging Rome and the ancient churches of the eastern Mediterranean on a level inconceivable just decades before. The bishops went on to unify their order, crystallizing around battles against heresy (Iconoclasm and Adoptionism). Bishops also strove to establish a "standard library" of canonical books in a series of great councils and other initiatives countering local episcopal independence. They believed that they were thereby furthering the aims of a "Roman catholic church." It even appears that Roman Catholicism was a Frankish invention. Yet a paradox emerges, in that bishops were prepared to oppose the popes themselves in pursuing their ideas. The centrality of Rome therefore remained an ambiguous ideal.[7] The importance of kingship to Frankish thinking, for example, was not shared by the popes, who clung to a distinctly Roman political tradition.[8]

Frankish kingship was sacralized by the close association of kings with bishops and their concerns. Kings announced new ideals and ambitious goals, located in a developing "sacral-imperial" symbolic world. The Carolingians developed a new style of power, invoking reform as the driving idea—especially in regard to justice.[9] Charlemagne forced men of local prominence to translate power between the royal center and localities, resulting in a highly effective configuration of power that Matthew Innes calls the *Pax Karolina*.[10] Carolingian royal law was shaped by episcopal initiatives, and the kingdom itself was considered an entity of religious importance. Such developments have often been ascribed to political doctrines stemming from St. Augustine.[11] A key argument here is that Gallo-Frankish episcopal tradition was the source of these values.

Fulrad of St. Denis, chaplain of Charlemagne's palace and abbot of the most important monastery of the Frankish realm, was a central figure in the period of transition under discussion. He had a hand in the Carolingian usurpation and served as ambassador between the Frankish court and the papacy during the crucial years when Charles erected an empire centered in the Austrasian heartland of the Carolingian family.[12] Perhaps more significant still was Ful-

7. Peter Classen, "*Causa Imperii:* Probleme Roms in Spätantike und Mittelalter," in *Ausgewälte Aufsätze von Peter Classen,* edited by Carl Joachim Classen, Johannes Fried, and Josef Fleckenstein, Vorträge und Forschungen 28 (Sigmaringen: 1983), 45–84; see esp. 48–51.

8. See for example, Walter Ullmann, "Der Grundsatz der Arbeitsteilung bei Gelasius I," in his *Jurisprudence in the Middle Ages: Collected Studies* (London: 1980), 41–70, esp. 43.

9. Fouracre, "Carolingian Justice," 771–803.

10. Innes, *State and Society,* 180–88.

11. The classic and influential statement of this view is: Arquillière, *L'Augustinisme politique,* 68–104.

12. Alain Stoclet, *Autour de Fulrad de Saint-Denis (v. 710–784),* Hautes études médiévales et modernes 72 (Geneva: 1993), 442–67.

rad's position at the head of St. Denis and his access to the king's ear.[13] It was Fulrad who gathered the keys of the Italian cities Pippin conquered in 756.[14] The Frankish episcopate, following the lead of men like Fulrad, enjoyed increasing prestige and could participate in affairs that reached far beyond Francia, a phenomenon Prinz interprets as the "instrumentalization" and "functionalization" of the Frankish episcopate by the monarchy. Like the rest of the nobility, bishops participated in a program of harsh estate exploitation on behalf of the royal fisc.[15] But the reverse is equally true: a redirection of monarchy by the bishops.

Bishops had been drawn from the greatest families since Roman times, and their churches were laden with wealth in the form of pious donations, collected over centuries.[16] Bishops were further rewarded by their king for participating in missionary warfare. After Charlemagne sacked the Avar stronghold, he sent part of its enormous treasure to Rome, dividing the rest between his nobles and bishops.[17] Bishops mobilized their vast material assets and their ancient intellectual and religious resources on behalf of the new regime.

As the temporal power of bishops reached a new plateau, so also did their religious power. Frankish society, so long characterized by diffuse localized power, was now asked to imagine the kingdom as a highly centralized, sacred entity. The religious tone represented more than a new appearance; it was a wide-ranging program to Christianize royal power, resulting in an early kind of state.[18] Like the Merovingian nobility, Carolingian nobles continued to be united by gregarious hunting and feasting rituals and a social economy of gift-exchange—but royal power was increasingly ambitious, claiming to fulfill the demands of justice and religious order, and thereby dominating and recruiting the nobility.[19] The state may be seen as "a power detached from society as a whole" that wields the language of command as an exclusive right.[20] Confronted by an emerging state, the local independence of nobles and bishops alike was compromised. As the

13. Josef Fleckenstein, "Fulrad von Saint-Denis," 380.

14. T. F. X. Noble, *The Republic of St. Peter: The Birth of the Papal State, 680–825* (Philadelphia: 1984), 92.

15. Prinz, "Fränkische Episkopat," 127–28.

16. Janet L. Nelson, "Making Ends Meet: Wealth and Poverty in the Carolingian Church," in *The Church and Wealth*, edited by W. J. Sheils and Diana Wood (London: 1987), 25–35.

17. "Dei dispensator magnam inde partem Romam ad limina apostolorum misit per Angilbertum dilectum abbatem suum; porro reliquam partem obtimatibus, clericis sive laicis" (Anno 796), *Annales regni Francorum*, edited by G. H. Pertz and Friedrich Kurze, MGH SRG in us. schol. (Hannover: 1895), 98.

18. Garrison, "The Franks as the New Israel," 135.

19. Fouracre, "Carolingian Justice," 800 and 830.

20. Clastres, *Society against the State*, 151–52.

Carolingian Empire was erected over the top of older Frankish social forms, it drew heavily on episcopal language and social ideals. Royal legislation expanded considerably under Charlemagne and was dominated by episcopal concerns. The Carolingian state was fabricated by redirecting and incorporating those ideals into a new kind of social power.

St. Denis and Sacred Images

Frankish bishops were drawn into a larger Mediterranean sphere of action shortly after the Carolingian usurpation. Under Stephen II (752–757), the "Republic of St. Peter," which the popes sought to preserve in central Italy, came under pressure from the Lombards.[21] Accompanied by his curia, Pope Stephen crossed the Alps, arriving at the royal villa in Ponthion early in 754.[22] The old Byzantine alliance, Rome's usual recourse in its conflict with the Lombards, was strained. Byzantium no longer seemed capable of protecting Rome. Relations were further interrupted by Byzantine iconoclasm. Shortly after Stephen arrived in Francia, Constantine V (741–745) assembled a council at the imperial palace of Hieria that condemned the use of icons.[23]

Pope Stephen wintered at the monastery of St. Denis, and there, having gained a promise from Pippin to come to his defense in Italy, the pope anointed him king of the Franks. Since the reign of the Merovingian Dagobert I, the monastery of St. Denis had formed the nucleus of a royal cult, offering perpetual prayers for the king's victory and salvation. It therefore seemed the most appropriate place to anoint King Pippin.[24] The pope was well aware of the abbey's importance, and of its patron St. Denis, whom the Franks believed had been the first bishop of Paris.

Independence from the Lombards and from the iconoclastic Byzantine em-

---

21. On numbering the popes named Stephen, see J. N. D. Kelly, *The Oxford Dictionary of Popes* (Oxford: 1986), 91. Scholars now follow the *Annuario Pontifico,* which since 1961 has listed this pope as Stephen II (III) (752–757). Ullmann listed him as Stephen III: *Short History of the Papacy,* 373. On the Lombard threat to Rome, see T. F. X. Noble, *The Republic of St. Peter,* 71–94; and Peter Classen, *Karl der Grosse, das Papsttum und Byzanz: Die Begründung des karolingischen Kaisertums,* Beiträge zur Geschichte und Quellenkunde des Mittelalters 9 (Sigmaringen: 1985), 11–14.

22. "Cum magno apparatu et multa munera" (Continuations: 36), Fredegar, *The Fourth Book of the Chronicle of Fredegar,* 104. See also Pius Engelbert, "Papstreisen ins Frankenreich," *Römische Quartalschrift* 88 (1993): 77–113; esp. 101–7, 88–92.

23. George Ostrogorsky, *History of the Byzantine State,* trans. J. Hussey (Oxford: 1968), 172–73; see also L. Rydén, "The Role of the Icon in Byzantine Piety," 41–52, esp. 41–43.

24. Pierre Riché, *The Carolingians,* 68–69; on the association of Reims with royalty and royal ceremonial, see Carlrichard Brühl, *Reims als Krönungsstadt des französosischen Königs bis zum Ausgang des 14. Jahrhunderts* (Frankfurt am Main: 1950).

peror was uppermost in Stephen's mind during his negotiations with Pippin.[25] Pippin honored his promise the following year.[26] Invading Italy in 755 and again in 756, he defeated the Lombard King Aistulf, forcing him to surrender the keys of various towns in central Italy; the keys were deposited on the altar of St. Peter's. During the siege of Pavia, Byzantine envoys arrived to inform Pippin that the lands he was surrendering to the pope belonged to the emperor. Pippin replied that he had come to Italy only on behalf of St. Peter. However, Pippin soon established diplomatic ties with Constantine V, apparently untroubled by iconoclasm or conflicting interests in Italy.[27]

Stephen's successor, Paul, followed up on this theme, sending Pippin a copy of the works of Pseudo-Dionysius sometime between 758 and 763, a rich gift that he knew would delight the Franks. The identification of St. Denis of Paris with Dionysius the Areopagite, disciple of the Apostle Paul, had been made as long ago as the early sixth century.[28] The pope sent these books as recognition of the ancient and apostolic origins of the Frankish Church.[29] In fact this "Dionysius" was a neoplatonic thinker who probably wrote in Syria late in the fifth century.[30] Pseudo-Dionysius was required reading for anyone involved in the debate over icons, and Pope Paul wanted to bring the Frankish Church into his struggle against iconoclasm. The fact that the books were in Greek, however, meant that for the time being the Franks could not read them.[31]

Within twenty years of Stephen's death in 757, the *Donation of Constantine* was probably produced in Rome, perhaps even at the papal court.[32] The connection to Rome cannot be established with certainty, and continues to rely on textual interpretation. The document seemingly sheds light on Roman thinking

25. Noble, *Republic of St. Peter,* 81.

26. McKitterick, *Frankish Kingdoms,* 48–50.

27. "Rex Pippinus legationem Constantinopolem ad Constantino imperatore pro amicitiis causa et salutem patrie sue mittens" (Continuations: 40), *Fourth Book of Fredegar,* 109.

28. The date depends on the age of the *Vita Genovefae,* the earliest source for the legend; see Levillain, "La crise des années 507–508," 556–58. In the earliest version of the legend, Denis was associated with Peter, rather than with Paul: Levillain, 556; see also Martin Heinzelmann and J.-C. Poulin, *Les vies anciennes de sainte Geneviève de Paris: Études critiques* (Paris: 1986).

29. G. Théry, "L'Entrée du Pseudo-Denys en occident," in *Mélanges Mandonnet: Études d'histoire littéraire et doctrinale du moyen âge,* Bibliothèque Thomiste 14 (Paris: 1930), 2:23–30.

30. The works are imbued with the influence of Plotinus and Proclus: Andrew Louth, *Denys the Areopagite* (Wilton, Conn.: 1989), 1–14; Malingrey, *Littérature grecque chrétienne,* 139–41; Lorenzo Valla was the first to express doubts about authenticity: Berthold Altaner, *Patrologie,* 454.

31. Riché, "Le renouveau culturel," 66–67.

32. Peter Llewellyn, "Le contexte romain du couronnement de Charlemagne: Le temps de l'Avent de l'année 800," MA 96, 5th ser. 4 (1990): 209–25; Raymond J. Loenertz, "En marge de Constitutum Constantini: Contribution à l'histoire du texte," *Revue des sciences philosophiques et théologiques* 59 (1975): 289–94.

as the popes forged their new Frankish alliance, abandoning Byzantium and its heretical emperors. Many scholars downplay the contemporary importance of this forgery, which claimed to come from the hand of Constantine the Great in the fourth century, and which only became widely known later in the Middle Ages.[33] The *Donation* imagined that when Constantine moved from Rome to his newly built capital in Constantinople, he gave up any claim over Rome and its environs, which he "donated" to the popes as the Vicars of the Apostles.[34] He granted to the bishops of Rome an imperial regalia, complete with crown, sceptre, and robes of purple.[35] The *Donation* therefore appears to be a manifesto of independence for the "Republic of St. Peter" from Byzantium.[36]

In a recent examination of the relevant documents, Johannes Fried suggests that the *Donation* is much later, and reflects a Frankish milieu in about 829/830, when opposition to Louis the Pious called for a reimagination of Rome and the church.[37] This would make the *Donation* comparable in milieu and purpose to the aims of the *False Decretals.* The interpretation pursued here instead ties the *Donation* to the struggle over iconoclasm and the developing idea of papal supremacy.

For the document has these further implications: The *Donation* portrayed Rome as the center of an iconophilic western church with its own ultra-imperial legitimacy. According to the *Donation of Constantine,* in an attitude of humility and respect, the Emperor Constantine held the bridle of Pope Sylvester's horse and went on to cede to him the city of Rome and the western empire.[38] According to the *Donation,* icons played a major role in Constantine's conversion to Christianity: the emperor was visited in a dream by Peter and Paul, whom he recognized the next day in icons shown to him by Pope Sylvester (such dreams were a standard iconophilic *topos*).[39] The *Donation of Constantine* is also relevant

---

33. On reception and study of these documents: Johannes Fried, *Donation of Constantine and Constitutum Constantini: The Misinterpretation of a Fiction and its Original Meaning,* Millenium-Studien/Millenium Studies 3 (Berlin: 2007), 11–33.

34. *Das Constitutum Constantini (Konstantinische Schenkung) Text,* ed. Horst Fuhrmann, Fontes iuris germanici antiqui 10 (Hannover: 1968), 81.

35. Raymond J. Loenertz, "*Constitutum Constantini:* Destination, destinataires, auteur, date," *Aevum* 48 (1974): 199–245; see 227; Nicolas Huyghebaert, "Une légende de fondation: Le Constitutum Constantini," MA 85, 4th ser. 34 (1979): 177–209.

36. Noble, *Republic of St. Peter,* 134–37; McKitterick points out that interpretation of the document hinges on its date, which is impossible to fix with any precision: *Frankish Kingdoms,* 48.

37. Fried, *Donation,* 88–109.

38. Study of the *Donation* has long been dominated by later medieval topics, despite Ernst Kantorowicz, "The 'King's Advent' and the Enigmatic Panels," 73–75.

39. "Et rursum interrogare coepimus eundem beatissimum papam, utrum istorum apostolo-

to the recruitment of the Frankish bishops during Rome's struggle against icon-oclasm. The popes abandoned Byzantium and sought to undermine the Byzan-tine emperor's singular political and religious claims.[40] The *Donation* imagined a division: there could be two empires and two Romes.

In 761 a synod was held in Rome under Pope Paul I (757–767) that reflected the new situation in Italy.[41] Held in a monastery that Pope Paul had built and dedicated to St. Stephen (the "proto-martyr") and St. Sylvester (the pope figur-ing so prominently in the *Donation*), the monks were enjoined to undertake per-petual psalmody "for the expansion and stability of the Republic."[42] The monas-tery of SS. Stephen and Sylvester was meant to be the centerpiece of a renewal of Rome. It was also a monument to Rome's resistance to iconoclasm. The monks housed in the monastery were, in fact, Greek iconophiles taking refuge in Rome.

The Frankish-Roman alliance diminished the influence and scope of Byzan-tine activities. By making Rome much less dependent on eastern help, Pippin's invasion of Italy weakened Byzantine influence over Roman policy, especially on the issue of iconoclasm.[43] Constantine V's ambassadors tried to sway the Franks on this issue when they met with Pippin III at the royal villa at Gentilly in 767. It is possible that Frankish clerics were already inclined to take an independent line that rejected the position of the iconoclastic emperor, and that was also at variance with the position of Rome.[44]

When Pippin died in 768, the kingdom was divided between his two sons, Carloman and Charles (Charlemagne). Shortly afterward, Frankish bishops were invited to a council in Rome, held under Pope Stephen III (768–772). This council had important implications for the Frankish bishops, both by involv-ing them directly in confronting eastern iconoclasm and by giving them their first opportunity to participate in a large and important council.[45] By uniting Frankish and Italian bishops, the Roman council of 769 was intended to em-

rum imaginem expressam haberet, ut ex pictura disceremus hos esse, quos revelatio docuerat. Tunc isdem venerabilis pater imagines eorundem apostolorum per diaconem suum exhiberi praecepit," *Constitutum Constantini,* 72–73. This is similar to a story in a letter of Pseudo-Ambrose, cited by Pope Hadrian in referring to the Council of Rome of 769: MGH Conc. 2.1:74–92; see 90.

40. On the religious claims of the eastern emperors, see Norman H. Baynes, "Eusebius and the Christian Empire," in his *Byzantine Essays and Other Essays* (London: 1969), 168–72; and Grillmeier, *Le Christ dans la tradition chrétienne,* 293–302.

41. Council of Rome (761), MGH Conc. 2.1:64–71.

42. "Pro dilatione et stabilitate rei publicae," Council of Rome (761), MGH Conc. 2.1:67.

43. Judith Herrin, "Constantinople, Rome and the Franks in the Seventh and Eighth Cen-turies," in *Byzantine Diplomacy: Papers from the Twenty-Fourth Spring Symposium of Byzantine Studies,* edited by J. Shepard and S. Franklin (Aldershot: 1992), 91–107; see 100–1.

44. Riché, "Le renouveau culturel," 67.

45. Council of Rome (769), MGH Conc. 2.1:74–92; Mansi, 12:701–22.

body a unified western church, which, acting in unison, could rebut the iconoclasm of the eastern church.[46]

Gathering in the imperial palace Hiereia on the Sea of Marmora in 754, a
Byzantine council tried to return the church to its original purity by destroying
the influence of icons and the "deceitful painting of likenesses." According to
the Council of Hiereia, Christianity was incompatible with the worship of mere
"creatures," images made by man from worldly materials. The only acceptable
images were those painted within the soul by the zealous believer who studies
the lives of the saints and practices virtue.[47] Only internal symbols were appropriate expressions of divine reality, the impress on the soul.

Twelve Frankish bishops traveled to Rome in 769, drawn from both sides
of the divided kingdom.[48] In addition to the problem of iconoclasm, Stephen
III (768–772) hoped to involve the Franks in his effort to depose the anti-pope
Constantine (767–769). For Pope Stephen, the iconoclasm of the bishops gathered at Hiereia departed from orthodoxy and tradition. "If we wish to be part-
ners of the saints," the Roman council declared, we should venerate "the relics
of the saints, not only of their bodies, but also of their vestments, the basilicae
named after them, and even their images and likenesses wherever they might
be depicted."[49] The council was not careful to distinguish veneration (*venerare*)
and adoration (*adorare*). When Pope Hadrian (772–795) later referred back to
the council, he said that "they stated that sacred images are to be venerated *and*
adored," and, later in the same text, that "they established that sacred images
are to be adored *and also* venerated."[50] And so they had.

Hadrian informs us about the council, often referring to it and citing lost
portions. According to his report, the adoration of images was vindicated at

46. Classen, *Karl der Grosse, das Papsttum,* 11–12 and 35–36, notes the importance of the council for Frankish-Roman relations, and the role of iconoclasm in those relations.

47. Rydén, "The Role of the Icon in Byzantine Piety," 41–42.

48. Classen, *Karl der Grosse, das Papsttum,* 12.

49. "Si ad sanctorum consortium venire optamus, profecto hic omnia in honore sanctorum
sive reliquias non solum corporum, set et vestimentorum sive basilicas nominibus eorum memo-
ratas seu etiam imagines et vultus illorum in quolibet loco depictos celeberrimo honore venerari
debemus," Council of Rome (769), MGH Conc. 2.1:87.

50. According to Ann Freeman, referring to a translation of the later Council of Nicaea (787):
"Hadrian had been scrupulous in using *venerare* and *veneratio* in reference to images, while the
translator of the Acta observed no such caution, using *adorare* and *adoratio* indiscriminately";
Ann Freeman, "Scripture and Images in the Libri Carolini," *Settimane* 41 (1994), 1:163–88; see
166–67. This is not accurate. Hadrian was not scrupulous in observing this distinction when he
referred to the Council of Rome: "Venerari et adorari sacras imagines in eorum concilio censu-
erunt"; "Adorari atque venerari sacras imagines statuerunt," Pope Hadrian, citing the Council
of Rome (769), MGH Conc. 2.1:89.

Rome in 769 as an integral and coherent part of the traditions of the universal church, established in the six great ecumenical councils. The bishops had declared that anyone who refused to adore Christ's image was casting doubt on the Incarnation (*humanatio*).[51] The council cited the writings of Pseudo-Dionysius to confirm the real connection between an image and what it represented: "In truth, visible things are images of invisible things."[52] Not only was there a genuine connection between the invisible and the visible, but for Pseudo-Dionysius, the visible sign was the only path by which the soul could travel toward the invisible. "In fact it is impossible for our mind to reach those incorporeal things of the heavenly army[53] . . . unless we can approach the beautiful invisible things by means of a visible, material effigy."[54] Hadrian's report indicates that at least as early as the council of 769, Frankish bishops were aware of the importance of their apostle, St. Denis, for the debate over religious images.[55]

The Franks were treated to an impressive display of Roman authority. As the council ended, Stephen gathered "all the priests and clerics, and all the people," barefoot and singing hymns in honor of St. Peter.[56] Frankish bishops were thus drawn into a larger world, but as an elite, feeling supremely confident of their apostolic claims through St. Denis; they clung to this tradition, which they increasingly considered as universal and Roman.

---

51. "Si quis alium terminum fidei sive symbolum aut doctrinam habet praeter quod traditum est a sanctis magnis et universalibus sex synodis et confirmatum est ab his sanctis patribus, qui in eis convenerunt, et non adorat imaginem sive figuram domini nostri Iesu Christi neque humanationem eius confitetur," Hadrian, citing the Council of Rome (769), MGH Conc. 2.1:89.

52. "In veritate et manifeste imagines sunt visibiles invisibilia," Pseudo-Dionysius, Letter 10, claiming to be a letter to St. John on Patmos, as cited at Rome (769), MGH Conc. 2.1:91. The letter may be conveniently consulted in *Pseudo-Dionysius: The Complete Works,* trans. Colm Luibheid (New York: 1987), 288–89.

53. Note that the Latin *militia* was used to translate the Greek neologism *hierarchia* of Dionysius.

54. "Etenim inpossible est nostra mente ad incorporea illa pertingere caelestis militiae initatione visionemque, nisi per elementorum poterimus per visibilem ad invisibilem pulcherrimamque attingi effigiem," Pseudo-Dionysius, *Celestial Hierarchy* (1.3), as cited at the Council of Rome (769), MGH Conc. 2.1:91; see also *Pseudo-Dionysius: Complete Works,* 146.

55. It is often assumed that Hilduin of St. Denis made the first translation sometime after 827, as argued by G. Théry, "L'Entrée du pseudo-Denys en occident," 25–27; and Jean Leclercq, "Influence and Noninfluence of Dionysius in the Western Middle Ages," in *Pseudo-Dionysius: Complete Works,* 25–32; see 26. But as early as 1923, Lehmann pointed out earlier important appearances of Dionysius in the west, and in Latin, including the Council of Rome in 769: Paul Lehmann, "Zur Kenntnis der Schriften des Dionysius Areopagita im Mittelalter," in his *Erforschung des Mittelalters: Ausgewälte Abhandlungen und Aufsätze,* 4:128–41 (Stuttgart: 1961).

56. Council of Rome (769), MGH Conc. 2.1:77–78.

Sources of Carolingian Sacral Kingship

Scholars have often looked to the ancient Germanic past to find the primeval origins of a sacred kingship that was later Christianized in the late eighth century. Most scholars have abandoned this avenue of discussion.[57] More persistent and influential is the view that Carolingian kingship, so deeply tinted in religious purple, should be seen as an expression of "political Augustinianism." According to this argument, medieval thinkers misunderstood Augustine and hoped to establish the "City of God" on earth. This political view was confirmed by the concise Augustinianism of Gregory the Great. But this influential thesis of H.-X. Arquillière should be reexamined.[58] In contrast, I have emphasized the conciliar and liturgical sources of Carolingian social doctrine, pointing to episcopal social thought as developed in Gallic, Merovingian, and early Carolingian councils, alongside the influential writings of Isidore of Seville and the persuasive theocratic model of the Visigothic kingdom.

One frequent supposition behind the thesis of political Augustinianism is that Augustine's writings against Donatism provided the basis for medieval political thought, rather than the complex views of the *City of God*. Indeed, as Robert Markus has shown, Augustine believed that the Donatist crisis required the church to call on the state to enforce religious doctrine and punish dissent. Yet Augustine's doctrine was complex and hardly triumphalist.[59] Francis Oakley has recently restated this view of the political Augustinism of Carolingian kingship: "the Augustine whom one encounters in the political thinking of the western (or Latin) Middle Ages is not the Augustine whom one encounters in the pages of the City of God." The view of politics in the City of God was after all "strikingly negative."[60] According to Augustine, rulers play a limited, useful role in imposing a tentative kind of peace, although the very need for them reflects the fallen state of mankind.

Going against the theory of a misreading of Augustine is the fact that Augus-

---

57. Goffart, "Two Notes on Germanic Antiquity," 9–30.

58. "Les théologiens, les synodes, les publicistes ont été frappés par cet Empire terrestre dont Charlemagne a voulu faire une sorte de Cité de Dieu," Arquillière, *L'Augustinisme politique,* 116. This is the view of Ganshof and McKeon as well: Peter McKeon, "The Empire of Louis the Pious: Faith, Politics and Personality," RB 90 (1980): 50–62; See also Walter Ullmann, *The Carolingian Renaissance and the Idea of Kingship* (London: 1969), 43. More cautious is J. M. Wallace-Hadrill, "The 'Via Regia' of the Carolingian Age," in his *Early Medieval History,* 181–200 (Oxford: 1975).

59. Robert A. Markus, *Saeculum: History and Society in the Theology of St. Augustine* (Cambridge: 1970), 133–53.

60. Francis Oakley, *Kingship: The Politics of Enchantment* (Oxford: 2006), 89.

tine's writings were widely admired and studied in detail. An example of such erudition may be seen in a massive compilation of passages from Augustine reflecting the saint's understanding of Paul, prepared in ninth-century Lyon. The compiler, probably Florus of Lyon, must have traveled widely from library to library to assemble his collection.[61] Florus also drew extensively on Augustine as he developed a theology of predestination.[62] The library of Lyon, with a specialism in law and its collection of books, whose origins extended far back in late antiquity, was the perfect place for a Carolingian scholar to study Augustine. However, Augustine was a source for almost everything but political concepts, and his writings were almost never quoted in Carolingian discussions of social structure and kingship. Frankish bishops viewed the political realm as transparent to religious concerns, and moreover considered the kingdom to be a crucial vehicle for Christian salvation. Such a formula would have flabbergasted Augustine. It seems that Frankish bishops understood Augustine very well, and removed him from political discussion in the most tactful possible way.

Frankish bishops believed that their society could be rectified by making it conform to a divine pattern, a concept drawn from their own traditions of social thought. Isidore, rather than Augustine, was the towering figure in this development. Bishops thought of royal and episcopal power as two aspects of a single problem. Carolingian sacral kingship derived from an ancient tradition that confronted social reality with acts of the imagination. What the bishops had imagined was coming true.

The integration of royal and episcopal power reflects the influence of an educated elite, acting in unison and manipulating a venerable intellectual and legal tradition that, under the Carolingians, became the very basis of royal claims to authority. Episcopal influence over royal legislation is strikingly evident from the very beginning of Charlemagne's reign. In the earliest of such documents, Charlemagne was proclaimed "king by the grace of God, *rector* of the Frankish kingdom, devoted defender of the holy church and its helper in all things." He acted as such a *rector* (guide or "straightener") by undertaking legislation in response to the "exhortation of the apostolic see and of all our faithful, and especially the bishops and other priests."[63] The bishops would benefit enormously

---

61. Célestin Charlier, "La compilation augustinienne de Florus sur l'Apôtre: Sources et authenticité," RB 57 (1947): 132–86.

62. Klaus Zechiel-Eckes, *Florus von Lyon als Kirchenpolitiker und Publizist: Studien zur Persönlichkeit eines karolingishcen "Intellektuellen" am Beispiel der Auseinandersetzung mit Amalarius (835–858) und des Prädestinationsstreits (851–855),* Quellen und Forschungen zum Recht im Mittelalter 8 (Stuttgart: 1999), 202–10.

63. "Karolus, gratia Dei rex regnique Francorum rector et devotus sanctae ecclesiae defen-

from this powerful partnership. Charlemagne confirmed older legislation on the obligation of the faithful to pay tithes to their churches and enforced these laws with new energy.[64]

Under Charlemagne, written law became a characteristic expression of royal power on a scale unlike the Merovingians or mayors of the palace. Although the Merovingian kings had issued a few edicts, a tremendous increase in the quantity of written law distinguishes Carolingian from Merovingian royal power.[65] The Carolingians found efficient means of publishing the law through the *missi,* but strangely, the texts of the capitularies were not carefully preserved. There is some evidence that the capitularies were deposited in a palace archive, but much of this law was lost due to neglect or inefficiency. The laws were inconsistent in form and vocabulary.[66] Despite these limitations, written law became, in the Carolingian program of royal power, the most prominent guarantee of justice and good government.[67] Charles sought to ensure that his *missi dominici* and judges would have copies of this law.[68]

Ganshof assumed that with the Carolingian capitularies, we have to do with the normative written law of a royal power, and in this sense, a direct inheritance of Roman traditions of law.[69] But the capitularies raise peculiar problems: it is difficult to distinguish them from other kinds of sources, such as episcopal councils, and questions are frequently raised about their origins, how they came into existence, and their effectiveness. At the death of Charlemagne the impact of capitularies was still in question.[70] Although royal law was still thought to emerge from the consensus of the people (*consensus omnium*), its character had

---

sor atque adiutor in omnibus. Apostolicae sedis hortatu, omniumque fidelium nostrorum, et maxime episcoporum ac reliquorum sacerdotum," *Karoli M. Capitulare primum* (769), MGH Capit. 1.1:44–46; see 44.

64. Giles Constable, *Monastic Tithes: From their Origins to the Twelfth Century* (Cambridge: 1964), 28–29.

65. Wormald offers an excellent survey of legal developments on the continent: Patrick Wormald, *The Making of English Law,* vol. 1, see esp. 43.

66. F. L. Ganshof, *Recherches sur les capitulaires* (Paris: 1958), 39–46; see also Collins, *Charlemagne,* 10–12.

67. Fouracre, "Carolingian Justice," 779.

68. Rosamond McKitterick, *The Carolingians and the Written Word* (Cambridge: 1989), 39; Ganshof, *Recherches,* 62.

69. Cf. "Notre texte est le premier à contenir à cet égard une disposition normative écrite, de portée générale," F. L. Ganshof, "Le droit romain dans le capitulaires et dans la collection d'Ansegise," in *Droit romain dans les capitulaires;* Ius romanum medii aevi, Pars I, 2 b *cc,* alphabeta (Milan: 1969), 1–43; this quote, 7.

70. Patzold, *Episcopus,* 61–64; councils and secular assemblies met at close to the same time and place, and it was possible for conciliar decisions to be cited in capitularies, while some capitulary decisions found their way into the councils: Patzold, 72.

changed.[71] Gone were the legislative reticence and specificity of the ancient Salic law, which carefully distinguished the theft of a sheep from the theft of "three she-goats."[72] As Fouracre says, "much of the *Lex Salica* is in fact concerned with compensation payments . . . many of a petty nature, but it is silent on other is-sues of major social importance, such as marriage, or the transfer of property."[73] Carolingian law set out to address these larger issues. Some capitularies were en-titled *Capitula legibus addita* to indicate that they were intended to supplement or complete the *Lex Salica*.[74]

Carolingian royal law, like episcopal law, now pursued whole categories of ac-tion and issued directives rather than defining remedies. Consider the sweeping horizon of the following law: "That bishops and presbyters should live according to the canons, and so teach others."[75] The vocabulary, content, and even the form of Charlemagne's legislation (in flexible, numbered, prescriptive *capitula*)[76] drew heavily on the norms of conciliar law. At Thionville in 805, a double capitulary was issued in which laws relevant to clerics alone (*infra aecclesiam*) were sepa-rated from those that applied to everyone (*ad omnes generaliter*).[77] Ganshof em-phasized the diverse content and lack of rational structure characterizing such legislation.[78] The capitulary addressed a number of topics, but more than half of its provisions were driven by ecclesiastical concerns. The "clerical" section con-tains 16 articles, while the "general" section contains 22. However, four of the latter drew upon episcopal concerns: item 2, on widows and orphans; 4, on pray-ing during famine; 16, on the oppression of the poor; and 17, on the building of private churches. Carolingian law represented a new direction, and had wholly different aims than the *Lex Salica*. It was political and religious. Still, the col-lection of Ansegis, abbot of St.-Wandrille, shows that there was no constant or consistent method of archiving the capitularies, and little to show that they had

71. Pétrau-Gay, *La notion de "lex,"* 201–9; see also Ganshof, *Recherches*, 30–34.

72. "Si quis agnum furaverit" (4.1), Pardessus' "Third Text," Pardessus, *Loi salique,* 67–112, 73; "Si quis tres capras furaverit," (5.1), 73.

73. Fouracre, "Carolingian Justice," 795.

74. Ganshof, *Recherches*, 74–75 and 92–101.

75. "Ut episcopi et presbiteris secundum canones vibant et itaque caeteros doceant," *Capitu-lare missorum generale* (802), MGH Capit. 1.1:91–99; see 93.

76. The format of numbered titles and rubrics was adopted even in the early versions of the Salic law: Pardessus, *Loi salique, 67*. Here I refer instead to the combination of content and form that links Carolingian legislation to episcopal law.

77. *Duplex capitulare missorum in Theodonis villa datum,* MGH Capit. 1.1:120–26. The "cleri-cal" section is: *Capitulare missorum in Theodonis villa datum primum, mere ecclesiasticum,* 121–22. The "general" section is *Capitulare missorum in Theodonis villa datum secundum, generale,* 122–26.

78. Ganshof, *Recherches*, 75–76.

kingdom-wide force. Rather than a clear picture of contemporary legal practice, the capitularies may reveal most about the social imagination, the mentality and concepts, of powerful men in the Carolingian order.[79]

In combatting paganism, the bishop could still call on the help of the local exponent of royal law, the *grafio,* "who is a defender of the church."[80] Under Charlemagne, however, royal power coalesced around missionary goals. Bishops were instructed to travel through their parishes each year "to teach and investigate the people, and to prohibit pagan observances."[81] Such an intensification of old ideals cut both ways. Although bishops had long offered up prayers for the aid of their kings, it was now decreed that no one should neglect this whenever a call for prayers was issued.[82] In royal hands, ancient episcopal imperatives took on a new, coercive quality; meanwhile, there is the striking fact that royal power was now obsessed by such topics.

The prospect of amplified power and wealth must have been dizzying. At Harestal in 779, Charlemagne issued a law augmenting episcopal wealth in the form of the "tenth," a donation of one-tenth of all income that had long been purely notional.[83] The capitulary also confirmed episcopal power over all the clerics in their parishes.[84] But the same capitulary sought to limit the right of asylum offered by churches. Murderers or others "who ought to die" were not to be excused merely by taking refuge in a church.[85] The laws issued at Heristal then veered to a discussion of criminal procedures, thereby blending episcopal and royal concerns in a way that was now typical. Declared during a period of famine and after a Saxon attack on Paderborn, the prologue stated explicitly that the goal of the capitulary was to return the kingdom to conformity with the will of God. The proper functioning of ecclesiastical hierarchies and duties was viewed as crucial to this effort.[86]

---

79. Patzold suggests that the basic content, rather than the precise text, was most important to the compilers: Patzold, *Episcopus,* 64–65.

80. "Decrevimus, ut secundum canones unusquisque episcopus in sua parrochia sollicitudinem adhibeat, adiuvante grafione qui defensor ecclesiae est, ut populus Dei paganias non faciat," *Capitulare primum,* 45. This was based upon *Karlmanni principis capitulare* (742), MGH Capit. 1.1:25.

81. "Plebes docere et investigare, et prohibere paganas observations," *Capitulare primum,* 45.

82. *Capitulare primum,* 46.

83. "De decimis, ut unusquisque suam decimam donet, atque per iussionem pontificis dispensentur" (Forma communis, 7), *Capitulare Haristallense* (779), MGH Capit. 1.1:46–51; see 48.

84. "Ut episcopi de presbiteris et clericis infra illorum parrochia potestatem habeant secundum canones" (Forma communis, 4), *Capitulare Haristallense,* 47.

85. "Ut homicidas aut caeteros reos qui legibus mori debent, si ad ecclesiam confugerint, non excusentur" (Forma communis, 8), *Capitulare Haristallense,* 58.

86. Patzold, *Episcopus,* 65–67.

The combination of royal and episcopal power soon resulted in specific, kingdom-wide directives. The traditional role of rallying a warband still remained a feature of Carolingian kingship.[87] Light raids for plunder were the most common form of war, a competition between the opposed elites of the Franks and their neighbors for trophies and wealth.[88] Charlemagne revamped the military organization of the Frankish kingdom, allowing him to field much larger armies, for longer periods, than his predecessors. The tasks to which he put these armies were in line with the doctrine of missionary warfare.

According to royal propaganda, Charlemagne's wars combatted injustice or expanded the church. Against the Saxons his military victories were always followed by "rebellion" whenever the Franks withdrew, provoking Charlemagne to decades of savagery.[89] In 772 he destroyed the Saxon's central cult-site, the Irminsul, but in a military action that did not have an impact like that of Boniface and the "Oak of Jupiter."[90] In 780, Charles again arrived in Saxony with a large army, whose success was judged by its salvific outcome, which by now had become central to Charlemagne's military policies; he "divided the country among his bishops, presbyters and abbots, so that they could baptize and preach there."[91] According to another record, the army assembled at Lippspringe, "where many of the North Saxons were baptized."[92] Warfare and Christianization were combined in campaigns culminating in atrocity and forced baptism.[93] In 783, Charles returned to Saxony, and "having made a slaughter, devastated the land."[94]

To aid these armies, and perhaps in response to a famine, a series of special prayers and masses were ordered in the *Capitulary for Bishops*.[95] Every bishop was to offer up three masses and to chant the Psalter three times, "one for the

---

87. On changes in military organization, see Innes, *State and Society*, 150–53; see also Reuter, "Plunder and Tribute," 79.

88. Reuter, "Plunder and Tribute," 91.

89. Kleinclausz, *Charlemagne*, 207–33.

90. "Carolus rex hostiliter ingressus est in Saxonia, et destruxit fanum eorum, quod vocabatur Hirminsuul" (Anno 772), *Chronicon Moissiacense*, ed. G. H. Pertz, MGH SS. 1:280–313; see 295.

91. "Divisitque ipsam patriam inter episcopos et presbyteros seu et abbates, ut in ea baptizarent et praedicarent" (Anno 780), *Annalium Lareshamensium pars altera*, ed. G. H. Pertz, MGH SS. 1:30–39; see 31; Kleinclausz, *Charlemagne*, 208–10.

92. "In quo loco multi aquilonales Saxones baptizati sunt" (Anno 780), *Annales Mettenses priores*, ed. B. von Simpson, MGH SRG in us. schol. (Hannover: 1905), 68.

93. Schutz, *The Carolingians in Central Europe*, 53–59.

94. "Karolus rex iterum in Saxonia, caede facta terram devastavit" (Anno 783), *Annales Alamannici*, ed. G. H. Pertz, MGH SS. 1:19–60; see 41.

95. *Capitulare episcoporum* (780), MGH Capit. 1.1: 51–52; the annals mention a famine (Anno 779): *Annalium Lareshamensium pars altera*, ed. G. H. Pertz, MGH SS. 1:31.

lord king, another for the army of the Franks, and a third for the present tribulation."[96] The concept of missionary warfare, and the central role of bishops in its
successful prosecution, here gave shape to royal legislation, "instituted through
the consensus of the bishops."[97]

The domination of Charlemagne's legislation by episcopal concerns can be
seen throughout his reign.[98] Perhaps the most important example of this influence is the famous capitulary of 789, the *Admonitio generalis,* a set of directives
proposing an ambitious program of church reform on a kingdom-wide scale.
These reforms expressed episcopal concern for cultural and moral integration,
and probably also reflect the importance of Alcuin, a leading figure in the intellectual life of the court in this period.[99] Although some of the better-known
initiatives proposed in the law were designed to promote book production and
education, the impulse behind the *Admonitio* was not humanistic, nor was it
simply an effort to create a literate administration.[100] The *Admonitio* was Charlemagne's attempt to foster the governmental aims of the most important clerics of his kingdom—an episcopal cultural manifesto issued under the aegis of
royal power. Magnou-Nortier has argued that the text of the edict shows traces
of later manipulation and interpolation to heighten this aspect.[101]

As bishops knew from their own experience, high intellectual accomplish-

96. "Unusquisque episcopus tres missas et psalteria tria cantet, unam pro domno rege, alteram pro exercitu Francorum, tertiam pro presenti tribulation," *Capitulare episcoporum* (780),
MGH Capit. 1.1:52.

97. "Capitulare qualiter institutum est in hoc episcoporum consensus," *Capitulare episcoporum* (780), MGH Capit. 1.1:52.

98. The body of such law cannot be thoroughly discussed here. Falling into the same category
as the *Amonitio Generalis* are the *Duplex legationis edictum* (789), MGH Capit. 1.1:62–64; *Karoli epistola de litteris colendis* (780–800), MGH Capit. 1.1:78–79; *Capitulare missorum generale*
(802), MGH Capit. 1.1:91–99; *Capitulare missorum item speciale* (802?), MGH Capit. 1.1:102–4;
Capitula a sacerdotibus proposita (802?), MGH Capit. 1.1:105–7; *Capitula de examinandis ecclesiasticis* (802?), MGH Capit. 1.1:109–11; *Capitula ecclesiastica ad Salz data* (803–804), MGH
Capit. 1.1:119–20; *Duplex capitulare missorum in Theodonis villa datum,* MGH Capit. 1.1:120–26;
Capitula excerpta de canone (806?), MGH Capit. 1.1:133–34; *Capitula de causis cum episcopis et
abbatibus tractandis,* (811), MGH Capit. 1.1:162–64; *Capitula e canonibus excerpta* (813), MGH
Capit. 1.2:173–75; *Capitula ecclesiastica* (810–813?), MGH Capit. 1.2:178–79; *Capitula missorum*
(813?), MGH Capit. 1.2:181–82; *Capitula de rebus ecclesiasticis* (787–813?), MGH Capit. 1.1:185–86.

99. Fouracre, "Carolingian Justice," 778–79.

100. *Admonitio generalis* (789), MGH Capit. 1.1:52–62; see 54; see also McKitterick, *Frankish
Kingdoms,* 145; and McKitterick, *Carolingians and the Written Word,* 20. The centrality of reform
to the *Admonitio* has been addressed by Giles Brown, who believes that the initiative was entirely
Charlemagne's: Brown, "Introduction: The Carolingian Renaissance," in *Carolingian Culture:
Emulation and Innovation,* edited by Rosamond McKitterick, 1–51, esp. 17–21 (Cambridge: 1994).

101. Élisabeth Magnou-Nortier, "La tentative de subversion de l'État sous Louis le Pieux et
l'oeuvre des falsificateurs," MA 105 (1999): 1:331–65 and 2:615–41. On the *Admonitio,* see 617–18.

ment was tied to the specific local achievements of isolated cultural centers.[102] A monastery or church needed the luck of possessing a good library and a remarkable scholar or teacher. The place could then hope to foster a school, great or small. Intellectual culture remained local and idiosyncratic.[103] Frankish bishops were now keen on forging broad intellectual consensus in their ranks, so as to act together in a worldwide context. A higher level of education and agreement on a central group of texts would be basic to such a project. Clerical education was an exercise of episcopal authority and a means of uniting the clergy around the theme of "Roman" orthodoxy. The *Admonitio* betrays the hand of a self-confident group of powerful individuals who had recruited their king for a project of cultural reform centering on ecclesiastical concerns.[104] It was therefore an important landmark of royal-episcopal cooperation.

The *Admonitio* applied the same terminology of rulership to kings and bishops. Both were rectors, *rectores,* of society.[105] Nevertheless, the law was far more concerned with episcopal rulership than with kingship. The *Admonitio* highlighted "Roman" canon law and episcopal prerogatives and sought to introduce "Roman chant" to the liturgy. The romanizing theme of liturgical reform was at the center of Charlemagne's perception of his role as a king, and he was closely involved in such efforts, with his characteristic concern with "authority, orthodoxy and correctness."[106]

Education was therefore at the center: "You should emend Psalms, notes, songs, handbooks, grammars, and catholic books in every monastery and episcopal region, because although someone might want to call on God, they look without profit in uncorrected books."[107] Impressive liturgical books from Rome were now desired as a pattern, even though they could not fit Frankish purposes without revision: the Gregorian Sacramentary known as the *Hadrianum* epito-

---

102. John J. Contreni, "Carolingian Biblical Studies," in *Carolingian Essays: Andrew W. Mellon Lectures in Early Christian Studies,* edited by Uta-Renate Blumenthal (Washington, D.C.: 1983), 71–98.

103. Anita Guerreau-Jalabert, "La 'renaissance carolingienne': Modèles culturels, usages linguistiques et structures sociales," *Bibliothèque des chartes* 139 (1981): 5–35; see also Pierre Riché, "Les centres de culture en Neustrie de 650 à 850," in *La Neustrie: Les pays au nord de la Loire de 650 à 850,* edited by Hartmut Atsma, 2:297–305, Beihefte der Francia 16 (Sigmaringen: 1989).

104. Guerreau-Jalabert, "La 'renaissance carolingienne,'" 9.

105. For Charlemagne, "rex et rector regni Francorum," *Admonitio generalis* (789) MGH Capit. 1:53. For the bishops, "Venerabiles pastores et rectores ecclesiarum Dei," *Admonitio generalis* (789) MGH Capit. 1:61.

106. Hen, *Royal Patronage,* 73.

107. "Psalmos, notas, cantus, compotum, grammaticam per singula monasteria vel episcopia et libros catholicos bene emendate; quia saepe, dum bene aliqui Deum rogare cupiunt, sed per inemendatos libros male rogant," *Admonitio generalis* (789) MGH Capit. 1:60.

mised the Roman ideal. This splendid gift from Pope Hadrian was deposited in the royal library, where it exerted its attraction for liturgical poets.[108] The Frankish bishops viewed the cultivation of such resources as a basic step in forging a kingdom-wide consensus, to ensure that all bishops would "[follow] canonical customs and [shine] in peaceful unity."[109]

The *Admonitio* emphasized episcopal government of monks and other clerics and the organization of bishops under metropolitans.[110] What Charlemagne had to gain from the bishops who composed the *Admonitio* was access to a wider sphere of action, from Rome to Byzantium, by participation in the Frankish-Roman ecclesiastical alliance forged at Rome in 769.[111] Royal law now backed up the episcopal reform movement; in response to this persistent conflation of ecclesiastic and royal concerns, Carolingian kingship was increasingly interpreted in a religious light. Royal involvement was crucial to standardizing clerical life, and, indeed, made such a novelty thinkable.[112] Not unlike his Merovingian predecessors, Charlemagne found that by furthering and adopting the aims of his bishops, and by sitting in their councils, he gained the allegiance of a powerful sector of society, men who could display royal power on a grand canvas and give a lofty religious tone, not only to Frankish kingship, but even to Frankish warfare.

The rise of the Carolingian state was accompanied by changes in the relation of the king to local nobles. The state also engaged in elaborate acts of self-justification and propaganda reflecting the themes of episcopal social thought. The Carolingian state gives the appearance of a thin, but brilliant band of action and language at the head of society rather than a thorough redirection of society as a whole. This should be described as a "thin" state, with a social doctrine concerned only with how nobles, bishops, and kings should behave and believe. The doctrine of sacred kingship was connected to the rise of the Carolingian family in the *Earlier Annals of Metz* and the *Royal Frankish Annals*.[113]

---

108. Hen, *Royal Patronage*, 74–75.

109. "Canonica instituta sequentes et pacifica unitate nitentes," *Admonitio generalis* (789) MGH Capit. 1:57.

110. *Admonitio generalis* (789) MGH Capit. 1; see especially 54.

111. This is open to widely varying interpretations; Prinz, "Fränkische Episkopat," 127–28, portrays the *Admonitio* as a royal initiative in which the king offered the bishops a wider sphere of action.

112. Josef Semmler, "Le souverain occidental et les communautés religieuses du IXe au début du XIe siècle," *Byzantion* 61 (1991): 44–70. For a similar phenomenon in England: Antonia Gransden, "Traditionalism and Continuity during the Last Century of Anglo-Saxon monasticism," JEH 40 (1989): 159–207.

113. Fouracre, "Carolingian Justice," 774; Rosamond McKitterick, "The Illusion of Royal Power in the Carolingian Annals," EHR 115 (2000): 1–20.

This may also be seen in Charlemagne's new edition of the Salic law, published about 798, known as the *Lex emendata*.[114] Here the old laws were neatly arranged under rubrics, and some changes were made to the Latin. In essence, Charlemagne republished the ancient law of the Salian Franks, going back to the time of Clovis, which had survived in a large number of divergent copies.[115] If the existence of so many copies reflects a practical need, then we have to imagine the persistence of archaic social forms after nearly 300 years.[116] Wormald is right to direct our attention instead to the function of this law as the guarantor of a social identity, especially in distinction to other peoples.

In some surviving copies of Charlemagne's edition the code was prefaced by a little essay (the "Great Prologue" or *Prologus majus*), which projected the new publication against the entire panorama of Frankish history.[117] The prologue recapitulated most of the older "Short Prologue" as found in the editions made under Pippin, and mentioned earlier. The origin of Frankish identity was still found in the invasion period, in a romantic sketch of the old Franks, "audacious, swift, and harsh," who abandoned barbarism, it was pointed out, by converting to a Christianity free of heresy.[118] The publication allowed Charlemagne to associate himself with archaic legal custom.[119] The law was still ascribed to the four men of old and to assemblies that had gathered the law under King Clovis.[120] Seated among his bishops, on the other hand, the legislative horizon was cloudless and round.

Bishops considered the "poor, orphans and widows" to be under their special care. The right of such persons to be defended or fed by the church was a major element in a theory of property securing episcopal control over the church's vast possessions. It is significant, therefore, that Charlemagne placed such persons under his special protection. Counts were ordered to give priority to legal cas-

---

114. *Lex salica a Carolo Magno emendata anno DCCLXVIII* (Pardessus' Fifth Text), Pardessus, *Loi salique*, 265–321. Associated with Charlemagne's edition is the *Prologus majus*: Pardessus, *Loi salique*, 344–45. See the discussion in McKitterick, *Carolingians and the Written Word*, 40–60.

115. See McKitterick's "Table A," *Carolingians and the Written Word*, 49–55.

116. It is impossible to decide conclusively about the practical use of these manuscripts, since they may represent only "intellectual motives": McKitterick, *Carolingians and the Written Word*, 45.

117. *Prologus majus,* in Pardessus, *Loi salique,* 344–45.

118. "Audax, velox et aspera, ad chatholica fide conversa et inmunis ab herese," *Prologus majus,* 344.

119. Mordek, "Karolingische Kapitularien," 46–47.

120. "Wisogastis, Bodogastis [Saligastis,] et Widogastis . . . qui per tres mallos convenientes, omnes causarum origines sollicite discuciendum," *Prologus majus,* 344–45.

es involving orphans.[121] He sought to ensure that those poor people "who have been tossed into the streets or crossroads" had their confessions heard.[122] His interest in the poor gradually deepened as time went on:

let no-one presume to injure widows, orphans or travelers in the holy churches of God, by fraud or rapine; because the lord emperor himself, after God and his saints, has been established as their protector and defender.[123]

As defender of the weak, Charlemagne tried to halt the oppression of "free poor men."[124] He instructed his royal agents (*missi*) to inquire everywhere into the treatment of widows and orphans.[125] The *missi* were to listen carefully whenever widows or orphans "cried out" at a public judgment,[126] and everyone was to give alms to the poor during a famine.[127] Such concerns were a regular feature of Charlemagne's legislation. The king offered what in a sense was not his to give: "the poor, orphans and widows should have the peace of the church of God." This ancient task of bishops now had the powerful backing of the royal "ban" (*bannum*).[128] Royal power was drawn into a world whose boundaries had been shaped and expanded by bishops over centuries. By legislating on these lines, the king not only broke free from the narrow confines of Frankish custom, but could also legislate beyond his own people. He legislated not merely for the Salian or Ribuarian Franks, but, as bishops long had done, for "all Christian people."[129]

121. "Ut comites pupillorum et orfanorum causas primum audient," *Duplex legationis edictum* (789), MGH Capit. 1.1:63.

122. "De pauperibus in plateis vel in quadruviis iacentibus: ut ad ecclesiam veniant et illorum confessiones donent," *Duplex legationis edictum* (789), MGH Capit. 1.1:64.

123. "Ut sanctis ecclesiis Dei neque viduis neque orphanis neque peregrinis fraude vel rapinam vel aliquit iniuriae quis facere presumat; quia ipse domnus imperator, post Domini et sanctis eius, eorum et protector et defensor esse constitutus est," *Capitulare missorum generale* (802), 93.

124. "De obpressionibus liberorum hominum pauperum, qui in exercitu ire debent et a iudicibus sunt obpressi," *Capitularia missorum specialia* (802), MGH Capit. 1.1:99–102; see 100; "Ut liberi homines pauperes a nullo iniuste opprimantur," *Capitulare missorum item speciale* (802?), MGH Capit. 1.1:104.

125. "Ut missi nostri, undecunque necesse fuerit, tam de iustitiis ecclesiarum Dei, viduarum, orphanorum, pupillorum et caeterorum hominem inquirant," *Capitulare missorum item speciale* (802?), MGH Capit. 1.1:104.

126. "De iustitiis aecclesiarum Dei, viduarum, orfanorum et pupillorum, ut in publicis iudiciis non dispiciantur clamantes sed diligenter audiantur," *Capitulare missorum in Theodonis villa datum secundum, generale* (805), MGH Capit. 1.1:122–26; see 122.

127. "Ut indigentibus adiuvare studeant de annona, ita ut famis periculum non pereant," *Capitula per episcopos et comites nota facienda* (805–808), MGH Capit. 1.1:141.

128. "Ut pauperes, orfani et viduae et ecclesiae Dei pacem habeant," *Capitulare missorum Aquisgranense primum* (810), MGH Capit. 1.1:152–54; see 154. On the *bannum* as the source of legislative authority, see Ganshof, *Recherches*, 29–30.

129. "Ut omnis populus christianus fidem catholicam et dominicam orationem memoriter teneat," *Capitulare missorum item speciale*, 103.

The sacral character of Carolingian kingship drew upon episcopal traditions, which became a primary intellectual resource of their king. While in other ways remaining similar to the decentralized Merovingian state, the Carolingian state, thought of as a "sacred kingdom," could now claim that its aims were the same as those of the church. The ideal of a sacred kingdom would mobilize and unite the most powerful men in Frankish society for several decades. Great kingdom-wide councils of bishops were an important vehicle for expressing the aims of the Carolingian state. Charlemagne, like all Carolingian kings, remained a Frankish warlord; when he turned from what he had learned or read to what he could do, the results were violent and unsparing.

In a special capitulary for the Saxon territories, Charlemagne made clear that the church "which was being constructed in Saxony" could be established by his army and imposed on a conquered people under the threat of death. This was "assented to by everyone":

7. If someone should burn the body of a dead man according to the rite of the pagans, reducing his bones to ashes, let him pay with his head.

8. If someone . . . among the Saxons should hide a person in their midst who wants to escape being baptized, and who despises baptism, wanting to remain a pagan, let him be put to death.

9. If someone should sacrifice a man to the devil, or make an offering to demons in the manner of pagans, let him be put to death.[130]

The Christian fanaticism of these laws cannot be reduced to an "ideological cover" for territorial ambitions. A new perspective has been offered by a study of Charlemagne's attempt to end Saxon burial customs.[131] A fundamental conceptual component of Carolingian kingship was its aggressive missionary tone, directed against the dark, chaotic regions of Germany. Frankish warfare was transformed not merely by technologies of supply and organization, but above all by a powerful moral rationale. Missionary warfare found it difficult to vanquish a people so distressingly similar to the ancient Franks: "audacious, swift, and harsh."

---

130. "7. Si quis corpus defuncti hominibus secundum ritum paganorum flamma consumi fecerit et ossa eius ad cinerem redierit, capitae punietur. 8. Si quis deinceps in gente Saxonorum inter eos latens non baptizatus se abscondere voluerit et ad baptismum venire contempserit paganusque permanere voluerit, morte moriatur. 9. Si quis hominem diabulo sacrificaverit et in hostiam more paganorum daemonibus obtulerit, morte moriatur," *Capitulatio de partibus Saxoniae* (775–790), MGH Capit. 1.1: 68–70; see 69.

131. Bonnie Effros, "*De partibus Saxoniae* and the Regulation of Mortuary Custom: A Carolingian Campaign of Christianization or the Suppression of Saxon Identity?" RBPH 75 (1997): 267–86.

The Council of Frankfurt

At Regensburg in 792, a council was held in which these new tendencies of Carolingian kingship coalesced. Only recently this city had been the seat of an independent Bavaria, but was now the center of intense missionary activity in the east and a royal center from which Charles issued with his armies.[132] The council addressed a Spanish heresy, Adoptionism, that had recently come to the notice of the Franks. The assembly burned the writings of its most prominent defenders, Felix of Urgel and Elipandus of Toledo.[133] Felix himself was summoned to the council, where he recanted. Regensburg was the forerunner of a similar project two years later at the Council of Frankfurt. The Council of Regensburg was a portent of the extent to which Frankish bishops, under the guidance of the Sacred Palace, were prepared to turn their missionary zeal toward the cultural integration of the Carolingian Empire.

At this time new compilations of conciliar law were made, gathering the oldest and most authoritative sources of the ancient church and Gallican law.[134] On a trip to Rome in 774, Charlemagne was given a version of the old collection of Dionysius Exiguus, known as the *Dionysio-Hadriana*.[135] It may be that Charles intended to make this a standard, official code of law for the kingdom, although other major collections circulated alongside it.[136] A compilation combining the *Dionysio-Hadriana* with the *Vetus Gallica* was the result of palace-directed reforms around the year 800.[137]

A basic impulse of this cultural movement was to tie the authority of all bishops to a centrally defined orthodoxy, thought of as "Roman."[138] Kingdom-

132. "Ad Reganesburg pervenit et . . . contra iamdictos Avaros esse potuissent" (Anno 788), *Annales regni Francorum,* 84.

133. "Apud Reginum Baioariae civitatem, in qua hiemaverat, residebat,—ubi congregato episcoporum concilio auditus est et errasse convictus" (Anno 792), *Annales regni Francorum,* 91. Noted also in the *Annales mettenses priores* (Anno 792), 79. The Council of Regensburg was also recalled in the *Annals of Maximinianus,* with its harsh conclusion: "libri plurimi Felicis sive Elipandi in eadem herese perduranti combusti sunt" (Anno 792), *Chronicon universale,* 1–25; see 21–22.

134. A collection, to be associated with the Carolingian Renaissance, emulated and expanded the scope of Dionysius Exiguus: Rudolf Schieffer, "Spätantikes Kirchenrecht," 164–91.

135. Wallace-Hadrill, *Frankish Church,* 212; Donald Bullough, "Roman Books and Carolingian *renovatio,*" in his *Carolingian Renewal: Sources and Heritage,* 1–38; see 14 (Manchester: 1991).

136. Yitzhak Hen, "Knowledge of Canon Law among Rural Priests: The Evidence of Two Carolingian Manuscripts from around 800," JTS 50 (1999): 117–34; see 118.

137. Hubert Mordek, "Dionysio-Hadriana und Vetus Gallica—historische geordnetes und systematisches Kirchenrecht am Hofe Karls des Grossen," ZSRG.K 55 (1969): 39–63.

138. Carolingian scholars dreamed that their own liturgy was the same as Roman liturgy:

wide efforts at integration, such as the Council of Frankfurt, were staged and directed from the royal palace to bring this about. By the 780s, the king's personal chaplain, installed in the palace chapel in Aachen, had risen to prominence as "Archbishop of the Sacred Palace," an institutional change reflecting Charlemagne's interventionism, especially in northeastern churches.[139] Because of his unique status and closeness to the king, the chaplain could organize efforts to regularize religious practice throughout the kingdom, especially by means of grand councils.[140] Around twenty kingdom-wide councils were held between 742 and 843.[141]

The Council of Frankfurt in 794 was a major expression of this cultural shift.[142] With this council, it has been suggested, the Carolingian project of combining royal and episcopal power coalesced (as a "crystallization point").[143] Two themes were pursued at Frankfurt, each of which deserves some mention here. First was the tangled problem of religous images, which resulted in the writing of the *Libri Carolini* by Theodulf.[144] This initiative fell apart before the council opened, although its rumblings could still be heard in 794.[145] Then came the battle against the Adoptionism of Felix of Urgel and Elipandus of Toledo, in

---

Bullough, "Roman Books," 8. The *Epistola generalis* (between 786 and 800) and many other texts urged that chanting be done according to Roman tradition: Iégor Reznikoff, "Le chant des gaules sous les carolingiens," in *Haut moyen-âge: Culture, éducation et société: Études offertes à Pierre Riché,* edited by Michel Sot, 323–42 (La Garenne–Colombes: 1990).

139. "Hildebaldus, sacri palatii archiepiscopus": Preface of the Council of Mainz (813), MGH Conc. 2.1:258–73; see also Lesne, *Hiérarchie épiscopale,* 72; Heuclin, *Hommes de Dieu,* 291.

140. Josef Fleckenstein, *Die Hofkapelle der deutschen Könige 1: Grundlegung—Die karolingische Hofkapelle,* Schriften der Monumenta Germaniae historica 16.1 (Stuttgart: 1959), 48–50.

141. Wilfried Hartmann and Detlev Jasper, "Formen und Wege mittelalterlicher Konzilsüberlieferungen," in *Mittelalterliche Textüberlieferungen und ihre kritische Aufarbeitung: Beiträge der Monumenta Germaniae Historica zum 31. deutschen Historikertag, Mannheim 1976,* 42–51; see 43–44 (Munich: 1976). The decisions of Carolingian councils were preserved in a very diffuse manner, ranging from letters of Boniface to the capitularies of the Carolingian kings: Hartmann, "La transmission et l'influence du droit synodal carolingien," RHDr 4th ser. 63 (1985): 483–97; see also Ann Freeman, "Theodulf of Orléans: a Visigoth at Charlemagne's Court," in *L'Europe héritière de l'Éspagne wisigothique,* edited by Jacques Fontaine and Christine Pellistrandi, 185–94, Collection de la Casa de Velázquez 35 (Madrid: 1992).

142. Council of Frankfurt (794), MGH Conc. 2.1:110–71.

143. As emphasized in a recent collection of essays on the Council: *Das Frankfurter Konzil von 794: Kristallisationspunkt karolingischer Kultur,* ed. Rainer Berndt, Quellen und Abhandlungen zur mittelrheinischen Kirchengeschichte 80; 2 vols. (Mainz: 1997). On the combination of royal and episcopal power in the Carolingian state, see Werner, *Naissance de la noblesse,* 360–78.

144. *Opus Caroli regis contra synodum (Libri Carolini),* ed. Ann Freeman, MGH Conc. 2, Suppl. 1 (Hannover: 1998). This edition, restoring the original title, replaces the older edition of Bastgen, although the work will continue to be known as the *Libri Carolini (Libri Carolini, sive Caroli Magni capitulare de imaginibus,* ed. Hubert Bastgen, MGH Conc. 2, *Supplementum*).

145. On the crumbling of this effort, see Ann Freeman, "Scripture and Images," 183–88.

which the imperial Carolingian episcopate sought to crush an alternative regional orthodoxy rooted in the continuity of an ancient see.[146]

Spanish affairs, Visigothic law, political ideas, and theology were conspicuous in the Frankish kingdom. After 711 many Visigothic clerics fled to the Frankish kingdom to escape the Moslem invasion, bringing with them their books, most notably the works of Isidore.[147] The exiles brought collections of Hispanic episcopal legislation, especially from the great see of Toledo. A compilation of these, known as the *Hispana,* enjoyed considerable authority among the Franks and stood alongside the *Dionysio—Hadriana* sent to Charlemagne's court by Pope Hadrian.[148] Further contact with Spanish affairs came with Charlemagne's ill-fated invasion of Spain in 778 and, more importantly, by the creation of a Frankish sphere of influence around Barcelona in the last decade of the eighth century. Another source of Spanish influence was the Christian territory of Asturias, which gradually established its autonomy from the Muslim emirates after a series of rebellions in the 740s.[149] Here the pugnacious monk Beatus of Liebana maintained contacts with Alcuin, drawing the Franks into Spanish theological controversies. The Council of Frankfurt reveals a sense of mastery following victories in Bavaria and against the Avars and the uncompromising attitude of Alcuin and other theologians gathered at Charlemagne's court.[150] These men could confirm their importance by identifying and attacking outsiders.

The intellectual influence of Spanish clerics was everywhere at the Council of Frankfurt in 794. The council was occasioned by the Adoptionist heresy of Elipandus of Toledo and Felix of Urgel, and by the controversy over religious images, which had taken a new and dramatic turn in 787, when the Second Council of Nicaea sanctioned the veneration of icons.[151] The Frankish bishops

---

146. Alba Maria Orselli, "Controversia iconoclastica e crisi del simbolismo in occidente fra VIII e IX secolo," in *Culto delle immagini e crisi iconoclasta* (Palermo: 1986), 93–116; see esp. 96.

147. Jacques Fontaine, "Mozarabie hispanique et monde carolingien: Les èchanges culturels entre la France et l'Espagne du VIIIe au Xe siècle," *Anuario de estudios medievales* 13 (1983): 17–46; see 29.

148. Gaudemet, *Sources du droit de l'Église,* 160; see also Abilio Barbero de Aguilera, *La sociedad visigoda y su entorno histórico* (Madrid: 1992), 88–92.

149. Collins, *Early Medieval Spain,* 228–30.

150. On the awkward position of Alcuin: Heuclin, *Hommes de Dieu,* 316–23; see also Donald Bullough, "Alcuin before Frankfort," *Frankfurter Konzil,* 2:571–85. According to John Marenbon, Alcuin was without influence, and responsible for almost nothing, until some time after the council: Marenbon, "Alcuin, the Council of Frankfort, and the Beginnings of Medieval Philosophy," *Frankfurter Konzil,* 2:603–15. See the discussion of Alcuin's impact in John C. Cavadini, *The Last Christology of the West: Adoptionism in Spain and Gaul, 785–820* (Philadelphia: 1993), 88–102.

151. On Frankfurt 794, see Hartmann, *Synoden der Karolingerzeit,* 105–15; and Classen, *Karl der Grosse, das Papsttum,* 35–36.

felt secure in their apostolic authority and intellectual ability to hand down universal teachings in theology.

Reprehensible Things

The 263 bishops gathered at II Nicaea (787) restored the cult of images in the eastern church after nearly forty years of official iconoclasm.[152] Pope Hadrian sent letters to the council expounding his doctrines on the veneration of saints and the use of images in worship, which were read aloud and approved. Because the council had involved the bishop of Rome as well as the ancient Mediterranean sees, II Nicaea (787) declared itself to be the Seventh Ecumenical Council. Hadrian had a hand in producing the definition (*Horos*) that was accepted by the council, and he certainly agreed with its results.[153]

Stating that "he who venerates the image venerates the person represented in that image," the Council of Nicaea urged a resumption of the artistic representation of Christ, Mary, and other saints. The council's decisions were consistent with a doctrine the popes had maintained in the face of eastern iconoclasm since the Council of Rome (769). It was again declared that Iconoclasm violated the doctrine of Incarnation. According to II Nicaea: "If anyone does not confess that Christ our God can be represented in his humanity, let him be anathema."[154]

The Franks received a Latin translation of the proceedings of II Nicaea and its rehabilitation of the veneration of icons.[155] The translation made it appear that II Nicaea had insisted that worship (*adoratio*) should be directed to religious images.[156] In spite of Hadrian's approval, the Franks viewed the council with suspicion.[157] The *Libri Carolini* was therefore the result of a misunderstanding,

152. For the background of these disputes, see Ambrosius Giakalis, *Images of the Divine: The Theology of Icons at the Seventh Ecumenical Council,* Studies in the History of Christian Thought 54 (Leiden: 1994), 1–21.

153. Council of Nicaea (787), Mansi, 12:951–1154; now see the new critical edition: *Concilium Universale Nicaenum Secundum Concilii actiones I–III,* vol. 3, *Acta Conciliorum Oecumenicorum sub auspiciis Academiae Scientiarum Bavaricae,* ed. Erich Lamberz, 2nd ser. pt.1 (Berlin: 2008). The *Horos* can also be found in *Nicée II, 787–1987: Douze siècles d'images religieuses—Actes du colloque international Nicée II . . . Octobre 1986,* ed. François Bœspflug and Nicolas Lossky (Paris: 1987), 31–35. A critical edition: Jean Baptiste, Cardinal Pitra, *Juris ecclesiastici Græcorum historia et monumenta,* 2 vols. (Rome: 1864–1868).

154. *Decrees of the Ecumenical Councils,* 136–37; Giakalis, *Images of the Divine,* 93–113.

155. Heinz Ohme, "Ikonen, historische Kritik und Tradition: Das VII. ökumenische Konzil (787) und die kirchliche Überlieferung," ZKG 110 (1999): 1–24.

156. G. Adriányi, "Rezeptionsprobleme bezüglich des Zweiten Konzils von Nizäa in der karolingischen zeit," in *Streit um das Bild: Das Zweite Konzil von Nizäa (787) in ökumenischer Perspective,* edited by Joseph Wohlmuth, 59–66, Studium Universale 9 (Bonn: 1989).

157. Erich Lamberz, "Studien zur Überlieferung der Akten des VII. Ökumenischen Konzils: Der Brief Hadrians I. an Konstantin VI. und Irene (JE 2448)," DA 53 (1997): 1–43.

in the view of Ann Freeman.[158] This assumes that a stable theological vocabulary distinguished worship or adoration (*adoratio*) from veneration (*veneratio*), but such was not the case. Pope Hadrian himself used the Latin terms interchangeably. A heightening of cultural and theological distinctions accompanied the Carolingian drive toward consensus, which is what gave these Latin words, and the entire issue, such a divisive quality. Theodulf, an intellectual luminary at Aachen, thereby found a ready means of playing a major role at the council to be held in Frankfurt.[159]

As the council was in preparation, the bishops began, without the lead of Rome, to prepare a counterblow against the eastern church, somewhat hobbled by the fact that their position on images was opposed to that of Hadrian.[160] According to the *Annals of Lorsch,* the Council of Frankfurt (794) was a "universal synod," meeting with the help and approbation of Pope Hadrian.[161] The *Moissac Chronicle* affirmed the universal nature of Frankfurt and recorded its attack on II Nicaea.[162] According to the *Earlier Annals of Metz,* the Council of Frankfurt rejected "what the pseudo-synod of the Greeks, falsely called the Seventh, enacted in regard to adoring images."[163] Such bitterness toward an orthodox ecumenical council is striking evidence of Frankish parochialism. Historical writing such as we find in these annals was never mere reportage, but was freighted with political interests. As Patzold rightly points out, the annals were part of complex debates and discussions among the powerful. The audience for such annals was not only monks and priests, but the palace and lay nobility.[164] Clearly there was a shared sense of outrage about the Byzantines.

The question of religious images touched on the overarching themes of a sa-

158. Ann Freeman, "Scripture and Images," 166–67.

159. Barbero de Aguilera, *La sociedad visigoda,* 122–23; Ann Freeman, "Carolingian Orthodoxy and the Fate of the Libri Carolini," *Viator* 16 (1985): 65–108; Freeman, "Further Studies in the Libri Carolini," *Speculum* 40 (1965): 203–89; Freeman, "Theodulf of Orléans and the Libri Carolini," *Speculum* 32 (1957): 663–705; see also Celia Chazelle, "Matter, Spirit and Image in the Libri Carolini," *Recherches Augustiniennes* 21 (1986): 163–84; Donald Bullough, "Alcuin and the Kingdom of Heaven: Liturgy, Theology and the Carolingian Age," in *Carolingian Essays,* 1–69, esp. 31–39.

160. Wilfried Hartmann, "Das Konzil von Frankfurt 794 und Nizäa 787," AHC 20 (1988): 307–24; Hans Barion, "Der Kirchenrechtliche Charakter der Konzils von Frankfurt 794," ZSRG.K 19 (1930): 139–70.

161. "In estivo tempore congregavit universalem synodum cum missis domni apostolici Adriani" (Anno 794), *Annales Laureshamenses,* 36.

162. "Allata est etiam in eadem synodo quaestio de nova Graecorum synodo, quam de adorandis sanctorum imaginibus Constantinopolim fecerant" (Anno 794), *Chronicon Moissiacense,* 301.

163. "Pseudosinodus Grecorum, quam falso septimam vocabant, pro adorandis imaginibus fecerunt, reiecta est a pontificibus" (Anno 794), *Annales Mettenses priores,* 80.

164. Patzold, *Episcopus,* 49.

cralized Carolingian state in which no line was drawn between imperial politics and religious politics; for this reason Charlemagne was ready to back the efforts of scholars like Theodulf with his own authority and resources.[165]

Theodulf theologized with a hammer. The *Libri Carolini* argued relentlessly against religious images, based on a theology of the Holy Spirit. Theodulf presented an enormous array of citations from late antique Christian authors, marking a sophisticated departure from the standards of Merovingian scholarship. He used Charlemagne's royal library, books in the monastery of St. Emmeram, and his own collection, probably brought from Spain. The rhetorical skill of the *Libri Carolini* parallels the revival by Carolingian scholars of dialectic, grammar, and the art of commentary.[166] Like many other bishops, Theodulf was cultivating patristic studies to a considerable degree, and in these regards was very characteristic representative of Carolingian educational ideals.[167]

The writings of Augustine, Isidore, and other authorities of the past were newly situated in this imperial-conciliar expression of power.[168] For Theodulf and his colleagues, the Carolingian Empire was the localization of universal authority:

If the bishops of two or three provinces gather together [Frankfurt?] and—strengthened by the institution of the ancient canons—they establish something in regard to dogma or preaching, which moreover does not deviate from the dogma of the ancient Fathers, what they do is catholic, and perchance can be called universal. This is because, although it were not performed by the bishops of the whole world, nevertheless, it did not deviate from the faith and tradition of everyone (*universorum*).

Now, if this synod [II Nicaea] lacked profane new voices, and was content with the

165. Jacques Le Goff, "Le Christianisme médiéval en occident du Concile de Nicée (325) à la Réforme (début du XVIe siècle)," in *Histoire des religions,* edited by Henri-Charles Puech (Paris: 1970–1976), 2:749–868, esp. 794; see also Werner Ohnsorge, "Orthodoxus Imperator: Vom religiösen Motiv für das Kaisertum Karls des Grossen," repr. in his *Abendland und Byzanz: Gesammelte Aufsätze zur Geschichte der byzantinisch-abendländischen Beziehungen und des Kaisertums,* 64–78 (Darmstadt: 1958); Ann Freeman, "Scripture and Images," 184–85.

166. Ann Freeman, Introduction to *Opus Caroli regis,* 50; Bernhard Bischoff, *Manuscripts and Libraries in the Age of Charlemagne,* trans. Michael Gorman (Cambridge: 1994), 98–100. On Theodulf's rhetoric: Freeman, "Theodulf of Orléans: A Visigoth," 189; Ann Freeman, Introduction to *Opus Caroli regis,* 56–60.

167. Michael E. Moore, "Carolingian Bishops and Christian Antiquity: Distance from the Past, Canon-Formation, and Imperial Power," in *Learned Antiquity: Scholarship and Society in the Near-East, the Greco-Roman World, and the Early Medieval West,* edited by Alaisdair A. MacDonald, Michael W. Twomey, and Gerrit J. Reinink, 175–84 (Leuven: 2003); Luitpold Wallach, "The *Libri Carolini* and Patristics, Latin and Greek," in his *Diplomatic Studies in Latin and Greek Documents from the Carolingian Age* (Ithaca: 1977), 59–122.

168. Moore, "Ancient Fathers," 335–40, suggests that a new imperial vision of the Christian past is reflected in the Libri Carolini.

dogma of the ancient fathers, it might be called universal. However, it was not content with the dogma of the ancient Fathers, and therefore cannot be called universal.[169]

The papal legates attending the council must have been aghast at the *Libri Carolini,* and they probably prevented the Franks from issuing the book under the authority of the council. Nevertheless, the Franks believed that they had overturned II Nicaea.[170]

An Angel, an Arrow, an Eagle

Felix of Urgel, whose see had also come under Frankish control, was summoned to the Council of Regensburg in 792. Defending his colleague Felix, Elipandus of Toledo sent two letters explaining his views on the nature of Christ.[171] The letters were read publicly before an assembly of presbyters, deacons, and other clerics, seated in a circle around their king (*in modum coronae*). When it had been read, Charlemagne leaped up from his throne in a rage:

How does it seem to you? It has been a year now since the insanity of this disease has been spreading out in a swelling ulcer of treachery. The error has grown especially in those regions at the extreme limits of our kingdom, and it is necessary with the censure of faith to cut it out by any means.[172]

This image of the old warrior Charlemagne enraged by a theological doctrine shows that he and his bishops had found a means of communication and joint action.

The unhappy Felix[173] was summoned a second time, to attend the Council of Frankfurt in 794. There are many points of contact between the council's at-

169. "Cum ergo duarum et trium provinciarum praesules in unum conveniunt, si antiquorum canonum institutione muniti aliquid praedicationis aut dogmatis statuunt, quod tamen ab antiquorum Patrum dogmatibus non discrepat, catholicum est, quod faciunt, et fortasse dici potest universale; quoniam, quamvis non sit ab universi orbis praesulibus actum, tamen ab universorum fide et traditione non discrepant," *Opus Caroli regis,* 557; "Nam si haec synodus vocum novitatibus careret et antiquorum patrum dogmatibus contenta esset, universalis dici poterat. Non autem antiquorum patrum dogmatibus contenta est, non igitur universalis dici potest," *Opus Caroli regis,* 557–58.

170. Council of Frankfurt (794), MGH Conc. 2.1:165.

171. Council of Frankfurt (794), MGH Conc. 2.1:111–19; 120–21.

172. "Cumque iubente rege publica voce recitata fuisset, statimque surgens venerabilis princeps de sella regia stetit supra gradum suum, adlocutus est de causa fidaei prolixo sermone et adiecit: 'Quid vobis videtur? Ab anno prorsus praeterito et ex quo coepit huius pestis insania tumescente perfidiae ulcu diffusius ebullisse, non parvus in his regionibus, licet in extremis finibus regni nostri, error inolevit, quem censura fidaei necesse est modis omnibus resecare,'" Council of Frankfurt (794), MGH Conc. 2.1:131.

173. This pun on the name Felix ("happy") was offered by Paulinus of Aquileia, Council of Frankfurt (794), MGH Conc. 2.1:135.

tack on Elipandus and the *Libri Carolini*. In both cases the Franks presented themselves as the chief defenders of "Roman" Catholicism.[174]

Since 711, nearly all of Spain had come under Muslim control, and Christians were forced to accommodate their new rulers. To other European Christians it seemed that the Visigoths had been punished by a judgment of God for their sins: Boniface, as was mentioned, had warned Aethelbald that he might face the same fate if he did not adhere to Christian norms.[175] After the passage of eighty years, the Spanish bishops now saw their Muslim milieu in a very different light, and had reached a *modus vivendi*. The immediate background of the Adoptionist controversy was this difference of perception between clerics within the Emirate and those without.[176]

Elipandus' see of Toledo lay within the Emirate of Cordoba. A Frankish missionary named Egila joined forces with the followers of Migetius, an inflexible opponent of conciliation with the Muslims and a thinker of doubtful orthodoxy. In contending with these men, Elipandus worked out his views on the nature of Christ, explaining that Christ had *adopted* human nature in the Incarnation. He first elaborated this doctrine in a letter to Migetius.[177]

The letter read before Charlemagne and the bishops assembled at Regensburg in 792 was probably the result of a council held in Toledo by Elipandus. It was directed from the bishops of Spain "to all the reverend fraternal bishops of Gaul, Aquitaine, and Austria."[178] Beatus of Liebana, one of the inflexibles, brought Elipandus to the attention of the Frankish Church. The Spanish bishops returned the favor by calling Beatus "that abominable presbyter of Asturias, pseudo-Christ and pseudo-prophet" with his "snake-like preaching of a pestilential dogma."[179] Spanish episcopal doctrine, the letter went on, was in full accord with patristic tradition, namely with Hilary, Ambrose, Augustine, Jerome, Fulgentius of Ruspe, Isidore, Eugenius, Ildefonse, and Julian.[180] It is interesting

---

174. Barbero de Aguilera, *La sociedad visigoda*, 118–21.

175. Boniface to King Aethelbald (746–747), *S. Bonifatii et Lullii epistolae*, Letter 73:151.

176. Cavadini, *Last Christology*, 10–23.

177. There is a useful summary in Collins, *Early Medieval Spain*, 208–10; see also Knut Schäferdiek, "Der adoptianische Streit im Rahmen der spanischen Kirchengeschichte," Part I—ZKG 80 (1969): 291–311; Part II—ZKG 81 (1970): 1–16; see Part I:297; Elipandus to Migetius, PL 96:864; see Cavadini, *Last Christology*, 22.

178. "Reverentissimis fratribus Galliae adque Equitanie adque Austrie cunctis sacerdotibus nos indigni et exigui Spanie praesules," Council of Frankfurt (794), MGH Conc. 2.1:111. This letter is discussed in Cavadini, *Last Christology*, 31–38.

179. "Nefandi Asturiensis presbyteri, pseudochristi et pseudoprophete, pestiferi dogmatis sermo viperous," Council of Frankfurt (794), MGH Conc. 2.1:111.

180. Council of Frankfurt (794), MGH Conc. 2.1:111.

how this list of authorities connected thinkers of the distant past to the traditions of Elipandus' own church in Toledo.[181] But the Franks were developing a different, imperial understanding of episcopal authority. The patristic basis of Elipandus' position earned him no sympathy from the Franks.[182]

Elipandus declared that his doctrines were supported by "an immense wave of Scripture."[183] He had inherited his theology from "our predecessors Eugenius, Ildefonse and Julian, bishops of the see of Toledo."[184] The center of his intellectual framework was Toledo and the traditions of the Visigothic church. Elipandus explained that his illustrious predecessors had enshrined their orthodox faith in the liturgy of Toledo.[185] Thus he tried to make clear that his theology was "strengthened by the assertions of the holy Fathers, in no way deviating from the vestiges of their decrees."[186]

As a bishop, Elipandus believed that he had an incontrovertible right to speak about the nature of Christ, and that the Council of Regensburg was abridging his episcopal rights. After all, many terms were applied to Christ in the Bible, so why should his own speech be condemned?

I doubt very much if it is contrary or a blasphemy to say that the Son of God was adopted in the form of a slave, because sometimes he is called a lion, sometimes a cub-lion, sometimes a calf, sometimes a sheep or a lamb . . . a sacrifice . . . a prince and a priest, a man and a prophet, a virgin, a flower, a root, a judge and a king, a just man and justice, apostle and bishop, an arm, a slave, ointment, pastor, boy, first-born, a door, an angel, an arrow, an eagle.[187]

181. Roger E. Reynolds, "The Visigothic Liturgy in the Realm of Charlemagne," *Frankfurter Konzil*, 2:919–45; see 920.

182. John C. Cavadini, "Elipandus and His Critics at the Council of Frankfort," *Frankfurter Konzil*, 2:787–807.

183. "His exemtis, que de inmenso scripturarum pelage," Council of Frankfurt (794), MGH Conc. 2.1:118.

184. "Item precessores nostri Eugenius, Hildefonsus, Iulianus, Toletane sedis antistites, in suis dogmatibus," Council of Frankfurt (794), MGH Conc. 2.1:113.

185. "Qui per adobtivi hominis passionem, dum suo non indulgit corpora," was a citation from the Mozarabic liturgy: Council of Frankfurt (794) MGH Conc. 2.1:113.

186. "His premissis sanctorum patrum sententiis assertionibus nostris roborati, in commune decrevimus ab eorum decretis nullo modo deviare vestigiis," Council of Frankfurt (794), MGH Conc. 2.1:114.

187. "Si contrarium est aut blasfemum dicere filium Dei secundum formam servi adobtibum, procul dubio, quod dici nefas est, et illut blasfemum erit, quod aliquando leo, aliquando catulus leonis, aliquando vitulus, aliquando ovis sive agnus, victima, hostia, sacrificium, olocaustum, pro diversa varietate causarum princeps et sacerdos, homo et profeta, virga et flos et radix, iudex et rex, iustus et iustitia, apostolus et episcopus, bracium, servus, unguentum, pastor, puer, primogenitus, ostium, angelus, sagitta, Aquila," Council of Frankfurt (794), MGH Conc. 2.1:118.

His language regarding the nature of Christ was biblical, traditional, and authentically patristic.[188] The perspective of Elipandus was grounded in the old Cyprianic model of local episcopal independence and authority. The Frankish bishops had abandoned the ancient concept of local authority in favor of kingdom-wide integration. According to Elipandus, Charlemagne had turned from religious and military triumph toward something unworthy of his fame. Indeed, Elipandus scoffed, "it is said that you compel many by the terror of power (*terror potestatis*), not by justice."[189]

Elipandus' letters triggered an intense reaction. Copies were sent to Pope Hadrian, who sent his own reply to the Spanish bishops. At the Council of Frankfurt, bishops from the Frankish territories in Lombardy produced their own response, as did the Frankish bishops. Finally, a letter was produced, perhaps by the palace chapel, to reflect Charlemagne's own answer to Elipandus. All these documents were part of a coordinated effort of the Frankish bishops, court intellectuals, and their king.

The bishops assembled in Frankfurt often mentioned the importance of Charlemagne's role, "sitting with and helping us."[190] Yet only conciliar authority could quash Elipandus' ideas and bind him with anathema. Charlemagne's letter explained to Elipandus that "the texts of your little books were read, with the careful counsel of many . . . by ecclesiastical doctors and the rectors of the Christian people."[191] According to the letter of Charlemagne, the Council of Frankfurt spoke for the entire church:

The most certain help of divine mercy will be here, where there is one charity and one confession of true faith for the whole church. You [Elipandus] adverted to the multitude of the Christian people and the unanimity of priestly council. If indeed we do

188. The "names of Christ" that Elipandus recorded were ancient and traditional. A full-scale *summa* of this tradition was compiled by Luis de León, *De los nombres de Cristo* (1583): "León y cordero; Puerta y Camino, y Pastor y Sacerdote, y Sacrificio y Esposo, y Vid y Pimpollo, y Rey de Dios y Cara suya, y Piedra y Lucero, y Oriente y Padre, y Principe de Paz y Salud, y así otros nombres sin cuento," *Obras completas castellanas de Fray Luis de León,* ed. Felix Garcia (Madrid: 1967), 1:401–864; see 425. Many of these names were recorded as early as the pseudo-Gelasian Decretal—overlapping Elipandus in naming Christ a "prophet, lion, flower, angel, lamb and priest"; Pseudo-Gelasius, *Das Decretum Gelasianum de libris recipiendis et non recipiendis,* ed. Ernst von Dobschütz, TU 38.4 (Leipzig: 1912), 3–4.

189. "Nam dicitur, quod terrore potestatis multos, non iustitia convinces," Council of Frankfurt (794), MGH Conc. 2.1:121.

190. "Adsedente et auxiliante nobis," Council of Frankfurt (794), MGH Conc. 2.1:143.

191. "Libelli vestri legeretur textus et perscrutante plurimorum consilio, quid in eo rectae fidaei sanctionibus consentiens inveniretur, fecimus sicut petistis, collectis undique, veluti praefati sumus, ecclesiasticis doctoribus et populi Christiani rectoribus," Council of Frankfurt (794), MGH Conc. 2.1:161.

not doubt that the Lord is present, according to his promise, in the holy and pious consensus of two or three, then how much more is he present where so many very holy fathers, so many venerable brothers, so many sons of the holy mother church gather in concord in his peaceful name.[192]

The Council of Frankfurt (794) and the *Libri Carolini* asserted that the Frankish Church could define orthodoxy based in part on expertise in patristics and in part on imperial coordination. Among the authors cited are Augustine, Ambrose, Gregory, Jerome, Leo, Cassiodorus, Isidore, Faustus, Hilarius, Cyril, and Athanasius.

Should we interpet all this as "political Augustinianism"? According to Charlemagne's letter, the City of Christ was centered in its bishops: the "fighters for our faith, the rectors throughout different sees of the City of Christ. Within its wall is the catholic faith."[193] Bishops guarded this City:

Over this City, the true Son of God himself . . . presides with royal power, and whose grace rules, defends, and exalts the whole structure of this City. Whoever wishes to come to this City, let him hurry, led by his faith, his hands very full of good works.[194]

Over this City the bishops had the power of inclusion and exclusion. Entry into the City could be gained only by traveling the *via regia* of orthodox faith, turning "neither right nor left."[195]

The Frankish bishops rebuked Elipandus for his argument from the traditions of Toledo. If his predecessors taught that Jesus was "adopted," then "it was clear what kind of predecessors you had, so that everyone may know why you were given over to the hands of the infidels."[196] The Muslim conquest of Spain was a punishment for the heterodoxy of Toledo!

192. "Certissimum itaque ibi erit divinae miserationis auxilium, ubi una est totius ecclesiae caritas et una verae fidaei confessio. Ad multitudinem populi Christiani et ad concilii sacerdotalis unanimitatem revertimini. Si enim duorum vel trium sancto pioque consensui secundum suam promissionem Dominum esse praesentem non dubitamus, quanto magis ubi tot sanctissimi patres, tot venerabiles fratres, tot filii piae matris ecclesiae in nomine illius pacifica conveniunt unanimitate," Council of Frankfurt (794), MGH Conc. 2.1:162.

193. "Hi sunt propugnatores fidaei nostae, hi sunt rectores per diversas sedes civitatis Christi. Cuius antemurale est fides catholica," Council of Frankfurt (794), MGH Conc. 2.1:160.

194. "Huius vero civitatis ipse Dei verus et proprius filius, Deus verus, homo verus, Iesus Christus, dominus noster, regali praesidet potentia, cuius gratia totam illius civitatis structuram regit, defendit et exaltat. Quisquis ad hanc civitatem, recta sibi praeviante fide, manus bonorum operum habens plenissimas, pervenire festinate," Council of Frankfurt (794), MGH Conc. 2.1:160–61.

195. "Et non declinemus ad dexteram neque ad sinistram, sed per viam regiam ad regem et redemptorem," Council of Frankfurt (794), MGH Conc. 2.1:159.

196. "Ut manifestum sit, quales habeatis parentes, et ut notum sit omnibus, unde vos traditi sitis in manus infidelium," Council of Frankfurt (794), MGH Conc. 2.1:145.

Theological unity was considered to be vital to the central task of the Frankish Church: missionary expansion to the east. Italian bishops, under Paulinus of Aquileia, connected the attack on Adoptionism to their missionary calling in terms quite similar to their counterparts in Bavaria:

Omnipotent God, by the declaration of his infinite power, subdues the barbaric nations so that in this way they might come to recognition of truth and know their true Creator and living God. Truly regenerated in the waters of baptism, they are gathered to the breast of mother church, so that they might complete what good pastor had promised, saying: And I will have other sheep, which are not from this flock.[197]

The Council of Frankfurt (794) was a decisive transfer of episcopal authority. No longer reflecting the regional collegiality of aristocratic networks or the local authority of regional traditions, this council assembled an imperial episcopate under the direction of the palace and its intellectuals.

The important role Charlemagne played in calling the Council of Frankfurt placed him squarely within the City of Christ, surrounded by his bishops. It was a grand position, providing orientation for his political action. The council was an institutional location for the reification of social ideals. The Frankish Church's involvement in worldwide struggles over theology lent a crucial theoretical basis for Charlemagne's territorial expansionism. Royal and episcopal interests coalesced around the themes of "reform" and "missionary activity."

The Caesar-Name

Charlemagne had united a vast territory for which some poets and scholars began to adopt the name *Europa*.[198] Even to a wary outsider like Elipandus it seemed that the Frankish realm should be called an empire.[199] Around the year 775, Charlemagne received a letter from from the otherwise unknown Cathwulf. It has been suggested that the author was a scholar attached to the Abbey of St. Denis.[200] It can also be said that Cathwulf's ideas are extremely close to

---

197. "Barbaras etiam nationes infinita Deus omnipotens ditioni eius potentia subdat, ut ex hac occasione ad agnitionem perveniant veritatis et cognoscant verum et vivum Deum creatorem suum. Regenerati siquidem unda baptismatis in graemio adgregentur matris ecclesiae, ut impleatur quod bonus pastor promiserat dicens: Et alias oves habeo, quae non sunt ex hoc ovili," Council of Frankfurt (794), MGH Conc. 2.1:141. Compare the *Libri Carolini,* 21.

198. Karl J. Leyser, "Concepts of Europe in the Early and High Middle Ages," *Past and Present* 137 (1992): 25–47; see 32–33.

199. "Et oratio servorum tuorum imperii vestri culmen exaltet," Council of Frankfurt (794), MGH Conc. 2.1:121.

200. A reconstruction of the place and author of the work: Joanna Storey, "Cathwulf, Kingship, and the Royal Abbey of Saint-Denis," *Speculum* 74 (1999): 1–21.

the Irish doctrine of the *Twelve Abuses*.[201] Charlemagne's victories were interpreted as a sign that God himself had exalted Charles to his kingship over Europe. Cathwulf urged him to glorify God for this blessing.[202] Cathwulf further reminded him:

you stand in His place, to rule and protect all His members, and an account will be sought from you on the day of judgment. And the bishop is next to you, standing in the place of Christ. Therefore diligently consider between you how to establish the law of God over the people of God.[203]

Walter Ullmann famously argued that the Franks saw themselves as "the people of God," as in some way the successors of the ancient Hebrews.[204] By the "people of God" Cathwulf meant the church, and his letter implied that the church could be identified with a kingdom.[205] Cathwulf's letter was consistent with the thinking of Boniface and other missionary bishops. The letter signaled the transfiguration of Frankish kingship, as it was invested with layer upon layer of significance.

On Christmas Day, 800, Charles was dressed in Roman imperial garments at the request of Pope Leo III. Wearing a long, sleeved tunic, over which was thrown a short military cloak (*chlamys*), Charles was crowned as "Emperor of the Romans."[206] No doubt Charlemagne wished to be seen as the equal of the Byzantine emperors, in line with the principle "two empires, two Romes." The coronation ritual was newly devised, but based on Byzantine accession ceremo-

201. Michael E. Moore, "La monarchie carolingienne et les anciens modèles irlandais," *Annales* 51 (1996): 307–32.

202. Cathwulf's Letter to Charlemagne: *Cathuulfus Carolo I Francorum regi prosperitatem gratulatur eumque ad uirtutem sequendam admonet,* edited by Ernst Dümmler, is printed in MGH Epp. 4.2:502–5; see 503. "Ipse te exaltavit in honorem glorie regni Europe"; see also McCormick, *Eternal Victory,* 360.

203. "Quod tu es in vice illius super omnia membra eius custodire et regere, et rationem reddere in die iudicii, etiam per te. Et episcopus est in secundo loco, in vice Christi tantum est. Ergo considerate inter vos diligenter legem Dei constituere super populum Dei," Cathwulf, MGH Epp. 4.2:503.

204. Walter Ullmann, *The Carolingian Renaissance*, 19–20; this was also the view of Wallace-Hadrill, *Frankish Church,* 226–57.

205. "Memor esto ergo semper, rex mi, Dei regis tui cum timore et amore," Cathwulf, MGH Epp. 4.2:503.

206. "Peregrina vero indumenta, quamvis pulcherrima, respuebat nec umquam eis indui patiebatur, excepto quod Romae semel Hadriano pontifice petente et iterum Leone successore eius supplicante longa tunica et clamide amictus, calceis quoque Romano more formatis induebatur" (c. 23), Einhard, *Vita Karoli Magni,* 28; Peter Classen, "*Romanum gubernans imperium:* Zur Vorgeschichte der Kaisertitulatur Karl des Grossen," DA 9 (1951): 103–21. Folz and others tend to follow the account of the *Annales Laureshamenses,* ed. G. H. Pertz, MGH SS 1 (Hannover: 1826), 22–30.

nies and thought of as old.[207] Political desires of the papacy, first made clear in the *Donation of Constantine,* must have played a central role in this innovation.[208] By means of this ceremony, the pope, as a Priest-king, anointed Charles as a King-priest, just as Samuel had anointed David.[209] The author of the *Royal Frankish Annals* believed the coronation was the revival of an ancient ceremony.[210] The "conceptual transfer" of episcopal concepts to royal power had reached a high point.[211] Thus ended a search going back to the Merovingian era, the writings of Isidore, and the Visigothic theocracy for mutuality and parallelism between royal and episcopal power.

Before long, Carolingian historians would discover an imperial quality to Charlemagne's predecessors going back to the mayors of the palace.[212] Henry Mayr-Harting has argued that Charlemagne adopted the title to make legitimate sense of his rule over the Saxons (since they had no kingship he could assume).[213] However, the Rome to which the Franks looked was the Rome of orthodoxy and the See of Peter. The Frankish Church, now identified with its society and hence the borders of Charlemagne's empire, could wield this orthodox tradition under its own authority. Bishops looked to the king and clerics of the palace chapel as the organizational center of this church.[214] The significance of Charles' coronation as emperor was soon brought home to the Frankish kingdom in an edict directed to the *missi dominici* in 802, the so-called *Programmatic Capitulary.* Every man, "whether an ecclesiastic or a layman," was required to take a new oath to Charles in his imperial *persona,* despite their previous oaths to him as king. With the coronation, Charles had reached for a new *nomen,* the "Caesar-name."[215] Characteristically, the first clause of the law insisted on justice and protection of the poor.[216]

---

207. On the importance of the Byzantine model: Van Caenegem, *De Instellingen,* 1:86–87; Tellenbach, *Römischer und christlicher Reichsgedanke,* 29–33; Robert Folz, *Le couronnement impérial de Charlemagne, 25 Décembre 800,* Trente journees qui ont fait la France 3 (Paris: 1964), 171.

208. Folz, *Le couronnement,* 128–33.

209. Classen, *Karl der Grosse,* 54–57; Folz, *Le couronnement,* 118–20.

210. "More antiquorum principum" (Anno 801), *Annales regni Francorum,* 112.

211. To refer once more to Assmann's term *"Umbuchung":* Assmann, *Herrschaft und Heil,* 50.

212. As in the *Annales Mettenses Priores;* see the commentary of Fouracre and Gerberding, *Late Merovingian France,* 340–43.

213. Henry Mayr-Harting, "Charlemagne, the Saxons, and the Imperial Coronation of 800," EHR 111 (1996): 1113–33.

214. Walter Ullmann, *Carolingian Renaissance,* 55–60.

215. "Preceptique, ut omni homo in toto regno suo . . . nunc ipsum promissum nominis cesaris faciat," *Capitulare missorum generale* (802), MGH Capit. 1.1:91–99; Collins, *Charlemagne,* 154; on the imperial titles adopted by Charles: Werner, *Naissance de la noblesse,* 280–82.

216. "Pauperibus, pupilis et viduis adque cuncto populo legem pleniter adque iustitia exhiberent secundum voluntatem et timorem Dei," *Capitulare missorum generale* (802) MGH Capit. 1.1:92.

By 800, the Franks had reestablished the organization of their church under archbishoprics. None of these bishops had the authority to call the series of great kingdom-wide councils that now took place. The king could do this, aided by the scholars and clerics gathered at his court in Aachen. This court, viewed as an ecclesiastical institution, was frequently referred to as "the Sacred Palace," from which issued calls for councils and circulars, such as those calling for the investigation of baptismal practice, eliciting answers from around the kingdom.[217] Frankfurt (794) affirmed the episcopal status of the palace chaplain, a post that upon Fulrad's death in 784 had been filled by the canonist Angilramn and then, from 791, by Hildebald of Cologne.[218] The Sacred Palace then staged a series of grand councils beyond anything attempted by the popes in Rome.

In 813, under the direction of the most important clerics of the kingdom, including Chaplain Hildebald, Arno of Salzburg, and Theodulf of Orléans, a series of five councils were held to address various issues of ecclesiastical and social reform in a highly coordinated way.[219] Held in Arles, Rheims, Mainz, Chalons, and Tours, the Five Councils of 813 attempted to bring as many bishops of the realm as possible into the discussion of topics issued by the Sacred Palace.[220] The idea for these councils had its inception in the disastrous and gloomy year 810, marked by eclipses and invasion by foreign enemies. Tribute was paid to the Norse in Frisia. Charles thought that he must act, and this was set in motion with a period of fasting and prayer for aid.

Two capitularies from this period document preparations for this impressive initiative: the *Capitula de causis cum episcopis et abbatibus tractandis* and the *Capitula tractanda cum comitibus episcopis et abbatibus.*[221] The *Moissac Chronicle* relates further that after the five councils met, the "bishops, abbots, counts and

---

217. Susan A. Keefe, "Carolingian Baptismal Expositions: A Handlist of Tracts and Manuscripts," in *Carolingian Essays,* 169–237; see esp. 174–75. Amalarius of Metz, the learned archbishop of Trier authored one of these replies, in 812: Wolfgang Steck, *Der Liturgiker Amalarius—Eine Quellenkritische Untersuchung zu Leben und Werk eines Theologen der Karolingerzeit,* Münchener theologische Studien, Hist. Abteilung 35 (Munich: 2000), 1–10.

218. "Deprecatus est eadem synodum, ut eo modo, sicut Angilramnum habuerat, ita etiam Hildeboldum episcopum habere debuisset, quia et de eodem, sicut et de Angilramnum, apostolicam licentiam habebat," Council of Frankfurt (794), MGH Conc. 2.1:171; see also Riché, *Carolingians,* 126.

219. Hartmann, *Synoden der Karolingerzeit,* 128–40.

220. Council of Arles (813), MGH Conc. 2.1:248–53; Council of Rheims (813), MGH Conc. 2.1: 253–58; Council of Mainz (813), MGH Conc. 2.1:258–73; Council of Chalon (813), MGH Conc. 2.1:273–85; Council of Tours (813), MGH Conc. 2.1:286–93.

221. *Capitula de causis cum episcopis et abbatibus tractandis,* (811), 162–64. The connection between the Five Councils and the troubles of 810 and these capitularies is discussed by Patzold, *Episcopus,* 74.

nobles of the Franks" came together in a great gathering at Aachen (*magnum conventum*), the result of which was a single, massive capitulary issued by the bishops. Selections from the canons were then issued as royal law.[222]

This procedure was an innovation by a church seeking the most effective means of forging a consensus among its members and of strengthening the ties between bishops and their king. The religious character of Charlemagne was evident to the bishops. The bishops who met in Mainz under Hildebald, Archbishop of Cologne, Richulf of Mainz, and Arno of Salzburg assembled after a three-day fast and prayers in the basilica of St. Alban the Martyr and announced that the council would profit the "Christian people."[223] The council thanked God that the church had "so pious and devoted a rector, revealing in their time a fountain of sacred wisdom."[224] The bishops understood Charlemagne's war-like expansion of Christianity as a tireless effort "to free the souls of many from the jaws of the dire dragon, and to recall them to the breast of the holy mother church."[225]

The Council of Arles found a direct precedent for its work 120 years earlier, in the theocratic Visigothic kingdom. What was presented as the preamble to the Council of Arles in 813 was in fact lifted from the records of the Fourteenth Council of Toledo, held in 693.[226] The Franks were still impressed by the profound record of Toledan councils, a prestigious model of episcopal power. The Five Councils of 813 (like Arno's Council of Reisbach in 798)[227] were further imbued with the spirit of the *Admonitio Generalis*. Bishops patiently listened to readings of the Rule of St. Benedict and of Gregory the Great's treatise on *Pastoral Care*.[228] Their ability to sit for long periods should be admired! Clerical education, the bishops declared, was the necessary basis for educating "all the people."[229] Plans were made to translate patristic homilies into "rustic Roman" and the Germanic language then known as Theodisca.[230]

---

222. The resulting documents were: *Karoli Magni capitula e canonibus excerpta* (813) MGH Conc. 2.1:294–97; and the *Concordia episcoporum* (813) MGH Conc. 2.1:297–301.

223. Patzold, *Episcopus,* 76.

224. "Consona voce gratias egimus Deo patri omnipotenti, quia sanctae eclesiae suae tam pium ac devotum in servitio Dei concessit habere rectorem, qui, suis temporibus sacrae sapientiae fontem aperiens," Council of Mainz (813), MGH Conc. 2.1:259.

225. "De fauce diri draconis multorum animas studet eripere et ad sinum sanctae matris eclesiae revocare," Council of Mainz (813), MGH Conc. 2.1:259.

226. Hartmann, *Synoden der Karolingerzeit,* 131; Council of Toledo (693), J. Vives, *Concilios visigóticos,* 482–521.

227. Council of Reisbach (798), MGH Conc. 2.1:196–201.

228. Rheims (813), MGH Conc. 2.1:255; Mainz (813), MGH Conc. 2.1:259; Chalons (813), MGH Conc. 2.1:274; Tours (813), MGH Conc. 2.1:287, 290.

229. "Universum populum docere," Council of Arles (813), MGH Conc. 2.1:250 (citing IV Toledo).

230. "Et ut easdem omelias quisque aperte transferre studeat in rusticam Romanam linguam

Reform of society was the ultimate goal. Although the Five Councils of 813 were held under the aegis of a triumphant Sacred Palace, the bishops evinced anxiety about the depth of Christianity in the hearts of the subjects of the Empire, particularly at the upper levels of society. One could not be purged of sin merely "by looking at a monastery," the bishops at Chalons sarcastically remarked: sins must be confessed to a priest and penance undertaken.[231] Only the purified life of a monk had religious significance. Here one sees a looming conflict between bishops, with their newly resplendent power in the countryside, even commanding tolls at bridges and markets, and the counts and other important nobles who felt this encroachment on their power, but who also wanted to "own" the church.[232]

Let there be peace and concord and unanimity among the Christian people, since we have one God and Father in the heavens and one mother church, one faith, one baptism.[233]

Such concord had not been realized because of dissension between bishops and counts. Both groups had the task of government. Together, the assembly at Chalon declared, bishops and counts should "rule the people of God under the dignity of the imperial apex."[234]

The councils of 813 insisted on the distinction of bishops as a separate group with a unique dignity and authority to rule the people of God. The counts were enjoined to obey them and seek their counsel.[235] The bishops also complained about laymen removing presbyters from churches in their territories without consultation.[236]

In spite of the bishops' recognition of a role for the lay nobility, their own functions and responsibilities were distinct and of greater importance. Bishops should have freedom to pursue these tasks: this they proclaimed as the "peace

---

aut Thiotiscam, quo facilius cuncti possint intelligere quae dicuntur," Council of Tours (813), MGH Conc. 2.1:288.

231. "Ut putent se sanctorum locorum sola visione a peccatis purgari," Council of Chalons (813), MGH Conc. 2.1:282.

232. Kaiser, "Royauté et pouvoir épiscopal," 1:152–59.

233. "Ut pax et concordia sit atque unanimitas in populo Christiano, quia unum Deum patrem habemus in caelis et unam matrem ecclesiam, unam fidem, unum baptisma," Council of Mainz (813), MGH Conc. 2.1:261.

234. "Si inter omnes fideles pax et concordia habenda est . . . multo magis inter episcopos et comites esse debet, qui post imperialis apicis dignitatem populum Dei regunt," Council of Chalons (813), MGH Conc. 2.1:277.

235. Council of Tours (813), MGH Conc. 2.1:290–91; see also Council of Arles (813): "Ut comites, iudices seu reliquus populus oboedientes sint episcopo," MGH Conc. 2.1:252.

236. Council of Arles (813), MGH Conc. 2.1:250.

of the church" (*pax ecclesiae*). The symbolic heart of this concept was the sacred confines of the basilica. Absolute separation of sacred from profane was called for:

THAT CHURCHES HAVE PEACE. Let no one presume to seize an accused person who has fled to a church, in order to hand him over to punishment or death, so the honor of God and his saints may be preserved. But let the rectors of churches strive to obtain peace, life and limb [for refugees]. Nevertheless they should legally make amends for what they did wrongly.[237]

Charlemagne had restricted the right of asylum, but the "peace of the church" here meant that secular powers should have no rights over the sanctified interior of a church, where the altar marked the axis of contact with the divine. The "peace of the church" meant that secular assemblies (*placita*) and bishops' councils should be distinguished: "We ordain that secular assemblies should not be held in churches, or in houses or halls attached to churches."[238] At Tours, the bishops distinguished between *two kinds* of government:

We heard that in many places secular assemblies are held in churches or their halls by counts and vicars. Lest this continue, it was interdicted with that divine authority which expelled the tradesmen from the temple, asserting that the house of God should be a house of prayer.[239]

Secular assemblies should not be held on Sundays, because they were occasions on which "some are sentenced to death or punishment."[240] Rather than engage directly in such "secular business," bishops and abbots were instructed to secure an advocate.[241] The only reason clerics might legitimately attend these assemblies was to defend orphans or widows.[242] Alongside these assertions were

---

237. "UT ECCLESIAE PACEM HABEANT. Reum confugientem ad eclesiam nemo abstrahere praesumat neque inde donare ad poenam vel ad mortem, ut honor Dei et sanctorum eius conservetur. Sed et rectores ecclesiarum pacem et vitam ac membra eis obtinere studeant; tamen legitime componant quod inique fecerunt," Council of Mainz (813), MGH Conc. 2.1:271.

238. "ITERUM DE PACE ECCLESIARUM. Praecipimus, ut in ecclesiis aut in domibus eclesiarum vel atriis placita saecularia minime fiant," Council of Mainz (813), MGH Conc. 2.1:271.

239. "Placita quidem saecularia in eclesiis vel in atriis eclesiarum a comitibus vicariisque usque modo multis in locis habita audivimus, sed, ne ultra fiant, interdicendum est, cum auctoritate dominica, quae expulsis de templo negotiatoribus asserens debere domum Dei domum esse orationis," Council of Tours (813), MGH Conc. 2.1:291.

240. "Ubi aliquis ad mortem vel ad poenam iudicetur," Council of Mainz (813), MGH Conc. 2.1:270.

241. "Per advocatos suos hoc faciat," Council of Mainz (813), MGH Conc. 2.1:264.

242. "Excepta defensione orfanorum aut viduarum," Council of Mainz (813), MGH Conc. 2.1:264.

many strictures on clerical behavior, emphasizing the distinction between clerics and laymen. Clerics were not to go hunting or attend feasts and entertainments. They were to renounce the world and rely upon "spiritual, not secular weapons."[243] The Five Councils of 813 were a remarkable restatement of episcopal social thought for a Carolingian imperial context.

The line that the Five Councils of 813 sought to draw between comital and episcopal authority was especially clear on the topic of the poor and defenseless. Bishops wanted the lay nobility to accept the episcopal ideals that motivated both episcopal and royal law. In a strident rhetoric of reform, the councils claimed that they stood beside the poor. In protecting the poor and travelers, they could "refresh them with corporeal and spiritual food."[244] Protecting the poor also legitimized the church's control over property. Julian Pomerius provided the terminology linking ecclesiastical property to protection of the poor. Pomerius, and not Augustine, provided the standard theory of property at the height of the Carolingian period.[245] Church property was the "patrimony of the poor," over which bishops were overseers, not owners.[246]

Let bishops exercise the greatest care and concern for the poor. Let them dispense the ecclesiastical property accumulated by churches with wary circumspection, as the ministers of God, not as pursuers of filthy lucre. It is to be used not as though it were their own [property], but as something committed to them to dispense.[247]

Everyone who controlled wealth should attempt to aid the poor. It was hateful to God, the bishops said, that the rich have so much and do not help the miserable and penniless.[248] The greatest violators of the rights of the poor, and the least willing to help them, were the "counts, vicars, judges, and *centenarii* [who] take the goods of the poor by force or sell them in an evil way or by trickery."[249]

243. "Nos autem, qui saeculum relinquimus, id modis omnibus observare volumus, ut arma spiritalia habeamus, saecularia dimittamus," Council of Mainz (813), MGH Conc. 2.1:266.

244. "Peregrini et pauperes convivae sint episcoporum, cum quibus non solum corporali, sed spirtali reficiantur alimento," Council of Tours (813), MGH Conc. 2.1:287.

245. David Ganz, "The Ideology of Sharing," 17–30; see esp. 18 (Cambridge: 1995).

246. "Quia res eclesiae, quibus episcopi non ut propriis, sed ut commendatis uti debent, pretia sunt peccatorum, patrimonia pauperum, stipendia fratrum in commune viventium"; citing Julian Pomerius, *De vita contemplativa* (2.9); Council of Chalons (813), MGH Conc. 2.1:275.

247. "Episcopi quidem maximam curam et sollicitudinem circa pauperes habeant et res ecclesiasticas eclesiis collatas cauta circumspectione dispensent quasi Dei ministri, non quasi turpis lucri sectatores, illisque ita utantur non ut propriis, sed ut sibi ad dispensandum commissis," Council of Tours (813), MGH Conc. 2.1:287.

248. "Quoniam impium est et Deo odibile eos, qui divitiis affluunt nimiisque opibus abundant, non adiuvare miseros et indigentes," Council of Tours (813), MGH Conc. 2.1:291.

249. "Ne comites vel vicarii seu iudices vel centenarii sub mala occasione vel ingenio res

Powerful nobles were systematically subjecting free men to their control as they expanded their estates: Men "known to be free" were falling "under the power of the powerful."

Perhaps we can hear little more than a "theme of justice" expressing the ambitions of Carolingian government.[250] The councils stressed that episcopal government was independent, that it gathered property on behalf of the poor, and that it represented a higher moral and social order than the counts. Although counts were charged with dispensing justice, it was bishops who had a real concern for justice for the weak:

We intend that bishops should have the power to provide ecclesiastical property, to rule and govern and to dispense in accordance with the authority of the canons, and that in their duties laymen obey the bishops in ruling the churches of God, and defending widows and orphans.[251]

If there were to be peace between counts and bishops, it would have to be on the basis of aristocratic obedience to bishops and to the principles of episcopal government. Thus we can see the importance of the "ideological underpinnings of doctrines of property and the power it entailed."[252]

The alliance of missionary bishops with their king was based on his inclusion within the church, and on his promotion of episcopal projects and ideals. The larger goal of evangelizing and reforming the kingdom begun by the "episcopal revolution" of Boniface and Pippin had seemed, under Charlemagne, on the point of transforming the world. Frankish conquests allowed a vast expansion of episcopal activity east and north. The power and reach of bishops expanded along with the Empire, giving them a highly visible role in the intellectual life of the universal church. The round of assemblies held in 813 attempted to further bind episcopal power to the leadership of the Sacred Palace.

What has been described here is the elaboration of a body of concepts about the nature of society. Bishops focused on what they wished to change, on their own claims to power, and were much less concerned to describe the actual conditions and functioning of their society. Obviously, they were bound by ties of

---

pauperum emant nec per vim tollant," Council of Arles (813), MGH Conc. 2.1:253; compare also Council of Mainz (813), MGH Conc. 2.1:262.

250. Fouracre, "Carolingian Justice," 782–83.

251. "Ut episcopi potestatem habeant res ecclesiasticas praevidere, regere et gubernare atque dispensare secundum canonum auctoritatem, volumus, et ut laici in eorum ministerio oboediant episcopis ad regendas ecclesias Dei, viduas et orphanos defensandos," Council of Mainz (813), MGH Conc. 2.1:262.

252. Ganz, "Ideology of Sharing," 30.

family and friendship with other members of the nobility. The secular nobility had scarcely been included in the austere intellectual structures of the sacralized imperial state. Bishops had control over enormous properties, assembled over the centuries, aquired as donations from nobles, kings, and queens. In principle these lands were inalienable, but the needs of defense and management led to the large-scale distribution of property to the nobility in the form of *beneficia* or *precaria*. Nobles came to acquire rights over those lands after long occupation, which caused church lands and their episcopal overseers to become enmeshed in complex relations and bonds of loyalty with the secular nobles.[253]

The writings of St. Augustine offered little support for the bishops' desire for a total triumph for religious ideals in the Carolingian kingdom. Instead, in their councils bishops reemphasized the most ancient traditions of episcopal government, their authority as patrons of the poor and as overseers of the property of the poor, and their unique status as rectors of the "Christian people." They did so even as they became more deeply involved in the countryside and the tangle of duties and responsibilities that sprouted like weeds from the fields their peasants farmed and the slopes on which their animals were pastured. Above these disorderly fields rose a perfect vision of the Frankish kingdom as a theopolitical order.

253. Susan Reynolds, *Fiefs and Vassals: The Medieval Evidence Reinterpreted* (Oxford: 1994), 77–80.

[8]

A KINGDOM OF THE
FAITHFUL

WITH THE REIGN of Louis the Pious, the religious ideal of kingship and the vision of the Frankish empire as a sacred kingdom reached a radical high point—with ambiguous results, however, in the period of civil wars that clouded the last years of Louis's rule. The governing elites, both the warrior nobility and the bishops themselves, accepted the hieratic vision of a sacred kingdom and the holy purposes of the Carolingian state, a fact that embittered every conflict. Just as "mirrors of bishops" had long ago devised the model of an ideal bishop, so now "mirrors of princes" were frequently written to educate kings in their religious and governmental duties.

The tightly unified imperial church continued to meet in grandiose councils, bringing together all the important Frankish bishops and uniting them around the ideal of combatting heresy and reforming the church and kingdom. But signs of strain began to emerge. A fanatical tone can be detected in the anti-Semitic imperialist writings of Agobard. Meanwhile, a rebellious message broke through the smooth surface of conciliar tradition in the Council of Paris (829). The sole surviving record, significantly, reflects the ideal of an exclusively religious doctrine of the state and an ideology of kingship looking back to the theocratic views of Isidore of Seville and the Visigothic Church. The social model presented at Paris reflects serious challenges during a time when the emperor faced continual conflict. The "sacred kingdom" concept called for unity. The ideal of kingship was heightened at a moment when it seemed least applicable, as the pious emperor Louis saw the Carolingian Empire torn apart by his sons. The council was an effort by powerful and highly placed individuals to develop a solution to the disunity and confusion of the period.[1]

Pharaonic Kingship

Visigothic Spain had long ago shown that under the cooperative government of king and bishop, the kingdom could become a holy structure. With Pippin's anointing, it seemed to Frankish bishops that their kingdom, unified and following their guidance, had also become a sacred entity. The destruction of the Visigoths in 711 did not dim the hopes attached to this model as Visigothic conciliar law, the writings of Isidore of Seville, and men inspired by this cultural message made their way into the Frankish world.[2] Like their Visigothic counterparts, the bishops of Francia could identify with the aims of a sacralized kingdom.[3] The reign of Charlemagne seemed to prove the rightness of this model. The Empire's steady expansion and the round of councils uniting its bishops were two sides of a religious project. Kingship was apprised as a Christian institution, and thinkers began to elaborate on this theme in handbooks known as "mirrors of princes."[4] As we shall see, conciliar authority was further developed as a mode of political instruction and political action, culminating in the lightning and thunder of the Council of Paris in 829.

Charlemagne's tireless energy helped to hold his far-flung dominions together. The terror he inspired gave force to the institutions through which he governed, such as the *missi dominici,* local agents of royal power with significant authority to implement his laws.[5] As Matthew Innes has shown, the *missus dominicus* was a trustworthy figure with local prestige and far-reaching connections. Count Rupert was one such man, descendent of a family notable in the Middle Rhine since the Merovingian period. Unlike his ancestors, who were above all local patrons, Rupert "was first and foremost an agent of the political centre."[6]

Charlemagne thus recruited, around his empire, an elite group of counts and archbishops capable of mediating between the centers of power and the various

---

1. Patzold suggests that there was an "advisor-crisis": Patzold, *Episcopus,* 511.
2. Fontaine, "Mozarabie hispanique," 29–30.
3. Werner, *Naissance de la noblesse,* 371.
4. See the overview of Hans Martin Klinkenberg, "Über karolingische Fürstenspiegel," *Geschichte in Wissenschaft und Unterricht* 7 (1956): 82–98; see also Michel Senellart, *Les arts de gouverner,* 88–89.
5. McKitterick, *Frankish Kingdoms,* 93–97.
6. Innes, *State and Society,* 194.

regions of the empire. Unlike the Merovingian state, which it resembled in so many other ways, the Carolingian state had extensive and clearly announced aims. These were religious aims quite unlike the aims of a modern state. The Carolingian state did not fully develop or exercise a capacity to carry out its aims with coercive power. This is paralleled by the fact that pure force was scarcely addressed in the many sources of political thought that have been analyzed here. For Gregory of Tours, as we saw, political violence was usually the mark of moral and political failure. It might seem, therefore, that these statements of sacralized purpose were remote from the "real" nature of the state. This is to take for granted that the history of political power has to do only with the "rise of secular sovereignty." This is an anachronistic perspective: kings, bishops, and the nobility all possessed power and responsibility. Kings and bishops each claimed to govern the same society, and they did so through their mutual recruitment in common purposes. The language of legitimacy took for granted the concept of righteous power. The aims of the Carolingian state were pious. Scholars such as Hraban Maur concluded that biblical scholarship was the most important type of reading for kings, and Louis, like Charlemagne before him, was part of an intimate learned circle of men devoted to such topics.[7]

In the midst of this system of consensus and negotiation, a new political order had emerged, adorned with imperial themes and claiming to bring the sublime to earth in tireless expressions of sacrality. The historical vision supporting the Carolingian state looked back, not to the Roman Empire, but beyond it to the sacred kingship of Israel.[8] The bishops, so central to erecting this fragile structure, were soon overshadowed by the domineering way the king had seized on their ideas and projects. Just how fragile this structure was became clear during the reign of Charles' son, Louis the Pious (814–840). Upon his accession, Louis immediately set to work establishing the continuity of his reign with that of Charlemagne. Louis wished to be seen as a man "crowned by divine command, ruling the Roman Empire, the most serene Augustus."[9] His inheritance of this crown was by no means a given. Louis had to secure control of the palace at Aachen, and to present to his contemporaries the face of a renewed role for royal power.[10] In a

---

7. Mayke De Jong, "The Empire as *ecclesia*: Hrabanus Maurus and Biblical *historia* for Rulers," in *Uses of the Past,* 191–226; see 196–201.

8. On the concept of "Rome": Tellenbach, *Römischer und christlicher Reichsgedanke,* 21. On the Biblical time-horizon: Orlandis, "Bible et royauté," 51–57.

9. *Capitula legi addita* (816), MGH Capit. 1.2:267–69; see 267.

10. Matthew Innes, "Charlemagne's Will: Piety, Politics and the Imperial Succession," EHR 112 (1997): 833–55; see 845.

world that suddenly seemed tipped on its side by the death of Charlemagne, the bishops took up their ancient preoccupation with kingship in a new tone of anxiety and radicalism.

Handbooks for the instruction of princes typically focused on the personal qualities of a prince or king and evoked the problem of justice, frequently drawing a connection between royal justice and the prosperity and safety of the realm. One such writer of the ninth century offered a gloomy warning to the unidentified prince whom he addressed: "A kingdom may be transferred from one people (*gens*) to another people, because of injustices, injuries, outrages and diverse sorrows."[11] A king who rules without justice, the author went on, "proves that he is not a king, but a tyrant."[12]

Despite Louis' claim that he ruled a *Roman* Empire, his bishops continued to focus on the older problem of kingship that underlay it. In formulating their ideas, bishops turned to a number of sources, including writings from Visigothic Spain and Ireland. Irish traditions, in particular, provided a rich store of thought about kingship. Alcuin, for example, drew upon an Irish work, Pseudo-Cyprian's *Twelve Abuses of the World,* in an important discussion of royal authority.[13] Alcuin drew a connection between the fertility of nature and good kingship:

We also read that in the goodness of a king lies all the prosperity of a people, the victory of its army, the temperence of the weather, the abundance of the land, the blessing of sons, the health of the people. It is an awesome thing to rule all the people. A king (*rex*) receives his title from ruling (*regendo*), and the one who rules well the people subject to him has a good reward from God: that is, the heavenly kingdom. Someone who will earn a celestial kingdom in exchange for an earthly one reigns quite happily on earth. He should at once petition God with prayers and vigils, and cry out not just for himself, but for the prosperity of all the people. Likewise the princes and judges of a people should exceed them in justice and piety. May they be like fathers to widows, ophans, and the wretched, because the equity of princes is the exaltation of the people.[14]

11. "Regnum a gente in gentem transfertur propter iniusticias et iniurias et contumelias et diversos dolos," Rudolf Schieffer, "Zwei karolingische Texte über das Königtum," DA 46 (1990): 1–17. This quote, 8–9, is from Schieffer's first text, edited from Ms. Gotha, Forschungsbibliothek, Cod. Memb. II 189, fol. 1r–5r.

12. "Quia quisquis sine illa imperat, non regem, se (ti)rannum se esse comprobat," Schieffer, "Zwei karolingische Texte," 12.

13. *Pseudo-Cyprianus De XII abusivis saeculi,* ed. S. Hellmann, TU 34 (Leipzig: 1909).

14. "Legimus quoque, quod regis bonitas totius est gentis prosperitas, victoria exercitus, aeris temperies, terrae habundantia, filiorum benedictio, sanitas plebis. Magnum est totam regere gentem. A regendo vero rex dicitur; et qui bene regit subiectum sibi populum, bonam habet a Deo retributionem: regnum scilicet caeleste. Valde feliciter regnat in terra, qui de terreno regno

The text also contains an oblique reference to Isidore's views on kingship. As mentioned earlier, Isidore had derived the word king (*rex*) from doing rightly (*recte agendo*). Alcuin instead raised the topic of the benefits to a ruler if he rules well (*bene regere*). This he interpreted in terms of the ancient episcopal obligation of protecting the poor, orphans, and widows, now thought of as a duty of the king. A new theme arose, however, in making this duty an expression of royal justice. Like Boniface and Cathwulf, Alcuin's concern was for the People of God (*populus Dei*), and he saw kings and bishops as playing a central role in its expansion and its well-being.[15] Alcuin therefore found an important explanation of kingship in an Irish tradition he thought compatible with Scripture and the nature of social reality.[16] It was also possible to find precedents in the Old Testament for such a "pharaonic" kingship, in the connection between royal justice, the fertility of people and crops, the kingdom's prosperity.[17]

Like his close advisor Alcuin, Charlemagne also believed in the link between a king's promotion of justice and religion and his ability to protect the realm. In 807 he wrote to Bishop Ghaerbald to set in motion a series of processions and vigils in response to troubles afflicting the kingdom:

because in an unusual and unaccustomed way, sterility of the land may be seen everywhere, and to threaten hunger. The intemperance of the weather is very harmful to the crops, there is pestilence in some places, and there are continuous, intractable wars with pagan peoples around our marches.[18]

---

merebitur caeleste. Orationibus vero et vigiliis eo instantius ad Deum insistere debet, quo non pro se solummodo, sed pro totius gentis prosperitate Deum deprecari debet. Similiter principes et iudices populi in iustitia et pietate populo praesint. Viduis, pupillis, et miseris sint quasi patres; quia aequitas principum populi est exaltation," MGH Epp. 4, no. 18 of Alcuin's letters, 49–52; see 51–52. The passage is closely related to the "ninth abuse" of Pseudo-Cyprian; see Hans Hubert Anton, "Pseudo-Cyprian: De duodecim abusivis saeculi und sein Einfluss auf den Kontinent, insbesondere auf die karolingischen Fürstenspiegel," in *Die Iren und Europa im früheren Mittelalter,* edited by Heinz Löwe, 568–617 (Stuttgart: 1982); see also Wallace-Hadrill, *Early Germanic Kingship,* 56.

15. I Deug-Su, *L'Opera agiografica di Alcuino,* Biblioteca degli "Studi Medievali" 13 (Spoleto: 1983): 69–71. On the connections between Pseudo-Cyprian, Cathwulf and Alcuin, see Anton, *Fürstenspiegel,* 104–7.

16. Anton, "Pseudo-Cyprian," 585. Wallace-Hadrill maintained that Alcuin pursued a political Augustinianism: "The *Via Regia* of the Carolingian Age," 189.

17. The term "pharaonique" is Jean Devisse's: "Le sacre et le pouvoir," 27; see also E. O. James, "The Sacred Kingship and the Priesthood," in *The Sacral Kingship,* 63–70, Studies in the History of Religions 4 [Supplements to NVMEN] (Leiden: 1959).

18. "Quod insolito more et ultra consuetum ubique terrae sterelitas esse et famis periculum imminere videtur, aëris etiam intemperies frugibus valde contraria, pestilentia quoque per loca, et paganorum gentium circa marcas nostras sedentia bella continua," Charlemagne, Letter to Ghaerbald (807), *Karoli ad Ghaerbaldum Episcopum Epistola,* MGH Capit. 1.1:244–46, quoting 245.

Charlemagne's letter poignantly shows how permanent troubles, combined with rumors of new ones, could loom into a perception of kingdom-wide malaise and danger.

The Royal Road

In the last years of Charlemagne's life, an attempt was made to summarize the principles of Carolingian sacral kingship. The *Via regia* of Smaragdus was written for Charlemagne's son Louis the Pious, king of Aquitaine from 781 until Charles' death in 814.[19] The brief work was meant as a handbook to guide the young king through the distractions and dangers of government. Smaragdus took his title from a passage in the Book of Numbers (21:22), a phrase already developed by John Cassian.[20] The book was doggedly ethical, and appears to have been written, in large part, to show how Louis himself could achieve personal salvation. The concept of kingship was developed as a ministry.[21] As in Alcuin's *Liber de virtutibus et vitiis,* which influenced Smaragdus' work, the aim was to show the universality of Christian norms. The prince must "submit totally to the Christian moral law."[22] In this, the *Via regia* was consistent with the conflation of religious and political concerns toward which bishops had worked for decades.

Smaragdus, abbot of St.-Mihiel, and Benedict of Aniane, Louis' close adviser after his accession in 814, illustrate the emergence of monastic reform and monastic thinkers in Carolingian politics.[23] These men also show the growing influence of Spanish thinkers at the court of Louis the Pious, a factor also among the palace intellectuals of Charlemagne. Here one may add the name of Agobard of Lyon. One of the earliest acts of Louis was to issue laws offering his special "defense and protection" to those who had fled to the Franks from the "power of the Saracens."[24]

19. Smaragdus, *Via regia,* PL 102:931–70. On Smaragdus, see Brunhölzl, *Histoire de la littérature latine,* vol. 1.2:192–97; see also Otto Eberhardt, *Via Regia: Der Fürstenspiegel Smaragds vons St. Mihiel und seine literarische Gattung,* Münstersche Mittelalter-Schriften 28 (Munich: 1977), and Anton, *Fürstenspiegel,* 132–89.

20. Adalbert de Vogüé, "Pour comprendre Cassien," in his *De Saint Pachôme à Jean Cassien: Études littéraires et doctrinales sur le monachisme égyptien à ses début,* 303–29; see 312, Studia Anselmiana 120 (Rome: 1996).

21. Wallace-Hadrill, *Frankish Church,* 239–40.

22. Brunhölzl, *Histoire de la littérature latine,* vol. 1.2:195.

23. See T. F. X. Noble, "The Monastic Ideal as a Model for Empire: The Case of Louis the Pious," RB 86 (1976): 235–50.

24. "Quod eosdem homines sub protectione et defensione nostra receptos in libertate conservare decrevimus," *Constitutio de Hispanis in Francorum regnum profugis prima* (815) MGH Capit. 1.2:261–62; see 261. Their occupation of uncultivated land was also protected: *Constitutio Hludowici de Hispanis secunda* (816), MGH Capit. 2.1:263–64.

As mentioned earlier, Charlemagne's letter to Elipandus had described the path of orthodoxy as a "royal road" (*via regia*) leading the believer toward the "City of Christ." This was a social concept: the City of Christ could be identified with the reformed kingdom and church of the Frankish Empire. Irish traditions similarly spoke of the need "to establish the law of God over the people of God," as Cathwulf explained in his letter to Charlemagne.[25] This "royal road" was the central image of Smaragdus' *Via regia*. His use of this terminology was part of a theological and social outlook centered in the conciliar activity of 794 and 813.

Smaragdus, like the bishops who assembled in 813, found important sources for his view of kingship in Visigothic Spain. The writings of Isidore, the Mozarabic liturgy, and Visigothic canon law provided a vocabulary for conceptualizing the kingdom as a religious structure.[26] The "royal road" signified Roman and Frankish orthodoxy. In Smaragdus' hands, however, the *via regia* underwent two major conceptual transformations. Smaragdus attempted first to formulate a Christian ethics specifically appropriate to powerful laymen, and second to lay down the norms of Christian kingship.

Kingship had a divine origin. Like Isidore, Smaragdus argued that the king's baptism, anointing, and crowning were closely related events:

He anointed your head with the oil of sacred chrism, and worthily adopted you as a son. He established you as king of the people of the earth, and ordained that you become the heir of His own Son in heaven. Enriched by these sacred rewards, you rightly wear the diadem of a king.[27]

For Smaragdus the king was a religious figure in his own right. Christian behavior was vital to the royal function: the king should "hurry down the royal road to the kingdoms of heaven."[28] Smaragdus often returned to the parallel between the kingship of Christ and earthly kingship. By seeking his own salvation, Smaragdus believed, the king would thereby also emulate Christ, the divine model of kingship.

The supposition animating this densely written little work is that the sub-

25. "Ergo considerate inter vos diligenter legem Dei constituere super populum Dei," Cathwulf, Letter to Charlemagne, MGH Epp. 4.2:502–5; see 503. Cathwulf's letter resonates strongly with the *Collectio canonum hibernensis*.

26. Eberhardt, *Via Regia*, 127, 507.

27. "Caput tuum oleo sacri chrismatis linivit, et dignanter in filium adoptavit. Constituit te regem populi terrae, et proprii Filii sui in coelo fieri jussit haeredem. His etenim sacris ditatus muneribus rite portas diademata regis," Smaragdus, *Via regia*, PL 102:931–70; see col. 933.

28. "Quia cum sis rex in terra, ad coelorum properans regna per regiam debes currere viam," Smaragdus, *Via regia*, PL 102:934.

lime could be located in human institutions by reshaping them in accordance with Christian principles. Characteristic of this argument is the way the commandment to love one's neighbor was extended by Smaragdus into a principle of government. The "neighbor" was interpreted in a universal way to mean "every faithful Christian."[29] The king's Christian duty to offer charity and love was thus extended into a social principle and a manner of governing. At this point, Smaragdus arrived at a restatement of what might be called the "promise" of Carolingian kingship: that the kingdom could be a vehicle for man's rectification and salvation. Love as a "royal virtue" could reform the kingdom—ending heresy and conflict by bringing about consensus (*concordia mentium*).

Smaragdus also connected royal goodness, success in warfare, and the beneficence of nature. Passages from Deuteronomy and Leviticus were quoted to show that if the king would obey the "mandates of the the Lord," his kingdom would be blessed with rainfall and bountiful crops.[30] If the king would stop the practice of taking and keeping slaves, for example, then his military efforts would be rewarded with victory. Smaragdus supported this view with a savage illustration from Ezechiel: "you will eat the flesh of the strong, and drink the blood of the princes of the earth" (Ezech. 39:17–20).[31] Binding these ideas together was the notion that the kingdom was a religious structure, a "kingdom of the faithful." Smaragdus hoped that God would favor the rule of a truly Christian prince: "may He place the necks of your enemies to be trampled underfoot, and under your leadership, may He defend the kingdom of the faithful from the snares of its enemies."[32]

Protection of the poor, orphans, and widows had long been the signature claim of episcopal government, forming the basis of bishops' assertion of a right to control and dispense ecclesiastical property without interference from lay authority. Care for the poor had also been inscribed in Charlemagne's capitularies. For Smaragdus, this duty was especially borne by the king. The king's Christian virtue could preserve peace by restraining the power of the mighty and giving aid to the destitute.[33] Upon occupying the imperial throne, Louis likewise gave

29. "Nos vero proximum, fidelem omnem dicimus Christianum, qui non solum rationabiliter proximus, sed et fideliter frater vocatur," Smaragdus, *Via regia,* PL 102:936.

30. Smaragdus, *Via regia,* PL 102:937–38.

31. Smaragdus, *Via regia,* PL 102:69.

32. "Inimicorum colla plantis tuis calcanda substernat, et fidelium regna ab inimicorum insidiis te dominante, defendat," Smaragdus, *Via regia,* PL 102:941.

33. "Coercet potentiam divitum, refovet inopiam pauperum," Smaragdus, *Via regia,* PL 102:947.

the poor a prominent place in his legislation. Protection of the poor was now a measure of royal justice.

Governing Those Beneath Them

The new emperor was compelled to fight in various quarters of the kingdom, and behind the orderly facade presented by official chronicles, one can see Louis securing his hold on the kingdom.[34] Potential opponents such as Adalhard were sent into exile, and Wala, Charlemagne's cousin, was forced to enter the abbey of Corbie as a monk. Louis also sent his *missi* throughout the realm "to render justice and relieve the oppression of the people," although the nature of this oppression was not described. Such "oppressions" and other troubles mentioned in the sources are often difficult to tie to specific historical events.[35] Unlike his father, who had spent so much of his life on horseback, endeavoring constantly to expand the Empire, Louis turned most of his efforts toward internal consolidation. Yet the very act of slowing external campaigns meant that the task of governing the kingdom and pacifying the nobility became more difficult. Possessing considerable resources, the nobility were at the same time being called to ever greater tasks on behalf of the kingdom.[36] Without a continuous supply of land and booty from outside the realm, scarce internal resources had to satisfy the warrior elite. The "oppressions" that concerned Louis and his bishops were partly due to the resulting intensification of estate exploitation.[37]

The emperor instructed his nobles to protect those who came before a court "unable to fight because they are timid, or weak or ill."[38] The sacred nature of Carolingian kingship was unrelentingly on display during the reign of Louis, so it is not surprising to find an episcopal vocabulary of sacred power threaded throughout his legislation. As the "most Christian and most pious emperor," he issued laws confirming episcopal prerogatives and property, adding the weight of royal power to the "tradition of the holy fathers," such as the oft-mentioned words of Julian Pomerius.[39] Laws extended the royal *bannum* to protect priests

34. Against the Danes and Saxons (Anno 814, Anno 815): *Annales regni Francorum,* 141.

35. Élisabeth Magnou-Nortier, "Les évêques et la paix," 33–50; see 34.

36. Werner, *Naissance de la noblesse,* 430–31.

37. Timothy Reuter, "The End of Carolingian Military Expansion," in *Charlemagne's Heir: New Perspectives on the Reign of Louis the Pious (814–840),* edited by Peter Godman and Roger Collins, 391–405; see esp. 405 (Oxford: 1990).

38. "Hoc et de timidis adque inbecillibus sive infirmis qui pugnare non valent, ut nullatenus propter hoc iustitias suas careant, censuimus faciendi," *Capitula legi addita* (816), MGH Capit. 1.2:267–69; see 268.

39. "Quia iuxta sanctorum patrum traditionem novimus 'res ecclesiae vota esse fidelium,

in their churches,[40] and sought to secure a careful hearing in the courts for "widows, orphans and the poor."[41] Louis instructed his *missi* to "aid and relieve" this same triad of marginal persons if they suffered unjust oppression.[42]

By thus endeavoring to end oppression, Louis not only displayed the continuity of his rule with that of Charlemagne, but also showed that he established justice, balancing the government of the realm in "a very level pair of scales."[43] Like his father, Louis found that only the ancient themes of episcopal government could support the fragile, but brilliant placard of an imperial and sacral state that had been "added to" older Frankish law and social forms. An assembly of bishops, abbots, counts, and "the rest of the people" at the palace of Aachen in 818 or 819 saw their decisions and laws as something added on to the Salian Law.[44] Although I describe such themes as thin and fragile, they are vital to understanding a political culture that mobilized the most powerful men in the kingdom, precisely because of its sacrality.[45] All of this was choreographed by a king whose capability is sometimes overlooked.[46]

Louis recognized the importance of church reform to a sacralized state structure. Convoking a great council seemed an urgent first step, which Louis undertook with the Council of Aachen in 816.[47] Louis gave his backing to an extensive range of reforms guided by Benedict of Aniane. It is not known who completed the task of compiling patristic and other writings used in the final version of the records of Aachen 816, but it may have been Amalarius of Metz.[48] Using the pal-

---

pretia peccatorum et patrimonia pauperum,'" *Capitulare ecclesiasticum* (818–819), MGH Capit. 1.2:275–80; see 275.

40. "Sanguinis effusio in ecclesiis facta cum fuste, si presbiter fuerit, triplo conponatur," *Capitula legibus addenda* (818–819), MGH Capit. 1.2:281.

41. "De viduis et pupillis et pauperibus. Ut quandocumque in mallum ante comitem venerint, primo eorum causa audiatur et definiatur," *Capitula legibus addenda* (818–819), MGH Capit. 1.2:281.

42. "De pauperibus et viduis et pupillis iniuste oppressis, ut adiuventur et releventur," *Capitulare missorum* (819), MGH Capit. 1.2:288–91; see 289.

43. "Et regni gubernaculis aequissimo libramine tenere," *Hludowici prooemium generale ad capitularia tam ecclesiastica quam mundana* (818–819), MGH Capit. 1.2:273–75; see 274.

44. "Cum venerabilibus episcopis et abbatibus atque comitibus vel cum reliquo populo in Aquisgrani palatio promulgavit atque legis Salicae addere," *Capitula legibus addenda* (818–819), 280.

45. A similar suggestion was made a century ago by Arthur Kleinclausz, *L'empire carolingien: Ses origines et ses transformations* (Paris: 1902), 263–73.

46. McKitterick, *Frankish Kingdoms*, 124.

47. Council of Aachen (816), MGH Conc. 2.1:307–464.

48. Ansegesis or Benedict of Aniane are also possible candidates; see Charles de Clercq, "La législation religieuse franque depuis l'avènement de Louis le Pieux jusqu'aux Fausses Décrétales," *Revue de Droit Canonique* 4 (1954): 376. The clearest evidence, which names Amalarius of Metz, is also the latest: Hartmann, *Die Synoden der Karolingerzeit,* 159.

ace library, the compiler gathered texts from a wide range of patristic authors, "having an abundance of books before my hands, drawing on canonical authority and the words of the holy fathers."[49] The aim of the Council of Aachen was not to legislate on the ancient model of Gallic and Merovingian canon law, but to publish a law book (*codex*) under conciliar authority. The codex, in this case, was to be a detailed set of regulations for clerics living communally, whether cathedral clerics (canons), monks, or nuns. The law book produced at Aachen in 816 was nothing other than a specialized *florilegium* showing the flexibility of Carolingian conciliar authority.[50]

In 813, the Five Councils had coordinated all the bishops of the kingdom in a carefully staged ritual of consensus. Aachen 816 likewise brought together as many bishops as possible, alongside abbots and important clerics, at Aachen, which was becoming the seat of the empire.[51] The concept of reform was characteristically ambiguous, however. The goal was partly to compile authoritative rules, a "form of institution drawn from the sacred canons and the words of the holy fathers."[52] The council was also intended as a major expression, early in the reign of a new king, of combined royal and ecclesiastical power, with a newly prominent role for monasteries. As so often since the time of Pippin and Carloman, this combined power was affirmed by directing it toward reform and the "correction of the holy church of God."[53] The council preamble depicted a joyous scene as the assembly rose to recognize the role of the emperor:

Filled with deepest joy by this admonition, the holy assembly, raising their hands toward heaven and thanking the Creator of all things, blessed the One who had put before them a prince so pious and so kind-hearted toward his holy church, most wise about every necessity, and a very devoted leader.[54]

---

49. "Eius [sc. Louis] videlicet liberalissima largitione copiam librorum prae manibus habentes, ex canonica auctoritate et sanctorum patrum dictis," Council of Aachen (816) MGH Conc. 2.1:313. It is likely that Amalarius would have used the palace library. What is known about this library is described in Bischoff, *Manuscripts and Libraries,* 56–92.

50. McKitterick, *Frankish Kingdoms,* 112–18.

51. Josef Semmler, "Die Beschlüsse des Aachener Konzils im Jahre 816," ZKG 74 (1963): 15–82; see 16.

52. "Ex eisdem sacris canonibus et sanctorum patrum dictis institutionis formam," Council of Aachen (816), 312.

53. "Emendatione sanctae Dei ecclesiae," Council of Aachen (816), 312.

54. "Ad quam etiam admonitionem sacer conventus intimo gaudio repletus, expansis in caelum manibus, creatori omnium gratias agens benedixit, quippe qui talem tam pium tamque benignum ecclesiae suae sanctae principem cunctisque eius necessitatibus sapientissimum ac devotissimum praetulerit procuratorem," Council of Aachen (816), MGH Conc. 2.1:312–13.

The reformers assembled at Aachen in 816 (and again in 817)[55] hoped to make the Rule of Benedict a standard for cloistered monks.[56] A copy of Benedict's Rule was obtained from Monte Cassino, thus assuring the reform's authenticity by an act of pious *ressourcement.* The monasteries of Rome also served as models.[57] This is only part of the story, however, because statements from the Rule of St. Benedict were scattered throughout a compendium that also drew from the homilies and *Pastoral Care* of Gregory the Great, as well as Jerome and Augustine. The works of Gregory, moreover, were entirely drawn from the *Sententiae* of Taio of Saragossa (fl. 651–after 656), a pupil of Isidore.[58] The compilers also relied on Isidore, especially the *De ecclesiasticis officiis,* and Julian Pomerius' *De vita contemplativa,* from which extensive passages were cited. The influence of Spanish authors (Isidore and Taio of Saragossa) at Aachen 816 may have resulted from the role played there by clerics of Spanish origin, such as Smaragdus himself, Benedict of Aniane, and Agobard of Lyon.[59] In assessing the role of patristics at the Council of Aachen, it seems clear that the authors cited at Aachen were considered figures of a distant past: canonical sources established with the aid and resources of royal power. Both Charlemagne and Louis established important libraries in the palace in Aachen and promoted the gathering of libraries in monasteries and cathedrals.[60] The reforms at Aachen are thus related to the "centralization-tendency" of bishops who attempted to emulate the liturgy of Rome.[61]

Aachen 816 gave due attention to the power and scope of episcopal authority. The bishops confirmed their government over monks and nuns and detailed how all clerics should live, including themselves, which is why Isidore's discussion of the tonsure was quoted at length.[62] The concept of episcopal government was approached, characteristically, through a discussion of church property, viewed as the property of the poor. The crucial passage in this regard was from Julian Pomerius, by now a standard description of the connection between care for

55. Council of Aachen (817), MGH Conc. 2.1:464–66.

56. Josef Semmler, "Benedictus II: Una regula—una consuetudo," 1–49.

57. Semmler, "Die Beschlüsse," 25–28.

58. Hartmann, *Die Synoden der Karolingerzeit,* 158. Taio of Saragossa, *Sententiae,* PL 80:723–990. The influence of Taio's compendium is noted by Evans, *Thought of Gregory the Great,* 145; and Collins, *Early Medieval Spain,* 73.

59. Barbero de Aguilera, *La sociedad visigoda,* 120–21; Hartmann, *Die Synoden der Karolingerzeit,* 157.

60. Bischoff, *Manuscripts and Libraries,* 56–75 and 76–92.

61. Semmler points to the *Vereinheitlichungstendenzen* of Carolingian bishops: Semmler, "Die Beschlüsse," 59.

62. Council of Aachen (816), MGH Conc. 2.1:318.

the poor and episcopal power. Julian said that the property of the church is "the prayers of the faithful, the ransom of sinners, and the patrimony of the poor," which bishops must oversee and properly distribute.[63] Proper distribution entailed supporting clerics, maintaining the physical plant of the church, aiding the poor, and ransoming captives.[64] Pomerius thus offered a prime theoretical support for episcopal government.

May they govern those who are beneath them, and provide for the poor, taking into account all the necessities and advantages of the Church by administering it faithfully. Because of their faithful administration, let them deserve to be rewarded ineffably by Him whose ministers they are known to be.[65]

Bishops were not to expect material rewards for overseeing church property, but only the ineffable reward of salvation. But another reward was the confirmation of episcopal government as a righteous form of power. In laws issued early in Louis' reign, special protection was demanded for widows, orphans, the poor, and priests. At comital courts, these weaker members of society, who had no natural defenders, were to be protected by an advocate.[66]

The Kingdom as Christ

In the *Ordinatio imperii* of 817, Louis sought to lay down the succession to the Empire, designating his oldest son Lothair as chief heir, giving him the imperial title and dividing the kingdom between Lothair and his brothers, who were designated "sub-kings." Looking back to the reign of Charlemagne as a peaceful time of order, the *Ordinatio* sought to codify the sources of secure government and divine approval.[67] The document gives every appearance of an intact and integrated kingdom, a vision of imperial harmony, and yet this was a period of crisis, in which rebellion and resistance arose in many quarters.[68] The *Ordinatio*

63. Julianus Pomerius, *De vita contemplativa* 2.9 (PL 59:454); "Non ut possessores, sed ut procuratores facultates ecclesiae possidebant. Et idcirco scientes nihil aliud esse res ecclesiae, nisi vota fidelium, pretia peccatorum, et patrimonia pauperum; non eas vindicaverunt in usus suos, ut proprias, sed ut commendatas pauperibus diviserunt," At Aachen, only the portion "nisi vota fidelium. . . . patrimonia pauperum" was cited; Council of Aachen (816) MGH Conc. 2.1:398.

64. "Ut his et milites Christi alerentur, ecclesiae exornarentur, pauperes recrearentur et captivi pro temporum oportunitate redimerentur," Council of Aachen (816) MGH Conc. 2.1:398.

65. "Et subditos gubernent et pauperes foveant cunctisque utilitatibus ac necessitatibus ecclesiae fideliter administrando consulant, quatenus de fideli administratione ab ipso, cuius ministri esse noscuntur, ineffabiliter remunerari mereantur," Council of Aachen (816) MGH Conc. 2.1:398.

66. *Capitula legibus addenda* (818–819), MGH Capit. 1.2:280–85; see 281.

67. Patzold, *Episcopus,* 511.

68. Peter McKeon, "817: Une année désastreuse et presque fatale pour les Carolingiens," MA 84, 4th ser. 33 (1978): 5–12.

was promulgated with religious solemnity after a period of fasting and prayer.[69] Louis used the edict to express his ideal of a Christian empire, linking imperial unity to peace in the kingdom and protection of the church.[70] The empire was described as though it could express God's will without mediation: human law and custom are in God's hands, and by obeying them, one obeys God. To disobey would incur his wrath.[71] Louis' sons were required to prevent the oppression of churches and the poor, because to allow it would be tyranny (*tyrannis*).[72]

Thegan, who recounted with benefit of hindsight the events of 817, told of immediate dissatisfaction on the part of the younger sons.[73] Bernard, Louis' nephew and king of Frankish lands in Italy, rebelled.[74] Louis reacted violently and quickly. Bernard was arrested and his eyes put out after a trial at Aachen. Louis' half-brothers were seized, forcibly tonsured, and imprisoned in monasteries, a punishment that the bishops facilitated.[75] Bernard died shortly after his punishment. The issue of succession and division of the realm here followed the pattern established by Pippin and Charlemagne, of giving the crowns of dependent kingdom-regions to royal sons. Louis himself had been king of Aquitaine in his youth.[76] The *Ordinatio* insisted, however, that this should now amount to a hierarchy of kings, with only one of the sons getting the imperial title.[77]

69. "Ieiuniis et orationibus et elemosinarum largitionibus," *Ordinatio imperii* (817), MGH Capit. 1.2:270–73; see 271.

70. See the discussion and bibliography provided in Egon Boshof, "Einheitsidee und Teilungsprinzip Ludwigs des Frommen," in *Charlemagne's Heir*, 177–80; Wallace-Hadrill, *The Barbarian West, A.D. 400–1000: The Early Middle Ages*, 2nd ed. (New York: 1962), 123. For Arquillière, the *Ordinatio* was a triumph of "les impérialistes," safeguarding the unity of the empire by placing it largely in one man's hands; Arquillière, *L'Augustinisme politique*, 123.

71. McKeon, "The Empire of Louis the Pious," 54–55. According to the *Ordinatio Imperii*: "Ut amore filiorum aut gratia unitas imperii a Deo nobis conservati divisione humana scinderetur, ne forte hac occasione scandalum in sancta ecclesia oriretur et offensam illius in cuius potestate omnium iura regnorum consistunt incurreremus," *Ordinatio imperii* (817), MGH Capit. 1.2:270–71.

72. "Ut aliquis illorum propter cupiditatem rerum terrenarum, quae est radix omnium malorum, aut divisor aut obpressor ecclesiarum vel pauperum extiterit aut tyrannidem, in qua omnis crudelitas consistit," *Ordinatio imperii* (817), MGH Capit. 1.2:272.

73. "Ceteri filii ob hoc indignati sunt," Thegan, *Vita Ludovici imperatoris,* in *Quellen zur Karolingischen Reichsgeschichte,* edited by Renhold Rau, Ausgewählte Quellen zur deutschen Gesschichte des Mittelalters 5 (Darmstadt: 1955–1960), 1:213–53; see 230; see also Patzold, *Episcopus,* 231.

74. Innes, "Charlemagne's Will," 847.

75. "Episcopos synodali decreto depositos monasteriis mancipari" (Anno 818), *Annales regni Francorum,* 148.

76. On the relation of these "regional" kingships to the imperial idea, see Henry Mayr-Harting, "Charlemagne," 1113–33; see 1124.

77. T. F. X. Noble, "The Revolt of King Bernard of Italy in 817: Its Causes and Consequences," SM Ser. 3.15 (1974): 315–26; see esp. 325–26.

The *Ordinatio imperii* also proposed a new way of understanding the kingdom. It has been argued that the *Ordinatio* was Augustinian in inspiration; it is more accurate to say that it was a revolutionary extension of episcopal ideals.[78] The non-Augustinian nature of those ideals may be seen in its underlying concepts. The *Ordinatio* portrayed the Empire as a holy structure, which must be united "lest the unity of the empire conserved for us by God be split apart by human division."[79] Further, the Empire was conflated with the church. The *Ordinatio* concerned "what is expedient for the empire, for conserving uninterrupted peace among [the sons], and for the defense of the entire church."[80]

Augustine's writings offered little support for such concepts.[81] For Augustine, the appearance of Christian emperors only offered the prospect that the emperor himself could be saved, and even that seemed tenuous because of the struggle for power inherently involved in becoming and remaining emperor. The Roman Empire remained a human and hence "mixed" construction that could not correspond to the City of God.[82] The Christian emperors did not inspire Augustine to abandon the radical antinomies that he saw extending from worldly existence into the afterlife; indeed, he wrote his *City of God Against the Pagans* while such emperors governed. Augustine pointed out that despite the rule of the Theodosius, the status of the world and earthly dominion remained the same. A Christian emperor might go to heaven, but "all the other things of this life, be they great or small . . . he bestows upon good and evil men alike. . . . And among these things is imperial sway, also, of whatever scope."[83] While Augustine believed that the state might serve as a tool of discipline for the church, this did not sanctify the state.[84]

The *Ordinatio imperii* reflected currents of episcopal thought that, as has been shown, arose in the missionary atmosphere of imperial expansion toward the east and looked back especially to the writings of Isidore. This perspective was being expanded and radicalized in the hands of a new generation of bishops, such as Agobard of Lyon, a bishop of Spanish origin.[85] Agobard is one of

---

78. Noble argues for Augustinianism: "Revolt of King Bernard," 320–21.

79. "Gratia unitas imperii a Deo nobis conservati divisione humana scinderetur," *Ordinatio imperii* (817), MGH Capit. 1.2:270.

80. "Quae capitula propter utilitatem imperii et perpetuam inter eos pacem conservandam et totius ecclesiae tutamen," *Ordinatio imperii* (817), MGH Capit. 1.2:271.

81. Senellart, *Les arts de gouverner,* 75–83.   82. Markus, *Saeculum,* 59–61.

83. Augustine, *City of God* (5.26), 235.   84. Markus, *Saeculum,* 133–53.

85. On Agobard, see Egon Boshof, *Erzbishof Agobard von Lyon: Leben und Werk,* Kölner historische Abhandlungen 17 (Cologne: 1969), and Adrien Bressolles, *Doctrine et action politique d'Agobard,* vol. 1, *Saint Agobard, évêque de Lyon (769–840),* L'Église et L'État au moyen-âge 9 (Paris: 1949).

the most complex and difficult of Carolingian personalities, yet his influence is probably to be seen in the *Ordinatio* itself. Agobard was radical and idiosyncratic, yet like all extremists, he was responding to a current in his world; his writings are therefore of great importance for the student of Carolingian bishops. This is especially true since, as will be shown, bishops were adopting a more radical position *en masse* as they sought to assert their authority in a rapidly changing world. The radicalization emerged in a time of doubt and crisis. Omens added to the sense of danger. Louis was nearly killed when a portico at Aachen collapsed, wounding a number of his companions.[86]

Shortly after the *Ordinatio imperii* was issued in 817, Agobard wrote a book urging a complete change of the Empire's legal structure. Attacking the principle that each distinct "people" should be governed by its own law, Agobard urged that Frankish law should be the only law. Agobard's attack on Burgundian law, *Against the Law of Gundobad,* illuminates the theoretical background of Louis' kingship.[87] Agobard attended the assembly at which the *Ordinatio* was issued, and was the leading figure in a group intent on preserving imperial unity.[88] The unity of the kingdom was, for Agobard, an imitation of the unity of Christ. The roots of this far-reaching concept lay in Isidore of Seville's concept of a Catholic kingdom. Like Isidore, Agobard believed that because Christ was a king and priest, so the Christian kingdom was rightly governed by king and priest.

To describe how unity could arise out of human diversity, Agobard employed the unusual term *concorporatio,* "being gathered into one body."[89] The Incarnation and Christ's mission meant that "for all the nations of the world [there is] one hope . . . one charity born in all, one will, one burning desire."[90] Agobard elaborated the varieties of condition, sex, and quality that are mingled in Christian unity: by praying to one God, all are brought together, "poor and rich, untaught and learned, weak and strong, the humble worker and the sublime emperor."[91] He underscored this concept of union with the striking eucharistic

---

86. McKeon, "817: Une année désastreuse," 5–6.

87. *Adversus legem Gundobadi,* in Agobard of Lyon, *Opera Omnia,* edited by L. Von Acker, CCCM 52 (Turnhout: 1981), 17–28.

88. Boshof, *Erzbishof Agobard von Lyon,* 19, describes Agobard as the head of a "Reichseinheitspartei."

89. Boshof, *Erzbishof Agobard von Lyon,* 43–44.

90. "Annuntiataque est ab eis omni creaturae, id est cunctis nationibus mundi, una fides indita per Deum, una spes diffusa . . . in cordibus credentium, una caritas nata in omnibus, una uoluntas, accensum unum desiderium," Agobard, *Adversus legem Gundobadi,* 19.

91. "Unum Patrem Deum inuocant, seruus et dominus, pauper et diues, indoctus et eruditus, infirmus et fortis, humilis operator et sublimis imperator," Agobard, *Adversus legem Gundobadi,* 20.

image that "we are one bread, one body of Christ, indeed we are one Christ."[92] For Agobard, Christian unity was a decisive reality that had direct consequences for political culture and social policy. Like Isidore, Agobard's vision of an integral Christian society led him to attack the Jews with special virulence, to the point of obsession, since he grounded all social and political life in the unifying power of Christianity.[93] Christian society was a holy body of untold dimension and worldwide scope. This was a radical restatement of Visigothic theocracy and Isidore's "Christological sociology."

The unity of the Empire must be maintained at all costs. In this, Agobard's *Against the Law of Gundobad* is closely related to the *Ordinatio imperii*: both works emphasized imperial unity.

Augustine believed that human structures were mortal and impure (*permixta*), while Agobard wanted to help the Frankish kingdom realize itself as a holy entity. Like Augustine, he believed that there was a gulf dividing mankind, and that each side of this chasm could be thought of as a "city":

Here there assuredly ought to be a discrimination and a division between two kingdoms, that is, of Christ and of the devil, between the city of God and the city of the devil, which constitute two peoples. For the city of God contains the people of increase, and the city of the devil the people of perdition. While it is impossible for humans to discern who belongs to the city of God, and who to the city of the devil, at least they know who [belongs to each city] most evidently by their particular fruits. The Apostolic letters teach through [such] evidence they should reject those who are separate from the body of Christ.[94]

Agobard's "City of God" was non-Augustinian. His terminology does not, in fact, come from Augustine, but from Tyconius, whom Agobard might have read either in the original or in citations contained in Beatus of Liebana's *Com-*

92. "Quoniam unus panis, unum corpus Christi, immo unus Christus," Agobard, *Adversus legem Gundobadi*, 20.

93. Boshof, *Erzbishof Agobard von Lyon*, 43–44. Agobard attacked the Jews in a series of works: *De baptismo mancipiorum Iudaeorum* (*Opera Omnia*, 113–17); *Contra praeceptum impium de baptismo iudaicorum mancipiorum* (*Opera Omnia*, 183–88); *De insolentia Iudaeorum: De iudaicis superstitionibus et erroribus* (*Opera Omnia*, 189–95): and *De cauendo conuictu et societate iudaica* (*Opera Omnia*, 229–34).

94. "Hic profecto debet esse discretio et diuisio inter regnum et regnum, id est Christi et diaboli, inter ciuitatem Dei et ciuitatem diaboli, que faciunt duas plebes. Nam ciuitas Dei continet populum adquisitionis, ciuitas diaboli populum perditionis. Quod si hominibus impossibile est, omnes discernere, qui sint de ciuitate Dei, qui uero de ciuitate diaboli, saltem quos euidentissime ex fructibus propriis cognoscunt, et litterae apostolice a corpore Christi separatos docent, reiciant de testimonio," Agobard, *Adversus legem Gundobadi*, 22.

mentary on the Apocalypse.[95] Gregory the Great also developed the concept that Christ and Satan divide humanity between them, contrasting the Body of Christ with its obscene parallel, the Body of Satan. Gregory likewise conceived of each side as a City (*civitas Dei/civitas diaboli*).[96] Agobard's "City of God" was closer to the "City of Christ" described in Charlemagne's letter to Elipandus, a shift in language and concepts highlighting an extremely optimistic understanding of society and politics.

Agobard laid out his plans for standardizing and integrating the Empire so that the Empire could become a better representation of Christ's body. The Burgundians should abandon Gundobad's law code—because it was made by a heretic—and accept Frankish law. This would lift them out of their "squalid misery" somewhat.[97] Agobard was thinking not of the *Lex Salica,* but of what he called the *Lex Francorum,* the expansive style of royal law, with its universal claims and religious content. As an abstraction, the term seems momentous.

The chief failing of the code was its reliance on trial by battle, forcing even the old and sick to fight over vile things, "a terrible error and a confused order."[98] The laws of Gundobad were heretical because by relying upon duels, they sanctioned murder: although the Burgundians believed that such fighting revealed the will of God, Agobard pointed out, "this is not law, but murder" (*non est lex, sed nex*).[99] The will of God is quite hidden—*occultissima.* If the good always won such struggles, then "Herod would not have killed John, but John would have killed Herod"—Saracens would not have captured Jerusalem, Goths would not have conquered Rome.[100] Victory does not always go to the innocent, and so we can neither understand nor predict how God will dispense human history.

If Agobard believed that the concept of imperial unity, the *Ordinatio imperii,* had solved the problem of how to preserve the unity of the church, he was soon disappointed. The rebellion of Bernard of Italy threatened to overturn the

---

95. Beatus of Liebana, *Obras Completas de Beato de Liebana,* ed. Joaquin Gonzalez Echegaray, Alberto del Campo, and Leslie G. Freeman (Madrid: 1995), 11–12; see also Boshof, *Erzbishof Agobard von Lyon,* 48–52.

96. Michael Fiedrowicz, *Das Kirchenverständnis Gregors des Grossen: Eine Untersuchung seiner exegetischen und homiletischen Werke,* Römische Quartalschrift für christliche Altertumskunde und Kirchengeschichte, Suppl. 50 (Freiburg: 1995), 260–66.

97. "Si autem placeret domino nostro sapientissimo imperatori, ut eos transferret ad legem Francorum, et ipsi nobiliores efficerentur, et hec regio ab squaloribus miseriarum quantulumcumque subleuearetur," Agobard, *Adversus legem Gundobadi,* 23.

98. "Hic est pessimus error et ordo confusus," Agobard, *Adversus legem Gundobadi,* 23.

99. Agobard, *Adversus legem Gundobadi,* 26.

100. "Occultissima Dei dispensatione," Agobard, *Adversus legem Gundobadi,* 24.

Ordinatio almost at once. In the years after 817, Agobard wrote a brief work, *On the Privilege and Law of the Bishop,* which betrayed the deep anxiety he felt in this tense period. Therein he reflected on the meaning of episcopal office and its role in history.[101] Bishops had a crucial part to play in what Agobard believed was the end-time of history. He described himself and his readers as being "under pressure" from unheard-of and deplorable evils characterizing the end of the world, troubles "our ancestors and fathers did not know."[102] In the days of the early church, the world was youthful, but now it is old, tottering toward death.[103] The troubles afflicting the kingdom meant that soon the "Adversary who is now bound in the Abyss will be loosed to wage war on all men."[104]

The role of the priesthood had been, from its inception, to maintain a struggle now culminating in the Apocalypse: "we were chosen for the ministry of ordaining and ruling the Churches in these terrible times."[105] What struck Agobard as convincing proof that the world was ending was the violation of ecclesiastical order by the nobility. Wealthy laymen built private churches and hired priests to serve in them. These priests, far from remaining obedient to their bishop, became part of the layman's household, waiting tables, pouring wine, leading dogs, or guiding horses that women were riding.[106] Agobard contrasted this privatization of the sacred with the dignity of the bishop's unique governing authority. One can detect a heightening of distinctions as Agobard "walked the boundary," so to speak, of episcopal power in the countryside.

Agobard cited the story of King Ozias, from the Book of Chronicles, who arrogated the right to burn incense in the temple. He was met at the altar by the high priest Azarias, with eighty priests, *"viri fortissimi,"* who told him "it does not pertain to your office, Ozias, to offer incense to the Lord, but to the priesthood, that is the sons of Aaron, who were consecrated for this ministry:

101. *De privilegio et iure sacerdotii,* in Agobard of Lyon, *Opera Omnia,* CCCM 52, 53–69.

102. "Nuper dum in unum positi conloqueremur, maxime de pressuris, odiis et dispectione Ecclesiarum atque clericorum . . . que ignorauerunt antecessores et patres nostri," Agobard, *De privilegio et iure sacerdotii, Opera Omnia,* CCCM 52, 53–69.

103. "Mundus in annis prioribus uelut in iuuentute uiguit. At nunc ipsa sua senectute deprimitur, et quasi ad uicinam mortem molestiis crescentibus urguetur," Agobard, *De privilegio et iure sacerdotii,* CCCM 52, 64. Agobard relies on Bede, *De temporum ratione* 66, CCSL 123B (Turnhout: 1977), 263–460.

104. "Aduersum quos ille, qui nunc ligatus est in abysso, solutus, totis uiribus permittetur belligerare," Agobard, *De privilegio et iure sacerdotii,* CCCM 52, 65.

105. "Qui in his pessimis temporibus ordinandi et regendi Ecclesias ministerium sortiti sumus," Agobard, *De privilegio et iure sacerdotii,* CCCM 52, 63.

106. "Aut ad mensas ministrent, aut saccata uina misceant, aut canes ducant, aut caballos, quibus femine sedent, regant," Agobard, *De privilegio et iure sacerdotii,* CCCM 52, 62.

leave the sanctuary."[107] King Ozias was struck with leprosy when he refused to leave. The high priest at the head of his eighty followers provided Agobard with an image of episcopal conciliar authority, which had been violated by the nobles with their private churches. The line of priests, from the time of the sons of Adam, was established as a distinct group with sacred duties. No laymen, not even a king, could organize or instruct this priesthood. The borders of the sacred marked out a zone of freedom from lay control. Episcopal government of church land and clerics was threatened by the bonds of obligation attached to private churches, funded as they were by the provision of *beneficia*—that is, lands to which obligations were inherently attached. To Agobard, this seemed to be a recent evil. A noble might approach his bishop and say, "I have a cleric whom I raised for myself from my own serfs, whether holders of benefices or villagers, either obtained from this or that man, or from such-and-such village: I want you to ordain him as a presbyter for me."[108]

Powerful manorial establishments had long offered a challenge to episcopal government by incorporating church lands, churches, and clerics within a vassalic system. As Susan Reynolds has remarked, the duty of laymen to protect churches and their property often led to control and dominance of those same churches. This still did not affect the theoretical and real freedom of ecclesiastical property, and thus it is not right to speak of *proprietary churches*.[109] Agobard was most concerned with the obedience of clerics to their bishop. According to Agobard, any departure from this would transgress the boundaries of sacred space and categories of persons. Agobard believed that the king would have to accept the boundaries of authority and the sacred before they could have any force.

The problem of establishing an imperial succession threatened to upset the sources of Louis' own authority. Recent analysis views the empire as a complex arrangement of independent regional powers, connected by means of concerted action and rituals of reconciliation that tied region to region and ultimately to royal centers of power.[110] Charlemagne had also faced the problem of arranging

107. "Non est tui officii, Ozia, ut adoleas incensum Domino, sed sacerdotum, hoc est filiorum Aaron, qui consecrati sunt ad huiuscemodi ministerium: egredere de sanctuario," from II Par. 26:16–20, as cited by Agobard, *De privilegio et iure sacerdotii,* CCCM 52, 59–60.

108. "Habeo unum clericionem, quem mihi nutriui de seruis meis propriis, aut beneficialibus, siue pagensibus, aut obtinui ab illo uel illo homine, siue de illo uel illo pago: uolo ut ordines eum mihi presbiterum," Agobard, *De privilegio et iure sacerdotii,* CCCM 52:62. On the ambiguity of the term *servus,* see Hans-Werner Goetz, "Serfdom and the Beginnings of a 'Seigneurial System' in the Carolingian Period: a Survey of the Evidence," EME 2 (1993): 29–51.

109. Reynolds, *Fiefs and Vassals,* 61.

110. Innes, *State and Society,* 195–96.

the status of various family members and determining how his crown and wealth would be inherited.[111] This meant excluding some family members, reducing the stems of the family deemed capable of power.[112] At the top level of the Carolingian system, just below the emperor, were regional kingships, given to the emperor's family members, while the imperial title was put in the hands of Louis. In the *Ordinatio imperii* Louis connected a just and peaceful succession and God's benevolence toward the realm, at the same time highlighting the theme of imperial unity. While adopting the cultural and political doctrines of his bishops, Louis also sought to forge a synthesis between those doctrines and the principles of succession developed by Charlemagne.[113] His position was a difficult one, raising the possibility of conflict between the imperial titles Louis loved to elaborate and his role as defender of the church, with the domestic and familial roots of royal power. Because of this conflict, Louis, at two important junctures, endured the public humiliation of penance at the hands of his bishops.

At Attigny, in 822, Louis the Pious publically confessed his wrongful imprisonment of his brothers and the destruction of Bernard of Italy. He also undertook a public penance.[114] This seems to have been a carefully prepared ceremony of reconciliation: in the previous year, Louis had freed Adalhard and Wala from exile. According to Agobard of Lyon, reflecting on these events years afterward, Louis was not at all a weak figure at Attigny, but the potent head of his church, convoking and directing the council. Agobard credited him with the reform legislation enacted there. In short, Louis "strenuously [provided] for everything useful to the people committed to his care." Divine grace showed him what had to be done, and he "faithfully announced it with his own mouth." This is why he deserved to be called "our sacred and religious lord emperor."[115] For Thegan, another contemporary observer, Louis' penance was a way of strengthening the religious sources of his authority, and in no way a public humiliation. Certain-

111. Innes, "Charlemagne's Will," 833.

112. Airlie, "Narratives of Triumph," 117.

113. Innes, "Charlemagne's Will," 841–43.

114. De Clercq, "La législation religieuse franque," *Revue de Droit Canonique* 5 (1955): 5–7. On the concept of public penance, see Rob Meens, "Paenitentia publica en paenitentia privata: Aantekeningen bij de oorsprong van de zogeheten Karolingische dichotomie," in *Die Fonteyn der Ewiger Wijsheit: Opstellen aangeboden aan prof. dr A. G. Weiler,* edited by P. Bange and P. M. J. C. de Kort, 65–73, Middeleeuwse Studies 5 (Nijmegen: 1989).

115. "In illis dibus, quando sacer et religiosus domnus noster imperator euocato conuentu in Attiniaco agebat, strenue prouidens de omnibus utilitatibus commissorum sibi populorum . . . quod utique laudabiliter inspirante Dei gratia queseuit, eleganter inuenit, fideliter ore su annuntiauit," *De dispensatione ecclesiasticarum rerum,* in Agobard of Lyon, *Opera Omnia* CCCM 52:119–42; see 121.

ly it was no check on his actions. According to Thegan, Louis continued per-secuting his relatives immediately after the council,[116] despite the fact that for such activities he was compelled to "[give] much to the poor for the purgation of his soul."[117]

Agobard used the occasion to speak against the misuse of church land. He recorded the speech of Adalhard, abbot of Corbie, before the council:

> Whatever your wisdom may learn for guarding against sin and avoiding danger, for building up religion, illuminating doctrine, strengthening faith, and cultivating the devotion to sanctity, declare it confidently and may you not doubt that the lord em-peror will be ready to satisfy God. Since the sacred scriptures teach us that sins lead to infelicities, disturbances, devastations and sterility for the people, [the emperor] is taking care, with the greatest concern, that by establishing good and destroying evil . . . the kingdom committed to him might prosper, and with God's help he might have the strength to govern.[118]

Like Pseudo-Cyprian, Cathwulf, and Alcuin, Adalhard saw the kingdom as a perfectable instrument of Christian salvation, and thought that this salvific function should be pursued in the context of church reform. Finally, there was the striking detail that Louis' ability to govern was tied to the prosperity of the realm and to nature's fruitfulness. Adalhard had been a victim of Louis' purge, and had returned from exile just prior to the council at Attigny.[119] Agobard por-trayed Louis as capable of living up to the ideals of the *Ordinatio imperii.* At the same time, this was an insistence that Louis must live up to them. Attigny was the most dramatic example yet of the impact of episcopal political ideas on royal action. Was Louis simply being crafty, enduring this ritual humiliation with no intention of fulfilling the demands made on him? While Louis sought to recon-cile or silence his victims by an appeal to sacred kingship, some of them, such as Wala (later abbot of Corbie), were only inspired to make more extreme statements

116. This seems to be the perspective of Thegan, who shows that Louis continued all the ac-tivities for which he had done penance; *Vita Ludovici imperatoris,* PL 106:417.

117. "Ob hanc causam multa dedit pauperibus propter purgationem animae suae," Thegan, *Vita Ludovici imperatoris,* PL 106:416–17.

118. "Quicquid utile potuerit reperire sagacitas uestra ad cauenda peccata, ad uitanda pericula, ad erigendam religionem, ad inlustrandam doctrinam, ad corroborandam fidem, ad excolendum studium sanctitatis, confidenter edicite, et ad explenda pariturum Deo Domnum imperatorem minime dubitetis. Qui, quoniam, ut Scripture sacre docent, peccata contrahunt infelicitates, per-turbationes, clades et sterilitates im populos, tota sollicitudine curat, ut, bona quidem statuendo, mala uero destruendo, optineat una uobiscum apud Dominum, ut, remotis aduersis casibus, reg-num sibi commissum prospere, Deo fauente, ualeat gubernare," Agobard, *De dispensatione eccle-siasticarum rerum,* CCCM 52:122.

119. Hartmann, *Die Synoden der Karolingerzeit,* 166.

of the centrality and independence of the church.[120] Given the activities and opinions of powerful men like Wala, it is clear that for understanding the reign of Louis the Pious, ideology is "evidence at least as important as *Realpolitik*."[121]

The Universal Church of Gaul

Three years after Attigny, Louis was given the opportunity to engage in a larger sphere of activity by presiding over a Frankish Church representing western, Roman orthodoxy, even against papal opposition. The issue was again iconoclasm. The Franks were drawn into the affair by Michael the Amorian, the Emperor of Byzantium. Some discussion is necessary of the complex events leading to the Council of Paris in 825.

Before dawn, on Christmas morning of 820, Emperor Leo V appeared at his palace chapel to attend the liturgy. A conspiracy was underway, led by Michael the Amorian, who was in prison at the time. As Leo entered the chapel, soldiers disguised as clerics attacked and dismembered the emperor. Michael was retrieved from his cell and, still wearing leg-irons, was acclaimed emperor (Michael II, 820–829). Although he was supported by many iconophiles, Michael II soon pursued a moderate version of iconoclasm. A civil war was staged by a rival claimant to the throne, Thomas the Slav, and in the wake of a costly victory, Michael was forced to emphasize the continuity of his regime with Leo's.[122]

Leo had rejected the Second Council of Nicaea in 787, and looked back to the *Horos* declared by the iconoclastic council of Hiereia in 754.[123] This *horos* formed the basis for the compilation of dossiers of texts supporting iconoclasm, activity that culminated in the Council of St. Sophia in 815. Michael's iconoclasm was much more wavering than Leo's.[124] He attempted to conciliate the iconophiles, but would not tolerate important or vigorous opponents. The patriarch Nicephorus was exiled to a monastery and replaced when he and other orthodox bishops refused to meet with iconoclastic bishops.[125] Pope Eugenius was sympathetic to

120. Magnou-Nortier, "La tentative de subversion," 334 and 347.

121. Radbertus recorded the oppositional views of Wala: David Ganz, "The *Epitaphium Arsenii* and Opposition to Louis the Pious," in *Charlemagne's Heir*, 537–50.

122. This account follows Warren Treadgold, *The Byzantine Revival, 780–842* (Stanford: 1988), 196–262.

123. Rydén, "The Role of the Icon in Byzantine Piety," 41–42. The Greek and Latin versions of II Nicaea are conveniently provided in N. P. Tanner, *Decrees of the Ecumenical Councils, Nicaea I to Lateran V* (London: 1990), 1:133–38.

124. See also the useful summary in R. Davis, *The First Seven Ecumenical Councils (325–787): Their History and Theology,* Theology and Life Series 21 (Collegeville, Minn.: 1990), 290–322.

125. P. J. Alexander, *The Patriarch Nicephorus of Constantinople: Ecclesiastical Policy and Image Worship in the Byzantine Empire* (Oxford: 1958), 147–48.

the iconophiles, and by accepting and helping the exiles, he could keep the pot boiling in Byzantium, as had his predecessors Paul and Hadrian. Michael believed that the Franks might be useful in this conflict.

In 824, Michael sent an embassy to Louis the Pious to gain support for his policy on images.[126] The embassy conveyed a letter laying out the parameters of the emperor's moderate iconoclasm.[127] The letter also offered a mendacious version of events leading to Michael's accession and victory over Thomas the Slav.[128] According to this tale, the Patriarch, Antonius I Kassimatas (821–834), along with assembled "senators and princes," elected Michael to the throne. His throne was therefore established by the "consensus of all." The letter asserted that all power is derived from Christ, "the arranger of all good things."[129] For their part, the Franks were well aware that Michael got his throne by means of a murderous conspiracy.[130]

Michael's letter was carefully crafted to elicit Frankish sympathy, and on this slender basis, the Franks accepted that the Emperor had come around to a position like that promoted at the Council of Frankfurt. Michael attempted to limit his attack to the "excesses" of the iconodules. Those who worshipped images were termed "aliens to apostolic traditions" and "inventors of evil things."[131] These remarks were aimed at Pope Eugenius II, whose sympathies lay with the exiled iconophiles.

Shortly after receiving the embassy, Louis ordered several important bishops to prepare a response. Heading the commission were Jonas of Orléans, Amalarius of Metz, Freculf of Lisieux, and Halitgar of Cambrai. These bishops organized a search for patristic references, basing their work on earlier research conducted under Charlemagne, in an attempt to delineate a "royal road" of compromise between iconoclasm and iconodulism.[132]

126. Freeman, "Carolingian Orthodoxy," 100–101.

127. *Michaelis et Theophili imperatorum Constantinopolitanorum epistola ad Hludowicum imperatorem directa,* MGH Conc. 2.2:475–80.

128. Treadgold, *Byzantine Revival,* 244–45; Ostrogorsky, *History of the Byzantine State,* 203–6, takes this version more seriously.

129. "Cumque proelium committeremus, ipse dominus Deus noster, qui semper adiutor et protector imperii nostri est, misit principem militiae virtutis suae, sicut legitur fecisse Iesu Nave, et dissolvit ac dissipavit virtutem eorum et praevelere nos fecit adversus eum," *Michaelis et Theophili imperatorum epistola,* 477.

130. "Adlatum est et de morte Leonis Constantinopolitani imperatoris, quod conspiratione quorundam optimatum suorum et praecipue Michahelis comitis domesticorum" (Anno 821), *Annales regni Francorum,* 155.

131. Note the combination of political and religious concerns: "Alieni de apostolicis traditionibus facti et neque paternos terminos custodientes, facti sunt inventores malarum rerum," *Michaelis et Theophili imperatorum epistola,* 478.

132. Council of Paris (825), MGH Conc. 2.2:473–551; See 482.

Not unlike the Council of Aachen in 816, the Council of Paris in 825 deployed conciliar authority toward the production of a book.[133] The greater part of the council's "proceedings" constituted an anthology on the subject of images. These were arranged in seventy-one *capitula* so that the form, if not the content, had a conciliar appearance.[134] Although the gathering in Paris in 825 is better described as a kind of colloquium on the problem of images, the bishops and their emperor insisted on its conciliar status.[135] It was a carefully orchestrated presentation of western orthodoxy as embodied by the bishops of Louis' empire, centering on the controversy over images and the production of a monument of Catholic doctrine repulsing both Eastern iconoclasm and Roman iconophilism.[136] The *Libellus synodalis,* the main document of the council, is a messy, rough-edged production. It is a collection of documents resulting from research directed by the bishops, then stitched together as though awaiting some further step. The uniqueness of the codex recording the council bears a strange resemblance to the lack of circulation of the *Libri Carolini*.[137] In both cases the Frankish Church made universal claims on the topic of icons, but documents making these claims were not circulated.

It has been argued that the bishops at Paris 825 did not make use of the *Libri Carolini,* but based their work on the *Capitulare adversus synodum,* a now lost predecessor of the *Libri Carolini*.[138] The lines of connection to the Council of Frankfurt in 794 were also personal. Jonas of Orléans, for example, had gone to Spain, perhaps in an official capacity, during the struggle with Adoptionism, before succeeding Theodulf as the bishop of Orléans in 821.[139]

133. *Conventus Parisiensis, De Causa imaginum:* Jacques Sirmond, *Conciliorum antiquorum Galliae a Iac,* 106–38.

134. The formal elements of the council, as presented in the main document associated with it, the *Libellus synodalis Parisiensis,* MGH Conc. 2.2:475–532, are complex. It may be schematized as follows: (1) letter from the Byzantine Emperors, 475–80; (2) address to Louis the Pious from the bishops, 481–84; (3) 71 *capitula,* consisting of quotations from the Fathers, fully half of which are from Augustine, 484–506; (4) first postscript, 506–7; (5) continuation of quotations, now unnumbered, 507–20; (6) second postscript. Introduction to three treatises, 520–23; (7) "Ratio," 524–26; (8) "Auctoritas," 526–29; (9) "Consilium," 529–32. Preserved in the same manuscript: a letter from Louis to Hieremias and Jonas of Orleans, a letter from Louis to Pope Eugenius II, and finally an Epitome of the Libellus synodalis. It impossible to say who wrote these, according to the editor Werminghoff: Council of Paris (825), MGH Conc. 2.2:475.

135. The form led its editor Werminghoff to characterize it as "non verum concilium, sed magis colloquium de imaginibus," Council of Paris (825), MGH Conc. 2.2:474.

136. Council of Paris (825), MGH Conc. 2.2:473–551; see also Wallace-Hadrill, *Frankish Church,* 266.

137. Freeman, "Carolingian Orthodoxy," 65–66.

138. Freeman, "Carolingian Orthodoxy," 102; see also Wallach, *Diplomatic Studies,* 1–2, 28.

139. Karl Amelung, *Leben und Schriften des Bischofs Jonas von Orléans* (diss., Programm des

Facing papal opposition, the bishops assembled at Paris were forced to consider the relationship between competing authorities. The hope Michael's letter inspired was that the churches of east and west could be rejoined in common orthodoxy through the cooperation of the Frankish and Byzantine emperors. The obstinance of the pope threatened to bring this to nothing. But how could he be corrected?[140]

In a preface to the council, the bishops sketched the history of Frankish involvement in the iconoclast controversy, particularly the events surrounding the Second Council of Nicaea in 787. The letter on images Pope Hadrian had sent to Nicaea was read and contrasted with the Council of Frankfurt, which had declared the adoration of images to be unholy (*adorare vero nefas sit*). Strikingly, Hadrian's letter was dismissed because the patristic testimony it brought forward was "badly out of tune" and "hardly pertinent."[141]

The *capitula* the bishops compiled were chosen to attack iconophilism (as idolatry) and iconoclasm at the same time. The centerpiece was Gregory the Great's letter to the iconoclast Serenus. Gregory explained that images were useful for providing instruction to the illiterate.[142] Having illustrated the proper use of images, the Council of Paris went on to present a vast dossier of patristic citations against idolatry and image worship of the kind that had confronted the late antique church.[143]

The bishops then turned their attention to the proper object of worship. Here, citations from Augustine were advanced, stressing the *latreia* due to God alone. The cross was described as the best symbol to use in Christian worship. Only the cross had a direct connection with Christ, and only the cross played a role in the sacraments, when an invisible cross was traced on the forehead and the breast at baptism. Only the cross was universal, unlike portrayals of saints, which differed from place to place.[144] The bishops also endeavored to make Augustine's theory of signs relevant to a discussion of religious images.

Wirzthumschen Gymnasium in Dresden, Leipzig University, 1888), 4–6; see also the resume in Brunhölzl, *Histoire de la littérature latine*, vol. 1.2:155–59.

140. Alain Dubreucq, "Fils de l'Église: genèse et développement d'une conception chrétienne du pouvoir royal," in *Clovis*, 2:85–102; see 97.

141. "Inseruit etiam in eadem epistola quaedam testimonia sanctorum patrum, quantum nobis datur intelligi, valde absona et ad rem, de qua agebatur, minime pertinentia," Council of Paris (825), MGH Conc. 2.2:481.

142. Council of Paris (825), MGH Conc. 2.2:487; see also Ann Freeman, "Scripture and Images," 170.

143. Council of Paris (825), MGH Conc. 2.2:489–99.

144. Council of Paris (825), MGH Conc. 2.2:503–6.

This section ended with a letter from "Louis to Emperor Michael," making clear the rather astonishing ambitions of the Council of Paris.[145] Louis addressed the "emperors of the eastern Romans" as his brothers, who ought to be admitted to the "intimate interior of our heart."[146] Gone was the attack on Byzantine emperors as inheritors of a pagan empire, as in the *Libri Carolini.* Bishops were now content to hear the emperors describe themselves as the "faithful emperors of the Romans."[147] The parallelism of the two empires was stressed as Louis and his bishops turned their attention to a critical and delicate issue: the correction of the pope.

Papal resistance to the Frankish position on images (which might be called "Frankish Iconoclasm") seemed apocalyptic. It was implied that division of the church had arisen because the end of time was approaching. After rehearsing the preeminence of the apostolic see, and its authority for the whole world, the problem of correcting the pope was approached, and very tentatively. The proper thing, said Louis' letter to Michael, might be to keep silent out of respect for the pope's sublime position. The cares of the realm, however, prevented Louis from convoking a council uniting the east and west. Further, the pope was making unification impossible. His errors on the topic of images made it impossible for the church in the east to accept his authority, even though he held the keys of St. Peter.[148] It is clear that the whole weight of the Council of Paris was directed against the pope. The council reflects a tremendous degree of confidence on the part of the Frankish bishops due to their participation in a project of orthodox universalism under imperial leadership.[149]

The arguments against the pope's position were laid out in three independent treatises closing the *Libellus synodalis:* "Reason," "Authority," and "Counsel." The three treatises were a summation of sources for the Frankish position and were offered as three avenues along which papal error might be corrected.

Reason (*ratio*) was described as intellectual moderation, necessary to properly interpret patristic statements and to recognize the need for unity. Intellectual moderation would use religious images discreetly.[150] Reason was available

---

145. Council of Paris (825), MGH Conc. 2.2:520–23.

146. "Necessitatem fratrum nostrorum, totius scilicet imperii Orientalium Romanorum, ad intima cordis nostri viscera admittere debemus, quorum inviolabilem caritatem," Council of Paris (825), MGH Conc. 2.2:521.

147. "Fideles in ipso Deo imperatores Romanorum," *Michaelis et Theophili imperatorum epistola,* 475.

148. Council of Paris (825), MGH Conc. 2.2:522–23.

149. Dubreucq also connects this audacious tone to the impact of imperial-episcopal cooperation: Dubreucq, "Fils de l'Église," 97.

150. Council of Paris (825), MGH Conc. 2.2:524–25.

to all, and it especially informed the Frankish Church. To portray Frankish unanimity and the possible unification with the east, every Latin term for inclusivity was put in play—*cunctus, omnis, totius, universa,* producing a confection difficult to translate.

And therefore the entire assembly of priests and every senate of the whole people or empire of the Franks, and the universal church through all of Gaul, with the other provinces put under its imperium with the aid of God. . . .

sought to overcome a disunion whose source could only be demonic. Once again the Franks defended "Roman" catholicism even against Rome:

They cry out to heaven with one mouth and one heart, to unfailingly impose the judgement of God Almighty upon us, whether by the authority of the highest apostles in the whole globe of lands, by whose doctrines and counsel the entire world is swayed, we may not struggle to return your discord to true concord.[151]

The pope should heed the "line of truth" to be found in the chain of patristic quotations the bishops had assembled, including the authoritative words of Dionysius, Clement, and Peter. Peter had caused Gaul to be evangelized, and the Franks were the heirs of this "line of truth." The apostles of Gaul—Dionysius, Hilary of Poitiers, and Martin of Tours—passed on to the Gallic Church their learning and their *magisterium*. In other words, the bishops at Paris in 825 were prepared to employ Cyprianic concepts of episcopal independence in a quite radical way, claiming the mantle of Peter in a bid to correct the pope.

The treatise on "Authority" (*auctoritas*) recapitulated Gregory's moderate position on images and asserted that such an authority should be interpreted correctly. The final treatise, "Counsel" (*concilio*), asserted the ability of the eastern and western churches, united under their emperors, to offer counsel to the pope. The document argued that the discord, murders, and vandalism carried out by proponents of iconoclasm were the result of a diabolical force attempting to divide the church.[152] It was implied, too, that the pope might be the cause of further violence and unrest if he persisted.

The hesitancy and the roughness of the council's documents show that the Franks were not in fact prepared to press home their universalist claims against

---

151. "Vociferantur enim in caelum uno ore et uno corde omnipotentis Dei iudicium inevitabiliter nobis incumbere, si auctoritate summorum in toto orbe terrarum apostolorum, quorum doctrinis et consilio universus flectitur mundus, discordiam vestram ad veram concordiam non certamus reducere," Council of Paris (825), MGH Conc. 2.2:525.

152. Council of Paris (825), MGH Conc. 2.2:532.

papal opposition, occasioning much wavering and inconsistency of argumenta-
tion. There were other ambiguities in the Frankish position, as well. By casting
doubt on the veneration of images of saints, the Council of Paris problematized
an old and established tradition of Frankish devotion toward the saints and their
images.[153] The bishops' vision of the Carolingian kingdom as a vehicle for salvation, moreover, was not compatible with an austere doctrine on images.

Like his father Charlemagne, Louis appeared at the head of his unified bishops, bringing together the moral and intellectual resources of his kingdom.
Again like his father, he oversaw a council that made an abortive claim to represent Roman catholicity against the pope himself. It was an impressive effort
of coordinated study and a dramatic spectacle of cultural integration. But the
cooperation of Louis and his bishops was not long-lived. Troubling signs that
had emerged at Attigny in 822 soon came back in force and led to a breakdown
of episcopal-royal cooperation.

Vassals and Bishops

In 823, a year after Louis' penance at Attigny, he had a child by his second
wife, Judith of Bavaria. Judith and her supporters began to press Louis to make
room for this son, the future Charles the Bald, by granting him a portion of the
kingdom.[154] Lothar and critics such as Agobard later decried the new arrangement as a violation of the oath Louis had made in the *Ordinatio imperii*. The
move seemed to cast doubt on Louis' allegiance to imperial unity. With caution
and due attention to legality, Louis sought to enter his son Charles in the hierar-
chal arrangement of his family members and their respective powers. He chose
as the setting for this significant event a series of great episcopal councils. As in
813, a round of coordinated councils were planned, to be held in four cities in
829, gathering all the great metropolitan and episcopal sees of the kingdom.[155]
The most important of these, and the only one whose records are extant, was
held in Paris.[156] These councils were the centerpiece of the most significant reform effort since 816, and seem to have been a direct response to a sense of crisis.[157] The Council of Paris in 829 reflects the fact that Louis felt he could rely
on his bishops to support a new political order.

---

153. See, for example, Peter Brown, *The Cult of the Saints: Its Rise and Function in Latin Christianity* (Chicago: 1981), 120–27.
154. Janet L. Nelson, *Charles the Bald* (London: 1992), 87.
155. De Clercq, "La législation religieuse franque," *Revue de Droit Canonique* 5 (1955): 29.
156. Riché, *Carolingians*, 149–51. For the records of the council, see Council of Paris (829),
MGH Conc. 2.2:596–680.
157. Nelson, *Charles*, 81.

Élisabeth Magnou-Nortier has argued in a major study of the council and its documents that the council records must be read with considerable caution, because they survive only in a heavily manipulated form, rewritten and interpolated.[158] This view has not been supported by further scholarship, and is disputed by Gerhard Schmitz.[159] According to Magnou-Nortier's interpretation, the falsification of the conciliar record reflects the aims of a subversive group of bishops who wished to destabilize imperial rule in favor of an episcopal regime.[160] Instead, we should see the council as the culmination of many years of development in the shared and widely disseminated social doctrines of the Carolingian Empire, which placed bishops at the head of society to guide and save the people.[161] The council was not the radical statement of outsiders, as has often been suggested, but was a prominent and imposing statement of old doctrine sharpened by old grievances. Steffen Patzold has demonstrated the connection between Paris (829) and the long-nurtured model of the bishop as the mediator between God and man, *mediator inter Deus et homines*.[162]

In the period of crisis that stretches from 829 until Louis' death in 840, bishops made increasingly strident assertions of their central position in the sacred kingdom. The Council of Paris represents the prominence of views held by reform-minded clerics. It would be impossible to say how extensive this party, so similar in its views to Agobard, might have been.[163] Even if the surviving council-record was produced by some supposed group of tendentious outsiders, the "alternative" council seems to reflect the actual views of the bishops who assembled in Paris. The successful promotion of this record of the Council of Paris, to the exclusion of all other records of the councils held in 829, suggests that conciliar authority had escaped the hands of the emperor. Nothing so comprehensive had been declared about the role of the bishops, but none of the claims were new. In the view of Magnou-Nortier, the date of these documents cannot be fixed with any certainty, but must be later than 829, and possibly after 833.[164]

Many of the bishops who had gathered at Paris in 825 were also at Paris in 829, above all Jonas of Orléans and Agobard of Lyon, who arrived with his suf-

158. Magnou-Nortier, "Tentative de subversion," 339–40.

159. Gerhard Schmitz, "Echte Quellen—falsche Quellen," 275–300.

160. Magnou-Nortier strongly emphasizes that the goal of the forgers was to replace the traditional concept of the Carolingian state with rule by bishops, "qui ressemble à une tyrannie": Magnou-Nortier, "Tentative de subversion," 623.

161. Patzold, *Episcopus,* 510.

162. Patzold, *Episcopus,* 149, citing Council of Paris (829), MGH Conc. 2.2:594.

163. Schmitz, "Echte Quellen," 292–93.

164. Magnou-Nortier, "Tentative de subversion," 623.

fragans.[165] These two men dominated the proceedings, and Jonas was charged with preparing the final documents of the council.[166] The council had its origins in a palace assembly during the winter of 828, at which basic questions were raised because of the sense of crisis enveloping the kingdom. The court gave explicit instructions to the bishops: that they should assemble and determine how to return the kingdom to God's favor, to examine how the *ordines* of society had strayed from their assigned tasks.[167] Louis indicated in a prefatory letter for the council that the ongoing project of church reform, and the councils in which it was carried out, were necessary to propitiate God, whose anger was evident in social upheavals and enemies surrounding Louis' throne. At the time of the council Louis was making military preparations to counter a rumored invasion.[168] The emperor's effort to propitiate an angry God was the central reason for calling the council.[169] The letter ended with a dramatic reminder of Louis' situation: "Let all men throughout our entire kingdom who are required to accompany the army, be well prepared with horses, arms, clothing and food."[170] Nevertheless, the bishops made it clear that they intended to admonish and correct a king they held partially responsible for the troubles he faced.

The reason a council could placate an angry God, the authors believed, was that the council was a penitential act for the king, and by extension, for the entire kingdom. The first notes sounded in the Council of Paris were recognizably a reference to Louis' penance at Attigny. Agobard's voice echoes here. Louis and Lothair were told that Christ had committed the government of the kingdom to them by "His hidden dispensation" (*occulta dispensatio*).[171] The bishops then went on to offer biblical examples of "princes who by the inspired advice

165. Hartmann, *Die Synoden der Karolingerzeit,* 179.

166. Wallace-Hadrill, *Frankish Church,* 240; Magnou-Nortier, however, feels that Jonas cannot be implicated in the forged versions, because of his well-known loyalty to Louis: Magnou-Nortier, "Tentative de subversion," 362.

167. Patzold, *Episcopus,* 152.

168. Council of Paris (829), MGH Conc. 2.2:601. The rumor was unfounded: "Sed ubi vana esse compererat, quae de Nordmannis fama disperserat" (Anno 829), *Annales regni Francorum,* 177.

169. "Deumque tota devotione deposcere, ut nobis propitiari," *Epistola generalis* to the Council of Paris (829), MGH Conc., 2.2:599; see also Magnou-Nortier, "Tentative de subversion," 338.

170. "Ut omnes homines per totum regnum nostrum, qui exercitalis itineris debitores sunt, bene sint praeparati cum equis, armis, vestimentis et victualibus," *Epistola generalis* in Council of Paris (829), MGH Conc., 2.2:601. Louis had believed that a Norse invasion was imminent, but this turned out to be a rumor; "Sed ubi vana esse compererat, quae de Nordmannis fama disperserat" (Anno 829), *Annales regni Francorum,* 177.

171. "Quam Christus, qui . . . gloriosis Augustis, regendam tuendamque committere occulta sua dispensatione voluit," Council of Paris (829), MGH Conc., 2.2:607.

of heaven" were converted, such as the king of Nineveh, who "was a man turned from his evil ways and from iniquity."[172] The Book of Jonah told how this king had put on sackcloth as a result of Jonah's preaching (Jon 3:5–7). The bishops' allusion was to the penance and "conversion" of a king. Penance by the whole kingdom had long been considered the best way to avert God's anger, and this propitiation was to be organized by bishops. As governors of their parishioners, bishops held themselves responsible for purging the Empire of its sins, *restoring* imperial stability:

We decree with a mutual will and a mutual consensus, that each of us should, by word and example, more attentively strive to urge the people of our parishes to better things, and to admonish them to withdraw from evil and turn with all their hearts to God: And God, whom they made angry at themselves by sinning, they are hard pressed to conciliate by the worthy payment of penance and by gifts of alms, and furthermore, on behalf of the life of the most pious Emperor Louis, who is dear to God, the safety of his wife and children, and the stability of the empire entrusted to him.[173]

It is by no means clear that the authors were intent on subversion. The bishops called for a perpetual campaign of preaching to turn the Lord's anger from the people of God.[174] The tone of the council is very similar to the admonitions and "mirrors of princes" that flourished in this troubled era, with their longing for order and their obsessive concern for justice.[175]

The records of the Council of Paris took the form of a great treatise, by now expected of a major council.[176] Unlike previous councils, however, the Council of 829 seems to have been entirely concerned with social and political matters. The treatise was divided into three books: one on the principles of episcopal gov-

172. "Idem Deo pleni principes caelitus inspirati consulto ad Deum congruam dignamque conversionem iudicaverunt esse faciendam iuxta illud regis Ninnivitae, quo legitur: Convertatur vir a via sua mala et ab iniquitate," Council of Paris (829), MGH Conc., 2.2:607.

173. "Statuimus pari voto parique consensu, ut unusquisque nostrum dictis et exemplis plebes parroechiae suae adtentius ad meliora incitare studeat easque, ut se a malis cohibeant et ad Deum ex toto corde convertant, sollicite admoneat; Deumque, quem peccando sibi iratum fecerant, digna paenitentiae satisfactione et elemosinarum largitione sibi placabilem facere satagant necnon et pro vita piissimi Deoque amabilis Hludowici imperatoris, coniugis prolisque eius incolomitate imperiique sibi commissi stabilitate," Council of Paris (829), MGH Conc., 2.2:612.

174. "Cum itaque praedicatoribus sine cessatione populo Dei praedicare necesse sit . . . tum maxime id eis facere necesse est, quando iram Domini contra populum Dei meritis exigentibus grassari perspexerint," Council of Paris (829), MGH Conc., 2.2:613.

175. Senellart, *Les arts de gouverner,* 49–51; Wallace-Hadrill, *Frankish Church,* 240.

176. According to Magnou-Nortier, two distinct positions can be detected in the council records, although prominence went to the views of the "Isidoreans": Magnou-Nortier, "Tentative de subversion," 357.

ernment, one on royal power, and one on the duties of the nobility.[177] In this arrangement, one is reminded of the social concerns of Agobard, but also, as an important backdrop, the political doctrines of Smaragdus. Jonas of Orléans was also interested in providing an ethical code for the nobility, which he had done on his own, before the council opened, in his *De institutione laicali*. In about 831, Jonas went on to write a companion book for kings, *De institutione regia*, addressed to Pippin I of Aquitaine.[178] In the latter work, Jonas emphasized the ministerial nature of kingship and its grounding in justice. "The royal ministry is to govern the people of God, and to rule with equity and justice, so that he will be devoted to peace and concord."[179] Because of the failure of the ideals embodied in the *Ordinatio imperii,* the council's attention was turned toward outlining a social framework for the kingdom, which, like all Carolingian social thought, was exclusively concerned with the duties of those at the top of society.

Patzold suggests that we can know in some detail who attended the council based on a charter of Inchad of Paris, listing twenty-four archbishops and bishops. Ebo of Rheims attended with seven suffragans, Aldrich of Sens with six suffragans, Ragnoard of Rouen with three suffragans, Landram of Tours with one. Also present were bishops Amatheus, Theodesclus, and Fulchar, from unknown sees, and the prominent abbots Wala of Corbie and Hilduin of St. Denis. Jesse of Amiens, Adelelm of Chalons, Inchad of Paris, Ebo of Rheims, Landram of Tours, Ragnoard of Rouen: these men were well-connected with the court, representing a new generation of northern bishops not present at the Five Councils of 813. Most had served as ambassadors, *missi dominici,* or palace chaplains, and all can be connected to earlier reform programs.[180]

Although the Council of Paris (825) had ransacked many of Augustine's writings, searching for every mention of sign, symbol, picture, or image, in its discussion of social reality the bishops at Paris in 829 abandoned Augustine completely. They instead followed Agobard's reading of Tyconius (or Beatus):

177. Patzold, *Episcopus,* 153.
178. The *De institutione regia* of Jonas of Orléans, in the edition of Luc d'Achery, may be consulted in PL 106:279–306. For a newer critical edition and study: Jean Reviron, *Les idées politico-religieuses d'un évêque du IXe siècle: Jonas d'Orléans et son "De institutione regia": Étude et texte critique,* L'Église et l'état au moyen Âge 1 (Paris: 1930); see also Brunhölzl, *Histoire de la littérature latine,* 1.2:157–58, and De Clercq, "La législation religieuse franque," *Revue de Droit Canonique* 5 (1955): 43.
179. "Regale minsterium est populum Dei gubernare et regere cum equitate et justitia, ut pacem et concordiam habeat studere," Reviron, *Les idées politico-religieuses,* 145.
180. Patzold, *Episcopus,* 160–61.

First, therefore [it should be said] that the universal holy Church of God is certainly believed to be one body, and its head is Christ. . . . Therefore whoever through unlawful things changed himself from a member of Christ, to a member of the devil, should know that he is not in the Body of Christ, but in the body of the devil.[181]

The sacralized social body was portrayed as a tangible reality, in a way quite unlike St. Augustine's more nuanced, and politically difficult, view. Nor should the admonitory quality of the bishops' dicta be overlooked, since they drew their social boundaries with Louis the Pious in mind.

The bishops then focused their attention on their society viewed as the Body of Christ, identified with the Frankish kingdom. They cited the well-known words of Pope Gelasius: "there are two august imperial powers by whom this world is chiefly ruled; the sacred authority of bishops and royal power."[182] The bishops' understanding of Gelasius, however, was closer to Isidore's transposition of late antique social categories than it was to Gelasius himself. As discussed earlier, Isidore did not see royal power, in Gelasian terms, as representing an independent secular world, but rather as one pole of a Christological interpretation of an integrated Christian society, governed by king and priest. The Council of Paris followed Isidore in this logic. Disregarding the difference between their categories and those of Gelasius, the bishops introduced Gelasius under this rubric:

THAT THE BODY OF THE CHURCH IS PRINCIPALLY DIVIDED BETWEEN TWO SPECIAL PERSONAGES. And so we know first of all, that the body of the entire holy Church of God is divided into two special personages, namely the priestly and the royal.[183]

This transposition of Gelasius' categories, from "the world" to "the Church" meant that the bishops here reasserted a sociology, going back to Isidore, granting them a status equivalent to that of kings.[184] This restatement of episcopal

---

181. "Primum igitur, quod universalis sancta Dei ecclesia unum corpus manifeste esse credatur eiusque caput Christus. . . . Quisquis ergo per aliqua inlicita ex membro Christi se fecit membrum diaboli noverit se non in corpore Christi, sed in corpore esse diabolic," Council of Paris (829), MGH Conc., 2.2:610.

182. "De qua re Gelasius Romane sedis venerabilis episcopus ad Anastasium imperatorem ita scribit: Duae sunt quippe, inquit, imperatrices augustae, quibus principaliter mundus hic regitur, auctoritas sacrata pontificum et regalis potestas," as cited at the Council of Paris (829), MGH Conc., 2.2:610.

183. "QUOD EIUSDEM ECCLESIAE CORPUS IN DUABUS PRINCIPALTER DIVIDATUR EXIMIIS PERSONIS. Principaliter itaque totius sanctae Dei ecclesiae corpus in duas eximias personas, in sacerdotalem videlicet et regale," Council of Paris (829), MGH Conc., 2.2:610.

184. Dubreucq, "Fils de l'Église," 98.

sociology was significant, considering the troubles Louis was facing after 829. It has been argued that such a doctrine, representing the views of an Isidorean faction, implied that the empire should become an instrument in the hands of the bishops.[185] The bishops here restated in a vigorous and forceful way a group of concepts fundamental to the principles of Carolingian kingship. Rather than an act of subversion, the council highlighted the principle of a sacred state, and did not shrink from raising this ideal against an emperor who had not lived up to his own precepts. The path forward, according to the bishops, lay in a mutual recognition of duties and a cooperation of king and bishop.[186]

The first and largest section of the treatise concerned episcopal government. Bishops were admonished to set themselves apart from society at large, as successors of the apostles, fulfilling a vital governmental function.[187] Bishops, like the Carolingian kings, were anointed at their ordinations.[188] The authors could therefore apply to bishops the phrase "Do not touch my anointed," because the "Lord's anointed" (*Christi domini*) was in fact the priesthood.[189] As an anointed "person," the bishop stood beside his king at the pinnacle of society. Retrieving an old tradition, the bishops stressed that, like kings, they could also be compared to David.[190] Far from being an innovation, this concept had been raised long ago at the Council of Marseilles in 533.[191] Anointing as an assumption of majesty, and the comparison of the anointed person to David, have commonly been thought of as distinctly royal imagery.[192] As will be seen, kingship was still viewed as a religious institution, but it is going too far to say that unction had conferred upon kings a "quasi-divine status."[193] The king was a layman whose status was sacralized through his association with the church and his duty to

185. Magnou-Nortier, "Tentative de subversion," 345.

186. Patzold, *Episcopus,* 159.

187. "Apostoli, quorum successores sunt episcope," Council of Paris (829), MGH Conc., 2.2:630.

188. Janet L. Nelson, "National Synods, Kingship as Office, and Royal Anointing: An Early Medieval Syndrome," in Nelson, *Politics and Ritual,* 239–57; see 249–50.

189. "Christos Domini sacerdotes appellari dubium non est, de quibus in psalmo divina voce canitur: Nolite tangere christos meos et in prophetis meis nolite malignari," Council of Paris (829), MGH Conc., 2.2:625.

190. "Sicut per Sahul reprobi praelati, ita et per David subiecti sunt humiles significati," Council of Paris (829), MGH Conc., 2.2:625.

191. "Videte, fratres, unde in libro Regum legimus de duobus regibus Saul et Dauid; sed si de eorum uitam pensamus, possumus aliquid ad nostram imitationem collegi. Iste prior et presens regnum perdedit et caelestem amisit, ille sequens et presentem habuit et caelestem adeptus est," Marseilles (533), CCSL 148A:96.

192. See for example Wallace-Hadrill, "The *Via Regia* of the Carolingian Age"; see also Anton, *Fürstenspiegel,* who argues (51 and elsewhere), that David represented *Herrschertum.*

193. Reviron, *Les idées politico-religieuses,* 81.

defend and help the church.[194] It is important to stress the fact that bishops here drew on an ancient tradition granting them a role parallel to that of the king, and that frequently employed the same imagery.

One feature of this relationship was the bishops' insistence that they were rectors (*rectores*) with power to judge the people given to their care—and that bishops were not subject to royal judgment. The council cited Emperor Constantine from the *Ecclesiastical History* of Eusebius (as translated by Rufinus): "God established you as priests and gave you the power of judging us; and therefore we are rightly judged by you, but you are not to be judged by human powers."[195] Bishops held the keys of St. Peter, and so were the "gatekeepers of heaven."[196] Episcopal power transcended the power of kings:

> what they establish on earth is also established in heaven, and what they undo on earth is also undone in heaven, and whose sins they remit are taken from them. It is established that they are vicars of the apostles and the windows of the world.

This unearthly power was the basis of episcopal legislative authority, and thus even emperors must "ask the priests for law."[197]

The bishops excoriated those of their number preoccupied with "earthly actions." The Council of Paris (829) was unique in being the first extended discussion of the daily activities of bishops, whose control of farmland and laborers was now seen as a troubling aspect of episcopal government.[198] Previous councils had emphasized episcopal government in an urban setting, with only a glance at the rural parishes falling inside his orbit. The Five Councils of 813 had gone furthest in this regard. At Paris, episcopal involvement in a manorial economy was addressed directly and contrasted forcefully with the urban ideal of the bishop. This concern had been raised nine years earlier in a document called *A Relation of the Bishops to Louis the Emperor,* a basic set of clerical precepts.[199] The bishops declared:

194. Le Goff, "Le roi dans l'occident," 16.

195. "In ecclesiastica historia Constantinus imperator episcopis ait: Deus vos constituit sacerdotes et potestatem vobis dedit de nobis quoque iudicandi; et ideo nos a vobis recte iudicamur, vos autem non potestis ab hominibus iudicari," citing Rufinus, *Ecclesiastica historia* 10.2), Council of Paris (829), MGH Conc., 2.2: 625.

196. "Ianitores caelestis aulae," Council of Paris (829), MGH Conc., 2.2:612.

197. "Quibus et in evangelio a Domino tanta confertur potestas, ut quae statuerint in terra statuta sint et in caelo et quae solverint in terra soluta sint et in caelis et quorum reiserint peccata remittantur eis. Hos quippe constat vicarios esse apostolorum et luminaria mundi," Council of Paris (829), MGH Conc., 2.2:605, citing Agg. 2:12 "Interroga sacerdotes legem"; see also Patzold, *Episcopus,* 154–55.

198. This was part of their incorporation in the imperial aristocracy: Werner, *Naissance de noblesse,* 371–73.

199. *Episcoporum ad Hludowicum imperatorem relatio* (820), MGH Capit. 1.2:366.

the priests of the Lord . . . should not be sent from their own churches, in a very un-lawful enterprise, to external accomplishments, because then the *opus divinum* is ne-glected, and infants typically die without the grace of baptism and men without con-fession; the danger of whose case is piteously bent back against those who call them from their churches, and against the bishops, who ought to act on their behalf.[200]

Bishops were engaged in estate exploitation and employed the lands entrusted to them in seigneurial exchanges of land and obligations.[201] The council addressed the increasing problem of pressure exerted by the *potentes,* the powerful and wealthy nobility that had not been fully integrated in the sacralized kingdom-concept.[202] The Council of Paris stressed that bishops were only administrators, not owners of church land. The nobility showed too little interest in salvation, while bishops showed too much interest in worldly gain: "It is an amazing thing: the world does not have enough ambition, and the church of Christ has too much."[203] Such preoccupations caused some bishops to neglect their parishes.

Yet we have learned that certain members of our order are frequenting remote places, neglecting their clerics and leaving the see of their own city, not out of necessity or utility, but rather most often out of avarice and for their own delight. Because of this, the divine cult is set aside, preaching to the people and caring for their subjects; and hospitality is neglected.[204]

"Hospitality" in this context meant the broad episcopal duty to provide for every-one in need, especially travelers and the poor.[205] Bishops were failing properly to govern the canons, monks, and nuns of their territories. The Council of Aachen

200. "Ut sacerdotes Domini . . . a suis eclesiis tam inlicito ausu ad exteriora peragenda non mittantur, quia proinde et opus divinum neglegitur et infantes sine baptismi gratia et homines sine confessione mori solent. Cuius causae periculum et in eos qui a suis eclesiis eos advocant et in episcopos, quorum vicem agere debent, miserabiliter retorquetur," *Episcoporum ad Hludowi-cum imperatorem relatio* (820), MGH Capit, 1.2:367.
201. Kaiser, "Royauté et pouvoir épiscopale," 152–57.
202. The constant refrain in Carolingian legislation that the poor must be protected from the powerful seems to show the disharmony between the *potentes* and imperial order; Stephen Weinberger, "La transformation des *Potentes* dans la Provence médiévale (IVe–XIe s.)," MA 97, 5th ser. 5 (1991): 159–69; see 164.
203. "Mira namque res: ambitio mundialis satis non habet, et ecclesia Christi nimium habet," Council of Paris (829), MGH Conc., 2.2:625.
204. "Conperimus etiam quosdam socios ordinis nostri non causa necessitatis aut utilitatis, se potius avaritiae et propriae delectationis saepissime, propria civitatis suae sede relicta cleroque neglecto, remociora loca frequentare, de qua re et distitutio divini cultus et praedicatio in plebi-bus et cura subiectorum postponitur et hospitalitas neglegitur," Council of Paris (829), MGH Conc., 2.2:627.
205. "Cum ergo hospitalitas in tremendi examinis die ab aeterno iudice sit remuneranda," Council of Paris (829), MGH Conc., 2.2:621.

in 816 had provided detailed rules for this governance. By means of their care and direction, the "Council of Paris" explained, bishops were to prevent "both orders" (canons and monks) from "falling into the mousetrap of the devil."[206]

Episcopal participation in seigneurial management was troubling, because the tendency of such bishops was to violate the boundaries of episcopal exclusivity, looking and behaving like the nobility. "No one is worthy of the kingdom of God," the Evangelist had warned, "who puts his hand to the plow and looks back."[207] Such concerns perverted the bishop's duty to protect the poor, because estate exploitation forced people into poverty. The oppression of the poor, which councils had complained of for centuries, was becoming systemic, and involved bishops as well as laymen. One particular method of exploitation was to create local monopolies over agricultural products. By setting prices at will, and fiddling with weights and measures, lords could squeeze profits from their peasants and serfs.[208]

As had the Council of Aachen in 816, the "Council of Paris" cited Julian Pomerius on episcopal administration, but at greater length:

knowing that the property of the church is nothing other than the prayers of the faithful, the ransom of sinners, and the patrimony of the poor, let them not lay claim to it for their own use, as their own, but portion them out as things commended to the poor.[209]

The authors envisioned the careful inspection and management of estates by a bishop and his clerics alone, without lay managers and their rapacious methods.[210] These lay estate managers were "ferocious ministers" (*atroces ministri*) through whom lords (including bishops) thrust their people into poverty. The poor "dare to take nothing from the fruit of their own harvests and their vine-

---

206. "Quia persepe hac occasione multos utriusque ordinis, canonici videlicet et monastici, viros muscipulam diaboli incurrisse cognovimus," Council of Paris (829), MGH Conc., 2.2:640.

207. "Nemo mittens manum suam in aratro et respiciens retro, aptus est regno Dei," Lk. 9:62, cited at Council of Paris (829), MGH Conc., 2.2:630.

208. "Et adflictionem atque obpressionem ingentem pauperibus inrogat, quod quidam non solum clerici, sed et laici dominici praecepti transgressores effecti minorem modium atque sestarium in vendendo atque commondando maioremque in recipiendo habent," Council of Paris (829), MGH Conc., 2.2:644.

209. "Et idcirco scientes nihil aliud esse res ecclesiae nisi vota fidelium, pretia peccatorum et patrimonium pauperum, non eas vidicaverunt in usus suos ut proprias, sed ut commendatas pauperibus diviserunt," Julian Pomerius, *De vita contemplativa* (2.9), as cited at Council of Paris (829), MGH Conc., 2.2:623.

210. "Didicimus sane quorundam relatu nonnullos coepiscoporum in peragrandis parroechiis suis non solum consacerdotibus, verum etiam quibusdam aliis fidelibus, quibus consultum ferre debuerant, honeri existere et ob hanc causam multos in sui detractionem detestationemque pertrahere," Council of Paris (829), MGH Conc., 2.2:632–33.

yards, but are compelled to leave untouched and deliver everything, whatever it is, to their lords."[211]

Although the bishops at Paris pictured every basilica as normally having lands and people (including slaves)[212] under its control, these lands were to be governed differently than lay estates.[213] Protection of the poor lay at the heart of episcopal claims to control property in a different way, and under a different law, than lay property. This was enfeebled when bishops engaged in the same abuses as laymen, such as loan-sharking. To dramatize this problem, the bishops offered an imaginary conversation between a moneylender and a poor man attempting to buy food: "If you want to buy it, bring the price and take it." To which the pauper says, "I don't have the money with which to buy it. I beg of you, that you pity me, lest I die of starvation, and extend a loan to me."[214] The moneylender then makes a loan against the next harvest, to be "violently extracted" in the autumn.

The bishops requested royal action to help end these abuses, and much of the first treatise admonished the king to do this. Before turning to a discussion of kingship itself, the bishops paused to remark that "because of usurious and unequal weights and measures, and the oppression of the poor, there is a commotion of the land, in fact there is a trial and weakening of the kingdom, and lamentation of all its inhabitants."[215] The sounds of rebellion that could be heard were therefore attributed to the Emperor's failure to protect the poor. This treatise ended by elaborating the importance of public penance for grave sins, strongly implying that the Emperor might be expected to endure such a penance once again.[216]

The Justice of a King

The council turned from its complaints about episcopal discipline and government to a treatise detailing the duties and function of royal power. Citing Isidore of Seville, the bishops pointed out that a king is so called because he rules correctly (*Rex a recte agendo vocatur*), and may be called king if he rules piously,

211. "Ita ut nihil sibi suaeque coniugi ac liberis de fructu messium vinearumque suarum usurpare audeant, sed omne, quicquid illud est, dominis suis ex integro custodire et reddere compellantur," Council of Paris (829), MGH Conc., 2.2:644.

212. Goetz, "Serfdom and the Beginnings of a 'Seigneurial System,'" 39.

213. "Ut singulae basilicae, plebes et res, quibus consistere possint," Council of Paris (829), MGH Conc., 2.2:642.

214. "'Si vis emere, fer pretium et tolle.' Cui pauper: 'Non est mihi', inquid, 'quicquam praetii, quo emere id, quo indigeo, valeam. Sed peto abs te, ut miserearis mei et quomodocumque vis, mihi quod peto, ne fame peram, mutuum porridge,'" Council of Paris (829), MGH Conc., 2.2:646.

215. "Quod propter usuras et inaequales mensuras staterasque dolosas atque obpressiones pauperum commotio terrae, immo periclitatio et infirmatio regni luctusque omnium habitatorum," Council of Paris (829), MGH Conc., 2.2:647.

216. Council of Paris (829), MGH Conc., 2.2:648–49.

justly, and mercifully. If he does not, then he is no king, but a tyrant.[217] Tyrants were sent to punish sin, and their government was as much a part of the divine plan as is the rule of the good king.[218]

The doctrine of the divine establishment of all power, good and bad, was a poor aid to understanding when the empire was being torn apart by the sons of Louis. The council quoted the dictum of Paul, who stood behind so much of what the Fathers had to say about government: "who resists a power ordained by God particularly resists the orderly government of God" (Rom. 13:2). Patristic political thought had no room for competing authorities, offered no way of distinguishing a true king from a tyrant. But Frankish bishops wanted to know how to identify a true king, because they viewed the kingdom as a moral entity that could be made consonant with the will of God. They rejected patristic social thought even while reciting it.

The bishops sought standards by which to judge kingship, and found them in a work attributed to Cyprian, but in fact an anonymous Irish work of the seventh century, the *Twelve Abuses of the Age*.[219] The political thought of the *Twelve Abuses* (which Alcuin may have known, as mentioned above), tied the seasonal and fruitful harmony of nature to the beneficial effect of a rightly ordered kingdom reflecting God's power over the earth. Kings must conform to the Creator's design: from that conformity would flow fruitfulness of every kind, the greatest sign of which was peace. The king who accomplished peace was a just king, and a king who ruled *recte,* but the king who failed was a blight on his people:

Truly the justice of a king is to oppress no one unjustly by his power, to judge a man and his peer without regard to persons, and those dear to him, to be a defender of travelers, orphans, and widows, to repress crime, punish adulteries, not to exalt evil men . . . to wipe the impious from the earth, not suffering parricides and perjurers to live, to defend churches, to nourish the poor with alms, to establish the just over the business of the realm . . . to defend the homeland strongly and justly against adversaries, to live in God in all matters. . . .

---

217. "Rex a recte agendo vocatur. Si enim pie et juste et misericorditer regit, merito rex appellatur; si his caruerit, non rex, sed tyrannus est," Council of Paris (829), MGH Conc., 2.2:649. The bishops cited Isidore; see Reydellet, *La royauté dans la littérature latine,* 576.

218. "Quapropter quisquis ceteris mortalibus temporaliter imperat non ab hominibus, sed a Deo sibi regnum commissum credat. Multi namque munere divino, multi etiam Dei permissu regnant. Qui pie et iuste et misericorditer regnant sine dubio per Deum regnant; qui vero secus, non eius munere, sed permissu tantum regnant," Council of Paris (829), MGH Conc., 2.2:655. This follows Isidore's *Sententiae* (3.48): "Reges quando boni sunt muneris est Dei, quando uero mali, sceleris est populi," cited in Reydellet, *La royauté dans la littérature latine,* 579.

219. Pseudo-Cyprian, *Pseudo-Cyprianus De XII abusivis saeculi,* 1–2.

[When this is not done,] the peace of the people is violated, and troubles are stirred up in the kingdom, all fruits of the land are diminished and the people are bound in servitude . . . invasions of armies destroy the provinces, tear apart the herds of cattle and flocks of sheep. Spring and winter storms abort the fecundity of the land and the fruits of the sea. Sometimes the lightening-blasts incinerate grain-fields and the flowers of trees and vines. Why, the injustice of a king's present authority casts a shadow over everything, not only for now, but even over our sons and grandsons, since they will have the kingdom after us.[220]

A good king could establish peace, an expansive idea much more complex and comprehensive than our modern negative and restricted concept. The *Twelve Abuses*, as cited at Paris, went on to describe this kind of peace:

The peace of the people is the protection of the homeland, immunity [from public impost or duty] of the people, the protection of the nations, the cure of weakness, the joy of men, temperate weather, serenity of the sea, fecundity of the earth, solace of the poor, inheritance of sons, and the people's hopes for future beatitude.[221]

Peace, fecundity, strength, a beneficent climate, security from enemies, religious salvation, and care for the poor—such were the blessings of royal justice.

It is noteworthy that much older strains of Irish social theology, with roots in an ancient understanding of pharaonic kingship, were so compatible with Frankish ideals of good kingship, which identified the aims of royal power with episcopal goals.[222] Since the king was deputed to do God's work, he ought to make

220. "Iustitia vero regis est neminem iniuste per potentiam obprimere, sine acceptione personarum inter virum et proximum suum iudicare, advenis et pupillis et viduis defensorem esse, furta cohibere, adulteria punire, iniquos non exaltare, inpudicos et istriones non nutrire, impios de terra perdere, parricidas et periurantes vivere non sinere, ecclesias defendere, pauperes elemosynis alere, iustos super regni negotia constituere. . . . patriam fortiter et iuste contra adversarios defendere, per omnia in Deo vivere. . . . Qui vero secundum hanc legem non dispensat, multas nimirum adversitates imperii tolerat. Idcirco enim saepe pax populorum rumpitur et offendicula etiam de regno suscitantur, terrarum quoque fructus diminuuntur et servitia populorum praepediuntur, multi etiam dolores prosperitatem regni inficiunt, carorum et liberorum mortes tristitiam conferunt, hostium incursus provintias undique vastant, bestiae armentorum et pecorum greges dilacerant, tempestates veris et hiemis terrarum fecunditatem et maris ministeria prohibent et aliquando fulminum hictus segetes et arborum flores et paminos exurunt. Super omnia vero regis iniustitia non solum praesentis imperii faciem fuscat, sed etiam filios suos et nepotes, ne post se regni hereditatem teneant, obscurat," Pseudo-Cyprian, *De XII abusivis saeculi,* c. 9; as cited at Council of Paris (829), MGH Conc., 2.2:650.

221. "Pax populorum est, tuamentum patriae, inmunitas plebis, munimentum gentis, cura languorum, gaudium hominum, temperies aeris, serenitas maris, terre fecunditas, solatium pauperum, hereditas filiorum et sibimetipsi spes futurae beatitudinis," Pseudo-Cyprian, *De XII abusivis saeculi,* c. 9, as cited at Council of Paris (829), MGH Conc., 2.2:650.

222. The Pseudo-Cyprianic *De XII abusivis saeculi* looks back to a seemingly archaic Irish

God's causes his own. This is why his duty included taking up the *causa paupe-rum*—he must end oppression of the poor.[223] According to the Council of Paris, the king "ought to be first of all the defender of the church, and of the servants of God, of widows, orphans, and, moreover, of the other poor, including all the destitute."[224] As Louis faced rebellion and invasion, his bishops produced a stri-dently expressed, wholly religious foundation for his throne, which strongly con-nected his royal function with what had long been seen as a basic episcopal duty (care for the poor); moreover they suggested that he had not fulfilled this duty.

The bishops had assembled in Paris, Jonas and Agobard among them, as the *rectors* of society, confident of their potency as the Vicars of the Apostles, and con-fident, too, in their ability to govern and teach, an order of men distinct from the rest of society, and in their purity and connection to God having a duty to guide and correct society.[225] As we have seen, the production of the interpolated and re-written conciliar record was by no means the "entrée en scène de l'episcopat franc comme corps organisé," but the radicalization of episcopal positions formulated over decades and rooted in the late antique past.[226] The adoption of a more aggres-sive tone by the bishops was a response to political crisis and can be dated at least from the assembly in Attigny (822).[227] Louis turned to the bishops for help in pro-pitiating the deity and strengthening the kingdom through ecclesiastical reform. They in turn required more of him as the crisis deepened.

---

vernacular work, the *Audacht Morainn;* see *Audacht Morainn,* ed. Fergus Kelly (Dublin: 1976); Dáibhí Ó Cróinín, *Early Medieval Ireland* (London: 1995), 77–78.

223. "Scire etiam debet, quod causa, quam iuxta minsterium sibi commissum administrat, non hominum, sed Dei causa existit, cui pro ministerio quod suscepit, in examinis tremendi die rationem redditurus est. Et ideo oportet, ut ipse, qui iudex est iudicum, causam pauperum ad se ingredi faciat et diligenter inquirat, ne forte illi, qui ab eo constituti sunt et vicem eius agere de-bent in populo, iniuste aut neglegenter pauperes oppressiones pati permittant," Council of Paris (829), MGH Conc., 2.2:652.

224. "Ipse enim debet primo defensor esse ecclesiarum et sevorum Dei, viduarum, orfano-rum ceterorumque pauperum necnon et omnium indigentium," Council of Paris (829), MGH Conc., 2.2:651.

225. Patzold, *Episcopus,* 510.

226. Étienne Delaruelle, "En relisant le 'De institutione regia' de Jonas d'Orléans: L'entrée en scène de l'episcopat carolingien," in *Mélanges d'histoire du Moyen Âge: Dédiés à la mémoire de Louis Halphen,* 185–92; see 186 (Paris: 1951).

227. Theodor Schieffer, "Die Krise des karolingischen Imperiums," 1–15.

[9]

THE END OF UNITY
The Abomination of Desolation

IN THIS FINAL CHAPTER, the significance of conciliar law comes to the fore once again. The division of the Carolingian Empire upon the death of Louis the Pious meant the end of its stridently proclaimed and religiously interpreted politico-religious unity. These dramatic changes were reflected, as on a seismometer, in councils that record the development of new, unprecedented lines of political thought. The division of the empire called for the reconceptualization of monarchical government. This chapter includes close readings of little-studied council records, such as Aachen (836) and Yütz-bei-Diedenhofen (844). In these and other documents, we see the problem of sheer power and military force addressed directly for the first time as a topic relevant to understanding royal and noble power. Significantly, the warrior nobility were included in descriptions of the political order for the first time. Sheer power broke out from beneath the smooth surface of a very old ideology and impinged mightily on the political blindness of the bishops.

The age-old ideals of imperial unity and royal-episcopal cooperation were broken into flinders. Not surprisingly, the bishops also began to speak, in their council records and other documents, of the problem of tyranny. In the aftermath of 843, in the kingdom of Charles the Bald, the formidable archbishop Hincmar endeavored to formulate a new conceptualization of the kingdom and to redefine the relationship of kings, bishops, and warriors. For the first time since the rise of the Carolingian state, a sharp theoretical (and real) divide had opened between royal power and the episcopal voice of the councils.

Three Necessary Things

Therefore, as sacred eloquence testifies, it is proper for those who would dominate to have three necessary things: terror, certainly; orderly government; and love. Unless a prince is both loved and feared, his orderly government (ordinatio) will not be able to stand.[1]

Thus an anonymous ninth-century treatise, "The Discipline of Princes" (De disciplina principum), quoted Pseudo-Cyprian to instruct one of Louis the Pious' sons about the harsh requirements of kingship. The Carolingian theorist and his Irish source almost seem to anticipate Machiavelli's reflections on the preferability of force or love (o la forza o l'amore) in securing princely domination.[2] The De disciplina principum, however, suggests the need to combine terror and love in the service of a sacred social order (ordinatio), because "imperial and royal power are ordained by God."[3] The conjuncture of terror and love seems significant in a text directed to a Carolingian prince. The author may well have reflected on the political outcome of the Ordinatio imperii of 817. The orderly government Louis laid down in that document was an attempt to reflect God's intentions for the empire: it was a careful arrangement of familial power-sharing that took every contingency into account, as Rosamond McKitterick has pointed out, except the birth of Charles the Bald.[4] In the end, the document could not prevent the Carolingian family from competing for power.

Beginning with the Council of Paris in 829, new sources of political and social understanding were sought by bishops caught up in the turmoil of Louis the Pious' last years.[5] The gathering of intellectual resources set in motion by Charlemagne's Admonitio generalis nourished these speculations: our anonymous author could draw with equal facility upon recent and ancient sources: Al-

1. "Tria ergo necessaria, sicut sacra testantur eloquia, eos, qui dominantur, habere oportet: terrorem scilicet, ordinationem et amorem. Nisi enim ametur princeps et metuatur, ordinatio illius constare nullatenus poterit," Rudolf Schieffer, "Zwei karolingische Texte," 15. This is from Schieffer's second text, contained in Vatican, Cod. Regin. lat. 407, fol. 90v–92r. The source of this text is Pseudo-Cyprianus De XII abusivis saeculi, 43–44.

2. Niccolò Machiavelli, Discorso fatto al magistrato dei dieci sopra le cose di Pisa, in Arte della guerra e scritti politici minor, edited by S. Bertelli (Milan: 1961), 13.

3. "Potestas imperialis et ragalis ideo a deo ordinata est," Schieffer, "Zwei karolingische Texte," 15.

4. McKitterick, Frankish Kingdoms, 136.

5. The text reflects the influence of Paris (829): Schieffer, "Zwei karolingische Texte," 14; see also See Anton, "Pseudo-Cyprian," 568–617.

cuin, Bede, Pseudo-Cyprian, Rufinus, and Ambrose.[6] Ominous political events, such as the penance of the emperor and the empire's division by fraternal warfare, seemed to call for a new terminology with which to explain them: but why terror? Terror had long been a term for bad power, the *potentiae terror* against which bishops sought to protect the weak.[7] As was mentioned at the outset of this study, Hilary of Arles extolled his hero, Honoratus, as one who chose "to rule with love rather than dominate by terror."[8] Elipandus had reproached Charlemagne for settling a question of theology with the terror of his power (*terror potestatis*).[9]

It has been shown how bishops sought to apply ancient categories to the problem of social change and noble domination of rural churches. As these troubles were compounded by civil war, the uncertainty of bishops mounted to anxiety that they were witnessing not only the eclipse of a social order, but perhaps even the end of the world. It is this fear that summoned *terror* to the aid of *ordinatio*. The composers of the Council of Paris also felt the need of "imperial terror" (*terror imperialis*).[10] The context of the *De disciplina principum* was one of conflict and civil war: "the crown of victory is only pledged in battles."[11]

The political theology of the Carolingian Empire had warily avoided the problem of force. The Carolingian usurpation and the subsequent anointing of Pippin III were seen as a resolution to this problem, confining force within the boundaries of a sacralized symbolic order.[12] Bishops thereby helped their kings erect or "add" a sacral state at the head of the Frankish kingdom, and had made this little realm of words and law into a powerful instrument for organizing the intellectual and military force of the kingdom. At the uppermost reaches of this state stood the thinnest and most transparent level of all: the concept of a new Roman Empire.[13] More influential was the idea that the Frankish world was a Christian empire.

6. Schieffer, "Zwei karolingische Texte," 14.

7. Werner, *Naissance de la noblesse,* 243. According to "Terror, Terrorismus," GGB 6:323–443, terror became a political concept only in the early modern period. However, here we have a political usage in the Carolingian period.

8. "Studebat praeterea amore potius regere quam terrore dominari" (28.2), Hilary of Arles, *Vie de Saint Honorat,* 148.

9. "Nam dicitur, quod terrore potestatis multos, non iustitia convinces," Council of Frankfurt (794), MGH Conc. 2.1:121.

10. Hans Hubert Anton, "Zum politischen Konzept karolingischer Synoden und zur karolingishcen Brüdergemeinschaft," HJ 99 (1979): 55–132; see 73.

11. "Corona victoriae non promittitur nisi certantibus," Schieffer, "Zwei karolingische Texte," 17.

12. A liturgical procedure was therefore prior to the ethical concept of *regimen:* compare Senellart, *Les arts de gouverner,* 42.

13. Mayer felt that native Frankish ideals overcame this Roman construct: Theodor Mayer,

To understand why the unified Empire could be so eagerly disassembled, and how, in the three new kingdoms succeeding it, there could be so much continuity with the empire of Charlemagne and Louis, one must recognize that the "Roman" Empire of the Franks was a very tenuous extension of an old tradition of social thought. Like so many of the royal concepts we have traced, the concept of "Rome" was also grounded in liturgical imagery.[14] The divisions of 843 reflected an attempt to equally divide the empire's resources and took account of patterns of aristocratic landholding.[15] It is sometimes argued that the sacred Carolingian state was in direct conflict with older forms of social organization—basic sources of motivation—such as the "blood-brother relationship" or "lordly ethic."[16] Recently it has been more fully recognized that the lordly ethic was acted out on a Carolingian stage in which religious motivations counted, alongside familial politics, vassalic loyalties, and strategies of landholding.[17] All of these were put under strain in a period of civil war. Bishops, meanwhile, sought to craft responses to a world in which their own power, and their ideals, appeared to be in jeopardy. As we shall see, their most poignant response was to retell the entire history of the priesthood from the beginning of time, and in doing so, to develop a wholly new theory of property, no longer based on their defense of the poor, but on the assertion that bishops uniquely represented God's interests in the world.

Bishops increasingly perceived a chasm between royal and episcopal power. They now found it necessary to take account of one sector of society, the powerful nobility (*potentes*), that had scarcely been reckoned with in the political theology of the Carolingian order.[18] Innes has argued forcefully for the priority of local arrangements in understanding the Frankish kingdoms. If "regional elites were what held the polity together," then the reemergence of smaller kingdoms in the Frankish world was not really the end of a political order, but a complex reconfiguration arising from local interests that remained in place.[19] Clearly the changes and violent events that took place affected contemporaries as a series of upheavals, even if in hindsight it seems to us they were not decisive. Magnou-

---

"Der Vertrag von Verdun," in *Der Vertrag von Verdun 843: Neuen Aufsätze zur Begründung der europäischen Völker- und Staatenwelt,* edited by Theodor Mayer, 5–30 (Leipzig: 1943).

14. Tellenbach, *Römischer und christlicher Reichsgedanke,* 34.

15. Innes, *State and Society,* 210.

16. On the conflict with a "Herrscherethik": Anton, "Zum politischen Konzept," 70; on the imagined conflict with "blutsbrüderlichen Beziehungen": 98.

17. Innes, "Charlemagne's Will," 850.

18. Weinberger, "La transformation des *Potentes*," 162–63.

19. Innes, *State and Society,* 195–210; quoting 165.

Nortier speaks of "hypertrophy" as imperial order collapsed in an atmosphere of intellectual subversion and political resistance.[20] Nevertheless, all the parties involved addressed themselves to the sacred kingdom, either to claim it as their own, or to show that their acts of subversion were guided by the highest ideals of the Carolingian state.

Carolingian Tyranny

New social terms and concepts percolated in the last troubled years of Louis' regime in the effort to understand a changed reality. The concept of tyranny, for example, came into prominence in the decade and a half from 829 to 843 to explain the problem of competing authorities and military powers. In the paroxysm of treason, royal rebellion, and civil war it seemed that "tyrants" were set loose in the kingdom. Just prior to the Council of Paris in 829, Agobard wrote a brief pamphlet to persuade Louis not to abandon the *Ordinatio imperii*.[21] In it, he warned Louis that breaking his oath would be to tempt God, with dire consequences for the kingdom. Indeed, the year after the council a revolt arose within the palace, assisted by sons of Louis: Pippin of Aquitaine and Louis the German. Judith, reviled by her enemies as "the scarlet woman of Babylon," took refuge in a monastery, and Louis was put under house arrest. Lothair temporarily took control and ruled in Louis' name. It was a brief humiliation, from which Louis recovered at an assembly of supporters in Nijmegen.[22]

The records of the Council of Paris resonated with contemporary relevance for the world of power.[23] The council had highlighted the idea of propitiation and returned again to the vocabulary of Pseudo-Cyprian to explain recent events. The council had been called because God was clearly angered: "Who is there who does not believe that God is offended by our depraved actions and is provoked to anger?" God's wrath could be seen in the death of animals, in pestilence among men, and in "sterility of all fruits." The people were being thrust into poverty:[24]

Nor do we doubt that it has happened because of His just vengeance, since scandals often arise in this kingdom from tyrants, who strive to tear apart the peace of the Christian people and the unity of the empire by their own depravity. Nevertheless it

---

20. Magnou-Nortier, "Tentative de subversion," 639.

21. Agobard, *De divisione imperii*, in *Opera Omnia*, CCCM 52:245–50.

22. McKitterick, *Frankish Kingdoms*, 170–71.

23. Magnou-Nortier argues that this is one among many interpolations: Magnou-Nortier, "Tentative de subversion," 339.

24. "Quis enim non sentiat Deum nostris pravissimis actibus esse offensum et ad iracundiam provocatum," Council of Paris (829), MGH Conc. 2.2:599.

must be reckoned as due to our sins, that the enemies of the name of Christ in the past year in this kingdom engaged in depredations, cruelly and eagerly burning churches and capturing Christians, and murdered the servants of God with impunity. This happened by the just judgment of God, so that, because we failed in everything, we are lashed internally and externally at the same time.[25]

Tyrants, in this usage, were those with military power who employed it in ways detrimental to the peace and unity of the empire. The document is totally coherent with the rest of Paris (829) and should be viewed as a product of the same group of highly placed bishops. The word "tyranny" now had a different sound. As Suzanne Teillet has shown, for Christian authors of the invasion period, *tyrannus* had a specifically religious meaning, indicating the persecuting or heretical emperors in contrast to a *princeps religiosus*.[26] Ambrose used *tyrannus* in such a way that it's impossible to tell whether he is speaking about Satan or a human, but evil persecutor of Christians.[27] Boethius, drawing on classical political theory, had applied the concept of tyranny to his oppressor, the Ostrogothic king Theodoric.[28] The authors of the documents associated with the Council of Paris had emphasized Isidore's ethical concept of kingship and his contrast with tyranny.[29]

This religious overtone may be detected in the Carolingian notion of tyranny, as well, as it was applied to the sons of Louis the Pious.[30] Agobard of Lyon, the most ardent proponent of imperial unity, was alarmed by the revolt against the emperor.[31] He blamed Judith's sexual power for the fact that Louis had abandoned his public duties in favor of a lascivious private life, something

25. "Nec illud etiam dubitamus ex iusta vindicta illius evenire, quod sepe scandala per tyrannos in hoc regno exsurgunt, qui pacem populi Christiani et unitatem imperii sua pravitate nituntur scindere. Nam et illud nihilominus peccatis nostris deputandum est, quod inimici Christi nominis praeterito anno in hoc regnum ingressi depraedationes, incendia ecclesiarum et captivationes Christianorum et interfectiones servorum Dei audenter et inpune, immo crudeliter fecerunt. Agitur siquidem iusto iudiciuo Dei ut, quia in cunctis delinquimus, interius simul et exterius flagellemur," Council of Paris (829), MGH Conc. 2.2:599–600.

26. Teillet, *Des Goths à la nation gothique,* 88–96.

27. Ambrose, *De officiis,* ed. and trans. Ivor J. Davidson (Oxford: 2001), 1:238.

28. Pierre Courcelle, "Le tyran et le philosophe d'après la 'Consolation' de Boèce," in *Passaggio dal mondo antico,* 195–224. On the classical tradition of tyranny, see "Tyrannis, Despotie," in GGB, 6:651–706; esp. 658–60.

29. Anton, "Zum politischen Konzept," 70–71.

30. It was at about this time (830) that the "So-called Roman Penitential" of Halitgar declared that "We ought to offer [the sacrament] for good rulers; on no account for evil rulers" (text amended by the editor); J. T. McNeill and H. M. Gamer, *Medieval Handbooks of Penance: A Translation of the Principal libri poenitentiales and Selections from Related Documents* (New York: 1990), 309. The canon was perhaps drawn from the "Preface of Gilda," Medieval Handbooks, 178.

31. Boshof, *Erzbishof Agobard von Lyon,* 233–41.

"the young laughed at, and the old sorrowed over."[32] By turning inward, Louis had laid himself open to reproach and mockery, and hence to rebellion. At the same time, Louis failed to advance the great mission of the empire: to expand the church by means of missionary warfare. As emperor, Louis had a sacred duty to extend the borders of the Empire—to send armies against "external peoples." For Agobard the imperial idea was rooted in the missionary ideals of the late eighth and early ninth centuries:

Armies should be sent against external peoples, and the emperor himself ought to fight against the barbaric nations, so that he might subjugate them to the faith, by extending the borders of the kingdom of the faithful—thus the universal church prays ... for emperors.[33]

The church prayed for the subjection of barbarians to a Christian emperor, Agobard pointed out, but instead, the empire was being "barbarized." Agobard's neologism (*barbarizari*) reflected his horror of competing powers.[34] By breaking apart the unity of the empire, the rebels were making the empire seem just like the tribes of Germany. The result would be (as the interpolation in the records of Paris 829 also declared) that the Frankish kingdom would either be conquered or "divided among many tyrants." For Agobard, Louis himself was not a tyrant, but a moral failure. The troubles of the kingdom were yet another sign of what Agobard seems constantly to have dreamed of in those turbulent years— that the Antichrist might soon be loosed.[35] Division of the Empire was viewed against an apocalyptic horizon, gaining clarity whenever order and right were violated.[36] Louis survived the rebellion of 830, as has been noted. But a rift had opened, from 829 onward, in the close cooperation between king and bishop.

32. "Quam rem inridebant minores, dolebant maiores," Agobard, *Liber apologeticus I,* in *Opera Omnia* CCCM 52:307–12; quoting 309.

33. "Cum enim deberent exercitus mitti aduersus exteras gentes, et ipse imperator aduersus barbaras nationes dimicare, ut eas fidei subiugaret ad dilatandum terminum regni fidelium—sic namque orat uniuersalis Ecclesia in solemnibus illis oracionibus, diebus passionis dominice, pro imperatoribus." Agobard then went on to quote a prayer for the emperor from the Gelasian Sacramenty; Agobard, *Liber apologeticus I:*310.

34. "Ut christianissimo imperatori barbari subiciantur, non ut subiecti conturbentur et barbarizentur," Agobard, *Liber apologeticus I:*311. While "to barbarize" had long been used as an abusive description of bad grammar or rhetoric, this was the first use of the verb, now passive, to mean "to become like the barbarians." This is a significant neologism, reflecting the political pressures of the time; see Charles du Fresne du Cange, *Glossaria medii aevi,* 5 vols. (Paris: 1678–1688), art. "barbarizo."

35. "Vnde constat, quia, nisi Deus subuenerit, aut exteris dabitur regnum, aut in multos tyrannos dispertietur, aut forsitan Antichristo, cui praeparabitur," Agobard, *Liber apologeticus I:*311.

36. Boshof, "Einheitsidee und Teilungsprinzip," 161–89.

In 833, a more serious rebellion and civil war began. Pope Gregory IV crossed the Alps in the company of Lothair and sought to intervene for the sake of peace, but to no avail.[37] Lothair seized the throne after Louis was abandoned by the nobility and the bishops at the Field of Lies. Soon thereafter the emperor was compelled to do penance, for a second time, by an assembly held in 833 in Compiègne. In the church of St. Médard in Soissons, Louis held a list of his crimes in his hand, prepared by the assembled bishops, and lay outstretched on the floor before the altar, tearfully begging for penance and forgiveness. Public penance was imposed because of the public and serious nature of his offenses, which were a scandal (*scandalum*) to the church.[38] Such a penance dictated that the emperor, deprived of arms and honor, would wear the clothing of a penitent for the rest of his life, precluded from engaging in public life and incapable of functioning as king.[39] With the imposition of hands, the bishops established the status of such a person, making him a penitent just as they established the orders of the church.[40]

Agobard, for a second time, was present as penance was imposed on Louis the Pious. Here indeed was a subversion of the regime, but carried out in the name of its own principles. The "clique of Agobard and Wala" cannot be thought of as marginal.[41] After the rebellion of 830, as mentioned, Agobard insisted that the emperor send armies against the external enemies of the realm, and that he fight in person. At Louis' second penance at Compiègne, Agobard participated in the removal of Louis' weapons and armor, especially his sword-belt, the *cingulum militiae*. The *cingulum* was a premier marker of noble status, and Louis had to be physically restrained as the bishops removed it.[42] In their relation of the proceedings, the bishops asserted that as Vicars of Christ, they held the keys of heaven, and had the capacity to interpret God's will and to judge kings. Pierre

37. Engelbert, "Papstreisen ins Frankenreich," 101–7.

38. On the concept of "scandal," see Anton, "Zum politischen Konzept," 107.

39. Mayke De Jong, "Power and Humility in Carolingian Society: The Public Penance of Louis the Pious," EME 1 (1992): 29–52; see 29–30 and 36–43; see also De Jong, *The Penitential State: Authority and Atonement in the Age of Louis the Pious, 814–840* (Cambridge: 2009).

40. A ninth-century ritual of penance is preserved in a penitential ascribed to Isaac of Langres, who claimed only to preserve an older penitential of Boniface: Robert Folz, "La pénitence publique au IXe siècle d'près les canons de l'évêque Isaac de Langres," in *L'encadrement religieux des fidèles au moyen âge et jusqu'au concile de Trente: Actes du 109e congrès national des Sociétés Savants, Dijon 1984,* Histoire médiévale et philologie 1 (Paris: 1985), 331–43.

41. This seems the implication of Magnou-Nortier, "Tentative de subversion," 623–25; however, the event shows how strong was the momentum in favor of Agobard.

42. Werner, *Naissance de la noblesse,* 222–23; On the removal of secular clothing: Folz, "La pénitence publique," 336–37.

Riché believes that the bishops had taken the notion of tyranny elaborated at the Council of Paris in 829 and condemned Louis as a tyrant, and that they believed that they had a right to unseat a tyrannical king. Public penance was the institutional means chosen for a novel procedure.[43] However, the deposition of Louis was carried out within the framework of penitential discipline. He was judged to have betrayed his *ministerium* and to have ruined the social order he had lain out in the *Ordinatio imperii*.[44] In this event, the bishops displayed their crucial participation in establishing the imperial *ministerium,* whether it be to support, to validate, or to invalidate the office of the king.[45] The assembly at Paris had, after all, adopted the patristic notion that tyrants were sent to punish the sins of the people, and had to be suffered.[46] The bishops did not claim the right to make and unmake kings, but rather held that it was their prerogative to interpret the will of God, whose judgment would be disclosed in historical events.[47]

Louis himself, somewhat ironically, had given tyranny a prominent place in Carolingian political language. In the *Ordinatio imperii,* Louis admonished his sons not to engage in "tyranny, in which every kind of cruelty is present."[48] The Council in 829 apprised the notion of tyranny not based on classical political theory, but on a reading of Isidore. The classical notion was ambiguous, an ambiguity reflected in Isidore's discussions of kingship and tyranny: the "Council of Paris" quoted Isidore in saying that a king was so called "by doing rightly" (*rex a recte agendo*).[49] If he did not "do rightly," then he no longer deserved the name "king," but was a tyrant. Recognizing the ambiguity of classical usage, Isidore remarked in the *Etymologiae* that "strong kings" were originally called tyrants: only later was the term restricted to "bad kings."[50] It is intriguing to

43. Riché, *Carolingians,* 156.

44. De Jong, "Power and Humility," 40–41.

45. Patzold, *Episcopus,* 521.

46. "Quapropter quisquis ceteris mortalibus temporaliter imperat non ab hominibus, sed a Deo sibi regnum commissum credat. Multi namque munere divino, multi etiam Dei permissu regnant. Qui pie et iuste et misericorditer regnant sine dubio per Deum regnant; qui vero secus, non eius munere, sed permissu tantum regnant," Council of Paris (829), MGH Conc., 2.2:655.

47. De Clercq, "La législation religieuse franque depuis l'avènement de Louis le Pieux jusqu'aux Fausses Décrétales," *Revue de Droit Canonique* 5 (1955), 271.

48. "Tyrannidem, in qua omnis crudelitas consistit," *Ordinatio imperii,* MGH Capit. 1:270–73; see 272.

49. Council of Paris (829), MGH Conc., 2.2:649, citing Isidore, *Etymologiae IX* (1.29); see Reydellet, *Royauté dans la littérature latine,* 576. On the classical tradition about tyranny, see Hannah Arendt, "What is Authority?" in her *Between Past and Future: Eight Exercises in Political Thought* (Harmondsworth: 1977), 91–141; and "Tyrannis, Despotie," in *GGB,* 6:662.

50. "Fortes enim reges tyranni uocabantur. . . . Iam postea in usum accidit tyrannos uocari pessimos atque improbos reges," Isidore, *Etymologiae IX* (9.3), cited in Reydellet, *La royauté,* 581.

consider the possibility that by following Isidore in this, the bishops acted from an old Frankish preoccupation with how one came to earn the name (*nomen*) of king. Remember that the mythic origins of the Carolingian dynasty lay in the embassy, discussed earlier, said to have asked the pope who should have the *nomen* of king. The reply made it appear that the exercise of power was sufficient to deserve the name. The Council of Paris put this question on a very different footing. It was no longer sufficient to have power—what kings and tyrants had in common was precisely power. Kingship now concerned royal justice, the extent to which a king governed justly (*recte*).

Failure of the Two Orders

In the end, Louis recovered from this second rebellion, despite its gravity, by allying himself with his two youngest sons against Lothair. In 834, the first phase of his restoration involved the crucial support of loyal bishops, who gathered a crowd of warriors outside the ancient abbey of St.-Denis, where an emotional homecoming was staged:

When they had received their king, the many people who were there now wanted to go in force against Lothair in favor of the father. They rushed with the bishops and all the clergy into the basilica of St.-Denis, devotedly offered praises to God, placed a crown and weapons on their king, and then strenuously debated what to do next.[51]

Modern scholarship has reversed the view, so convincingly portrayed by Nithard, that Louis was incapacitated and weak in his final years.[52] There are many signs that even after suffering the blow at St. Médard, Louis remained confident that his fortunes would brighten. When this happened, he resumed all his governmental functions with great vigor.[53] His restoration was accompanied by a purge of bishops who had betrayed him, including Ebbo of Rheims and Agobard of Lyon. At an assembly in Thionville in 833, Louis' half-brother Drogo (archbishop of the Sacred Palace) presided over a public ceremony in which Louis was crowned again. It is indeed astonishing how the radicalism of the Council of Paris seemed to come to nothing.[54] The assembly, which included a large num-

51. "Plebs autem non modica que praesens aderat et jam jamque Lodhario pro patre vim inferre volebat, rege recepto, basilicam sancti Dyonisii una cum episcopis et omni clero confluunt, laudes Deo devote referunt, coronam et arma regi suo imponunt et ad cetera deliberaturi contendunt" (1.4), Nithard, *Histoire des fils de Louis le Pieux,* ed. P. Lauer (Paris: 1964), 18.

52. "Ingruente senili aetate et propter varias afflictiones poene decrepita imminente" (1.6), Nithard, *Histoire,* 28.

53. Janet L. Nelson, "The Last Years of Louis the Pious," in *Charlemagne's Heir,* 147–59.

54. De Clercq, "La législation religieuse," *Revue de Droit Canonique* 5 (1955), 274–75.

ber of bishops (nine archbishops and thirty-five bishops), signed documents asserting that Louis had been wrongly deposed. With this ceremony of reversal the "global pronouncements" issued in the name of the council appear to have had only a momentary resonance.[55] Having dramatically vaunted their power to preside over Louis' deposition, the bishops now suffered an equally dramatic reversal of fortune, and were forced to either swear allegiance to Louis or face deposition themselves. Thus was revealed the tenor of a deep and long-lasting change in the Carolingian order, established in the period 820–830, as the social order came to be conceptualized in terms of episcopal-royal interaction and cooperation. Penance, excommunication, and reconciliation were now central to the understanding of the Empire.[56]

In 835 Louis had Agobard deposed as bishop of Lyon and put Amalarius of Metz in charge of the church of Lyon. Amalarius had spent part of his youth in the court school and had long been known to Louis, but his administration ran into fierce opposition from the devoted followers of Agobard among the clergy of Lyon, particularly Deacon Florus.[57] Amalarius was a significant choice, as Louis here drew on the connections between kingship and liturgy. Amalarius was a theorist of liturgical poetry and action, whose strange analogical approach was unusual, and provided a good way for his enemies to attack him.[58] Florus would eventually stage a successful attack on Amalarius at the Council of Quierzy (838), and these old accusations continue to shape how Amalarius is viewed by modern historians. Amalarius was devoted to the analogical method. When he replied to the baptismal inquiries of Charlemagne, his treatise highlighted the importance of the number seven of the scrutinies, because seven is a number reflecting the universal: "Thus John wrote to the seven churches which are in Asia."[59]

As a conflict of powers in the kingdom began to unfold, Amalarius must have looked back with conservative affection to the liturgy as the homeland of his religious aspirations and the source for royal theology. He well understood the liturgical dimension of kingship as established by the anointing ritual. According to Amalarius, those who understood the Bible understood the ritual of

55. Patzold, *Episcopus*, 195; "Globalaussagen": Anton, "Zum politischen Konzept," 95.

56. This change would last right into the Ottonian period: Patzold, *Episcopus*, 543.

57. Klaus Zechiel-Eckes, *Florus von Lyon*, 22–27.

58. Steck, *Der Liturgiker Amalarius*, 24.

59. "Sicut Iohannes scribit septem ecclesiis quae sunt in Asia," Amalarius of Metz, *Responsio*, in his complete works: *Amalarii episcopi Opera liturgica omnia*, edited by Johann Michael Hanssens, *Studi e Testi* 138, 139–40 (Vatican City: 1948–1950), 1:236–51; this quote, 240.

anointing as an ultra-royal act. "Why priests and kings were anointed we know from the Old Testament."[60] The ancient kings of Israel knew that through the oil of anointing they received "a royal and priestly mystery."[61] The liturgical resonance of kingship could still be asserted, according to Amalarius.

His great masterpiece was a treatise compiling all the analogical meanings of the *Ordo* of the Roman Mass—the *Liber Officialis,* dedicated to Louis the Pious in 823, and then revised and reissued in 831 and 835.[62] Here Amalarius developed an original synthesis of the liturgical themes that had long formed the symbolic underpinnings of the Carolingian state. The circular clerical tonsure was now understood not as a royal sign, but as a sign of circumspect reason, *ratio*—which had to do with the mind, and not with the stature of bishops in the kingdom. Amalarius was fascinated with the ritual of anointing. He noted that during the anointing of Aaron's head (described in Psalm 13:2), the oil poured all the way down to Aaron's beard. Thus the ritual of anointing indicated the entire head and its priority. "The bishop is the Vicar of Christ, and this is why his head is anointed."[63] The bishop was anointed on the head because he was the head of the church.[64]

The writings of Amalarius reflect a degree of anxiety about the stature of tradition. Amalarius attempted to find the origins, authenticity, or meaning of every ritual and garment of the priesthood. Often he had to rely upon analogical meanings, and this is the real source of his method. During the ordination of a bishop, for example, a copy of the Evangelists was held above the candidate's head. This custom was not prescribed by ancient authority, by apostolic tradition, nor by canonical authority. Yet the ritual was fitting, Amalarius argued: it served as a warning that the new bishop would now live under the yoke of the *Evangelium.* Amalarius reflects a level of anxiety about sources of authority in this period. He hunted for the meaning of the rituals of the Mass with a certainty that he could certainly find them: to Amalarius' mind, there were no arbitrary traditions: "We know that nothing should be done in the church, imitating our fathers according to their constitution, unless it is wholly established

---

60. "Unde sacerdotes et reges unctos esse novïmus in veteri testament," Amalarius, *Responsio,* 247.

61. "Intelligat baptizatus regale ac sacerdotale mysterium se accepisse," Amalarius, *Responsio,* 247.

62. The work met with resistance and was condemned by Florus of Lyon: Brunhölzl, *Histoire de la littérature latine,* vol. 1.2:188.

63. Amalarius, *Liber Officialis* (II.14.6), 2:234.

64. "Imitando illu qui caput est totius ecclesiae," Amalarius, *Liber Officialis* (II.14.6), 2:235.

and is rational."[65] Thus his method: a restless search for meaning in the liturgy, which he called a method of "knocking and seeking" (*pulsandi et quaerendi*).[66]

The method of the *Liber Officialis* was condemned in 838, although Amalarius had carefully revised his book after observing the customs of Rome in 835. With his sophisticated style of liturgical reasoning, Amalarius of Metz seems to reflect the continued importance of liturgy to imperial politics. Liturgy and its correct performance had linked Frankish bishops, monasteries, and kings for almost a century.

In 836, Louis summoned a council at Aachen, the records of which provide a glimpse into the bishops' first reaction to the defeat of Agobard.[67] The influence of Paris (829) can be traced in many later synods, even when long passages from Paris were not quoted.[68] Strangely enough, this council, headed by Jonas of Orléans, was not disposed to back away from the principles of the Council of Paris, even as it acquiesed in the imposition of royal power over the episcopal order.[69] Reciting Paul's dictum (as had the Council of Paris) that "whoever resists a power given by God resists the order established by God" (Rom. 13:2), the bishops anathematized clerics who had broken their fidelity to Louis, and deprived them of their ecclesiastical grades.[70] There is no doubt that the angry emperor cast a significant shadow over the proceedings.

Under the leadership of Jonas of Orléans, the Council of Aachen nevertheless clung to the very ideas that had put them in conflict with Louis.[71] Aachen (836) relied closely on Paris (829) and was an extension of the same project of reform.[72] The fact that the bishops at Aachen decided to produce yet another major statement on the nature of royal power and its relation to the episcopate

65. "Sciumus enim nichil agere in aecclesia imitando patres nostros secundum constitutionem illorum nisi omnia ordinate et rationem habentia," Amalarius, *A Lost Work by Amalarius of Metz: Interpolations in Salisbury, Cathedral Library, Ms. 154,* ed. Christopher A. Jones, Henry Bradshaw Society, Subsidia II (London: 2001), 183.

66. Amalarius, *A Lost Work,* 183.

67. Council of Aachen (836), MGH Conc. 2.2:704–67.

68. On the reception and wide influence of Paris (829): Patzold, *Episcopus,* 513.

69. On the relation between Paris (829) and Aachen (836), see Anton, "Zum politischen Konzept," 74–75.

70. "Si quispiam episcoporum aut quilibet sequentis ordinis ecclesiastici deinceps timore aut cupiditate aut qualibet suasione a domino et orthodoxo Hludowico imperatore defecerit. . . . gradum proprium canonica atque synodali sententia amittat," Council of Aachen (836), MGH Conc. 2.2:710.

71. Magnou-Nortier has argued that the so-called forgers of Paris (829) could not have included Jonas, and yet the council held under his direction in Aachen was very closely related to Paris (829) in terms of content and spirit; Magnou-Nortier, "Tentative de subversion," 362 and 628–29.

72. Patzold, *Episcopus,* 211–18.

was a sign of intransigence. Explicit references to the Council of Paris in 829 were threaded throughout the legislation at Aachen, beginning with the preface, which introduced, as had the bishops at Paris, Gelasius' statement about the "two persons" with an Isidorean interpretation: "that the norm of all religion and of ecclesiastical discipline consists in two persons, to wit, the episcopal and the imperial."[73] It is worth mentioning in this context that, by interpreting Gelasius in this way, episcopal social thought was in no way dominated by either the imperial or the papal idea. The bishops were not concerned to place emperor and pope as the "two persons" at the head of society, but rather to explain their own episcopal status vis-à-vis the king. As at the Council of Paris, each of these "two persons, that are principal in this world" was the subject of a separate treatise.[74] The council thus returned to Gelasius' original terminology in which "the world" was the subject of division.[75]

A description of episcopal and royal offices was necessary, the Council of Aachen explained, because of the "mutability of the times and the confusion of orders."[76] Their treatises on royal and episcopal power attempted to repair the confusion of orders by reaching back to the "ancient fathers." The sentiment had an ancient ring, recalling as it did the prefaces of so many Merovingian councils. Recollection and renewal were the pathway back to a time of stability and order. The bishops declared that they sought nothing new, but only to recover an ancient order "handed over to oblivion."[77] Social confusion and rebellion were thus the disastrous results of communal forgetfulness. The council insisted that a discussion of the "life and doctrine of priests" was something that concerned "the priests, princes and all the people" because both bishops and kings had abandoned their proper roles in Christian society: indeed, "both orders had failed."[78]

---

73. "Normam universae religionis atque aecclesiasticae disciplinae in duabus consistere personis, pontificali videlicet atque imperiali, de qua re Gelasius Romane sedis venerabilis episcopus ad Anastasium scripserit," Council of Aachen (836), MGH Conc. 2.2:705.

74. "De duabus siquidem personis, quas principales in hoc mundo esse non dubium est, sacerdotalem prout . . . brevitate adneximus," Council of Aachen (836), MGH Conc. 2.2:706.

75. Anton, "Zum politischen Konzept," 77–78.

76. "Temporum varietate et ordinum confusione perplura," Council of Aachen (836), MGH Conc. 2.2:706.

77. "Non aliquid novum querentes nec contra veritatis religionem quid statuentes, sed statuta antiquorum patrum innovantes, quae per desidiam quorundam labefactari visa sunt in quocumque ordine ac propter inusitatum vel inveteratum usum oblivioni tradita," Council of Aachen (836), MGH Conc. 2.2:706.

78. "In utroque ordine partim defecisse," Council of Aachen (836), MGH Conc. 2.2:714.

It failed among priests, as the authority of the priestly ministry slipped, to the extent that there was less devotion among them than was proper. It failed among princes, especially among those whom you sought to rear benevolently, and whom you even raised on high, because the affection of many was inconstant, their iniquity great, their charity grown cold.[79]

The blame was here laid squarely on the rebellious sons of Louis and their followers. Considering how consistent the Council of Aachen was with the Paris council of 829, however, it seems that Louis was subjected to admonition as much as his rebellious sons. There is, for example, a reference at Aachen to one of the crimes for which Louis had made his penance at Compiègne in 833: that he had made war during the season of Lent. At Aachen he was asked to protect the peace of that sacred season.[80]

Many of the canons promulgated at Aachen were drawn from the Council of Paris or from the *Relatio episcoporum*. Far from abandoning the admonitory tone of Paris, the bishops at Aachen recapitulated all the crucial points made there: Isidore's argument that a king (*rex*) is so called from acting rightly (*recte agendo*), and that otherwise he should be called a tyrant;[81] the notion that protection of the poor is part of the king's *ministerium*;[82] that bishops, as the gatekeepers of heaven, were judges even of emperors;[83] and finally, that bishops should not be preoccupied with rural pursuits.[84] The fact that Louis, having been restored to his throne, was again warned about tyranny and reminded of his recent penance reinforces the impression that the penance and deposition of 833 did not result from an accusation of tyranny. Rather, the bishops believed that

79. "In sacerdotibus enim defecit, auctoritate sacerdotalis ministerii labente, quantum in ipsorum studio aliquid minus fuit quam conveniret; in principibus, scilicet in illis, quos vos benivola intentione enutrire studuistis atque sublimastis, non permanente dilectione, sed habundante iniquitate et refrigescente multorum caritate," Council of Aachen (836), MGH Conc. 2.2:714.

80. "Absque inevitabili necessitate sanctum tempus quadragesimae liceat ecclesiasticis viris sub quiete agere, quatenus tempus illud, quod purificatio debet esse aliorum temporum, non inquietetur inquietudine perturbationum," Council of Aachen (836), MGH Conc. 2.2:722.

81. "Rex . . . a recte agendo vocatur. Si enim pie et iuste et misericorditer regit, merito rex appellatur; si his caruerit, non rex, sed tirannus est," Council of Aachen (836), MGH Conc. 2.2:715 (citing the *Relatio episcoporum*).

82. "Ne forte illi, qui ab eo constituti sunt et vicem eius agere debent in populo, iniuste aut neglegenter pauperes oppressiones pati permittant. [In fact everyone should do this:] multo magis de ministerio sibi divinitus commisso," Council of Aachen (836), MGH Conc. 2.2:716.

83. Citing the speech of Constantine, just as did the Council of Paris; Council of Aachen (836), MGH Conc. 2.2:717.

84. "Comperimus etiam quosdam socios ordinis nostri non causa necessitatis . . . sed potius avaritiae et propriae delectationis saepissimae, propria civitatis suae sede relicta cleroque neglecto, remotiora loca frequentare," Council of Aachen (836), MGH Conc. 2.2:708.

because he had broken his oath, Louis was subject to the "just judgment of God," which included the appearance of tyrants in the Frankish kingdom. So much agreement with the bewildering documents from Paris reinforces the impression that conciliar law after 829 did not simply reflect an official pro-imperial doctrine, but was a demonstration of episcopal doctrine regarding the sacralized state. It could be said that the bishops here exploited the gap that always existed between theory and *praxis* in Carolingian law.[85] McKitterick has argued that the Carolingian royal capitularies represent an effort at unity and standardization through the medium of legal texts.[86] But those capitularies were confronted by a counter-law: the Council of Aachen does not appear to have served the "precise functioning of an official apparatus."[87] Quite to the contrary, Aachen presented another manifesto—calling imperial *praxis* to account.

Sacrifice and Property

Associated with the Council of Aachen in 836 was a further treatise, issued under conciliar authority as a letter to the rebellious Pippin of Aquitaine. The letter is closely related to the *De institutione laicali* of Jonas of Orléans, who must have had a hand in writing it. Although claiming to draw on "both Testaments and the words of the holy Fathers," the letter was almost exclusively a commentary on passages from the historical books of the Bible.[88] Given the circumstances in which it was produced, this letter is precious, because one can see in it how bishops read and interpreted the Bible in light of specific historical pressures. De Jong has shown that Hraban Maur and others likewise produced exegetical treatises they felt would have a bearing upon current pressing problems.[89] Placed in this context, the council should be seen, not as a distant "normative" statement, but instead as an earnest attempt to address royal power with a highly relevant body of advice. Because the letter was directed to Pippin, the bishops could analyse the relation of episcopal and royal power more directly than they might have done in a letter addressed to Louis the Pious. The letter to Pippin sought to show the basis of ecclesiastical property, and of the exclusive

85. Sellert, "Aufzeichnung des Rechts und Gesetz," 100–1.

86. McKitterick, *Carolingians and the Written Word,* 36.

87. Sellert quotes Max Weber's description of state law as rationalization: "Herstellung innerlicher Rechtssicherheit im Interesse eines präzisen Funkionierens des amtlichen Apparates," Sellert, "Aufzeichnung des Rechts und Gesetz," 100.

88. "Ex utriusque testamenti paginis et sanctorum patrum dictis," Council of Aachen (836), MGH Conc. 2.2:731.

89. Mayke De Jong, "The Empire as *ecclesia:* Hrabanus Maurus and Biblical *historia* for Rulers," in *Uses of the Past,* 196–201.

right of bishops to govern that property. Pippin was obviously considered one of those "not caring for ecclesiastical dignity, but wishing rather to satisfy their own desire, taking for themselves the holy goods offered to God."[90]

For the bishops assembled at Aachen, there were no theoretical limits to the church's claim to land and wealth. They pointed out that some might "insanely" argue that there was a natural limit:

Why would God, as the rectors of churches declare, command that these things be offered to Him, especially since all things that are on the earth belong to Him, and He created them for the use of men?[91]

The first point to be addressed, therefore, was the fact that "all the kingdoms of the world and all the goods of the earth are God's and are offered to Him out of His own."[92] Faced with expropriations of church land arising from civil war, and from the disruption of arrangements of power and land in the countryside, the bishops were intent upon claiming their right to hold land permanently and without interference. In so doing they went much further than had previous councils toward making a universal claim to govern. Although the council cited, as had the Council of Paris in 829, Julian Pomerius' dictum that church property was the "patrimony of the poor," this conceptual function of the poor was bolstered by a wide-ranging argument about the origins of the priesthood. The bishops believed that controlling land was part of the religious function of the priesthood.

Many citations of the Old Testament were deployed to justify ecclesiastical ownership of land. In line with Visigothic exegetical tradition, the bishops pointed out that "those things which happened among the carnal people [the ancient Jews] as a prefiguration, were written down for our correction; for us who will see the end of time."[93] All the biblical descriptions of the ancient Jewish cult were thus applicable to the Christian Church. The Tabernacle, for example, was a "type" of the church, and hence all the gifts and sacrifices made there

90. "Sunt etiam quidam dignitatem ecclesiasticam non curantes, immo suam cupiditatem explere volentes sibique in Deo oblatis sacratisque rebus aferendis," Council of Aachen (836), MGH Conc. 2.2:731.

91. "Et ubi Deus haec, quae ecclesiarum rectores opponunt, iussit sibi offerri, presertim cum omnia, quae in terris sunt, sua sint et ille ea ad usus hominum creaverit?" Council of Aachen (836), MGH Conc. 2.2:731.

92. "Primum quidem, quod omnia terrarum regna et omnia bona terrae Domini sint et ex suis sua sibi offerantur," Council of Aachen (836), MGH Conc. 2.2:731.

93. "Qualiter templum illum Iudaicum typum gesserit ecclesiae catholicae," Council of Aachen (836), MGH Conc. 2.2:759.

were meant to show how the contemporary church was to be supported.[94] For the first time, justification for episcopal control of land was found in an exegesis of the Old Testament. The argument for the ownership of buildings and estates was thus brought into line with arguments for other features of episcopal social thought on the structure of society and the function of priests and of kings. As a feature of Christian society prefigured in the history of the Jews, episcopal control of property was also "ordained" as part of God's plan for the world.

The Bible was equally turned to as a history book, telling the origin and development of the cult out of which Christianity arose. The bishops' letter to Pippin was a reflection on the history of religion. This was a story of material increase, as the cult was elaborated and its furnishings multiplied. The origin of church property was in sacrifice: "The origin should be remembered, that religion was begun, without an altar, by Abel the Just."[95] The only material feature of that first offering was the sacrifice itself. The cult first acquired a location with Noah, who built an altar and there sacrificed cattle.

Altars, the Ark, the Tabernacle, and eventually the Temple—all were elaborations, by divine command, of the original sacrifice Abel made under the open sky. With such locations, ever more stable and elaborate, the transition was made from sacrifice to property. The history of religion was recounted with the goal of showing how contemporary kings, such as Pippin, should offer material wealth to the church as a continuation of sacrifices the Lord ordained from the very beginning of religion. The more that devotion was shown by such sacrifices, the more pleased was the Lord. Abraham, the bishops explained, received the Lord's blessing because of his willingness to sacrifice Isaac. As a result:

his seed was blessed by God, to be propagated and multiplied, and to be given the mightiest kingdoms of the earth, and triumph over its enemies. This blessing is offered not only to his own seed, which is Christ, but to the peoples (*gentes*), which is to say to us.[96]

The lesson of Jewish history was that the divine cult should be honored with gifts, rather than robbed of what it owns. Rulers ought to follow the example of

---

94. "Tabernaculum Domini, quod typum gerebat futurae ecclesiae Christi," Council of Aachen (836), MGH Conc. 2.2:743.

95. "Memorata igitur origo et religio primum coepit sine altari ab Abel iusto," Council of Aachen (836), MGH Conc. 2.2:733.

96. "Et a Deo benedici semenque suum propagari ac multiplicari eique amplissima regna terrae dari et de hostibus suis triumphum sibi praeberi necnon et in suo semine, quod est Christus, gentes, quae nos sumus, benedici," Council of Aachen (836), MGH Conc. 2.2:734.

Isaac, who erected altars and made offerings.[97] Abraham gave a tenth (*decimas*) of his goods to Melchisidech the High Priest, an archetype of Christ. Abraham is imitated by those who give a tenth of their wealth to bishops.[98] Pursuing the theme of material increase, the bishops explained that the cult was "amplified" by Jacob, who erected an altar and offered sacrifice at the spot where, in a dream, he saw angels ascending and descending a ladder reaching into heaven, calling it a gate of heaven (*porta caeli*):

> Whence today the Christian religion, following the example of the ancient tradition of the fathers, builds and dedicates houses in honor of God, erects altars, pours oil upon them and annoints them with sacrosanct chrism, and sings the melody of Jacob to Christ with words and deeds. [The Christian religion] takes up the offerings and vows of precious and diverse things from the faithful for the glory and honor of divine worship, takes up donations for the use of priests and the other ministers of Christ, and for the reception and support of the poor.[99]

The accumulation of property was thus vital to the episcopal function. At the most fundamental level, it allowed the priesthood to provide a gateway to heaven by "amplifying" the cult in the form of church-building. Property allowed for the sustenance of the poor, but even more emphasis was placed on the ability of the priesthood to protect society as a whole by means of liturgy and prayer. Moses, it was pointed out, built an altar to the Lord for the protection and liberation of the people of God. Rulers should be aware that if church property is taken, military disaster and conquest by their enemies will result.[100] Priests should be honored because "clearly it is they who placate the fury of the Lord by their prayers, that the misfortune sent by the Lord against the people may be ended."[101]

Just as princes gave property to Moses to achieve victory in battle, so Chris-

---

97. Council of Aachen (836), MGH Conc. 2.2:735.

98. "Quem imitantur qui sacerdotibus Christi ob illius amorem et honorem decimas dant," Council of Aachen (836), MGH Conc. 2.2:734.

99. "Unde hodie quoque Christiana religio, exemplum sumens ex antiqua patrum traditione, domos in honorem Dei aedificat ac dedicat, et altaria erigit eisque oleum superfundit ac sacrosancto chrismate ea perunguit et de factis dictisque eiusdem Iacob moelodiam Christo canit et a fidelibus oblationes et vota et pretiosarum diversarumque rerum ad decorem et honorem divini cultus, sacerdotum ceterorumque ministrorum Christi usus pauperumque receptionem ac recreationem suscipit donaria," Council of Aachen (836), MGH Conc. 2.2:736–37.

100. "Qui altaria Domini obruendo dehonorant et dehonorando obruunt, ne, si quando adversus hostes suos arma corripiunt, se ipsos eisdem hostibus suis triumphum exhibeant," Council of Aachen (836), MGH Conc. 2.2:737.

101. "Patet quippe, quod hi, per quorum orationem furor Domini placari et a populo plaga Dei potest cessari," Council of Aachen (836), MGH Conc. 2.2:743.

tians should give to those who pray for them.[102] The bishops warned King Pippin that because of the sins of the Jewish priests, kings, and people, the Temple of Solomon had burned, the city of Jerusalem was destroyed, the Temple treasure carried off, and the people led into captivity.[103] As at the Council of Paris in 829, the bishops sought to show the necessity of right action by bishops and kings, and of joining together in propitiation for sin.

The bishops then listed the gifts that God wanted the priesthood to receive: "houses and fields and servants."[104] These properties were the exclusive domain of ecclesiastical law:

Consider, prudent listener and diligent reader, how the divine cult should be augmented. God earlier had commanded that his tabernacle be presented with precious things, with cattle, gold and silver, gems and silk, and other diverse riches. Even back then houses and fields began to be consecrated to the Lord, and those things which are consecrated to the Lord pertain to the law of priests.[105]

In a remarkable reading of Leviticus, the animals sacrificed in the Temple were made to represent the chattel grazing in the bishops' own fields! The king should emulate the people of God, who gave "houses, fields, slaves, and what is more, cities and suburban sanctuaries." This was done so that "the ministers of their sanctuaries might engage in the sacred cult more freely, more readily and worthily, that they might carry out their service without making excuses."[106]

Examples from the New Testament were advanced at the end of the work,

---

102. On Moses as a model for the role of prayer in battle, see Schapiro, *Words and Pictures,* 17–26.

103. "Propter peccata quoque sacerdotum et regum tociusque populi idem templum, quod in magna gloria a Salomone Domino fuerat conditum . . . a Chaldeis fuit incensum atque dirutum et Hierosolymorum urbs destructa populusque in Babylonicam captivitatem deductus et vasa domus Domini et quaeque in thesauris domus Domini Domino fuerant consecrata et sanctificata in Babylonem sunt translata," Council of Aachen (836), MGH Conc. 2.2:753.

104. "Quod ergo Dominus ad sanctuarium suum inter ceteras species, quas dinumerare longum est, domos et agros et servos sibi offerre preceperit," Council of Aachen (836), MGH Conc. 2.2:744.

105. "Considera, prudens auditor et diligens lector, qualiter augeatur cultus divinus. Superius namque pretiosa quaeque in pecudibus, in auro et argento et gemmis et serico et ceteris diversis speciebus sibi Dominus suoque sancto tabernaculo iusserat offerri, hic autem iam inchoantur et domus et agri Domino consecrari, et ea, quae Domino consecrantur, ad ius peritineant sacerdotum," Council of Aachen (836), MGH Conc. 2.2:741.

106. "Quod Deus idcirco populo suo de hereditate possessionum suarum domos et agros et mancipia, insuper etiam, quod maius est, civitates et suburbana sactuario suo famulantibus dare preceperit, ut ministri sanctuarii sui instantius honestiusque atque inexcusabilius sacrum suum cultum exercere suumque famulatum potuissent liberius explere," Council of Aachen (836), MGH Conc. 2.2:744.

further supporting the concept of ecclesiastical property. Following the book of Acts, the bishops explained how members of the primitive church sold all they possessed and laid it at the feet of the apostles. Far from seeing this as evidence for communal ownership, the story was taken as proof that "from the beginning the new-born church began to take up the offerings of the faithful."[107] The bishops identified the history of the church's expansion with its accumulation of property, pointing out that as the successors of the apostles evangelized the world, the church was enriched by donations from Constantine and other kings, gradually reaching a sublime position (*ad alta*).[108] Pippin was enjoined to defend and enrich the church as his ancestors had done, because "exalting the holy church of God, and with God's protection, they extended and made the kingdom unconquerable far and wide in a terrible circuit against all the nations."[109] The history of the divine cult was thus brought forward to the reign of Charlemagne, to which contemporaries already looked back as a model of victorious expansion that years of rebellion threatened to destroy.

The Council of Paris had approached the delicate topic of episcopal estate exploitation with some concern. The contingencies of seigneural management seemed unavoidable, yet perverted the basis of ecclesiastical property as the patrimony of the poor. The development of this new economy also led to a tangle of obligations and rights. At Aachen in 836, therefore, the bishops set out to provide new grounds for the clerical right to property and the prerogative of bishops to govern that property without interference. By thus addressing Pippin, the bishops hinted that Louis the Pious was incapable of defending their interests in Aquitaine, or in the heart of his kingdom.

Division of the Empire

A crucial source for the period 830–843 is the brooding, tragic work of Nithard, a noble participant in the events he described. He followed his father as lay abbot of the monastery of St.-Riquier (Centulum) and wrote his *Histories* at

---

107. "In primordio nascentis ecclesiae coepit eadem ecclesia vota fidelium suscipere," Council of Aachen (836), MGH Conc. 2.2:765.

108. "Qualiter denique ecclesia Christi per successores apostolorum . . . sub orthodoxis imperatoribus et, ut de multis unum ponamus, Constantino necnon regibus aliis ac principibus ceterisque fidelibus sua vota Deo offerentibus eamque ecclesiam diversis donariis incrementantibus atque ad alta sublimantibus excreverit," Council of Aachen (836), MGH Conc. 2.2: 765–66.

109. "Perpendatis, qualiter progenitores vestri et ditando atque exaltando sanctam Dei ecclesiam regnum hoc longe lateque dilataverint gloriosumque ac cunctis in circuitu nationibus terribile atque, Domino se protegente, insuperabile fecerint," Council of Aachen (836), MGH Conc. 2.2:767.

Charles the Bald's request. Although he repeatedly declared that he was unwilling to write the book, he persevered because of a fear that someone might record these events "inaccurately." It was a partisan work taking the point of view of Charles the Bald's party, and yet shows the signs of nuance and doubt that mark a reflective and honest account.[110] This is part of its value, because the attitude of the high Frankish nobility toward the throne and toward the bishops can rarely be seen. It also reveals the kind of arguments made concerning the basis and legitimacy of governments. Nithard was intensely aware that he was writing the history of a collapsing regime. Although Louis inherited the realm and its ideals, the destruction of imperial unity by his sons led, Nithard observed, to daily deterioration of public well-being.[111]

In his last years, Louis struggled against repeated rebellions of his sons, aligning himself first with one and then with another. He simultaneously tried to provide a large and stable kingdom for his youngest son, Charles the Bald.[112] In 840, the old emperor, wasted with illness, died near Ingleheim, and his three sons fought to claim their shares of the Frankish kingdom. Charles and Louis allied against Lothair. Lacking the imperial crown, and having been given his portion of the realm in violation of the *Ordinatio imperii,* Charles had to carefully establish the justice of his cause and the injustice of Lothair's attempt to consolidate the Empire. In this, episcopal support was crucial. Only the bishops knew how to judge these bloody events; only they could interpret God's will as expressed in history.[113] The struggle among the three sons culminated in the battle of Fontenoy in 841, which Nithard described as a vast slaughter (*ingens cedes*). The outcome was interpreted by Charles and Louis as a judgment by God, an interpretation carefully prepared ahead of time.

The following Sunday, masses were held on the very battlefield, and the bishops assembled before the army to interpret the slaughter. The soldiers were evidently concerned that they had sinned by waging a fratricidal war against other Christian Franks; the moral boundaries of warfare had blurred:

---

110. Janet L. Nelson, "Public *Histories* and Private History in the Work of Nithard," in her *Politics and Ritual in Early Medieval Europe,* 208 (London: 1986).

111. "Res autem publica, quoniam quisque cupiditate illectus sua querebat, cotidie deterius ibat" (1.3), Nithard, *Histoire,* 12.

112. A useful summary is provided in Nelson, *Charles the Bald,* 75–131.

113. Hermann Dörries, "Die geistigen Voraussetzungen und folgen der karolingischen Reichssteilung 843," in *Der Vertrag von Verdun,* 150–80; see 151.

After this, the kings and the peoples, sorrowing over their brother and the Christian people, began to question the bishops as to what they should do about this affair. Hence all the bishops, in one spirit, gathered in council, and it was determined in the public meeting that they fought for justice and equity alone, and this manifest thing was accomplished by a judgement of God. Therefore every minister of God should be considered as exempt [sc. "from penance"], the instigator as well as the performer.[114]

Charles the Bald and Lothair were thus locked in a struggle that went beyond the use of weapons to a battle in the realm of symbols. With the aid of his bishops Charles sought to dominate the understanding of history by controlling the interpretation of events as they unfolded and by shaping how they would be remembered.[115] The *Annals of St. Bertin* recalled that by attacking his father, Lothair had "transgressed the law of nature."[116] These histories bear the marks of episcopal dominance over the interpretation of God's will inscribed in events. In the case of Nithard we can see the wide acceptance, even among the warrior nobility, of a lofty role for bishops in the interpretation of history and reconciliation between God and man.[117]

All this was meant to show that Lothair was not living up to the sacred nature of Carolingian kingship. In the fall of 841, Lothair planned another campaign against Charles. Bishop Emmon of Noyon (840–859) was sent to remind Lothair that Louis the Pious' arrangements for the kingdom had been vindicated by a judgment of God on the battlefield. Furthermore, "if he wished to forget all these things, he should stop his persecution the holy church of God, and show pity for the poor, widows, and orphans" and above all, "should not again force the Christian people to gather in mutual slaughter."[118] In Nithard's account, Lothair was consistently cruel and untrustworthy. The complaint that Lothair harmed the poor, orphans, and widows reveals the the continued relevance of episcopal vocabulary and intellectual resources to Carolingian kingship.

114. "Post haec, reges populique, super fratre populoque christiano dolentes, percontari episcopos coeperunt, quid agere super hoc negotio deberent. Quam obrem unanimes ad concilium omnes episcopi confluunt inventumque in conventu publico est quod pro sola justicia et aequitate decertaverint et hoc Dei juditio manifestum effectum sit ac per hoc inmunis omnis Dei minister in hoc negotio haberi, tam suasor quam et effector, deberetur" (3.1), Nithard, *Histoire*, 82.

115. See the comments of Nelson, *Charles the Bald*, 8–9.

116. "Iura naturae transgressus" (Anno 840), *Annales Bertiniani*, MGH SS 1, 419–515; see 437.

117. Patzold, *Episcopus*, 239–41.

118. "Et, si horum omnium recordare nolit, cesset a persecutione sancte Dei ecclesie, misereatur pauperum, viduarum orfanorumque, et regnum a patre suo sonsensu sibi datum ut ingrediatur omittat ne forte iterato populum christianum ad cedem mutuam confluere compellat" (3.3), Nithard, *Histoire*, 92.

At Aachen in 842, after Lothair's defeat, Charles and Louis the German turned to their bishops to find out what to do with his kingdom and people:

Indeed it seemed that first they should submit the matter to the bishops and priests, of whom a large number were present, so that by their counsel, as though by the divine will, the origin and authority of these things could be determined.[119]

A catalogue of Lothair's crimes followed: oath-breaking, murder, adultery; "the church endured crimes of every kind":

Moreover he knew how to govern the republic, nor could they find any vestige of good will in his government. For these reasons, it was not wrong, they asserted, but rather due to a just judgment of God omnipotent that he had fled first the battlefield and then his own kingdom.[120]

The condemnation of Lothair was a negative image of Carolingian kingship. The bishops extracted a promise from the brothers: "the bishops and priests declared: 'We ask, admonish, and order you on divine authority to take over this kingdom and to rule it in accordance with the will of God.'"[121] In 843, with the Treaty of Verdun, the three brothers divided the Empire into three kingdoms. Charles the Bald received Aquitaine, and, eventually, the West Frankish kingdom, Lothair the Middle Kingdom reaching into Italy, and Louis the old mission-fields of the East.[122] A crucial feature of this division was the ability of each king to gain the allegiance of important nobles in their regions. The final shape of the three kingdoms was the result of maneuvers and intrigues among the nobility and the three brothers.[123]

---

119. "Et quidem primum visum est ut rem ad episcopos sacerdotesque, quorum aderat pars maxima, conferrent, ut illorum consultu veluti numine divino harum rerum exordium atque auctoritas proderetur" (4.1), Nithard, *Histoire,* 116.

120. "Insuper autem neque scientiam gubernandi rem publicam illum habere nec quoddam vestigium bone voluntatis in sua gubernatione quemlibet invenire posse ferebant. Quibus ex causis non inmerito, sed justo Dei omnipotentis judicio primum a proelio et secundo a proprio regno fugam illum inisse aiebant" (4.1), Nithard, *Histoire,* 118.

121. "Et auctoritate divina, ut illud suscipiatis et secundum Dei voluntatem illud regatis, monemus, ortamur atque praecipimus" (4.1), Nithard, *Histoire,* 118.

122. On the division of the empire as a "product of Frankish consensus politics": Nelson, "Public *Histories,*" 219–21.

123. Nelson, *Charles the Bald,* 133–34. The procedure of division is described in Peter Classen, "Die Verträge von Verdun und von Coulaines 843 als politische Grundlagen des westfränkischen Reiches," HZ 196 (1963): 1–35.

Authority and Power

The day of Louis' death marked the end (with a single exception, as will be seen) of imperial councils uniting bishops from the entire area of Frankish control.[124] There was a return, in a sense, to the Merovingian model of councils giving shape to the territory of the king who convoked them. In West Francia the reign of Charles the Bald was marked by a steady stream of episcopal activity. In part this can be attributed to the influence of Hincmar, the remarkable archbishop of Rheims, who was broadly informed, extremely active, and difficult to sway from his goals.[125] Charles rallied formidable intellectual resources to his cause: Lupus of Ferrières, the layman Nithard, and Hincmar—and relied on this circle of intellectuals to help him establish a new political order.[126] The persistence of conciliar activity in the kingdom of Charles the Bald can also be explained by this king's interest in maintaining as much continuity as possible with his ancestors. As Janet Nelson has pointed out, moreover, it was in the lands that formed Charles' portion where ecclesiastical institutions could rely upon centuries of acculturation to Christianity.[127]

The first council under Charles the Bald was held in Germigny-des-Prés in 843. This gathering of fifty bishops and abbots met, in part, to survey the ground between the young king and his clerics.[128] It was also a "gathering of the people" of Charles' kingdom. The council addressed the expropriation of ecclesiastical property that had animated the Council of Aachen, "to repair what had happened out of the harshness of the negligent or the violence of civil war."[129] Like an orchestra retuning its instruments, the bishops prepared to reclaim as much power as possible in the new order of things.

Louis' death and the problem of royal continuity dominated discussion in 843 at a council held at Coulaines.[130] Relations between king and noble had, in the decade following the Field of Lies and the deposition of Louis, again become a subject of discussion, and the meeting at Coulaines sought episcopal partici-

124. Thomas Bauer, "Koninuität und Wandel synodaler Praxis nach der Reichsteilung von Verdun: Versuch einer Typisierung und Einordnung der karolingischen Synoden und *concilia mixta* von 843 bis 870," AHC 23 (1991): 11–115; see 27–29.

125. On Hincmar, see Jean Devisse, *Hincmar: Archévêque de Reims, 845–882,* Travaux d'histoire ethico-politique 29, 3 vols. (Geneva: 1975).

126. Nelson, "The Intellectual in Politics," 1–14.

127. Nelson, *Charles the Bald,* 65f.

128. Council of Germigny-des-Prés (843), MGH Conc. 3:1–7.

129. "Ob incuriam negligentium aut propter civilis belli transacti violentiam iuvante Christo in melius reformare," Council of Germigny-des-Prés (843), MGH Conc. 3:3.

130. Council of Coulaines (843), MGH Conc. 3:10–17.

pation in a treaty (*foedus concordiae*) providing the basis for a West Frankish kingdom by bringing noble maneuvering to an end.[131] The record of the proceedings was issued in the "voice" of Charles, and considering the presence of nobles, should perhaps be thought of as a *concilia mixta*.[132] It is likely, as Janet Nelson has argued, that Hincmar was responsible for the final documents.[133] The three parties at Coulaines—king, nobles (*fideles*), and bishops—sought to protect their own interests in this official reintegration of the new kingdom.[134] The nobles had made difficult and dangerous choices about which brother to support during the period of civil war, and the council ratified and celebrated their choice as the right one.[135] But bishops remained at the center of any effort to express a meaningful social and moral order.

By their reconciliation, it was hoped, society could be bound by a "chain of charity" (*caritatis vinculum*).[136] To express the unity it hoped to achieve, the assembly evoked the most potent image of Carolingian political language, identifying a unified and catholic society with the Body of Christ. Each of the three principals of the assembly (bishops, nobles, and king) declared that they would not undermine the other two:

> not speaking as an exchange of diverse persons: speaking one time as the royal sublimity, now as the episcopal authority, now in the interests of the nobility (*fideles*), but according to the Apostle, as one man in the body of one church, under the one head Christ, and "the individuals are members of one another" (Rom. 12:5). It is beneficial to everyone that we all speak unanimously with one voice, through Him and in Him, and of whom it is said: "it is not you who speak, but the Spirit of your Father, who speaks through you" (Mat. 10:20).[137]

The most striking feature of this passage was that Charles the Bald and the assembly could think of their kingdom as the unified Body of Christ, having just

131. Classen, "Die Verträge von Verdun und von Coulaines 843," 25.
132. Bauer, "Koninuität und Wandel," 38–39 and 55–59.
133. Nelson, "The Intellectual in Politics," 9–14.
134. Anton, "Zum politischen Konzept," 80–81.
135. Innes, *State and Society*, 205–10.
136. Council of Coulaines (843), MGH Conc. 3:17. The council thus used the same terms that had been used long before, when missionary clerics had explained to the Bavarians sometime after 740 that they should obey their priests, and be bound to them by a *vinculis caritatis*.
137. "Non loquentes diversarum inmutatione personarum, ut modo regalis sublimitas, modo episcopalis auctoritas, modo autem fidelium loquatur commoditas; sed secundum apostolum sub uno *capite* Christo, ut revera [sc. = res vera] unus homo in unius *ecclesie corpore, singuli autem alter alterius membra,* quod prosit omnibus, omnes unanimiter una voce loquamur, per eum et in eo, qui dixit et de quo dictum est: *Non vos estis, qui loquimini, sed spiritus patris vestri, qui loquitur in vobis,*" Council of Coulaines (843), MGH Conc. 3:15.

divided the Empire, and despite the fact that Charles did not wear the imperial crown.[138] It should again be emphasized that bishops continued to think of
their society as a sacred body, governed by king and priest as representatives of
the priesthood and royalty of Christ.[139] The disappearance of a fragile imperial
theme was no impediment to reasserting social meaning in the wake of civil war.

The problem of reconciling a restless nobility, however, now forced its recognition as a potent element in society, a recognition that could potentially dis-
rupt the bishops' social model.[140] The council's language placed these warriors
squarely within the church, as the faithful (*fideles*) governed by king and bishop:
thus "Charles defused faction within the realm by mobilizing . . . the force of
aristocratic opinion and ecclesiastical authority."[141] The three elements of society were carefully distinguished, and each was assigned a characteristic quality.
Charles explained that the arrangement would allow "our honor and the royal
power to remain undisturbed, through the counsel and help of episcopal authority and the unanimity of the faithful."[142]

The anxious insistence on continuity at Coulaines derived from the unprecedented problem of establishing a new kingdom. This was a problem not only
for Charles the Bald. The following year, in 844, the three brothers (Charles the
Bald, Louis the German, and Lothair) came together at Yütz bei Diedenhofen.
There, under Drogo of Metz, was held the last council to unite clerics from the
three kingdoms.[143] Drogo was in a unique position to preside over such a council—he was uncle of the three brothers, and as archbishop of the Sacred Palace
under Louis had been the most important cleric in the empire. He had also been
named papal vicar for Europe north of the Alps, and thus was an embodiment
of traditional order.[144] Amalarius of Metz was also present. Meanwhile, each
brother sought to claim continuity with his father, and to give the appearance
that he adhered to the *Ordinato imperii*.[145] The assembly at Yütz had another

138. Anton, "Zum politischen Konzept," 83.

139. Johannes Fried, "Der karolingische Herrschaftsverband im 9. Jh. zwischen 'Kirche' und
'Königshaus,'" HJ 235 (1982): 1–43.

140. Anton argues that this represents the reemergence of older sources of social order, now
thinly disguised in the colors of the Carolingian state: Anton, "Zum politischen Konzept," 84–85.

141. Nelson, "The Intellectual in Politics," 6.

142. "Et sic consilio atque auxilio episcopalis auctoritas et fidelium unanimitas, ut noster
honor et potestas regia inconvulsa permaneat," Council of Coulaines (843), MGH Conc. 3:16.

143. Council of Yütz bei Diedenhofen (844), MGH Conc. 3:27–35. On this council, see De
Clercq, "La législation religieuse franque depuis," *Revue de Droit Canonique* 5 (1955): 287–88.

144. Wallace-Hadrill, *Frankish Church*, 269.

145. "Unde inmensas domino deo nostro laudes referimus, qui et corda vestra ad intentionem
similem excitavit et post vestigia patrum vestrorum," Council of Yütz bei Diedenhofen (844),
MGH Conc. 3:30.

function, however, which was to ratify the end of the civil war and to clarify that each brother was to have his kingdom.

Looking back to the Council of Paris in 829, the bishops were prepared to admonish and correct their kings, remarking that because bishops were established as Christ's Vicars, it was necessary to "ask the priests for law."[146] The council rebuked their kings for having "cut apart, disturbed, and afflicted the church committed to your government" in a civil war that weakened their ability to rule in the present and to gain salvation in the future.[147] The bishops specifically complained that in the wake of the civil war, a number of episcopal sees lay vacant, and that the proceeds of their lands and income were directed toward the three brothers' efforts at kingdom-building.[148] The council seems to mark the end of the constant theme of unity that had been raised so often in the Carolingian councils.[149] From the perspective of Drogo and the other bishops, the misuse of ecclesiastical land had perverted the proper Christological structure of society, as the three brothers ought to know:

Because you know quite well that the church is properly ordered, by the One who alone is both a king and a priest by merit, in such a way that [the church] is governed by episcopal authority and royal power.[150]

As at Coulaines, the bishops again distinguished between power and authority, but this time more strictly. Faced with the problem of describing three new kingdoms with a political terminology formulated during the expansion of a single empire, the bishops transformed the language of social unity. The problem of description was exacerbated by the existence of three kings, who had appeared to be tyrants while Louis was alive. Each of the brothers, moreover, was guilty of having despoiled the church to provide himself with armies and buy the affections of a hard-bargaining nobility. The bishops assembled at Yütz, as had the councils of Aachen and Coulaines, looked back to the Council of Paris

146. "*Interroga sacerdotes legem* meam et *Interroga patres tuos et adnuntiabunt tibi,* a nobis, quamquam indignis, Christi tamen vicariis." Council of Yütz bei Diedenhofen (844), MGH Conc. 3:30.

147. "Vestra discordia esse discissam et perturbatam atque afflictam, videtur nobis, si et in praesenti feliciter regnare et in futuro cupitis esse salvi et ab hac eadem ecclesia vobis ad gubernandum commissa," Council of Yütz bei Diedenhofen (844), MGH Conc. 3:30.

148. "Ut sedes, quae vestra discordia ulterius nec nominanda sine sacro episcopali ministerio et sine episcopis viduatae manent," Council of Yütz bei Diedenhofen (844), MGH Conc. 3:31.

149. Anton, "Zum politischen Konzept," 87–88.

150. "Quia bene nostis ab illo, qui solus merito et rex et sacerdos fieri potuit, ita ecclesiam dispositam esse, ut pontificali auctoritate et regali potestate gubernetur," Council of Yütz bei Diedenhofen (844), MGH Conc. 3:31.

in 829 as a primary description of social structure. The shifts in language, although subtle, were nevertheless definitive.

By distinguishing the *authority* of bishops and the *power* of kings, the bishops emphasized a qualitative disjuncture between the two governing "persons" at the head of society—and thereby reversed the categories as they had been assigned, long ago, in the *Edict of Guntram* of 585. The statement was far from Isidore's assertion that bishops possessed a "dignity of power." In effect, the bishops were forced to acknowledge the power of the three kings, despite the fact that, during the civil war, they were tyrants, not deserving the *nomen* of king. The bishops at Yütz were powerless to attempt anything so bold as the penance imposed on Louis the Pious.

The bishops could, however, sweep aside any suggestion that a king could assume both royal and priestly dignity. Only Christ could do so. The Council of Yütz thus distinguished between the "actual" Christ, who was king and priest, and the Christological nature of Frankish society, merely governed by kings and priests. The bishops, with great economy, advanced a series of disunities and separations. The Christ who died on the cross was distinguished from the mundane society whose members now seemed, in the wake of civil war, an imperfect version of the Body of Christ. Authority was distinguished from power, and a social and moral border was drawn between bishops and kings. In this sense, the break in royal-episcopal unity at the Council of Yütz was rooted in the social thought of the Council of Aachen in 836.[151] The transformation of the Empire in the civil war called forth a new conceptualization of episcopal power.

Arguments were advanced at Yütz in order to distinguish the royal and episcopal "persons." The kings were upbraided for having upset the episcopal order, despite the fact that bishops were endowed with a religious potency not shared by royal power. All this was expressed in a formula that, unlike earlier episcopal social thought, highlighted what divided, rather than linked, the ruling "persons" in Frankish society: the relation between episcopal authority and royal power was compared to the distinction between soul and body.[152] Just as the soul, being more precious, should dominate the body, so, the bishops cautiously implied, bishops should have precedence over kings. Kings should therefore not presume to let bishoprics stand vacant.[153] To the kings' concerns for stabil-

151. The taxonomy proposed by Bauer does not affect the interest or importance of this synod; Bauer, "Koninuität und Wandel," 32–33.

152. On the Council of Yütz, see further Anton, *Fürstenspiegel und Herrscherethos,* 231–34.

153. "Ut sedes, quae vestra discordia ulterius nec nominanda sine sacro episcopali ministerio et sine episcopis viduatae manent," Council of Yütz bei Diedenhofen (844), MGH Conc. 3:31.

ity, in other words, the bishops opposed their own need for stability and peace.

Similarly, the bishops complained, laymen were put at the head of monasteries, "against all authority and reason and custom of your fathers or preceding kings."[154] In this connection, the bishops brought forward another new image of disjuncture, absent from previous councils: Matthew's story of Jesus, holding up a coin with its image of the emperor, saying "render unto Caesar what is Caesar's, and to God the things that are Gods" (Mat. 22:21).[155] This phrase neatly expressed the division between the property rights of bishops and laymen. In this sense Hincmar, who may well have attended the council, understood the words of Jesus, as will be seen shortly. It is certainly significant that at the Council of Yütz the bishops turned to the New Testament for a description of social order, in a way rarely done before. The Old Testament, throughout the Carolingian period, had provided the language and *topoi* of episcopal discussions of the nature of society. In the Pentateuch a treasury of stories, images, and vocabulary had been found to express the meaning and purpose of Christian institutions. The New Testament, with its antagonistic comparisons of the Roman Empire to the kingdom of Christ, was a rich source for a language of contrast between the holy and mundane, particularly in regard to social structures. Succeeding councils, such as Ver later the same year, Meaux-Paris in 845/846, Anjou in 850, Quierzy in 853, and Valence in 855, now turned to the New Testament to establish the church's priority and prerogatives against the encroachment of worldly power.

As had the Council of Aachen, the bishops at Yütz explained that pious princes of the past had built up the church, while "less religious" princes had not. The three kings were warned that they would be subject to divine vengeance because the church had fallen "into destruction, not in building, in the time of your reign."[156] The problem was not merely the active seizure of land by the kings themselves, but the fact that the three brothers allowed their noble *fideles* to overturn the carefully made arrangements of prestige and control in the countryside. The kings were urged to recall their hope for salvation, in the present and for eternity, and the generosity of their forefathers toward the holy churches.[157] Unlike their ancestors, the brothers allowed violent thefts of ecclesiastical prop-

154. "Contra omnem auctoritatem et rationem ac patrum vestrorum seu regum precedentium consuetudinem," Council of Yütz bei Diedenhofen (844), MGH Conc. 3:32.

155. "Quae dei sunt, deo et, quae sunt caesaris, caesari reddant," as cited at Council of Yütz bei Diedenhofen (844), MGH Conc. 3:32.

156. "Et metu ultionis divinae dicimus, in vestri regiminis tempore in destructionem, non in aedificationem," Council of Yütz bei Diedenhofen (844), MGH Conc. 3:32–33.

157. "Venerabiliter admonemus et devotissime obsecramus, ut memores salutis vestrae,

erty, which the bishops likened to "rending the tunic of Christ." The phrase drove home the point that the social order Carolingian bishops had portrayed so often, in the great series of councils beginning with Frankfurt in 794, was now broken. It was broken by a social group all but invisible to previous councils—the warriors (*milites*) whose services were so much in demand by warring kings.[158]

The bishops insisted that local commissions be established for the "restoration of places"[159] and ended with a plea for the revival of "ancient custom through your power and through the office of the executors of your power" (*ministerium ministrorum*).[160] The three kings, one may legitimately suppose, were not pleased by this council of bishops, led by the powerful Drogo of Metz, himself a bastard son of Charlemagne.[161] As mentioned above, Lothair and Louis the German had less to worry about from bishops in their kingdoms, especially if they could be kept from acting in concert with bishops of the western kingdom. It was perhaps a mistake they could not help making in that first year after the Treaty of Verdun, but it was a mistake they did not repeat.

Vobis et Nobis

In Ver-sur-Launette at the end of 844, an assembly gathered in the kingdom of Charles the Bald, bringing together "the bishops and the other faithful (*fideles*)."[162] As at Coulaines, the Council of Ver was a discussion of the terms on which the kingdom could be reconstituted in the wake of significant upheaval. While the Council of Coulaines and, to some degree, the Council of Yütz had attempted to redeploy the language of the imperial councils, this was not attempted at Ver, despite the fact that the council was called to declare that "discord, from which every evil emanates, had been set aside."[163] The bishops intend-

---

presentis scilicet et aeterne, memore etiam largitatis progenitorum vestrorum erga sanctas ecclesias," Council of Yütz bei Diedenhofen (844), MGH Conc. 3:33.

158. "Ante oculos reducentes tunicam Christi, qui vos elegit et exaltavit, quam nec milites ausi fuerunt scindere," Council of Yütz bei Diedenhofen (844), MGH Conc. 3:33. Although the word *miles, milites* had appeared in previous councils, it was almost without exception in the context of the phrase *milites Christi,* that is clerics, or more particularly monks. Here it means fighting men.

159. "Episcopi providentia, in cuius parrochia consistunt, adiuncto sibi aliquo abbate viro religioso studeatur, qualiter restauratio locorum et studium ac custodia . . . ministretur," Council of Yütz bei Diedenhofen (844), MGH Conc. 3:34.

160. "Per potestatem vestram et per ministerium ministrorum dominationis vestrae secundum antiquam consuetudinem," Council of Yütz bei Diedenhofen (844), MGH Conc. 3:35.

161. On Drogo, see Riché, *Carolingians,* 148–49 and 157–58.

162. "Gratias omnipotenti deo referimus, inclyte rex Karole, nos episcopi et ceteri fideles," Council of Ver-sur-Launette (844), MGH Conc. 3:36–44; see 38.

163. "Quod deposita discordia, unde tot mala processerunt," Council of Ver-sur-Launette (844), MGH Conc. 3:38.

ed to show how discord could be laid to rest, especially regarding ecclesiastical land. As in earlier episcopal discussions of church property, much more was at stake than the land itself. The seizure of property was only the symptom of a greater problem: "that the order (*status*) of the church was violently confused because of the magnitude and multitude of our sins."[164]

The Council of Ver promulgated a series of canons urging the return of monastic lands from Charles' followers to episcopal government and addressed the problem of "vacant" sees—above all Rheims, where Lothair had restored Ebbo as archbishop, an appointment the West Frankish bishops contested.[165] The king was also asked to discipline his followers by threatening them with loss of position.[166] The council then came "to the last portion of our admonition." It is one of the most remarkable passages in Carolingian conciliar law, speaking in the wounded and confused tone of men witnessing the end of a social order:

what we here propound will have been given by God—so you, your nobles, and the other faithful should take up what we say with devotion. We see that the anger of God threatens ourselves and all of you (*vobis et nobis*), because of rapine and other threatening crimes, but most of all because the properties of the church, which kings and other Christians dedicated to God to sustain the servants of God and the poor, for receiving strangers, for the redemption of hostages, and for the foundation of the churches of God, are now detained for secular use (*in usu saecularium*).[167]

Those unfulfilled duties had for centuries defined the function of episcopal government. The church's straitened circumstances had not, moreover, resulted from external invasion, but from an internal breakdown of social order, a civil war—"nay, more than civil," said the bishops, quoting a phrase from Lucan's *Pharsalia*.[168] The conflict among the three brothers had violated old cus-

---

164. "Ut de statu ecclesiae, qui vehementer magnitudine ac multitudine peccatorum nostrorum confusus est," Council of Ver-sur-Launette (844), MGH Conc. 3:39.

165. Ebbo, deposed by Louis the Pious, was reinstated by Lothair upon Louis' death: Nelson, *Charles the Bald*, 107.

166. Council of Ver-sur-Launette (844), MGH Conc. 3:41.

167. "Veniemus nunc ad ultimam partem admonitionis nostre; quam qua intentione fundimus, dederit deus, ut vos ac proceres caeterique fideles ea devotione suscipiatis. Videmus enim iram dei nobis et vobis imminere cum pro rapinis et immanibus aliis sceleribus, tum etiam maxime, quod ecclesiae facultates, quas reges et reliqui christiani deo voverunt ad alimentum servorum dei et pauperum, ad exceptionem hospitum, redemptionem captivorum atque templorum dei instaurationem, nunc in usu saecularium detinentur," Council of Ver-sur-Launette (844), MGH Conc. 3:42–43.

168. "Immo plus quam civilem," Council of Ver-sur-Launette (844), MGH Conc. 3:40; a reference to Lucan's "plus quam civilia" *Bellum civile* (1.1); see Lucan, *The Civil War (Pharsalia)*, edited and translated by J. D. Duff, Loeb Classical Library 220 (Cambridge, Mass.: 1928), 2.

toms by which such conflicts had traditionally been settled.[169] The collapse of royal and episcopal cooperation in governing the unified Body of Christ was a source of deep regret:

And indeed, if the church suffered these things under pagans, it would demand patience. Now, however, we are oppressed by our sons, that is to say by those to whom we or our predecessors gave birth in Christ, making them Christians by our ministry, and hence we retain no consolation in patience, since we dread their destruction. Indeed no one, however impudent will dare deny that "the possessions of the church are the prayers of the faithful, the patrimony of the poor, the redemption of souls."[170]

The bishops thought of the twenty-one-year-old king and his nobles as their "sons" whom they had instructed and were now rebuking. Yet the issue was serious enough. The Council of Yütz and the Council of Ver-sur-Launette both had mentioned the example of Ozas, who was struck down for having touched the Ark of the Covenant. The bishops at Ver explained: "Someone might laugh at this, except, we say with the deepest sadness, because of their actions, certain oppressors of churches meet a worthy demise even in our time."[171]

Although the council, as noted above, recited Julian Pomerius' dictum that church possessions are the patrimony of the poor, it is not surprising that the bishops, along the lines of the Council of Aachen in 836, went further: church land and property were the "possessions of God"; those who took them were hence actually robbing God.[172] This marked a boundary between two radically different kinds of property, based on the property theory propounded at Aachen in 836. Whereas the bishops at Aachen had insisted that all property was God's, the bishops at Ver asserted that some property was properly turned to mundane uses. Their insistence on the division between sacred and mundane spheres in society was reflected in a theory of property, as well. Unlike the Council of Aachen, these bishops saw a theoretical limit to ecclesiastical ownership: "Render to God what is his own, so that you might possess what is yours in peace,

---

169. Nelson, *Charles the Bald,* 115.

170. "Et quidem, si haec a paganis pateretur ecclesia, pacientiam flagitaret; nunc autem oppressi a filiis nostris, hoc est ab his, quos vel nos vel decessores nostri in Christo genuimus, christianos eos nostro mynisterio facientes, nullam patientiae consolationem recipimus, quoniam de illorum interitu formidamus. Certe, quod nullus quamquam inpudentissimus negare audebit, *possessio ecclesie votum est fidelium, patrimonium pauperum, redemptio animarum*"; based upon Julian Pomerius, *De vita contemplativa* II, 9, Council of Ver-sur-Launette (844), MGH Conc. 3:43.

171. "Rideat hoc aliquis, nisi, quod summo dolore dicimus, quidam oppressores ecclesiae dignum suis moribus exitum nostro etiam tempore invenerunt," Council of Ver-sur-Launette (844), MGH Conc. 3:43.

172. "Possessiones dei," Council of Ver-sur-Launette (844), MGH Conc. 3:44.

and avoid eternal torments. . . . Secular men possess secular honors, ecclesiastical honors are apportioned to ecclesiastical men."[173] The *honor* of each side—royal grants of public duties and prerogatives—were to be conceived separately.[174] Charles the Bald was faulted for taking bad counsel from his nobles (*perversorum consilia*) while rejecting the bishops "salutary counsels" (*nostris salutaribus consiliis*).[175] It is impossible to know what exactly the bishops were threatening in the final, bitter sentence of the Council of Ver-sur-Launette, though it certainly appears to threaten penance for the young king: "If, on the other hand, you have contempt for us, or rather for the God who speaks through us, then out of the necessity of fulfilling our ministry, we should be compelled to do what we don't wish to do."[176] The Council of Ver took so radical a stand that in the view of Lot and Halphen, it had almost no resonance in contemporary records or later councils.[177] More to the point, we find in these texts the saturation of political thought and action by the categories of episcopal judgement and governance over the rituals of penance, confession, excommunication, and reconciliation.[178]

In the end, the reconciliation of Charles the Bald with his bishops involved important concessions on each side. In place of the deposed Ebbo, Charles chose Hincmar as the new archbishop of Rheims, thereby forming an alliance of great importance to the future of his reign. It was Hincmar whose historical vision, centering on the city of Rheims rather than Aachen, provided crucial intellectual resources for the legitimacy of a West Frankish kingdom.[179] In 848, Charles was anointed and crowned as king of the western Frankish kingdom at Orléans, in a ritual composed for the occasion (but not by Hincmar).[180] Charles was

173. "Reddite deo sua, ut vestra cum pace possideatis, tormenta evadatis aeterna. . . . Saeculares honores saeculares possideant, ecclesiasticos ecclesiastici sortiantur," Council of Ver-sur-Launette (844), MGH Conc. 3:44.

174. Werner, *Naissance de la noblesse*, 179–84; see also Anton, "Zum politischen Konzept," 84–85; and Janet L. Nelson, "Kingship, Law and Liturgy in the Political Thought of Hincmar of Rheims," in *Politics and Ritual*, 133–71; esp. 147.

175. Council of Ver-sur-Launette (844), MGH Conc. 3:44.

176. "Sin autem nos, immo deum per nos loquentem, contempseritis, necessitate implendi ministerii, quod nollemus, facere compellemur," Council of Ver-sur-Launette (844) MGH Conc. 3:44.

177. Ferdinand Lot and Louis Halphen, *Le règne de Charles le Chauve (840–877)* (Paris: 1909), 126–29.

178. Patzold rightly highlights the *Deutungshoheit* of the bishops over these rituals and their outcomes: Patzold, *Episcopus*,512.

179. Nelson, "Kingship, Law," 147–48; Nelson, *Charles the Bald,* 145–46.

180. Nelson, "Inauguration Rituals," 62–63; Louis Levillain, "Le sacre de Charles le Chauve à Orléans," *Bibliothèque de l'École des Chartes* 64 (1903), 31–53; see 33; Guy Lanoë, "L'*ordo* de couronnement de Charles le Chauve à Sainte-Croix d'Orléans (6 Juin 848)," in *Kings and Kingship in Medieval Europe,* ed. Anne J. Duggan, 41–68, King's College London Medieval Studies 10 (London: 1993).

consecrated by the assembled bishops as a kind of priest-king, in a ceremony re-sembling the ordination of a priest.[181] The king and his bishops stood together at the head of a kingdom conceived of as the Body of Christ, as Charles was en-dowed with diadem, sceptre, and throne.[182]

Before receiving this unction, with its allusion to a Christological social structure, Charles was compelled to take an oath before an assembly in Beau-vais in which he conceded to demands Frankish councils had made regarding episcopal government and property rights.[183] He promised to punish "oppres-sors of our churches" and to respect his father's charters and arrangements, to take counsel from his bishops, and to help them preserve "ecclesiastical law and canon law."[184] The key phrase in the Oath of Beauvais was a mutual promise binding Charles and the West Frankish bishops:

Because neither in my person nor in my order—unless by chance, God forbid, did I in the past act manifestly against God and you so that I should be canonically con-demned, against me and my order may you not act so damnably, for whatever past causes, in such a way that dishonor or damnation might come to me.[185]

This article of the Oath of Beauvais reinforces the impression that Charles had been threatened with an imposition of penance or excommunication by the Council of Ver-sur-Launette. The most striking feature of the article is its firm distinction between two orders—one composed of bishops and their follow-ers, the other of the king and his nobles. The relation between bishop and king had come to resemble the sharp contrast between ecclesiastical and secular land imagined decades earlier by Wala.[186]

Although Charles' oath and his anointing ceremony had ostensibly settled the issues separating him from his bishops, the latter soon found that Charles would do nothing about church land except as a result of constant pressure. Believing that earlier councils had been ignored, late in 845 the West Frankish bishops assembled first in Meaux because of an incursion of Northmen along

181. "Sacroque crismate delibutum et benedictione episcopali solemniter consecrant" (Anno 848), *Annales,* ed. G. H. Pertz, MGH SS 1:443; see Levillain, "Le sacre de Charles," 49.

182. Robert Folz, "Les trois couronnements de Charles le Chauve," *Byzantion* 61 (1991): 93–111; see 95.

183. De Clercq, "La législation religieuse franque," *Revue de Droit Canonique* 5 (1955): 293.

184. Council of Beauvais (845), MGH Conc. 3:47–55; see 54–55.

185. "Quod in mea persona nec in meo ordine—nisi forte, quod absit, inantea contra deum et contra vos manifeste fecero, ut damnari canonice debeam—adversum me et meum ordinem ita dampnabiliter non faciatis pro quacumque preterita causa, ut mihi dehonoratio aut dampnatio veniat," Council of Beauvais (845), MGH Conc. 3:54.

186. Anton, "Zum politischen Konzept," 74, 119–21.

the Seine, moving to Paris when the invaders had withdrawn.[187] Hincmar of Rheims and Wenilo of Sens were present, both of whom arrived with their suffragan bishops.[188]

The long preface to the council declared the bishops' intention to summarize councils held since the death of Louis the Pious, a time when "the church was fatigued by diverse and adverse vexations."[189] In response to these vexations, bishops had attempted in every possible way to make their case to the princes, the powerful, and even to the poor, "in speech, in writing, in public and private persuasion," to no avail.[190] Above all there were the councils—Coulaines, Yütz, and Ver—that were not "presented to the ears of the prince and the people because of the envy and malice of the Devil or his ministers."[191] The bishops had thus pursued every avenue of political influence and discourse open to them. The twin evils of civil war and Viking invasions were symptoms, according to the bishops at Meaux, of ignoring the councils and abandoning God's will:

Therefore it happened, as was needful, that when obedience was not given to divine commands, the Lord sent *from the North,* whence as the prophet said, *evil is spread out,* "apostles" that we were worthy of, namely the cruel and monstrous Northmen, persecutors of Christians, who came all the way to Paris, as the Lord commanded.[192]

The kingdom was therefore faced with a clear sign of divine displeasure.[193] The reforms proposed by the council would restore the kingdom's obedience to the will of God, as expressed in councils. The bishops had assembled at Meaux as *"unworthy, nevertheless vicars of Christ,* the successors of the Apostles."[194] The

187. Lot and Halphen, *Le règne de Charles le Chauve,* 136–39.

188. Council of Meaux-Paris (845/846), MGH Conc. 3:61–132. On this council, see de Clercq, "La législation religieuse franque," *Revue de Droit Canonique* 5 (1955): 294–306; and Hartmann, *Synoden der Karolingerzeit,* 208–17.

189. "Postquam ab ipsis pie memorie Hludowidi divini augusti temporibus ecclesia diversis et adversis ceperat vexationibus fatigari," Council of Meaux-Paris (845/846), MGH Conc. 3:81.

190. "Hoc verbis, hoc scriptis, hoc publicis, hoc privatis suasionibus," Council of Meaux-Paris (845/846), MGH Conc. 3:82.

191. "Sed invidia ac malicia diaboli seu ministrorum eius nondum principis et populi auribus propalatum," Council of Meaux-Paris (845/846), MGH Conc. 3:82.

192. "Inde vero, quia, sicut necesse fuerat, divinis iussionibus non est secuta obediencia, dedit dominus *ab aquilone,* unde iuxta prophetam *pandetur malum,* dignos meritis nostris apostolos, crudeles scilicet et inmanissimos christianitatis persecutores Normannos, qui usque Parisius venientes, quod iussit dominus," Council of Meaux-Paris (845/846), MGH Conc. 3:82.

193. Simon Coupland, "The Rod of God's Wrath or the People of God's Wrath? The Carolingian Theology of the Viking Invasions," JEH 42 (1991): 535–54.

194. "Licet *indigni, Christi tamen vicarii* et apostolorum ipsius successores" (quoting the preface of the Council of Yütz, MGH Conc. 3:30): Council of Meaux-Paris (845/846), MGH Conc. 3:84.

council reaffirmed the most important canons of earlier West Frankish councils, demanding a restitution of ecclesiastical land and insisting on the prerogatives of episcopal government.

The bishops confirmed and intensified the decisions of earlier councils. Thus the complaint made at the Council of Yütz about lay abbots was reaffirmed with genuine bitterness. Such abbots were part of an

abomination of desolation, not only of religion . . . not only of such substituted and apocryphal rectors [the lay abbots] but also of the king and the kingdom, and the first men of the kingdom, through this detestable "dis-ordination" of partisans.[195]

The council anathematized such abbots "by the judgment of the Holy Spirit."[196] Under the direction of Hincmar of Rheims, a formidible legal scholar, the bishops entered into details of ecclesiastical landholdings and considered the legal ramifications of various kinds of tenure—*precariae, allodes,* and *beneficiae,* in a new way.[197] They were especially (and no doubt rightly) concerned that tenants of the lands bishops gave as benefices would come to think that they should be able to pass them on to their children, and were afraid the land would insensibly pass from the hands of the church. Their hope was to have such matters determined by a commission, made up of "powerful and faithful *missi,*" with authority to investigate misappropriations of church land throughout the kingdom.[198] The theory of property voiced at the Council of Aachen in 836 had shifted, at the Council of Ver-sur-Launette, toward an exclusionary claim for episcopal government. At the Council of Meaux-Paris, the bishops said that those who took the goods of the church, which were the only sustenance of the poor, were thus to be considered murderers of the poor (*necatores pauperum*).[199] The bishops thus revived a canon from the Council of Orléans in 549, having its origin in the mid-fifth century. The concept had not found its way into canon law for

195. "Vere enim ista est abominatio desolationis . . . non solum subditorum et talium apocriphorum rectorum, verum et regis et regni atque regni primorum huic detestabili inordinationi fautorum." The phrase "abomination of desolation" is from Mk. 13:14; Council of Meaux-Paris (845/846), MGH Conc. 3:90. *Inordinatio* "disorder" is a play on words with *ordinatio,* "ordination."

196. "Iudicio sancti spiritus praesenti decreta auctoritate anathematizetur," Council of Meaux-Paris (845/846), MGH Conc. 3:91.

197. Council of Meaux-Paris (845/846), MGH Conc. 3:95–96.

198. "Monenda est sollertia regia, ut strenuos et fideles missos per regnum sibi commissum dirigat; et investigent ac diligenter inbrevient res ecclesiasticas," Council of Meaux-Paris (845/846), MGH Conc. 3:104.

199. Council of Meaux-Paris (845/846), MGH Conc. 3:94 (citing Council of Orléans (549): CCSL 148A:148–69).

the preceding two centuries.[200] This was a conservative—one might even say a scholarly—reference to pre-Carolingian canon law, reflecting the influence of Hincmar. It also reflects a conservative basis for the property theory expounded at Meaux-Paris, reaching back to find the origins of church land-tenure in the fact that such land was the property of the poor. The bishops darkly condemned harsh exploitation on rural estates:

As despoilers of ecclesiastical properties, who are known not only to seize such properties even against authority, but, in truth, to cruelly plunder, some with collective effort even despoil, devastate and crush without pity the poor and also those nearby and in the vicinity; let the rapacious, who according to the Apostle are excluded from the kingdom of God, make satisfaction for their public and criminal sin with public penance. And if they do not wish to do this, and are not exhorted or compelled by royal power, may the terrible Apostolic dictum be hurled at them.[201]

The bishops issued an anathema against lay abbots, many of whom were favored by the king with this position because of their great importance. Nithard himself, the learned warrior, historian, and staunch supporter of Charles the Bald, was one such lay abbot. The bishops at Meaux-Paris were aware that they faced a feature of royal power directly opposed to their own conceptions of proper social order. Despite the fact that Nithard, and perhaps many of his fellow lay abbots, were aware of the majesty surrounding bishops, who alone could interpret the "just judgments of God," they were not eager to relinquish privileges granted by their king that they had sacrificed so much to earn. Eventually he would die in battle, fighting for Charles in Aquitaine, in 845. This was not merely a clash of ideas, nor even of social forces, but a struggle among individuals acting under tremendous political and social strains.[202]

The collapse of Carolingian unity and the rise of three successor kingdoms was accompanied by a breakdown in the unity of royal and episcopal power. In the summer of 846, Charles held a "national" assembly at the royal palace in Epernay. Of the eighty-three canons promulgated by the bishops at Meaux-

200. The phrase *necatores pauperum* had last been used at the Council of Chalon-sur-Saôn (647–653) CCSL 148A:304.

201. "Ut pervasores rerum ecclesiasticarum, qui easdem res vel contra auctoritatem non solum retinere, verum et crudeliter depopulari noscuntur, quidam etiam et facultates ecclesie in diversa conlaboratione et reditibus eas expoliant, sed et pauperes atque vicinos et cirummanentes inmisericorditer expoliant, devastant et opprimunt, ut rapaces, qui secundum apostolum a regno dei excluduntur, ex criminali et publico peccato publica penitentia satisfaciant. Quodsi hoc agere noluerint et potestate regia ad hoc exortati vel coacti non fuerint, proferatur contra eos apostolica terribilis sentientia," Council of Meaux-Paris (845/846), MGH Conc. 3:113.

202. Nelson, "The Intellectual in Politics," 2–5.

Paris, only the mildest nineteen were accepted by the assembly and affirmed as royal law.[203] In this way, the tradition of royal-episcopal cooperation characterizing the Carolingian kingdom from the time of Pippin and Boniface was finally broken in favor of lay abbots and other nobles gathered in the royal palace. Bishops could no longer expect that their law would be taken up and enforced by their king.

As the unified Empire of the Carolingians came to an end, bishops continued to think about the nature of royal power and to draw on a conciliar tradition they were in the process of expanding. They were uniquely able to provide the intellectual setting for political hope. In the reconfiguration of power among the Franks and the appearance of a new political order, warlords had once again emerged "from a thousand lairs," their loyalty to the sacred kingdom often tentative or compromised.[204] As we have seen, the role of episcopal law in the period 829 to 845 was flexible and subject to textual manipulation to intensify a specific doctrine of the state. In the last years of Louis the Pious, this law played a role in the collapse of imperial unity and in the reestablishment of political order by a renewed and sensitively adjusted statement of the "sacred kingdom" ideal. This can only be viewed as subversive if we believe that kings had an exclusive right to possess the state, and to shape it in the law: "a written, systematised law representing a permanent 'objective' statement of abstract justice . . . bounded by the requirements of continuity, predictability, and conformity with explicit norms." But the Carolingian monarchs had not produced such a law.[205]

Nor had these kings, for all their power, given shape to the Carolingian state by themselves, even in the many negotiations of power they made with nobles around the kingdom. Playing a role in discussions at the highest level of power, bishops had managed to enunciate a set of goals that seemed not only meaningful, but vital, for the small group of the kingdom's most powerful men. Bishops were uniquely placed to offer a vision for the kingdom with their mastery of law and their theological vision, anchored in a sacred history. In their councils, bishops pointed to their intellectual and moral resources time and again as the only conceptual walls that could shelter a social order and preserve the bonds of charity between men.

Nelson is right to insist that in the councils we are able to trace the impact

---

203. Hartmann, *Synoden der Karolingerzeit*, 216f.

204. Duby, *Three Orders*, 151.

205. Janet L. Nelson, "On the Limits of the Carolingian Renaissance," in *Politics and Ritual*, 49–67; this quote, 62.

of intellectuals on the Carolingian Empire, whether calmly promulgating their ideas in the hearing and presence of the king or stridently raising them as a counter-law opposed to current *praxis*. Certain individuals can be identified in this role: the abbots Wala and Hilduin, Ebbo of Rheims, Jonas of Orléans, Halitgar of Cambrai, Frechulf of Lisieux, Aldrich of Sense, Hugbert of Mieux, and others. These men were well known to the emperor, serving as his chaplains, missi dominici, and emissaries.[206] Bishops shifted their ancient social vocabulary in light of new social realities, without ceasing to claim a governmental and legislative prerogative, and calling the state to the task of expanding the church and promoting salvation. It is right to say that "social change is symbol change."[207] The bishops, with their ability to peer into the other world, could assemble these symbols, and ring their changes, where others could only see slaughter, suffering, or political opportunity.

206. Patzold, *Episcopus,* 512.
207. Smith, "Influence of Symbols upon Social Change," 144.

CONCLUSION

Yoking the Bull

*A*N ANCIENT POLITICAL QUESTION arose for the Carolingians, as it
does still today: is it possible to yoke the bull of power? This study has
examined the social and political doctrines of bishops from the Gallic Church
of the fourth century to the Frankish Church of the mid-ninth century, a period of some five hundred years. In relying on conciliar records I have not tried
to write a history of conciliar law, but rather to trace the formation of an intellectual elite within a warrior society, and to describe how this elite built and
maintained its power and functionality across periods of profound change. I
have also shown how, on this basis, bishops helped to shape the development
of the Carolingian state, through a steady conversation with kings, about the
meaning and purposes of royal power.

The conceptual transformation of kingship, set in motion with the baptism
of King Clovis, continued to have sway long afterward, as Carolingian power
declined in the tenth century. The "anointing of King Clovis" was further developed as a symbol for concepts of kingship.[1] At the heart of this social and
intellectual change lay the episcopal council: the primary vehicle of communication and organization among bishops, the premier display of their moral
and governmental power, and a forum for their intellectual work and concept-
formation. The council was a moment of contact with the Holy Spirit and thus
the wellspring of episcopal religious power and ritual prestige.

1. Philippe Gabet, "Constantin et Clovis, développements et transformations rémois aux IXe
et Xe siècles," in *Clovis,* 2:73–81.

The council was a vehicle for building moral and political consensus in the small circle of the Gallic regional aristocracy and, later, among important Frankish nobles. Ultimately this aspect gave way to imperial organization, and yet bishops were able to define political concepts in the new regime. Councils gave them a unique ability to speak. In face-to-face meetings, certain bishops could assume leadership through the combined force of their institutional prestige, their closeness to power, and their ability to articulate ideas, to wield the tradition, and exert their personal qualities. One can point to Caesarius at the Council of Orange in 529, Boniface at the *Concilium Germanicum* in 742, Agobard and Jonas at the Council of Paris in 829, and Hincmar at the Council of Meaux-Paris in 845. Conciliar records should not lightly be dismissed as "normative sources." They should be read alongside other sources to develop a fuller picture of the figure of the bishop, and of the historical actions erected on that image. The worldly power of bishops was heightened by the spiritual and legal dimension of their authority.[2] The councils reflect the pressures of social change and are tied to their historical moment, representing the response of well-placed intellectuals who participated in these events at the highest level.[3] From unrecorded discussions and debates the final record presented a seamless, concordant, unanimous statement. It is evident that these clear statements reflected a worldview that the councils were at the same time actively creating.[4] This worldview was of great importance in the history of Carolingian Europe. A symbolic realm of discourse influenced the political, military, and economic actions not only of bishops, but of all those who wished to play a role at the royal or imperial level. Councils presented the episcopal worldview as specific recommendations or complaints, backed up not only with the social, familial, political, and intellectual weight of the bishops themselves, but also by the religious nature of conciliar authority, endowed with the authority of the Holy Spirit.

Episcopal social thought had the attention of contemporaries. The learned laywoman Dhuoda, writing in 841, thus explained to her son that bishops were endowed with a capacity to govern because they occupied a pinnacle at once religious and intellectual:

it is the responsibility of bishops to reveal each man to others, and our responsibility to observe and to obey those bishops.

2. Patzold, *Episcopus,* 520.
3. Nelson, "The Intellectual in Politics," 2–5.
4. Mary Douglas, *How Institutions Think* (Syracuse: 1986), 16.

Bishops, after the model of the true and sublime Lord, are the bearers of authority above, below, within, and outside. They have authority above for the reason that they give protection by looking out afar, as they take up a point of observation at a distance. For through their learning and by the example of their chastisement, the Lord gathers us together from far-off lands.[5]

Echoes of conciliar documents in Dhuoda's handbook show that the doctrines "plowed through" by councils of bishops circulated widely, perhaps in written form, but certainly in sermons the noblewoman heard on Sundays. Nithard, another layman and member of a well-placed family, assumed that bishops were the appropriate judges of historical action—they spoke with the voice of the Holy Spirit. As Steffen Patzold has demonstrated, the power and grandeur of the image of the bishop was still intact in the social imagination of the tenth century. Writing in the 930s, for example, Rather of Verona made the strongest possible claims for episcopal prestige and dignity: bishops could be called "gods, lords, or Christs"; "they are the heavens, they are the angels, the patriarchs, prophets, apostles, evangelists . . . they are kings, they are princes, judges." Rather of Verona's stunning praise of bishops is just a chapter in the long-enduring history of the importance of bishops, going back to the fifth century.[6] I have tried to show that this was due, not merely to the fact that bishops were well-connected nobles in clerical garb, but also because bishops sought to be disjoined from the society around them. Their combination of earthly power and otherworldly distance helps explain how bishops could question the possibility and meaning of kingship. Viewing the problem of kingship from the standpoint of old and well-developed theories of episcopal power, bishops came to believe that kingship could become a form of "clean power," opening the possibility that these two social functions could exist in mutuality.[7] Nevertheless a major gap existed between king and bishop. Bishops could mediate between God and humanity, and were admitted to the sphere of the sacred. Bishops controlled sacred space and the functioning of ritual.[8] These privileges were maintained even against the king.

In the course of the centuries here discussed, bishops acted in dramatically

5. Dhuoda, *Handbook for William: A Carolingian Woman's Counsel for Her Son,* trans. Carol Neel (Lincoln: 1991), 39.

6. For a text and translation of Rather of Verona's *Praeloquia:* Patzold, *Episcopus,* 17–18.

7. "Clean power" is a phrase of Peter Brown's, referring to the power of saints: Brown, *Cult of the Saints,* 102–3. On mutuality or "dualism" in the concept of political theology, see Assmann, *Herrschaft und Heil,* 28.

8. Patzold, *Episcopus,* 529.

changing contexts, accommodating different kings, the alternation of dynasties, and the transformation of social and economic forms. They participated in the expansion of the Frankish Empire and the restoration of political order after the death of Louis the Pious. All these changes were confronted by bishops from within the collegial atmosphere of the episcopal council, where they acted, thought, and argued together.

Throughout this half-millennium bishops continuously maintained their status and social function, explained in a stable and continuous vocabulary. This vocabulary emerged from the legislation of previous councils, from the Bible, and from the liturgy. During Charlemagne's reign, traditionally considered a turning point in European political history, liturgy was subject to reforming and Romanizing changes. It nevertheless remained consistent with Merovingian liturgy by including many blessing rituals, stressing episcopal government over major features of daily life. Through these blessings, bishops could foster and protect the hopes of their people. Also consistent with the Gallic and Merovingian past was the self-perception of Carolingian bishops, who continued to assert their status through specialized clothing and hairstyle. Bishops never wavered in their effort to occupy the center of society, even as that society was transformed. The occupation of the center (or *apex*, as bishops liked to say) was intimately tied to the central place of bishops in the maintenance of the cult. The bishop was a military, diplomatic, and governmental figure, controlling vast lands and the people working on them—and also a ritual expert, capable of restoring water to the primeval purity it had at Creation.

Episcopal influence over royal activity cannot be calculated with precision. Frankish kings, who remained war-leaders, would have continued to seek the domination of their neighbors. Yet bishops invested Frankish warfare with a sublime value that warriors could not self-provide. Bishops linked the warriors' ethic of loyalty, and their need for plunder and support, to a divine mission— which explains more fully the sweeping expansion of the Carolingian Empire. Like Charlemagne before him, Louis the Pious did not pursue a policy of organizing a state church system—on the contrary, his bishops pursued a *Königspolitik,* a policy of organizing royal power.[9] This was "the king in service of the church, not the *Reichskirche* in service of the king."[10] The impact of episcopal ideals had a profound effect on royal law, pointing to the fact that the aims of

9. Cf. Patzold, *Episcopus,* 23, and Monika Suchan, *"Kirchenpolitik des Königs oder Königspolitik der Kirche,"* ZKG 111 (2000): 1–27.

10. Patzold, *Episcopus,* 24.

the Carolingian state were turned toward a concern with righteous power. Royal action, by cooperating in the development of a sacralized state, was granted new realms to conquer.

Bishops adopted images from the liturgy, and themes developed in their legal tradition, to fashion a body of social thought that resonated throughout the Carolingian period. It can be said that the Carolingian Empire was imagined before it was created. However, the bishops were not wed to the Empire they helped create. Their intellectual resources were invested in the concept of the kingdom as the People of God, or as the Body of Christ, at whose head stood a Christian king, paralleled by and cooperating with his bishops. This social structure, the bishops saw, might have a different appearance at different times. Bishops were above all intent on the continuity and purity of their own status and governing role.

Kingship was thereby linked to the governing role of bishops, an institution playing a major role in intellectual life through its ancient historical and legal resources. The religious aura of Carolingian kingship was inherently Christian, rooted in analogies conflating the kingdom—the Church—the Body of Christ. Since Christ was king and priest, so the church, the Body of Christ, was rightly governed by king and bishop. Kingship was reinterpreted, and its goals and purposes redefined, in line with a political myth, backed up by a program of historical reinterpretation.

With the division of the Carolingian Empire, all parties turned to bishops' councils as a source of stability. This sparked the kind of rancor inevitable among people with competing interests who need one another. In selecting Hincmar for the See of Rheims, Charles the Bald showed strategic brilliance, for in Hincmar he found an ally who could fulminate with telling effect against his episcopal colleagues and Emperor Lothair. But this alliance was bought at a price. In the wake of the Empire's partition, Hincmar gave Charles' kingship an awkward contractual basis with the Oath of Beauvais. Hincmar could also, as the young king soon found out, pour his wrath on Charles' head as amply as he would pour the chrism of unction in Charles' second anointing of 869. Although Hincmar tried to revive the vocabulary of the Carolingian Empire to describe the relationship of king and bishop, his perspective was rooted in councils that, beginning with the Council of Aachen in 836, had highlighted the division between royal and ecclesiastical spheres, and between secular and church lands.

With Hincmar the old model of royal and episcopal cooperation in governing the Body of Christ was reconceptualized. The Body of Christ was now seen as the cooperation of two independent social groups: clerics united under their (arch)bishop, and nobles under their king. Between the two groups was a gulf of function and capacity. Each group was endowed with its own law. When Charles the Bald had clerics tried before his own court rather than by Hincmar's, the bishop reacted bitterly—clerics should be tried by legitimate accusers, by the primate of the province, and before a synod. He protested that even the heathen are judged by their own laws: "the ploughman, the swineherd, and the shepherd have their own law," but this had been denied to churchmen, against every custom of Christian princes.[11] That clerics should not be tried in secular courts was one of Hincmar's constant concerns, one that also troubled the composers of the *False Decretals*.[12] The king's function, Hincmar explained, was to defend the Church's liberties and property. This implied that the king should obey conciliar legislation:

Because after that unction by which, with the rest of the faithful, you deserve to achieve what blessed Peter the Apostle says, that "you are a chosen generation, a royal priesthood" (1 Peter 2:9): you achieved royal dignity by an episcopal and spiritual unction and blessing rather than by earthly power: you ought to attend with a subtle mind, since you are not exempt from the determination of the Holy Spirit, which is made known by synodal authority, "If someone, he said, shall go against his own declaration or signed document, he will deprive himself of honor."[13]

Hincmar thus presented the Oath of Beauvais to Charles in a way strongly reminiscent of how earlier bishops had flung the *Ordinatio imperii* in the face of Louis the Pious. Hincmar certainly believed that royal anointing gave Charles a kind of priestly status. This was an ambivalent status, however, because while Charles had gained a priestly quality, he did not have episcopal power. The king's anoint-

---

11. "Ego vero verbis non possum exprimere quanta constringar in mente angustia, quoniam per ora multorum audio volitare, quia homines omnium gentium, etiam et Judaei Christianae legis inimici, passim legum suarum judicantur judicio: bubulcus quoque et subulcus, atque opilio habent legem: et contra omnem consuetudinem Christianorum principum," Hincmar, *Expositiones pro ecclesiae libertatum defensione,* PL 125: 1041–42; see col. 1055.

12. Hincmar, *Expositiones,* PL 125: 1047; see also *Decretales pseudo-Isidorianae et capitula Angilramni,* ed. Paul Hinschius (Leipzig: 1863), 33.

13. "Quia enim post illam unctionem qua cum caeteris fidelibus meruistis hoc consequi, quod beatus Petrus apostolus dicit, 'Vos genus electum, regale sacerdotium' (1 Pet. 2) episcopali spirituali unctione, ac benedictione regiam dignitatem potius quam terrena potestate consecuti estis: attendere subtili intellectu debetis, quoniam ad definitionem sancti Spiritus, quam synodali auctoritate protulit, excepti non estis: 'Si quis, inquit, contra suam professionem vel subscriptionem venerit, ipse se honore privabit,'" Hincmar, *Expositiones* (PL 125: 1040).

ing was really no different than the baptismal unction of "the rest of the faithful." As a kind of priest, the king was subject to synodal authority—and Hincmar even implied that he had conferred kingship on Charles by anointing him.

On the other hand, Hincmar compromised on the issue of ecclesiastical land. Like the bishops at Germigny, Ver-sur-Launette, and Yütz-bei-Deidenhofen, Hincmar was prepared to concede royal claims to ecclesiastical land, so long as it remained firmly in episcopal control. Beyond that, the bishop of Rheims felt that such an arrangement reflected royal-episcopal cooperation in governing the Body of Christ. Church land was usefully and properly employed as benefices for military service, so long as its primary function of providing for the poor had been arranged. Having provided for the poor, the bishop should:

give a benefice for military service, either to the sons of fathers who benefitted the same church or to fathers who can usefully succeed them, because, as a certain man wrote, "unless the calf is nourished, the bull will not be yoked to the plow." On the other hand, he ought to render to Caesar what is Caesar's and to God what is God's—having set aside the benefices of this kind that are necessary to the ministry of the church and to himself, and without which we ought not exist, [from the remainder] are to be given, as the Lord commands: "Thou shalt not muzzle the mouth of the ox that treadeth out the corn." (1 Cor 9:9)[14]

Hincmar wanted to yoke the bull of military violence. The fighting nobility had to be cultivated by the church for its own protection. Wealth controlled by bishops could be divided in two: one part fulfilled the church's duty toward the poor and strangers, the other providing military service to the king. The first part is "what is God's," and the second, "what is Caesar's."

Hincmar's social vocabulary was still based on Isidore's vision of the kingdom as the Body of Christ. The breakup of the Empire, however, had driven a conceptual wedge between bishop and king. Long afterward bishops would continue to look to royal power as a vital guarantor of episcopal participation in the social order. They did not abandon their own capacity to rule, and in later centuries were still drawing on the legal tradition described here, along with their

---

14. "Porro episcopis dispositis quae sunt ecclesiae ac suis, ecclesiasticorum nihilominus, et pauperum hospitumque subsidiis, cum de rebus ecclesiae propter militiam beneficium donat, aut filiis patrum qui eidem ecclesiae profuerunt, et patribus utiliter succedere potuerunt; quoniam, ut quidam scripsit, nisi vitulus nutriatur, bos aratro non jungitur: aut talibus dare debet qui idonei sint reddere Caesari quae sunt Caesaris, et quae sunt Dei Deo: exceptis hujusmodi beneficiis quae ministris ecclesiae, et sibi necessariis, sine quibus esse nec debemus. . . . tribuenda sunt, jubente Domino: 'Non obturabis os bovi trituranti'" (1 Cor. 9:9), Hincmar, *Expositiones* (PL 125:1050).

capacity as governors to bring social thought to bear on the problem of power.

It has been argued that the "Peace of God" councils of the tenth century were essentially an effort by bishops to substitute for royal power. Appearing first in Auvergne and Aquitaine, where royal power had not been felt for many decades, the Peace of God movement was a remarkable innovation, particularly in the way bishops organized popular support against the knights. To the contrary, it can be said that the Peace of God councils were rooted in the patterns of episcopal action and social thought described here, conservatively maintained over centuries. Throughout the tenth century, councils of bishops feared that the sins of society had awakened the anger of God, followed by punishment, to be seen in the sterility of crops, destruction of cities, monasteries burned by violent men of power.[15] In vain they called on kings to live up to their duties. For centuries bishops had insisted on the royalty of the priesthood. In protecting the poor, orphans, and widows at the peace councils, bishops reasserted their most ancient and important prerogatives.[16]

The protection of the unarmed was a major accomplishment, but it was not a novelty forced on the bishops by social collapse, as Georges Duby argued.[17] It was grounded in Gallic and Merovingian canon law, and in a series of Carolingian councils: Riesbach in 798, the Five Councils of 813, and the Council of Paris of 829, in which bishops connected the royalty of bishops to their protection of the marginal, oppressed, and orphaned. The peace movement was taken up by one council after another, from the ancient city of Arles to northern France.[18] It is not surprising, then, that at the Council of Charroux in 989, "laypeople of both sexes" would look to a council of bishops as the best forum in which social order might be reasserted. It was essential to social stability that protection be offered to the poor. There can be neither social order nor peace when the strong are allowed to take "sheep, oxen, asses, or pigs from peasants or other poor people."[19]

AEQUO ANIMO

15. Henri Maisonneuve, *La Morale chrétienne d'après le conciles des Xe et Xie siècles,* Analecta Mediaevalia Namurcensia 15 (Louvain: 1962), 2.

16. Werner, *Naissance de la noblesse,* 248.

17. Duby, *Three Orders,* 135.

18. Harding, *Medieval Law,* 70.

19. Council of Charroux (989) Mansi, 19:89–90.

BIBLIOGRAPHY

Sources

Councils and Conciliar Documents
(only councils cited in the text are listed)

Arles (314) [Concilium Arelatense]. CCSL 148:3–25; in Munier, *Concilia galliae A. 314–A. 506.* CCSL 148; see "Other Sources."

The so-called "Council of Cologne" (346) [Concilium Coloniae Agrippinae]. CCSL 148: 26–29.

Arles (353) [Concilium Arelatense]. CCSL 148:30.

Paris (360/361) [Concilium Parisiense]. CCSL 148:32–34.

Valence (374) [Concilium Valentinum]. CCSL 148:35–45.

Trier (386) [Concilium Trevirense]. CCSL 148:47–48.

Nîmes (394 or 396) [Concilium Nemausense]. CCSL 148:49–51.

Turin (398) [Concilium Taurinense]. CCSL 148:52–60.

Riez (439) [Concilium Regense]. CCSL 148:61–75.

Orange (441) [Concilium Arausicanum]. CCSL 148:76–93.

Vaison-la-Romaine (442) [Concilium Vasense]. CCSL 148:94–104.

The so-called "Second Council of Arles" (c. 442–506) [Concilium Arelatense secundum nuncupata]. CCSL 148:111–30.

Arles (449-461) [Concilium Arelatense]. CCSL 148:131–34.

Council in a Place Unknown: Epistola synodica episcoporum Galliae ad Leonem Papam post concilium incerto in loco adunatum (451). CCSL 148:107–10.

Angers (453) [Concilium Andegavense]. CCSL 148:137–39.

Tours (461) [Concilium Turonense], CCSL 148:142–49.

Vannes (461–491) [Concilium Veneticum]. CCSL 148:150–58.

Arles (c. 470) [Concilium Arelatense]. CCSL 148:159–60.

Statuta ecclesiae antiqua (c. 475). CCSL 148:162–88. See *Les Statuta ecclesiae antique.* Edited by Charles Munier. Bibliothèque de l'Institut de droit canonique 5. Paris: 1960.

Agde (506) [Concilium Agathense]. CCSL 148:189–228.

Orléans (511) [Concilium Aurelianense]. CCSL 148A:3–19; see *Concilia Galliae A. 511–A. 695,* edited by De Clercq. CCSL 148A. See "Other Sources."

Épaone (517) [Concilium Epaonense]. CCSL 148A:20–37.

Arles (524) [Concilium Arelatense]. CCSL 148A: 42–46.

Carpentras (527) [Concilium Carpentoratense]. CCSL 148A:47–52.

Orange (529) [Concilium Arausicanum]. CCSL 148A:53–76.

Valence (529) [Concilium Valentinum]. CCSL 148A:82–83.

Marseilles (533) [Concilium Massiliense]. CCSL 148A:84–97.

Orléans (533) [Concilium Aurelianense]. CCSL 148A:98–103.

Clermont (535) [Concilium Claremontanum seu Arvernense]. CCSL 148A:104–12.

Orléans (538) [Concilium Aurelianense]. CCSL 148A:113–30.

Orléans (541) [Concilium Aurelianense]. CCSL 148A:131–46.

Orléans (549) [Concilium Aurelianense]. CCSL 148A:147–61.

Synod of Bishop Aspasius (551) [Concilium Aspasii episcopi metropolitani Elusani]. CCSL 148A:162–65.

Paris (552) [Concilium Parisiense]. CCSL 148A:166–69.

Arles (554) [Concilium Arelatense]. CCSL 148A: 170–73.

Paris (556–573) [Concilium Parisiense]. CCSL 148A: 204–10.

Diocesan Synod of Auxerre (561–605) [Synodus Dioecesana Autissiodorensis]. CCSL 148A:264–72.

Tours (567) [Concilium Turonense]. CCSL 148A:175–99.

Lyon (567–570) [Concilium Lugdunense]. CCSL 148A:200–3.

Braga (572) [Concilium Bracarense Secundum]. See Martin of Braga: *Martini . . . opera omnia,* edited by Claude W. Barlow, 116–23, under "Other Sources."

Paris (573) [Concilium Parisiense]. CCSL 148A: 211–17.

Berny (580) [Concilium Brennacense]. CCSL 148A:220.

Mâcon (581–583) [Concilium Matisconense]. CCSL 148A:222–30.

Valence (583–585) [Concilium Valentinum]. CCL 148A: 234–36.

Mâcon (585) [Concilium Matisconense]. CCSL 148A: 237–50.

Toledo (589) [Toletana Synodus Tertia]. See J. Vives, *Concilios visigóticos,* 107–45.

Paris (614) [Concilium Parisiense]. CCSL 148A:274–85.

Council in a Place Unknown (after 614) [Concilium Incerti Loci]. CCSL 148A: 286–89.

Clichy (626–627) [Concilium Clippiacense]. CCSL 148A:290–97.

Clichy (636) [Concilium Clippiacense]. CCSL 148A:300. Council records do not survive.

Toledo (633) [Concilium Toletanum IV]. J. Vives, *Concilios visigóticos,* 186–225.

Chalon-sur-Saôn (647–653) [Concilium Cabilonense]. CCSL 148A:302–10.

Bordeaux (662–675) [Concilium Modogarnomense seu Burdegalense]. CCL 148A: 311–13.

Jean-de-Losne (673–675) [Concilium Latunense]. CCSL 148A:314–17.

Toledo (693) [Synodus Toletana XVI]. J. Vives, *Concilios visigóticos,* 482–521.

Concilium Germanicum (742). MGH Conc. 2.1:1–4.

Lestinnes (743) [Concilium Liftinense]. MGH Conc. 2.1:5–7.

Soissons (744) [Concilium Suessionense]. MGH Conc. 2.1: 33–36.

Rome (745) [Concilium Romanum]. MGH Conc. 2.1: 37–44.

Frankish Council (747) [Concilium in Francia Habitum]. See Boniface to Archbishop Cuthberht of Canterbury (747). *Die Briefe des Heiligen Bonifatius und Lullus.* In *S. Bonifatii et Lullii epistolae,* edited by M. Tangl. Letter 78:161–70. MGH Epistolae Selectae 1. Berlin: 1916. See "Other Sources."

Ver (752) [Capitula synodalia data apud Vermeriam]. Mansi, 12:113–18.

Ver (755) [Capitula synodi Vernensis]. Mansi, 12:117–26.

Ascheim (754–763) [Concilium Ascheimense]. (Dated by Werminghoff to "756 or 755–760"). MGH Conc. 2.1:56–58; Mansi, 12:667–74.

Rome (761) [Concilium Romanum]. MGH Conc. 2.1:64–71.

Attigny (762 or 760–762) [Concilium Attiniacense]. MGH Conc. 2.1: 72–73; Mansi, 12:661–64.

Rome (769) [Concilium Romanum]. MGH Conc. 2.1:74–92. Mansi, 12:701–22.

Dingolfing (c. 770) [Concilium Dingolfingense]. MGH Conc. 2.1:93–97.

Neuching (772) [Concilium Neuchingense]. MGH Conc. 2.1:98–105.

Frankish Council (c. 779–780) [Concilium in Francia Habitum]. MGH Conc. 2.1:108–9.

Nicaea (787) [Concilium Nicaenum II]. Concilium Universale Nicaenum Secundum Concilii actiones I–III. Edited by Erich Lamberz. Acta Conciliorum Oecumenicorum sub auspiciis Academiae Scientiarum Bavaricae 2d ser. vol. 3, pt. 1. Berlin: 2008. An older edition will be found in Mansi, 12:951–1154.

Frankfurt (794) [Concilium Francofurt]. MGH Conc. 2.1:110–71.

Banks of the Danube (796) [Conventus Episcoporum ad Ripas Danubii]. MGH Conc. 2.1:172–76.

Reisbach (798) [Concilium Rispacense]. MGH Conc. 2.1:196–201.

Reisbach/Freising/Salzburg (800) [Concilia Rispacense/Frisingense/Salisburgense] MGH Conc. 2.1: 205–19.

Aachen (800) [Concilium Aquisgranense]. MGH Conc. 2.1:220–25.

Salzburg (807) [Concilium Salisburgense]. MGH Conc. 2.1:234.

Arles (813) [Concilium Arelatense]. MGH Conc. 2.1:248–53.

Rheims (813) [Concilium Remense]. MGH Conc. 2.1:253–58.

Mainz (813) [Concilium Moguntinense]. MGH Conc. 2.1:258–73.

Chalon (813) [Concilium Cabillonense]. MGH Conc. 2.1: 273–85.

Tours (813) [Concilium Turonense]. MGH Conc. 2.1: 286–93.

Aachen (816) [Concilium Aquisgranense]. MGH Conc. 2.1:307–464.

Aachen (817) [Concilium Aquisgranense]. MGH Conc. 2.1:464–66.

Frankish Council (818/819–829) [Concilium in Francia Habitum]. MGH Conc. 2.2: 593–95.

Attigny (822) [Concilium Attiniacense]. MGH Conc. 2.2: 468–72.

Paris (825) [Concilium Parisiense]. MGH Conc. 2.2:473–551.

Paris (829) [Concilium Parisiense]. MGH Conc. 2.2:596–680.

Compiégne (833) [Concilium Compendiense]. See *Episcoporum de poenitentia* under "Other Sources." See also the relation by Agobard. *Cartula de Ludouici imperatoris poenitentia,* in Agobard, *Opera Omnia,* 321–24.

Aachen (836) [*Concilium Aquisgranense*]. MGH Conc. 2.2:704–67.

Ingelheim (840) [*Concilium Ingelheimense*]. MGH Conc. 2.2: 791–814.

Germigny-des-Prés (843). MGH Conc. 3:1–7.

Coulaines (843). MGH Conc. 3:10–17.

Yütz bei Diedenhofen (Thionville) (844). MGH Conc. 3:27–35.

Ver-sur-Launette (844). MGH Conc. 3:36–44.

Beauvais (845). MGH Conc. 3:47–55.

Meaux-Paris (845/846). MGH Conc. 3:61–132.

Charroux (989). Mansi, 19:89–90.

Royal Law and Royal Documents

Childeberti I regis praeceptum (511–558). MGH Cap. 1.1:2–3.

Guntchramni regis edictum (585). MGH Cap. 1.1:10–12.

Childeberti secundi Decretio (594–596). MGH Cap. 1.1:15–17.

Chlotharii II edictum (614). MGH Cap. 1.1:20–23.

Dagoberctus I. rex Desiderium, thesaurarium suum, poscentibus civibus abbatibusque Cadurcensibus ecclesaie Cadurcensis episcopum consituit (629). MGH Dip. 1:15.

Dagoberctus I. rex monasterio Resbacensi, a Dadone referendario et fratribus eius Adone et Radone in fisco Meldensi constructo privilegium liberatis atque immunitatis concedit (635). MGH Dip. 1:16–18.

Karlmanni principis capitulare (742). MGH Capit. 1.1:24–26.

Karlmanni principis capitulare liptinense (743). MGH Capit. 1.1:26–28.

Pippini principis capitulare suessionense (744). MGH Capit. 1.1:28–30.

Karoli M. Capitulare primum (769). MGH Capit. 1.1:44–46.

Capitulatio de partibus Saxoniae (775–790). MGH Capit. 1.1:68–70.

Capitulare Haristallense (779). MGH Capit. 1.1:46–51.

Capitulare episcoporum (780). MGH Capit. 1.1:51–52.

Karoli epistola de litteris colendis (780–800). MGH Capit. 1.1:78–79.

Capitula de rebus ecclesiasticis (787–813?). MGH Capit. 1.1:185–86.

Admonitio generalis (789). MGH Capit. 1.1:52–62.

Duplex legationis edictum (789). MGH Capit. 1.1:62–64.

Capitulare missorum generale (802). MGH Capit. 1.1:91–99.

Capitularia missorum specialia (802). MGH Capit. 1.1:99–102.

Capitulare missorum item speciale (802?). MGH Capit. 1.1:102–4.

Capitula a sacerdotibus proposita (802?). MGH Capit. 1.1:105–7.

Capitula de examinandis ecclesiasticis (802?). MGH Capit. 1.1:109–11.

Capitula ecclesiastica ad Salz data (803–804). MGH Capit. 1.1:119–20.

Capitula per episcopos et comites nota facienda (805–808). MGH Capit. 1.1:141.

Duplex capitulare missorum in Theodonis villa datum (805). MGH Capit. 1.1: 120–26. in two sections: *Capitulare missorum in Theodonis villa datum primum. mere ecclesiasticum.* MGH Capit. 1.1:121–22; and *Capitulare missorum in Theodonis villa datum secundum, generale.* MGH Capit. 1.1:122–26.

Capitula excerpta de canone (806?). MGH Capit. 1.1:133–34.

Karoli ad Ghaerbaldum Episcopum Epistola (807). MGH Capit. 1.1:244–46.

Capitulare missorum Aquisgranense primum (810). MGH Capit. 1.1:152–54.

Capitula ecclesiastica (810–813?). MGH Capit. 1.2:178–79.

Capitula de causis cum episcopis et abbatibus tractandis (811). MGH Capit. 1.1:162–64.

Karoli Magni capitula e canonibus excerpta (813). MGH Conc. 2.1:294–97.

Concordia episcoporum (813). MGH Conc. 2.1:297–301.

Capitula e canonibus excerpta (813). MGH Capit. 1.2:173–75.

Capitula missorum (813?). MGH Capit. 1.2:181–82.

Constitutio de Hispanis in Francorum regnum profugis prima (815). MGH Capit. 1.2:261–62.

Constitutio Hludowici de Hispanis secunda (816). MGH Capit. 2.1:263–64.

Capitula legi addita (816). MGH Capit. 1.2:267–69.

Ordinatio imperii (817). MGH Capit. 1.2:270–73.

Hludowici prooemium generale ad capitularia tam ecclesiastica quam mundana (818–819). MGH Capit. 1.2:273–75.

Capitulare ecclesiasticum (818/819). MGH Capit. 1.2:275–80.

Capitula legibus addenda (818–819). MGH Capit. 1.2:280–85.

Capitulare missorum (819). MGH Capit. 1.2:288–91.

Capitula de iustitiis faciendis (ca. 820). MGH Capit. 1.2:295–96.

Episcoporum ad Hludowicum imperatorem relatio (820). MGH Capit. 1.2:366–68.

Capitula ab episcopis Attiniaci data (822). MGH Capit. 1.2:357–58.

Admonitio ad omnes regni ordines (823–825). MGH Capit. 1.2:303–7.

Other Sources

Agobard of Lyon. *Opera Omnia.* Edited by L. Von Acker. CCCM 52. Turnhout: 1981.

Amalarius of Metz. *A Lost Work by Amalarius of Metz: Interpolations in Salisbury. Cathedral Library. Ms. 154.* Edited by Christopher A. Jones. Henry Bradshaw Society Subsidia II. London: 2001.

Amalarius of Metz. *Amalarii episcopi Opera liturgica omnia.* Edited by Johann Michael Hanssens. *Studi e Testi* 138, 139, 140. Vatican City: 1948–1950.

Ambrose of Milan. *De officiis.* Edited and translated by Ivor J. Davidson. 2 vols. Oxford: 2001.

Annales Alamannici. Edited by G. H. Pertz. MGH SS. 1:19–60.

Annales Bertiniani. Edited by G. H. Pertz. MGH SS 1:419–515.

Annales Laureshamenses. Edited by G. H. Pertz. MGH SS 1:122–40.

Annales Laurissenses minores. Edited by G. H. Pertz. MGH SS 1:112–23.

Annales Mettenses Priores. Edited by B. von Simpson. MGH SRG in us. schol. Hannover: 1905.

Annales regni Francorum. Edited by G. H. Pertz and Friedrich Kurze. MGH SRG in us. schol. Hannover: 1895.

Annalium Laureshamensium pars altera. Edited by G. H. Pertz. MGH SS. 1:30–39.

Annals of Maximinianus: see *Chronicon universale.*

Anonymus Valesianus: see *Excerpta Valesiana.*

Anonymus Valesianus II. Ch. 79–96: texte et commentaire. Edited by Wouter Bracke. Bologna: 1992.

Audacht Morainn. Edited by Fergus Kelly. Dublin: 1976.

Augustine. *The City of God Against the Pagans.* Translated by R. W. Dyson. Cambridge: 1998.

Beatus of Liebana. *Obras Completas de Beato de Liebana.* Edited by Joaquin Gonzalez Echegaray, Alberto del Campo and Leslie G. Freeman. Madrid: 1995.

Bede. *De temporum ratione.* Edited by W. Jones. CCSL 123B. Turnhout: 1977.

———. *Venerabilis Baedae Historiam ecclesiasticam gentis Anglorum, Historiam abbatum, Epistolam ad Ecgberctum, una cum Historia abbatum auctore anonymo.* Edited by Charles Plummer. Oxford: 1896.

The Bobbio Missal: A Gallican Mass-book (MS. Paris. Lat. 13246) Text. Edited by E. A. Lowe. Henry Bradshaw Society 58. London: 1920.

Boethius. *Philosophiae consolationis libri quinque.* Edited by Karl Büchner. Editiones Heidelbergensis 11. Heidelberg: 1977.

Boniface. *Die Briefe des Heiligen Bonifatius und Lullus. (S. Bonifatii et Lullii epistolae).* Edited by Michael Tangl. MGH Epistolae Selectae 1. Berlin: 1916.

Caesarius of Arles. *Sancti Caesarii Arelatensis Sermones.* Edited by D. Morin. 2 vols. CCSL 103, 104. 2nd ed. Turnhout: 1953.

Canones suppositii ad finem canonum concilii arelatensis. In *Concilia Galliae A. 314–A. 506.* Edited by Charles Munier. CCSL 148:25.

Les canons des conciles mérovingiens (VIe–VIIe siècles). Translated by J. Gaudemet and B. Basdevant. SC 353. 354. 2 vols. Paris: 1989.

Cathwulf. Letter to Charlemagne: *Cathuulfus Carolo I Francorum regi prosperitatem gratulatur eumque ad uirtutem sequendam admonet.* Edited by Ernst Dümmler. MGH Epp. 4.2:501–5.

Chronicon Moissiacense. Edited by G. H. Pertz. MGH SS 1, 280–313.

Chronicon universale—741, cum continuatione (annalibus Maximinianus). Edited by G. Waitz. MGH SS 13. Hannover: 1881, 1–25.

Codigo de Alarico II: Fragmentos de la "Ley Romana" de los Visigodos conservados en un codice palimpsesto de la Catedral de Leon. 1896. Reprint, León: 1991.

Collectio canonum hibernensis: *Die irische Kanonensammlung.* Edited by H. Wasserschleben. 1885. Reprinted Aalen: 1966.

Conciles Gaulois du IVe siècle. Edited by Jean Gaudemet. SC 241. Paris: 1977.

Concilia Galliae A. 314–A. 506. Edited by Charles Munier. CCSL 148. Turnhout: 1963.

———. *511–A. 695.* Edited by Charles de Clercq. CCSL 148A. Turnhout: 1963.

Conciliorum oecumenicorum decreta. Edited by Joseph Alberigo. Third edition. Bologna: 1973.

Concordia Episcoporum (813). Edited by Albertus Werminghoff. MGH Conc. 2.1:297–301.

Constantius of Lyon. *Vie de Saint Germain d'Auxerre.* Edited by René Borius. SC 112. Paris: 1965.

Conversio Bagoariorum et Carantanorum. Edited by Milko Kos. Razprve Znanstvenega Drustva Ljubljani 11., Historicni Odsek 3. Ljubljana: 1936.

Die Conversio Bagoariorum et Carantanorum *und die Brief des Erzbischofs Theotmar von Salzburg.* Edited by Fritz Losek. MGH Studien und Texte 15. Hannover: 1997.

Corpus benedictionum pontificalium. Edited by E. Moeller. CCCM 162, 162A, 162B, 162C. 4 vols. Turnhout: 1971–1979.

Councils and Ecclesiastical Documents relating to Great Britain and Ireland. Edited by A. W. Haddan and W. Stubbs. 3 vols. Oxford: 1871.

Cresconius. *Die concordia canonum des Cresconius. Studien und Edition* 1–2. Edited by Klaus Zechiel-Eckes. Freiburger Beiträge zur mittelalterlichen Geschichte 5. Frankfurt: 1992.

Cyril of Jerusalem. *St. Cyril of Jerusalem's Lectures on the Christian Sacraments: The Procatechesis and the Five Mystagogical Catecheses.* Edited by F. L. Cross. London: 1951.

Decretales pseudo-Isidorianae et capitula Angilramni. Edited by Paul Hinschius. Leipzig: 1863.

De S. Memorio et sociis MM. AASS. Septembris. Edited by J. Pinius and J. Limpenus. 3:70–72.

Dhuoda. *Handbook for William: A Carolingian Woman's Counsel for Her Son.* Translated by Carol Neel. Lincoln: 1991.

Dionysius Exiguus: *Die Canonessammlung des Dionysius Exiguus in der ersten Redaktion.* Edited by Adolf Strewe. Arbeiten zur Kirchengeschichte 16. Berlin: 1931.

Diplomata Regum Francorum e Stirpe Merowingica. Edited by G. H. Pertz. MGH Dip. 1.

Donation of Constantine. *Das Constitutum Constantini (Konstantinische Schenkung).* Edited by Horst Fuhrmann. Fontes iuris germanici antiqui 10. Hannover: 1968.

Drew, Katherine Fischer. *The Laws of the Salian Franks.* Philadelphia: 1991.

Einhard. *Einhardi vita Karoli magni.* Edited by O. Holder Egger. MGH SRG in us. schol. Hannover: 1911.

Elipandus. *Elipandi epistolae.* PL 96: 839–88.

Enchiridion patristicum. Edited by M. J. Rouët de Journel. 2nd ed. Freiburg: 1962.

Episcoporum de poenitentia, quam Hludovicus imperator professus est: Relatio Compendiensis. Edited by Alfred Boretius and Victor Krause. MGH Capit. 1:51–55.

Epistola synodica episcoporum Galliae ad Leonem Papam post concilium incerto in loco adunatum (451). In *Concilia Galliae A. 314–A. 506.* Edited by Charles Munier. CCSL 148:107–10.

Eucherius of Lyon. *De laude eremi.* PL 50:701–12.

———. *Instructiones ad Salonium.* Edited by C. Wotke. CSEL 31:1. Vienna: 1894.

Eutropius. "Sur quelques textes littéraires relatifs aux grandes invasions." In *De similitudine carnis peccati,* edited by Pierre Courcelle. RBPH 31 (1953): 23–37.

Excerpta Valesiana. Edited by Jacques Moreau. Leipzig: 1968.

Expositio antiquae liturgiae gallicanae. Edited by E. C. Ratcliff. Henry Bradshaw Society 98. London: 1971.

Fredegar. *The Fourth Book of the Chronicle of Fredegar with its Continuations.* Edited by J. M. Wallace-Hadrill. London: 1960.

Gennadius. *De viris inlustribus.* Edited by E. C. Richardson. TU 14.1. Leipzig: 1896.

Die Gesetze des Karolingerreiches, 714–911. Edited by Karl August Eckhardt. Schriften der Akademie für Deutsches Recht, Gruppe V: Rechtgeschichte; Germanenrechte. Texte und Ubersetzungen Bd. 2. 2 vols. Weimar: 1934.

Gregory of Tours. *Gregorii episcopi Turonensis: Libri historiarum X.* Edited by Bruno Krusch and Wilhelm Levison. MGH: SRM 1.1. Hannover: 1951.

Gregory the Great: *Grégoire le Grand. Régle pastorale.* Edited by Bruno Judic and Floribert Rommel. SC 381, 382. 2 vols. Paris: 1992.

Hilary of Arles. *Hilaire d'Arles: Vie de Saint Honorat.* Edited by Marie-Denise Valentin. SC 235. Paris: 1977.

Hilary of Poitiers. *Collectanea antiariana parisina.* In *S. Hilarii episcopi Pictaviensis Opera.* Edited by Alfredus Feder. CSEL 65. Vienna: 1916.

———. *Contre Constance.* Edited by André Rocher. SC 334. Paris: 1987.

———. *Hilary of Poitiers' Preface to his Opus historicum: Translation and Commentary.* Edited and translated by P. Smulders. Leiden: 1995.

Hincmar of Rheims. *Opusculum in causa Hincmari Laudensis.* PL 125:290–494.

———. *Expositiones pro ecclesiae libertatum defensione.* PL 125: 1041–42.

Hippolytus of Rome. *La tradition apostolique de saint Hippolyte: Essai de reconstitution.* Edited by B. Botte. Munster: 1963; SC 11 (Paris: 1984).

Isidore of Seville. *Isidore de Séville. Traité de la nature.* Edited by Jacques Fontaine. Paris: 2002.

———. *Etymologiae IX.* Edited by Marc Reydellet. Paris: 1984.

———. [Isidoro de Sevilla]. *De ortu et obitu patrum: Vida y muerte de los santos.* Edited and translated by C. Chaparro Gómez. Paris: 1985.

———. *Sancti Isidori episcopi Hispalensis: De ecclesiasticis officiis.* Edited by Christopher M. Lawson. CCSL 108. Turnhout: 1989.

———. *The Letters of St. Isidore of Seville.* Edited and translated by G. B. Ford. 2nd ed. Amsterdam: 1970.

Jerome. *Letter to Fabiola.* In *Sancti Eusebii Hieronymi epistulae.* Edited by Isidor Hilberg. Pars 1, 586–615. CSEL 54. Vienna: 1910.

Jonas of Orléans. *De institutione regia.* PL 106:279–306. See also Reviron, Jean.

Julian of Toledo. *Historiae Wambae regis.* Edited by W. Levison. MGH SRM 5: 486–535.

Julian Pomerius. *De vita contemplativa.* PL 59:415–520.

Juris ecclesiastici Graecorum historia et monumenta. Edited by Jean Baptiste, Cardinal Pitra. 2 vols. Rome: 1864–1868.

Justinian. *Imp. Iustiniani Institutionum libri quattuor.* Edited by P. Eduard Huschke. Leipzig: 1911.

Le leggi dei Longobardi: Storia. memoria e diritto di un popolo germanico. Edited by Claudio Azzara and Stefano Gasparri. Le Fonti 1. Milan: 1992.

Leges Baiwariorum/Lex Baiwariorum. Edited by E. Freiherr von Schwind. MGH. Leges 1. *Legum nationum Germanicarum* Leg. 5.2.

Legis romanae Wisigothorum fragmenta ex codice palimpsesto sanctae legionenensis ecclesiae. Edited by Francisco de Cardeñas y Espejo. Madrid: 1896.

Lex Baiuvariorum. In *Die Gesetze des Karolingerreiches, 714–911*. Edited by Karl August Eckhardt. 2:78–187.

Lex Baiuvariorum: Lichtdruckwiedergabe der Ingolstädter Handschrift des Bayerischen Volksrechts. Edited by Konrad Byerle. Munich: 1926.

Lex Ribuaria. Edited by F. Beyerle and R. Büchner. MGH Leges. 3.2. Hannover: 1954.

Lex Ribuaria. In *Die Gesetze des Karolingerreiches. 714–911*. Edited by Karl August Eckhardt. 1:137–207.

Lex romana Visigothorum. Edited by Gustav Haenel. Leipzig, 1849.

Lex Salica. In *Die Gesetze des Karolingerreiches, 714–911*. Edited by Karl August Eckhardt. 1:2–99.

Lex Salica: 100 Titel Text. Edited by Karl August Eckhardt. MGH Leg. 4.2. Hannover: 1962.

Lex Salica. *Loi salique ou recueil contenant les anciennes rédactions de cette loi et le texte connu sous le nom de Lex emendata*. Edited by Jean Marie Pardessus. Paris: 1843.

Le Liber Ordinum en usage dans l'église wisigothique et mozarabe d'Espagne du cinquième au l'onzième siècle. Edited by M. Ferotin. Monumenta ecclesiae liturgica 5. Paris: 1904.

Liber Sacramentorum Gellonensis. Edited by A. Dumas. CCSL 159. Turnhout: 1981.

Libri Carolini. See also *Opus Caroli regis Libri Carolini (Libri Carolini, sive Caroli Magni capitulare de imaginibus*. Edited by Hubert Bastgen. MGH Conc. 2, *Supplementum*.

Lucan. *The Civil War (Pharsalia)*. Edited and translated by J. D. Duff. Loeb Classical Library 220. Cambridge, Mass.: 1928.

Martin of Braga. *Martini episcopi Bracarensis opera omnia*. Edited by Claude W. Barlow. Papers and Monographs of the American Academy in Rome 12. New Haven: 1950.

Maximus of Turin. *Contra paganos*. Edited by A. Spagnolo and C. H. Turner. In "Maximus of Turin Against the Pagans: Contra paganos." JTS 17 (1916): 321–37.

Mayer, Josephine. *Monumenta de viduis diaconissis virginibusque tractantia*. Florilegium patristicum 42. Bonn: 1938.

McNeill, J. T., and H. M. Gamer. *Medieval Handbooks of Penance: A Translation of the Principal libri poenitentiales and Selections from Related Documents*. New York: 1990.

Merlin, Jacques. *Conciliorum quatuor generalium: Niceni, Constantinopolitani, Ephesini, et Calcedonensis*. 2 vols. in 1. Cologne: 1530.

Michaelis et Theophili imperatorum Constantinopolitanorum epistola ad Hludowicum imperatorem directa. MGH Conc. 2.2:475–80.

"Missale Gothicum": A Gallican Sacramentary. MS. Vatican. Regin. Lat. 317. Edited by H. M. Bannister. Henry Bradshaw Society 52, 54. 2 vols. London: 1916–1917.

Monumenta eucharistica et liturgica vetustissima: Pars 1. Edited by Johannes Quasten. Bonn: 1935.

Nithard. *Histoire des fils de Louis le Pieux*. Edited by Ph. Lauer. Paris: 1964.

Notitia Arnonis und Breves notitiae: Die Salzburger Güterverzeichnisse aus der zeit 800. Sprachlich-historische Einleitung. Edited by Fritz Losek. Salzburg: 1990.

Notitia Arnonis. Edited by W. Hauthaler. Salzburger Urkundenbuch 1. Vienna: 1910.

Opus Caroli regis contra synodum (Libri Carolini). Edited by Ann Freeman. MGH Conc. 2. Suppl. 1. Hannover: 1998.

Ordines Coronationis Franciae: Texts and Ordines for the Coronation of Frankish and French Kings and Queens in the Middle Ages. Edited by Richard A. Jackson. 2 vols. Philadelphia, 1995–2000.

Ordo de celebrando concilio. Edited by Charles Munier. PL *Supplementum* 4:1865–1876.

Pactus Legis Salicae. Edited by Karl August Eckhardt. II.1, *65 Titel-Text*. Göttingen: 1955.

Pactus Legis Salicae. Edited by Karl August Eckhardt. I.2, *Systematischer Text*. Göttingen: 1957.

Pirmin. *Scarapsus*. In *Die Heimat des Hl: Pirmin des Apostels der Alamannen*. Edited by Gall Jecker. Beiträge zur Geschichte des alten Mönchtums und des Benediktinerordens 13. Münster in Westf.: 1927.

Pitra, Cardinal: see *Juris ecclesiastici Græcorum historia*.

Plummer, Charles, ed. *Two of the Saxon Chronicles Parallel*. Oxford: 1892.

Prosper of Aquitaine. *Sententiae*. PL 51:427–96.

Pseudo-Cyprian. *Pseudo-Cyprianus De XII abusivis saeculi*. Edited by S. Hellmann. TU 34. Leipzig: 1909.

Pseudo-Dionysius. *The Complete Works*. Translated by Colm Luibheid. New York: 1987.

Pseudo-Gelasius. *Das Decretum Gelasianum de libris recipiendis et non recipiendis*. Edited by Ernst von Dobschütz. TU 38.4. Leipzig: 1912.

Pseudo-Jerome. *Ps.-Hieronymi De septem ordinibus ecclesiae*. Edited by P. Athanasius Walter Kalff. Diss., Bayerischen Julius-Maximilians-Universität Würzburg, 1935.

Reviron, Jean. *Les idées politico-religieuses d'un évêque du IXe siècle: Jonas d'Orléans et son "De institutione regia": Étude et texte critique*. L'Église et l'état au moyen Âge 1. Paris: 1930.

Salonius of Cologne. *Expositiones mysticae in parabolas Salomonis et in Ecclesiasten*. PL 53:967–1012.

Sidonius Apollinaris. *Sidoine Apollinaire: Poèmes. Lettres*. Edited by André Loyen. 3 vols. Paris, 1960–1970.

Sirmond, Jacques. *Conciliorum antiquorum Galliae a Iac: Sirmondo S.I. editorum Supplementa*. Paris: 1666.

Sisebut. Letter to Adualuald. King of the Lombards (c. 616–620). Edited by Ernst Dümmler. MGH Epp. 3.1:671–75.

Sisebut. Letter to Eusebius (c. 614-620). Edited by Ernst Dümmler. MGH Epp. 3.1:670.

Smaragdus. *Via regia*. PL 102:931–70.

Sulpicius Severus. *Sulpice Sévère: Vie de Saint Martin*. Edited by Jacques Fontaine. SC 133–135. 3 vols. Paris: 1967–1969.

———. *Sulpici Severi Dialogi*. Edited by Giuseppe Augello. Palermo: 1969.

Tacitus. *The Annals of Tacitus*. Edited by Henry Furneaux. 2d ed. 2 vols. Oxford: 1896.

Taio of Saragossa. *Sententiae*. PL 80:723–990.

Tanner, Norman P., ed., trans. *Decrees of the Ecumenical Councils. Vol. I, Nicaea I to Lateran V*. London: 1990.

———. *Decrees of the Ecumenical Councils.* 2 vols. Washington, D.C.: 1990.

Tertullian. *De Baptismo.* In *Quinti Septimi Florentis Tertulliani Opera.* Edited by August Reifferscheid and Georg Wissowa, part 1, 201–18. CSEL 20. Vienna: 1890.

———. *Tertullien: Apologétique.* Edited by Jean-Pierre Waltzing. Paris: 1998.

———. *Q. Septimi Florentis Tertulliani De corona/Tertullien: Sur la couronne.* Edited by Jacques Fontaine. Érasme 18. Paris: 1966.

Thegan. *Thegani Vita Ludovici imperatoris.* In *Quellen zur Karolingischen Reichsgeschichte.* Edited by Reinhold Rau. Ausgewählte Quellen zur deutschen Gesschichte des Mittelalters 5. 3 vols. Darmstadt; 1955–1960.

Theodoriciana: see Anonymus Valesianus.

The Theodosian Code and Novels and the Sirmondian Constitutions. Edited and translated by Clyde Pharr. The Corpus of Roman Law (Corpus Juris Romani) 1. Princeton: 1952.

Tomus Leonis. In *Conciliorum oecumenicorum.* Edited by Joseph Alberigo. 77–82.

Valerianus of Cimiez. *Epistola ad monachos.* PL 52:755–58.

Vincent of Lérins. *The Commonitorium of Vincentius of Lerins.* Edited by Reginald Stewart Moxon. Cambridge: 1915.

Vita Alpini. AASS. *Septembris.* Edited by J. Pinius and J. Limpenus. 3:85–89.

Vita Austrigisilus. episcopi Biturigi. Edited by Bruno Krusch. MGH SRM 4, 188–208.

Vita Lebuini antiqua. Edited by A. Hofmeister. MGH SS 30.2:789–95. Leipzig: 1934.

Vita Sancti Bonifatii: see Willibald.

Vita Sancti Germani: see Constantius of Lyon.

Vita Sancti Magni Confessoris: see Otloh of Saint-Emmeran.

Vives, José. *Concilios visigóticos e hispano-romanos.* España Cristiana. Textos 1. Madrid: 1963.

Willibald. *Vita sancti Bonifatii archiepiscopi Moguntini.* Edited by Wilhelm Levison. MGH SRG in us. schol. Hannover: 2003.

Wilmart, André. *Precum libelli quattuor aevi Karolini.* Rome: 1940.

Literature

Adams, J. N. *The Text and Language of a Vulgar Latin Chronicle (Anonymus Valesianus II).* University of London, Institute of Classical Studies Bulletin Supplement 36. London: 1976.

Adriányi, G. "Rezeptionsprobleme bezüglich des Zweiten Konzils von Nizäa in der karolingischen zeit." In *Streit um das Bild: Das Zweite Konzil von Nizäa (787) in ökumenischer Perspective,* edited by Joseph Wohlmuth, 59–66. Studium Universale 9. Bonn: 1989.

Aigran, René. *L'Hagiographie: Ses sources, ses méthodes, son histoire.* Paris: 1953.

Airlie, Stuart. "Narratives of Triumph and Rituals of Submission: Charlemagne's Mastering of Bavaria." *Transactions of the Royal Historical Society* 6th ser. 9 (1999): 93–119.

Alexander, P. J. *The Patriarch Nicephorus of Constantinople: Ecclesiastical Policy and Image Worship in the Byzantine Empire.* Oxford: 1958.

Alföldi, Andreas. "Zum Speersymbol der Souveränität im Altertum." In *Festschrift Percy Ernst Schramm,* edited by Peter Classen and Peter Scheibert, 1:3–6. 2 vols. Wiesbaden: 1964.

Altaner, Berthold. *Patrologie: Leben, Schriften und Lehre der Kirchenväter.* Third edition. Freiburg: 1951.

Amelung, Karl. *Leben und Schriften des Bischofs Jonas von Orléans.* Diss., Programm des Wirzthumschen Gymnasium in Dresden, Leipzig University, 1888.

Amory, Patrick. "The Meaning and Purpose of Ethnic Terminology in the Burgundian Laws." EME 2 (1993): 1–28.

Andersen, Ernst. *The Renaissance of Legal Science after the Middle Ages: The German Historical School no Bird Phoenix.* Copenhagen: 1974.

Angenendt, Arnold. *Das Frühmittelalter: Die abenländische Christenheit von 400 bis 900.* Stuttgart: 1990.

———. "Pirmin und Bonifatius: Ihr Verhältnis zu Mönchtum, Bischofsamt und Adel." In *Mönchtum: Episkopat und Adel zur Gründungszeit des Klosters Reichenau,* edited by Arno Borst, 251–304. Vorträge und Forschungen 20. Sigmaringen: 1974.

———. "Princeps imperii—Princeps apostolorum: Rom zwischen Universalismus und Gentilismus." In *Roma—Caput et fons: Zwei Vorträge über das päpstliche Rom zwischen Altertum und Mittelalter,* edited by Arnold Angenendt and Rudolf Schieffer, 7–44. Opladen: 1989.

Anton, Hans Hubert. *Fürstenspiegel und Herrscherethos in der Karolingerzeit.* Bonner Historische Forschungen 32. Bonn: 1968.

———. "Der König und die Reichskonzilien im westgotischen Spanien." HJ 92 (1972): 257–81.

———. "Pseudo-Cyprian: De duodecim abusivis saeculi und sein Einfluss auf den Kontinent, insbesondere auf die karolingischen Fürstenspiegel." In *Die Iren und Europa im früheren Mittelalter,* edited by Heinz Löwe, 568–617. Stuttgart: 1982.

———. "Zum politischen Konzept karolingischer Synoden und zur karolingischen Brüdergemeinschaft." HJ 99 (1979): 55–132.

Arendt, Hannah. "What is Authority?" In her *Between Past and Future: Eight Exercises in Political Thought,* 91–141. Harmondsworth: 1977.

Arnold, Carl Franklin. *Caesarius von Arelate und die gallische Kirche seiner Zeit.* Leipzig: 1972.

Arquillière, H.-X. *L'Augustinisme politique: Essai sur la formation des théories politiques du moyen-âge.* L'Église et l'etat au moyen âge 2. Paris: 1934.

Assmann, Jan. *Herrschaft und Heil: Politische Theologie in Altägypten, Israel und Europa.* Munich: 2000.

Atsma, Hartmut, ed. *La Neustrie: Les pays au nord de la Loire de 650 à 850.* Beihefte der Francia 16. 2 vols. Sigmaringen: 1989.

Audin, Pierre. "Cesaire d'Arles et le maintien de pratiques paiennes dans la Provence du VIe siècle." In *La Patrie gauloise d'Agrippa au VIème siècle: Actes du Colloque, Lyon 1981,* 327–338. Lyon: 1983.

Auf Der Maur, Ivo. "Iroschottische Mönche: Peregrinari pro Christo." *Studien und Mitteilungen zur Geschichte des Benediktiner-ordens* 94 (1983): 497–503.

Babut, E.-Ch. "Saint Martin de Tours." *Revue d'histoire et de littérature religieuses*. New Series 1 (1910): 466–87 and 513–41; New Series 2 (1911): 44–78, 160–82, 255–75, 431–63, and 513–43; New Series 3 (1912): 120–59, 240–78, and 289–329.

Bailey, T. *The Processions of Sarum and the Western Church*. Pontifical Institute for Medieval Studies, Studies and Texts 21. Toronto: 1971.

Banniard, Michel. *Genese culturelle de l'Europe: Ve–VIIIe siècle*. Paris: 1989.

———. "Seuils et frontières langagières dans la Francia romane du VIIIe siècle." In *Karl Martell*, 171–91.

Bardy, Gustave. *La conversion au christianisme durant les premiers siècles*. Théologie 15. Paris: 1947.

———. *Littérature latine chrétienne*. Paris: 1929.

Barion, Hans. *Das fränkisch-deutsche Synodalrecht des Frühmittelalters*. 1931. Reprint, Kanonistische Studien und Texte 5.6. Amsterdam: 1963.

———. "Der Kirchenrechtliche Charakter der Konzils von Frankfurt 794." ZSRG.K 19 (1930): 139–70.

Barnes, Barry. *The Nature of Power*. Cambridge: 1988.

Barnes, Timothy D. *Athanasius and Constantius: Theology and Politics in the Constantinian Empire*. Cambridge, Mass.: 1993.

———. *Constantine and Eusebius*. Cambridge, Mass.: 1981.

———. *Tertullian: A Historical and Literary Study*. 2nd ed. Oxford: 1985.

Bartelink, G. J. M. *De Geboorte van Europa: Van laat-romeins imperium naar vroege middeleeuwen*. Muiderberg: 1989.

———. *Het vroege Christendom en de antieke Cultuur*. Muiderberg: 1986.

Bartlett, Robert. "Symbolic Meanings of Hair in the Middle Ages." *Transactions of the Royal Historical Society* 6th ser. 4 (1994): 43–60.

Basdevant-Gaudemet, Brigitte. "La Bible dans les canons des conciles mérovingiens." In *Église et Autorités: Études d'histoire du droit canonique médiéval*, 201–12. Cahiers de l'Institut d'Anthropologie Juridique 14. Limoges: 2006.

———. "L'évêque, d'après la législation de quelques conciles mérovingiens." In *Clovis*, 1:471–94.

Batiffol, Pierre. "La liturgie du sacre des évêques dans son évolution historique." *Revue d'histoire ecclésiastique* 23 (1927): 733–63.

———. *Saint Grégoire le Grand*. 3rd ed. Paris: 1928.

Bauer, Thomas. "Koninuität und Wandel synodaler Praxis nach der Reichsteilung von Verdun: Versuch einer Typisierung und Einordnung der karolingischen Synoden und *concilia mixta* von 843 bis 870." AHC 23 (1991): 11–115.

Baynes, Norman H. *Constantine the Great and the Christian Church. Second Editon.* The Raleigh Lecture on History 1929. London: 1972.

———. "Eusebius and the Christian Empire." In his *Byzantine Essays and Other Essays*, 168–72. London: 1969.

Beaujard, Brigitte, et al. *Province ecclésiastique de Lyon (Lugdunensis prima)*. TCCG 4. Paris: 1986.

Beck, Heinrich, Detlev Ellmers, and Kurt Schier, eds. *Germanische Religionsgeschichte:*

Quellen und Quellenprobleme. Ergänzungsbände zum Reallexikon der germanischen Altertumskunde 5. Berlin: 1992.

Beck, Henry G. *The Pastoral Care of Souls in South-East France during the Sixth Century.* Analecta Gregoriana 51. Rome: 1950.

Bell, Brenda M. "The Contribution of Julius Caesar to the Vocabulary of Ethnography." *Latomus* 54 (1995): 753–67.

Bellomo, Manlio. *The Common Legal Past of Europe, 1000–1800.* Translated by Lydia G. Cochrane. Washington, D.C.: 1995.

Benoît, André, and Charles Munier. *Die Taufe in der Alten Kirche (1.–3. Jahrhundert).* Translated by Annemarie Spoerri. Traditio christiana 9. Bern: 1994.

Benson, R. L. "Provincia = Regnum." In *Prédication et propagande au moyen âge: Islam, Byzance, Occident,* edited by George Makdisi, Dominique Sourdel, and Janine Sourdel-Thomine, 41–69. Penn-Paris-Dumbarton Oaks Colloquia 3. Paris: 1983.

Berman, Harold J. *Law and Revolution: The Formation of the Western Legal Tradition.* Cambridge: 1983.

Beskow, Peter. *Rex Gloriae: The Kingship of Christ in the Early Church.* Translated by E. Sharpe. Uppsala: 1962.

Betz, Werner. "Karl der Grosse und die Lingua Theodisca." In *Karl der Grosse: Lebenswerk und Nachleben,* edited by W. Braunfels, 2:300–306. Dusseldorf: 1965.

Bévenot, Maurice. "A Bishop is Responsible to God Alone (St. Cyprian)." *Recherches de science religieuse* 49 (1951): 397–415.

Biarne, Jacques, et al., eds. *Provinces ecclésiastiques de Vienne et d'Arles (Viennensis et Alpes graiae et poeninae).* TCCG 3. Paris, 1986.

Bischoff, Bernhard. *Manuscripts and Libraries in the Age of Charlemagne.* Translated by Michael Gorman. Cambridge: 1994.

Blanc, Odile. "Historiographie du vêtement: un bilan." In *Vêtement,* 7–33.

Blázquez, José María. "El monacato de los siglos IV, V y VI como contracultura civil y religiosa." In *Intelectuales, ascetas y demonios al final de la Antigüedad,* 221–55. Madrid: 1998.

Blumenthal, Uta-Renate, ed. *Carolingian Essays: Andrew W. Mellon Lectures in Early Christian Studies.* Washington, D.C.: 1983.

Boespflug, François, and Nicolas Lossky, eds. *Nicée II, 787–1987: Douze siècles d'images religieuses—Actes du colloque international Nicée II . . . Octobre 1986.* Paris: 1987.

Bogatryev, P. G. *The Functions of Folk Costume in Moravian Slovakia.* Translated by R. G. Crum. Approaches to Semiotics 5. Mouton–La Haye: 1971.

Bord, J. B. *L'extrême onction d'après l'épître de saint Jacques (V.14.15), examinée dans la tradition.* Museum Lessianum—Section théologique. Brussels: 1923.

Boshof, Egon. "Einheitsidee und Teilungsprinzip Ludwigs des Frommen." In *Charlemagne's Heir,* 177–80.

———. *Erzbischof Agobard von Lyon: Leben und Werk.* Kölner historische Abhandlungen 17. Cologne: 1969.

Bosl, Karl. "Potens und Pauper: Begriffsgeschichtliche Studien zur gesellschaftlichen Differenzierung im frühen Mittelalter und zum 'Pauperismus' des Hochmittelalters." In *Alteuropa und die moderne Gesellschaft: Festschrift für Otto Brunner,* edited by Alexander Bergengruen and Ludwig Deike, 60–87. Göttingen: 1963.

Bouffartigue, Jean. "L'Empereur Julien et les barbares: Réalisme et illusion." In *Haut moyen-âge: Culture, éducation et société—Études offertes à Pierre Riché,* edited by Michel Sot, 49–58. La Garenne–Colombes: 1990.

Bouhout, P. "Explications du rituel baptismal à l'époque carolingienne." *Revue des études augustiniennes* 24 (1978): 278–301.

Bouman, C. A. *Sacring and Crowning: The Development of the Latin Ritual for the Anointing of Kings and the Coronation of an Emperor before the Eleventh Century.* Bijdragen van het Instituut voor Middeleeuwse geschiedenis der Rijks-Universiteit te Utrecht 30. Groningen: 1957.

Bourdieu, Pierre. *Homo Academicus.* Translated by Peter Collier. Stanford: 198.

Boureau, Alain. "Les théologiens carolingiens devant les images religieuses. La conjuncture de 825." In *Nicée II,* 247–62.

Bourgain, Pascale, and Martin Heinzelmann. "Courbe-toi, fier Sicambre, adore ce que tu a brûlé: Á propos de Grégoire de Tours. Hist. II: 31." *Bibliothèque de l'École de Chartes* 154 (1996): 591–606.

Bowes, Kim. *Private Worship, Public Values, and Religious Change in Late Antiquity.* Cambridge: 2008.

Bowersock, Glen W. *Julian the Apostate.* Cambridge, Mass.: 1978.

Bowlus, Charles R. "Die militärische Organisation des karolingischen Südostens (791–907)." *Frühmittelalterliche Studien* 31 (1997): 46–69.

Braudel, Fernand. *La méditerranée et le monde méditerranéen a l'époque de Philippe II.* 2 vols. 2nd ed. Paris: 1966.

Braun, J. *Die liturgische Gewandung im Occident und Orient: Nach Ursprung und Entwicklung. Verwendung und Symbolik.* Freiburg im Breisgau: 1907.

Bremmer, J. N. "The Birth of the Term 'Magic.'" *Zeitschrift für Papyrologie und Epigraphik* 126 (1999): 1–12.

Brennecke, Hanns Christof. "Hilarius von Poitiers." *Theologische Realenzyklopädie* 15:315–22. 36 vols. Berlin, 1977–2004.

———. "Synodum congregavit contra Euphratam nefandissimum episcopum: Zur angeblichen Synode gegen Euphrates." ZKG 90 (1970): 176–200.

Bressolles, Adrien. *Doctrine et action politique d'Agobard,* Vol. 1. *Saint Agobard, évêque de Lyon (769–840).* L'Église et L'État au moyen-âge 9. Paris: 1949.

Brettler, Marc Zvi. *The Creation of History in Ancient Israel.* London: 1995.

Breukelaar, Adriaan H. B. *Historiography and Episcopal Authority in Sixth-Century Gaul: The Histories of Gregory of Tours Interpreted in their Historical Context,* Forschungen zur Kirchen- und Dogmengeschichte 57. Göttingen: 1994.

Brouwer, Christian. "Egalité et pouvoir dans les 'Morales' de Grégoire le Grand." *Recherches augustiniennes* 27 (1994): 97–129.

Brown, Giles. "Introduction: The Carolingian Renaissance." In *Carolingian Culture: Emulation and Innovation,* edited by Rosamond McKitterick, 1–51. Cambridge: 1994.

Brown, Peter. *The Cult of the Saints: Its Rise and Function in Latin Christianity.* Chicago: 1981.

——. *The Making of Late Antiquity.* Cambridge, Mass.: 1978.

——. *Poverty and Leadership in the Later Roman Empire.* Menahem Stern Jerusalem Lectures. Hannover: 2002.

——. *Power and Persuasion in Late Antiquity: Towards a Christian Empire.* Madison: 1992.

——. *The Rise of Western Christendom: Triumph and Diversity, A.D. 200–1000.* 2nd ed. Oxford: 2003.

Brühl, Carlrichard. *Reims als Krönungsstadt des französosischen Königs bis zum Ausgang des 14. Jahrhunderts.* Frankfurt am Main: 1950.

Brunhölzl, Franz. *Histoire de la littérature latine du moyen âge.* Translated by Henri Rochais. 3 vols. Turnhout: 1990–1996.

Buc, Philippe. *The Dangers of Ritual: Between Early Medieval Texts and Social Scientific Theory.* Princeton: 2001.

——. "Political Rituals and Political Imagination in the Medieval West from the Fourth Century to the Eleventh." In *The Medieval World,* edited by Peter Linehan and Janet L. Nelson, 189–213. London, 2001.

Bullough, Donald. "Alcuin and the Kingdom of Heaven: Liturgy, Theology and the Carolingian Age." In *Carolingian Essays,* 1–69.

——. "Alcuin before Frankfort." In *Frankfurter Konzil,* 2:571–85.

——. "Roman Books and Carolingian *renovatio.*" In his *Carolingian Renewal: Sources and Heritage,* 1–38. Manchester: 1991.

Cabrol, Fernand. *Liturgical Prayer: Its History and Spirit.* Translated by a Benedictine of Stanbrook. London: 1925.

Callewaert, Camillus. "De dalmatica." In *Sacris Erudiri: Fragmenta liturgica collecta a monachis Sancti Petri Aldenburge in Steenbrugge ne pereant,* edited by Camillus Callewaert, 219–22. Steenbrugge: 1940.

——. "La mét dans l'étude de la liturgie." In *Sacris Erudiri: Fragmenta liturgica collecta a monachis Sancti Petri Aldenburge in Steenbrugge ne pereant,* edited by Camillus Callewaert, 25–40. Steenbrugge: 1940.

Cameron, Averil. "How did the Merovingian Kings Wear their Hair?" RBPH 43 (1965): 1203–16.

Campbell, Brian. *The Writings of the Roman Land Surveyors.* Journal of Roman Studies Monograph No. 9. London: 2000.

Cañal, Carlos. *San Isidoro: Exposición de sus obras é indicaciones acerca de la influencia que han ejercido en la civilización española.* Seville: 1897.

Canning, Joseph. *A History of Medieval Political Thought, 300–1450.* London: 1996.

Cappuyns, D. M. "L'origine des 'Capitula' d'Orange 529." *Recherches de théologie ancienne et médiévale* 6 (1934): 121–42.

Caravita, Gregorio. *Teoderico: I Goti a Ravenna V–VI secolo.* Rimini: 1993.

Cardot, Fabienne. *L'Espace et le pouvoir: Étude sur l'Austrasie mérovingienne.* Histoire ancienne et médiévale 17. Paris: 1987.

Carrias, Michel. "Vie monastique et règle à Lérins au temps d'Honorat." RHEF 74 (1988): 195–211.

Cavadini, John C. "Elipandus and His Critics at the Council of Frankfurt." In *Frankfurter Konzil.* 2:787–807.

————. *The Last Christology of the West: Adoptionism in Spain and Gaul, 785–820.* Philadelphia: 1993.

Cerfaux, Lucien. "Le peuple de Dieu." In *Populus Dei: Studi in onore del Card. Alfredo Ottaviani per il cinquantesimo di sacerdozio: 18 marzo 1966,* edited by H. Cazelles and Roland de Vaux, Communio 10 and 11 (Rome: 1969): 2:803–926. .

————. "Regale sacerdotium." Reprinted in *Recueil Lucien Cerfaux,* 2:283–315. Gembloux: 1954–1985.

————. "Le titre *Kyrios* et la dignité royale de Jésus." In *Recueil Lucien Cerfaux,* 1:1–63. Gembloux: 1954–1985.

Chadwick, Henry. "Bishops as Monks." *Studia Patristica* 24 (Louvain: 1993): 45–61.

————. *Priscillian of Avila: The Occult and the Charismatic in the Early Church.* Oxford: 1976.

Champagne, J., and R. Szramkiewicz. "Recherches sur les conciles des temps mérovingiens." RHDr 49 (1971): 7–49.

Charlemagne's Heir: New Perspectives on the Reign of Louis the Pious (814–840). Edited by Peter Godman and Roger Collins. Oxford: 1990.

Charlier, Célestin. "La compilation augustinienne de Florus sur l'Apôtre: Sources et authenticité." RB 57 (1947): 132–86.

Chaume, Maurice. "Le mode de constitution et de délimitation des paroisses rurales aux temps mérovingiens et carolingiens." *Revue Mabillon* 27 (1937): 61–73.

Chauvot, Alain. "Images positives, images négatives des Barbares dans les sources latines à la fin du Ve siècle et au début du VIe siècle après J.-C." In *Clovis,* 1:3–14.

Chazelle, Celia. "Matter, Spirit and Image in the *Libri Carolini.*" *Recherches Augustiniennes* 21 (1986): 163–84.

Chevalier, Ulysse. *Poésie liturgique du moyen âge: Rythme et histoire.* Paris: 1893.

Classen, Peter. "*Causa Imperii.* Probleme Roms in Spätantike und Mittelalter." In *Ausgewälte Aufsätze von Peter Classen,* edited by Carl Joachim Classen, Johannes Fried, and Josef Fleckenstein, 45–84. Vorträge und Forschungen 28. Sigmaringen: 1983.

————. *Karl der Grosse, das Papsttum und Byzanz: Die Begründung des karolingischen Kaisertums.* Beiträge zur Geschichte und Quellenkunde des Mittelalters 9. Sigmaringen: 1985.

————. "*Romanum gubernans imperium.* Zur Vorgeschichte der Kaisertitulatur Karl des Grossen." DA 9 (1951): 103–21.

————. "Die Verträge von Verdun und von Coulaines 843 als politische Grundlagen des westfränkischen Reiches." HZ 196 (1963): 1–35.

Clastres, Pierre. "La question du pouvoir dans les sociétés primitives." In his *Recherches d'anthropologie politique,* 103–9. Paris: 1980.

————. *Society Against the State.* Translated by Robert Hurley. New York: 1989.

Claussen, M. A. *The Reform of the Frankish Church: Chrodegang of Metz and the Regula Canonicorum in the Eighth Century.* Cambridge: 2004.

Clovis. Clovis: Histoire et mémoire. Edited by Michel Rouche. 2 vols. Paris: 1997.

Coens, M. "Saint Boniface et sa mission historique." *Analecta Bollandiana* 73 (1955): 462–95.

Collins, Roger. *Charlemagne.* Toronto: 1998.

———. *Early Medieval Spain: Unity in Diversity. 400–1000.* Houndmills/Basingstoke: 1983.

———. "Julian of Toledo and the Royal Succession in Late Seventh-Century Spain." In *Early Medieval Kingship*, 30–49.

———. "Theodebert I. 'Rex Magnus Francorum.'" In *Ideal and Reality*, 7–33.

Congar, Yves. *L'ecclésiologie du haut moyen âge de Saint Grégoire le Grand à la désunion entre Byzance et Rome.* Paris: 1968.

Constable, Giles. *Monastic Tithes: From their Origins to the Twelfth Century.* Cambridge: 1964.

Contreni, John J. "Carolingian Biblical Studies." In *Carolingian Essays*, 71–98.

Coppens, J. *Le sacerdoce chrétien: Ses origines et son développement.* Analecta lovaniensia biblica et orientalia Ser. 5. Fasc. 4–5. Leiden: 1970.

Cordwell, J. M., and R. A. Schwartz, eds. *The Fabrics of Culture: The Anthropology of Clothing and Adornment.* The Hague: 1979.

Coupland, Simon. "The Rod of God's Wrath or the People of God's Wrath? The Carolingian Theology of the Viking Invasions." JEH 42 (1991): 535–54.

Courcelle, Pierre. "Nouveaux aspects de la culture lérinienne." *Revue des études latines* 46 (1968): 379–409.

———. "Le tyran et le philosophe d'après la 'Consolation' de Boèce." In *Passaggio dal mondo antico*, 195–224.

Cramer, Peter. *Baptism and Change in the Early Middle Ages, c. 200–c. 1150.* Cambridge: 1993.

Cristiani, Léon. "Essai sur les origines du costume ecclésiastique." *Orientalia christiana periodica* 13 (1947): 69–80.

———. *Lérins et ses fondateurs.* Paris: 1946.

Cubitt, Catherine. *Anglo-Saxon Church Councils c. 650–850.* London: 1995.

Daly, William M. "Caesarius of Arles: A Precursor of Medieval Christendom." *Traditio* 26 (1970): 1–28.

Daniélou, Jean. *The Angels and Their Mission.* Translated by D. Heimann. Westminster, Md.: 1987.

———. *Message évangélique et culture hellénistique aux IIe et IIIe siècles.* Bibliothèque de théologie 2. Paris: 1961.

———. *Théologie du Judéo-Christianisme.* Tournay: 1958.

Dannheimer, Hermann. *Lauterhofen im frühen Mittelalter. Reihengräberfeld—Martinskirche—Königshof.* Materialhefte sur Bayerischen Vorgeschichte 22. Oberpfalz: 1968.

Da Silva-Tarouca, Carlos. *Fontes historiae ecclesiasticae medii aevi in usum scholarum selegit.* Rome: 1930.

Dauge, Yves Albert. *Le Barbare: Recherches sur la conception romaine de la barbarie et de la civilisation*. Collection Latomus 176. Brussels: 1981.

Davis, R. *The First Seven Ecumenical Councils (325–787): Their History and Theology*. Theology and Life Series 21. Collegeville, Minn.: 1990.

de Aguilera, Abilio Barbero. *La sociedad visigoda y su entorno histórico*. Madrid: 1992.

De Clerck, Paul. "Les origines de la formule baptismale." In *Rituels: Mélanges offerts à Pierre-Marie Gy. O.P.*, edited by Paul De Clerck and Éric Palazzo, 199–213. Paris: 1990.

De Clercq, Charles. "La législation religieuse franque depuis l'avènement de Louis le Pieux jusqu'aux Fausses Décrétales." *Revue de Droit Canonique* 4 (1954): 371–404; 5 (1955): 5–55, 269–306, 390–429; 6 (1956): 145–62, 263–89. This work was completed by: "La législation religieuse franque depuis Fausses Décrétales jusqu'aux la fin du IXe siècle," 8 (1958): 122–58.

De Jong, Mayke. "The Empire as *ecclesia:* Hrabanus Maurus and Biblical *historia* for Rulers." In *Uses of the Past,* 191–226.

———. "Monastic Prisoners or Opting Out? Political Coercion and Honour in the Frankish Kingdoms." In *Topographies of Power,* 291–328.

———. *The Penitential State: Authority and Atonement in the Age of Louis the Pious, 814–840.* Cambridge: 2009.

———. "Power and Humility in Carolingian Society: The Public Penance of Louis the Pious." EME 1 (1992): 29–52.

De Jong, Mayke, Frans Theuws, and Carine van Rhijn, eds. *Topographies of Power in the Early Middle Ages.* The Transformation of the Roman World 6. Leiden: 2001.

De Jouvenel, Bertrand. *On Power: The Natural History of Its Growth.* Translated by J. F. Huntington. 1948. Reprint, Indianapolis: 1993.

Delaruelle, Étienne. "En relisant le 'De institutione regia' de Jonas d'Orléans: L'entrée en scène de l'épiscopat carolingien." In *Mélanges d'histoire du Moyen Âge: Dédiés à la mémoire de Louis Halphen*, 185–92. Paris: 1951.

De León, Luis. *De los nombres de Cristo* (1583). In *Obras completas castellanas de Fray Luis de León,* edited by Felix Garcia, 1:401–864. Madrid: 1967.

De Lubac, Henri. *Corpus mysticum: L'Eucharistie et l'église au moyen âge. Étude historique.* 2nd rev. ed. Paris: 1949.

De Montauzan, Germain. "Saint-Eucher: Évêque de Lyon et l'école de Lérins." *Bulletin historique du diocèse de Lyon* 2 (1923): 81–96.

De Nie, Giselle. "Le Corps, la fluidité et l'identité personnelle dans la vision du monde de Grégoire de Tours." In *Aevum inter utrumque,* edited by Marc van Uytfanghe and Roland Demeulenaere, 75–87. Steenbrugis: 1991.

De Pange, Jean. "Doutes sur la certitude de cette opinion que le sacre de Pépin est la première époque du sacre des rois de France." In *Mélanges d'histoire du Moyen Âge dédiés a la mémoire de Louis Halphen,* edited by Charles-Edmond Perrin, 557–64. Paris: 1951.

De Vaux, Roland. *Ancient Israel: Its Life and Institutions.* Translated by John McHugh. Grand Rapids: 1997.

De Vogüé, Adalbert. *Histoire littéraire du mouvement monastique dans l'antiquité.* 12 vols. thus far. Paris: 1991–.

———. "Pour comprendre Cassien." In his *De Saint Pachôme à Jean Cassien: Études littéraires et doctrinales sur le monachisme égyptien à ses début,* 303–29. Studia Anselmiana 120. Rome: 1996.

De Vries, Jan. *Altgermanische Religionsgeschichte.* Grundriss der germanischen Philologie 12,1. 2 vols. 3rd ed. Berlin: 1970.

De Waele, Ferdinand Joseph M. *The Magic Staff or Rod in Graeco-Italian Antiquity.* Ghent: 1927.

Deane, H. A. *The Political and Social Ideas of St. Augustine.* New York: 1963.

Deanesly, Margaret. *The Pre-Conquest Church in England.* An Ecclesiastical History of England 1. London: 1961.

Degenhart, F. *Studien zu Julianus Pomerius.* Eichstätt: 1905.

Demandt, Alexander. *Geschichte der Spätantike: Das Römsiche Reich von Diocletian bis Justinian.* Munich: 1998.

Devisse, Jean. *Hincmar: Archévêque de Reims, 845–882.* Travaux d'histoire ethico-politique 29. 3 vols. Geneva: 1975.

———. "L'influence de Julien Pomère sur les clercs carolingiens: De la pauvreté au Ve et IXe siècles." RHEF 56 (1970): 285–95.

———. "Le sacre et le pouvoir avant les carolingiens, l'héritage wisigotique." In *Le Sacre des rois: Actes du Colloque international d'histoire sur les sacres et couronnements royaux.* Reims: 1975; Paris: 1985, 27–38.

Dierkens, Alain. "Carolus monasteriorum multorum eversor et ecclesiasticarum pecuniarum in usus proprios commutator? Notes sur la politique monastique du maire du palais Charles Martel." In *Karl Martell,* 277–94.

———. "Christianisme et 'paganisme' dans la Gaule septentrionale aux Ve et VIe siècles." In *Die Franken und die Alemannen bis zur "Schlacht bei Zülpich" (496/97),* edited by Dieter Geuenich. Ergänzungsbände zum Reallexikon der germanischen Altertumskunde 19. Berlin: 1998.

———. "The Evidence of Archaeology." In *The Pagan Middle Ages,* edited by Ludo J. R. Milis, translated by Tanis Guest, 39–64. Woodbridge: 1998.

Diesner, H. J. *Isidor von Sevilla und seine Zeit.* Berlin: 1973.

Dietrich, Claude. "Untersuchungen zum Untergang des Westgotenreiches (711–725)." HJ 108 (1988): 329–58.

Dill, Samuel. *Roman Society in Gaul in the Merovingian Age.* London: 1926.

Dold, Alban. "Alte, teilweise unbekannte Väterfragmente auf dem Doppelblatt N I 6 Nr. 9 der Universitätsbibliothek Basel." RB 63 (1953): 239–45.

Döpp, Siegner, and Wilhelm Geerlings, eds. *Lexikon der antiken christlichen Literatur.* Freiburg: 1998.

Dörries, Hermann. "Die geistigen Voraussetzungen und folgen der karolingischen Reichsteilung 843." In *Vertrag von Verdun,* 150–80.

Douglas, Mary. *How Institutions Think.* Syracuse: 1986.

Doujat, Jean. *Histoire du droit canonique.* Paris: 1685.

Doyle, Daniel Edward. *The Bishop as Disciplinarian in the Letters of St. Augustine.* Patristic Studies 4. New York: 2002.

Drewal, H. J. "Pageantry and Power in Yoruba Costuming." In *Fabrics of Culture,* 189–230.

Drinkwater, John, and Hugh Elton, eds. *Fifth-Century Gaul: A Crisis of Identity?* Cambridge: 1992, 144–55.

Du Cange, Charles du Fresne. *Glossarium mediae et infimae latinitatis.* Edited by D. P. Carpenter and G. A. L. Henschel. 10 vols. in 5. Graz: 1954.

Dubreucq, Alain. "Fils de l'Église: genèse et développement d'une conception chrétienne du pouvoir royal." In *Clovis.* 2:85–102.

Duby, Georges. *The Early Growth of the European Economy: Warriors and Peasants from the Seventh to the Twelfth Century.* Translated by H. B. Clarke. Ithaca: 1978.

———. *The Three Orders: Feudal Society Imagined.* Translated by Arthur Goldhammer. Chicago: 1980.

Duchesne, Louis. *Christian Worship, Its Origin and Evolution: A Study of the Latin Liturgy up to the Time of Charlemagne.* Translated by M. L. McClure. 5th ed. London: 1931.

———. *L'Église au VIème siècle.* Paris: 1925.

———. *Fastes épiscopaux de l'ancienne Gaule.* 3 vols. 2nd ed. Paris: 1907–1915.

Dudden, F. Homes. *The Life and Times of St. Ambrose.* 2 vols. Oxford: 1935.

Dufour, Jean. *Les Évêques d'Albi, de Cahors, et de Rodez, des origines à la fin du XIIe siècle.* Mémoires et documents d'histoire médiévale et de philologie 3. Paris: 1989.

Dumézil, Georges. *Mitra–Varuna: An Essay on Two Indo-European Representations of Sovereignty.* Translated by Derek Coltman. New York: 1988.

Dupraz, Louis. *Contribution à l'histoire du Regnum Francorum pendant la troisème quart du VIIe siècle (656–680).* Fribourg: 1948.

Durliat, Jean. "Les attributions civiles des évêques mérovingiens: l'exemple de Didier, évêque de Cahors (630–655)." *Annales du Midi* 91 (1979): 237–54.

Durst, Michael. "Nizäa als 'autoritative Tradition' bei Hilarius von Poitiers." In *Stimuli: Exegese und ihre Hermeneutik in Antike und Christentum. Festschrift für Ernst Dassmann,* edited by Georg Schöllgen and Clemens Scholten, 406–22. Jahrbuch für Antike und Christentum. Erganzungsband 23. Munster: 1996.

Dutripon, François Pascal. *Bibliorum sacrorum concordantiae.* 1880. Reprinted Hildesheim: 1976.

Duval, Yvette, Paul-Albert Février, and Jean Guyon, eds. *Provinces ecclésiastiques d'Aix et d'Embrun (Narbonensis secunda et Alpes Maritimae).* TCCG 2. Paris: 1986.

Eberhardt, Otto. *Via Regia: Der Fürstenspiegel Smaragds vons St. Mihiel und seine literarische Gattung.* Münstersche Mittelalter-Schriften 28. Munich: 1977.

Eck, Werner. "Der Einfluss der konstantinischen Wende auf die Auswahl der Bischöfe im 4. u. 5. Jahrhundert." *Chiron* 8 (1978): 561–85.

Effros, Bonnie. "*De partibus Saxoniae* and the Regulation of Mortuary Custom: A Carolingian Campaign of Christianization or the Suppression of Saxon Identity?" RBPH 75 (1997): 267–86.

———. "Monuments and Memory: Repossessing Ancient Remains in Early Medieval Gaul." In *Topographies of Power*, 93–118.

Eichmann, E. "Königs- und Bischofsweihe." *Sitzungsberichte der Bayerischen Akademie der Wissenschaften: Philosophisch-philologische und historische Klasse* 6 (1928): 1–71.

Eliade, Mircea. *The Myth of the Eternal Return, or, Cosmos and History*. Translated by Willard Trask. 2nd rev. ed. Bollingen Series 46. Princeton: 1971.

———. *The Sacred and the Profane: The Nature of Religion*. Translated by Willard Trask. New York: 1959.

———. *Shamanism: Archaic Techniques of Ecstasy*. Translated by Willard Trask. Bollingen Series 76. Princeton: 1964.

Elbern, V. H. "Liturgisches Gerät des Frühmittelalters als Symbolträger." *Settimane* 23 (1976): 1:349–81.

Ellard, G. *Ordination Anointings in the Western Church before 1000 A.D.* Cambridge: 1933.

Elze, Reinhard. "Le consacrazione regie." *Settimane* 33 (1987): 1:43–55.

Engelbert, Pius. "Papstreisen ins Frankenreich." *Römische Quartalschrift* 88 (1993): 77–113.

Enright, Michael J. *Iona, Tara and Soissons: The Origin of the Royal Anointing Ritual*. Arbeiten zur Frühmittelalterforschung. Schriftenreihe des Instituts für Frühmittelalterforschung der Universität Münster 17. Berlin: 1985.

Esders, Stefan. *Römische Rechtstradition und merowingische Königtum: Zum Rechtscharakter politischer Herrschaft in Burgund im 6. und 7. Jahrhundert*. Veröffentlichungen de Max-Planck-Instituts für Geschichte 134. Göttingen: 1997.

Étaix, Raymond. "Le texte complété du sermon 178 de saint Césaire d'Arles." *Sacris Erudiri* 34 (1994): 59–66.

Ethnogenese und Überlieferung: Angewandte Methoden der Frühmittelalterforschung. Edited by Karl Brunner and Brigitte Merta. Veröffentlichungen des Instituts für Österreichische Geschichtsforschung 31. Vienna: 1994.

Evans, G. R. "Eutyches, Nestorius and Chalcedon." In *The First Christian Theologians: An Introduction to theology in the Early Church*, edited by G. R. Evans, 243–47. Oxford: 2004.

———. *The First Christian Theologians: An Introduction to Theology in the Early Church*. Oxford: 2004.

———. *The Thought of Gregory the Great*. Cambridge: 1986.

Evans-Pritchard, E. E. *The Divine Kingship of the Shilluk of the Nilotic Sudan*. The Frazer Lecture 1948. Cambridge: 1948.

Ewig, Eugen. "Milo et eiusmodi similes." In *Sankt Bonifatius Gedankgabe zum zwölfhundersten Geburtstag*, 412–40. 2nd ed. Fulda: 1954.

———. "Saint Chrodegang et la reforme de l'église franque." In his *Spätantikes und Fränkische Gallien: Gesammelte Schriften (1952–1973)*, edited by Hartmut Atsma, 2:232–259. Beihefte der Francia 3. Munich: 1976–1979.

Faivre, Alexandre. *Naissance d'une hiérarchie: Les premières étapes du cursus clérical*. Théologie historique 40. Paris: 1977.

————. *Ordonner la fraternité: Pouvoir d'innover et retour à l'ordre dans l'Église anci-enne.* Paris: 1992.

Fauvarque, Bertrand. "Eschatologie: Conversion et mission à la fin de l'Empire romain." *MScR* 53 (1996): 13–26.

Ferreiro, Alberto. "'Frequenter Legere': The Propagation of Literacy, Education, and Divine Wisdom in Caesarius of Arles." *JEH* 43 (1992): 5–15.

Fichtenau, Heinrich. *The Carolingian Empire: The Age of Charlemagne.* Translated by Peter Munz. New York: 1964.

Fiedrowicz, Michael. *Das Kirchenverständnis Gregors des Grossen: Eine Untersuchung seiner exegetischen und homiletischen Werke.* Römische Quartalschrift für christliche Altertumskunde und Kirchengeschichte, Suppl. 50. Freiburg: 1995.

Fisher, J. D. C. *Christian Initiation: Baptism in the Medieval West. A Study in the Dis-integration of the Primitive Rite of Initiation.* Alcuin Club Collections 47. London: 1965.

Flachenecker, Helmut. "Der Bischof und sein Bischofssitz: Würzburg—Eichstätt—Bamberg im Früh- und Hochmittelalter." *Römische Quartalschrift* 91 (1996): 148–81.

Fleckenstein, Josef. "Fulrad von Saint-Denis und der fränkische Ausgriff in den süddeutschen Raum." In *Zur Geschichte der Alemannen,* edited by W. Müller, 354–400. Wege der Forschung Band C. Darmstadt: 1987.

————. *Die Hofkapelle der deutschen Könige 1: Grundlegung—Die karolingische Hofka-pelle.* Schriften der Monumenta Germaniae historica 16.1. Stuttgart: 1959.

Flint, Valerie. *The Rise of Magic in Early Medieval Europe.* Princeton: 1991.

Folz, Robert. *Le couronnement impérial de Charlemagne, 25 Décembre 800.* Trente journ-ees qui ont fait la France 3. Paris: 1964.

————. "La pénitence publique au IXe siècle d'près les canons de l'évêque Isaac de Langres." In *L'encadrement religieux des fidèles au moyen âge et jusqu'au concile de Trente: Actes du 109e congrès national des Sociétés Savants, Dijon 1984,* 331–43. His-toire médiévale et philologie 1. Paris: 1985.

————. "Les trois couronnements de Charles le Chauve." *Byzantion* 61 (1991): 93–111.

Fontaine, Jacques. *Isidore de Séville et la culture classique dans l'Espagne wisigothique.* 2 vols. Paris: 1959.

————. "Mozarabie hispanique et monde carolingien: Les èchanges culturels entre la France et l'Espagne du VIIIe au Xe siècle." *Anuario de estudios medievales* 13 (1983): 17–46.

Fontaine, Jacques, and J. N. Hillgarth, eds. *Le Septième siècle. Changements et continui-tés/The Seventh Century. Change and Continuity.* Proceedings of a joint French and British Colloquium at the Warburg Institute 8–9 July 1988. Studies of the Warburg Institute 42. London: 1992.

Fouracre, Paul. *The Age of Charles Martel.* Harlow: 2000.

————. "Carolingian Justice: The Rhetoric of Improvement and Contexts of Abuse." *Settimane* 42 (1995): 2:771–803.

————. "Merovingian History and Hagiography." *Past and Present* 127 (1990): 3–38.

————. "'Placita' and the Settlement of Disputes in Later Merovingian Francia." In

The Settlement of Disputes in Early Medieval Europe, edited by W. Davies and Paul Fouracre, 23–43. Cambridge: 1986.

Fouracre, Paul, and Richard A. Gerberding. *Late Merovingian France: History and Hagiography, 640–720.* Manchester: 1996.

Frakes, Robert M. *Contra Potentium Iniurias: The Defensor civitatis and Late Roman Justice.* Münchner Beiträge zur Papyrusforschung und antiken Rechtsgeschichte 90. Munich: 2001.

Frank, H. *Die Klosterbischöfe des Frankenreiches.* Beiträge zur Geschichte des Altenmönchtums und das benediktiner Ordens 17. Münster im Westf.: 1932.

Das Frankfurter Konzil von 794: Kristallisationspunkt karolingischer Kultur. Edited by Rainer Berndt. Quellen und Abhandlungen zur mittelrheinischen Kirchengeschichte 80. 2 vols. Mainz: 1997.

Fransen, Gérard. *Les collections canoniques.* Typologie des sources du moyen âge occidental 10. Turnhout: 1973.

Franz, Adolph. *Die kirchlichen Benediktionen im Mittelalter.* 2 vols. Freiburg im Breisgau: 1909.

Freeman, Ann. "Carolingian Orthodoxy and the Fate of the Libri Carolini." *Viator* 16 (1985): 65–108.

———. "Further Studies in the *Libri Carolini.*" *Speculum* 40 (1965): 203–89.

———. "Scripture and Images in the Libri Carolini." *Settimane* 41 (1994): 1:163–88.

———. "Theodulf of Orléans and the *Libri Carolini.*" *Speculum* 32 (1957): 663–705.

———. "Theodulf of Orléans: A Visigoth at Charlemagne's Court." In *L'Europe héritière de l'Éspagne wisigothique,* edited by Jacques Fontaine and Christine Pellistrandi, 185–94. Collection de la Casa de Velázquez 35. Madrid: 1992.

Fried, Johannes. *Donation of Constantine and Constitutum Constantini: The Misinterpretation of a Fiction and its Original Meaning.* Millenium-Studien/Millenium Studies 3. Berlin: 2007.

———. "Der karolingische Herrschaftsverband im 9. Jh. zwischen 'Kirche' und 'Königshaus.'" HJ 235 (1982): 1–43.

Funkenstein, Amos. *Heilsplan und natürliche Entwicklung: Formen der Gegenwartsbestimmung im Geschichtsdenken des hohen Mittelalters.* Munich: 1965.

Fustel de Coulanges, Numa Denys. *La Gaule romaine.* Completed from the author's manuscript by Camille Jullian. Paris: 1994.

Gabet, Philippe. "Constantin et Clovis, développements et transformations rémois aux IXe et Xe siècles." In *Clovis,* 2:73–81.

Gamber, Klaus. *Codices liturgici latini antiquiores.* Spicilegii Friburgensis subsidia 1. Freiburg: 1963.

———. *Die Messfeier nach altgallikanischem Ritus.* Studia patristica et liturgica quae edidit Institutum Liturgicum Ratisbonense 14. Regensburg: 1984.

Ganshof, F. L. "Le droit romain dans le capitulaires et dans la collection d'Ansegise." In *Droit romain dans les capitulaires,* 1–43. Ius romanum medii aevi, Pars I, 2 b *cc.* alpha-beta. Milan: 1969.

———. *Een Historicus uit de VIe Eeuw. Gregorius van Tours:* Mededelingen van de

Koninklijke vlaamse Academie voor Wetenschappen. Letteren en schone Kunsten van België. Klasse der Letteren 28, no. 5. Brussels: 1966.

———. *Recherches sur les capitulaires.* RHDr 1957: 1 and 2; Paris: 1958.

Ganz, David. "The *Epitaphium Arsenii* and Opposition to Louis the Pious." In *Charlemagne's Heir,* 537–50.

———. "The Ideology of Sharing." In *Property and Power in the Early Middle Ages,* edited by Wendy Davies and Paul Fouracre, 17–30. Cambridge: 1995.

García Moreno, Luis A. *Historia de España visigoda.* Madrid: 1989.

Garnsey, Peter. *Social Status and Legal Privilege in the Roman Empire.* Oxford: 1970.

Garrison, Daniel. "The *Locus Inamoenus:* Another Part of the Forest." *Arion,* 3rd ser. 2.1 (Winter 1992): 98–114.

Garrison, Mary. "The Franks as the New Israel? Education for an Identity from Pippin to Charlemagne." In *The Uses of the Past in the Early Middle Ages,* edited by Yitzhak Hen and Matthew Innes, 114–161. Cambridge: 2000.

———. "The *Missa pro principe* in the Bobbio Missal." In *The Bobbio Missal: Liturgy and Religious Culture in Merovingian Gaul,* edited by Yizhak Hen and Rob Meens, 187–203. Cambridge: 2004.

Gaudemet, Jean. "Charisme et droit: Le domaine de l'évêque." ZSRG.K 74 (1988): 44–70.

———. *L'Église dans l'empire romain (IVe–Ve siècles).* Paris, 1958.

———. *Église et Cité: Histoire du droit canonique.* Paris: 1994.

———. "La législation des conciles gaulois du IVe siècle." In *Proceedings of the Third International Congress of Medieval Canon Law.* Strasbourg. Sept. 3–6, 1968, edited by Stephen Kuttner, 1–13. Monumenta Iuris Canonici ser. C. Subsidia 4. Vatican City, 1971.

———. *Les sources du droit de l'Église du IIe au VIIe siècle.* Paris: 1985.

———. "Survivances romaines dans le droit de la monarchie franque du Vème au Xème siècle." *Tijdschrift voor Rechtsgeschiedenis/Revue d'histoire du droit* 23 (1955): 149–206.

Gauthier, Nancy. *L'Évangélisation des pays de la Moselle: La province romaine de Première Belgique entre antiquité et moyen âge (IIIe–VIIIe siècles).* Paris: 1980.

———. *Province ecclésiastique de Trèves (Belgica Prima).* TCCG 1. Paris: 1986.

Geary, Patrick. *Before France and Germany: The Creation and Transformation of the Merovingian World.* Oxford: 1988.

Gerberding, Richard A. "716: A Crucial Year for Charles Martel." In *Karl Martell,* 205–16.

Giakalis, Ambrosius. *Images of the Divine: The Theology of Icons at the Seventh Ecumenical Council.* Studies in the History of Christian Thought 54. Leiden: 1994.

Gillett, Andrew. "The Purposes of Cassiodorus' *Variae.*" In *After Rome's Fall,* 37–50.

Gilliard, Frank D. "Senatorial Bishops in the Fourth Century." *Harvard Theological Review* 77 (1984): 153–75.

Glassie, Henry. *Passing the Time in Ballymenone.* Bloomington: 1982.

Gobry, Ivan. *Les moines en occident.* 3 vols. Paris: 1985–1987.

Godding, Robert. *Prêtres en Gaule mérovingienne.* Subsidia Hagiographica 82. Brussels, 2001.

Goetz, Hans-Werner. "Serfdom and the Beginnings of a 'Seigneurial System' in the Carolingian Period: a Survey of the Evidence." EME 2 (1993): 29–51.

Goffart, Walter. *The Narrators of Barbarian History (A.D. 550–800): Jordanes, Gregory of Tours, Bede, and Paul the Deacon.* Princeton: 1988.

———. "Two Notes on Germanic Antiquity Today." *Traditio* 50 (1995): 9–30.

Goldschmidt, Rudolf Carel. *Paulinus' Churches at Nola.* Amsterdam: 1940.

Gottlieb, Gunther. "Die formalen Bestandteile in der Überlieferung der gallischen Konzilien des 4. und 5. Jahrhunderts." AHC 16 (1984): 254–63.

Gousset, Marie-Thérèse. "La Représentation de la Jérusalem céleste à l'époque carolingienne." *Cahiers archéologiques* 33 (1974): 47–60.

Gransden, Antonia. "Traditionalism and Continuity during the Last Century of Anglo-Saxon monasticism." JEH 40 (1989): 159–207.

Gregorio magno e il suo tempo XIX incontro di studiosi dell'antichità cristiana. . . . Roma 9–12 maggio 1990. Studia Ephemeridis "Augustinianum" 33, 34. 2 vols. Rome: 1991.

Greenway, G. W. *Saint Boniface.* London: 1955.

Griffe, Élie. *La Gaule chrétienne à l'époque romaine.* 3 vols. 2nd ed. Paris: 1964–1966.

Grillmeier, Aloys. *Le Christ dans la tradition chrétienne.* Translated by Sister Pascale-Dominique. *Vol. 2.1, Le Concile de Chalcédoine (451): réception et opposition (451–513).* Paris: 1990.

Gryson, Roger. *Le prêtre selon Saint Ambroise.* Universitas Catholica Lovaniensis—Dissertationes Series tertia 11. Louvain: 1968.

Guenée, Bernard. *Histoire et culture historique dans l'Occident médiéval.* Paris: 1980.

Guerreau-Jalabert, Anita. "La 'renaissance carolingienne': Modèles culturels. usages linguistiques et structures sociales." *Bibliothèque des chartes* 139 (1981): 5–35.

Gussone, Nikolaus, and Heiko Steuer. "Diadem." In *Reallexikon der germanischen Altertumskunde,* 5:351–75. Berlin: 1973–.

Gy, Pierre-Marie. *La liturgie dans l'histoire.* Paris: 1990.

Hack, Achim Thomas. "Zur Herkunft der karolingischen Königssalbung." ZKG 110 (1999): 170–90.

Hadot, Pierre. "La fin du paganisme." In *Histoire des religions,* edited by Henri-Charles Puech, 2:81–113. Paris: 1970–1976.

———. "De Tertullien à Boèce: Le développement de la notion de personne dans les controverses théologiques," in *Problèmes de la personne: Colloque du Centre de Recherches de Psychologie comparative,* edited by Ignace Meyerson, 123–34. École Pratique des Hautes Études—Sorbonne: Congrés et colloques 13. Paris: 1973.

Halbwachs, Maurice. *On Collective Memory.* Translated by Lewis A. Coser. Chicago: 1992.

Hanson, R. P. C. *The Search for the Christian Doctrine of God: The Arian Controversy, 318–381.* Edinburgh: 1993.

Harding, Alan. *Medieval Law and the Foundations of the State.* Oxford: 2002.

Harper, John. *The Forms and Orders of Western Liturgy from the Tenth to Eighteenth Century.* Oxford: 1991.

Harries, Jill. *Law and Empire in Late Antiquity.* Cambridge: 1999.

————. *Sidonius Apollinaris and the Fall of Rome, AD 407–485.* Oxford: 1994.

Harries, Jill, and Ian Wood, eds. *The Theodosian Code: Studies in the Imperial Law of Late Antiquity.* London: 1993.

Hartmann, Wilfried. "Das Konzil von Frankfurt 794 und Nizäa 787." AHC 20 (1988): 307–24.

————. *Die Synoden der Karolingerzeit im Frankenreich und in Italien.* Konziliengeschichte Reihe A: Darstellung. Paderborn: 1989.

————. "La transmission et l'influence du droit synodal carolingien." RHDr 4th ser. 63 (1985): 483–97.

Hartmann, Wilfried, and Detlev Jasper. "Formen und Wege mittelalterlicher Konzilsüberlieferungen." In *Mittelalterliche Textüberlieferungen und ihre kritische Aufarbeitung: Beiträge der Monumenta Germaniae Historica zum 31. deutschen Historikertag. Mannheim 1976,* 42–51. Munich: 1976.

Hauck, Albert. *Die Bischofswahlen unter den Merovingern.* Erlangen: 1883.

————. *Kirchengeschichte Deutschlands.* 5 vols. 5th ed. Leipzig: 1935.

Hauck, Karl. "Lebensformen und Kultmythen in germanischen Stammes- und Herrschergenealogien." *Saeculum* 6 (1955).

Heather, Peter. *Goths and Romans, 332–489.* Oxford: 1991.

Hedeager, Lotte. "Migration Period Europe: The Formation of a Political Mentality." In *Rituals of Power from Late Antiquity to the Early Middle Ages,* edited by Frans Theuws and Janet L. Nelson, 15–57. Leiden: 2000.

Heidrich, Ingrid. "Synode und Hoftag in Düren im August 747." DA 50 (1994): 415–40.

Heijmans, Marc. *Arles durant l'antiquité tardive: De la* Duplex Arelas *à l'*Urbs Genesii. Rome: 2004.

Heinzelmann, Martin. "The 'Affair' of Hilary of Arles (445) and Gallo-Roman Identity in the Fifth Century." In *Fifth-century Gaul,* 239–51.

————. "L'aristocratie et les évêchés entre Loire et Rhin jusqu'à la fin du VIIe siècle." RHEF 62 (1976): 75–90.

————. *Bischofsherrschaft in Gallien: Zur Kontinuität römischer Führungsschichten vom 4. bis zum 7. Jahrhundert—Soziale, prosopographische und bildungsgeschichtliche Aspekte.* Beihefte der Francia 5. Munich: 1976.

————. *Gregor von Tours (538–594), "Zehn Bücher Geschichte": Historiographie und Gesellschaftskonzept im 6. Jahrhundert.* Darmstadt: 1994.

Heinzelmann, Martin, and J.-C. Poulin. *Les vies anciennes de sainte Geneviève de Paris: Études critiques.* Paris: 1986.

Heitz, C. "L'architettura dell'età carolingia in relazione alla liturgia sacra." In *Culto Cristiano: Politica imperiale carolingia.* Todi: 1979, 337–62.

————. "Symbolisme et architecture: Les nombres et l'architecture religieuse du haut moyen âge." *Settimane* 23 (1976), 1:387–420.

Hen, Yitzhak. *Culture and Religion in Merovingian Gaul, A.D. 481–751.* Cultures, Beliefs, and Traditions 1. Leiden: 1995.

————. "Knowledge of Canon Law among Rural Priests: The Evidence of Two Carolingian Manuscripts from around 800." JTS 50 (1999): 117–34.

——. *Roman Barbarians: The Royal Court and Culture in the Early Medieval West.* Houndmills/Basingstoke: 2009.

——. *The Royal Patronage of Liturgy in Frankish Gaul to the Death of Charles the Bald (877).* Henry Bradshaw Society Subsidia III. London: 2001.

Hen, Yitzhak, and Matthew Innes, eds. *The Uses of the Past in the Early Middle Ages.* Cambridge: 2000.

Herlihy, Daniel. *Medieval Households.* Cambridge, Mass.: 1985.

Herrin, Judith. "Constantinople, Rome and the Franks in the Seventh and Eighth Centuries." In *Byzantine Diplomacy: Papers from the Twenty-Fourth Spring Symposium of Byzantine Studies,* edited by J. Shepard and S. Franklin, 91–107. Aldershot: 1992.

——. *The Formation of Christendom.* Princeton: 1987.

Hess, Hamilton. *The Canons of the Council of Sardica A.D. 343: A Landmark in the Early Development of Canon Law.* Oxford: 1958.

Heuclin, Jean. *Aux origines monastiques de la Gaule du nord: Ermites et reclus du Ve au XIe siècle.* Lille: 1998.

——. "Le clergé mérovingien et carolingien: Instrument de christianisation?" MScR 53 (1996): 27–42.

——. "Le concile d'Orléans de 511. Un premier concordat?" In *Clovis,* 1:435–50.

——. *Hommes de Dieu et fonctionnaires du roi en Gaule du Nord du Ve au IXe siècle (348–817).* Villeneuve-d'Ascq [Nord]: 1998.

——. "Identité et rôle du clergé à l'époque du Bréviaire d'Alaric." In *Bréviaire d'Alaric,* 57–71.

Hillgarth, J. N. "Ireland and Spain in the Seventh Century." *Peritia* 3 (1984): 1–16.

——. "The Position of Isidorian Studies: A Critical Review of the Literature 1936–1975." SM 3rd ser., vol. 24 (1983): 817–905.

Hoeflich, Michael H. "The Concept of Utilitas Populi in Early Ecclesiastical Law and Government." ZSRG.K 67 (1981): 36–74.

Honoré, Tony. *Law in the Crisis of Empire, 379–455 A.D.: The Theodosian Dynasty and Its Quaestors.* Oxford: 1998.

Hoyoux, J. "Reges criniti: Chevelures. tonsures et scalps chez les mérovingiens." RBPH 26 (1948): 479–508.

Hubert, Henri, and Marcel Mauss. "Esquisse d'une théorie générale de la magie." *Année sociologique* 7 (1902–1903): 1–146.

Hubert, Jean. "La topographie religieuse d'Arles au VIe siècle." *Cahiers archéologiques* 2 (1947): 17–27.

Huyghebaert, Nicolas. "Une légende de fondation: Le Constitutum Constantini." MA 85. 4th ser. 34 (1979): 177–209.

I Deug-Su. *L'Opera agiografica di Alcuino.* Biblioteca degli "Studi Medievali" 13. Spoleto: 1983.

Imbart de la Tour, Pierre. *Les paroisses rurales dans l'ancienne France du IVe au XIe siècle.* Paris: 1898.

Innes, Matthew. "Charlemagne's Will: Piety, Politics and the Imperial Succession." EHR 112 (1997): 833–55.

————. *State and Society in the Early Middle Ages: The Middle Rhine Valley, 400–1000.* Cambridge: 2000.

Instinsky, H. U. *Bischofsstuhl und Kaiserthron.* Munich: 1955.

Isaacs, M. E. *Sacred Space: An Approach to the Theology of the Epistle to the Hebrews.* Journal for the Study of the New Testament. Supplement Series 73. Sheffield: 1992.

Jahn, Joachim. *Ducatus Baiuvariorum: Das Bairische Herzogtum der Agilolfinger.* Monographien zur Geschichte des Mittelalters 35. Stuttgart: 1991.

James, Edward O. "Bede and the Tonsure Question." *Peritia* 3 (1984): 85–98.

————. *Europe's Barbarians A.D. 200–600.* Harlow: 2009.

————. "Gregory of Tours and the Franks." In *After Rome's Fall,* 51–66.

————. "The Sacred Kingship and the Priesthood." In *The Sacral Kingship,* 63–70. Studies in the History of Religions 4 [Supplements to NVMEN]. Leiden: 1959.

Jarnut, Jörg. *Agilolfingerstudien: Untersuchungen zur Geschichte einer adligen Famile im 6. und 7. Jahrhundert.* Monographien zur Geschichte des Mittelalters 32. Stuttgart: 1986.

————. "Bonifatius und die fränkischen Reformkonzilien (743–748)." ZSRG.K 66 (1979): 1–26.

————. "Genealogie und politische Bedeutung der agilolfingischen Herzöge." *Mitteilungen des Instituts für Österreichische Geschichtsforschung* 99 (1991): 1–22.

Jarnut, Jörg, Ulrich Nonn, and Michael Richter, eds. *Karl Martell in seiner Zeit.* Beihefte der Francia 37. Sigmaringen: 1994.

Jasper, Detlev, and Horst Fuhrmann. *Papal Letters in the Early Middle Ages.* Washington, D.C.: 2001.

Joannou, Périclès-Pierre. *La legislation imperiale et la christianisation de l'empire romain (311–476).* Orientalia christiana analecta 192. Rome: 1972.

Jolowicz, Herbert Felix. *Historical Introduction to the Study of Roman Law.* Cambridge: 1932.

Jones, Cheslyn, et al., eds. *The Study of Liturgy.* London: 1992.

Jourjon, Maurice. "À propos du conflit entre le Pape Léon e Hilaire, évêque d'Arles." In: *La Patrie gauloise d'Agrippa au VIème siècle: Actes du Colloque. Lyon: 1981,* 267–71. Centre d'Études Romaines et gallo-romaines 3. Lyon: 1983.

Judic, Bruno. "Grégoire le Grand et le pouvoir royal." *Studia Patristica* 33 (Louvain: 1997): 434–40.

Jullian, Camille. *Gallia: Tableau sommaire de la Gaule sous la domination romaine.* Paris: 1892.

Jungmann, J. A. *The Early Liturgy to the Time of Gregory the Great.* Translated by F. A. Brunner. University of Notre Dame Liturgical Studies 6. Notre Dame: 1980.

Jussen, Bernhard. "Der 'Name' der Witwe: Zur 'Konstruktion' eines Standes in Spätantike und Frühmittelalter." In *Veuves et Veuvage dans le haut moyen âge,* edited by M. Parisse, 137–75. Paris: 1993.

————. "On Church Organization and the Definition of an Estate: The Idea of Widowhood in Late Antique and Early Medieval Christianity." *Tel Aviver Jahrbuch für deutsche Geschichte* 22 (1993): 25–42.

———. "Über 'Bischofsherrschaften' und die Prozeduren politisch-sozialer Umordnung in Gallien zwischen 'Antike' und 'Mittelalter.'" HZ 260 (1995): 673–718.

Juster, Jean. "La condition légale des Juifs sous les rois Visigoths." In *Études d'histoire juridique offertes à Paul Frédéric Girard*, 2:275–335. Paris: 1913.

Kaiser, Reinhold. *Bischofsherrschaft zwischen Königtum und Fürstenmacht: Studien zur bischöflichen Stadtherrschaft im westfranzösischen Reich im frühen und hohen Mittelalter.* Pariser historische Studien 17. Bonn: 1981.

———. "Bistumsgründungen im Merowingerreich im 6. Jahrhundert." In *Beiträge zur Geschichte des Regnum Francorum: Proceedings of a Colloquium for the 75th Birthday of Eugen Ewig 28 May 1988,* edited by R. Schieffer, 9–35. Sigmaringen: 1990.

———. "Royauté et pouvoir épiscopal au nord de la Gaule (VIIe–IXe siècles)." In *La Neustrie,* 1:143–160.

Kantorowicz, Ernst. "The 'King's Advent' and the Enigmatic Panels in the Doors of Santa Sabina." In his *Selected Studies,* 37–75. Locust Valley, N.Y.: 1965.

Kardong, Terrence G. "Benedict's Insistence on Rank in the Monastic Community: RB 63:1–9 in Context." *Cistercian Studies Quarterly* 42 (2007): 243–65.

Kasper, Clemens M. *Theologie und Askese: Die Spiritualität des Inselmönchtums von Lérins im 5. Jahrhundert.* Beiträge zur Geschichte des alten Mönchtums und des Benediktinertums 40. Munster: 1990.

Keefe, Susan A. "Carolingian Baptismal Expositions: A Handlist of Tracts and Manuscripts." In *Carolingian Essays,* 169–237.

Kelly, Henry Asgar. *The Devil at Baptism: Ritual, Theology, and Drama.* Ithaca: 1985.

Kelly, J. N. D. *Jerome: His Life. Writings and Controversies.* London: 1998.

———. *The Oxford Dictionary of Popes.* Oxford: 1986.

Kempf, F. "Primatiale und episkopal-synodale Struktur der Kirche vor dem gregorianischen Reform." AHC 16 (1978): 27–66.

Kern, Fritz. *Kingship and Law in the Middle Ages.* Translated by S. Chrimes. Oxford: 1939.

———. "Recht und Verfassung im Mittelalter." HZ 120 (1919): 1–79.

Kéry, Lotte. *Canonical Collections of the Early Middle Ages (ca. 400–1140): A Bibliographical Guide to the Manuscripts and Literature.* Washington, D.C.: 1999.

Kierkegaard, Søren. *Papers and Journals: A Selection.* Translated by Alastair Hannay. London: 1996.

King, P. D. "The Barbarian Kingdoms." In *The Cambridge History of Medieval Political Thought. c. 350–c. 1450,* edited by J. H. Burns, 123–53. Cambridge: 1991.

———. *Law and Society in the Visigothic Kingdom.* Cambridge Studies in Medieval Life and Thought 3rd ser., vol. 5. Cambridge: 1972.

Klauser, Theodor. *A Short History of the Western Liturgy: An Account and Some Reflections.* Translated by J. Halliburton. 2nd ed. Oxford: 1979.

———. *Der Ursprung der bischöflichen Insignien und Ehrenrechte.* In *Gesammelte Arbeiten zur Liturgiegeschichte. Kirchengeschichte und christlichen Archäologie,* edited by Ernst Dassmann, 195–211. Jahrbuch für Antike und Christentum. Ergänzungsband 3. Münster: 1974.

Klein, Herbert. "Salzburg an der Slawengrenze." *Südostdeutsches Archiv* 11 (1968): 1–14.

Kleinclausz, Arthur. *Charlemagne.* Paris: 1977.

———. *L'empire carolingien: Ses origines et ses transformations.* Paris: 1902.

Klingshirn, William E. *Caesarius of Arles: The Making of a Christian Community in Late Antique Gaul.* Cambridge Studies in Medieval Life and Thought 22. Cambridge: 1994.

———. "Charity and Power: Caesarius of Arles and the Ransoming of Captives in Sub-Roman Gaul." *Journal of Roman Studies* 75 (1985): 183–203.

———. "Defining the *Sortes Sanctorum:* Gibbon, Du Cange, and Early Christian Lot Divination." JECS 10 (2002): 77–130.

Klinkenberg, Hans Martin. "Über karolingische Fürstenspiegel." *Geschichte in Wissenschaft und Unterricht* 7 (1956): 82–98.

Knight, Jeremy K. *The End of Antiquity: Archaeology, Society and Religion A.D. 235–700.* Stroud: 1999.

Kolon, P. Benedikt. *Die Vita S. Hilarii Arelatensis: Eine eidographische Studie.* Rhetorische Studien 12. Paderborn: 1925.

Koselleck, Reinhart. "Social History and *Begriffsgeschichte.*" In *History of Concepts: Comparative Perspectives,* edited by Iain Hampsher-Monk, Karin Tilmans, and Frank Van Vree, 23–35. Amsterdam: 1998.

Krusch, Bruno. *Die Lex Bajuvariorum: Textgeschichte, Handschriftenkritik und Enstehung.* Berlin: 1924.

Kulikowski, Michael. *Late Roman Spain and Its Cities.* Baltimore: 2004.

Kurtscheid, Bertrandus, and Felix Antonius Wilches. *Historia iuris canonici.* 2 vols. Rome: 1943–1951.

L'Orange, H. P. *Studies in the Iconography of Cosmic Kingship in the Ancient World.* Oslo: 1953.

Labhart, Verena. *Zur Rechtssymbolik des Bischofsrings.* Rechtshistorische Arbeiten 2. Cologne: 1963.

Labrousse, Mireille. *Saint Honorat: Fondateur de Lérins et évêque d'Arles.* Bégrolles-en-Mauges: 1995.

Lamberz, Erich. "Studien zur Überlieferung der Akten des VII. Ökumenischen Konzils: Der Brief Hadrians I. an Konstantin VI. und Irene (JE 2448)." DA 53 (1997): 1–43.

Lamoreaux, John C. "Episcopal Courts in Late Antiquity." JECS 3 (1995): 143–67.

Lampe, G. W. H. *The Seal of the Spirit: A Study in the Doctrine of Baptism and Confirmation in the New Testament and the Fathers.* 2nd ed. London: 1967.

Lanoë, Guy. "L'*ordo* de couronnement de Charles le Chauve à Sainte-Croix d'Orléans (6 Juin 848)." In *Kings and Kingship in Medieval Europe,* edited by Anne J. Duggan, 41–68. King's College London Medieval Studies 10. London: 1993.

Lapierre, J.-W. *Essai sur le fondement du pouvoir politique.* Aix-en-Provence: 1968.

Lawrence, C. H. *Medieval Monasticism: Forms of Religious Life in Western Europe in the Middle Ages.* 2nd ed. London: 1989.

Lebecq, Stéphane. "Variations sur l'image du Barbare vu par ses contemporains et par les historiens: le cas Childeric." In *Le Barbare, le primitif, le sauvage: neuf études,* edited by Jacques Boulogne and Jacques Six, 89–108. Études Inter-ethniques New Series 10. Villetaneuse: 1995.

Le Bras, Gabriel. *Études de sociologie religieuse.* 2 vols. Paris: 1955–1956.

———. *Introduction à l'histoire de la pratique religieuse en France.* 2 vols. Paris: 1942–1945.

Leclercq, Jean, F. Vandenbroucke, and L. Bouyer, eds. *A History of Christian Spirituality.* Vol. 2, *The Spirituality of the Middle Ages.* Translated by The Benedictines of Holme Eden Abbey. London: 1968.

Légasse, Simon. *Naissance du baptême.* Lectio divina 153. Paris: 1993.

Le Goff, Jacques. *The Birth of Europe.* Translated by Janet Lloyd. Malden, Mass.: 2005.

———. "Le Christianisme médiéval en occident du Concile de Nicée (325) à la Réforme (début du XVIe siècle)." In *Histoire des religions,* edited by Henri-Charles Puech, 2:749–868. Paris: 1970–1976.

———. "Le roi dans l'occident médiéval: caracteres originaux." In *Kings and Kingship in Medieval Europe,* edited by Anne J. Duggan, 1–39. King's College London Medieval Studies 10. London: 1993.

Lehmann, Paul. "Zur Kenntnis der Schriften des Dionysius Areopagita im Mittelalter." In his *Erforschung des Mittelalters: Ausgewälte Abhandlungen und Aufsätze,* 4:128–41. Stuttgart: 1961.

Le Jan, Régine. "La sacralité de la royauté mérovingienne." *Annales: Histoire, Science Sociales* 58 (2003): 1217–41.

Lesne, Émile. *La Hiérarchie épiscopale: Provinces, métropolitains, primats en Gaule and Germanie 742–882.* Mémoires et travaux des facultés Catholiques de Lille 1. Lille: 1905.

———. *Histoire de la propriété ecclésiastique en France. Vol. 1, Époques Romaine et Merovingienne.* Mémoires et travaux des facultés Catholiques de Lille 4. Lille: 1910.

Letinier, Rosine. "Le rôle politique des conciles de l'Espagne wisigothique." RHDr 75 (1997): 617–26.

Levillain, Louis. "La crise des années 507–508 et les rivalités d'influence en Gaule de 508 à 514." In *Mélanges offerts à M. Nicolas Iorga par ses amis de France et des pays de langue française,* 537–67. Paris: 1933.

———. "Le sacre de Charles le Chauve à Orléans." *Bibliothèque de l'École des chartes* 64 (1903): 31–53.

Levison, Wilhelm. *England and the Continent in the Eighth Century.* Oxford: 1946.

———. "Die Iren und die Fränkische Kirche." HZ 109 (1912): 1–22.

Lévi-Strauss, Claude. *Tristes Tropiques.* Translated by John Weightman and Doreen Weightman. New York: 1975.

Lévy-Bruhl, Lucien. *La Mentalité primitive.* 2nd ed. Paris: 1922.

Leyser, Conrad. *Authority and Asceticism from Augustine to Gregory the Great.* Oxford: 2000.

———. "Expertise and Authority in Gregory the Great: The Social Function of *Peritia.*" *Gregory the Great: A Symposium,* edited by John Cavadini, 38–61. Notre Dame: 1995.

———. "'Let Me Speak, Let Me Speak': Vulnerability and Authority in Gregory's Homilies on Ezekiel." In *Gregorio magno,* 2:169–82.

———. "Shoring Fragments against Ruin? Eugippius and the Sixth-Century Culture of the Florilegium." In *Eugippius und Severin: Der Autor, Der Text und der Heilige,* edited by Walter Pohl and Maximilian Diesenberger, 65–75. Forschungen zur Geschichte des Mittelalters 2. Vienna, 2001.

———. "'This Sainted Isle': Panegyric, Nostalgia, and the Invention of Lerinian Monasticism." In *The Limits of Ancient Christianity: Essays on Late Antique Thought and Culture in Honor of R. A. Markus,* edited by William E. Klingshirn and Mark Vessey, 188–206. Ann Arbor, 1999.

Leyser, Karl J. "Concepts of Europe in the Early and High Middle Ages." *Past and Present* 137 (1992): 25–47.

Lheureux-Godbille, Catherine. "Barbarie et hérésie dans l'oeuvre de saint Ambroise de Milan (374–397)." MA 109 (2003): 473–92.

Lietzmann, Hans. *Mass and Lord's Supper: A Study in the History of the Liturgy.* Translated by Dorothea H. G. Reeve. Leiden: 1972, fasc. 8.

Little, Lester K. *Benedictine Maledictions: Liturgical Cursing in Romanesque France.* Ithaca: 1993.

Lizzi, Rita. "I vescovi e i *potentes* della terra: definizione e limite del ruolo episcopale nelle due *partes imperii* fra IV e V secolo d.c." In *L'Évêque dans la cité du IVe au Ve siècle: Image et autorité,* edited by E. Robillard and C. Sotinell, 81–104. Rome, 1987.

Llewellyn, Peter. "Le contexte romain du couronnement de Charlemagne: Le temps de l'Avent de l'année 800." MA 96. 5th ser. 4 (1990): 209–25.

Loenertz, Raymond J. "*Constitutum Constantini:* Destination, destinataires, auteur, date." *Aevum* 48 (1974): 199–245.

———. "En marge de Constitutum Constantini: Contribution à l'histoire du texte." *Revue des sciences philosophiques et théologiques* 59 (1975): 289–94.

Loseby, S. T. "Bishops and Cathedrals: Order and Diversity in the Fifth-Century Urban Landscape of Southern Gaul." In *Fifth-Century Gaul: A Crisis of Identity?* edited by John Drinkwater and Hugh Elton, 144–55. Cambridge: 1992.

Lot, Ferdinand, and Louis Halphen. *Le règne de Charles le Chauve (840–877). Part 1, 840–851.* Paris: 1909.

Louth, Andrew. *Denys the Areopagite.* Wilton, Conn.: 1989.

Loyen, André. "Les débuts du royaume wisigoth de Toulouse." *Revue des études latines* 12 (1934): 406–15.

———. "Le rôle de saint Aignan dans la défense d'Orléans." *Comptes rendus de l'Académie des Inscriptions et Belles-Lettres* (1969): 64–74.

Lupoi, Maurizio. *The Origins of the European Legal Order.* Translated by Adrian Belton. Cambridge: 2000.

Maassen, Friedrich. *Geschichte der Quellen und der Literatur des canonischen Rechts im Abendlande bis zum Ausgang der Mittelalters.* Vol. 1, 1870. Reprinted Graz: 1956. Only Vol. 1 was ever published.

Mabillon, Jean. *De liturgia gallicana libri tres.* Paris: 1685. Reprinted in PL 72: 99–448.

———. *De re diplomatica libri VI* (Paris: 1681)

Macaigne, R. *L'Église mérovingienne et l'état pontifical.* Paris: 1929.

MacCormack, Sabine G. *Art and Ceremony in Late Antiquity*. Berkeley: 1981.

———. "Loca Sancta: The Organization of Sacred Topography in Late Antiquity." In *The Blessings of Pilgrimage*, edited by R. Ousterhout, 7–40. Illinois Byzantine Studies 1. Urbana: 1990.

Machiavelli, Niccolò. *Arte della guerra e scritti politici minor*. Edited by S. Bertelli. Milan: 1961.

MacMullen, Ramsay. *Christianity and Paganism in the Fourth to Eighth Centuries*. New Haven: 1997.

Magnou-Nortier, Élisabeth. "La christianisation de la Gaule (VIe–VIIe siècles): Esquisse d'un bilan et orientation bibliographique." MScR 53 (1996): 5–12 [*Christianisation en Gaule de Clovis à Charlemagne*].

———. "Les évêques et la paix dans l'espace franc (VIe–XIe siècles)." In *L'Éveque dans l'histoire de l'Église. Actes de la 7me rencontre d'histoire religieuse—Fontevrault Abbey*, 33–50. Angers: 1984.

———. "Remarques sur la genèse du *Pactus Legis Salicae* et sur le privilège d'immunité (IVe–VII siècles)." In *Clovis*, 1:495–538.

———. "La tentative de subversion de l'État sous Louis le Pieux et l'oeuvre des falsificateurs." MA 105 (1999): 1:331–365; MA 105 (1999): 2:615–41.

Maisonneuve, Henri. *La Morale chrétienne d'après le conciles des Xe et XIe siècles*. Analecta Mediaevalia Namurcensia 15. Louvain: 1962.

Mâle, Émile. *La fin du paganisme en Gaule et les plus anciennes basiliques chrétiennes*. Paris: 1950.

Malingrey, Anne-Marie. *La littérature greque chrétienne*. Paris: 1996.

Mane, P. "Émergence du vêtement de travail à travers l'iconographie médiévale." In *Vêtement*, 93–122.

Marcone, Arnaldo. "Late Roman Social Relations." In *The Cambridge Ancient History*. Vol 13, *The Late Empire, A.D. 337–425*, edited by Averil Cameron and Peter Garnsey, 338–70. Cambridge, 1998.

Marenbon, John. "Alcuin, the Council of Frankfort, and the Beginnings of Medieval Philosophy." In *Frankfurter Konzil*, 2:603–15.

Markus, Robert A. "From Caesarius to Boniface: Christianity and Paganism in Gaul." In *Septième siècle*, 154–72.

———. *Gregory the Great and His World*. Cambridge: 1997.

———. "The Sacred and the Secular: From Augustine to Gregory the Great." JTS 36 (1985): 84–96.

———. *Saeculum: History and Society in the Theology of St. Augustine*. Cambridge: 1970.

Marriott, Wharton B. *Vestiarum Christianum: The Origin and Gradual Development of the Dress of Holy Ministry in the Church*. London: 1868.

Martindale, J. R. *The Prosopography of the Later Roman Empire*. Vol. 3a. Cambridge: 1992.

Mathisen, Ralph W. "D'Aire-sur l'Adour à Agde: Les relations entre la lois séculière et la loi canonique à la fin du royaume de Toulouse." In *Bréviaire d'Alaric: Aux origines du Code civil*, edited by Michel Rouche and Bruno Dumézil, 41–52. Paris: 2008.

———. "Barbarian Bishops and the Churches 'in barbaricis gentibus' during Late Antiquity." *Speculum* 72 (1997): 664–95.

———. "Clovis, Anastase et Grégoire de Tours: consul, patrice et roi." In *Clovis,* 1:395–407.

———. *Ecclesiastical Factionalism and Religious Controversy in Fifth-Century Gaul.* Washington, D.C.: 1989.

———. "Hilarius, Germanus and Lupus: The Aristocratic Background of the Chelidonius Affair." *Phoenix* 33 (Toronto: 1979): 160–69.

———. *Roman Aristocrats in Barbarian Gaul: Strategies for Survival in an Age of Transition.* Austin: 1993.

———. "The 'Second Council of Arles' and the Spirit of Compilation and Codification in Late Roman Gaul." JECS 5 (1997): 511–54.

Matthews, John F. *Laying Down the Law: A Study of the Theodosian Code.* New Haven: 2000.

———. *The Roman Empire of Ammianus.* Baltimore: 1989.

———. *Western Aristocracies and Imperial Court, A.D. 364–425.* Oxford: 1975.

Maurer, E. M. "Symbol and Identification in North American Indian Clothing." In *The Fabrics of Culture,* 119–42.

Maurin, Louis, and Jean-Luc Boudartchouk. *Province ecclésiastique d'Eauze (Novempopulana).* TCCG 13. Paris: 2004.

Mauss, Marcel. "Une catégorie de l'esprit humain: la notion de personne, celle du 'moi': Un plan de travail." Huxley Memorial Lecture 1938. *Journal of the Royal Anthropological Institute* 68 (1938): 263–81.

———. "Fait social et formation du caractère (1938): Notes inédites de Marcel Mauss transcrites et présentées par Marcel Fournier." *L'ethnographie* 93 (1997): 7–14.

———. "Théorie générale de la magie." See Hubert, Henri.

Mayer, Theodor. "Der Vertrag von Verdun." In *Vertrag von Verdun,* 5–30.

Mayer, Theodor, ed. *Der Vertrag von Verdun 843: Neuen Aufsätze zur Begründung der europäischen Völker- und Staatenwelt.* Leipzig: 1943.

Mayr-Harting, Henry. "Charlemagne, the Saxons, and the Imperial Coronation of 800." EHR 111 (1996): 1113–33.

Mazzini, I. M. "Lettura del concilio di Arles." VC 27 (1973): 282–300.

McCormick, Michael. "Clovis at Tours, Byzantine Public Ritual and the Origins of Medieval Ruler Symbolism." In *Das Reich und die Barbaren,* edited by Evangelos K. Chrysos and Adreas Schwarcz, 155–80. Vienna: 1989.

———. *Eternal Victory: Triumphal Rulership in Late Antiquity, Byzantium and the Early Medieval West.* Cambridge: 1986.

———. "The Liturgy of War in the Early Middle Ages: Crisis, Litanies, and the Carolingian Monarchy." *Viator* 15 (1984): 1–23.

———. "An Unknown Seventh-Century Manuscript of the Lex romana Visigothorum." *Bulletin of Medieval Canon Law* New Series 6 (1976): 1–13.

McKenzie, J. L. *Dictionary of the Bible.* New York: 1965.

McKeon, Peter. "817: Une année désastreuse et presque fatale pour les Carolingiens." MA 84. 4th ser. 33 (1978): 5–12.

————. "The Empire of Louis the Pious: Faith, Politics and Personality." RB 90 (1980): 50–62.

McKitterick, Rosamond. *The Carolingians and the Written Word.* Cambridge: 1989.

————. *The Frankish Kingdoms under the Carolingians, 751–987.* London: 1983.

————. *History and Memory in the Carolingian World.* Cambridge: 2004.

————. "The Illusion of Royal Power in the Carolingian Annals." EHR 115 (2000): 1–20.

————. "Knowledge of Canon Law in the Frankish Kingdoms before 789: The Manuscript Evidence." JTS 36 (1985): 97–117.

McLynn, N. B. *Ambrose of Milan: Church and Court in a Christian Capital.* Transformations of the Classical Heritage 22. Berkeley: 1994.

McNally, R. "Christus in the pseudo-Isidorian *Liber de ortu et obitu patriarchum.*" *Traditio* 21 (1965): 167–83.

Meens, Rob. "Paenitentia publica en paenitentia privata: Aantekeningen bij de oorsprong van de zogeheten Karolingische dichotomie." In *Die Fonteyn der Ewiger Wijsheit: Opstellen aangeboden aan prof. dr A. G. Weiler,* edited by P. Bange and P. M. J. C. de Kort, 65–73. Middeleeuwse Studies 5. Nijmegen: 1989.

Mikat, Paul. "Zu Bedingungen des frühchristlichen Kirchenrechts." ZSRG.K 64 (1978): 309–20.

Minnerath, Roland. *Histoire des conciles.* Paris: 1996.

Mitchell, L. L. *Baptismal Anointing.* Alcuin Club Collections 48. London: 1966.

Modzelewski, Karol. "*Legem ipsam vetare non possumus:* Il re codificatore dinanzi alla forza della consuetudine." *Bulletino dell'Istituto storico italiano per il Medio Evo* 101 (1997–1998): 1–12.

Mohrmann, Christine. *Liturgical Latin, its Origins and Character: Three Lectures.* Washington, D.C.: 1957.

Mollat, Michel. *The Poor in the Middle Ages: An Essay in Social History.* Translated by Arthur Goldhammer. New Haven: 1986.

Mommsen, Theodor E. "St. Augustine and the Christian Idea of Progress: The Background of the City of God." In his *Medieval and Renaissance Studies,* edited by Eugene F. Rice, Jr., 265–98. Ithaca: 1959.

Monachino, Vincenzo. *S. Ambrogio e la cura pastorale a Milano nel secolo IV.* Milan: 1973.

Monod, Gabriel. *Études critiques sur les sources de l'histoire mérovingienne: Première partie. Introduction—Grégoire de Tours—Marius d'Avenches.* Paris: 1872.

Moore, Michael Edward. "The Ancient Fathers: Christian Antiquity, Patristics and Frankish Canon Law." In *Millenium: Jahrbuch zu Kultur und Geschichte des ersten Jahrtausends n. Chr./Yearbook on the Culture and History of the First Millennium C.E.,* 7 (2010): 293–342.

————. "Bede's Devotion to Rome: The Periphery Defining the Center." In *Bède le Vénérable entre tradition et postérité,* edited by Stephane Lebecq, Michel Perrin and Olivier Szerwiniack, 199–208. Lille: 2005.

————. "Carolingian Bishops and Christian Antiquity: Distance from the Past. Canon-Formation. and Imperial Power." In *Learned Antiquity: Scholarship and So-*

ciety in the Near-East, the Greco-Roman World, and the Early Medieval West, edited by Alaisdair A. MacDonald, Michael W. Twomey, and Gerrit J. Reinink, 75–184. Leuven: 2003.

———. "The King's New Clothes: Royal and Episcopal Regalia in the Frankish Empire." In *Robes and Honor: The Medieval World of Investiture,* edited by Stewart Gordon, 95–135. New York: 2000.

———. "La monarchie carolingienne et les anciens modèles irlandais." *Annales* 51 (1996): 307–32.

———. "The Spirit of the Gallican Councils." AHC 39 (2007): 1–52.

Moorhead, John. *Ambrose: Church and Society in the Late Roman World.* London: 1999.

———. *The Roman Empire Divided.* Harlow: 2001.

Mordek, Hubert. "Dionysio-Hadriana und Vetus Gallica—historische geordnetes und systematisches Kirchenrecht am Hofe Karls des Grossen." ZSRG.K 55 (1969): 39–63.

———. "Il diritto canonico fra tardo antico e alto medioevo." In *La cultura in Italia fra tardo antico e alto medioevo,* 1:149–164. Rome: 1981.

———. "Kanonistische Aktivität in Gallien in der ersten Hälfte des 8. Jahrhunderts: Eine Skizze." *Francia* 2 (1974): 19–25.

———. "Kapitularien und Schriftlichkeit." In *Schriftkultur und Reichsverwaltung unter den Karolingern: Referate des Kolloquium der Nordrhein-Westfälischen Akademie der Wissenschaften am 17./18. Februar 1994 in Bonn,* edited by Rudolf Schieffer, 34–66. Abhandlungen der Nordrhein-Westfälischen Akademie der Wissenschaften 97. Opladen: 1995.

———. "Karolingische Kapitularien." In *Überlieferung und Geltung normativer Texte des frühen und hohen Mittelalters: Vier Vorträge, gehalten auf dem 35. deutschen Historikertag 1984 in Berlin,* edited by Hubert Mordek, 25–50. Quellen und Forschungen zum Recht im Mittelalter 4. Sigmaringen: 1986.

———. *Kirchenrecht und Reform im Frankenreich: Die Collectio vetus Gallica: die älteste systematische Kanonensammlung des fränkischen Gallien: Studien und Edition.* Berlin: 1975.

———. "Kirchenrechtliche Autoritäten im Frühmittelalter." In *Recht und Schrift im Mittelalter,* edited by Peter Classen, 237–55. Vorträge und Forschungen 23. Sigmaringen: 1977.

Moreau, Jacques. "La lutte entre le christianisme et le paganisme gréco-romain dans la Guale du nord-est." In *Rome et le christianisme dans la région rhenane: Colloque du Centre de recherches d'histoire des religions de l'Université de Strasbourg, 19–21 mai, 1960,* 109–26. Paris: 1963.

Moreira, Isabel. *Dreams, Visions, and Spiritual Authority in Merovingian Gaul.* Ithaca: 2000.

Morhain, E. "Origines et histoire de la Regula Canonicorum de S. Chrodegang." In *Miscellanea Pio Paschini: Studia di storia ecclesiastica,* 1:175. Rome: 1948.

Morton, Catherine. "Marius of Avenches, the 'Excerpta Valesiana,' and the Death of Boethius." *Traditio* 38 (1982): 107–36.

Munier, Charles. "L'Ordo *De celebrando concilio* wisigothique." *Revue des sciences religieuses* 37 (1963): 250–71.

———. *Les Statuta ecclesiae antiqua.* Paris: 1960.

Murray, Alexander Callander, ed. *After Rome's Fall: Narrators and Sources of Early Medieval History: Essays Presented to Walter Goffart.* Toronto: 1998.

———. "Immunity, Nobility, and the Edict of Paris." *Speculum* 69 (1994): 18–39.

———. "Post vocantur Merohingii: Fredegar, Merovech, and 'Sacral Kingship.'" In *After Rome's Fall,* 121–52.

Nathan, Geoffrey. "The Rogation Ceremonies of Late Antique Gaul: Creation, Transmission and the Role of the Bishop." *Classica et Mediaevalia* 49 (1998): 275–303.

Nelson, Janet L. *Charles the Bald.* London: 1992.

———. "The Intellectual in Politics: Context, Content and Authorship in the Capitulary of Coulaines, November 843." In *Intellectual Life in the Middle Ages: Essays Presented to Margaret Gibson,* edited by Lesley Smith and Benedicta Ward, 1–14. London, 1992.

———. "Kingship, Law and Liturgy in the Political Thought of Hincmar of Rheims." In her *Politics and Ritual,* 133–71.

———. "The Last Years of Louis the Pious." In *Charlemagne's Heir,* 147–59.

———. "Making Ends Meet: Wealth and Poverty in the Carolingian Church." In *The Church and Wealth,* edited by W. J. Sheils and Diana Wood, 25–35. London: 1987.

———. "National Synods, Kingship as Office, and Royal Anointing: An Early Medieval Syndrome." In her *Politics and Ritual,* 239–57.

———. "On the Limits of the Carolingian Renaissance." In her *Politics and Ritual,* 49–67.

———. *Politics and Ritual in Early Medieval Europe.* London: 1986.

———. "Public *Histories* and Private History in the Work of Nithard." In her *Politics and Ritual,* 195–237.

———. "Symbols in Context: Rulers' Inauguration Rituals in Byzantium and the West in the Early Middle Ages." In her *Politics and Ritual,* 259–307.

Nicholas, Barry. *An Introduction to Roman Law.* Oxford: 1962.

Noble, T. F. X. "The Monastic Ideal as a Model for Empire: The Case of Louis the Pious." RB 86 (1976): 235–50.

———. *The Republic of St. Peter: The Birth of the Papal State, 680–825.* Philadelphia: 1984.

———. "The Revolt of King Bernard of Italy in 817: Its Causes and Consequences." SM Ser. 3.15 (1974): 315–26.

Noche, Carla. *Vestis Varia: L'immagine della veste nell'opera di Origene.* Studia Ephemeridis Augustinianum 79. Rome: 2002.

Ntedika. J. *L'Évocation de l'au-delà dans la prière pour les morts: Étude de patristique et de liturgie latines (IVe–VIIIe s.).* Recherches africaines de théologie 2. Louvain: 1971.

Oakley, Francis. *Kingship: The Politics of Enchantment.* Oxford: 2006.

Ó Cróinin, Dáibhi. *Early Medieval Ireland.* London: 1995.

Ohme, Heinz. "Ikonen, historische Kritik und Tradition: Das VII. ökumenische Konzil (787) und die kirchliche Überlieferung." ZKG 110 (1999): 1–24.

Ohnsorge, Werner. "Orthodoxus Imperator: Vom religiösen Motiv für das Kaisertum

Karls des Grossen." In his *Abendland und Byzanz: Gesammelte Aufsätze zur Geschichte der byzantinisch- abendländischen Beziehungen und des Kaisertums,* 64–78. Darmstadt: 1958.

Oldoni, Massimo. "Gregorio di Tours e i 'Libri Historiarum': Le fonti scritte." In *Gregorio di Tours,* 251–324. Convegni del centro di studi sulla spiritualità medievale 12. Spoleto: 1977.

Orlandis, José. "Bible et royauté dans les conciles de l'Espagne wisigotho-catholique." AHC 18 (1986): 51–57.

———. *La conversión de Europa al Cristianismo.* Madrid: 1988.

Orlandis, José, and D. Ramos-Lisson. *Die Synoden auf der Iberischen Halbinsel bis zum Einbruch des Islam (711).* Konziliengeschichte Reihe A: Darstellung. Paderborn: 1981.

Orselli, Alba Maria. "Controversia iconoclastica e crisi del simbolismo in occidente fra VIII e IX secolo." In *Culto delle immagini e crisi iconoclasta,* 93–116. Palermo: 1986.

Ostrogorsky, George. *History of the Byzantine State.* Translated by J. Hussey. Oxford: 1968.

Otto, Rudolf. *The Idea of the Holy: An Inquiry into the Non-Rational Factor in the Idea of the Divine and its Relation to the Rational.* Translated by John W. Harvey. Oxford: 1931.

Ozoline, Anastasia. *Trésors de la Gaule chrétienne: Histoire et restauration des reliques textiles de saint Césaire d'Arles (470–542).* Arles: 2008.

Palanque, J.-R. "La date du transfert de la préfecture des Gaules de Trèves à Arles." *Revue des études anciennes* 36 (1934): 359–65.

———. "Du nouveau sur la date du transfert de la préfecture des Gaules de Trèves à Arles?" *Provence historique* 23 (1973): 29–38.

Pardessus, Jean Marie. *Loi salique ou recueil contenant les anciennes rédactions de cette loi et le texte connu sous le nom de Lex emendate.* Paris: 1843.

Parsons, David. "Some Churches of the Anglo-Saxon Missionaries in Southern Germany: A Review of the Evidence." EME 8 (1999): 31–67.

Paschoud, François. "Le mythe de Rome à la fin de l'empire et dans les royaumes romano-barbares." In *Passaggio dal mondo antico,* 123–38.

Passaggio dal mondo antico al medio evo da Teodosio a san Gregorio Magno (Rome: April 25–28, 1977). Atti dei convegni Lincei 45. Rome: 1980.

Pastoureau, M., ed. *Le Vêtement: Histoire, archéologie, et symbolique vestimentaires au moyen âge.* Paris: 1989.

Patzold, Steffen. *Episcopus: Wissen über Bischöfe im Frankenreich des späten 8. bis frühen 10. Jahrhunderts.* Mittelalter-Forschungen 25. Ostfildern: 2008.

Paxton, Frederick S. *Christianizing Death: The Creation of a Ritual Process in Early Medieval Europe.* Ithaca: 1990.

Pearson, Kathy Lynne Roper. *Conflicting Loyalties in Early Medieval Bavaria: A View of Socio-Political Interaction, 680–900.* Aldershot: 1999.

Pelikan, Jaroslav. *The Christian Tradition: A History of the Development of Doctrine.* Vol. 1, *The Emergence of the Catholic Tradition (100–600).* Chicago: 1971.

Pelliciari, Luisa. *Sulla natura giuridica dei rapporti tra Visigoti e impero romano al tempo*

delle invasioni del Vo secolo. Publicazioni della facoltà de giurisprudenza della università di Modena 3. Milan: 1982.

Penco, Gregorio. "Monasterium—Carcer." *Studia Monastica* 8 (1966): 133–43.

Peters, Edward. *The Shadow King: Rex Inutilis in Medieval Law and Literature 751–
1327.* New Haven: 1970.

Pétrau-Gay, Jean. *La notion de "lex" dans la coutume salienne et ses transformations dans
les capitulaires.* Grenoble: 1920.

Pétychaki-Henze, Maria. "Les fonctions sociales des mythes politiques." In *Mythe et
politique: Actes du Colloque de Liège 14–16 septembre 1989,* edited by François Jouan
and André Motte, 249–59. Liège: 1990.

Philippson, Paula. "Genealogie als mythische Form (Studien zur Theogonie des Hesiod)." In her *Untersuchungen über den Griechischen Mythos,* 7–42. Zurich: 1944.

Pietri, Charles. "L'espace chrétien dans la cité: Le *vicus christianorum* et l'espace chrétien de la cité Averne (Clermont)." RHEF 66 (1980): 177–209.

———. "La politique de Constance II: Un premier 'césaropapisme' ou l'*Imitatio Constantini.*" In *Christiana Respublica: Éléments d'une enquête sur le christianisme
antique,* 1:281–346. 3 vols. Collection de l'École française de Rome 234. Rome:
1997.

———. *Roma Christiana: Recherches sur l'Église de Rome, son organisation, sa politique,
son idéologie de Miltiade à Sixte III (311–440).* Bibliothèque des Écoles françaises
d'Athènes et de Rome 224. 2 vols. Rome: 1976.

Pietri, Luce. *La ville de Tours du IVe au VIe siècle: Naissance d'une cité chrétienne.* Collection de l'École française de Rome 69. Rome: 1983.

Plumpe, Joseph C. "Pomeriana." VC 1 (1947): 227–39.

Pohl, Walter. "Tradition, Ethnogenese und literarische Gestaltung: Eine Zwischenbilanz." In *Ethnogenese und Überlieferung,* 9–26.

Pontal, Odette. *Histoire des conciles mérovingiens.* Paris: 1989.

Porter, W. S. *The Gallican Rite.* London: 1958.

Prévot, Françoise. "Sidoine Apollinaire et l'Auvergne." RHEF 79, no. 203 (1993): 243–59.

Pricoco, Salvatore. *L'isola dei santi: Il cenobio di Lerino e le origini del monachesimo gallico.* Filologia e critica 23. Rome: 1978.

Prigent, Pierre. *Apocalypse et liturgie.* Cahiers théologiques 52. Paris: 1964.

Prinz, Friedrich. "Aristocracy and Christianity in Merovingian Gaul: An Essay." In
*Gesellschaft—Kultur—Literatur: Rezeption und Originalität im wachsen einer eu-
ropäischen Literatur und Geistigkeit. Beiträge Luitpold Wallach gewidmet,* edited by
Karl Bosl, 153–65. Monographien zur Geschichte des Mittelalters 11. Stuttgart: 1975.

———. "Die bischöfliche Stadtherrschaft im Frankenreich vom 5. bis zum 7. Jahrhundert." HZ 217 (1973): 1–35.

———. "Der fränkische Episkopat zwischen Merowinger- und Karolingerzeit." *Settimane* 27 (1981) 1:102–33.

———. *Frühes Mönchtum im Frankenreich: Kultur und Gesellschaft in Gallien, den Rheinlanden und Bayern am Beispiel der monastischen Entwicklung (4. bis 8. Jahrhundert).* Munich: 1965.

————. *Herrschaft und Kirche: Beiträge zur Entstehung und Wirkungsweise episkopaler und monastischer Organisationsformen.* Stuttgart: 1988.

————. "King, Clergy and War at the Time of the Carolingians." In *Saints, Scholars, and Heroes: Studies in Medieval Culture in Honor of Chas. W. Jones,* edited by M. King and W. Stevens, 1:301–29. Collegeville: 1979.

————. *Klerus und Krieg im früheren Mittelalter: Untersuchungen zur Rolle der Kirche beim Aufbau der Königsherrschaft.* Monographien zur Geschichte des Mittelalters 2. Stuttgart: 1971.

————. "Il monachesimo occidentale." In *Passaggio dal mondo antico,* 415–34.

————. "Monastische Zentren im Frankenreich." SM. Ser. 3.19 (1978): 571–90.

Quesnel, Pasquier. *Ad S. Leonis Magni Opera Appendix 2.* Paris: 1675.

Ramelli, Ilaria. "Alcune osservazioni sulle origini del cristianesimo in Spagna: la tradizione patristica." *Vetera Christianorum* 35 (1998): 245–56.

Ramsey, Boniface. *Ambrose.* London: 1997.

Rapp, Claudia. *Holy Bishops in Late Antiquity: The Nature of Christian Leadership in an Age of Transition.* Berkeley: 2005.

Reallexikon der germanischen Altertumskunde. 18 vols. Berlin: 1973–.

Reimitz, Helmut. "*Omnes Franci:* Identifications and Identities of the Early Medieval Franks." In *Franks, Northmen, and Slavs: Identities and State Formation in Early Medieval Europe,* edited by Ildar H. Garipzanov, Patrick J. Geary, and Przemslaw Urbanczyk, 51–68 (Turnhout: 2008).

Reuter, Timothy. "The End of Carolingian Military Expansion." In *Charlemagne's Heir,* 391–405.

————. "Plunder and Tribute in the Carolingian Empire." *Transactions of the Royal Historical Society* 5th ser. 35 (1985): 75–94.

Reydellet, Marc. "Pensée et pratique politiques chez Grégoire de Tours." In *Gregorio di Tours,* 173–205. Convegni del centro di studi sulla spiritualità medievale 12. Spoleto: 1977.

————. *La Royauté dans la littérature latine de Sidoine Apollinaire à Isidore de Séville.* Bibliothèque des Écoles Françaises d'Athènes et de Rome 243. Rome: 1981.

Reynolds, Roger E. "The Pseudo-Hieronymian 'De septem ordinibus ecclesiae': Notes on its Origins, Abridgments, and Use in Early Medieval Canonical Collections." RB 80 (1970): 238–52.

————. "The Visigothic Liturgy in the Realm of Charlemagne." In *Frankfurter Konzil,* 2:919–45.

Reynolds, Susan. *Fiefs and Vassals: The Medieval Evidence Reinterpreted.* Oxford: 1994.

————. "Our Forefathers? Tribes, Peoples, and Nations in the Historiography of the Age of Migrations." In *After Rome's Fall: Narrators and Sources of Early Medieval History—Essays Presented to Walter Goffart,* edited by Alexander Callander Murray, 17–36 (Toronto: 1998).

Reznikoff, Iégor. "Le chant des gaules sous les carolingiens." In *Haut moyen-âge: Culture, éducation et société: Études offertes à Pierre Riché,* edited by Michel Sot, 323–42. La Garenne–Colombes: 1990.

Richard, R. P. Ch.-L. *Analyse des conciles généraux et particuliers, contenant leurs canons sur le dogme, la morale, et la discipline tant ancienne que moderne.* 4 vols. Paris: 1772.

Riché, Pierre. *The Carolingians: A Family who Forged Europe.* Translated by Michael Idomir Allen. Philadelphia: 1993.

———. "Les centres de culture en Neustrie de 650 à 850." In *La Neustrie,* 2:297–305.

———. *Éducation et culture dans l'Occident barbare. Vie–VIIIe siècle.* Paris: 1995.

———. "Le renouveau culturel à la cour de Pepin III." *Francia* 2 (1974): 59–70.

Ricoeur, Paul. "Ipséité, altérité, socialité." *Archivio di filosofia* 54 (1986): 17–33.

Ritter, Hans Werner. *Diadem und Königsherrschaft: Untersuchungen zu Zeremonien und Rechtsgrundlagen des Herrschaftsantritts bei den Persern, bei Alexander dem Grossen und im Hellenismus.* Vestigia 7. Munich: 1965.

Roach, M. E., and J. B. Eicher. "The Language of Personal Adornment." In *The Fabrics of Culture,* 7–21.

Rose, Els. "Liturgical Commemoration of the Saints in the *Missale Gothicum* (Vat. Reg. Lat. 317): New Approaches to the Liturgy of Early Medieval Gaul." VC 58 (2004): 75–97.

———. "Liturgical Latin in the Bobbio Missal." In *The Bobbio Missal: Liturgy and Religious Culture in Merovingian Gaul,* edited by Yizhak Hen and Rob Meens, 67–78. Cambridge: 2004.

———. "Liturgical Latin in the *Missale Gothicum* (Vat. Reg. lat. 317): A Reconsideration of Christine Mohrmann's Approach." *Sacris Erudiri* 42 (2003): 97–121.

Rosenwein, Barbara. *Negotiating Space: Power, Restraint, and Privileges of Immunity in Early Medieval Europe.* Ithaca: 1999.

———. "Worrying about Emotions in History." *American Historical Review* 107 (2002): 821–45.

Rouche, Michel, and Bruno Dumézil, eds. *Le Bréviaire d'Alaric: Aux origines du Code civil.* Paris: 2008.

Rousseau, Philip. *Ascetics, Authority, and the Church in the Age of Jerome and Cassian.* Oxford: 1978.

———. "In Search of Sidonius the Bishop." *Historia* 25 (1976): 356–77.

Ruggini, Lellia Cracco. "Prêtre et fonctionnaire: L'essor d'un modèle épiscopal aux IVe–Ve siècles." *Antiquité tardive—Antigüedad Tardía—Late Antiquity—Spätantike—Tarda Antichità* 7 (1999): 175–86.

Russell, James C. *The Germanization of Early Medieval Christianity: A Sociohistorical Approach to Religious Transformation.* New York, 1994.

Rydén, L. "The Role of the Icon in Byzantine Piety." In *Religious Symbols and their Functions,* edited by H. Biezais, 41–52. Scripta Instituti Donneriani Aboensis 10. Stockholm, 1979.

Sagüés, J. G. "La doctrina del Cuerpo mistico en San Isidoro." *Estudios eclesiásticos* 17 (1943): 227–257, 329–360, and 517–546.

Saramago, José. *The History of the Siege of Lisbon.* Translated by Giovanni Pontiero. New York: 1989.

Saupe, Heinrich Albin. *Der indiculus superstitionum et paganiarum: Ein Verzeichnis heidnischer und abergläubischer Gebräuche und Meinungen aus der Zeit Karls der Grossen, aus zumeist gleichzeitigen Schriften erläutert.* Program des städtischen Realgymnasiums 551. Leipzig: 1891, 3–34.

Sawyer, P. H., and I. N. Wood, ed. *Early Medieval Kingship.* Leeds: 1979.

Schäferdiek, Knut. "Der adoptianische Streit im Rahmen der spanischen Kirchengeschichte." Part I—ZKG 80 (1969): 291–311; Part II—ZKG 81 (1970): 1–16.

———. *Die Kirche in den Reichen der Westgoten un Suewen bis zur Errichtung der westgotischen katholischen Staatskirche.* Arbeiten zur Kirchengeschichte 39. Berlin: 1967.

———. "Das sogenannte zweite Konzil von Arles und die älteste Kanonessammlung der arelatenser Kirche." ZSRG.K 71 (1985): 1–19.

Schapiro, Meyer. *Words and Pictures: On the Literal and the Symbolic in the Illustration of a Text.* Approaches to Semiotics Paperback Series 11. The Hague: 1973.

Schatz, Klaus. "Œcuménicité du concile et structure de l'Église à Nicée II et dans les Livres Carolins." In *Nicée II,* 263–270.

Scheibelreiter, Georg. *Der Bischof in merowingischer Zeit.* Veröffentlichungen des Instituts für österreichische Geschichtsforschung 27. Vienna: 1983.

Schieffer, Rudolf. "Spätantikes Kirchenrecht in einer rätischen Sammlung des 8. Jahrhunderts." ZSRG.K 66 (1980): 164–91.

———. "Zwei karolingische Texte über das Königtum." DA 46 (1990): 1–17.

Schieffer, Theodor. "Die Krise des karolingischen Imperiums." In *Aus Mittelalter und Neuzeit: Festschrift für G. Kallen,* edited by Josef Engel and Hans Martin Klinkenberg, 1–15. Bonn: 1957.

———. *Winfrid-Bonifatius und die christliche Grundlegung Europas.* 2nd ed. Darmstadt: 1980.

Schlesinger, Walter. "Zur politischen Geschichte der fränkischen Ostbewegung vor Karl dem Grossen." In his *Althessen im Frankenreich,* 9–6. Nationes 2. Sigmaringen: 1975.

Schmidt-Wiegand, Ruth. *Fränkische und frankolateinische Bezeichnungen für sociale Schichten und Gruppen in der Lex Salica.* Nachrichten der Akademie der wissenschaften in Göttingen, philologisch-historische Klasse, Jahrg. 1972, no. 4. Göttingen: 1972.

Schmitt, Jean-Claude. *La raison des gestes dans l'Occident médiéval.* Paris: 1990.

Schmitz, Gerhard. "Echte Quellen—falsche Quellen. Müssen zentrale Quellen aus der Zeit Ludwigs des Frommen neu bewertet werden?" In *Von Sacerdotium und Regnum: Geistliche und weltliche Gewalt im frühen und hohen Mittelalter—Festschrift für Egon Boshof,* edited by Franz-Reiner Erkens and Hartmut Wollf, 275–300. Cologne, 2002.

Scholz, Sebastian. "Die Rolle der Bischöfe auf den Synoden von Rome (313) und Arles (314)." In *Köln: Stadt und Bistum in Kirche und Reich des Mittelalters. Festschrift für Odilo Engels zum 65. Geburtstag,* 1–21. Kölner historische Abhandlungen 39. Cologne: 1993.

Schramm, Percy Ernst. *Herrschaftszeichen und Staatssymbolik: Beiträge zu ihrer Geschichte vom dritten bis zum sechzehnten Jahrhundert.* Schriften der Monumenta Germaniae historica 13. 3 vols. Stuttgart: 1954–1956.

Schröder, Franz Rolf. *Germanentum und Hellenismus: Untersuchungen zur germanisch-en Religionsgeschichte.* Heidelberg: 1924.

Schüssler, Heinz Joachim. "Die fränkische Reichsteilung von Vieux-Poitiers (741) und die Reform der Kirche in den Teilreichen Karlmanns und Pippins. Zu den Grenzen der Wirksamkeit des Bonifatius." *Francia* 13 (1985): 47–112.

Schutz, Herbert. *The Carolingians in Central Europe, their History, Arts and Architecture: A Cultural History of Central Europe, 750–900.* Cultures, Beliefs and Traditions 18. Leiden, 2004.

Schwartz, Eduard. *Aus den Akten des Concils von Chalkedon.* Abhandlungen der Bayerischen Akademie der Wissenschaften, Philosophisch-philologische und historische Klasse 32/2. Munich: 1925.

———. *Kaiser Constantin und die Christliche Kirche: Fünf Vorträge.* Leipzig: 1913.

Selb, Walter. "Episcopalis audientia von der Zeit Konstantins bis zur Nov. XXXV Valentiniens II." *ZSRG.R* 84 (1967): 162–217.

Sellert, Wolfgang. "Aufzeichnung des Rechts und Gesetz." In *Das Gesetz in Spätantike und Frühen Mittelalter,* edited by W. Sellert, 67–102. Abhandlungen der Akademie der Wissenschaften in Göttingen, Phil.-hist. Klasse, 3rd Folge 196. Göttingen: 1992.

Semmler, Josef. "Die Aufrichtung der karolingischen Herrschaft im nördlichen Burgund im VIIIe Jahrhundert." In *Langres et ses évêques. VIIIe–XIe siècles: aux origines d'une seigneurie ecclésiastique: actes du colloque Langres-Ellwangen 28 Juin 1985,* edited by J. Semmler, 19–41. Langres: 1986.

———. "Benedictus II: Una regula—una consuetudo." In *Benedictine Culture 750–1050,* edited by W. Lourdaux and D. Verhelst, 1–49. Mediaevalia Lovaniensia Ser. 1, Studia 11. Louvain, 1983.

———. "Die Beschlüsse des Aachener Konzils im Jahre 816." *ZKG* 74 (1963): 15–82.

———. "Le souverain occidental et les communautés religieuses du IXe au début du XIe siècle." *Byzantion* 61 (1991): 44–70.

Senellart, Michel. *Les arts de gouverner: Du regimen médiéval au concept de gouvernement.* Paris, 1995.

Senn, Frank C. *Christian Liturgy, Catholic and Evangelical.* Minneapolis: 1997.

Simonetti, Manlio. "L'incidenza dell'Arianesimo nel rapporto fra Romani e barbari." In *Passaggio dal mondo antico,* 367–79.

Sirks, A. J. Boudewijn. "The Summaria Antiqua Codicis Theodosiani in the ms. Vat. Reg. Lat. 886." *ZSRG.R* 113 (1996): 243–67.

Smith, Jonathan Z. "The Influence of Symbols upon Social Change: A Place on Which to Stand." In *Map Is Not Territory: Studies in the History of Religions.* Studies in Judaism in Late Antiquity 23. Leiden: 1978, 129–46.

Somerville, Robert, and Bruce C. Brasington. *Prefaces to Canon Law Books in Latin Christianity.* New Haven: 1998.

Sot, Michel. "Le baptême de Clovis et l'entrée des Francs en romanité." *Bulletin de l'Association Guillaume Budé* (1996: fasc. 1): 64–75.

Sotinel, Claire. "Le personnel épiscopal: Enquête sur la puissance d l'évêque dans la cité." In *L'Évêque dans la cité du IVe au Ve siècle: Image et autorité,* edited by E. Robillard and C. Sotinel, 105–126. Rome: 1987.

Spencer, Mark. "Dating the Baptism of Clovis, 1886–1993." EME 3 (1994): 97–116.

Stancliffe, Clare. "Kings who Opted Out." In *Ideal and Reality,* 154–76.

Steck, Wolfgang. *Der Liturgiker Amalarius—Eine Quellenkritische Untersuchung zu Leben und Werk eines Theologen der Karolingerzeit.* Münchener theologische Studien. Hist. Abteilung 35. Munich: 2000.

Stein, Peter. *Roman Law in European History.* Cambridge: 1999.

Stenton, Frank. *Anglo-Saxon England.* 3rd ed. Reprinted Oxford: 1989.

Sternberger, Dolf. "Der alte Streit um den Ursprung der Herrschaft." *Schriften.* Vol. 3, *Herrschaft und Vereinbarung,* 11–27. Frankfurt am Main: 1980.

Stevens, C. E. *Sidonius Apollinaris and his Age.* Oxford: 1933.

Stewart, Columba. *Cassian the Monk.* New York: 1998.

Stiegler, Anton. *Der kirchliche Rechtsbegriff: Elemente und Phasen seiner Erkenntnisgeschichte.* Munich: 1958.

Stock, Brian. *The Implications of Literacy: Written Language and Models of Interpretation in the Eleventh and Twelfth Centuries.* Princeton: 1983.

Stocking, Rachel. *Bishops, Councils, and Consensus in the Visigothic Kingdom, 589–633.* Ann Arbor: 2000.

Stoclet, Alain. *Autour de Fulrad de Saint-Denis (v. 710–784).* Hautes études médiévales et modernes 72. Geneva: 1993.

Storey, Joanna. "Cathwulf, Kingship, and the Royal Abbey of Saint-Denis." *Speculum* 74 (1999): 1–21.

Straw, Carole. "Gregory's Politics: Theory and Practice." In *Gregorio magno,* 1:47–63.

———. *Gregory the Great: Perfection in Imperfection.* Berkeley: 1988.

Stroheker, Karl Friederich. *Der senatorische Adel im spätantiken Gallien.* Tübingen: 1948.

Stulz, Heinke. *Die Farbe purpur im frühen Griechentum: Beobachtet in der Literatur und in der bildenden Kunst.* Beiträge zur Altertumskunde 6. Stuttgart: 1990.

Suchan, Monika. "Kirchenpolitik des Königs oder Königspolitik der Kirche." ZKG. 111 (2000): 1–27.

Sullivan, Richard E. "Carolingian Missionary Theories." *Catholic Historical Review* 62 (1956): 273–95.

Tabacco, Giovanni. *The Struggle for Power in Medieval Italy: Structures of Political Rule.* Translated by Rosalind Brown Jensen. Cambridge: 1989.

Taylor, Henry Osborn. *The Mediaeval Mind: A History of the Development of Thought and Emotion in the Middle Ages.* 2 vols. 3rd ed. New York: 1919.

Teillet, Suzanne. *Des Goths à la nation gothique: Les origines de l'idée de nation en Occident du Ve au VIIe siècle.* Paris: 1984.

Tellenbach, Gerd. *Römischer und christlicher Reichsgedanke in der Liturgie des frühen Mittelalters.* Sitzungsberichte der Heidelberger Akademie der Wissenschaften. Philosophisch-historische Klasse 1. Heidelberg: 1934.

Testard, Maurice. "Observations sur le passage du paganisme au christianisme dans la monde antique." *Bulletin de l'Association Guillaume Budé* (1988; fasc. 2): 140–61.

Théry, G. "L'Entrée du Pseudo-Denys en occident." In *Mélanges Mandonnet: Études d'histoire littéraire et doctrinale du moyen âge,* 2:23–30. Bibliothèque Thomiste 14. Paris: 1930.

Theuws, F. C. "Centre and Periphery in Northern Austrasia (6th–8th centuries): An Archaeological Perspective." In *Medieval Archaeology in the Netherlands: Studies Presented to H. H. von Regteren Altena,* edited by J. Besterman, J. Bos and H. Heidinga, 41–69. Aasen: 1990.

——. "The Integration of the Kempen Region into the Frankish Empire (550–750): Some Hypotheses." *Helinium* 26 (1986): 121–36.

——. "Maastricht as a Centre of Power in the Early Middle Ages." In *Topographies of Power,* 155–216.

Thomas, Heinz. "Frenkisk: Zur Geschichte von *theodiscus* und *teutonicus* im Frankenreich des 9. Jahrhunderts." In *Beiträge zur Geschichte des Regnum Francorum: Proceedings of a Colloquium for the 75th Birthday of Eugen Ewig 28 May 1988,* edited by R. Schieffer, 67–95. Sigmaringen: 1990.

Thouvenot, R. "Saint Augustin et les Païens (d'après *Epist.* XLVI et XLVII)." In *Hommages à Jean Bayet,* edited by Marcel Renard and Robert Schilling, 682–90. Collection Latomus 70. Bruxelles-Berchem: 1964.

Timpe, Dieter. "Tacitus' Germania als religionsgeschichtliche Quelle." In *Germanische Religionsgeschichte: Quellen und Quellenprobleme,* edited by Heinrich Beck, Detlev Ellmers, and Kurt Schier, 434–85. Ergänzungsbände zum Reallexikon der germanischen Altertumskunde 5. Berlin: 1992.

Treadgold, Warren. *The Byzantine Revival, 780–842.* Stanford: 1988.

Trout, Dennis E. *Paulinus of Nola: Life, Letters, and Poems.* Berkeley: 1999.

Trichet, L. *Le costume du clergé: Ses origines et son évolution en France d'après les règlements de l'église.* Paris: 1986.

——. *La Tonsure: Vie et mort d'une pratique ecclésiastique.* Paris: 1990.

Tuan, Yi-Fu. *Topophilia: A Study of Environmental Perception, Attitudes, and Values.* Englewood Cliffs, N.J.: 1974.

Turner, C. H. "Arles and Rome: The First Developments of Canon Law in Gaul." JTS 17 (1916): 236–47.

Ullmann, Walter. *The Carolingian Renaissance and the Idea of Kingship.* London: 1969.

——. *Gelasius I (492–496): Das Papsttum an der Wende der Spätantike zum Mittelalter.* Päpste und Papsttum 18. Stuttgart: 1981.

——. "Der Grundsatz der Arbeitsteilung bei Gelasius I." In his *Jurisprudence in the Middle Ages: Collected Studies,* 41–70. London: 1980.

——. "Public Welfare and Social Legislation in the Early Medieval Councils." In *Councils and Assemblies,* 1–39. Studies in Church History 7. Cambridge: 1971.

——. *A Short History of the Papacy in the Middle Ages.* New York: 1982.

Van Caenegem, R. C. *De Instellingen van de Middeleeuwen: Geschiedenis van de westerse Staatsinstellingen van de Ve tot de XVe Eeuw.* 2 vols. Ghent: 1967.

Van Dam, Raymond. *Leadership and Community in Late Antique Gaul.* Berkeley: 1985.

Van Den Eynde, Damien. *Les normes de l'enseignement chrétien dans la littérature patristique des trois premiers siècles.* Universitas catholica Lovaniensis. Dissertationes Ser. 2.25. Paris: 1933.

Vanhengel, M. P. "Le Rite et la formule de la chrismation postbaptismale en Gaule et en Haute-Italie du IVe au VIIIe siècle d'apres les sacramentaires gallicans: Aux origines du rituel primitif." *Sacris Erudiri* 21 (1972/73): 209–12.

Vanneufville, Eric. "L'Église en Provence du Ve au VIIIe siècles." MScR 53 (1996): 61–81.

Van Uytfanghe, M. "Les *Visiones* du très haut Moyen Age et les récentes 'expériences de mort temporaire': Sens ou non-sens d'une comparison. Première partie." In *Aevum inter utrumque,* 447–81.

Vessey, Mark. "The Origins of the *Collectio Sirmondiana:* A New Look at the Evidence." In *Theodosian Code: Studies,* 178–99.

Vetere, Benedetto. *Strutture e modelli culturali nella società merovingia: Gregorio di Tours—una testimonianza.* Università degli studi di Lecce, Saggi e Ricerche 3. Lecce: 1979.

Vigouroux, F. *Dictionnaire de la Bible.* 5 vols. Paris: 1907–1912.

Vinogradoff, Paul. *Roman Law in Mediaeval Europe.* London: 1909.

Vismara, Giulio. *La Giurisdizione civile dei vescovi (secoli I–IX).* Pubblicazioni dell'Istituto di Storia del Diritto Italiano 18. Milan: 1995.

Vogel, Cyrille. *Medieval Liturgy: An Introduction to the Sources.* Translated by William G. Storey and Niels Krogh Rasmussen. Washington, D.C.: 1986.

Voigt, K. *Die karolingische Klosterpolitik und der Niedergang des westfränkischen Königtums: Laienäbte und Klosterinhaber.* Kirchenrechtliche Abhandlungen 90 and 91. 1917. Reprinted Amsterdam: 1965.

Vollrath, Hannah. *Die Synoden Englands bis 1066.* Konziliengeschichte Reihe A: Darstellungen. Paderborn: 1985.

Von Campenhausen, Hans Urs. *Ecclesiastical Authority and Spiritual Power in the Church of the First Three Centuries.* Translated by J. A. Baker. Stanford: 1981.

Von Der Nahmer, Dieter. "Martin von Tours: Sein Mönchtum—seine Wirkung." *Francia* 15 (1987): 1–41.

von Padberg, Lutz E. *Mission und Christianisierung: Formen und Folgen bei Angelsachsen und Franken im 7. und 8. Jahrhundert.* Stuttgart: 1995.

———. "Odin oder Christus? Loyalitäts- und orientierungskonflikte in der frühmittelalterlichen Christianisierungsepoche." *Archiv für Kulturgeschichte* 77 (1995): 149–278.

Waché, Brigitte. *Monseigneur Louis Duchesne (1843–1922): Historien de l'Église, directeur de l'École française de Rome.* Rome, 1992.

Waldmüller, Lothar. "Salzburg als Zentrum der bairischen Slawenmission des achten Jahrhunderts." In *Bavaria Christiana: Zur Frühgeschichte des Christentums in Bayern. Festschrift Adolf Wilhelm Ziegler,* 111–27. Beiträge zur altbayerischen Kirchengeschichte 27. Munich: 1973.

Wallace-Hadrill, J. M. *The Barbarian West, A.D. 400–1000: The Early Middle Ages.* 2nd ed. New York: 1962.

————. *Early Germanic Kingship in England and on the Continent.* The Ford Lectures 1970. Oxford: 1971.

————. *The Frankish Church.* Oxford: 1983.

————. "Fredegar and the History of France." *Bulletin of the John Rylands Library, Manchester* 40 (1958): 527–50.

————. "Gothia and Romania." *Bulletin of the John Rylands Library, Manchester* 44 (1961): 213–37.

————. *The Long-Haired Kings.* Toronto: 1982.

————. "The *Via Regia* of the Carolingian Age." In his *Early Medieval History,* 181–200. Oxford: 1975.

Wallach, Luitpold. "The *Libri Carolini* and Patristics, Latin and Greek." In his *Diplomatic Studies in Latin and Greek Documents from the Carolingian Age,* 59–122. Ithaca: 1977.

Walters, Dafydd. "From Benedict to Gratian: The Code in Medieval Ecclesiastical Authors." In *Theodosian Code: Studies,* 200–16.

Waszink, J. H. "Pompa Diaboli." In his *Opuscula selecta,* 288–316. Leiden: 1979.

Wataghin, Gisela Cantino. "La conversion de l'espace: quelques remarques sur l'établissement matériel chrétien aux IVe–Ve siècles, d'après l'exemple de l'Italie du Nord." In *Clovis.* 1:127–39.

Watson, Alan. "Uses and Abuses of Law in History." In his *Ancient Law and Modern Understanding: At the Edges,* 1–19. Athens, Ga.: 1998.

Wattenbach, W., E. Dümmler, and Franz Huf. *Deutschlands Geschichtsquellen im Mittelalter.* 2 vols. Kettwig: 1991.

Webster, Jane. "Sanctuaries and Sacred Places." In *The Celtic World,* edited by Miranda J. Green, 445–64. London: 1995.

Weidemann, Margarete. *Kulturgeschichte der Merowingerzeit nach den Werken Gregors von Tours.* Römisch-germanisches Zentralmuseum Monographien 3. 2 vols. Bonn: 1982.

Weinberger, Stephen. "La transformation des *Potentes* dans la Provence médiévale (IVe–XIe s.)." MA 97. 5th ser. 5 (1991): 159–69.

Weiss, Rolf. *Chlodwigs Taufe: Reims 508. Versuch einer neuen Chronologie für die Regierungszeit des ersten christlichen Frankenkönigs unter Berücksichtigung der politischen und kirchlich-dogmatischen Probleme seiner Zeit.* Geist und Werk der Zeiten. 29. Bern: 1971.

Weissensteiner, Johann. "Cassiodors Gotengeschichte bei Gregor von Tours und Paulus Diaconus? Eine Spurensuche." In *Ethnogenese und Überlieferung,* 123–28.

Wenskus, Reinhard. "Religion abâtardie: Materialien zum Synkretismus in der vorchristlichen politischen Theologie der Franken." In *Iconologia Sacra, Mythos, Bildkunst und Dichtung in der Religions- und Sozialgeschichte Alteuropas. Festschrift für Karl Hauck,* edited by Hagan Keller and Nikolaus Staubach, 179–248. Arbeiten zur Frühmittelalterforschung 23: Berlin, 1994.

Werner, Joachim. "Childerics Pferde." In *Germanische Religionsgeschichte,* 145–61.

Werner, Karl Ferdinand. "Die 'Franken': Staat oder Volk?" In *Die Franken und die Alemannen bis zur "Schlacht bei Zülpich" (496/97),* edited by Dieter Geuenich, 95–101.

Ergänzungsbände zum Reallexikon der Germanischen Altertumskunde 19. Berlin: 1998.

———. "La place du VIIe siècle dans l'évolution politique et institutionnelle de la Gaule franque." In *Le Septième siècle,* 173–211.

———. *Naissance de la noblesse: L'essor des élites politiques en Europe.* Paris: 1998.

Widengren, Geo. *Sakrales Königtum im Alten Testament und im Judentum.* Franz Delitzsch-Vorlesungen 1952. Stuttgart: 1955.

Williams, Daniel H. *Ambrose of Milan and the End of the Nicene-Arian Conflicts.* Oxford: 1995.

Willis, G. G. *A History of Early Roman Liturgy to the Death of Pope Gregory the Great.* Henry Bradshaw Society 1. London: 1994.

Wilmart, André. "Un florilège carolingien sur le symbolisme des cérémonies du baptême, avec un Appendice sur le lettre de Jean Diacre." In *Analecta Reginensia: Extraits des manuscrits latins de la reine Christine conservés au Vatican, 174.* Studi e Testi 59. Rome:1933.

———. *Precum libelli quattuor aevi Karolini.* Rome: 1940.

Windemuth, Marie-Luise. *Das Hospital als Träger der Armenfürsorge im Mittelalter.* Sudhoffs Archiv 36. Stuttgart: 1995.

Wolff, Hans Julius. *Roman Law: An Historical Introduction.* Norman: 1978.

Wolfram, Herwig. "Baiern und das Frankenreich." In *Die Bajuwaren von Severin bis Tassilo, 488–788: Gemeinsame Landaustellung des Freistaates Bayern und des Landes Salzburg. Rosenheim/Bayern/Mattsee/Salzburg 19. Mai bis 6. November 1988,* edited by Hermann Dannheimer and Heinz Dopsch, 130–35. Munich: 1988.

———. *History of the Goths.* Translated by T. J. Dunlap. 2nd ed. Berkeley: 1988.

———. *The Roman Empire and Its Germanic Peoples.* Translated by Thomas Dunlap. Berkeley: 1997.

Wood, Ian. "The Code in Merovingian Gaul." In *Theodosian Code: Studies,* 161–77.

———. "Constructing Cults in Early Medieval France: Local Saints and Churches in Burgundy and the Auvergne, 400–1000." In *Local Saints and Local Churches in the Early Medieval West,* edited by Alan Thacker and Richard Sharpe, 155–87. Oxford: 2002.

———. "The Ecclesiastical Politics of Merovingian Clermont." In *Ideal and Reality,* 34–57.

———. "Gregory of Tours and Clovis." RBPH 63 (1985): 249–72.

———. "Kings, Kingdoms and Consent." In *Early Medieval Kingship,* 6–29.

———. *The Merovingian Kingdoms, 450–751.* London: 1994.

———. "The Secret Histories of Gregory of Tours." RBPH 71 (1993): 253–70.

———. "Topographies of Holy Power in Sixth-Century Gaul." In *Topographies of Power,* 137–54.

Wormald, Patrick. "Bede, the *Bretwaldas* and the Origins of the *Gens Anglorum*." In *Ideal and Reality,* 126–27.

———. *The Making of English Law: King Alfred to the Twelfth Century.* Vol. 1. *Legislation and its Limits.* Oxford: 1999.

Wormald, Patrick, Donald Bullough, and Roger Collins, eds. *Ideal and Reality in*

Frankish and Anglo-Saxon Society: Studies Presented to J. M. Wallace-Hadrill. Oxford: 1983.

Zanella, Gabriele. "La legittimazione del potere regale nelle 'Storie' di Gregorio di Tours e Paolo Diacono." SM ser. 3, vol. 31 (1990): 55–84.

Zechiel-Eckes, Klaus. *Florus von Lyon als Kirchenpolitiker und Publizist: Studien zur Persönlichkeit eines karolingishcen "Intellektuellen" am Beispiel der Auseinandersetzung mit Amalarius (835–858) und des Prädestinationsstreits (851–855).* Quellen und Forschungen zum Recht im Mittelalter 8. Stuttgart: 1999.

Ziegler, A. K. "Pope Gelasius I and His Teaching on the Relation of Church and State." *Catholic Historical Review* 27 (1942): 412–37.

Zimmermann, Michael. "Les sacres des rois wisigoths," in *Clovis* 2:9–28.

INDEX

A Sacred Kingdom: Bishops and the Rise of Frankish Kingship, 300–850 was designed in Adobe Garamond Premier Pro and typeset by Kachergis Book Design of Pittsboro, North Carolina. It was printed on 60-pound House Natural Smooth and bound by Sheridan Books of Ann Arbor, Michigan.